SIXTH EDITION

Organization Theory

A Strategic Approach

B. J. Hodge

William P. Anthony

Lawrence M. Gales

Prentice
Hall

Upper Saddle River, New Jersey 07458

Library of Congress Cataloging-in-Publication Data

Hodge, Billy J.
    Organization theory: a strategic approach / B. J. Hodge, William P. Anthony, Lawrence
M. Gales. — 6th ed.
        p. cm.
    Includes bibliographical references and index.
    ISBN 0-13-033064-7
        1. Organization. 2. Management. I. Anthony, William P. II. Gales, Lawrence M.,
1950– III. Title.

HD31 .H542 2002
658.4 — dc21

2001058794

Acquisitions Editor: Melissa Steffens
Editor-in-Chief: Jeff Shelstad
Editorial Assistant: Kevin Glynn
Senior Marketing Manager: Shannon Moore
Marketing Assistant: Christine Genneken
Managing Editor (Production): John Roberts
Production Editor: Kelly Warsak
Permissions Coordinator: Suzanne Grappi
Associate Director, Manufacturing: Vincent Scelta
Production Manager: Arnold Vila
Manufacturing Buyer: Michelle Klein
Cover Designer: Bruce Kenselaar
Composition: BookMasters, Inc.
Full-Service Project Management: BookMasters, Inc.
Printer/Binder: The Maple Press Company
Cover Printer: LeHigh Press

Credits and acknowledgments borrowed from other sources and reproduced, with permission, in this textbook appear on appropriate page within text.

Pearson Education LTD.
Pearson Education Australia PTY, Limited
Pearson Education Singapore, Pte. Ltd.
Pearson Education North Asia Ltd
Pearson Education, Canada, Ltd
Pearson Educación de Mexico, S.A. de C.V.
Pearson Education — Japan
Pearson Education Malaysia, Pte. Ltd

10 9 8 7 6 5 4 3
ISBN 0-13-033064–7

Contents

PART II: THE CONTEXT OF ORGANIZATIONS   49

Preface

In the Preface to the fifth edition we wrote that a basic fact of organizational life is that things change. We did not realize at that time how much things would change, not only in the world of organizations and management, but also in the world of higher education. The electronic information age is truly upon us. This new edition is consistent in both theme and content with many of the changing nature of organizations and management today. While we made extensive changes to this text, the strategic focus and the theoretical frameworks presented in this sixth edition can be directly traced through the previous five editions.

The material in this text is intended to be a primer in organization theory for upper-division undergraduate and introductory-level MBA students—the future managers and leaders of organizations. The sixth edition continues the reengineering begun in the previous edition. The tone and direction are focused on managerial application—how the student as a potential future manager can use the knowledge of organization theory to be a better manager and organization member. The sixth edition of *Organization Theory: A Strategic Approach* continues to present a balance of theory, research, and practice. Theory and research are necessary to provide coherence, certainty, and predictability in an otherwise incoherent, uncertain, and unpredictable world. However, in presenting theory and research, we have maintained a belief that they should provide practical value to the inhabitants of organizations—the managers and members of organizations. To accomplish this balance, we have provided numerous examples from organizations to illustrate the theories, concepts, and research findings throughout the text.

The changes in this sixth edition are extensive. We continue working to improve readability and increase emphasis on practical application. We have drawn on the experience of many successful old-line and new high-tech firms to give a broad cross-section of examples. Updated cases begin and end each chapter. Numerous "real life" examples are spread throughout the chapters. The clustering of chapters has been revised to enhance the logical flow of material. The thirteen chapters are divided into four parts: "Introduction," "The Context of Organizations," "Managing the Organizational Context," and "Organizational Processes." We have created greater integration among the topics and issues covered in the text so that the reader can more easily relate material introduced in early chapters to material covered later.

Part I of the text contains Chapters 1 and 2. These two chapters provide the basic framework for the text. Chapter 1 provides a historical background for understanding the development of organization theory, introduces a variety of theoretical perspectives, and presents the strategic approach. Chapter 1 also presents the subject of organizational structure—the basic building blocks of the organization. In this chapter, we also introduce the contingency theory framework for organizations that is central to the strategic approach. To understand the appropriate form of organization (structure and design) one must understand the conditions or context in which the organization exists. Chapter 2 presents the basic elements of structure so that the reader can think about how structure should vary with differing contextual conditions.

Part II introduces the contextual dimensions: organizational goals, environment, technology, size and life cycle. From a contingency perspective, these are the factors that must be considered in making judgments about structure. The examination of goals in Chapter 3 has been expanded to include a discussion of ethics and ethical goals. In light of the many troubling events in the business world lately, we felt that a discussion of ethics was especially important. Although the environment has been a central focus of previous editions, this new edition gives even greater attention to that subject, emphasizing the global nature of the business environment for nearly every business. Chapter 4 discusses methods describing the environment, whereas strategic management of the environment is the focus of Chapter 5. Chapter 6 shifts attention to technology. We present three traditional views of organizational technology based on the works of Woodward, Perrow, and Thompson. The traditional views are augmented by contemporary views of technology that examine shifts to services, demands for flexibility, and increasing automation and computerization. Part II concludes with discussion of the two related topics of organizational size and organizational life cycles. These topics have received extensive coverage in the business press due to the proliferation of mergers at the same time that many large organizations are downsizing. Coinciding with these trends are difficulties that some large, prominent organizations are encountering as they enter mature stages of their development.

The contextual conditions presented in Part III are the variables that managers must consider in determining the best-fitting structures, designs, and governance systems. Chapter 8 explores organizational design as a strategic response to the organizational context. The focus is on how people are grouped together in departments or divisions. The chapter also examines some recent trends in design, including virtual organizations, federal organizations, and two Asian forms—the Japanese *keiretsui* and the Korean *chaebol*. Organizational economics, an area of increasing importance in the field of organization theory, is presented in Chapter 9. Using agency theory and transaction costs economics, we examine organizational control, transactions, and boundaries.

The theme of Part IV is organizational processes. Organizational culture, introduced in Chapter 10, discusses those factors that make each organization distinctive and unique. We focus on both the observable and unobservable elements of culture. Chapter 11 introduces organizational information processing and decision making. With the advent of inexpensive high-speed computing and sophisticated telecommunications, organizations can be overwhelmed by information. Thus, managing information is a critical—some would say central—task of organizations. But information is not a final destination. Information is fuel for the decision processes that are also discussed in this chapter. The concepts of bounded rationality and garbage can decision making described in Chapter 11 provide a glimpse of the political side of organizations that, along with power, are the subjects of Chapter 12.

The final chapter introduces organizational innovation, change, and renaissance, subjects that we have implicitly discussed throughout the text. Chapter 12 specifically examines a variety of organizational change perspectives. We conclude with some speculation about the nature of organizations of the twenty-first century and how organization theory can help managers.

The text concludes with four extensive, integrative organizational cases, one of which—Wal-Mart—is a revision of an earlier case. The remaining cases provide an array of new and old firms in manufacturing and service. The purpose of these cases is twofold: (1) to demonstrate the applicability of organization theory concepts and principles to real-life organizations; and (2) to permit the student to use these concepts and principles as problem-solving tools.

As with any complex endeavor, many people deserve thanks for their help and support in making this sixth edition possible. Though too numerous to mention, we give thanks to our colleagues and students at Florida State University and the University of Cincinnati. Special thanks are due to Melissa Steffens, our editor at Prentice Hall Business Publishing. Specific reviewers for the edition include Dr. Marianne W. Lewis, University of Cincinnati; Dr. Hoyt Hayes, Columbia College; Dr. M. Suzanne Clinton, Cameron University; Dr. Robert H. Bennett III, University of South Alabama; and Dr. Richard M. Hodgetts, Florida International University.

Finally, it is to our families that we dedicate this edition. Without their love, help, inspiration, and support this venture would not have been possible, and it is to our children and grandchildren who will become the makers and members of future organizations.

PART

I

Introduction

What are organizations, and why are they an important subject to study? As we will begin to see in Chapter 1, organizations are ubiquitous. They affect nearly every aspect of human existence—birth, growth, development, education, work, social relations, health, and even death. Yet the average person's understanding of the complexities of organizations and organizational life is typically quite limited. Thus, first among our goals is to provide a basis for understanding organizations. An understanding of organizations serves as a stepping-stone to our second goal, which is to provide a foundation for working successfully in organizations and for participating in or initiating efforts to change and adapt organizations to new conditions.

Organization theory and management theory are closely related concepts. A manager must understand the workings of an organization to be effective in the managerial role. Therefore, an understanding of organization theory serves as a foundation for studying management. The concepts that underlie organization theory developed hand in hand with management concepts. As people understood more about how organizations operate, they learned how managers could operate more efficiently. Moreover, although the development of organization theory is rather eclectic, it is closely related to management theory. Concepts, ideas, and research from such diverse areas as economics, engineering, psychology, sociology, social psychology, and political science appear in organization theory literature.

How do we gain an understanding of these concepts? How can we place boundaries on them and arrange them in some logical fashion? To answer these questions we use a combination of strategy and systems approaches. We examine issues in the context of real organizations and real events. We begin addressing these issues in this first chapter and return to them periodically throughout the text.

The first chapter addresses three groups of critical questions: (1) What is organization theory, how does it relate to management, and how did the field develop? (2) What is an organization, why is it important, and how can it be studied? (3) What is a strategic systems approach to organizations?

Chapter 2 introduces the subject of organizational structure—the basic building blocks of the organization. The text takes a contingency approach: The appropriate form of organization (structure and design) depends on the conditions or context in which the organization exists. Understanding the basic elements of structure presented in Chapter 2 provides the reader with a framework for thinking about how structure varies with differing contextual conditions. Part Two then introduces the contextual dimensions of organizational goals, environment, technology, size, and life cycle. These are the contingency factors that must be considered in making judgments about structure.

In Part Three of the text we return to focusing on the organization itself as a means for managing the organizational context. Attention is directed toward the strategic design of organizations and nonstructural means for controlling and managing the organization. We finally examine culture, the last step in managing the context. Culture has been described as the glue that holds an organization together.

Part Four explores three critical organizational processes. First, we examine the nature of information and decision making in organizations. Three models of decision making are presented and critiqued. Up to this point we will have largely regarded organizations as rational and purposeful entities. With our examination of decision making we open up the possibility that organizations and managers sometimes act (make decisions) in ways that do not fit with a rational view of the world. Chapter 12 extends the analysis by presenting a political view of organizations. Finally, we conclude the text by discussing the processes of innovation, change, and organizational renaissance. But like any long journey, the study of organizations must begin with a sturdy foundation.

CHAPTER

Organization Theory and the Manager

1

CASE: THRIFTY HARDWARE COMPANY: ON-THE-JOB TRAINING*

It was early in the morning on March 4, and Mike Lawrence was both excited and concerned as he unlocked the door to Thrifty Hardware Company (Thrifty for short) in northwest Detroit. The night before, he and his ailing father had signed papers transferring ownership of Thrifty to Mike. Mike had grown up in the family's retail hardware business, working summers and weekends during the school year and becoming his father's assistant after graduating from college.

As he walked into the store and turned on the lights, he was soon greeted by his arriving employees. That thought, "employees," felt strange to Mike. He had known and worked with most of the workers for several years (their average tenure on the job was four years), but he had never thought of them as his "employees." Mike felt a new twinge of responsibility, which he had not felt in the past, to his eight full-time and three part-time employees.

By 8:00 A.M. the store was ready to open for business. Thrifty was a full-service hardware, lumber, and building supply store. The store carried nearly 20,000 different items from everything for minor household repairs to those needed for major renovations. The business had grown steadily through the late 1960s to the present at rates well above inflation and the industry average, and was currently doing just over $1,000,000 annually. The primary customers were local homeowners and small businesses. As Mike's father, Irv, always said, "Hardware is recession-proof. In good times you sell the frills, and in tough times when people can't afford new things or plumbers and electricians, you sell them the things they need to 'do it yourself.'"

Mike wasn't too concerned about how to run the business. As his father's assistant, he had done almost everything and knew almost everything there was to know about hardware, lumber, and building supplies. Mike had run the business when his father took rare vacations or days off and had been in charge for the last two weeks while his father was in the hospital. Doing weekly and seasonal ordering, he had dealt with most of the more than 20 major suppliers. He had coordinated the small amount of advertising that they had done. And his major responsibility as his father's assistant had been to take care of the store's financial management, which involved dealing with the banks and credit card companies; managing payroll, accounts receivable and accounts payable; and preparing the books for the accountant. It was this last task that took Mike to his office early on March 4.

Once he was in his office, Mike again felt that vague uneasiness that had kept him awake the night before and had troubled him as he opened the store in the morning. As he stared at the ledger, he realized what was weighing so heavily on his mind. He had been his father's assistant, but now he had no assistant. No one else knew all the ins

---

*This case is based on an actual event. Names of the people involved have been changed.

and outs of the business. What would happen if he got sick, or wanted to take a day off or go on a vacation? Sure, he had heard his father's stories of working seven days a week, ten hours a day. It also occurred to Mike that his father hadn't started taking vacations until Mike was 20 years old and could run the business. Mike knew that he couldn't run the business like that. He had to have an assistant. The more he thought about who to pick as an assistant, the more he began to see that what he needed was more than just an assistant. He started to think about an organizational plan. He spent the rest of the morning writing notes, talking with each of his employees, and just wandering around the nearly 20,000 square feet of sales floor and warehouse space. By the end of the workday Mike felt that an organizational plan was coming together. As his employees were leaving the store, he asked them to show up early the next day for a breakfast staff meeting. The workers looked quizzically at Mike because they'd never before had a staff meeting.

That night, after finishing the bookkeeping that he had avoided all day, Mike went to bed and slept soundly. At the staff meeting the next morning he announced his new organizational plan. First, he made Ben Slater his assistant and the store manager. Ben had been with Thrifty the longest of any of the salespeople and seemed to be the brightest and most responsible of the employees. Mike would begin today to train Ben about all the critical managerial responsibilities.

Mike then assigned each of the other full-time employees to manage specific departments. For example, Paul Schultz was responsible for the plumbing and electrical departments. He was to become completely knowledgeable about each product they sold in these two departments, each wholesaler that supplied merchandise, how and when to order, and what sold and what didn't sell. Similar responsibilities were created for lumber, paint, tools, and each additional product area.

This plan would relieve Mike of the day-to-day tasks of ordering, dealing with wholesalers, and being the primary source of product and "how-to" information. Major decisions about ordering new products or dropping slow sellers would be made by a group composed of the department head, Mike, and Ben. Bea Simms, the head cashier, also became the bookkeeper.

After dividing tasks among the employees, Mike then described what he saw as his job. He would supervise and coordinate everyone's work. He would determine Thrifty's direction, make the major decisions for the business, and provide employees with information and feedback about their jobs. Mike knew that if the company were to grow and prosper, he could not be bogged down by the day-to-day minutiae. Mike then laid out Thrifty's strategy:

- They would be a full-service hardware, lumber, and building supply company. This meant that they would stress customer service and a wide variety of products and services. Thrifty would be the premier hardware, lumber, and building supply company in its market area.
- They would treat each customer fairly and honestly. They would never sell inferior quality products and they would never use hard-sell tactics to sell something that the customer didn't want. Employees would keep in mind that it is the customer who pays their wages.
- Each employee would be respected for his or her unique contributions to the business and would be treated with fairness and respect.

Mike closed the meeting by stating that this was only the beginning. They should all expect more changes, and he welcomed suggestions from employees. As the meeting broke up, Mike felt pretty good about what had been accomplished. He thought he had laid the groundwork for the smooth operation of the business.

Although the business, in general, was running smoothly, a number of unexpected events did cause some problems. First, at 3:00 A.M. on June 1, a drunk driver rammed through the plate glass windows in the front of the store, doing over $20,000 damage to the building, fixtures, and merchandise. Fortunately, the police called Ben Slater, who arrived on the scene to begin boarding up the storefront. Then, in July, Thrifty's major hardware wholesaler burned to the ground. The immediate question that Mike faced was how to replace this supplier—quickly. Without a dependable supply of merchandise, the business would suffer and customers would go elsewhere. In the short run, he turned to several small local wholesalers. In the long run, the crisis turned into a positive event. Mike reevaluated how the store bought merchandise, and he made a major decision to join a wholesale cooperative. The major comprehensive suppliers in the hardware industry, ACE, True Value, ServiStar, and HWI, are all dealer-owned cooperatives. This change allowed him to concentrate the store's buying with far fewer wholesalers, making ordering easier and more efficient.

In September, Paul Schultz, the plumbing and electrical department manager, resigned. Next to Ben Slater, Schultz was the most competent and reliable employee. Mike knew it would be difficult to replace Schultz; but because of the changes that Mike started making in March, he knew he could clearly define the skills and responsibilities that were part of Paul's job. Finally, in November, several local auto plants announced layoffs or temporary shutdowns because car sales were slow. Mike was concerned because so many of his customers were autoworkers. Nonetheless, Mike was optimistic. The business had weathered previous economic slowdowns, increased competition, and major changes in the local neighborhood.

As the year drew to a close, Mike sat in his office and reflected on events since he had taken over Thrifty. Business had been good despite all the turmoil. Sales had increased at an annual rate of 17 percent, which was well above the rate of inflation. Profits had also increased significantly. The switch to the new wholesale cooperative had resulted in lower costs. Most important to Mike was that he now felt comfortable that he could take a few days off after the first of the year and know that the company could go on without him. What Mike did not realize was that in the last nine months he had learned a great deal about organizations.

The previous case is a real-life example of the importance of understanding the nature of organizations. Although Thrifty Hardware Company may not be the largest or most sophisticated organization, this case illustrates several key points about the nature of organizations that will be examined in greater detail in this chapter and throughout the text. First, organizations are made of *people,* whether it is the handful of employees at Thrifty or the thousands of employees at General Motors. Second, Mike learned that *division of labor* among members of the organization is critical. Everyone does not have the same task. A third aspect of organizations that Mike came to understand was the importance of *goals* to organizations. Understanding and improving the operation of Thrifty required Mike to explicitly understand each of these three elements of organization, and that is where our study of organizations begins.

ORGANIZATIONS

Nearly every aspect of our daily life is affected in some way by organizations. Work, school, family, health care, religion, entertainment—nearly every facet of life takes place in, is regulated by, or is the result of organizations and organizational action. In fact, the very concept of modern civilized society is based on the premise that people work together in formal or informal groups to complete tasks that individuals alone could not perform. Perhaps because organizations are everywhere and we are so involved in them, we give little thought to what organizations really are and how they work. Yet, most of us work in organizations. We depend on them for our livelihood and for most of the products and services we need to live. If, like Mike Lawrence in the introductory case, we wish to understand, manage, and improve the situations we face in organizations, it is necessary to study organizations.

Unlike Mike Lawrence's on-the-job education about organizations, this book takes a systematic look at organizations. Our intention is to first examine the concept of *organizations* and then explore how they are designed, how they function, and how they change over time. Our examination of organizations focuses mainly on business organizations although the basic concepts and relationships we present can be applied to nearly all complex organizations. Throughout our examination we are most concerned with explaining and understanding how organizations can operate more efficiently and effectively. We are especially concerned with what managers can do to make organizations operate better.

Organizational Challenges

Today's organizations face several key challenges. Even rich and powerful companies with long traditions are not immune to obstacles in meeting these challenges: Witness the recent problems faced by such industry giants as Kodak, General Motors, IBM, Sears, and countless dot-com Internet companies. While these companies face many varied challenges, five major areas represent recurrent themes in this text:

1. Managing organizations in a global environment
2. Designing and structuring (or restructuring) organizations
3. Improving quality, empowering organization members, and enhancing competitiveness
4. Reducing complexity, increasing speed, and reacting to environmental changes
5. Providing ethical and moral management of the organization

The Global Challenge

Virtually all businesses are affected in one way or another by a host of global issues, ranging from tariffs, to the relocation of American firms offshore, to import/export restrictions. Even Mike Lawrence had to consider global markets when he made decisions about the merchandise he bought for his store. Some foreign producers simply made better or cheaper products than his domestic suppliers.

Currently, mere geographical borders are no protection from the effects of actions taken by businesses and governments all around the world. In the United States the automotive industry certainly felt the full effects of foreign competition from which it is only now recovering, and some even doubt that it has. Almost every business is affected in some way by the seemingly constant crises in the Middle East, perhaps the most notable of which surrounds the importation of oil, the literal as well as the symbolic lubricant of U.S. industry.

Even the fast food industry that supplies many of our daily meals (some say too many!) is drastically affected. At one time, this industry relied heavily on "locally grown" beef and potatoes. The hamburger you ate just a few years ago came from the meat of one animal that was more than likely raised on a farm located perhaps only a few miles away. Today, however, that pattie is composed of an admixture of meat from many animals that might be bought from all over the world and that are the subject of a wide variety of government regulations and even cultural issues.

Today, the global meat industry and its customers are in the crosshairs of a major outbreak of foot-and-mouth disease that is affecting meat products from Europe. This highly contagious disease affects cloven-hoofed animals such as cows, hogs, and sheep. It is very easily contracted because the virus can be transmitted by footwear, vehicles, and even the wind. Although there is no evidence that the disease is harmful to humans, it spreads so rapidly that entire herds and flocks must be destroyed in order to contain it.

The U.S. Department of Agriculture has implemented a ban on European Union livestock and meat. This action comes in response to the outbreak of the disease in Great Britain and Northern Ireland that has made the leap to France. These countries are destroying entire herds in a frantic effort to control spread, and travelers from the European Union can be subjected to disinfection of their footwear if they have been on a farm.

One of America's favorite fast food chains, McDonald's, is initiating its own efforts to keep its products free from mad cow disease, another disease that affects cattle. The company has established a deadline for its suppliers to document that they have fed their animals in accordance with federal rules and regulations designed to stop the spread of mad cow disease. Because of its position, McDonald's actions have had a ripple effect through the meatpacking industry. Even the Livestock Marketing Association has suggested that its members require documentation from producers or risk being unable to sell to slaughterhouses. One need only look at a few newspapers or newsmagazines over the past few years to see how dramatically the world political and business landscape has changed. Communism has fallen in most of eastern Europe. The shift to market economies in these countries presents businesses with opportunities, but political instability also creates great risk. In western Europe the formation of a unified economic market has caused great concern for many businesses, particularly firms outside the European community. Several events in Asia may have important implications for business organizations. Recent turbulence in Japan's economy has made the task of balancing trade more difficult. Because of their own recession, the Japanese are spending less on American products.

The economic and political situation in China is equally uncertain. As China has become more open and adopted a more market-based economy, it has become an increasingly important trade partner for western business. Yet, human rights organizations throughout the world have pressured the Chinese to grant greater political freedoms in exchange for favorable trade relations. Additionally, in 1997 the former British colony of Hong Kong, a major Asian economic center, reverted to the People's Republic of China. No one knows what long-range impact this change will have on Hong Kong–based businesses.

Finally, adoption of the North American Free Trade Agreement (NAFTA) and recent revisions in the General Agreement on Tariffs and Trade (GATT) will reduce trade barriers between the United States and its trading partners throughout the world. This, too, will create new opportunities for American businesses, but it is also likely to increase competition. Many businesses may expand the scope of their operations; some will relocate to take advantage of lower costs of doing business; and some will be challenged by new competitors.

The point is that no business, big or small, can ignore events throughout the world. Thus, as we examine organizations in this text, we will repeatedly make reference to organizations in their global environments.

Designing and (Re)Structuring

General Motors (GM), IBM, Unisys, Compaq Computer, . . . the list goes on. All of these firms are cutting back on personnel and changing the way they are organized. They are cutting the number of top managers, middle managers, support staff, and even production workers to become leaner and more efficient. To accommodate these cuts, organizations are implementing new structures. Even Mike Lawrence had to restructure Thrifty so it would run smoothly in the absence of his father. Despite these trends toward downsizing and restructuring, many firms have yet to reap anticipated benefits. We will examine the designing, downsizing, and restructuring trends at several junctures in the text to try to understand why firms may need to design, downsize, and restructure, how they should go about this process, and what firms should expect from these actions.

Quality, Empowerment, and Competitiveness

Few subjects have received more attention in the business press in recent years than the Total Quality Management (TQM) movement. Basically, this is a concept, an approach, and a philosophy that are aimed at maximizing productivity while simultaneously minimizing costs. It is proactive in maintaining that quality can be managed and is a process for doing so. It involves everyone in the organization and requires conformance to standards so that the end result of effort is managed quality.

The Malcolm Baldrige National Quality Award is given annually to U.S. companies to recognize their excellence and quality achievement. This award is intended to promote awareness of quality and its importance in a firm's being competitive and sharing information about its success with other U.S. organizations in the categories of manufacturing, service, and small business.

Among the firms honored with the Baldrige Award are Motorola, Cadillac Motor Car Division, AT&T, and Ames Rubber Corporation. The receipt of the award surely counts as a mark of excellence and a commitment to the constant pursuit of the management of total quality in the organization. Indeed, the acceptance and implementation of the Baldrige criteria provide possibly the best basis for the installation and maintenance of a Total Quality Management program for any business striving for quality improvement and maintenance.

So, you can see, the total management of quality is a philosophy, an approach, and a commitment that have broad implications for organizations, and we will examine these in several chapters, including those dealing with goals, technology, structure, work groups, and culture.

Along with the total quality movement, managers have come to realize that one route to streamlined operation and greater employee involvement is to *empower* employees. The result is that employees lower in the organizational hierarchy are now being given responsibility for making decisions about a variety of job-related issues. While this may seem to be an obvious way to run an organization, it challenges traditional thinking about power, authority, and hierarchy in organizations. As we examine total quality, we will also look at issues related to empowerment at several points in our exploration of organizations.

Both Total Quality Management and empowerment are seen as tools organizations can use to become more competitive. This serves to highlight the point that businesses in almost all markets are facing increasingly fierce competition. That competition is the result of many factors including increasingly open global markets in nearly every industry, ruthless cost cutting on the part of some companies, lower economies of scale in some basic industries, such as steel, and changing consumer attitudes about price and value.

Complexity, Speed, and Responsiveness

Not only is the world changing as we noted earlier, but it appears that these changes are happening with greater speed than ever before.[1] High-speed, high-capacity computing; advanced telecommunications; and worldwide electronic media coverage have all increased the speed with which information is transmitted. The increasing rapidity of information transfer requires that organizations be structured in ways that maximize their ability to handle information. Such innovations as ***just-in-time (JIT)*** manufacturing and inventory control systems and ***computerized integrated manufacturing systems (CIMS)*** make use of this abundant information. However, speed and responsiveness require more than bigger and faster computers. Organizations must get the right information in the right form to the appropriate people in a timely fashion. We will examine the impact on organizations of this abundant information and these demands for speed and responsiveness at several points in the text. Most specifically, we will address these issues in chapters dealing with the environment, technology, structure, information, and culture.

Moral and Ethical Management

Cynics may argue that *business ethics* is an oxymoron. We, along with numerous corporate leaders, believe that is not the case. Ethical behavior and traditional business objectives and operations can and, we maintain, should be consistent. The scandals that involved former president Bill Clinton highlight how moral standards and behavior can permeate not only political circles but business circles as well. The alleged contributions to Clinton's presidential library fund on behalf of international businessman Marc Rich by his ex-wife, Denise, in return for a presidential pardon for Rich are a case in point. Even though presidential pardons are generally agreed to be legal, there are broad-based concerns about whether this pardon and others granted by Clinton in his last days in office were ethical.

Chapter 3 will introduce an ethical framework for guiding the management of organizations. Periodically we will return to this ethical framework to guide discussions of issues such as decision making, downsizing, and organizational politics.

Organizations: A Definition

Humans have probably always lived in organized groups. Tasks such as hunting, food gathering, protection, and migration could be more effectively and efficiently carried out in such groups. Groups of individuals working together could accomplish goals that no individual alone could realize. Complicated tasks could be divided among several people, and people who possessed special skills, knowledge, or other attributes could work in areas that provided the best match between the individual and the group's needs. The modern organization is, in reality, an extension of the specialization and division of labor that existed in early social groups. This leads us to a preliminary definition of organizations stated on page 10.

DEFINITION

An organization is defined as two or more people working together cooperatively within identifiable boundaries to accomplish a common goal or objective. Implicit in this definition are several important ideas: Organizations are made up of people (i.e., members); organizations divide labor among members; and organizations pursue shared goals or objectives.

Organizations are made up of people. Although this seems rather obvious and simplistic, to understand and appreciate the human component is important because of the complexity of social relationships and variability or diversity in humans. The human component makes organizations among the most complex systems[2] and presents managers and organizational researchers with some of their most critical challenges. Organizations such as Thrifty Hardware Company or General Motors must attract, motivate, and retain the right people. We will return to the "people" issue repeatedly throughout our investigation of organizations.

Second, when people work together a number of things become necessary. We need to *divide labor among people,* and as noted earlier, we may seek people with specialized skills or knowledge. The eighteenth-century economist and philosopher Adam Smith used the example of a pin factory to point out the value of division of labor and specialization.[3] Not all members of the organization should necessarily carry out the same tasks. For example, in Smith's pin factory, it was more efficient for laborers to specialize in specific parts of the pin production process instead of each person creating one pin from start to finish. In the introductory case, Mike Lawrence found it useful to divide responsibilities among his employees so that each one managed a different department and had specialized knowledge about its products, suppliers, and customer needs.

As we begin to divide labor and seek specialization among organizational members, it also becomes necessary to make certain that everyone continues to work toward the common goals of the organization. *Coordination and control of actions* among organization members become imperative. At Thrifty the responsibility for coordination was largely Mike's. Without coordination and control some workers may intentionally or unintentionally engage in activities that do not contribute to the organization's goals or that may interfere with them. Some people may pursue actions that further their own interests and others may simply freeload—not contribute their fair share of effort—yet still expect to share in the organization's outcomes. Moreover, some operations within organizations may require precise timing or scheduling so that actions of different workers or departments fit together. For example, Mike Lawrence found that the timing of ordering was critical. Thursday through Monday was the period of heaviest customer traffic. It was critical that orders be placed so that merchandise arrived before these busy periods. Otherwise, important merchandise might not have been on display and employees would have had to divert their attention from customers to stocking tasks. Similarly, an automaker must ensure that assembly workers carefully coordinate their actions so that their assembly efforts result in the efficient and effective production of a car. To exercise coordination and control, members of the organization need a formal structure that specifies roles, responsibilities, and relationships among organizational members. We will have more to say about the topic of structure shortly.

Third, *organizations have identifiable boundaries*. Defining an organization's boundaries may appear to be a simple matter. Most people think of membership as the characteristic that defines the boundaries of an organization. Employees in a business, volunteers in a voluntary organization, or students in an academic institution would all appear to be within the boundaries of those organizations. Closer inspection of the boundary issue, however, makes this determination less clear-cut.

Two critical organizational tasks help us to define two different approaches to delineating an organization's boundaries. The first approach to boundaries emphasizes people and membership while the second approach emphasizes where activities take place.[4]

We already noted that organizations are made up of people, and one important task is to bring into the organization necessary employees or members willing to exchange their contributions for wages or other rewards. This task is, in part, consistent with a definition of organizational boundaries that emphasizes membership—employees, volunteers, or students. The organization's boundary is defined by those people who are official organizational members. But what about the recent trend toward using contracted labor, temporary workers, or consultants? For example, Florida's governor Jeb Bush has proposed a plan to reduce by 25 percent the state's permanent workforce over a 5-year period. This move is aimed at saving the state a considerable sum of money in the form of personnel costs (not only salaries, but matching funds for Social Security and the funding of retirement benefits). The work done by these "displaced" employees would be done through contract services and temporary employees who would not receive the benefits received by permanent employees. Perhaps some of these employees might even be rehired by the state to serve as consultants—and even occupy their old desks!

These changes raise two important questions. Are these contractors and temporary workers members of the organization? Where is the boundary? The answers are not clear. Basing our definition of organizational boundaries on membership suggests that these people are not true members of the organization. Yet, clearly, the work these people do for the organization is often equal in importance to that carried out by true members—and sometimes of even greater importance.

A second critical task for an organization is to determine which activities it should attempt to perform and which ones it should leave to other organizations in the external environment. This is commonly referred to as the make-buy decision.[5] For example, General Motors must decide whether it should make or buy certain components, such as shock absorbers or spark plugs. While GM has decided to make many of its component parts, some competitors have decided to buy those parts from supplier companies in the external environment. This approach to organizational boundaries emphasizes activities rather than people. Accordingly, boundaries are defined by those activities that the organization chooses to pursue, regardless of whether the workers who perform the tasks are regular employees or contract laborers.

Thus, we are left with two ways of describing organizational boundaries; one emphasizing people in the organization and the other emphasizing activities that the organization conducts. Although these two views are not mutually exclusive (i.e., applying one approach does not rule out applying the other), they are not necessarily complementary views. How we choose between these two views of boundaries depends largely on the organizational question or problem we seek to answer. For example, questions dealing with positions, communication, hierarchy, or politics may be best addressed using membership as the boundary criterion. Relationships between departments, between the organization and outside customers or suppliers, and even between the organization and its employees typically focus on activities as boundary criteria.

The fourth part of our definition of an organization states that *organizations are purposeful, goal-seeking work arrangements*. They are not just temporary or transient collections of people. Organizations exist to pursue commonly held goals. Part of Mike Lawrence's strategy was a list of specific goals that his business should achieve that included serving customers, making money, and behaving ethically. In Chapter 3 we will examine in detail organizational goals. We will see, however, that the combination of the human aspect of organizations and the goal-seeking or purposeful nature of organizations may be a source of problems. We will eventually have to deal with problems of determining who sets organizational goals and what happens when goal consensus is absent. Thus, even the seemingly simple notion of organizational goals is not as simple as it would appear.

We began with a simple definition of an organization as two or more people working together to accomplish a common goal. As we began to explore this definition, we came to the realization that organizations are *not* simple. Therefore, we may need a more comprehensive definition. Even though debates exist about each part of the definition of an organization, it is still useful to rework our original definition. Our refined, more complete, definition of organizations is highlighted in the box following:

DEFINITION

Organizations are human systems of cooperation and coordination assembled within identifiable boundaries to pursue shared goals or objectives.

To sharpen and improve our understanding of organizations and organizational activity, researchers and managers must develop explanations of how organizations form, function, change, and survive. Such explanations are the domain of organization theory that we discuss in this text.

ORGANIZATIONS AS SYSTEMS

Our definition of an organization also includes the term *systems*.[6] Systems theory provides a simple way to model organizations by focusing on the structure and relationships or interdependence among parts of the organization. A systems approach conveys the idea that organizations are made up of parts and that the parts interact with each other to accomplish the organization's goals. For example, at Thrifty Hardware the business must obtain inputs from the external environment. These inputs include merchandise to sell, employees, labor, and bank financing. The internal processes at Thrifty include receiving and stocking merchandise, marketing, selling, maintenance, and other activities necessary to support the day-to-day conduct of business. On the output side Thrifty must sell its goods to customers, respond to government agencies that tax or regulate the business, and deal with unexpected events, such as the drunk driver who crashed through the front window.

General Motors presents a more complex example. The purchasing department must obtain such inputs as steel, tires, paint, wire, fabrics, and many components necessary to produce an automobile. The personnel department must attract workers who have the necessary skills and then must develop training, compensation, and administrative systems to retain and motivate those employees. Production must take the material and human inputs and produce automobiles. Marketing must develop advertising, promotional, product, and sales strategies that facilitate the sale of the cars that the production subsystem produces. In a typical organization many departments or units must interact to accomplish the firm's objectives.

Critical relationships or interdependencies may exist among these departments. At GM, production and personnel must work together to ensure that the organization has enough workers with the appropriate skills required by the production subsystem. Purchasing and production must plan carefully to guarantee flows of raw materials necessary to produce products. Oversupplies of raw materials can be costly, tying up capital and requiring storage. Innovative systems, such as just-in-time inventory control, change the nature of interdependence between production and purchasing and make coordination even more critical. Production and marketing must work together to plan how much of each product to produce to match expected demands and scheduled promotions. If the marketing department aggressively promotes a new product before production is fully operating, the unexpected demand may place undue stress on production. Similar types of coordination must take place even at Thrifty Hardware. Retailers often face serious problems when they create marketing promotions and then the manufacturers fail to ship the advertised products. The results of poor coordination among interdependent departments could be overworked employees, equipment breakdowns, defective products, unfilled orders, unhappy customers, and lost profits.

Two additional and related characteristics of systems are ***holism*** and ***synergism.*** First, *holism means that a system should be considered as a functioning whole. Changes in any one part of the system are likely to have an impact throughout the system.* If the purchasing department has difficulty obtaining raw materials, the production department will probably also suffer because it has no raw materials to convert to outputs. Or if the organization implements a just-in-time inventory system, it is likely to have profound impact on the need for communication between purchasing and production. Thus, one should consider performance in all components of the organization when changes affect any one component. Second, *synergism* refers to the interactive effect of the parts of the system working together. *The sum of the interaction of the component parts of the organization working together is greater than the effect of the parts working separately,* or as it is commonly described, 2 + 2 = 5. As each part of the system performs its role, it enhances the performance of other parts. Just as a basketball team is more than five players playing as individuals, so is an organization more than just the sum of its parts. In fact, this is usually why the parts are brought together in the first place. The organization creates separate departments in purchasing, production, personnel, and marketing because of the specialized knowledge and skills that each area requires. It is, however, only through the coordinated interaction of these departments that the organization is able to achieve its goals.

Closed and Open Systems

Systems theorists differentiate between ***closed systems*** and ***open systems.*** Closed systems are self-perpetuating and receive no outside energy or resources. They have no need to interact with their environments. As closed systems run out of energy, they enter a state of collapse called ***entropy.*** A major advance in the study of organizations was the realization that organizations are *not (and cannot be)* closed systems because they depend on their external environments for energy. Open systems can avoid entropy, and create a state called ***negative entropy,*** by importing energy in the form of physical, human, and financial resources. The approach presented in this book emphasizes how organizations as open systems attempt to manage relationships with their environments.

Open systems models acknowledge that organizations must receive energy (***inputs***) in the form of important resources from their external environments. For example, Thrifty Hardware Company receives merchandise, labor, and customers from its outside environment. General Motors receives parts from independent suppliers, labor from the labor market, and capital from investors and lenders. Additionally, Thrifty and General Motors sell their ***output*** to customers who are also external to the company. Sales of products and services produce cash flow and provide additional energy for the system. Many other facets of the external environment are critical to any organization's existence, and we will explore them in detail in Chapter 4.

Figure 1-1 graphically presents the three parts of a basic open systems model: inputs, throughputs or transformation processes, and outputs. Several subsystems are also associated with these three activities and are included in the diagram.

The input and output portions of the open systems model are critical because they represent the organization's interface with the external environment. Together, these input and output functions are part of the ***boundary spanning*** subsystem.[7] Input subunits of the organization are responsible for importing resources and information into the organization. In a typical business, these activities may include purchasing, receiving, personnel recruiting, and market research as well as links to investors and bankers. Output units are responsible for disseminating information about the organization and disposing of the firm's outputs. These functions may include advertising, public relations, and sales. An in-depth discussion of these activities is presented in Chapter 4, but for now the important point is that these activities require that organizational members interact extensively with people or organizations in the external environment. GM must interact with suppliers, advertising agencies, dealers, journalists, investors, bankers, government agencies, and myriad other external factors. Even a small business like Thrifty must interact with a subset of these external constituents. Remember that the external environment is a source of both energy and uncertainty for an organization, and the organization must have mechanisms for dealing with its environment if it is to survive.

FIGURE 1-1   The Open Systems Model

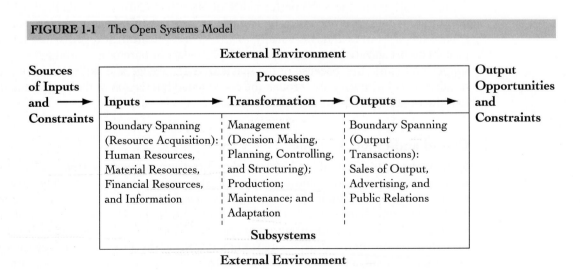

The remaining process in the systems model is the throughput process. Several important activities take place in relation to throughput. First, the ***production subsystem*** is responsible for transformation of the organization's inputs into outputs. This is the means that the organization uses to take the raw materials, labor, capital, and information that it has received in the input process and convert them into outputs. In the case of a manufacturing company such as General Motors, steel, plastics, tires, batteries, glass, and countless other inputs are converted into vehicles. The transformation for a service organization such as Thrifty is less clear. Its transformation process involves the linking of customers to various services. For example, Thrifty acquires merchandise from wholesalers and then sells that merchandise to customers. The production subsystem is responsible for preparing the merchandise for sale and actual selling to customers. We will further investigate activities of the production subsystem under the heading of technology in Chapter 6.

Other activities and systems are necessary to support the transformation process as shown in Table 1-1. Organizations must balance the need for stability and predictability with the need to adapt to the changing external environment. Stability and predictability are the responsibility of two key subsystems. First, as we saw in the case of Mike Lawrence, ***management*** is responsible both for coordinating and controlling activities of the various subsystems, and for setting the organization's strategic goals, design, structure, and policies. These functions provide for predictable and stable interactions within the organization. Second, smooth, trouble-free operation is the responsibility of the ***maintenance subsystem.*** Activities in this subsystem include maintenance of the organization's human resources through personnel administration, maintenance of production facilities by people responsible for the cleaning and repair of equipment, and operation of support facilities, such as a legal department, clinics, information systems, and other functions necessary, but not central, to actual production of the desired outputs.

TABLE 1-1   Subsystems and Functions

Subsystem	Function
Boundary Spanning	Input: Human Resources, Purchasing, Market Research, Investor Relations, Environmental Scanning. Output: Sales, Marketing/Advertising, Public Relations, Lobbying.
Production	Produces the goods and services that make up the organization's outputs. Examples include assembly line workers, sales staff (in a sales organization), and service providers.
Maintenance	Supports the organization by ensuring that all subsystems and physical facilities operate smoothly. Examples include plant operations, legal staff, custodians, human resource administration, and other support staff.
Adaptation	Accountable for helping the organization change to meet new opportunities and threats in environment. Includes research and development, engineering, market research, and other departments responsible for innovation and change.
Management	Responsible for ensuring that all other subsystems work smoothly together. Directs, controls, and coordinates actions of other subsystems. Sets organizational goals and strategy. Examples include top management team, department heads, and supervisors.

Countering the need for stability and predictability is the organization's need to respond to the changing demands of the external environment, the domain of the ***adaptation subsystem.*** Departments such as research and development (R&D) and market research try to create innovations and help the firm adapt to change. In Chapter 5 we explore how organizations adapt to conditions in the external environment. Often, the organization itself needs to change to accommodate changed conditions in the environment. These changes may include activities such as production innovations, changes in the technology of the transformation process, and changes in the organization's structure and design. Chapter 13 deals more extensively with the processes of innovation, organizational change, and learning.

A STRATEGIC SYSTEMS APPROACH

The open systems model provides the first step in developing an organizing framework for this text—what we refer to as a ***strategic systems approach.*** The open systems model identifies or implies the existence of several key components of organizations. The next step is to systematically identify organizational dimensions. For example, the open systems model makes explicit the fact that organizations must interact with their external environment. But what other components of an organization's context or situation are critical? We must now begin to identify the set of features that scholars and managers must recognize if they are to understand the complex relationships that exist in operating organizations.

Managers select organizational structures to respond to specific conditions that the organization faces. These conditions are called the ***organizational context*** or ***contingency factors*** and include the organization's goals, environment, technology, size, and culture. Each of these contextual factors is discussed in subsequent chapters. The important point for now is that the essence of the strategic systems approach to organizations is that managers must attempt to maximize the fit between their choice of structure and the context that their organization faces.[8] Thus, Mike Lawrence at Thrifty, just like his counterparts at GM, IBM, and other organizations, tries to structure the organization to fit the various conditions it faces. Our task is to describe these different structural dimensions of the organization, the various contingency conditions or contextual factors, and how they all fit together. This is no easy task. Although the logic of strategically adapting the organization to its context is appealing, a variety of factors both internal and external to the organization make this task more difficult and complicated than we expect.

Our definition of an organization states that division of labor is a key factor in distinguishing organizations from random collections of people. Moreover, the open systems model identifies a number of key subsystems that are part of an organization. Implied in both the definition and the open systems model is the notion of ***structure.*** Organizational structure describes the internal relationships, division of labor, and means of coordinating activity within the organization. Structure includes such things as where decisions are made (degree of centralization), how labor is divided and departments are formed (differentiation), and the extent to which rules, policies, and procedures govern activities (formalization). One of the first things Mike Lawrence did when he took over Thrifty was to create a formal structure. Chapter 2 examines in detail organization structure. We return to structure and the related topic of design in Chapter 8. For now it is sufficient to note that managers select or attempt to change organization structure to fit their personal preferences and the conditions the organization faces.

It is critically important for managers to structure the organization so that internal activities are coordinated and controlled. But because organizations are open systems affected by the uncertainties, constraints, and resources available in the external environment, the structure must also be designed so that managers can control or adapt to these external conditions.

The conclusion of this approach is that the choice of an organization's structure should be ***contingent,*** or dependent, on the context that the organization faces. Some contextual conditions require one type of structural response by the organization while other conditions require different structural responses. Thus, *there is no one best or most appropriate way for all organizations to structure and organize. The best-fitting structure depends on the context that the organization faces.* That is, it depends on the organization's environment, technology, goals or objectives, size, and culture. As a result, we would hardly expect Thrifty Hardware Company to have the same type of structure as General Motors, or even another retailer such as Wal-Mart. Moreover, while not all ways of organizing and structuring are equally good, there may be more than one good way for an organization to structure or organize. This idea is referred to as ***equifinality.*** Thus, we will identify different types of structural configurations that work in specific situations and those that are not likely to work. More important, we will examine *why* those structures work or do not work. We will use *theory* to guide our study of these issues.

DEFINITION

Contingency means that one thing depends on something else. The contingency approach states that there is no one best or most appropriate way for *all* organizations to structure and organize. The best-fitting structure depends on the context that the organization faces.

Thus, an open systems view of organizations emphasizes that organizations are open to influence and uncertainty in the environment in which they exist. Additionally, when determining how best to manage the organization, managers must consider other factors such as organizational size, technology, goals, and culture. The strategic systems approach to organization theory states that managers should consider these contextual factors when they determine the strategies for managing the firm.

The reader should be cautioned, however, that this strategic systems approach does not mean that managers will necessarily correctly survey conditions, perceive their context, and make the best decisions about organizational issues such as structure, design, and management. Other factors such as change, uncertainty, bounded rationality, faulty perceptions, and organizational politics may intervene and affect outcomes. In sum, we suggest that management decisions are likely to be better if guided by the strategic systems approach—but there is no guarantee.

DEFINITION

The strategic systems approach to organization theory states that managers should consider contextual factors when they determine the strategies for managing the firm.

ORGANIZATION THEORY AND MANAGERIAL PRACTICE

You may still be asking yourself why we need theory to examine organizations. Theory is necessary to provide a *systematic* exploration of our topic. ***Theory*** can be defined as an explanation of some phenomenon, and it consists of principles that state relationships observed in association with that phenomenon.[9] Organization theory can be thought of as a set of related concepts, principles, and hypotheses about organizations that is used to explain components of organizations and how they relate to each other. The systems model previously presented is an example of a ***descriptive theory***.[10] It attempts to describe the nature of the relationship among the various subsystems of the organization and the environment. The goal of descriptive theory is simply to describe why and how something happens. Descriptive theory provides a means for better understanding the phenomenon of interest—in this case, organizations. Better understanding may, in turn, lead to better management. On the other hand, ***prescriptive*** or ***normative theory*** specifically suggests how things should be or what can be done about conditions identified by descriptive theory. Prescriptive theory informs managers about what they should do. The *should* in prescriptive theory is typically directed at improving various aspects of the organization: efficiency, competitiveness, profitability, adaptability, work satisfaction, or other aspects of general effectiveness. Although debate has raged about the relative merits of each approach, a general knowledge of both is necessary for us to understand organizations and how they work. We balance our approach to organization theory between descriptive and prescriptive theories. However, because this book is aimed at future managers in organizations, we concentrate on prescriptive or normative theories that suggest what managers *can* do.

A BRIEF HISTORY OF ORGANIZATION THEORY

In this section we briefly trace the development of organization theory in order to appreciate the present state of knowledge of organizations. Although we stress organization theory in this discussion, there is some overlap with the evolution of management study. Many concepts of organization are traceable to antiquity. There is mention of organizations and organizing in ancient China and Greece. There are even references to division of labor and delegation in the Old Testament. However, modern organizations and the systematic study of them really began with the Industrial Revolution.

Division of Labor

As we noted earlier in this chapter, one of the first contributors to what is now known as organization theory was the economist Adam Smith (1723–1790), who demonstrated the greater efficiency that could be gained through division and specialization of labor. Through specialization and division of labor among ten people, a shop could produce as many as 48,000 pins per day.[11] This work laid the foundation for later organizational and industrial theorists such as Max Weber and Frederick Taylor who advocated narrowing the scope of workers' jobs so that specialization could be developed and efficiency enhanced.

Weber and the Rules of Bureaucracy

The German sociologist Max Weber (1864–1920) was arguably the most influential early contributor to the theory of organizations. His monumental work presented bureaucracy as the ideal form of organization. It was common in the 1800s for organizations to be simply extensions of families. Hiring and promotions were typically based on favoritism. Subjectivity took precedence over objectivity. As organizations grew larger during the Industrial Revolution, the inefficiencies of the typical organization of the day became apparent. The bureaucracy, proposed by Weber as a rational, efficient alternative, included the following characteristics:

- Division of labor was arranged so that each worker's authority and responsibility were clearly defined and were legitimate, official responsibilities.
- Positions or offices were organized in a hierarchy of authority that established a clear chain of command.
- Personnel were selected based on technical competence as established by examination, training, or education.
- Individual performance was guided by strict rules, discipline, and controls. These rules were impersonal and uniformly applied. A system of written documentation was used to record the rules and compliance with them.
- Administrative officials were not owners of the means of production. Equipment and privileges belonged to the position or office, not the person holding the position or office.
- Administrators were career officials and worked for a fixed salary.[12]

Although Weber's contributions to organization theory were immense, they went almost unnoticed in the United States until 1940. When the search for explanations of how large organizations work began in earnest, attention focused on Weber and his work.[13]

The Classical School

The organizational and management writers grouped under this common heading look at organizational issues from two different directions. Frederick W. Taylor focused on rationalizing jobs beginning at the lowest levels of the organization. Henri Fayol, on the other hand, focused on providing a rational model for top management of an organization. Their approaches have two things in common: (1) they proposed *one best way to manage* and (2) they attempted to develop *rational* techniques that would help in building the structure and processes necessary to coordinate action in an organization.

Today, readers of Taylor's ***Principles of Scientific Management*** may think of them as dehumanizing and exploitative of workers. That was not at all his intent. Taylor and his followers believed that the key to efficient management and positive labor relations was the scientific study of jobs performed by workers to discover wasteful steps. Furthermore, Taylor sought to simplify tasks so that workers could be easily trained to master their jobs. He believed that workers were primarily motivated by money and that, if they were narrowly specialized and had simple, narrowly defined jobs, they would be better able to pursue monetary reward. Taylor also believed that management could maximize its return on labor through his system of scientific management because of its emphasis on efficiency. Like Weber's emphasis on competence, Taylor advocated an objective system that rewarded productive labor.

At about the same time that Taylor and his followers were developing principles of scientific management, Henri Fayol was beginning his study of organizations in France. Unlike Taylor, Fayol concentrated his efforts on explaining the workings of the administrative levels of organizations. He maintained that it was possible to develop a set of universally applicable principles (i.e., one best way) that could be used to improve management practices.

According to Fayol, two management functions, ***coordination*** and ***specialization,*** are critically important.* Some disagreement exists about the exact number of principles that Fayol and his colleagues proposed as instruments for coordination and control. It is generally agreed that coordination is achieved through adherence to four of Fayol's principles. First, the ***scalar principle*** stated that coordination would be aided by a hierarchial distribution of authority in organization. Authority and control in an organization should be distributed in a pyramid-like structure. Second, the principle of ***unity of command*** stated that workers should only have to respond to one superior. Having to respond to more than one superior would be confusing and a potential source of conflict. Third, significant attention was focused on ***span of control,*** identifying the optimal number of subordinates that a supervisor could efficiently and effectively supervise. Fourth, the ***exceptions principle*** stated that routine events or issues should be handled by lower-level employees. This would allow top administrators to deal with unusual problems or exceptions.

Specialization, the second management function, was achieved by virtue of how departments were formed and jobs were grouped. The ***departmentalization principle*** stated that similar tasks or functions should be grouped within the same department or unit. Fayol was also responsible for differentiating between ***line*** and ***staff functions,*** another form of specialization. Line functions are those that contribute directly to the pursuit of primary organizational goals. Support activities (e.g., legal departments, information systems departments) are staff functions. According to Fayol, because staff functions are peripheral to the organization's primary goals, they should be subordinated within the organization's scalar authority structure.

Emphasis on a rational authority structure for organizations and attempts to devise a single best way to manage eventually led to the demise of the classical theorists. First, a number of researchers in what has been labeled the Human Relations School began examining the social or human aspects of organizations and shifted the focus from normative (what they thought organizations should be) to descriptive (what organizations really were like). They also began focusing on worker satisfaction, believing that the key to organizational effectiveness was a satisfied workforce. Second, contingency theorists, who viewed organizations as open systems, began to see that variations in the organizational context (i.e., variations in environment, size, and technology) would require variations in both structure and management practice.

The Human Relations School

The human relations approach to organizations explored the role of groups and social processes in organizations. Although several researchers have contributed to this perspective, perhaps the most notable works are the Hawthorne studies at Western Electric by Roethlisberger and Dickson[14] and works by Elton Mayo.[15] These studies questioned the rational, efficiency-oriented scientific management views of work. Rather, these researchers found that group interactions and social climate were also important to job performance. Other works of note in this school include Chester Barnard's book *The Functions of the Executive*[16] and Douglas McGregor's book *The Human Side of Enterprise.*[17] One point that these works emphasized was that the focus on efficiency may have been somewhat misdirected. In general, these works contested the idea that organizations were machine-like entities. They emphasized that organiza-

---

*This interpretation is based largely on Scott's (1992) writings on Fayol.

tions were composed of people who had roles and responsibilities beyond their work organizations. Moreover, within organizations, people had multiple and sometimes conflicting roles and objectives. While the classical theorist viewed organizations as well-oiled machines, the human relations theorist viewed organizations as shifting coalitions of people with multiple and divergent needs. According to the Human Relations School, there is more to organizational effectiveness, as we will see in Chapter 3, than efficiency.

Contemporary theorists who have adopted aspects of the Human Relations School emphasize such features as informal structure, power, and political behavior in organizations (Chapter 12), and organizational culture (Chapter 10). The human relations perspective augments our investigation of numerous issues throughout the text.

The Contingency School

As its name implies, the Contingency School maintains that relationships among organizational characteristics, especially the relationships between structure and size and technology and environment, are contingent or dependent on the situation or context. Contingency theorists reject the one-best-way model of organizing proposed by earlier theorists. Thus, theorists and managers must understand the organization's context in order to prescribe the appropriate structure. The works of contingency theorists have a decidedly rational overtone and have resulted in extensive investigations of organizational technology (the work process), the external environment, goals, organizational size, and how these contextual factors are related to organizational structure. The basic premise of contingency theories is that different structural configurations are appropriate for different contextual conditions. As interpreted by managers, contingency theory suggests that they should attempt to assess the contextual conditions and select the appropriate structure and design for the organization. However, as we will see, the world of organizations is complex and uncertain. Selecting the appropriate structure and design may be much more difficult and problematic than contingency theorists indicate.

Although several contemporary approaches to organizational theory dispute many contingency theory propositions and the research support for their assertions is only modest, contingency theory has played a dominant role in organization theory in recent years. This perspective will guide much of our early discussion of environment, goals, technology, size, and structure. We will point out contradictions and differing perspectives throughout the chapters and use contingency theory as a jumping off point to explore alternative viewpoints of organizations.

CONTEMPORARY PERSPECTIVES

Recently, several new ways of viewing organizations have emerged. Some of these approaches have tried to deal with the shortcomings of contingency theory, while others take different views of organizations. Four of the more widely studied perspectives are organizational economics approaches, institutional theory, ecological perspectives, and holistic or cultural views of organizations.

Organizational Economics

Two theories based in industrial and organizational economics are transaction cost economics[18] and agency theory.[19] Although subtle differences distinguish these two approaches, their central focus is similar. Both view organizations as bundles of transactions or contracts binding workers and owners together. According to agency theory, the primary interests of owners (called *principals*) and workers (called *agents*) are essentially different. Owners seek to maximize their return on investment by the most efficient use of the organization (including the workers). Agents, on the other hand, seek to minimize their efforts and maximize their remuneration. To protect their interests, principals will use various forms of contracts and organizing to ensure that agents carry out their jobs.

Transaction cost economics explores transactions that take place both inside and outside the organization. These include transactions between owners and managers, managers and subordinates, suppliers and producers, and sellers and buyers. Both agency and transaction cost perspectives view the primary reason for organizing as being the reduction of uncertainty that exists in typical transactions. Agency and transaction cost theorists believe that it is human nature to act in a selfish and opportunistic fashion. Accordingly, the primary task of managers and owners of organizations is to create structure to ensure that others (e.g., employees, customers, or suppliers) do not act selfishly and opportunistically. We examine transaction and agency ideas at several points throughout the text.

Institutional Theory

The perspectives presented up to this point have been infused with nearly machinelike, rational interpretations of organizations. Alternative views have emerged that treat organizations as complex groupings of sometimes conflicting rules, goals, and behaviors. Institutional theorists argue that social reality is constructed by organizational members. "The process by which actions are repeated and given meaning . . . is defined as institutionalization."[20] Institutional theory approaches to organizations emphasize the similarities among organizations. Rather than proceeding through a detailed rational assessment of a problem, organizational members bend to social pressures to conform to conventional or *institutionalized* beliefs. The result is that managers tend to imitate past practices and practices of other successful organizations.[21] We turn to the institutional perspective periodically to help explain certain seemingly nonrational actions of organizations.

Cultural Perspectives

The cultural perspective is, in many ways, an extension of the institutional perspective. Most other theories of organizations make many rational and simplifying assumptions about organizations. We assume that the formally structured organization that managers create *is* the organization. Additionally, many of those perspectives take a *reductionist* view of organizations. That is, they focus on only small portions of the organization at any given time. Contingency theorists largely direct attention to structure, environment, technology, and size. Organizational economics attends to transactions or contracts. Cultural approaches differ in that they are concerned with the whole organization and with informal aspects of the organization.[22] The culture is the result of organizational ideologies that produce people's norms, values, and beliefs. It is these norms, values, and beliefs that energize and direct people's actions within the organization and that provide a rationale for those actions. However, the cultural perspective differs from the institutional perspective in that it emphasizes how different and unique organizations are. We delve into the topic of culture in greater depth in Chapter 10.

Ecological Perspectives

Up to this point, we have examined individual organizations. Two perspectives, community ecology[23] and population ecology,[24] look at groups of organizations. Community ecology approaches to organizations assume that groups of organizations can work together to control uncertainty in their environments. For example, groups of retailers or manufacturers can present a united front and influence government intervention through lobbying. Industry associations can reduce uncertainty by setting specific standards. In Chapter 5 we explore numerous other ways that organizations can attempt to control their environments through joint efforts.

Population ecologists suggest that these efforts to control environmental uncertainty may be either ineffective or deal with the wrong elements of the environment. This perspective simply states that organizations cannot, in general, determine all of the important environmental threats that need to be managed. Instead, it is the environment that selects which types of organizations will persist in the long run. Thus, population ecology focuses on organizational births and deaths. We explore this controversial view of organizations and environments in more detail in Chapter 5.

ORGANIZATION THEORY, THE MANAGER, AND THE FUTURE

From the discussion thus far we can see how organization theory has evolved through the various schools of thought and that there is still potential for controversy about which ideas from these schools serve today's manager best. Then there is the question of why organization theory itself should be included on a manager's agenda in the first place. Perhaps a brief listing of some of the issues facing today's manager and what can be expected in the future can help remove these reservations.

Managers in today's organizations are facing a vast array of highly complex problems and issues that were not on their predecessors' agenda. A brief glance at a newspaper, a magazine, or a snippet of nightly television news programs will give the reader/viewer a sense of the enormity of daily challenges. Headlines and "lead-ins" seemingly deal routinely with Middle Eastern oil issues, conflicts in that region, a turbulent global economy that can seem rudderless at times, mergers between economic giants, and the failures so prevalent among Internet companies that once appeared so promising. Even political controversy affects all manners of choices and organization life. These events have caused governmental intervention (as in the cases of Microsoft and Napster), a host of lawsuits (as in the case of tobacco companies), and civil rights demonstrations (as in the case of the 2000 presidential election in Florida).

Managers are faced with the necessity to retrench, restructure, and streamline organizations (and even change their missions in some cases) in response to these and other perhaps equally powerful environmental forces if they and their organizations are to survive. It is axiomatic that these managers must make difficult choices in their attempts to satisfy various organization constituencies, each with a desire for immediate results. It is obviously easy to see the necessity for these choices to be consistent with one another, to reflect organization values, and provide the guidelines for future choices that will doubtless have to be made in conditions that will likely remain turbulent and uncertain.

It is thus a given condition that management choices be based on a set of ideas, principles, and concepts that can form a tight-knit decision framework. Unless managers truly understand their organizations and how they work in today's global environment, chances are good that their choices will not fit the requirements just mentioned. Armed with an understanding of organizations and how they work, however, managers can at least appreciate the need for good, consistent, integrating decisions. That's what organization theory can provide.

By adopting the concepts of a strategic explanation of organizations and how they work, managers not only can understand but can also significantly influence the direction and force of their organizations. This is true of all types of organizations, from large conglomerates, to governmental agencies, to military operations, to the mom-and-pop farm. No organization and its managers are immune to the host of environmental forces prevalent today; everyone is affected, either directly or indirectly.

This book is devoted to an explanation of organization concepts that, we believe, can provide the conceptual framework to support the type of quality decisions managers must make in the unprecedented conditions of today that will likely prevail in at least the foreseeable future. So an understanding of past efforts to explain organization behavior can set the stage for not only dealing with present decision issues, but for also preparing the manager to appreciate the future and how it can affect today's and tomorrow's organization choices that will be made in ever-more complex organizations that must learn from and adjust to their environments.

Questions for Discussion

1. How do you think a thorough knowledge of organization theory would help today's managers do a better job? Would this information be of most benefit to lower, middle, or top management? Why? What is the value to you of studying organization theory?

2. The subject of this book is organization *theory*. What do you think should be the relationship between theory and managerial practice (what managers do)?

3. Why is it useful to think of organizations as systems? What is the basic difference between an open systems and closed systems view of organizations? Why is it that organizations must be viewed as open systems?

4. Why is a sense of history important to the study of any field? How can understanding the historical development of organization theory help you better understand organizations and organization theory?

5. In this chapter we list five challenges to today's organizations. Select one of these challenges, and find an example of this challenge in the business press (i.e., *Fortune, Business Week, Forbes, The Wall Street Journal,* etc.). Explain how organization theory can help you better understand this issue.

References

1. Tom Peters, *Thriving on Chaos* (New York: Alfred A. Knopf, 1987).

2. Daniel Katz and Robert L. Kahn, *The Social Psychology of Organizations,* 2nd ed. (New York: John Wiley & Sons, 1978).

3. Adam Smith, *Selections From the Wealth of Nations,* ed. by George J. Stigler (New York: Appleton-Century-Crofts, 1957).

4. W. Richard Scott, *Organizations: Rational, Natural, and Open Systems,* 3rd ed. (Upper Saddle River, NJ: Prentice Hall, 1992).

5. Oliver Williamson, "The Economics of Organizations: The Transaction Cost Approach," *American Journal of Sociology* 87 (1981): 548–77.

6. See note 2; See note 4.

7. J. Stacey Adams, "The Structure and Dynamics of Behavior in Organizational Boundary Roles," in *Handbook of Industrial and Organizational Psychology,* ed. by M. D. Dunnette (Chicago: Rand McNally, 1976), 1175–99.

8. Tom Burns and George M. Stalker, *The Management of Innovation* (London: Tavistock, 1961); Joan

Woodward, *Management and Technology* (London: H.M.S.O., 1958). Paul R. Lawrence and Jay W. Lorsch, *Organization and Environment: Managing Differentiation and Integration* (Boston: Graduate School of Business Administration, Harvard University, 1967). Michael L. Tushman and David A. Nadler, "Information Processing as an Integrating Concept in Organizational Design," *Academy of Management Review* 3 (1978): 613–24.

9. H. M. Blaylock, *Theory Building* (Upper Saddle River, NJ: Prentice Hall, 1971).

10. Arthur G. Bedeian and Raymond F. Zammuto, *Organizations: Theory and Design* (Chicago: The Dryden Press, 1991).

11. See note 3. Adam Smith, *An Inquiry into the Nature and Causes of the Wealth of Nations,* vol. 39 of *Great Books of the Western World* (1776; reprint, Chicago: Encyclopaedia Britannica, 1952). See note 4.

12. A. M. Henderson and Talcott Parsons, eds. and trans., *Max Weber: The Theory of Social and Economic Organization* (New York: Free Press, 1947). See note 4.

13. Daniel A. Wren, *The Evolution of Management Thought* (New York: Ronald Press, 1972), 230.

14. F. J. Roethlisberger and William J. Dickson, *Management and the Worker* (Cambridge, MA: Harvard University Press, 1939).

15. Elton Mayo, *The Social Problems of an Industrial Civilization* (Boston: Graduate School of Business Administration, Harvard University, 1945).

16. Chester Barnard, *The Functions of the Executive* (Cambridge, MA: Harvard University Press, 1958).

17. Douglas McGregor, *The Human Side of Enterprise* (New York: McGraw-Hill, 1960).

18. See note 5. William Ouchi, "Markets, Bureaucracies and Clans," *Administrative Science Quarterly* 25 (1980): 129–41.

19. Eugene Fama, "Agency Problems and the Theory of the Firm," *The Journal of Political Economy* 88 (1980): 288–307.

20. See note 4.

21. Walter W. Powell and Paul DiMaggio, eds., *The New Institutionalism in Organizational Analysis* (Chicago: University of Chicago Press, 1991). Lynne G. Zucker, *Institutional Patterns and Organizations: Culture and Environments* (Cambridge, MA: Ballinger, 1988).

22. Linda Smircich, "Concepts of Culture and Organizational Analysis," *Administrative Science Quarterly* 28 (1983): 339–58. Harrison M. Trist and Janice M. Beyer, *The Cultures of Work Organizations* (Upper Saddle River, NJ: Prentice Hall, 1993). Joanne Martin, *Cultures in Organizations: Three Perspectives* (New York: Oxford University Press, 1992).

23. W. Graham Astley, "The Two Ecologies: Population and Community Perspectives on Organizational Evolution," *Administrative Science Quarterly* 30 (1985): 224–41. W. Graham Astley and Andrew H. Van de Ven, "Central Perspectives and Debates in Organizational Theory," *Administrative Science Quarterly* 28 (1983): 245–73.

24. Howard E. Aldrich, *Organizations and Environments* (Upper Saddle River, NJ: Prentice Hall, 1979). Michael T. Hannan and John Freeman, "The Population Ecology of Organizations," *American Sociological Review* 82 (1977): 929–64.

*Hot Doughnuts Now**

For more than 60 years, Krispy Kreme doughnut shops have announced to their customers that a fresh batch of doughnuts was on the way by flashing a red neon sign that reads "Hot Doughnuts Now." This sign signals that these deep-fried delicious morsels are coming down the conveyor belt and are ready for the sugar coating that gives them the name, Krispy Kreme. Watching for this sign to be lit and queuing up to begin to enjoy the inviting taste of these "Kremey" goodies has become a sort of southern "tradition."

It all began in 1933 when Vernon Rudolph, the company's founder, bought the assets of a French chef in Paducah, Kentucky, and opened a doughnut shop that would be the first Krispy Kreme shop. After only a short time, however, Rudolph decided that this market was too limited, and he moved his operations to Nashville, Tennessee, in search of more customers while other family members opened shops in Charleston, West Virginia, and Atlanta, Georgia. After a short time selling his doughnuts to local grocery stores, Rudolph decided to look for "sweeter pastures" and packed up his doughnut-making equipment, his secret recipe, and the name "Krispy Kreme Doughnuts" and began his search.

Rudolph finally decided on Winston Salem, North Carolina, which was then beginning to find its place as an economic force in the Southeast. Although its base was primarily textiles and tobacco, Rudolph thought there was room there for doughnuts, too, and he guessed right. He and two partners, whom he brought with him from Nashville, used their last $25 to rent a building in the historic district of Old Salem. With a loan from a local grocer, the three purchased the ingredients and began to make and deliver doughnuts in Rudolph's old car, from which he removed the back seat to make room for the doughnut racks. This was in 1937, and the business was about to begin flourishing as word about Krispy Kremes spread throughout the community.

Recognizing the potential market for "hot" doughnuts, Rudolph decided to open a shop to meet what he saw as a "drive-through" demand. He cut a hole in the wall of the shop and began selling his doughnuts to customers who were glad to get them fresh from the fryer. This was the beginning of the service window that marks all Krispy Kreme shops. Believing that there was a demand for other varieties, Rudolph soon introduced cake doughnuts, cinnamon buns, jelly-filled doughnuts, and 20 related items that are now available at all shops.

Now Krispy Kreme is going national. After years of success as a regional chain, the company has decided to expand its operations from Key West to Alaska. In keeping with this strategic decision, the company has issued an initial public offering (IPO) that raised $75 million for operations and expansion. It also entered into agreements with well-known leaders in the restaurant business as well as with KreMaritta, which is associated with Jimmy Buffett and is a part of his Margaritaville Holdings. These moves are calculated to at least double the 150 or so outlets by 2005.

In selecting its developers, the company sought out respected members of the restaurant industry who had extensive operating experience as well as a thorough understanding of the brand and product. As a result, these developers have successfully opened stores in Chicago, Las Vegas, Detroit, Houston, the Pacific Northwest as well as two kiosks in Manhattan. These developers, in turn, have entered into arrangements with others to continue the expansion program.

Scott Livengood, who is president of Krispy Kreme, appears to be delighted at the rate of growth and success of the expansion program. He believes that the experience, entrepreneurship, and organizational infrastructure brought by these new developers are the foundation of a solid program to bring Krispy Kreme to a larger part of the American market. It seems that a lot of folks have a sweet tooth for doughnuts, especially if they're hot.

Local competition thus appears to be facing a potent new force in the doughnut market. Supermarkets that once made and sold their own doughnuts are now not only seeing increased competition from Krispy Kreme but, in some cases, have ceased making doughnuts and are, instead, stocking Krispy Kreme. This apparently is being done not only in the name of cost saving but also to capitalize on Krispy Kreme's growing fame as the doughnut maker of choice among today's consumers who have come to expect familiarity with products they buy. Now not only do they expect to find the same quality, product, and service with their burgers, they can also expect to find the same in their doughnuts, wherever Krispy Kremes are sold, and the area is getting bigger by the day.

Soon the sign, "Hot Doughnuts Now," might beckon from a Krispy Kreme near you and you will be able to indulge yourself in a little bit of doughnut delight while you enjoy watching the doughnuts being made in the doughnut theater where the entire production process is visible. This unique experience will only add to the overall mystique that is Krispy Kreme. ∎

*This case is based on information contained on the following Web sites: www.krispykreme.com and www.findarticles.com.

QUESTIONS FOR DISCUSSION

1. How do you think changing food preferences and perceptions can affect Krispy Kreme's growth plans? How might the company deal with these changes?

2. Some directors and officers have a financial interest in some franchises. Do you see any ethical/moral issues with this arrangement? Explain.

3. Krispy Kreme faces competition from other doughnut retailers, fast food restaurants, coffee shops, grocery stores, and others. What are some unique ways you would suggest for dealing with this competition, which is likely to intensify? How can a knowledge of organization theory help with this problem?

4. The company's growth plans appear to depend heavily on opening new stores, but factors beyond its control can influence this strategy's success. What might some of these factors be, and how can a knowledge of organization theory help deal with this potential problem?

CHAPTER 2

Structure and Design — Basic Organizational Building Blocks

CASE: A LIMITED VIEW*

At one time, The Limited was a leader in fashion retailing. For a company with once what appeared to be a limitless future, The Limited saw a change in its fortunes during the mid 1990s. The trouble, perhaps, could be traced to founder Leslie Wexner's almost unbridled belief in entrepreneurship. Thus, the situation of the country's largest specialty store conglomerate was a surprise to Wexner. Although there were many reasons for The Limited's difficulty, including a general sluggishness in the whole fashion industry, some of the problems could be traced to the company's structure.

Wexner believed that all of The Limited's division managers should operate their divisions virtually free of interference — their only guideline was to see how quickly they could get their respective divisions to the $1 billion mark in sales. However, this simple guideline provided the platform for infighting among the divisions. Falling sales figures in all the divisions indicated that managers had lost sight of changing customer needs and habits. Wexner admits that his "hands-off" philosophy is largely to blame, and he acknowledges that his penchant for decentralization and freedom for his managers resulted in too little support from the top. So in order to reshape the organization, he instituted monthly meetings in which his division heads can share problems, solutions, and ideas in general. This was done so that the once completely autonomous divisions could begin to build a general consensus and appreciation for the company as a whole.

Although this new approach took some getting used to, a concern seemed to be developing for a holistic approach to managing the entire company instead of allowing each division head to run his or her division somewhat in isolation. At the center of this attempt to broaden management's perspective was the return to defining clearly who the customer is and to building a total marketing approach suitable not only for the whole company but for each division. In the late 1990s, The Limited reappraised its activities, resulting in a reduction from 12 retail businesses to the 5 that include Express, Lerner New York, Lane Bryant, Structure, and The Limited.

Previous success had dulled management's view of their customers and of what they looked for in a store. Customers, now older, more affluent, and perhaps more sophisticated, were turning to other outlets for quality and fashion. By the mid 1990s, even the look of the stores seemed out of date. This was especially the case with The Limited stores division.

---

*This case is largely based on the following articles: Susan Caminiti, "Can The Limited Fix Itself?" *Fortune* (October 17, 1994): 161–162, 166, 168, 170, and 172; Laura Bird, "Limited Considers Splitting Operations into Two Publicly Traded Companies," *Wall Street Journal* (March 29, 1995), A3; "World-classretailer — America's best-kept secret," *Retail Week* (August 4, 2000), 14; Ann Tsao, "The Limited Puts Structure on the Express Track," BusinessWeek Online (March 23, 2001), Retrieved May 23, 2001, from the World Wide Web: www.businessweek.com/investor/content/mar2001/pi20010323_099.htm; Kelly Barron, "Limited Expectations," *Forbes* (March 5, 2001): 145–146; "Limited to Sell Lane Bryant," *Stores* (April 2001): 18; Debbie Gebolys, "Economy Blamed for Limited Slump," *Columbus Dispatch* (May 22, 2001), C1.

At the same time, the chic sportswear division, Express, was also having problems staying focused on its customers. Instead of its original emphasis on young fashion, Express turned its attention to designer clothes for older customers with similar disappointing results. Now Express has returned to young sporty merchandise and has emerged as The Limited's most successful division.

Wexner launched a 5-year reorganization of The Limited which involved the centralization of operations, installation of new executives, elevation of performance goals, and closing or spinning off of chains (creating Intimate Brands in 1995, which includes Bath & Body Works, White Barn Candle Co., and Victoria's Secret). By the year 2000, The Limited seemed to be well on the way to making a successful comeback.

Wexner initially developed strategies for reorganization by looking outside the retail field to see whether he could transplant ideas from the industrial world into his struggling retail giant. He visited General Electric's Jack Welch and Pepsi's Wayne Galloway to learn how these proven leaders of huge nonretail organizations operate. Their approach to decentralization might possibly fit (or be made to fit) The Limited's vast organization.

From these visits Wexner brought back the idea of putting more structure into finance meetings, for example, establishing a more or less standard way to present findings and to review results. This plan for working as a group in a structured way rather than as a loose collection of independent managers has taken hold in The Limited. The basic approach has been to get managers to think brandwide instead of in terms of private labels. This strategy would give management a broader, more integrated way to manage.

Computer analyses have helped improve the methodology for marketing goods. These analyses center on the coordination of ordering, production, and sales efforts, a condition not previously possible. The rush to move managers around different divisions of the company (sort of robbing Peter to pay Paul) has slowed. That practice had resulted in management voids or talent gaps in divisions throughout the company.

Wexner's reorganization of The Limited has refocused the company as having a core base in fashion and clothing, yet in this realm the company continues to struggle. After reporting disappointing results at the end of 2000, the company has recently announced plans to sell Lane Bryant, its plus-size women's apparel division. It also plans to relaunch its ailing men's clothing division, Structure, under its most successful chain, Express. Some attribute The Limited's troubles to an industrywide slowdown as a result of the recent recession in the American marketplace. Others believe the company cannot fully recover from the mid 1990s when it became too vast with its many acquisitions. As Kelly Barron described it, "[The] Limited grew to be too many different things, no one of them particularly special." Whatever happens, the look of The Limited (and we are not just talking about clothing styles) is likely to continue changing into the future.

This case points out some of the difficulties faced by a large and complex organization as it attempts to deal with changing customer demographics and a dynamic environment. It highlights the role of organization structure, differentiation, integration, and the necessity for adaptation, all concepts discussed in Chapter 2. Keep The Limited organization in mind as you read the chapter and see whether the contents of the chapter help you understand the importance of structure and design as basic organizational building blocks.

THE NATURE OF STRUCTURE AND DESIGN

As we stated in the first chapter, one of the first consequences of organizing is the need to divide labor and then coordinate the diverse departments, work units, or groups that have been created. Some theorists suggest that structure results from choices about technology;[1] others suggest that structure is developed in reponse to environmental conditions that the organization faces;[2] still others say that structure is the result of specific strategies (i.e., goals) that the organization seeks to pursue.[3] Whichever view one subscribes to, the first step is to understand the concept of structure and the elements of which it is composed.

The division of labor and subsequent coordination involve both the structure and design of the organization. Although these two terms—*structure* and *design*—are widely used in the organization theory literature, there is a lack of consistency and clarity in how they are used. When we speak of structure we are referring to the sum total of the ways in which an organization divides its labor into distinct tasks and then coordinates them.[4] Some theorists also refer to structure as the arrangement of roles (i.e., jobs) within the organization. The arrangement of roles is consistent with the division of labor and coordination. The design of an organization can have two meanings because the word can be used as a noun describing the appearance of the organization or as a verb describing the process of setting up (i.e., designing) or changing (i.e., redesigning) the organization.[5] In this chapter our primary focus will be on the appearance of the organization. We return to design configurations once again in Chapter 8.

DEFINITION

Structure refers to the sum total of the ways in which an organization divides its labor into distinct tasks and then coordinates them.

Structure Versus Design

The concepts of structure and design are closely related. Some confusion exists in the literature on the topic, and the terms are often used interchangeably. The definition of structure recognizes two key elements: differentiation and integration. Differentiation involves breaking up the work to be done into an array of tasks. Integration refers to the necessary coordination among these various tasks to ensure that the overall goals of the organization are achieved. The structure of the organization is usually depicted through the formal organizational chart. This chart displays the authority relationships (who reports to whom, or the chain of command); formal communication channels; formal work groups, departments, or divisions; and formal lines of accountability.

Organization design, on the other hand, is a broader concept that includes structure but also encompasses other concepts. Design parameters include such things as unit grouping, unit size, planning and control systems, behavioral formalization (rules, policies, and procedures), decision-making and centralization-decentralization issues.[6] Thus, design is an umbrella concept that includes both process and structural issues. Think of structure as the skeleton. It is the framework to which muscles, nerves, blood vessels, and other components are attached. These items make the structure come alive.

Formal Versus Informal Organization

In examining organization structure and design, we often speak of the formal organization. Organizations create an officially sanctioned structure known as the formal organization or de jure organization. This is the organization as it is depicted by a formal organizational chart as shown in Figure 2-1. The lines that connect each point on the chart show the authority or reporting relationships that exist in the organization. Typically, each point represents a position in the organization occupied by one person. For the sake of economy, a point may be used to represent an entire unit or department. Also, not all subordinate positions in the organization are shown. In Figure 2-1, for example, each department head would have a similar complement of supervisors as those shown, and each supervisor would have a number of subordinates. Each horizontal level of points in the chart represents a level of authority in the organization. All the department heads in this example would have essentially the same level of authority.

A formal organizational chart presents the official structure explicitly authorized by the organization. The official structure is made of the officially designated roles and relationships that exist independently of the individual person who occupies the role or the people who form relationships. This is only half the story, for superimposed on these relationships are informal or de facto relationships that are not necessarily sanctioned by the organization although they might be perceived to actually exist (see Figure 2-2). In the informal structure it is impossible to separate the roles and relationships from the people. Personal characteristics and patterns of social relationships that may not be captured in the formal structure are ever present and important to the informal structure.[7] The informal organization is a result of the political nature of organizations and evolves

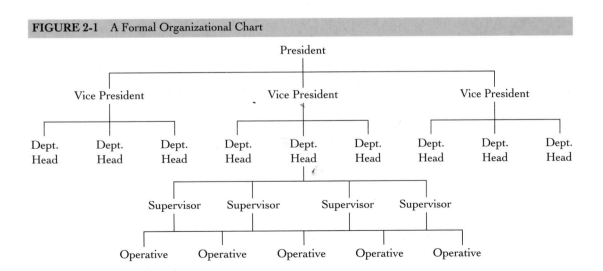

FIGURE 2-1   A Formal Organizational Chart

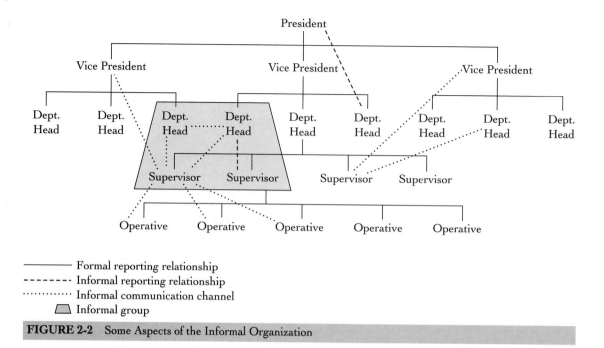

Formal reporting relationship
- - - - - Informal reporting relationship
· · · · · · · · Informal communication channel
Informal group

FIGURE 2-2 Some Aspects of the Informal Organization

from the people working there rather than from being officially established. This informal organization usually comes about, in part, because of flaws, vagueness, incompleteness, or inefficiencies in the formal design, or because of changes in conditions the organization faces. The focus in this chapter is on the formally established organization. In Chapter 12 we shift the focus to the political nature of organizations and examine the informal organization.

DIFFERENTIATION AND INTEGRATION: KEY ELEMENTS OF STRUCTURE

As noted in Chapter 1, the very reason for organizations to exist is so they can perform tasks more effectively and efficiently than individuals working alone. All organizations must split up their work into units called tasks. This division of labor into tasks is called differentiation. In most organizations today it is physically impossible and economically infeasible for one individual to do all the tasks. To carry out its mission more efficiently, an organization will divide its work into many tasks and allocate those tasks among workers. In this way workers can specialize in their more narrowly and specifically designated task. For example, a large corporation like General Motors has differentiated tasks so that assembly people build cars; clerical workers do typing and filing; managers manage; lawyers write contracts and represent the company in legal proceedings; and top management sets the strategic direction for the firm. Within each of these groupings, tasks are further differentiated. At an assembly facility, some workers may be responsible for only narrow portions of the assembly process—for example, attaching wheels, wiring engines, or painting the cars. In fact, one of the key issues facing many organizations, including automakers, is how much tasks should be differentiated.

Just as organizations split up work, they must also coordinate this work. This coordination is called integration.* Basically, integration involves the various means that organizations use to pull together the highly differentiated tasks into cohesive output.

As we will see in subsequent sections, differentiation and integration are key elements of organizational structure. The degree of differentiation and the methods of integration provide great insight into the structure of an organization.

Nature and Process of Differentiation

Three basic types of differentiation occur in organizations. Organizations can be subdivided horizontally into an increasing number of distinct positions at the same level, vertically into increasing levels of hierarchy, and spatially by increasing numbers of distinct locations dispersed in space.[8] Although we did not use the term *differentiation* in the discussion of bureaucracies in Chapter 1, the narrowly defined tasks and narrowly defined areas of decision-making responsibility that are key components of bureaucratic organizations are prime examples of horizontal and vertical differentiation.

Horizontal differentiation refers to the division of work to be done into tasks and subtasks at the same organizational level. Horizontal differentiation is represented by the number of different individuals or units at the same level of an organization. One group of researchers refers to horizontal differentiation as the degree of occupational specialization, the specific professional activity, and the professional training required for specific tasks.[9] Thus, with increasing task specialization, increasingly specific professional credentials or certification, and increasingly focused training, we will see increasingly high levels of horizontal differentiation. In fact, some authors have used the term *specialization* instead of horizontal differentiation to describe this dimension of structure.[10] Figure 2-3 illustrates horizontal differentiation.

A modern hospital provides an excellent example of an organization that incorporates each of these aspects of horizontal differentiation. Among doctors and medical support personnel there is a high degree of specialization: cardiologists, gastroenterologists, orthopedists, X-ray technicians, critical care nurses, lab technicians, and so on. Each of these task areas is specifically described and each is distinct from the other. Each area requires specific training, and each requires certification and credentials for the individual practitioner.

The horizontal division often represents a strategic decision on the part of the organization. For example, the division of a college into separate departments may be done to provide the college with greater specialized expertise or greater flexibility. Some colleges of business may divide the task of educating students into the following highly differentiated departments: management, operations management, accounting, finance, marketing, information systems, and quantitative analysis. Management faculty

---

*Sometimes the same or similar terms in the organizational literature are used to express more than one idea. Integration is one such term. In the present context, the term is used to describe methods or structures used to coordinate tasks. Integration, particularly vertical, horizontal, backward, and forward, is also used to describe a firm's entry into different parts of the value-added chain of resource acquisition, production, distribution, and sales. For example, an automobile manufacturer that enters the steel fabrication business in order to supply its manufacturing facilities is involved in backward integration. A developer and distributor of shoes, such as Nike, that enters the retail business is said to be involved in forward integration. Finally, a manufacturer that adds more products to its line is involved in horizontal integration, also known as diversification. For example, Johnson & Johnson's acquisition of Neutrogena diversifies Johnson & Johnson into new areas of soap and beauty products. When discussing this type of integration, we will always use the terms *backward, forward,* or *horizontal integration,* or *diversification.* We take up these strategies in detail in Chapter 5.

Low Horizontal Complexity

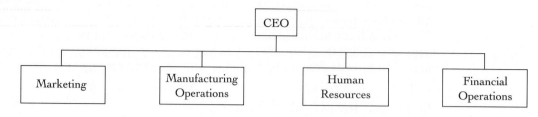

High Horizontal Complexity

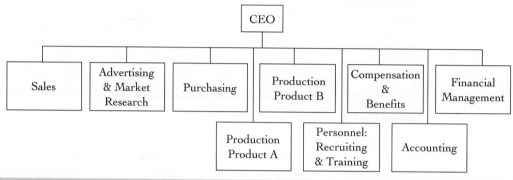

FIGURE 2-3 Horizontal Differentiation

would only teach management courses; accounting faculty would only teach accounting; and so forth. Each department would be narrowly specialized, a structure that should lead to high levels of specific expertise in the narrow field. Another college may decide to divide the task more broadly into the following set of departments: organizational and operations management, accounting and financial systems, and marketing. In the more broadly defined departmental arrangement, faculty would teach a wide range of courses. For example, in the combined accounting and financial systems department, a given faculty member may teach both financial accounting and finance courses. The broader task groupings may involve less specific expertise in a narrowly defined field, but such groupings would allow the departments to be more flexible and responsive to changing conditions. A sudden increase in demand for accounting courses could be met by shifting personnel from teaching finance to teaching accounting.

In the past decade the trend has been toward less specialization or horizontal differentiation. The term that reflects this is *broadbanding*. This refers to collapsing a large number of distinct tasks into a smaller number of positions. Each position or job involves a broad range of tasks and requires a broad range of skills. For example, a computer manufacturer may have used many discrete jobs to build computers. Each individual worker may have been responsible for only one or a few tasks in the process of building the computer. With broadbanding, individuals are trained to carry out many tasks so that one individual or a small team could be responsible for the entire task of building the computer. This gives the organization much more flexibility in assigning work. However, it has the potential disadvantage of having employees who are jacks of all trades, and masters of none.

Vertical differentiation refers to the division of work by level of authority, hierarchy, or chain of command.[11] This is often referred to as the scalar process.[12] Here work is divided on the basis of the authority each unit or person has over each other unit or person in the organization. Vertical differentiation is represented by the number of different levels in an organization. Figure 2-4 shows levels of vertical differentiation.

Like many other large corporations, the Union Pacific Railroad Corporation was extremely vertically differentiated. Before its 1988 reorganization, Union Pacific had nine layers of management in just its Operations Department. Each higher level had more authority. However, numerous problems can develop with extreme vertical differentiation: communication through the levels of hierarchy is slow; decision making bogs down; and top management may be detached from day-to-day events lower in the organization. Because of these problems, CEO Michael Walsh reorganized the Operations Department by reducing the number of layers from nine to five.[13] This has been a common tactic of large organizations as they downsize and remove layers of management to cut cost. This results in a flattened organization — fewer levels of management, with each level having more people.

FIGURE 2-4   Vertical Differentiation

Low Vertical Complexity (Flat)

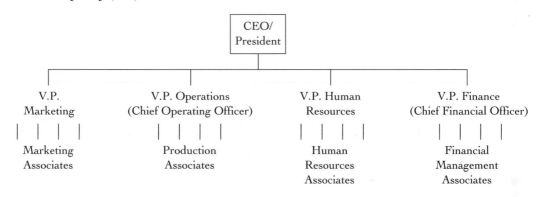

High Vertical Complexity (Tall)

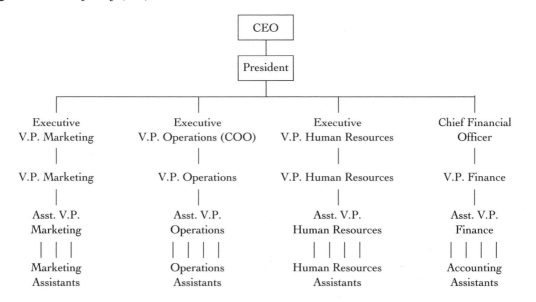

Spatial differentiation or dispersion can be both horizontal and vertical. This aspect of differentiation involves the geographical location of different organizational activities—typically the case with multinational companies that have operations in several different countries. An automobile manufacturer may have an engine-building facility in one locale and a final vehicle assembly facility in another. For example, many component parts for the Honda cars manufactured in Marysville, Ohio, are made at Honda facilities in Japan. A grocery store chain may have distribution facilities throughout the country. Finally, a computer manufacturer may have its assembly operation in a separate facility from its administrative offices. Each of these is an example of spatial dispersion or differentiation. Figure 2-5 shows a spatially dispersed organization.

The level of complexity of an organization is largely determined by the amount of horizontal, vertical, and spatial differentiation that exists in it.[14] Complexity is often related to organizational size, but it need not be. Large organizations are often more vertically and horizontally differentiated than small ones. As we will see shortly, the trend in many organizations is to reduce both vertical and horizontal complexity. Conversely, some small organizations may be very complex. For example, a medical clinic may have narrowly specialized tasks and a clearly and steeply differentiated hierarchy. The point is that although size is often associated with complexity, this is not always the case.

Current Trends in Differentiation

A source of debate among both organizational scholars and managers has been the question of how narrowly tasks should be differentiated. Early in the history of organizational studies, Weber's bureaucratic model and Frederick W. Taylor's system called Scientific Management suggested that tasks should be highly differentiated—broken down into their least common denominator. Weber believed that narrowly defined tasks and responsibilities would lead to an organization that operated with machine-like precision. Taylor believed that narrow, simplified tasks would be easy to master.

FIGURE 2-5 Spatial Differentiation or Dispersion

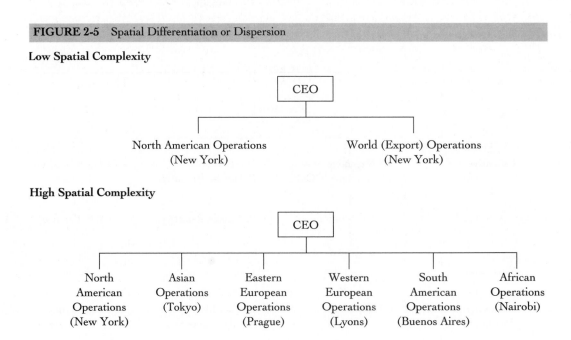

Low Spatial Complexity

High Spatial Complexity

EXHIBIT 2-1

Managing the Mobile Office[15]

With the advent of powerful and inexpensive notebook computers, cellular phones, fax machines, beepers, and an array of electronic and telecommunications devices, the traditional corporate office is becoming a vague memory in many leading corporations. In some cases, decisions to set up home and mobile offices were motivated by such natural disasters as the Los Angeles earthquake and Hurricane Andrew. Companies needed quick, on-the-spot responses to emergency situations. Temporary mobile offices met the challenge. However, with the widespread availability of telecommunications, home and mobile offices have become workplace trends of the late 1990s and the new millennium. According to the International Telework Association and Council, over 19.6 million people worked as telecommuters in 1999 and this number increased in 2000.

A typical worker stationed in a home-based mobile office travels to customers or clients and logs in sales or service calls on a laptop computer. When the employee returns home each day, he or she transmits information back to the home office. In some cases, employees may receive parts or merchandise and store them in their home office for future delivery to customers. Some companies claim that mobile offices increase by 15 percent to 20 percent the amount of time employees spend with customers or clients. Home-based mobile offices also reduce commuting time, an advantage to both employees and employers. In fact, some companies use the home office as an incentive to attract and retain valued employees.

Coordinating the activities of mobile office employees can be a bit of a trick. Some mobile employees return to branch offices or headquarters on a periodic basis for meetings and training. Most coordination takes place over the various telecommunications mechanisms and lacks a personal touch. Also, some mobile employees feel disenfranchised because they no longer have an office in the organization. In many organizations, the size and location of an office is still seen as an important perquisite and symbol of power.

The home-based mobile office is not without problems. Some employers (and employees) worry about overwork. When the office is in your home, it is sometimes difficult to know when to stop working. Experts have also stated concern about the safety of home offices. While the government has issued and regulated safety standards in the traditional workplace, these standards are not regulated in the home office. Recently, there was much controversy in Congress to clarify whether OSHA (Occupational Safety and Health Administration) holds employers responsible for health and safety violations in the home office. In the case of office work at home, it seems that employee privacy is the dominant issue, and OSHA will not inspect these home offices.

The trend toward home-based mobile employees is bound to grow in the new millennium. The new freedom and flexibility offered by mobile technologies, however, will require new integrating skills for managers who coordinate mobile workers.

Workers, even those who were poorly educated or not particularly bright, could become expert in narrow, simplified tasks. Highly differentiated tasks had the added benefit that when workers were poor performers or unreliable they could easily be replaced because the tasks were easily learned. Weber's principles of bureaucracy and Taylor's Scientific Management were driving forces in the industrialization of North America and western Europe in the first half of the twentieth century. Many leading manufacturing firms designed horizontally narrow, specialized tasks. Similarly, these same organizations created multilevel structures with steep vertical hierarchies.

Recently, managers and theorists alike have questioned the value of high degrees of differentiation. Theorists, researchers, and practitioners suggest that in many situations, narrow, simple tasks are demotivating and not necessarily as efficient as once believed. In addition, high levels of complexity may result in employees who lack a vision of the overall organizational goals and purpose. We explore the issue of goals in greater detail in Chapter 3. For example, it is difficult for a person in a large organization doing a highly specialized task to identify with the overall organizational goals. This is typical of the situation that exists in traditional automobile assembly plants.

As a result, many organizations are broadening tasks to include operations that were formerly divided among several workers—broadbanding, as discussed previously. For example, when General Motors created its Saturn Division, the plant was designed with many fewer job titles than typical GM plants. Each worker does the work formerly divided across many different tasks in a typical GM plant. This trend has been replicated at many Ford and Chrysler facilities, too.

Similarly, many organizations are delayering their hierarchies (pushing decision making down and broadening employee responsibilities) in much the same way as Union Pacific. Many reasons are given for this movement away from highly vertically and horizontally differentiated organizations. Although these broader tasks require more training, judgment, skill, and education than narrow, simple tasks, they are easier to integrate. As we will see shortly, they provide greater flexibility in responding to changing conditions.[16] Reducing complexity also facilitates communication.

In addition to the tedium and inefficiencies that sometimes result with high differentiation, many organizations find that highly differentiated tasks are often difficult to coordinate. That is, the more the organization subdivides its work horizontally, vertically, or spatially, the more it must adopt techniques or structural mechanisms to coordinate those activities. We now turn our attention to integration, the structural mechanisms for coordinating.

The Role of Integration

At the same time an organization differentiates itself, it must also integrate the activities, tasks, and sets of tasks performed throughout the organization into a coordinated whole. This coordination is the prime responsibility of people in managerial positions. The very functions of management—decision making and influence—imply coordinating and integrating activities in the organization. In addition to the management functions that integrate the differentiated parts of the organization, integration can be achieved through four broad categories of integrating structures. Keep in mind that it is management that creates or changes the organizational structure by designating levels of both differentiation and integration. Table 2-1 summarizes these integrating structures.

Formalization

One method for ensuring that individuals and departments performing highly differentiated tasks coordinate their activities is through the creation of formal rules, policies, and procedures. Introduction of these guides is referred to as formalization. Organizations typically create elaborate employee manuals, job descriptions, and other written documents to direct employee behavior. The greater the reliance on these written documents, the higher is the level of formalization.

Inherent in the use of formalization to integrate tasks is a number of assumptions about people.[17] The organization that relies heavily on formalization is assuming that employees may lack the information, knowledge, skills, judgment, or self-control nec-

TABLE 2-1 Integrating Structures	
Integrating Structure	**Characteristics**
Formalization	Rules, policies, and procedures
Centralization	Locus of decision making
Spans of Control	Number of subordinates supervised
Standardization: Process, Input, and Output	Setting standards to guide processes, acquisition of inputs, or desired outputs

essary to coordinate diverse sets of tasks in the organization. On the other hand, when management assumes that employees are informed, knowledgeable, and skilled, possessing good judgment and self-control, management is likely to forgo formalization. Rather, management assumes that employees will do the right thing without the necessity of formal rules, policies, or procedures.

Spatial dispersion also affects the use of formalization. When all the operations of an organization are located under one roof, management can rely on face-to-face interactions and informal relationships to enforce expected ways of behaving. When operations are dispersed among several locations, then rules, policies, and procedures are necessary to ensure coordination.

Formalization often presents an interesting conundrum to managers. Some managers think that the way to integrate highly uncertain tasks is through rules, policies, and procedures. At first glance this may seem to be a logical way to guide employees through uncertain situations. It will create certainty and predictability. However, once a manager begins this task, he or she will soon see the paradox. The more uncertain the task, the more rules, policies, and procedures are required to cover anticipated situations. But the very nature of uncertainty means that management cannot anticipate all possible situations or conditions. Thus, formalization typically is not the answer to uncertainty. Instead, managers try to rely on other means of integration for highly uncertain situations.

Centralization: The Decision-Making Locus

Organizations can integrate activities through the decision-making process. Of particular importance here is the place in the organizational hierarchy where decisions are made. Decision making can be either centralized, with decision-making authority vested in top management, or decentralized, with decision-making authority vested in lower-level employees. In a highly centralized organization the president may believe that she or he needs to be involved in nearly every decision of any consequence. The president or other top managers may believe that they are the only ones with the vision and skills necessary to make decisions. For example, the president of American Home Products, the large pharmaceutical and food products company (maker of Anacin, Chap Stick, and Robitussin), approves spending decisions involving as little as $1,500.[18] By contrast, many organizations today are granting authority to lower-level employees to spend money, change designs or procedures, and bend rules to meet customer demands. This is called empowerment and is becoming a common practice in organizations.

As in low levels of formalization, managers in decentralized organizations are assuming that lower-level employees have the information, knowledge, skills, and good judgment to solve problems as they encounter them. In many cases, particularly in organizations involved in highly specialized and technical fields, lower-level employees have more knowledge about products, processes, and problems than do top managers. Additionally, decentralized decision making may be quicker and can reduce the burden on top management. This allows the organization to be more responsive to changing conditions and may allow management to reduce the number of top managers necessary to run the organization. This is often a key part of downsizing as organizations eliminate home office staff positions and levels of management, transferring decision-making authority down to lower levels through the delegation process.

On the other hand, centralized decision making is typically necessary when a broader organizational perspective is needed. Lower-level employees in highly differentiated organizations may lack awareness of the more general organizational goals and may instead focus on the more localized concerns of their department or division. Under these conditions centralized decision making may be necessary. Moreover, centralized decision making can ensure consistency in the organization's actions. When decision making is decentralized, one department may treat employees, tasks, or customers in a different manner from the way they are dealt with in another department. Centralization can provide consistency in treatment, but pushing decisions up the hierarchy is usually a time-consuming process.

The degree of decision-making centralization is sometimes confused with vertical differentiation. Although it is common to find decentralized decision making in flat organizations and centralized decision making in tall organizations, that is not always so. Weber's ideal bureaucratic organization would be characterized by both vertical complexity and decentralized decision making. The rationale for this organizational configuration was that at each level employees should be competent to make decisions appropriate to their level (thus, no need to push routine decisions up the hierarchy). At the same time, the domain of responsibility at each level of the hierarchy was narrowly defined, necessitating a high degree of vertical complexity.

Span of Control

Another way to approach the issue of integration is through the span of control. The span of control refers to the number of immediate subordinate positions a superior position controls or coordinates. A manager who supervises seven subordinates has a span of control of seven, which would be narrow compared to a manager who supervises 20 subordinates. The job of the manager in the supervisory position is to integrate the activities and tasks of those in immediate subordinate positions. For example, the head teller in a branch bank would supervise all the tellers and coordinate their work. The head teller may be responsible for scheduling, ensuring that each teller's cash drawer balances at the end of the day, directing tellers to relevant rules and policies, and performing other tasks that ensure a smooth, coordinated operation.

Much of the early management literature discussed the ideal number of subordinates a manager should supervise. The old rule of thumb was that the ideal number of subordinates for a supervisor was five to seven. Supervising fewer than five subordinates was thought to be an inefficient use of supervisors. On the other hand, it would be difficult to coordinate the activities and monitor the actions of more than seven subordinates.

This thinking on spans of control, however, has been replaced by a different approach to determining the appropriate ratio of supervisors to subordinates. No rule-of-thumb number is specified as applicable for all managers and all situations. Rather, the approach taken now holds that the most workable span of control depends on a number of factors, including these:

- The ability and expertise of the manager in the integrating and controlling position
- The ability and expertise of subordinates
- The nature of the task being performed by subordinates (i.e., routineness of tasks and interrelatedness among subordinates of tasks performed)
- The spatial differentiation (i.e., geographical dispersion) of those in supervisory and subordinate positions
- The amount and type of interaction required by the supervisor position with higher-level positions

In general, the more competent the manager and subordinates, the less geographically dispersed managers and subordinates, and the less interrelated and more routine the tasks of the subordinate, the wider the span of control can be. Additionally, the less often the manager has to interact with his or her superiors and others in the organization, especially over routine matters, the greater the span can be. However, even this line of thinking is being challenged in many organizations today. For example, one line of research shows that highly professional subordinates (e.g., engineers, scientists, and accountants) require narrow spans of control because of their needs for frequent interactions with supervisors and for quick decisions.[19] Other trends toward greater delegation of responsibilities, professionalized workforces, and self-managing groups have motivated organizations to adopt broader spans of control. For example, a medium-sized electronics manufacturer in Florida recently doubled its average span of control from seven to 14 as a result of a restructuring. Two levels of supervision were eliminated.

Flat versus Tall Organizations   Another way of thinking about spans of control is the flatness or tallness of an organization. Earlier, Figure 2-4 contrasted flat and tall organizations. Organizations with broad spans of control tend to have few levels of hierarchy (less vertically complex) and are regarded as flat. Organizations with narrow spans of control tend to have more levels of hierarchy (more vertically complex) and are taller.

Standardization

Integration can be achieved through process, input, and output standardization. Table 2-2 summarizes and describes each of these. Each type of standardization attempts to reduce the uncertainty and unpredictability of organizational work.

One commonly used form of standardization is to standardize the task or process that workers perform. For example, fast food restaurants clearly define the process to

TABLE 2-2 Methods of Standardization	
Method of Standardization	**Example**
Process	Guidelines or instructions on how to produce output: Pizza Hut's instructions on how to make each type of pizza.
Inputs	
Raw Materials	McDonald's specifications on the type of ground beef to be used in hamburgers.
Human Resources	Specification of the type of training, certification, or degree required by job applicants: X-ray technicians must be trained and certified.
Outputs	Inspection of finished product to ensure that it meets specifications: Auto companies visually inspect finished products for flaws in fit and finish.

be used when making a burger or pizza, waiting on customers, or cleaning restrooms. Process standardization guarantees that tasks will be performed in the same way all the time. Fast food restaurants build their reputations on the consistency and predictability of their products. Process standardization is part of the reason for that consistency. Process standardization aids in integration by clearly outlining each task and how each task relates to other tasks. At a fast food restaurant, standardization creates consistency in how counter workers greet customers and enter orders, how grill workers fry the burgers and deliver them to counter workers, and how the counter worker delivers the order to the waiting customer. Standardization facilitates these interactions by making interactions uniform and by removing unnecessary interactions. The same type of standardization can smooth interactions on an assembly line or in an accounting firm.

Inputs can also be standardized to aid in task integration. Input standardization is an attempt to reduce uncertainty and unpredictability of tasks by standardizing the raw material and labor inputs. The raw materials or labor can be narrowly prescribed to reduce the potential variability in the work to be done. For example, many fast food restaurants deal with only one set of suppliers of raw materials (e.g., meat, hamburger buns, or cheese). This reduces the amount that subordinates and supervisors need to interact. Each batch of raw materials should be indistinguishable from past shipments. Thus, workers need not take any special actions or exercise any discretion in the handling of these raw materials. In fact, many fast food chains go to great lengths to contract with specific suppliers to ensure consistency of raw material inputs. Subordinates face fewer questions or issues about these raw materials. This was a key factor for McDonald's when it opened its first restaurant in Moscow. Obtaining potatoes and beef that met McDonald's standards was difficult initially. McDonald's eventually taught farmers to grow potatoes and raise beef that met its standards.

The organization could also standardize its personnel inputs, either through training within the organization or through careful selection of educated, trained, and/or certified employees. Many organizations put employees through rigorous training when they take on new jobs. Both McDonald's and Disney operate their own "universities" for training employees in standard ways of interacting with customers or carrying out tasks. Some organizations rely instead on an outside agent to train employees and require that employees for specific jobs have a specific degree (e.g., an MBA or an engineering degree) or certification (e.g., a certified public accountant, registered nurse, or X-ray technician). Many investment banking and consulting firms in the northeastern United States will hire only graduates of specific Ivy League MBA programs. Both on-the-job training and training outside the organization help ensure that employees have the necessary information and skills to perform their jobs. This reduces the burden on supervisors to integrate.

A final method of standardization is to standardize outputs. The organization may determine that all outputs should meet the same specifications. Products or services are not customized (or the degree of customization is very limited). Output standardization is typically achieved through inspection. One common way of standardizing output is through a Total Quality Management (TQM) program that empowers employees and work teams to be responsible for verifying product and service quality. Many major corporations and even nonbusiness organizations now have some sort of quality enhancement program aimed at developing and maintaining specific quality levels—standards.

Nonstructural Means for Integration

A number of other mechanisms can be used to provide integration in organizations. Although these are not, strictly speaking, structure, they are still important. The integrating positions of liaison roles, teams, information systems, and culture are briefly described below. We return to these subjects for more comprehensive treatment later in the text.

Liaison Roles

Organizations can create liaison roles or horizontal linking positions that link two units or departments at the same level of the organization. This is done when coordination and communication are necessary between two units. For example, an organization may create horizontally specialized departments to handle production and shipping. However, it may be necessary to coordinate these two departments so that each knows the other's capacity, capabilities, schedules, and other constraints. Each department would create a liaison role. The persons filling those positions would be responsible for maintaining connections between the two departments. Without the coordination and communication provided by a liaison role, each department would conduct itself without concern for the other. Production may produce more goods than shipping can effectively send out, or production may not schedule in such a way as to make the best use of the shipping department's capabilities. Thus, the liaison role can mediate potential conflicts and smooth interactions between groups.

Teams

Another way organizations are integrating work activities is by adopting a team-based form of organization. Employees and managers are organized into work and interunit teams in order to enhance communication, coordination, and control. Many organizations that have adopted TQM also adopt a team-based structure. The primary advantage of this approach is that it forces employees to think and act as a unit rather than as a set of individuals. They share information and a sense of collective responsibility for the work. Each person sees how his or her individual efforts affect those of the other team members.

As we have indicated elsewhere in this book, the Saturn unit of General Motors uses team-based management extensively to design and build the Saturn. This is completely different from the way American auto companies have traditionally operated. Usually highly specialized units do their own thing, and their work is integrated at the top of the various divisions. Of course, this takes much time as information is passed up and down the chain of command. Borrowing from the Japanese automakers, GM decided to use teams to shorten the time required to design the car and to achieve better coordination where the work is done in building the car. GM views the team-based concept as a huge success at the Saturn operation and is adopting it in its other divisions and plants.

Culture

Culture plays an extensive role in nearly every aspect of organizational life, and Chapter 10 discusses this subject in more depth. Organization culture is composed of the informal and unwritten values, norms, and behavior patterns that are commonly accepted and observed by members of an organization. Organizations can have thick or thin cultures. Organizations with thick cultures, such as IBM, strongly enforce a detailed culture through numerous informal sanctions. Thin culture organizations have hard-to-identify, loose cultures that are not strongly enforced. Thick cultures are a means to achieve integration because people buy into a common set of shared values and operate from a common frame of reference. Things are done a certain way, not necessarily because of a rule or policy, but simply because "that's the way we do things around here." Other behaviors are avoided because "we simply do not do those things here."

Information Systems

Finally, organizations can achieve integration through the way they structure their information system. This is the method they use to gather, process, analyze, and report the information necessary to operate the organization. It includes information on customers, operations, employees, and accounting. Who has access to this information and how it is used are key parts of the system. By structuring an information system that is comprehensive, user friendly, and automated, much information can be quickly provided to people throughout the organization on a timely basis. E-mail networks, video, conference calling, and local area networks are all examples of information systems that can significantly aid the organization in achieving integration.

Putting It All Together: Mechanistic and Organic Organizations

Thus far we have described attributes of organizational structure. These attributes tend to group together in coherent and systematic ways. It is not an accident that flat organizations tend to be characterized by low levels of vertical and horizontal complexity, by low levels of formalization, and by decentralized decision making. By contrast, it is also no accident that tall organizations tend to be characterized by high levels of vertical and horizontal complexity, by high levels of formalization, and by centralized decision making. These arrangements are logical and consistent. This, of course, does not prevent some organizations from developing structures that are illogical and inconsistent. The result, however, is likely to be an inefficient and ineffective organization.

Two prototypical organizational types have emerged: the mechanistic organization and the organic organization.[20] (The mechanistic organization is much the same as Weber's bureaucracy and is sometimes referred to as a machine bureaucracy.) These two prototypes represent extremes, and it is important to note that many organizations occupy the midrange on these structural attributes. Table 2-3 summarizes the collective attributes of these two types.

The contingency framework presented in the first chapter is based in part on the idea that these two extremes of organizational types, mechanistic and organic, are best suited for different organizational conditions. We identified five contextual factors—organizational goals, environments, technology, size, and culture—that must be considered in determining the most appropriate structural arrangement. In the following

TABLE 2-3 Mechanistic and Organic Organizations		
Structural Characteristic	**Mechanistic**	**Organic**
Complexity	High vertical and horizontal complexity	Low vertical and horizontal complexity
Formalization	High formalization	Low formalization
Centralization	High centralization	High decentralization
Spans of Control	Narrow spans of control	Broad spans of control
Standardization	High standardization	Low standardization

chapters we describe these contextual factors and discuss the appropriate structural responses. The reader must keep a few things in mind, however. First, the mechanistic and organic organizations are prototypes or ideals. Organizations vary from these extremes. Second, some organizations do not adopt the appropriate structural attributes for their context. As a result, they may be inefficient and ineffective. Third, in some situations there are nonstructural means for managing the context. Thus, an organization that appears to have an inappropriate structure for its context may still be efficient and effective because it has adopted other means for coping with the context.

SUMMARY

Organizations are not random collections of people. All organizations need structure to divide labor and then to coordinate the action of the work being done. Structure provides a systematic way of dividing labor (differentiation) and coordination (integration). Structure provides reporting relationships, formal communication channels, determination of task responsibility, and delegation of decision-making authority.

We are concerned with the issue of structure because appropriate structure is required for effective organizational operations. Structure should facilitate effective performance. Characteristics of appropriate structure include clear lines of authority and accountability, effective differentiation and integration, and well-developed and clear communication channels.

The reader must keep in mind three caveats at this point. First, as the contingency framework suggests, there is not one best way to structure an organization. The most appropriate structure for an organization depends on its context (goals, environment, technology, size, and culture). We explore the relationships between structure and context in the chapters that follow. Second, we have presented the formal structure of the organization—the structure that management has defined and that may be recorded in organizational charts. As we stated at the outset of this chapter, the formal structure is but one side of the organization. Existing simultaneously with the formal structure is an informal organization with reporting lines, communication channels, authority, power, and responsibilities that may be very different from the formal configuration. We explore the informal organization when we investigate power and the political nature of organizations. Third, structure (and design) does not just happen. People in organizations make decisions and select specific structural arrangements. The structure (and design) of an organization is an important strategic decision. One need only look at the extensive restructuring that is going on in many organizations to understand the important strategic role that structure plays.

This chapter has reviewed the important concepts involved with structure without actually indicating how these concepts fit together into specific design configurations. How, for example, shall we decide which tasks to group together into departments or divisions? In Chapter 8 we return to structure and describe various design configurations.

Questions for Discussion

1. What is the basic difference between structure and design?
2. Basically, what is shown on an organization chart?
3. What is the informal organization, and how is it related to the formal organization? Can there be a formal organization without an accompanying informal organization? Explain.

4. Why is differentiation necessary to build a formal organization structure?
5. What is integration, and how can it be achieved in a large organization?
6. Is spatial differentiation limited to large organizations? Explain.
7. How is the concept of span of control related to both integration and differentiation?
8. Distinguish between a mechanistic and an organic structure. When would you suggest that each be used? Can they be used together in the same organization? Explain.

References

1. T. Burns and G. M. Stalker, *The Management of Innovation* (London: Tavistock, 1961), 1.
2. P. R. Lawrence and J. Lorsch, "Differentiation and Integration in Complex Organizations," *Administrative Science Quarterly* 12 (1967): 1–47.
3. Alfred D. Chandler, Jr., *Strategy and Structure: Chapters in the History of the American Industrial Enterprise* (Cambridge, MA: M.I.T. Press, 1962).
4. Henry Mintzberg, *The Structuring of Organizations* (Upper Saddle River, NJ: Prentice Hall, 1979), 2; Richard H. Hall, *Organizations: Structures, Processes, and Outcomes* (Upper Saddle River, NJ: Prentice Hall, 1991).
5. Ibid., 65.
6. Ibid., 66–67.
7. W. Richard Scott, *Organizations: Rational, Natural, and Open Systems,* 3rd ed. (Upper Saddle River, NJ: Prentice Hall, 1992), 18.
8. See Hall in note 4.
9. Jerald Hage and Michael Aiken, "Relationships of Centralization to Other Structural Properties," *Administrative Science Quarterly* 12 (1967): 72–91.
10. R. L. Daft, *Organization Theory and Design,* 4th ed. (St. Paul, MN: West, 1992).
11. See Hall in note 4.
12. Keith Davis and John W. Newstrom, *Human Behavior at Work,* 7th ed. (New York: McGraw-Hill, 1985).
13. Daniel McHalba, "Building Steam: Union Pacific Changes Its Hidebound Ways Under New Chairman," *Wall Street Journal* (January 18, 1989), A10.
14. See Hall in note 4.
15. Sue Shellenbarger, "Overwork, Low Morale Vex the Mobile Office," *Wall Street Journal* (August 17, 1994), B1–B7; Steven Greenhouse, "Home Office Isn't Liability for Firms, U.S. Decides," *New York Times* (January 28, 2000), A13; Vivian Marino, "Telecommuting as Workplace Carrot," *New York Times* (July 9, 2000), Section 3, p. 6.
16. Bill Hendrick, "Saturn Plant Hits Bumps," *Atlanta Journal/Constitution* (January 10, 1993); Neal Templin, "A Decisive Response to Crisis Brought Ford Enhanced Productivity," *Wall Street Journal* (December 15, 1992), A1–A8; David Woodruff and Elizabeth Lesly, "Surge at Chrysler," *Business Week* (November 9, 1992): 89–96.
17. See Hall in note 4.
18. Elyse Tanouye and Greg Steinmetz, "Takeover Would Ease, Not End, American Home Products' Bind," *Wall Street Journal* (August 5, 1994), A1–A10.
19. Marshal Meyer, "Expertness and the Span of Control," *American Sociological Review* 33 (1968): 944–51.
20. See Hall in note 4. See note 1.

C A S E

*Shoot the Moon**

General Motors thought that it was, indeed, shooting the moon when it established its Saturn Division. This move, costing some $500 million, was a major thrust by GM to give Saturn a distinctive image apart from the stoic one that the car-buying public had of the parent company. The move came at a time when the American car-making industry was facing fierce competition from abroad, especially from Japan.

Saturn has been a big hit with its buyers, but it has been a costly venture. Some $5 billion, in both start-up costs and operating losses, have been poured into the project. These results were enough for GM to rethink its decision to set up the Saturn Division as a quasi-independent member of the company. It simply didn't appear economically feasible for Saturn to add the assembly plants that were needed to expand its product line.

During the mid 1990s, in a move to curb losses and yet continue to promote the Saturn line, GM decided to fold Saturn into its small-car group, organizationally. This decision was aimed at allowing Saturn to share both engineering and manufacturing costs with the parent company as well as to share economies of scale with other members of the newly established small-car group that includes the Chevrolet Cavalier and Pontiac Sunfire.

Saturn was to remain, essentially, a separate unit of the small-car group with its own labor agreement, organization structure, and marketing strategy, built around a strong emphasis on customer service, no-haggle pricing, and a stress on innovation.

Basically, then, GM was attempting to reabsorb Saturn into the GM organization while preserving the uniqueness of the division. Instead of its previous degree of independence, however, Saturn was to share in a more integrated effort by GM to tie Saturn to the parent company in a product sense—identifying Saturn with the GM line organizationally while at the same time retaining Saturn's marketing strategy that has produced valuable customer satisfaction with the product. As an indication of GM's intention in this regard, Saturn's president, Richard LeFauve, was appointed to head the expanded small-car division known as the Lansing Automotive Division.

The Saturn move is a part of GM's larger effort to reorganize its entire North American unit. The company also melded its luxury car divisions in order to reduce the number of chassis required for both divisions. It was also felt that this move would avoid the design problems experienced in the mid-size car products in past years. Even though these two divisions were to be closely tied organizationally, they would be run separately.

Thus, it appeared that GM was reversing a previous decision to decentralize by moving control of operations into a smaller number of divisions in the name of efficiency and faster product introduction.

So, after a massive effort to distance itself from GM, Saturn was "brought into the family" by GM. This was a move intended to achieve the best of both worlds—organizational control, economies of scale, and sharing of engineering and technology while preserving Saturn's niche in the small-car market.

Although there was an initial question of whether this organizational move would sully the Saturn image, Saturn was recently ranked as the top brand in customer satisfaction. Officials continue to insist that it is possible to reap the benefits of the parent company, GM, while still pursuing the marketing strategy that has made Saturn the popular car it is today. GM has continued to draw Saturn into its structure during the late 1990s and through the present by increasing investments and coordination between Saturn's sales, service, and marketing group with GM's North American groups.

Recent reports of financial losses at Saturn have raised questions as to the future of the GM division. However, GM continues its investment strategy and anticipates that Saturn will soon make a recovery. Only time will tell if these efforts will bring soaring success or bring GM back "down to earth." ∎

*This case is based on the following articles: Gabrilla Stern, "GM Puts Saturn in Small-Car Group, Shakes up North American Operation," *Wall Street Journal* (October 5, 1994), A4; Mike McKesson, "GM Reorganizes Units, Brings Saturn into Small-Car Group," *Tallahassee Democrat* (October 5, 1994), 10D; Bruce Horovitz, "Saturn Hopes Folksy Image Isn't Lost in Shuffle," *USA Today* (October 6, 1994), 1B; Warren Brown, "Investment Ties Saturn Closer to GM; Small-Car Maker's Sales Had Begun to Falter," *Washington Post* (April 26, 2000), E1; David Kiley "Huge Losses Could Jeopardize Future of GM's Saturn," *USA Today* (April 24, 2001), 1B.

QUESTIONS FOR DISCUSSION

1. How would you suggest that GM go about coordinating the Saturn Division with the rest of the small-car division? Would different techniques be needed to tie the small-car division to the parent company? Explain.

2. What do you see as the major problem(s) to be solved by this reorganization? What major problem(s) do you think it will create or aggravate?

3. What organizational factors suggest that Saturn will continue to be independent?

4. Will the spatial differentiation patterns in GM be disturbed by this move? Explain.

5. Suggest some integrating structures for the new move.

6. Would you expect the entire GM organization structure to be flatter or taller after this reorganization? Explain.

7. Is this move more toward a mechanistic or an organic structure? Explain.

PART

II

The Context of Organizations

hapter 1 introduced the basic concept of an organization—a group of people working together cooperatively within identifiable boundaries to accomplish a common goal. The open systems approach to organizations further refined this definition by establishing that organizations must interact with their environment. The contingency framework is built on this notion of an open system. According to contingency theory, there is not one best way to organize. Rather, there are many ways to organize, and some are better than others. But what is "better" and under what circumstances?

Chapter 2 elaborated on the structure of organizations. That discussion provided the foundation for understanding the building blocks of organizations. By introducing differentiation, integration, and other aspects of structure, the reader could begin to understand how organizations differ. Not all organizations look the same. In Part Two we focus on the organization's *context*—the set of circumstances that an organization faces. By looking at the context, we begin to investigate *why* organizations adopt different structures and how they attempt to create a better fit with their context. Understanding the context in which an organization exists is key to understanding why there is not one best way to organize. The best way to organize depends on the nature of the context an organization faces.

Recall that one basic part of the definition of an organization is that it is goal oriented. In Chapter 3 we examine the related subjects of goals, objectives, and strategies. The line of business and the manner in which an organization pursues that business are important contextual or contingency factors that shape the requirements for organizing. As a natural extension of our discussion of goals, we move on to issues of organizational effectiveness. It may seem that effectiveness is a straightforward issue, but, as you will learn, this is not the case.

The second contextual factor to be explored is the environment—the critical element in the open systems framework. Chapter 4 describes eight sectors of the environment and three general characteristics that are useful in characterizing environmental conditions. All organizations, even those in the same industry, face different environmental conditions. It is these different conditions that organizations must recognize and manage.

Chapter 5 is a slight departure from the examination of contextual factors. This chapter addresses how organizations learn about, respond to, and change the environment. Some of these responses to the environment are structural and fit with our contingency framework. However, there are also many other nonstructural mechanisms for managing the environment. These are also covered in Chapter 5.

Technology, as used in organization theory, refers to the knowledge, information, tools, and skills necessary to complete tasks. Chapter 6 presents three different ways of thinking about and analyzing technology in organizations. Technologies vary from one organization to another, and the different technologies any one organization uses also vary from department to department. These different technologies place different demands on organizations and require different ways of organizing.

Chapter 7 discusses two related contextual factors: organizational size and organizational life cycles. It may seem obvious that the ways to organize and manage small organizations differ from those that work best for large organizations. But what exactly is size? And why do large organizations require different methods of organizing? We have also been discussing organizations as if they were unchanging, static entities. You only need to pick up a copy of *The Wall Street Journal* or one of the major business periodicals to see that organizations undergo many changes. Some are planned—mergers, acquisitions, growth, divestitures, leader succession, and so on. Some are unplanned—hostile takeovers, bankruptcies, declines. All these changes require that the methods of managing and organizing also change. Our focus in Chapter 7 is the ongoing dynamic nature of organization. Later, in Chapter 13, we take up the subject of planned organizational change.

One contextual factor remains for later discussion—organizational culture. Because culture is an integrating, holistic element of organizations that includes factors such as structure and design, we save that discussion for Chapter 10.

Keep in mind as you read these five chapters that each of these factors—goals, environment, technology, size, and life cycle—places demands on the organization to be managed and organized in specific ways. That is key to the contingency framework.

CHAPTER

Organizational Goals and Effectiveness

CASE: SOUTHWEST AIRLINES

SOUTHWEST AIRLINES CO.[1] is the nation's low-fare, high Customer Satisfaction airline. We primarily serve short haul city pairs, providing single-class air transportation, which targets the business commuter as well as leisure travelers. The Company, incorporated in Texas, commenced Customer Service on June 18, 1971, with three Boeing 737 aircraft serving three Texas cities—Dallas, Houston, and San Antonio. At year end 2000, Southwest operated 344 Boeing 737 aircraft and provided service to 58 airports in 29 states throughout the United States. Southwest has the lowest operating cost structure in the domestic airline industry and consistently offers the lowest operating cost structure in the domestic airline industry and consistently offers the lowest and simplest fares. Southwest also has one of the best overall Customer Service records. LUV is our stock exchange symbol, selected to represent our home at Dallas Love Field, as well as the theme of our Employee and Customer relationships.[2]

One of the great business success stories of the 1980s and 1990s was not a high tech start up. Southwest Airlines has grown to be the fifth largest major U.S. airline, flying over 57 million passengers to 58 cities. Southwest maintains the highest customer satisfaction numbers and is rated by *Fortune* as one of the five best companies for employees. In addition, the company has been able to show profits for 28 consecutive years and growth in profits for nine years in a row, outperforming the S&P 500 for the year 2000. All of this has been accomplished in a highly competitive industry, fraught with many environmental threats (e.g., unpredictable weather, rising fuel costs, and hostile unions and passengers).

Southwest's extraordinary performance is no accident. Much credit for the company's success is given to the cofounder and CEO Herb Kelleher. He and his managers have created a clear mission and goals to guide employees.

Southwest is a bit different from its major competitors United Airlines, Delta, American, Northwest, and Continental. Although each of the competitors operates some short-haul commuter affiliates, they are full-service operators who use the hub-and-spoke system to shuttle passengers throughout the world. Southwest operates point-to-point flights within their market. Most of these flights are less than one hour in duration. For example, Southwest has 11 one-hour flights daily in each direction between Detroit and Chicago. Twenty-five minutes after landing in Detroit a plane is on its way back to Chicago with another load of passengers. Frequent, short flights with

---

[1]www.southwest.com/about_swa/airborne.htm
[2]Annual Report, 2000, Southwest Airlines Co.

quick turnaround have made Southwest a leader in efficiency. The dramatically lower fares and frequent flights take passengers not only from competing airlines but also attract fliers who would have used other modes of transportation.

To achieve high performance Southwest gets everyone, including passengers, into the act. The fare structure is generally quite simple with only two or three options (no first class or business class): advanced purchase fares, refundable fares, and senior or children's fares. Typically there is no disadvantage to buying a one-way ticket, unlike the practice of most airlines. Moreover, low fares do not require staying over a Saturday and the company does not charge for rebooking or exchanges.

Southwest has no reserved seats. Passengers are seated on a first-come-first-served basis, speeding passenger loading and reducing paperwork. In addition, 80 percent of passengers use "e-tickets," reducing costs associated with paper tickets. To keep costs down, Southwest does not offer meals on its flights. Maintenance and cleaning are standardized because all the planes in the fleet are 737s, which further reduces cost. Standardization of operations is much easier when employees do not need to think about the type of plane. Even Southwest's frequent flier program is simple. Rather than basing awards on miles flown, Southwest awards a free ticket for passengers who have flown eight round-trips. The plan simplifies record keeping and reduces passenger questions and uncertainty.

Southwest's attention to details and efficiency extends to recruiting. Recruiting focuses on values, attitudes, and fit. The prevailing value in the "People Department" (not Human Resources) is finding people who will *fit* Southwest's emphasis on teamwork, customer service, and positive attitude. With the exception of technical positions such as pilots and mechanics, skills are not the primary criterion for hiring. The belief is that skills can be learned; values and attitudes are much more difficult to develop.[3] Emphasis is placed on compassion and common sense among employees. Once hired, Southwest employees are subjected to extensive training in teamwork and customer service. As the company's annual report states: "*We believe that winning is a team effort.*"[4]

Despite the fact that Southwest is largely unionized, entry-level wages are somewhat below industry averages. The company also avoids lavish perquisites for executives. Southwest manages the salary gap through a profit-sharing plan that covers employees who have been with the company for at least 1 year. The plan requires employees to invest a portion of the profit sharing in Southwest stock. In the mid-1990s nearly 90 percent of employees owned stock and 11 percent of Southwest's stock was held by employees.[5] "Once hired, we provide a nurturing and supportive work environment that gives our Employees the freedom to be creative, have fun, and make a positive difference. . . . it's our Employees' sense of ownership, pride in team accomplishments, and enhanced job satisfaction that keep our Culture and Southwest Spirit alive and why we continue to produce winning seasons."[6]

The positive work environment and performance-based compensation plan have produced a workforce that is highly committed to the company. Turnover is low by industry standards; productivity is high; and customers are satisfied.

---

[3]Charles O'Reilly and Jeffery Pfeffer, "Southwest Airlines: Using Human Resources for Competitive Advantage (A)," (Palo Alto, CA: Graduate School of Business, Stanford University, 1994), 9–10.
[4]Annual Report, 2000.
[5]O'Reilly and Pfeffer, p. 11.
[6]Annual Report, 2000.

Southwest's ticker symbol is "LUV," which pays homage to the airport where the company was founded—Dallas Love Field. But the ticker symbol and the Southwest heart that adorns planes and advertising are both symbols of the company's commitment to employees and customers. These features are captured in the company's mission statement:

> The mission of Southwest Airlines is dedication to the highest quality Customer Service delivered with a sense of warmth, friendliness, individual pride, and Company Spirit.[7]

Southwest Airlines' extraordinary growth and success in the last 28 years has been no accident. It is the result of a clear development of a mission, goals, and objectives, and the reinforcement of actions that are consistent with the mission, goals, and objectives.

For more information on Southwest Airlines, visit their Web site: www.southwest.com and www.biz.yahoo.com/luv.htm.

As we see in this brief description of Southwest Airlines, the mission statement, goals, and objectives are intended to guide the company's overall direction as well as the actions of individual employees. It is essential for any organization to have a strong sense of its overall direction if all of its members and various stakeholders (i.e., groups with interests in the organization) are to know what is required and what to expect. The mission statement establishes the legitimacy and direction of the firm. The goals and objectives establish a standard by which one can judge the effectiveness and efficiency of the firm. However, as we will learn, the objectives of the firm are only one set of standards for judging effectiveness.

This chapter takes a look at the role that goals play in everyday organizational life. The material clearly shows the vital nature and place of goals and their relationship to the effectiveness of organizations.

ORGANIZATIONAL GOALS AND EFFECTIVENESS

A key part of our definition of an organization stated in Chapter 1 was that organizations have goals,* that they are purposeful collections of people who join together to achieve these goals. In this chapter we explore what that means. Goals are statements that identify an endpoint or condition that an organization wishes to achieve. On the surface, the idea that organizations have goals and that the members pursue those goals may seem obvious and straightforward. That, however, is not the case. As we dig below the surface and rhetoric of typical organizational goals, we begin to see problems. Organizations have many goals—some that are clear, some that are ambiguous, and some that contradict other goals. Moreover, many groups of people, both inside and outside the organization, have goals for an organization that may or may not be consistent with the official goals of the organization. Thus, even the seemingly simple idea that organizations have goals is, as we will see, deceptively complex.[1]

We begin by stating a general definition of goals, and then we examine different classes of goals or objectives in typical organizations. We next turn our attention to the

---

[7]Southwest Airlines, "Customer Service Commitment," March 13, 2000.
*In this book, goals, purposes, and objectives are used interchangeably.

process of managing goals in organizations, including setting goals, managing conflicting goals, and assessing goal attainment. Goal attainment provides us with a bridge to the second theme of this chapter—organizational effectiveness.

Like goals, organizational effectiveness is a complex and multifaceted issue. The problems that lie in answering the question of whether an organization is effective become apparent when we explore the concept of effectiveness. To a great extent, the answer to this question depends on *who* is asking the question and for *what purpose*. The rise of many Internet and dot.com businesses in the late 1990s and their subsequent fall in 2000–2001 demonstrates the complexity of determining goals and assessing effectiveness. Thus, we present several models of organizational effectiveness that may be useful for different purposes in assessing organizational effectiveness.

GOALS AND THEIR ATTAINMENT

An organization takes on an identity of its own as a result of its specific set of goals. Even companies in the same line of business look and act different partly because their goals differ. For example, compare General Motors' attempts to produce automobiles for every market niche from compact economy cars to luxury cars with BMW's focus on luxury sport sedans and sports cars. Although both Ericsson of Sweden and Nokia of Finland compete vigorously in telecommunications, the firms have pursued different goals. Ericsson has focused attention on building cellular and digital communications infrastructure and has recently deemphasized phone manufacturing. Nokia has focused its attention on developing innovative phones and communication devices. In general, an organization's goals or objectives serve three main purposes: (1) they establish the desired future state that the organization is trying to realize, thus setting **guidelines** for members of the organization to follow; (2) they provide a rationale for the organization's existence, what organizational theorists refer to as **legitimacy**; and (3) they provide a set of **standards** against which the organization's performance can be measured.[2]

DEFINITION

Organizational Goals: Statements that establish the desired future state an organization is attempting to achieve.

These three purposes of goals can be applied to three levels of the organization (summarized in Table 3-1). First, at the broadest and most general level, the level of the organization as a whole, overall goals are stated in **official goals** or **mission statements**. These are broad, general statements about future conditions and guiding principles, such as those of Southwest Airlines in the introductory case. Official goals or mission statements are often so broad that they can do little more than set a general tone for the organization, but that tone may be critically important to establishing a culture. **Operative goals**, derived from official goals, are more specific statements about what the organization, division, department, or business unit intends to do. Finally, **operational goals** are the most specific and narrowly stated goals of the organization. Operational goals, contained in documents such as job descriptions, state what specific individuals in the organization should be doing. Because our level of analysis is the

TABLE 3-1   Classification of Goals

Type of Goal	Focus	Purpose	Example
Official Goals, or Mission Statement	Establishment of broad strategy	Set guiding principles	Introduce new products; enter new markets
Operative Goals	Specific actions to enact strategy	Guide divisions, departments, or business units	Develop specific product; identify specific market to enter and take actions to realize that goal
Operational Goals	Individual jobs or tasks	Guide individuals' behaviors	Create job descriptions

organization, we focus on these first two levels of goals—official goals, or mission statements, and operative goals.

We must also examine a variety of other factors related to goals, including these:

- The beneficiaries of the organization
- The relevant time frame for specific goals
- The relative importance of specific goals

Primary and Secondary Beneficiaries

Organizations have a multitude of **stakeholders**—that is, groups of people affected by the success or failure of the organization. These groups can be divided into **primary beneficiaries** and **secondary beneficiaries**. The primary beneficiaries are those people the organization serves. For Southwest Airlines, the primary beneficiaries are the customers who purchase tickets and fly Southwest. Thus, a critical part of Southwest's mission is to provide services that ensure customer satisfaction: efficient, convenient, and inexpensive air travel. Without satisfied customers or clients, a business cannot exist for long.

In addition to the primary beneficiary group, all organizations must attempt to satisfy a secondary group. This group potentially gains satisfaction through association with the organization. For Southwest, this group includes employees, owners, suppliers, members of communities served by the airline, and many other groups. This leads us to an important problem faced by organizations. *Because organizations have multiple stakeholders (i.e., groups with interest in the success or failure of the organization), they will necessarily have multiple goals, some of which* may *be in conflict with one another.*[3] This has important implications for many aspects of organizations, including the assessing of effectiveness.

Short- and Long-Term Goals

Placing time dimensions on goals is also critical. Not all objectives are amenable to immediate satisfaction; some will take significantly longer to achieve than others. In fact, one method for dealing with complex, potentially competing goals is to sequence them with specific time frames. We can look at the various types of goals of an organization and establish some sort of time boundary for them.

Short-term goals[4] are those the organization hopes to accomplish within a year or other specific accounting cycle. Companies may, for example, seek annual increases in

---

EXHIBIT 3-1

Competing Goals at Procter & Gamble: What Works in Cincinnati May Not Work in Brussels

Like most consumer goods companies, Procter & Gamble (P&G) has tried to extend the global reach of its brands and products. Selling toothpaste, soap, detergent, disposable diapers, and its numerous other products globally has proved to be a daunting task for P&G.

To understand the difficulty that P&G is experiencing, it is important to look closely at the potential contradictions and paradoxes that globalization presents. P&G is known around its headquarters for its strong culture and dedicated employees. While employees may refer to themselves sarcastically as "Proctoids," there is a strong sense of commitment to the company and its way of doing business.

Until recently, the P&G way was to create products that could be produced and marketed worldwide. Little or no attention was directed at local differences or local competitors. From products to management, the prevailing belief was that if it worked in Cincinnati it should work in Brussels, Paris, Frankfurt, Tokyo, or wherever P&G did business. The result was that P&G was battered in many non–North American markets. For example, in many European markets P&G has been out maneuvered by Colgate-Palmolive, Unilever, Henkel, or other consumer products companies that have been more adaptable to local needs.

P&G's goals of developing a consistent management system and consistent products worldwide has conflicted with their desire to increase global market share. The conflict between consistency and local adaptation is common to most firms that attempt to do business in the global marketplace. Unfortunately, there is no simple solution concerning what should be globalized and what should be localized. The challenge of management is to figure out the correct balance to strike, and that balance is likely to vary by company, industry, and location.

---

sales, profits, new business, or productivity. For example, early in the history of Amazon.com the objective was to build traffic on the company's Web site. Like many of the early e-businesses, Amazon's focus was on "hits"—visits to the Web site. The belief was that visitors would eventually become shoppers and revenue would follow. Additionally, a short-term goal of many e-business start-ups in the 1990s was to attract venture capital and to eventually "go public" with an initial public offering (IPO). Typically absent from these early short-term goals was any discussion of profits. However, as many of the e-business start-ups of the 1990s learned, without profits (or even positive cash flow), the venture capital, loans, and equity eventually evaporate. The result was that many high-fliers of the 1990s Internet economy (e.g., e-Toys, BigWords.com, and Pets.com) have disappeared.

Long-term goals[5] are those that cannot be accomplished within the short run. These goals may be for periods of more than 1 year or one accounting cycle, but may be as long as 10 or 20 years, although rapid changes in environments may make it difficult or unwise to plan beyond a 3- to 5-year period. Whatever the length of the defined time period, long-term goals provide the overall direction for an organization beyond a single year or accounting period.

Jeff Bezos and the remaining e-business entrepreneurs are quickly learning that long-term viability is critical to survival. Grandiose growth plans are giving way to more carefully crafted business plans that focus on providing unique services particularly well-suited to the Internet and to managing personnel and supply chains for efficiency. Amazon and other e-businesses have downsized and scaled back plans to expand product lines and services. While it may eventually be important for Amazon to be a full-service Web retailer or for E*Trade to be a comprehensive Web-based financial services company, these may be long-term goals that cannot be achieved with success overnight.

GOALS AT THE HIGHEST LEVEL: THE ORGANIZATION'S MISSION

All organizations, whether they are businesses, not-for-profit organizations, or sociopolitical entities, have officially chartered purposes. ***Mission statements***, ***official goals***, or, as they are sometimes called, ***strategic objectives*** set forth those purposes. A statement is generally broad and general, but it states the direction the organization is taking and, often, the philosophy of the organization. For example, General Electric, under [former] CEO Jack Welsh, has stated that the company should be number one or number two in everything it does. If GE cannot achieve a number one or number two ranking, it will abandon those lines of business. Mission statements typically identify the product or service, market niche, production methods, and financial objectives of the organization. Welsh's goal of being number one or two motivated GE to sell its small appliance business to Black and Decker in the early 1980s. Other organizations, typically those in high technology or changing markets, use mission statements as the basis for setting specific goals for new product or service innovations. Some organizations include other classes of goals that go beyond the business of the organization to include objectives such as employee development and general social responsibility.

The mission statements of the two sample firms in Table 3-2 illustrate the diversity of these statements in two very different industries. They are important to establishing the general, long-term direction of these firms.

Clearly an electric power generating utility and an insurance and financial services company are very different. To some extent, those differences are expressed in the different goal statements of Reliant Energy and The Principal Financial Group. In addition to differences in business type, these mission statements express elements of a basic philosophy of the firm. At the top of Reliant Energy's statement is its goal to "maximize shareholder value" while meeting customer needs and providing rewarding careers for employees. The Principal Financial Group emphasizes stability, gradual change, and mutuality. In the absence of a profit motive (mutual companies are *not* in business to maximize shareholder value), the focus is placed on satisfying customers (who are also owners).

GOALS FOR ACTION: OPERATIVE GOALS

Operative goals are typically stated in terms of measurable outcomes. These goals cover all of the organization's subsystems described in Chapter 1. Different schemes have been developed for categorizing types or areas of operative goals.[6] Common to all of these is that they set standards and guide what people in the organization should be doing on a day-to-day basis. We use, with some modifications, Peter Drucker's eight key goal areas to delineate the scope of operative goals.[7]

Market Goals   Organizations may set goals to increase market share or to enter new markets. These goals may indicate new products to be developed or modifications to existing products. Such goals can serve as guidelines for product development, production, acquisitions, or divestitures, among others. Goals for increased market

TABLE 3-2 Sample Mission Statements	
Utility Company **Reliant Energy**	**Mutual Insurance Company*** **The Principal Financial Group**
Reliant Energy is an international energy delivery and energy services company. Reliant Energy's vision is to transform the company into a skills-based energy services provider deriving the majority of its earnings from competitive businesses with attractive growth rates and returns. We are focusing on key markets in the United States and Western Europe where industry restructuring is creating an attractive environment for our asset-backed energy trading and marketing strategy. We will become a skills-based company by focusing our capital and human resources on building our energy services business in the United States and Western Europe. This will require adjusting our existing portfolio to support the development of our energy services businesses. We will make . . . vital investments on a scale and at a pace that also allows us to meet our earnings target, which we recently adjusted upward to 10 to 12 percent annual growth in earnings per share.[†]	The Principal Financial Group is a diversified family of companies offering a wide range of insurance and other financial products and services for businesses, groups and individuals. For 114 years, stability and performance in a changing world have meant security and protection for millions of people. Helping people meet their financial needs is our goal. . . . Over time, *gradual change* and improvement produce *dramatic results.* The Principal provides *stability by balancing* financial risk with a sound investment policy. Our *philosophy of mutality* means we operate on *behalf of customers.*[‡]

*A mutual company operates on a different set of principles from a typical for-profit business. Mutual insurance companies are forms of cooperatives that are owned by the customers. Rather than trying to create wealth by amassing profits, these firms have as their primary goal benefit to customers through reduced costs of goods or services. Other examples of cooperative organizations include State Farm Insurance, Sunkist Oranges, and Recreational Equipment Incorporated (REI).

[†]*Source:* Annual Report, Reliant Energy, 1999.

[‡]Annual Report, Principal Financial Group, 1996. Note that Principal Financial Group announced plans in 2001 to convert from a mutual company to an investor-owned company.

share may include guidelines for advertising and promotion of products, pricing, packaging, and other actions aimed at getting further market penetration. Goals for new product niches may guide research and development or acquisitions.

Financial Performance Goals   Typical businesses are guided by specific objectives for profitability, cash flow, stock market performance, and other indicators of the organization's financial soundness. In the heyday of the dot.com Internet businesses, a key financial goal was market capitalization. Businesses may set goals of increasing profits or operating revenues of a specific amount. Investors and analysts pay particular attention to the degree to which businesses achieve these goals. The precipitous fall in the equity markets throughout the world in 2000–2001 was the result of firms failing to meet profit expectations. Top executive compensation and, increasingly, lower-level employee salaries and bonuses are often directly tied to a firm's financial performance.

Resource Goals   As noted in Chapter 1, because organizations are open systems, they are dependent on the external environment for important resources. They must obtain resources from outside, and resource goals state objectives for obtaining external financial, physical, and human resources. Businesses must attract financial resources from investors or financial institutions. Even nonprofit organizations are not immune to the task of obtaining financial resources. In nonprofit organizations a great deal of attention is typically directed to lobbying, fund-raising, and revenue-generating activities. Public television or radio stations, for example, continually ask viewers or listeners to contribute in fund-raising drives. Managers of public universities and other state agencies lobby state legislators in an effort to enhance their organization's share of revenues. In addition, business and nonbusiness organizations must obtain other resources from the environment. These include the raw materials needed to create outputs as well as the equipment and facilities necessary for the transformation process.

Innovation Goals   Another consequence of adopting an open systems view of organizations is the recognition that the environment is constantly changing. To meet those changing environmental demands, organizations must also change. Innovation goals may be objectives for changing virtually anything, including the products and services sold, the processes used to create those outputs, the people in the organization, and the organization itself. Clearly, innovation is critical to success in such high-tech industries as computer hardware, software, electronics, and telecommunications.[8] However, organizations in settings as diverse as retailing, automobile manufacturing, education, health care, and consumer products adhere to the belief that they must innovate in order to survive.[9] One reason for the difficulties faced by Xerox, GM, and Procter & Gamble is their failure in recent years to successfully innovate and meet changing environmental conditions.

Productivity Goals   Concerns for the quality, cost, and amount of output are included under productivity goals. An important issue facing nearly every organizations is how to simultaneously increase product or service quality while reducing waste and inefficiency. Many organizations have turned to ***Total Quality Management*** (TQM) as a means for creating specific productivity goals that address quality, cost, and amount of output. TQM involves the setting of extensive sets of goals, many of which go well beyond productivity. The interested reader can find many articles and books that specifically deal with TQM.

Management Development Goals   Not only must organizations think to the future when planning new products and services; they must also consider the managerial personnel and skills that will be necessary to lead the company in the future. The proliferation of inexpensive, rapidly changing computer and telecommunications technology, along with rapid changes in the broader business environment, place new demands on managers. Continuous training and development become critical as managers must develop new skills and acquire new information. Downsizing and the elimination of middle management in many organizations have also placed new demands on remaining managers. Organizations must also anticipate employment changes brought about by retirements, dismissals, promotions, or new opportunities. Organizations must develop comprehensive plans for attracting, retaining, training, promoting, and compensating managers. In fact, many organizational and management scholars have extended these development goals to all levels of organizations. These ideas form the foundation of strategic human resources management.[10]

EXHIBIT 3-2

The Rise and Fall of the Crest Empire[11]

For much of the 1960s through most of the 1990s, Procter & Gamble Crest brand of toothpaste dominated the market. The development of sodium fluoride as a decay-preventing additive gave P&G a clear competitive advantage. However, as the brand matured and P&G eventually lost patent protection, Crest faced increasing competition. Many brands were able to boast similar dental health advantages. At the same time, competitors like Colgate-Palmolive's Colgate Total brand and SmithKline Beecham's Aquafresh brand developed packaging and product innovations that P&G was late to recognize as threats. Moreover, Crest's market penetration outside North America has been disappointing. Early in 2001, Colgate dominated the U.S. market with a 37 percent share, compared to Crest's share of just over 27 percent.

Despite the fact that Crest is not one of P&G's 10 largest brands in sales volume, the company will devote considerable attention to innovations that they hope will restore the brand to its leadership position. One such innovation was the recently released Crest Whitestrips kits. The company has also developed new toothpaste formulations to compete more aggressively in the whitening market and other dental care niches. Brand loyalty is not what it once was. Consumers are more conscious of features and values. Innovation is more important than ever.

Visit www.pg.com for more information on recent innovations at Procter & Gamble.

Employee Performance and Attitudes   Obviously, organizations set specific goals for individual employees or groups of employees. These may include sales goals for salespeople, production goals for production employees, or recruiting goals for human resources managers. These goals are tied to the specific tasks that individuals or work units perform.[12] Like management development goals, these goals are part of a comprehensive strategic human resources system.

Perhaps less clear is the idea that organizations may have goals concerning employee attitudes. The fact is that many companies spend significant amounts of time and money assessing employee attitudes and attempting to create conditions conducive to development of more positive attitudes about work and the organization. These goals are motivated in part by the mistaken belief that happy workers are productive workers. In reality, the relationship between worker satisfaction and worker performance is far more complex and has been the focus of extensive research for many years. At a minimum, we can say that positive worker attitudes contribute to the quality of work life, and that may be a desirable end in itself. Thus, as we will see later in discussions of organizational climate and culture, goals for improved employee attitudes may be important to establishing internal organizational conditions.

In distinguishing between management development goals and employee performance and attitude goals, organizations must be careful to not create an overly stratified workforce. Identifying one group as "managers" and another as "employees" has the potential to create alienation and disharmony. Moreover, many organizations pursue "promotion from within" strategies. Employees at every level who show great potential are identified early for special training and grooming as future managers. Many organizations boast of managers or leaders who rose through the ranks from mailrooms, stockrooms, or other other low-level positions to assume leadership positions. Progressive management practice should focus on developing all employees to their fullest potential and should be concerned with the attitudes and performance of all employees.

Social Responsibility and Ethical Behavior   Organizations often expend considerable effort in pursuit of various ethics and social responsibility goals. McDonald's spends valuable corporate resources promoting recycling, nutritional education, and Ronald McDonald House. For many years, J.C. Penney has been guided by the Penney Way, which advocates the fair and equitable treatment of employees and customers. Early in its history, Ben & Jerry's Homemade, the Vermont-based ice cream maker, established social welfare as a central part of its mission. The company contributed to local social causes such as the welfare of small family farms, national causes such as food purity, and global causes such as world peace.[13]

Some businesses even make ethics and social responsibility fundamental to their entire approach to business, marketing themselves as "green" (i.e., environmentally responsible) or in other ways socially responsible. A case in point is The Body Shop International, the British franchisor of soap and cosmetic shops.[14] The company actively supports the animal rights movement and avoids using animal testing of its products. Instead, the company avoids testing by using ingredients that have been already established as safe. The Body Shop also extensively uses recycled materials in packaging and advocates recycling or reuse of containers. Last, the company has tried to stimulate local economies of poorer nations by producing and purchasing in those locales. Rather than paying at the lower local rates, the company has paid prices and wages comparable to those in Europe. Recently, a number of critics have challenged The Body Shop, suggesting, on the one hand, that some of its policies do not contribute to the well-being of local third world economies and, on the other hand, that the company's policies have detracted from its profitability.[15] This business is based not only on the profit motive, but, like a growing number of other firms, on "doing good." This leads us to examine the meaning of "doing good." For that we turn briefly to the issue of ethics.

Ethical Principles

Much of what organizational members do on a day-to-day basis involves ethics. Issues such as decisions about whom to lay off during downsizing, how to market products, how to dispose of potentially hazardous waste, or how many and what type of defects in products are acceptable involve ethical choices. In general, ethical dilemmas have the following five characteristics.[16]

1. *Actions taken have extended consequences.* For example, a decision to downsize a company affects those people who lose their jobs, the morale of workers remaining on the job, the community's tax base, the local economy, and so forth.

2. *Managers have alternatives and can make choices about which course of action to pursue.* There may be more than one way to reach a desired goal. Instead of downsizing, for example, a firm may decide to cut wages or worker hours across the board.

3. *Outcomes are mixed.* Not all of the consequences of most actions are totally positive or totally negative. We have noted the negative consequences of downsizing. Downsizing may, however, make a company more efficient and more competitive, thus saving the company from eventual failure.

4. *Consequences of actions are uncertain.* Managers making decisions about a problem like downsizing do not know for sure whether their actions will have the intended consequence. Were the right people laid off? Will layoffs really make the company more efficient? Most decisions that managers make are fraught with uncertainties.

5. *Decisions that managers make have personal implications; they affect people.*

Organizations use ethical codes or guidelines to social responsibility to help employees make difficult decisions. Many different frameworks cataloging different types of business ethics have been developed over the years. One of the most straight-forward is that presented by F. Neil Brady in his book *Ethical Managing: Rules and Results*.[17] Brady proposes an ethical framework that balances two views of ethics: **ethical utilitarianism** and **ethical formalism**. The two perspectives are described in Table 3-3.

Increasingly, organizations are using ethical codes to specify acceptable and desir-able conduct for employees and the organization. We revisit the issue of organizational ethics when we explore organizational culture in Chapter 10.

Purposes of Goals and Objectives

Clearly, goals and objectives at different levels serve different purposes. The broad, general aims expressed in a mission statement are different from the more specific operative goals. Nonetheless, a number of features of goals are common to, or overlap, both levels. These are discussed below.

Guidance or Direction   Official goals or mission statements give general **guidance** or **direction** to employees. Employees at each of the companies featured earlier are motivated to focus on different behaviors: efficiency contributes to greater profitability at Reliant Energy; customer service enhances the benefits provided to customer-owners of The Principal Financial Group; and product innovation at Procter & Gamble. Mission statements, however, are not specific enough to show individual employees how they should implement these guidelines in their day-to-day actions. The mission or goal statements help create a **culture** (the prevailing philosophy and values of the organization) that should support the achievement of these goals, and the operative goals provide more specific mechanisms for accomplishing them.

Motivation   The achievement of goals does not just happen *because* goals are set. The guidance component of goals tells employees what they should do and how to do it. The motivation component *encourages* workers to do those things. Frequently, goals are set to challenge employees, and often rewards accompany achievement of these goals. When General Motors created its Saturn Division, it was clear that to be competitive the division would need to be more productive and innovative than other GM divisions or the competition, and that profitability of the division would be sometime in the future. Although the Saturn cars initially were a sales success, the division lost $700 million in 1992. General Motors maintained goals of high product quality, high productivity, continuous improvement, and eventual profitability by offering bonuses when the division shows an operating profit. In 1992 the division did show its first operating profit and rewarded workers with $1,000 bonuses.[18] Although Saturn sales have slowed in recent years, GM has continued to reward workers in profitable years.

Legitimacy   A third purpose of goal statements is to create **legitimacy** for the organization. These statements communicate to people inside and outside the legitimate reason or justification for the organization's existence. Southwest Airline's mission statement emphasizes "Customer Service" and "Company Spirit." This legitimizes the company's extraordinary efforts aimed at ensuring satisfied customers. It gives employees permission to go to great lengths to meet customer needs. Similarly, the "Company Spirit" mission has given the company great latitude to act in ways that are not characteristic of competing airlines. Behaviors of flight attendants, ticket

TABLE 3-3   Two Views of Ethics

Utilitarian Ethics

- *Utilitarianism*, based on works of British philosopher Jeremy Bentham (1748–1832), means the ethical correctness of actions is judged by *consequences*. Utilitarian ethics are guided by the "greatest happiness" principle. This principle states that those actions that produce the greatest good for the greatest number of people are ethical. Actions that produce good outcomes, however defined, are ethical. Because consequences occur after a decision is made or an action is taken, one cannot judge the ethics, according to utilitarianism, until *after* the fact.
- Actions that produce pain or suffering are unethical. Acting in a selfish manner would be unethical because good outcomes would not be distributed to the greatest number of people.
- The process of ethical judgment is essentially that of cost-to-benefit analysis. Managers would weigh the costs (pain or suffering) against the anticipated gains (pleasure). If the positive outcomes outweigh the negative outcomes, then the action is deemed ethical.
- Utilitarianism tends to be flexible, situational, tolerant, and liberal. Individuals are left to judge what is best for them as long as those actions do not create pain and suffering for others. Utilitarianism emphasizes a rational decision process for arriving at ethical outcomes. Problems arise because people may not agree on whether certain outcomes are positive or negative and on whether certain groups of people are affected by actions of others.
- For example, a business manager may go through an elaborate cost-to-benefit analysis to determine whether to dump potentially toxic waste material into sewers. It may not be clear whether this action is legal. Factors to weigh would include the possible damage, the cost of fines if the action is found to be illegal, the potential loss of business, and the cost of alternative means of disposal. After weighing all of these factors, a manager would make a decision based on maximizing good outcomes (continued profitability of firm, maintaining jobs, providing goods and services) and minimizing bad outcomes (damage to the environment and threats to human health).

Ethical Formalism

- *Ethical formalism* is based largely on the writings of the eighteenth-century philosopher Emanuel Kant. Whereas utilitarian ethical judgments are tied to the consequences of actions, Kant believed that we can know what is ethical *before* we know the consequences. By the application of universally recognized rules or principles, we can know what actions are ethical. These rules or principles may be formally stated laws, doctrine, or widely held beliefs or values. For example, state legal codes forbid the taking of a life (defined variously as murder or manslaughter). Many religious or personal codes also forbid such action. Holders of these rules or values will attempt to apply them consistently and universally.
- Actions that violate laws, rules, and generally held values are unethical. Making oneself an exception to the rule is unethical.
- The process of ethical judgment is something Kant called *pure reason*. Ethical judgments are independent of what an individual or group thinks. We recognize the authenticity of an ethical law without necessarily agreeing with it. Ethical principles are absolute, universal, and consistent.
- Formalism emphasizes universal and consistent application of rules. Emphasis is placed on a prior knowledge of rules. Problems arise when rules are confusing or when sets of rules conflict with each other.
- For example, we may have universally applicable rules that state that businesses cannot dump toxic waste materials into the sewer system of the city. Without knowing the consequences of an action, the business manager knows beforehand that to dump toxic waste down the sewer is unethical. Knowledge of these rules or laws, not knowledge of potential consequences, will guide the manager's actions.

agents, and others are unusual by industry standards. Flight attendants have been known to climb into overhead bins to greet passengers and to lead cheers during flights. The mission statement or official goals state the legitimate intentions of the organization. Similarly, operative goals state the legitimate means that employees should use to achieve the official goals.

Standards   It would seem logical that if organizations set goals to legitimize, guide, and motivate, then these goals can be used as standards of achievement. Quantifiable goals, like Saturn's goal of profitability, can be clearly stated, and progress toward that goal can be measured. Thus, goals may serve as standards for performance. We return to this subject shortly when we discuss organizational effectiveness.

Structure and Design   The number, diversity, and complexity of an organization's goals should play an important role in decisions about how it should be structured or designed. For example, companies with goals to produce many different products or services may require types of structure and design different from those of companies that set goals to produce only a few related products or services. Organizations having goals that require extensive interaction between departments or divisions (a concept known as inter-dependence) require different structures or designs from those organizations in which departments or divisions can carry out tasks more or less autonomously. Organizations that have goals dealing with environmental scanning, adaptation, or manipulation will be structured in ways that maximize boundary-spanning activities and environmental planning. Thus, the nature of the goals an organization sets should be an important consideration in decisions about how the organization should be structured, as we noted in Chapter 2, or designed, as we see in Chapter 8.

Unification of Effort   Goals, especially broad goals, can serve to unify efforts among diverse groups inside and outside an organization. Certain goals can serve as overarching mechanisms to link disparate groups together. The 15 nations of the European Union (www.europa.eu.int/index_en.htm) had a long history of mistrust and animosity. After the devastation of World War II, leaders in several European nations realized that they needed a mechanism to align their potentially disparate interest if they had any hope of avoiding another war. After decades of negotiation, false starts, and then real progress, the European Union (EU) is a reality. Trade barriers among member nations have vanished. Movement between member countries is as simple for Europeans as movement between states is for Americans. Eleven member countries have adopted the euro as a common currency, with coins and bank notes issued in January 2002. The next step for the EU is expansion through inclusion of former Eastern Bloc member countries Poland, the Czech Republic, Hungary, Slovenia, and Estonia.

Companies frequently use the same technique by expressing broad goals that are difficult to oppose, for example, goals such as improving customer service or raising profits. (Unanimous support of goals is often rare in organizations as we will see shortly and again in Chapter 12.) Diverse groups in the organization can agree on these motherhood-and-apple-pie goals more easily than goals of retrenchment or downsizing.

Managing Goals and Objectives

In a perfectly rational world, managing the diverse goals of an organization might not be a significant problem. If everyone agreed on the goals and the relative importance of each goal, the organization would simply direct its efforts at sequentially fulfilling

---

EXHIBIT 3-3

Unification of Goals and Effort in the European Union

The mission of the European Union is to coherently organize relations among Member States and their people on the basis of solidarity. The five primary objectives are these:

1. Promote economic and social progress

2. Assert the identity of the European Union on the international scene through humanitarian aid, common foreign and security policy, involvement in mediating international crises, holding common positions in international relations

3. Introduce the concept of European citizenship as a complement to national citizenship

4. Maintain the free flow of people, goods, and capital among member nations

5. Develop and maintain European Union laws and institutions

---

these goals in order of importance. Organizations do not, however, operate in a perfectly rational world. Organizational reality is far more complex. The process of setting organizational goals is at best ambiguous and uncertain. Moreover, goal setting is a *political process* whereby individuals or groups may pursue self-interest rather than what is best for the organization as a whole. Different groups within and outside the organization, referred to as *coalitions* or *stakeholders*, may have different ideas about what are the most important goals to pursue. Stakeholders with interests in the organization (e.g., customers, suppliers, investors, and others) may also have different goals or different priorities for the organization. Instead of perfectly rational agreement on an organization's goals and priorities, organizations typically have many goals, some of which may conflict with others, and managers may disagree on the relative importance of these goals. After all, what seems perfectly rational to one person or group may appear to be misguided, wrong, or irrational to others. Finally, individuals and groups may operate on the basis of a hidden agenda. For example, a manager may advocate and pursue a particular goal because it enhances his or her self-interest rather than the organization's overall interests. That process is depicted in Figure 3-1. However, even Figure 3-1 gives the impression (sometimes a mistaken impression) that the goal-setting process yields one final set of objectives. Conflict may produce a disparate set of goals for the different coalitions and stakeholders.

Given these conditions of multiple and conflicting goals, how do managers proceed? Officially, organizations often have formal and explicit means for establishing goals whether by top management, by a vote of stockholders, by the board of directors, or by some other specified means. In actuality, the setting and managing of goals is often quite different from the formal means that the organization espouses. Internal politics is often the key to understanding the goal-setting and management process. Several techniques for managing goals are discussed in the following:

- If we acknowledge that the process of setting and managing goals in organizations is a political rather than a rational process, then it should become clear that the process of managing goals is one of managing conflict. When top managers responsible for goal setting disagree on an organization's goals, it is typical that the disagreeing parties will *negotiate* or *bargain* in an attempt to resolve differences. Negotiation may result in some goals being abandoned and others being pursued as the primary goals of the organization.

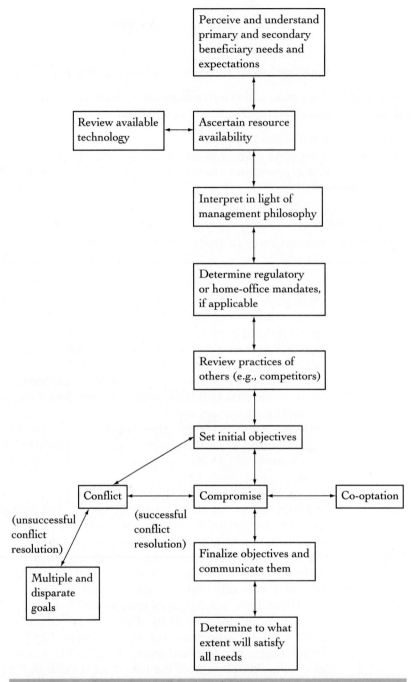

FIGURE 3-1 Determination of Goals and Objectives

Compromises may result when groups give and take. Some groups may come out as winners in negotiations while others are losers—a so-called win-lose negotiation. Occasionally, the bargaining process can be conducted in a way that promotes compromises or changes in the nature of the goals so that all parties regard themselves as winners—a win-win negotiation.

- Another consequence of the human and political nature of organizations is that members of the organization may be satisfied with something less than perfect or complete goal achievement. This phenomenon is referred to as **satisficing**.[19] Managers may set lofty goals for many aspects of the organization. Because some of these goals may be contradictory, it may be impossible to fully meet each of them. For example, in the early 1990s, Apple Computer set goals for increasing market penetration, sales, innovativeness, and profitability. The costs associated with market penetration, sales, and innovativeness caused serious declines in profits. To the extent that management was satisfied with less-than-expected profits would be an example of satisficing. Management has accepted a *satisfactory* level of performance rather than a *maximal* level of performance, although financial analysts and investors may not have been pleased. We explore the phenomenon of satisficing more extensively in the chapter on organizational decision making.

- Finally, two related ordering techniques for managing multiple and potentially conflicting goals are **setting priorities** and **sequencing** of events. In setting priorities, top management determines which of the diverse goals are most important to the organization. The Apple example above suggests that Apple management may have thought that satisfying customers through new, lower-priced products and developing greater sales volume were more important goals than satisfying investors. At the same time, Apple spent extensively on development of the Newton personal data device that was not profitable. Apple eventually abandoned the PDA (personal data appliance) market and devoted its attention to innovative desktop and laptop computers. Clearly, a publicly traded company cannot put too low a priority on investor satisfaction for long. The resulting decline in profitability caused turmoil at Apple that eventually led to the departure of CEO John Sculley.[20]

  Sequencing, on the other hand, assumes that all goals will eventually be met; however, some will be met before others. Apple management focused on first rebuilding its specialized market niches such as graphics and sound applications with the G3 line of computers; it then moved to innovative designs with the iMac line of computers and finally focused on educational markets. Although Apple has regained some market share, it remains to be seen if they move from the fringes of the personal computer market into the mainstream.

Organizational Goals: Summary and Recap

We began this investigation of organizational goals with the premise that organizations have goals. That is what, in part, differentiates an organization from an idle collection of people. The definition in Chapter 1 noted that *organizations are purposeful, goal-oriented entities.* As we started exploring the levels and diversity of goals that an organization may have, we began to see some problems with this idea of organizational goals. First, organizations may have multiple and conflicting goals that are broad or ambiguous so that maximization of all goals may be impossible. Next, we noted that organizations are made up of diverse internal and external constituent groups that may have different ideas about what the goals of the organization should be. This led us to the conclusion that organizational goals may not be rationally or logically constructed. Instead, organizations are political entities made up of diverse groups of people, and goals are the outcome of political processes such as bargaining, negotiating, wielding power, and dominating. Thus, we began with what seemed like a straightforward idea that organizations have goals, and now we have come to realize goals are really a complex issue. As a leading organizational scholar has noted, "The concept of goals is among the most important—and most controversial—concepts to be confronted in the study of organizations."[21]

EFFECTIVENESS

Hand in hand with any discussion of goals should go a treatment of the concept of organizational effectiveness. The preceding examination of organizational goals in some respects sets the stage for exploring effectiveness. One might reasonably assume that if an organization achieves its goals, then it is effective. We will learn, however, that effectiveness is more complicated than merely achieving goals (not that achieving goals is an easy task). Thus, we now turn our attention to the subject of effectiveness.

At some point in our study of an organization or a group of organizations we probably want to ask questions about *how well the organization is doing.* On the surface this question may seem innocent and direct. And at some levels the question is rather simple. Is the organization surviving? And if it is a business, is it making money? But as you may already have guessed from the previous examination of goals, the question of effectiveness is also not as simple as it might first seem. The collapse of many dot.com Internet businesses in 2000–2001 has highlighted the importance of this question. Initially many dot.com entrepreneurs convinced investors and others that standard measures of business performance were not relevant to the "new economy." Typically, many of these Internet businesses focused on "hits" or visits to their Web sites, regardless of whether the "hits" produced revenue. While many business analysts questioned the applicability of such measures of Internet traffic, they are not too different from audience share measures used in television.

The term *effectiveness* is itself unclear. Organizations may be more or less effective in a variety of different ways. Is effectiveness simply the amount of profits earned? Or is it the number of units produced or customers served? What about worker satisfaction? And what about definitions of *effectiveness* proposed by stakeholders of the organization? Are customers satisfied with the organization's products or services? Is the broader community satisfied with the manner in which the organization has conducted itself? Has the company polluted the air and water? Has the company provided some value to the community?

All of the above questions may be relevant to our assessment of an organization's effectiveness. Thus, the answer to our question—Is Organization X effective?—may partly depend on who is asking and the reason for the question. The implication is that there is a variety of ways in which to measure an organization's effectiveness. In the following sections we look at several approaches to the assessment of organizational effectiveness and discuss their applicability, strengths, and weaknesses.

Internal Effectiveness   Some of the earliest organizational theorists focused on internal effectiveness as the key to organizational effectiveness. Two different subgroups of theorists emerged and looked at different characteristics of organizational effectiveness, or "health": internal efficiency and human relations.

The *efficiency* approach to internal effectiveness, a legacy of the industrial engineering and time-motion studies of Frederick W. Taylor, measures the efficient use of resources.[22] An organization is effective to the extent that it maximizes outputs with respect to the costs of inputs and the costs of the transformation of those inputs into outputs. For example, automakers pay great attention to the cost of producing a given car. General Motors has been judged to be a less effective car maker because its costs of production are greater than those of Ford, Daimler-Chrysler, and Japanese rivals. Similarly, downsizing in many industries (e.g., Apple and IBM in the computer industry and Procter & Gamble in consumer products) has been aimed at reducing the cost of production to improve internal effectiveness. The underlying assumption is that an organization that more efficiently transforms inputs into outputs is more effective than an organization that is less efficient. Although that logic is appealing, effectiveness typically involves more than merely being efficient. Figure 3-2 shows the relationship between efficiency and effectiveness.

Internal efficiency may be an important element in organizational effectiveness, but it provides only a limited perspective on effectiveness. A company may greatly improve its internal efficiency by substituting lower quality inputs, cutting corners on production, or using less expensive but questionable means for disposing of waste materials. All these tactics may *reduce* overall effectiveness. Additionally, a company may be efficient in producing outputs, but there may be no market for those products.

The **Human Relations School** of organization theory, mentioned briefly in Chapter 1, provides the foundation for a second internal process view of organizational effectiveness. Theorists from this school are concerned with the **emotional** or **affective health** of an organization and have focused on internal stress and strain as indicators of effectiveness. An effective organization is characterized by smooth vertical and horizontal information flows, a near absence of conflict, and the presence of trust and benevolence. In sum, an effective organization is one in which workers are happy and satisfied.[23]

FIGURE 3-2   Efficiency and Effectiveness

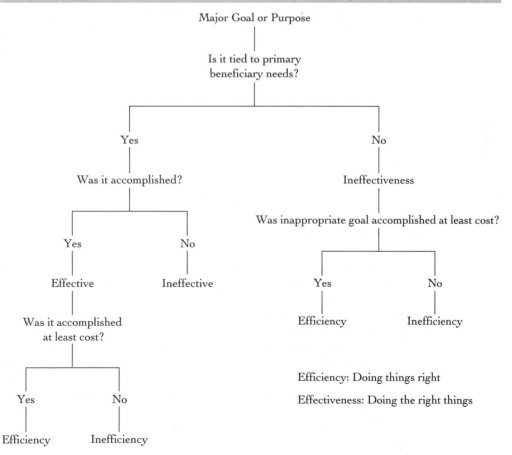

As is the case with efficiency, the human relations approach provides only a partial, and sometimes inaccurate, picture of organizational performance. Ample evidence suggests that worker happiness does not necessarily lead to productivity—let alone effectiveness. Happy workers may become complacent and fail to see the need to adapt to changing external conditions. Even if workers are happy and efficient, they may not be producing desired outputs. Moreover, the elimination of conflict may *reduce* effectiveness. Workers may fail to challenge inefficient or misdirected efforts, thus reducing effectiveness. You can begin to see that effectiveness is more complex than efficiency and worker satisfaction and a lack of conflict.

Goals and Effectiveness The ***goal approach*** defines effectiveness in terms of if and how well an organization accomplishes its goals. To the extent that an organization has defined its goals in ways that permit observation and measurement, effectiveness can be judged by the extent to which the organization meets its goals. The closer the organization comes to meeting its goals, the more effective it is. An advantage of the goal approach is that the effectiveness of each organization can be judged independently. The goal approach does not depend on comparative judgments of effectiveness. Investment analysts, to a great extent, use a version of the goal approach—Has a firm met its revenue and profit goals—although these goals are often imposed on the organization by the investment community.

Although this approach has a certain logical appeal, our earlier examination of goals should suggest to the reader that this approach is also problematic. First, if an organization has ill-defined, complex, or inappropriate goals, this approach may lead to erroneous conclusions. In the mid-1980s Kmart embarked on a goal of acquiring specialty store chains. It was successful in meeting that goal through several acquisitions: Builders Square building supply warehouse stores, Walden Books, Borders Books, Pace Membership Warehouse stores, Pay Less Drug Stores, Sports Authority, and OfficeMax. If Kmart's effectiveness were measured simply by its attainment of its acquisition goals, then Kmart would have been judged effective. However, by several other measures of effectiveness Kmart's performance clearly fell short. The company's profits and stock price fell; it lost market share to Wal-Mart in its primary market and was unable to compete effectively in the specialty markets; and eventually Kmart divested itself of most of the specialty business to refocus on its core discount store business.[24]

Second, an organization's goals may not represent the diverse interests of the many stakeholder groups (e.g., community, employee, government) that have interests in the organization. An organization's goal to grow and expand may conflict with the interests of the local community that fears the potential increases in traffic, congestion, and pollution. Wal-Mart has encountered just this sort of problem in a number of rural communities in which it desires to locate new stores.[25] Wal-Mart's goals include expanding into new, untapped markets. Yet many residents, especially in rural communities, fear that Wal-Mart's entry will degrade the quality of life in those communities. An organization's goals to streamline operations, increase productivity, and downsize may conflict with employees' goals to maintain a high quality of work life. A company may move production to another country to meet goals of low-cost labor. Federal, state, and local governments may object because such a move counters their goals of maintaining levels of employment and the tax base.

Third, the very nature of goals, that they may be ambiguous or conflict with one another, may mean that meeting some goals is not possible or that meeting some goals means that others will go unmet. We examined this problem earlier in the chapter in our discussion of goals. The point here is that it may be difficult to determine whether an organization has met its goals if the goals are ambiguous, and it may be difficult to judge effectiveness if goals are conflicting. Academic institutions typically set as a goal educating their students. In some technical or skill areas, assessment of educational effectiveness may be clear, but that is the exception rather than the rule. One only needs to look at the heated debates in civic and political circles concerning educational effectiveness to understand the difficulty of measurement.[26]

Thus, even though the practice of judging effectiveness by the degree to which an organization reaches goals is commonly used, it is a method that is problematic. A company that reaches its goals may not, in a more general sense, be effective.

Resources and Effectiveness   A basic premise of the open systems view of organizations presented in Chapter 1 is that organizations must acquire resources from the external environment. Materials and labor necessary to create the intended outputs of the organization are found in the external environment. The ***systems resource model*** claims that effectiveness is attained to the extent that the organization acquires from the environment those resources necessary to carry out its purpose. The reasoning behind this model is based on the belief that there is a clear connection between inputs to the system and its performance. An organization must have inputs to create outputs. For example, in the tight labor market of the late 1990s, many technology firms found it difficult to find skilled labor. Many North American technology firms turned to outsourcing in India to procure skilled workers. In the Czech Republic, the Škoda Automotive division of Volkswagen has had to import Polish laborers to perform much of the welding work because Czech workers were unwilling to tackle those jobs. Without sufficient human resources, these firms could not function and compete. Acquiring inputs, in this case labor inputs, is *necessary* for successful operation. The mere presence of this input is not, however, *sufficient* to guarantee the effective operation of the firm, and that is a significant weakness of the systems resource model of effectiveness. Many other factors may inhibit the performance of the franchise. Obtaining the highest quality inputs is no guarantee of superior performance. Sports teams packed with superstars have failed to win championships and those lacking superstar players have at times won championships.[27] Similarly, there is no guarantee that a business will make the best use of the inputs it acquires. While acquiring resources is clearly necessary and may be a precursor to success, resource acquisition alone does not give a comprehensive picture of organizational effectiveness.

Performance and Stakeholders   Satisfaction of key ***constituent groups*** or ***stakeholders*** represents another major method of assessing organizational effectiveness. The belief is that organizations are effective to the extent that the key groups of individuals (i.e., constituents or stakeholders) are at least minimally satisfied. Constituents or stakeholders are those groups of individuals with a definite and immediate interest in the organization's performance. Typical of these groups are stockholders, managers, employees (and perhaps their unions), creditors, suppliers, customers, regulators, and community members, to name just a few concerned groups. These groups attempt to influence the organization to perform in certain ways and judge effectiveness by the degree to which the organization responds to this influence. Shareholders seek to maximize their return on investment and judge effectiveness accordingly. Creditors judge effectiveness by the firm's creditworthiness and its ability to meet debt obligations. Employees judge effectiveness on the basis of job security and the quality of the work environment.

EXHIBIT 3-4

Satisfying Multiple Stakeholders: Customers, Investors, and Unions in the North American Automobile Industry

The modern automobile manufacturer is a great case study of the multiple and conflicting stakeholders, and the resulting difficulty of measuring performance. An obvious fact of life for a publicly traded company is that it must show profits in accordance with investor expectations. When profits fall short of expectations, investors will voice their dissatisfaction by selling shares (further driving down prices of the stock) or, if they hold sufficient shares, by taking action to replace management. The result is that the investors push management to operate more efficiently. At the North American auto companies, management has shifted manufacturing to Mexico, Brazil, and other low-wage locations. The companies have also turned to external suppliers for components once produced internally. Specialized suppliers can often produce high quality components at lower costs. In some auto plants, suppliers are co-located with the production facility and even install the component part on the car. For example, a producer of seats or instrument panels for Ford may actually install those parts on the Ford car at Ford's assembly plant.

While such cost savings may satisfy investors (and consumers if the result is lower retail pricing), the changes have not pleased the United Automobile Workers (UAW) union. Many jobs formerly held by unionized workers in the United States have been shifted to nonunion workers, often outside the United States and Canada (the areas covered by the UAW). The UAW has vigorously fought this trend and has enlisted politicians and others in the battle. The union and its allies argue that outsourcing and off-shore manufacturing weaken the businesses through loss of core competence and weaken the economy through loss of jobs. Politicians push for a stable economy (and votes).

Consumers are primarily concerned with value: Does the vehicle represent the best combination of price, features, and quality? Keep in mind that auto workers are consumers too. Consumers will vote with their dollars. In the early 1990s, when Ford redesigned the Taurus with recurrent themes based on the oval, customers balked at the unconventional design and turned to Honda Accords and Toyota Camrys. Although the UAW protested because the Hondas and Toyotas were produced in nonunion plants, consumers could at least point to the fact that the cars were made in the United States (Honda in Ohio and Toyota in Kentucky).

Investors continue to push for efficiency and profits; unions continue to push for job security; and consumers push for quality, features, and value. All the while, management must do its best to satisfy these diverse stakeholders. No easy task, to say the least.

Much like the problems of conflicting and inappropriate goals, stakeholders or constituent groups hold diverse expectations for a typical company. Often it is not possible to satisfy all the demands of all constituent groups. The resulting dilemma is which constituent groups are most important. Unfortunately, there is no clear answer to that question. The importance of any given constituent group will vary over time and circumstances and will be a function of the power that group holds over the organization.

Effectiveness: A Synthesis   You may be wondering, what is an effective organization? After exploring the previous views of effectiveness, you may have the uneasy feeling that there is no clear-cut, surefire way to comprehensively measure organizational effectiveness. And you are correct. Each of the previously mentioned views provides only a partial, skewed vision of effectiveness. That brings us to two additional perspectives on effectiveness. These perspectives do not propose different measures of effectiveness. Instead, they suggest different ways of using some of the previously stated methods.

The ***contradictions model*** of effectiveness states that the idea of trying to characterize a whole organization as totally effective or ineffective is problematic.[28] In any complex organization there may be parts of the organization that function well and suggest effectiveness while other aspects of that same organization perform poorly. The juxtaposition of effective and ineffective segments of an organization constitutes the contradictions to which this model refers. Is that organization effective? More important, as noted with goals and the goal approach, the effectiveness of some parts of an organization may mean that other parts will of necessity perform suboptimally. Satisfying certain key stakeholders may mean unsatisfactory performance in the eyes of others.

Four central assumptions drive the contradictions model:[29]

1. Organizations face complex environments that place multiple and conflicting demands and constraints on them. It may not be possible to succeed in meeting all the environmental conditions an organization faces.

2. Organizations have multiple, conflicting goals. It is impossible to maximize achievement of all goals.

3. Organizations face multiple internal and external stakeholders or constituent groups that make competing or conflicting demands. It may be impossible to satisfy all groups of people who express interest in a company.

4. Organizations must manage multiple and conflicting time demands. Satisfying short- or long-term demands at the expense of the other may result in suboptimal performance.

The contradictions model merely suggests that we make note of these potential contradictions in our assessment of performance and acknowledge that *any* assessment of performance must, of necessity, be constrained or limited.

The ***competing values model*** takes a different approach to dealing with the problems and limitations of effectiveness assessment.[30] The essential point of the competing values model is that no single measure of effectiveness is, by itself, satisfactory. Rather, different methods of assessing performance will be relevant for organizations having different underlying management values or orientations. The result is the set of four different approaches to effectiveness represented in Figure 3-3.

The appropriate measure of effectiveness for a given organization depends upon its focus (internally focused versus externally focused) and its desires for either control or flexibility. The combination of these two dimensions yields four distinct approaches to effectiveness. Organizations that best fit in the human relations quadrant are internally focused and desire flexibility. They seek to develop employees so that they reach their highest potential to contribute to the organization. The organization pursues worker satisfaction, high morale, and cooperation as means for helping employees develop. Methods for measuring effectiveness described earlier under the heading of Human Resources would apply in this case. Flexible, externally oriented firms are described as fitting the open systems model. The organization acknowledges that it is affected by events or conditions in the external environment, and it seeks to maintain flexibility in responding to the environment. This organization pursues resources to foster growth. The systems resources model described earlier would fit this quadrant. Organizations that seek stability and predictability in their internal operations are internally focused and oriented toward control. Efficiency would be an appropriate measure in this situation. Finally, the control-oriented, externally focused organization seeks to achieve the goals set by top management. Emphasis is on strategic planning

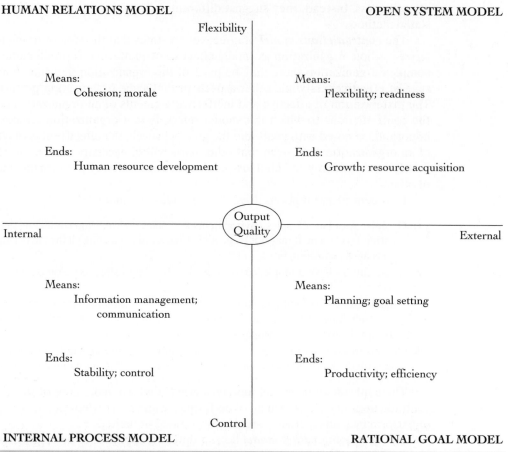

HUMAN RELATIONS MODEL

Flexibility

Means:
Cohesion; morale

Ends:
Human resource development

OPEN SYSTEM MODEL

Means:
Flexibility; readiness

Ends:
Growth; resource acquisition

Output Quality

Internal   External

Means:
Information management;
communication

Ends:
Stability; control

Means:
Planning; goal setting

Ends:
Productivity; efficiency

Control

INTERNAL PROCESS MODEL

RATIONAL GOAL MODEL

FIGURE 3-3   Competing Values Effectiveness Model

Source: Adapted from Robert E. Quinn and John Rohrbaugh, "A Spatial Model of Effectiveness: Toward a Competing Values Approach to Organizational Analysis," *Management Science* 29 (1983): 363–77.

and goal setting, and the measures of effectiveness would be the degree to which those goals are attained. This quadrant matches the goal model presented earlier.

The Balanced Scorecard   A variety of approaches to effectiveness have emerged in the 1990s that recognize the multidimensional nature of performance. Many of these approaches are direct products of the Total Quality Management (TQM) movement. One such approach is the **balanced scorecard** developed by Robert Kaplan and David Norton.[31] The balanced scorecard contains four dimensions of performance. To be successful, a firm must succeed in financial performance, internal operational performance, customer performance, and innovation and learning performance.

Financial performance measures include shareholder value, profitability, revenue growth, return on investment, and economic value added (EVA).

Internal operational measures assess levels of productivity, quality, and cycle time. All of these contribute to production cost.

Customer measures focus on customer satisfaction products and services, market share, and repeat business.

Innovation and learning are critical to the continuing success of the firm and focus on the organizational infrastructure and people. Assessment focuses on employee satisfaction, employee development, intellectual capital, and organizational innovation.

As Evans and Lindsay note, "A good balanced scorecard contains both leading and lagging measures and indicators. *Lagging measures* (outcomes) tell what has happened; *leading measures* (performance drivers) predict what will happen."[32] These measures should provide a comprehensive picture of performance over time. Measures of some performance elements (e.g., employee satisfaction, productivity, and quality) should be related to customer satisfaction and retention, which should in turn be related to financial performance and market share. Advocates of the balanced scorecard believe that understanding the relationships among the performance components is key to making informed decisions about strategy and operations.

Effectiveness: A Summary   We have presented a diverse set of approaches to measuring organizational effectiveness. This begs the question: Which approach is best? The answer to this question is not easy, but we can begin to answer it by asking a few others. First, why do we want to measure effectiveness? What is our objective? An investment analyst seeking to rate the investment potential of a given company will certainly use different criteria for effectiveness than will an employment specialist seeking to identify the best companies for which to work. Second, we may also need to set a time frame on our assessment. One lesson of works such as *In Search of Excellence*[33] is that organizations that are effective at one point in time are certainly not guaranteed effectiveness in the future. Many organizations that Peters and Waterman identified as excellent at the time the book was published are no longer in business or have fallen on hard times (e.g., Amdahl, IBM, Data General, and Wang Laboratories). Because organizations are open systems, they must deal with the external environment, and, as we learn in the next chapter, environments can change rapidly and unpredictably. Criteria for effectiveness that are appropriate today may not fit in the organizations of tomorrow. Finally, as the contradictions and competing values models suggest, different approaches to effectiveness may be appropriate for different types of organizations. Thus, we can answer our question, "Which model is best?" with a resounding, "It depends."

SUMMARY

Today's managers face an important assignment—setting goals or objectives that are aimed at satisfying the needs and desires of a complex set of constituents inside and outside the organization. Goals or objectives establish the desired future state that the organization is trying to achieve. Goals create legitimacy for the organization by providing the rationale for its existence. Goals guide members' actions and set standards against which the organization's performance can be measured.

Goals are multifaceted and may apply at different levels of the organization. Mission statements or official goals state the broad ambitions of the organization as a whole in rather general terms. Operative goals are more specific and may be tailored to individual departments, divisions, or work groups. Eight categories of operative goals were introduced (market, financial performance, resource, innovation, productivity, management development, employee performance and attitudes, and ethical or social responsibility goals). An area of goals to which organizations are devoting increasing attention is ethical behavior. Utilitarian (consequence-based) and formalist (rule-based) ethics provide two potentially complementary frameworks for viewing ethical problems in organizations.

Goals also vary by the intended beneficiaries (primary and secondary). Primary beneficiaries are those the organization intends to serve (e.g., customers). Secondary beneficiaries are those who benefit because of their association with the organization (e.g., employees, suppliers, or owners).

The organization must establish a hierarchy of short- and long-term goals. Some objectives may be critical to achieve quickly. Other goals may require more time or may be sequentially linked to the achievement of prior goals. An essential managerial task is assigning a time frame to the various goals an organization seeks to fulfill.

Goals serve a number of important functions for organizations. Employees look to goal statements for guidance and direction. Goals can motivate employees to achieve specific outcomes. The organization obtains legitimacy for its actions from its mission or goal statement. Goals provide standards for judging an organization's performance. However, as was noted in the discussion of effectiveness, one must be cautious in using goals alone to measure effectiveness. The organization must take into consideration the number, diversity, and complexity of goals when seeking to create an appropriate structure or design. Last, goals can serve as a rallying point to unify or consolidate organizational members.

With the diversity of goals and the potential for conflict among goals, the task of managing goals becomes critical. Several techniques for managing goals that include sequencing, setting priorities, satisficing, and bargaining or negotiation were explored. We concluded by noting that goals are a deceptively complex issue in organizations.

The manager's job does not end with the setting of goals or objectives. At some point people inside and outside the organization want to know how effective the organization is. The question of how effective an organization is becomes, like goals, deceptively difficult and complex. Several methods can be used, but none give a comprehensive picture of effectiveness. Internal approaches focus on efficiency and/or satisfaction of employees. These approaches typically ignore the external environment or external constituent groups. The goal approach judges effectiveness by the extent to which an organization achieves its stated goals. However, goals may be ambiguous, conflicting, or inappropriate. Thus, fulfilling goals may not indicate effectiveness. Acquiring resources is essential to an organization's effectiveness, and resource acquisition has been used as a measure of effectiveness. But even if an organization is successful acquiring resources, there is no guarantee that it will use those resources appropriately. Satisfying the diverse groups of stakeholders of an organization also may be used as an indicator of effectiveness. The problem is that, like goals, there are typically many stakeholders of an organization and their demands or requirements may conflict.

We concluded by presenting two models, the contradictions model and the competing values model, which try to accommodate the shortcomings in typical models of effectiveness. The contradictions model states that any model of effectiveness is inherently flawed. When using any model of effectiveness we must take into consideration our purpose and the limitations of the model. The competing values model is a contingency model that suggests different models of effectiveness for different types of organizations.

This chapter has analyzed organizational goals and effectiveness, two critical issues in the study of organizations. These two concepts, seemingly quite straightforward, turn out to be complex and difficult but essential to our understanding and management of organizations.

Questions for Discussion

1. Explain in detail the role of goals in the formation and operation of organizations.
2. What, if any, role do/should goals play in the downsizing of a major firm?
3. Explain the reasons for sequencing in the setting of mission, operative, and operational goals.
4. Write a long-term goal dealing with innovation for your university, and propose a derivative short-term goal for your department.
5. What can cause a conflict of organization goals? How would you propose to reconcile or resolve this conflict?
6. What role would you suggest that ethics play in both goal setting and goal measurement?
7. What role do goals play in legitimacy?
8. Define effectiveness and explain which organization members should be responsible for managing the organization to achieve it.
9. How can the contradictions model and the competing values model be used to determine organization effectiveness? Apply these models to measuring the effectiveness of your college or university.

References

1. W. Richard Scott, *Organizations: Rational, Natural and Open Systems,* 3rd ed. (Upper Saddle River, NJ: Prentice Hall, 1992); Amitai Etzioni, *Modern Organizations* (Upper Saddle River, NJ: Prentice Hall, 1964).
2. See Etzioni in note 1.
3. Richard H. Hall, *Organizations: Structures, Processes, and Outcomes,* 5th ed. (Upper Saddle River, NJ: Prentice Hall, 1991).
4. Leslie W. LaRue and Lloyd D. Byars, *Management: Theory and Application,* 4th ed. (Homewood, IL: Richard D. Irwin, 1986), 432–33.
5. Ibid.
6. Charles Perrow, "The Analysis of Goals in Complex Organizations," *American Sociological Review* 26 (1961): 854–66; Peter F. Drucker, *The Practice of Management* (New York: Harper & Row, 1973); Luther Gulick and L. Urwick, eds., *Papers on the Science of Administration* (New York: Institute of Public Administration, Columbia University, 1937).
7. Arthur G. Bedeian and Raymond F. Zammuto, *Organizations: Theory and Design* (Chicago: The Dryden Press, 1991); see Drucker in note 6.
8. G. Pascal Zachary, "Agony and Ecstasy of 200 Code Writers Beget Windows NT," *The Wall Street Journal* (May 26, 1993), A1, A6.
9. David Woodruff and Elizabeth Lesly, "Surge at Chrysler," *Business Week* (November 9, 1992): 88–96; Brian Dumaine, "How Managers Can Succeed Through Speed," *Fortune* (February 13, 1989): 54–59; Ronald Henkoff, "A High-Tech Rx for Profits," *Fortune* (March 23, 1992): 106–107; Lori Bongiorno,

"A Case Study in Change at Harvard," *Business Week* (November 15, 1993): 42.
10. Charles J. Fombrun, Noel M. Tichy, and Mary Anne Devanna, *Strategic Human Resources Management* (New York: Wiley, 1984); Anne B. Fisher, "Morale Crisis," *Fortune* (November 18, 1991): 70–80.
11. Randy Tucker, "P&G Struggles to Regain Toothpaste Lead," *The Cincinnati Enquirer* (April 7, 2001), C-1.
12. Myron Magnet, "The Truth About the American Worker," *Fortune* (May 4, 1992): 48–65.
13. See note 9.
14. William A. Sodeman, "The Body Shop International PLC," in *Business & Society,* 2nd ed., by Archie B. Carroll (Cincinnati, OH: Southwestern, 1993), 637–41.
15. Leslie Kaufman-Rosen, "Being Cruel to Be Kind," *Newsweek* (October 17, 1994); 51–52.
16. F. Neil Brady, *Ethical Managing: Rules and Results* (New York: Macmillan Publishing, 1990); Robert D. Hay, Edmund R. Gray, and Paul H. Smith, *Business and Society: Perspectives on Ethics & Social Responsibility* (Cincinnati, OH: Southwestern Publishing, 1989); Rogene A. Buchholz, *Fundamental Concepts and Problems in Business Ethics* (Upper Saddle River, NJ: Prentice Hall, 1989).
17. F. Neil Brady, *Ethical Managing: Rules and Results* (New York: MacMillan, 1990).
18. Neal Templin, "GM Unit Posts Operating Profit for First Time," *The Wall Street Journal* (June 14, 1993), A4.
19. James G. March and Herbert A. Simon, *Organizations* (New York: Wiley, 1958); Herbert A.

Simon, *Administrative Behavior,* 3rd ed. (New York: Free Press, 1976); Richard M. Cyert and James G. March, *A Behavioral Theory of the Firm* (Upper Saddle River, NJ: Prentice Hall, 1963).

20. Charles McCoy, "As Scully Leaves Apple, Image Lingers of a Leader Distracted by His Mission," *The Wall Street Journal* (October 18, 1993), B8.

21. See Scott in note 1, page 19.

22. See note 3; Daniel Katz and Robert L. Kahn, *The Social Psychology of Organizations,* 2nd ed. (New York: Wiley, 1978).

23. See note 3; Kim S. Cameron, "The Effectiveness of Ineffectiveness," in Barry M. Staw and L. L. Cummings, eds., *Research in Organizational Behavior* (Greenwich, CT: JAI Press, 1984), 235–86; J. Barton Cunningham, "Approaches to the Evaluation of Effectiveness," *Academy of Management Review* 2 (1977): 463–74.

24. Christina Duff, "Blue-Light Blues: K-Mart's Dowdy Stores Get a Snazzy Face Lift, but Problems Linger," *The Wall Street Journal* (November 5, 1993), 1–6.

25. Bob Ortega, "Aging Activists Turn, Turn, Turn Attention to Wal-Mart Protests," *The Wall Street Journal* (October 11, 1994), A1–A6.

26. William C. Symonds, "How to Fix America's Schools," *Business Week* (March 19, 2001): 66–80.

27. See Cameron (1984) in note 23.

28. See note 3.

29. See note 3, pp. 288–93.

30. Robert E. Quinn and John Rohrbaugh, "A Spatial Model of Effectiveness: Toward a Competing Values Approach to Organizational Analysis," *Management Science* 29 (1983): 363–77.

31. James R. Evans and William M. Lindsay, *The Management and Control of Quality,* 5th ed. (Cincinnati, OH: Southwestern College Publishing, 2002). Robert S. Kaplan and David P. Norton, *The Balanced Scorecard* (Boston: Harvard Business School Press, 1996).

32. See Evans and Lindsay in note 31.

33. Thomas J. Peters and Robert H. Waterman, Jr., *In Search of Excellence: Lessons from America's Best-Run Companies* (New York: Harper, Row & Co., 1982).

*Becoming the Next General Electric**

In the period from the mid-1980s to the new century, General Electric (GE) has undoubtedly been one of the most successful companies and its chairman, Jack Welch, has been one of the most admired executives. The company has strengthened its position in its core businesses such as power-generating equipment, aircraft engines, and lighting equipment; acquired new operations such as financial services; and, perhaps most important, shed underperforming businesses such as small appliances and televisions. The corporate landscape is littered with former competitors who tried to challenge GE in its key business areas, only to find the task insurmountable. Among "Blue Chip" companies, its growth and financial performance have been unparalleled.

One question often asked among management experts and financial analysts is who will be the next Jack Welch and what company will be the next GE. One CEO is already trying to claim that title: Dennis Kozlowski, head of Tyco International. In his words, "Hopefully, we can become the next GE."[1] You may ask, what is Tyco International, who is Dennis Kozlowski, and is there any merit to his claim?

Answering the first question may be the easiest. Tyco International is a $38 billion diversified industrial conglomerate with manufacturing and service subsidiaries in the electrical and electronic components business; the telecommunications and undersea cable communications systems business; the medical supplies and specialty products sector; fire detection, suppression, and electronic security systems business; and flow control and environmental consulting services area.

According to Tyco's corporate Web site, they are successful because they "adhere to basic strategies: we are a high-value producer, keeping our business simple and staying close to our markets and customers; we empower our employees through performance-based incentives and continuing education opportunities; we grow our business internally, while augmenting this growth through acquisitions."[2] But this only gives a small part of the picture. To really understand Tyco International and its goals and objectives, you have to understand L. Dennis Kozlowski and how he has managed Tyco International.

Kozlowski grew up in a blue-collar neighborhood of Newark, New Jersey, the son of a police detective. While a Seton Hall University finance and accounting student, he worked 30 hours a week and lived at home so he could afford tuition. Between working and studying, Kozlowski found time for flying lessons and now pilots corporate and personal aircraft. Upon graduation, he moved to New York and rose through the ranks of auditing and finance jobs at several companies before joining Tyco in 1975. At the time Tyco was a $15 million diversified manufacturing firm. But the company's CEO aspired to build the company to $1 billion through purchasing. Kozlowski's first order of business was to bring order and efficiency to existing acquisitions. He did this by cutting corporate staff by 85 percent and eliminating meetings. Those early lean trends became a hallmark of Kozlowski's management strategy. Today a corporate staff of only 140 supervises approximately 205,000 employees. Executives do not receive perks such as country club memberships or exclusive dining rooms. And Kozlowski works out of a modest two-story office in Exeter, New Hampshire (although the corporate headquarters is in Bermuda), in determined pursuit of growth.

Although Tyco International may be unknown to all but a few market analysts and students of business, the company's market capitalization (the value of its stock—one measure of size) is greater than that of high-visibility companies such as Boeing and Hewlett-Packard. The company has grown largely through acquisitions, including AMP (electrical connector maker), Kendall (medical supplies), Lucent Power Systems (telecommunications power supply systems and formerly part of Lucent Technology), ADT (home securities specialist), and most recently CIT Group (commercial finance). Kozlowski's strategy is to find unglamorous, fast-growing, undervalued firms. He strikes quickly, concluding acquisitions deals in 6 weeks rather than the customary 6 months that most experts think is necessary.

Tyco's game plan for acquisitions is straightforward. The company acts much like a mergers and acquisitions group. Tyco's operating managers scan the environment looking for likely takeover targets. Target firms are reviewed by managers of related Tyco business units to determine the fit. The firms that make it through this first review—about half of all prospects—are then subjected to "due diligence." Tyco managers pore over the books and closely examine operations, further reducing the list of prospects. Key to acceptance is that the target company must be able to immediately contribute to Tyco's earnings. Kozlowski doesn't buy on the basis of future potential. He seeks immediate results. Another key element is that Tyco does not pursue hostile takeovers. Even with these stringent criteria, Tyco acquires as many as 100 firms each year.

Implementation of the takeover is immediate. For example, Tyco cut 60 out of 66 vice presidents two days after acquiring AMP and embarked on an aggressive cost-cutting plan aimed at weeding out $1 billion in costs over an 18-month period. At CIT, Tyco immediately dumped over $4 billion in bad loans and refocused the company to finance many of Tyco's other units. CIT now writes loans and leases for several Tyco units, including the ADT home security division. The acquisition of Kendall was integrated with several other medical supply companies that the company already owned and has made Tyco competitive with the industry leader, Johnson & Johnson. In 1996 Tyco acquired Ruffies, the number 3 maker of trash bags. Through aggressive cost cutting and new product development, the unit moved to number 1 in the industry and tripled profit margins.

Kozlowski and Tyco have not been without controversy. The basic strategy of becoming a diversified conglomerate has a rather mixed track record. Although GE and Warren Buffet's Berkshire Hathaway have been successful, there's a longer list of failures including Westinghouse, LTV, ITT, and ATT. Over half of all mergers and acquisitions end in failures. Managing a diverse set of assets that includes electronics, electrical supplies, health care, home security and fire protection, industrial valves and flow controls, communications equipment, and now financial services requires constant attention. Even though Kozlowski grants managers significant autonomy, he is still a hands-on manager. He uses a computer-based information system to monitor performance and tells his managers that he wants to know immediately, and not by e-mail, if performance is below targets. He expects managers to call him directly to work out plans to turn around slumping units. On the other hand, Kozlowski aggressively uses a bonus system to reward successful managers. Meeting performance targets can result in bonuses that double executive salaries.

A second area of controversy has to do with accusations of accounting irregularities and use of questionable tax dodges to inflate earnings. Some analysts claimed that Tyco resorted to accounting gimmicks to pump up earnings. The Securities and Exchange Commission inquiry of July 2000 failed, however, to uncover any accounting problems. Also, Tyco's use of its Bermuda-based headquarters, acquired as part of the ADT deal, has allowed the company to avoid substantial U.S. tax liabilities. In fact, Tyco saves more in taxes—over $500 million—than some *Fortune* 500 firms earned in 2000. Although there is nothing illegal in Tyco's actions, some critics claim that the company's move offshore has cheated the American people out of tax revenues that are rightfully theirs.

Whether Tyco and Kozlowski reach the heights achieved by GE and Jack Welch is still open to question. But there is at least one area where Kozlowski has surpassed Welch. In 2000 Kozlowski's total compensation was $125.3 million, more than Jack Welch earned. ■

---

*This case is based on the following sources: William C. Symonds, "The Most Aggressive CEO," *Business Week* (May 28, 2001): 68–77; Yahoo financial; and www.tycoint.com.
[1]Symonds, 74.
[2]www.tycoint.com/main/business/welcome.

QUESTIONS FOR DISCUSSION

1. If Tyco International wants to challenge GE, what types of goals should it set?
2. How would you describe Tyco's current goals?
3. How can Tyco set goals for the diverse set of companies it owns?

CHAPTER

The Global Environment for Organizations

CASE: DRIVING A GLOBAL INDUSTRY

There was a time when people associated automobile manufacturers with particular countries. Ford and General Motors were viewed as quintessential American companies.[1] Henry Ford was part of the American entrepreneurial folklore and Alfred Slaon, the architect of the modern multidivisional General Motors Corporation in the 1920s, was viewed as a management pioneer. In recent years, people associated Saab and Volvo with Scandinavian pragmatism and safety; Mercedes Benz and BMW with precision German engineering and high performance; Renault, Peugeot, and Citroen with French quirkiness; Rolls Royce, Bentley, and Jaguar with British royalty; Fiat, Alfa Romeo, and Lancia with the Italian flair for design; and Toyota and Honda with the Japanese combination of quality and efficiency. But the automobile industry of the late twentieth century and early twenty-first century is truly global, and it is hard to think of national companies any longer.

Companies that were once thought of as "national" (and some were even government owned) are now becoming global beyond imagination. Think, for example, of the German company Volkswagen (VW) (www.vw.com/worldwide/?). Their core cars (Volkswagen, Audi, and Porsche) are produced in Austria, Finland, Mexico, and Brazil, as well as Germany. Additionally, the company owns Škoda of the Czech Republic, Seat of Spain, and Rolls Royce (although Volkswagen and BMW are engaged in heated controversy over the eventual rights to the Rolls Royce and Bentley names and assets) and has operations scattered around the globe.

And VW is not alone in its globalization. Perhaps the most dramatic attempt to expand a company's global presence was Daimler's merger with Chrysler. Daimler already had manufacturing facilities in the United States and Chrysler had a small presence in Europe, but the joining of the two companies (supposedly a merger of equals) potentially expanded markets for both companies. Chrysler would have an easier time distributing and selling products in Europe—Daimler's home market—and Daimler would potentially have a broader distribution network in the United States for Mercedes Benz cars.[2] (As we will see in Chapter 10, the competing cultures of Chrysler and Daimler have made this merger more difficult than company insiders expected.)

Similarly, Renault of France acquired a significant portion of Nissan. What makes this transaction unusual is that Renault is still partially owned by the French government. Moreover, one can hardly imagine two companies with different approaches to managing. Although Nissan has been saddled by mounting debt and has struggled

---

[1]Even early in their history, both GM and Ford had operations throughout much of the world. Ford had suppliers in Asia, South America, and Europe, and both companies had manufacturing in Europe as early as the 1930s.

[2]Alex Taylor, "Can the Germans Rescue Chrysler?" *Fortune* (European Edition) (April 30, 2001): 44–47.

unsuccessfully to keep up with Honda and Toyota, it still is associated with frugal Japanese management, tight links with suppliers, and focus on quality. Under years of government control, Renault built a reputation for ponderous bureaucracy, inefficiency, and poor product quality. Renault has recently undergone dramatic changes aimed at streamlining management, improving designs and decision making, and enhancing quality. Now *they* are viewed as potential saviors for the struggling Japanese manufacturer.

Those venerable American firms, General Motors and Ford, are now thoroughly global. Ford owns Jaguar, Volvo, Aston Martin, the Land Rover portion of Rover, and a significant portion of Mazda. In addition, Ford has extensive worldwide operations that manufacture under the Ford name in Europe, South America, and Asia. General Motors owns Saab, significant portions of Isuzu, Fiat, Fuji Heavy Industries (Subaru), Suzuki, and has held the German firm Adam Opel for many years.[3] Recently, General Motors entered into an agreement to manufacture Buick cars in China.

Many Japanese automakers moved production facilities to the United States and Europe in the 1980s and 1990s to deal with increasing political pressure over trade restrictions and increasing production costs in Japan. Toyota, Nissan, Honda, Mitsubishi, Isuzu, and Mazda have all had some production facilities in the United States during the last two decades. Honda even exports U.S.-made cars to Japan, and Toyota designs some models in this country specifically for the U.S. market.

Auto companies operating manufacturing facilities in foreign environments must weigh the advantages of their own management systems and expertise with the conditions in the local environment. The Toyota plant in Valenciennes, France, is a microcosm of how the automobile industry and people must adapt.[4] Toyota located a plant in France to take advantage of a position inside the European Union. However, adjusting to the French way was not easy for Toyota, nor was adjusting to Japanese management easy for the French. French workers, accustomed to drinking wine with their workday meals, needed to adapt to an alcohol-free environment and Toyota needed to justify to the government and employees why alcohol was forbidden. French managers, who typically had private office space, were forced to deal with the Japanese system that clustered many managers together in a large, open office space. But while the French workers need to make some concessions, adaptation was a two-way street. High unemployment in France made the location appealing to Toyota, but they needed to maintain a conciliatory approach to the sometime hostile French unions. The high unemployment also worked to dampen the zeal of many of the French unionists. One move that a few Japanese managers made that endeared them to the French was to learn the language.

GLOBAL TRENDS

The traditional powers in the automobile industry have been the Americans, Japanese, and Europeans. Although they have recently gone through a significant "shakeout" and restructuring, Korean manufacturers have made inroads in the market in the past decade. Hyundai, Kia (now owned by Hyundai), and Daewoo, once known mainly for inferior quality and designs that lagged behind industry standards, have recently made their presence felt in the global marketplace.

[3]Keith Bradsher, "Ford's 70-Year Itch Could Be Relieved," *The New York Times* (May 3, 2001), C1 & C3.
[4]John Tagliabue, "At a French Factory, Culture Is a Two-way Street," *New York Times* (February 25, 2001), 4.

At the same time that these firms are expanding their global presence, automobile markets are coming under increasing pressure. Concerns include overcapacity in production for American and European markets, lack of focus on emerging markets in Asia and Africa, insensitivity to needs for fuel efficiency and environmental compatibility, shifting economic conditions, and inattention to local and regional differences in consumer preferences, management practices, and sales/distribution processes. It is difficult to sell gas-guzzlers outside the United States when fuel prices can be two to three times as high in other countries. In several European countries diesel power is preferred because diesel fuel is significantly less expensive than gasoline. Thus, U.S. manufacturers must make somewhat different models for the European market. For example, Daimler-Chrysler produces diesel-powered minivans for the Austrian and German markets. It is also difficult to sell U.S.-style sport utility vehicles (SUVs) in Europe or Asia where roads, parking spaces, and garages (if they exist) are much smaller than in this country. Economic stagnation in much of Asia during the latter half of the 1990s eliminated some growth potential and placed heavy debt burdens on several Korean and Japanese firms.

Some automobile company executives once dreamed of creating "world cars" and "global companies" for a homogeneous automobile market; they are reocognizing that the global economy is truly differentiated. Management styles, operations, designs, marketing, and distribution must be modified for specific markets. Customs and regulations vary by country and region. Even in a mature industry like automobiles, the environment is complex and changing.

As the description of the world auto industry indicates, conditions change and evolve. Companies that were once dominant now struggle to compete. Members of the industry must continually monitor the environment if they are to stay in tune with conditions. And the environment they face has grown increasingly complex, crowded, and turbulent.

This chapter examines the nature of organizational environments and their components. A critical step to organizational success is a keen understanding of environments.

THE GLOBAL ENVIRONMENT FOR ORGANIZATIONS

The idea that organizations are *open systems* was presented in Chapter 1. Although the idea that organizations are affected by and must interact with the environment may seem obvious and straightforward, we see in this chapter just how complex and important the environment is to any organization. All organizations exist within an environment that affects their operations. For some organizations the environment is rather local, such as the neighborhood area for a family restaurant. For others, such as Ford, General Motors, Nokia, Ericsson, Motorola, Nike, or Reebok, the environment is essentially worldwide. The environment is the source of resources, including customers, necessary for survival. Both opportunities for success and threats to existence arise from the environment. Thus, we can begin to see the importance of understanding what factors constitute an organization's environment. In Chapter 5 we turn our attention to tactics that organizations can use to protect themselves from or harness the environment—in other words, how organizations try to manage the environment.

This chapter focuses on describing characteristics of environments. We explore all of those external conditions that could potentially affect an organization—the *organizational environment*.[1] The organizational environment is made up of those things *outside* the organization's boundaries. It comprises eight sectors or areas that are described in detail below. In addition to these eight specific sectors, one should keep in mind that organizations and their environments exist in a *global* context.

Organizations are affected by events throughout the world. When we consider each sector of the environment, we must not only look at local, regional, or national aspects of that sector, we must also consider the global implications. Obviously, it would be foolish to examine competition in the automobile industry if we did not include Japanese, European, and other producers. While this example is obvious, nearly every organization and every sector of the environment is, in some way, affected by events or conditions around the world. Thus, while some organizational theory texts choose to treat international or global business as a distinct sector of the environment, we take the approach that every sector has international or global aspects. To treat global or international forces as discrete or separate issues downplays their pervasiveness.

Although every organization exists within a general organizational environment, each organization is affected differently by that environment because organizations differ in size, industry, goals, technology, location, strategy, and many other ways. Elements of the environment centrally important to an automaker may be unimportant or only peripherally important to a bank or a shoe manufacturer. The term *task environment* refers to the specific parts of the environment that affect a given organization. Table 4-1 depicts the general organizational environment that potentially affects all organizations and suggests a task environment that could exist for a typical organization.

The Nature of the General Organizational Environment

The modern organization is shaped by components of its environment—from its purpose to the technology it employs, to the resources it needs, to its customers or clients, to its very definition of success. No organization can ignore its environment. In this section we systematically investigate sectors of organizational environments.

TABLE 4-1 Sectors of the General Environment

Sector of the Environment	Description
Industry Sector	Competitors and substitute products; the ease or difficulty of entering and leaving the industry
Cultural Sector	The local cultural and social conditions in the consumer and labor markets in which the firm operates
Legal and Political Sector	The political system, legal and political institutions, laws, and regulations that affect a firm
Economic Sector	The economic system and the general economic conditions that a firm faces
Technology Sector	The available and emerging technology that a firm can use to transform inputs into outputs
Human Resources Sector	The labor market, available skills, labor unions or organizations, and work ethic of available workers
Physical Resources Sector	Physical conditions (including weather, terrain, supply of natural resources, and natural catastrophes) that may affect an organization
Consumer and Client Sector	The market for the organization's outputs

The environment contains both *opportunities* and *threats*. Opportunities exist in the form of markets, resources, and other external conditions that the organization can exploit to grow and prosper. Threats, on the other hand, are forces in the environment that may constrain the organization, jeopardize growth or effectiveness, or even threaten the very survival of the organization. Threats, for example, may come from new competitors that challenge a firm's market niche or position, legal or political conditions that place new burdens on a firm, or changing demographic conditions that may erode a previous market base. However, it is important to keep in mind that each organization faces a distinct environment. Factors in the environment that threaten one organization may provide opportunities for another. An example of this dual nature (both opportunities and threats) should be useful.

Companies in a variety of industries are concerned about new environmental protection standards that became law in the United States in 1996 as a result of the Clean Air Act. The new stricter limits on toxic emissions for everything from manufacturing to operation of automobiles pose a serious threat to companies such as automakers, power generators, oil refiners, and chemical producers, to name a few. These companies must find new ways to produce their products that conform to the constraints emanating from the legal and political sector of the environment. If they fail to conform to these constraints, their very survival could be threatened. These same laws that place burdens on many companies may also provide opportunities for companies such as Catalytica, Inc., a small California firm that develops catalysts that control or speed up chemical reactions.[2] These catalysts help petroleum refiners and chemical manufacturers develop fuels and chemicals that meet new clean air standards. Thus, the threat to one set of firms provides an opportunity for Catalytica.

The message for managers is clear: They have little choice but to pay close attention to the environment and to devise mechanisms for coping with and even influencing that environment.* An organization that is out of touch with its environment would soon use up all its resources; would rely on dated, inaccurate information for decision making; and would lose contact with consumer wants and needs. In the long run an organization that fails to attend to its environment will not survive. To survive and prosper over time, organizations must react to and try to control the environment.

We begin by examining each of eight sectors of the general organizational environment. The reader should keep in mind that not all organizations are affected equally or in the same way by each of these sectors. We will have more to say about this issue shortly when we examine the task environment and **environmental complexity**. You should also remember that these sectors are not static. Rather, environmental sectors experience **turbulence** or **change**. For some organizations such as the railroads, environmental change is slow compared with the fast pace of change in the computer industry. Thus, it is important not only to identify various sectors that affect an organization but to monitor how those sectors change over time.

Environments also differ with respect to the availability of necessary resources and opportunities—what theorists have referred to as **munificence**.[3] For example, periods of low mortgage interest rates and high levels of employment produce a munificent environment for homebuilders and real estate companies trying to sell residential real estate. Market niches that are crowded by many competitors or that are shrinking

---

*In Chapter 5 we explore in detail specific mechanisms that organizations use to gain information and attempt to control the environment. We also introduce a theoretical perspective called population ecology that suggests that organizations are nearly powerless to adequately, systematically, and completely control their environments. Rather, it is the environment that does the controlling of organizations.

because of changing consumer preferences also demonstrate reduced munificence. Thus, after a period of early rapid expansion, cellular and digital phone manufacturers are experiencing declining munificence.

Finally, one must continue to keep in mind that we live in a global environment. Each of these eight sectors that we highlight has international ramifications. For some organizations, for example, Nike, Nokia, Toyota, or GM, the international ramifications are direct and immediate. They manufacture and market their products throughout the world. For others, like the hardware store featured in the introductory case for Chapter 1, the international ramifications are indirect and more remote. Some of the products they sell may be manufactured in other countries, and economic conditions in other countries may affect prices as well as local interest rates.

One need only look at the heated competition in the mobile phone industry to see the effects of competition. Extensive competition among Nokia, Ericsson, Motorola, and many other phone makers has dramatically driven down the cost of mobile phones at the same time that features, technical sophistication, and quality have made startling advances. As a result, Ericsson, once able to compete directly with industry leader Nokia, has turned much of its manufacturing to suppliers and has engaged in massive cost cutting and restructuring of its mobile phone business. Similar trends have occurred in other industries, for example, computers, as they mature.

The increased sophistication and proliferation of mobile phones affects related markets. Mobile phones now compete with personal data appliances (PDAs) such as Palm and Handspring. PDAs now have many phone features and mobile phones now have PDA features. Even laptop computers compete with mobile phones and PDAs.

Mobile phone manufacturing is also tightly linked with the telephone service providers such as MCI Worldcom, Verizon, AT&T in the United States, and countless other providers throughout the world. Mobile phone manufacturers compete vigorously to be the preferred hardware provider for particular service providers, since the service providers are often the ones who sell (or give away) phones as part of service contracts. The international mobile phone business is made more difficult by the different technical standards and transmission wavelengths that exist in different parts of the world. Phones made for the U.S. market will not necessarily work in all regions of the country or in other parts of the world. Several manufacturers are now producing new equipment with greater flexibility for use in different markets with different technical standards.

One of the interesting benefits of the mobile telephone revolution has been its adaptability to emerging markets such as China and Africa. Introduction of mobile phones into places that were never wired for traditional phone service is a far less costly approach to telecommunications. The cost of wiring for vast regions such as China or Africa is much more expensive than building transmission towers for mobile phones. Moreover, the technical infrastructure is easier to maintain. Mobile phone makers and service providers have competed aggressively for entry into these emerging markets.

As the preceding example indicates, competition today is an international phenomenon. The global marketplace accounts for a major part of the competitive environment for most moderate- to large-size organizations. One only needs to examine lists of major competitors in most industries to gain a sense of the globalization of the business environment. The example of the automobile industry in the introductory case illustrates this point. The pharmaceutical industry presents a similar picture. Because of extensive mergers and acquisitions, many firms cross national boundaries. Perhaps one of the best examples of this globalization is Aventis, SA, a French-based pharmaceutical company that resulted from a series of mergers and acquisitions that included

Marion-Merrill-Dow (a group of American drug companies), Rhone-Polenc (a French company), and Hoechst (a German chemical and drug firm). As a result, associating companies with particular countries is becoming increasingly difficult. Nearly every major industry is characterized in some way by globalization. As we examine other sectors of the environment (e.g., culture, markets, and regulations), we see that international aspects of environmental sectors make each sector more complex.

Although competition is an important aspect, there is more to the industry sector than competition. Michael Porter[4] has developed a useful framework that elaborates on industry competitiveness and provides a basis for analyzing the industry sector. He identifies five elements of the industry sector: (1) threats of new entrants, (2) substitutability threats, (3) rivalry among firms, (4) buyer bargaining power, and (5) supplier bargaining power. We will examine the first three of these elements in this section. Buyer bargaining power will be discussed in the section on the market sector, and supplier bargaining power will be presented in the section on the resource sector.

Threats from New Entrants   An important aspect of the industry sector is the relative ease or difficulty with which new firms can enter an industry. Porter calls this ***"threats from new entrants"*** while others speak of ***barriers to entry***. Several factors contribute to the ease or difficulty of entry, including economies of scale, capital requirements, product differentiation, switching cost, distribution channels, government policies, and various other cost disadvantages.

Economies of scale determine the minimum size at which a type of business can be efficiently run. High economies of scale (i.e., the requirement that a firm must be large in order to be competitive) reduce threats of new entrants. New methods of production and management have reduced economies of scale for some industries. Innovations and changes in management in the 1980s allowed companies like Nucor, a specialty steel producer, to be competitive at a smaller size than conventional wisdom suggested was possible. Nonetheless, certain types of business, such as automobile or chemical companies, must of necessity be large because economies of scale are very high.[5]

Closely related to economies of scale is the ***capital required*** to enter an industry. Significant investment in capital equipment and human resources raises barriers to entry. Businesses that require minimal capital investment to start remove one obstacle to entry. For example, building personal computers essentially involves purchasing off-the-shelf technology, then assembling and marketing it. Low-entry barriers result in greater competition because of the potential flood of new companies. Clearly, these companies require expertise in computer assembly and marketing—no small task—but the capital requirements for entry are comparatively low. These low-capital requirements explain in part the proliferation of such PC makers as Dell, Gateway, Compaq, Packard Bell, and no-name makers too numerous to list. By contrast, designing and building supercomputers requires significantly more capital investment in research and development and specialized assembly facilities. There are comparatively fewer supercomputer makers. (There is also a much smaller market for supercomputers.)

Highly ***differentiated products*** create the perception among customers and potential competitors of uniqueness and raise entry barriers. Patents, copyrights, proprietary knowledge, and brand loyalty can all contribute to product differentiation and raise entry barriers. For example, although toothpaste is relatively easy to make (low-capital barriers), a new company would have to compete with strong existing brands like Crest and Colgate that dominate the market. Sometimes firms will find ways to differentiate. The emphasis on features like baking soda and peroxide toothpastes promoted by several companies and natural toothpastes like Tom's of Maine are examples.

Switching costs refers to costs to buyers associated with shifting to products of a different producer. For example, new entries into computer manufacturing that chose to produce systems that do not use existing operating systems or application software would face high entry barriers. Potential customers would face the extra costs of acquiring software. These extra costs are the costs of switching to a new product and are a barrier to new entrants. The fact that most businesses have adopted Microsoft Windows–based software and hardware creates extraordinary costs to firms that switch to other operating systems and software. Not only is the investment in hardware and software lost, but firms would incur costs associated with training and developing new competencies. These costs to a potential user act as a barrier to would-be competitors to Microsoft. This explains some of the difficulty that Apple has faced in trying to compete in the personal computer industry.

Access to distribution channels can also lower barriers to entry. The presence of distribution channels removes one entry barrier. An organization that must establish a new distribution system for a new product will encounter an entry barrier. For example, when the Saturn, Lexus, Accura, and Infinity car lines were introduced, their respective companies established new networks of dealers to sell and service these cars. The cost of creating this dealer network raised entry barriers. This cost was one of the factors that discouraged Mazda from pursuing that same strategy. New entrants into the airline industry face two substantial distribution problems. They must acquire gates in airports, and they must establish an Internet presence through their own Web site and inclusion in systems of online travel services (e.g., Expedia and Travelocity) as well as convincing traditional travel agents to sell tickets. Interestingly, Southwest Airlines has successfully competed by finding gates at less crowded underutilized airports and has developed a simplified Web site and ticketing process to make it competitive.

In many industries *government policy* plays an important role in establishing or removing entry barriers. Governments create barriers or remove barriers through domestic and foreign policies, regulatory behavior, and as a customer. For example, government licensing of radio and television stations limits the number of new entrants and controls competition. The awarding of government contracts restricts entry and competition. Defense policy and government purchasing play important roles in defense industries. Without a government contract, it would make little sense to enter into the manufacturing of jet fighter aircraft. Similarly, governments can facilitate the development of industries and specific firms through policies. The governments of England, France, Germany, and Spain coordinated efforts to form Airbus Industries, a multinational maker of commercial aircraft. Governments can also restrict entry through controlled allocation of scarce resources such as oil drilling or timber rights on government property. Although the recent history of deregulation in industries such as utilities banking, and airlines has been mixed, the removal of government regulations in these industries through policy changes has removed some entry barriers.

Entry into foreign markets, either as a seller or manufacturer, may be restricted by government policy. During the height of the Cold War, U.S. firms were forbidden to sell certain types of products in specific countries. For example, until recently, U.S. companies could not sell computers to the former Soviet Bloc countries. Countries may also restrict foreign competitors from doing business in their country in order to protect domestic companies. Japan's policies of restricting foreign retailers and rice shipments are partially aimed at protecting small local retailers and rice farmers. Finally, government trade policies such as the North American Free Trade Agreement (NAFTA) and the General Agreement on Tariffs and Trade (GATT) reduce international barriers to trade. The effects of government go beyond barriers to or facilitation of entry. We return to the discussion of the role of government in the environment when we elaborate on environmental sectors later in this chapter.

Several other ***cost disadvantages***, which are unrelated to economies of scale, can also raise entry barriers. Potential new firms in an industry may lack proprietary knowledge (i.e., trade secrets) possessed by existing firms. Entry into a new industry may also require significant time to learn the intricacies of the new business. This learning process is referred to as a ***learning curve***. The learning curve reflects the idea that the more time an individual or firm practices a skill or gains experience, the easier (and/or cheaper) it is to do the task. The steepness of the learning curve an organization faces may be affected by the time at which a firm enters a new market. Companies that are ***first movers,*** the first firm to enter a market, face a steeper learning curve than later entrants into the field. This first mover strategy is referred to as an ***r-strategy***.[6] Later entries to the market can typically learn indirectly from the experience of the first movers and avoid problems and obstacles. The late entry strategy is referred to as a ***K-strategy***.

New firms may also face problems attempting to acquire scarce resources or favorable locations. For example, as the fast food market niche becomes more crowded with competitors, new entries are finding that existing franchises have already locked up prime locations.[7]

Each of the above seven factors can substantially raise (or lower) the entry barriers that potential new firms (or existing firms entering new markets) face. High entry barriers will reduce competitiveness by discouraging, or making difficult, entry into an industry. Two other industry characteristics that remain to be examined are substitutability from similar products or services and competitive rivalry among firms.

Substitutability Threats   The nature of an industry is affected by the extent to which substitute products or services exist. Competitiveness increases with the availability of substitute products. Substitutability plays an important role in competitiveness within the pharmaceutical industry. When a company patents a newly developed drug, the company gains some measure of protection from competition. Rival firms cannot produce copies of that same drug. However, nothing prevents a competitor from developing a substitute product to replace existing drugs. For example, one of the leading prescription drugs for the treatment of depression has been Prozac, produced by Eli Lilly. When Eli Lilly loses patent protection in the near future, they will face threats from makers of generic versions of Prozac. In recent years, Lilly has also faced competition from several other pharmaceutical companies that have produced other drugs in the same class of treatment (selective serotonin reuptake inhibitors or SSRIs) for clinical depression. Glaxo Smith Kline has heavily marketed Paxil and Phizer has promoted Zoloft.

To guard against threats of substitutability, these firms have sought other applications for these drugs such as treatment of premenstrual distress syndrome (Prozac), social anxiety (Paxil), and obsessive-compulsive disorder (several drugs). Also, firms will attempt modifications to products that extend their patent protection. For example, Eli Lilly has gained approval for a once-a-week dosage of Prozac.

Competitive Rivalry   Attempts by industry members to improve their position intensify rivalry within that industry. Several factors can contribute to this situation: large numbers of competitors, or competitors of nearly equal size; limited growth opportunities; high fixed operating costs; and high costs to exit the industry.

EXHIBIT 4-1

India's Pharmaceutical Copycats: Threats of Substitutability[8]

To the western pharmaceutical companies, the Indian firm Cipla is a pirate, a producer of copycat drugs, knockoffs of drugs such as Viagra, Prozac, Prilosec, and a vast array of drugs including AIDS treatments. Under India's current laws, Cipla is operating legally and bringing in revenues of $200 million per year. Estimates indicate that these same drugs sold at prices charged by U.S. and European firms would bring in over $4 billion.

In the United States, the cost of prescription medications has become a heated and controversial political and economic issue. Drugs for treatment of such common ailments as heart disease, gastrointestinal distress, heartburn, arthritis, allergies, and infections can not only drain the budgets of senior citizens on fixed budgets but can also threaten the economic health of many families who lack prescription insurance. Consider that a person with allergies may spend several dollars each day for antihistamines and inhalers. The situation becomes more dire when one considers treatments for diseases like AIDS, in which the bill for drugs can be tens of thousands of dollars per year for patients. For example, the antifungal drug fluconazole is used to treat a lethal brain infection—crytococcal meningitis. The cost of the daily treatment can range from $25 to $40. The price of this drug is clearly out of reach for patients in much of Asia, Africa, and South America. Cipla sells the same drug for 50 cents per pill in India. The company also sells several other AIDS drugs at similar discounts to American prices. A common AIDS "cocktail" that sells in the West for $1,000 per month is produced by Cipla and sells in India for $83 a month. Similar price differentials exist in nearly every class of drugs.

Pharmaceutical companies justify the high prices on the basis of the high development costs. Although it is difficult to clearly determine the cost of developing a drug due to the number of developments that never reach the market, a conservative estimate is $500 million and 17 years for a typical drug. The drug companies maintain that the costs they charge and the patent protection they seek are necessary to recover development costs and provide a fair return on investment to investors.

Companies such as Cipla are legally (in India) able to copy drugs because Indian law gives patent protection only to the processes used to produce products, not the products themselves. Cipla has reverse engineered drugs produced by leading pharmaceutical firms, thus eliminating the extensive development costs. Cipla maintains that its products are equal in quality to the "originals." Much of the information necessary to replicate the drugs is available from medical and pharmaceutical journals that cost Cipla $150,000 per year. Western firms complain that Indian laws give them little or no protection, and many American and European pharmaceutical firms have abandoned the Indian market.

The European and American firms claim they are losing more than $100 million per year in sales in India, although it is unlikely that those firms would be able to charge in India the prices they command in Europe and the United States. And therein lies the conundrum. The American and European firms complain that companies such as Cipla are stealing sales by using India's weak patent protection to copy patented pharmaceuticals. However, if the western firms attempted to market their drugs at or near the North American or European prices, they would price themselves out of the Indian market.

Not all western firms have abandoned the Indian market, but those who do remain must price their products aggressively. For example, the Swiss company Ciba-Geigy sells Voltaren in the U.S. market for $2 a pill, but because of competition from copycats, it sells the drug for 5 cents a pill in India.

But the implications for western pharmaceutical firms are more than just economics. The companies face serious ethical and public relations challenges. Much of the undeveloped or underdeveloped world cannot afford the high western prices of drugs. Yet these are the places where many diseases run rampant. The vast majority of AIDS cases are in Africa and infection rates in India and east Asia are quickly increasing. Moreover, many drug firms have abandoned or decreased development of treat-

(*continued*)

ments for tropical illnesses like malaria because of the difficulty they would face recouping their invest-ment. The issues are rather complex. For the western drug firms, the question often comes down to profits and continued success. Sales of drugs at "market" prices provide investors a return on invest-ment, cover the cost of development and production, and fuel future development. However, politi-cians, humanitarians, and health care workers see the issue as one of human welfare and view the big drug companies as greedy and uncaring. However the issues are argued, the situation is likely to change. India will need to comply with international patent and intellectual property rights rules by 2005 if it wants to be accepted into the World Trade Organization.

The airline industry is one with a high level of rivalry. The U.S. airline industry is dominated by a small number of large carriers (American Airlines, Delta, United, Northwest, and Continental). Yet, because each firm sees opportunities to expand at the expense of other firms and no single firm is dominant, rivalry among firms is extensive. Moreover, the airlines have high fixed costs that must be covered regard-less of how many passengers fly.[9] Add into this situation mergers and acquisitions, new entries in the discount niche such as Southwest and American Trans Air (ATA), and you have all the ingredients for high levels of competitiveness. Some of the com-petition is translated into price wars and some of it is focused on strategic positioning (e.g., differentiation, domination of hubs, or even the possibility of illegal acts such as collusion).

In addition to his identification of industry characteristics, Michael Porter also identifies three generic strategies for managing the industry sector: ***overall cost leader-ship***, ***differentiation strategy***, and ***focus strategy***. We discuss these as well other strate-gies for controlling environments in Chapter 5. Before examining strategies, however, we must complete our description of the environment. Thus, we now move to the sec-ond sector of the environment.

Cultural Sector

Organizations are embedded within a larger environment that extends far beyond a single industry. Perhaps the environmental sector that best represents that embedded-ness is culture.* Culture is the foundation that guides much of what happens in a social system. "Culture filters the ways in which people see and understand their worlds. Culture prescribes some behaviors and forbids others. Culture colors the emotional responses that people have to events."[10] Culture is the glue that holds a society together. It contains the values, norms, traditions, and artifacts of a society. Organi-zations and their members are both affected by and have an effect on culture.

---

*In this section we use the term *culture* to represent the values, norms, and beliefs of the larger society within which an organization exists. The term *culture* (more specifically, organizational culture) is also used to describe the values, norms, and beliefs that exist *within* an organization. Some overlap between the gen-eral use of the term and the organizational-specific use are apparent in concepts such as Japanese manage-ment. Chapter 10 specifically examines organizational culture.

Culture affects the way organizations operate. The societal values held by consumers, for instance, are determined to a great extent by the values society at large holds important.

Businesses entering new markets as both employers and vendors must consider the local culture. For example, in the United States consumers are used to shopping at all hours, any day of the week. However, U.S. firms doing business in other countries often confront different beliefs and values about the appropriate hours for conducting business. For example, Germany has laws that restrict the hours retail stores can be open.[11] Retail stores must close at 6:30 P.M. on most weekdays and 2 P.M. on Saturdays. In 1989 the laws were modified to allow businesses to remain open until 8:30 P.M. on Thursdays. Stores remain closed on Sundays. Similar laws are present in other European countries. These restrictive business hours were the result of several factors, including powerful unions trying to preserve leisure, religious institutions trying to preserve the Christian sabbath, and political institutions trying to preserve the unique local culture. One can imagine the difficulty American firms like Toys "R" Us, Kmart, or Wal-Mart might have operating under these constraints. However, to violate these laws and norms would not only result in legal challenges from the German government but would likely alienate and offend the local citizens—the customers these companies seek to attract. It is important to note that as the Germans become increasingly exposed to U.S. business either directly or through the new media, they are gradually changing some of these business practices.

Laws are not the only force that may dictate behavior, and restrictive retail business hours are only one example of cultural differences in business practices. Other examples, some more dramatic and fundamental, abound. Local cultures can affect such things as styles of dress, manners, conduct of negotiations, and even how business cards are exchanged. For example, many U.S. companies have recently adopted more casual dress codes for employees. IBM, which was long known for the conservative attire of its employees (e.g., blue suits and white shirts), adopted policies and practices that permitted employees to dress more casually. However, this trend has not taken hold at IBM Japan. This is in part because conservative business attire is a more generally and strongly held norm across nearly all Japanese firms. To the Japanese, appearance, or ***tatemae***, is critically important.[12]

Societal norms are the standards that mold the behavior, attitudes, and values of those members who constitute a society.[13] Norms come from laws, customs, religious teachings, and common practice. Members of the society take them into consideration in decisions about behaviors. Behaviors such as business hours, manners, speech, and dress reflect the prevailing culture of the community. Businesses must pay heed to the culture if they want to be part of that local community. The growing globalization of business has meant that many local cultures have been exposed to new and different ideas and practices, and many businesses have been exposed to new values, beliefs, and customs. In fact, many business organizations have themselves become microcosms of multiculturalism. ABB Asea Brown Boveri, a Swedish-Swiss maker of train engines, generators, and other large items, does business throughout the world and has taken great pains to establish a uniquely Swedish culture while at the same time accommodating the local culture in which the company's business units reside.[14] Similarly, when Honda first started building motorcycles and cars in the United States, it carefully modified its distinctive Japanese style of doing business to accommodate American values, beliefs, norms, and behaviors. In fact, Honda chose to locate in central Ohio because of the specific local culture and the resulting positive work ethic of the residents.[15]

Violating local norms or customs can be costly. The Disney Company decided to continue its long-standing prohibition against serving alcohol when it opened EuroDisney World in France. However, local customs supported consumption of alcohol. One result was that many French visitors to the park brought their own beverages, depriving Disney of much-needed concession revenues. Disney has since changed that policy to accommodate European tastes.[16]

As the examples above indicate, values, beliefs, norms, and behaviors, although durable, are not resistant to change. Businesses must monitor constantly to detect threats or opportunities from a changing environment. Clearly, producers of tobacco products have been adversely affected by changing attitudes toward the use of tobacco products. Conversely, changed attitudes about health, sports, and fitness, beginning in the 1970s, created new business opportunities for companies such as Nike and Reebok. Schools, churches, political institutions, and the media play critical roles in molding, transforming, and disseminating culture.[17]

These diverse examples illustrate that culture is a critical component of the environment with which managers must reckon. While we typically think of culture creating constraints on organizations, closer inspection suggests that culture may also be an important source of opportunities. We return to culture in Chapter 10 when we focus more specifically on the internal culture of individual organizations.

Legal and Political Sector

All organizations are affected to some degree by the diverse legal and political systems in their environments. The political system—the government, political, and legal processes—is an important variable in virtually all aspects of managerial decision making and activity. Like other aspects of the environment, the legal and political sector provides both constraints and opportunities to organizations.

The legal and political sector is important to the study of organizations because it is the source of laws and regulations that govern the operation of businesses. This sector includes local, regional, national, and international legal and political systems. In the case of an American firm, this could include city, county, state, and national laws and regulations. Additionally, a typical firm may also be affected by international agreements or the laws of other countries, especially if such a firm does business outside the United States or competes with foreign firms. For example, both Canada and France have "content laws" for music, movies, print, and broadcast businesses that require companies to ensure sufficient levels of Canadian or French content. In addition to the legal and regulatory functions of governments, they also affect organizations through the collection and provision of information, through research activities, and through governmental direct or indirect consumption.

Perhaps the most obvious impact of government is through its powers to tax and regulate. Governments often attempt to spur economic activity through tax cuts or suppress demand through the application of taxes. For example, local governments may offer tax abatements (i.e., elimination or reduction of taxes) to businesses willing to locate within the government's jurisdiction. In 1993 several states engaged in heated competition for new Mercedes Benz and BMW manufacturing facilities. The competing states typically offered elaborate plans that involved relief from property taxes for as long as 10 years.[18] As a result of these tax breaks, Alabama was able to lure a Mercedes Benz plant and South Carolina obtained a BMW plant. This use of taxation powers not only provides business opportunities for the targeted firms but may also provide benefits for supplier organizations selling to BMW or Mercedes Benz. Similarly, many U.S. companies have relocated to Puerto Rico because of specific federal tax advantages granted to Puerto Rican companies.[19] On the other hand, several states and the federal government have used nuisance taxes to inhibit consumption of certain products including tobacco, alcohol, and gasoline. Increases of taxes on cigarettes have had significant impact on the tobacco industry. Guzzler taxes on inefficient luxury cars suppressed the sales of those cars.

Managers need to become familiar with applicable laws and regulations because nearly every facet of their operation is affected by legal and political considerations. In the United States organizations must, for example, heed the Equal Employment Opportunities Commission (EEOC) personnel guidelines in hiring, training, promotion, compensation, and firing. The Americans with Disabilities Act (ADA), passed by Congress in 1992, not only set personnel standards for the employment of disabled Americans but also stated requirements for access by disabled individuals to all sorts of organizations. Businesses and other organizations are required to take into consideration the accessibility of their physical facilities to potential customers and employees. The Occupational Safety and Health Act (OSHA) sets requirements for the safe operation of facilities, including regulations protecting workers from exposure to toxic chemicals, dangerous noise levels, and other threatening conditions. The Securities and Exchange Commission (SEC) and the Internal Revenue Service (IRS) regulate the ways in which businesses are chartered, traded, monitored, and taxed. The above examples are only a few of the alphabet soup of laws, regulations, and government agencies that cover nearly every aspect of business operation.

Government's impact on business extends beyond domestic policy and domestic businesses. Another area of rapid change in recent years is international trade. The signing of NAFTA has removed or substantially reduced trade barriers among the United States, Canada, and Mexico.[20] Much debate raged over the anticipated impact of NAFTA on the three trade partners. Between December 1996 and December 1999, U.S. trade with Canada and Mexico tripled from a total of $14.3 billion per month (imports and exports) to $47.2 billion per month (in 1996 dollars).[21] In addition, Mexico has its first popularly elected president, Vicente Fox, from an opposition party. Since 1990, Mexican employment has increased by 22 percent, Canadian employment has increased by 10 percent and U.S. employment has increased by 7 percent. Recent discussions have focused on extending the free trade zone to all of North and South America.[22]

In Europe, the European Union (EU) plays an even more pervasive role in business and trade among the member nations. While the United States, Mexico, and Canada have not given up substantial autonomy with respect to trade and business issues, the 15 members of the EU have ceded considerable economic, labor, and trade authority in an effort to develop consistent rules among member nations. Thus, labor laws, environmental laws, agricultural regulations, and myriad other rules apply to all members of the EU. Trade barriers have been removed. People, assets, and capital can move freely among member countries. On January 1, 1999, 11 members adopted a common currency—the euro—that will replace their national currencies. On January 1, 2002 the euro began circulating. The adoption of this common currency is both an important economic issue and a symbolic statement. The common currency will facilitate trade and reduce transaction costs. It is also a statement of the shared destiny of the member nations.[23]

The 15 members of the European Union are Austria, Belgium, Denmark, Finland, France, Germany, Greece, Ireland, Italy, Luxemburg, the Netherlands, Portugal, Spain, Sweden, and the United Kingdom.

The 11 members agreeing to the common currency are Austria, Belgium, Finland, France, Germany, Ireland, Italy, Luxemburg, the Netherlands, Portugal, and Spain.

Several other countries are being considered for membership in the EU: Poland, the Czech Republic, Hungary, Slovenia, Turkey, Latvia, Lithuania, and Estonia.

For more information on the European Union, visit the Web site at www.europa.eu.int/index_en.htm

Shortly after NAFTA was signed into law, the leading trading nations of the world wound up 7 years of often intense and bitter negotiations over GATT.[24] The Uruguay Round of trade negotiations from 1986 to 1994 eventually led to the formation of the World Trade Organization (WTO). The WTO is an international quasi-governmental organization that deals with global rules for trade among nations. Its purpose is to facilitate the smooth and free flow of trade among nations through multilateral trade agreements that set the ground rules for trade. The organization administers trade agreements, acts as a forum for negotiations and settlement of disputes, reviews trade policies, and assists developing nations with trade policy issues.[25] It is this last area, assisting developing nations, that has resulted in the greatest controversy for the WTO. Many critics assert that the WTO may be acting to further corporate interest without representing the best interests of all residents of developing countries.

For more information on the WTO, visit the Web site at www.wto.org/index.htm.

Communications and transportation have made the world a much smaller place. The events of governments in far-flung corners of the globe can have extensive consequences on organizations. Few people would have predicted the downfall of the eastern European communist block including the former Soviet Union, reunification of Germany, disintegration of the former Yugoslavia, or many other startling events in the global political arena. Management has a responsibility to monitor its environment, familiarize itself with the political climate, and adjust to it. Opportunities also exist to influence the political system. Lobbying is a fact of political life; corporations and organizations attempt to influence government policy through lobbying. We examine lobbying and other means of environmental control in greater detail in Chapter 5.

The following section deals with the economic sector, a companion to the legal and political sector. In reality, these two elements of the environment are practically inseparable because actions taken in one generally have some impact on the other.

Economic Sector

Organizations exist within some form of economic system that exerts tremendous influence on them. There are, of course, many forms of economic order, ranging from mixed private-enterprise (i.e., capitalist) systems of North America, western Europe, and Japan to centrally planned economies like those of China, North Korea, and Cuba. In between, numerous economies are undergoing fundamental transformations from central planning to some form of market-based economy. Regardless of their form, however, all economic systems are concerned with resource allocation and distribution of goods and services. Market-based economies allocate through pricing. The vagaries of weather, physical catastrophes, or world events can cause havoc in markets for commodities such as oil, grains, or minerals. In market-based economies, prices, to a great extent, should reflect the relative supply and demand. U.S. oil companies, for example, prospered during oil embargoes of the 1970s because of the high price of oil but suffered more recently because of the glut of oil on the world market and the resulting price competition. Centrally planned economies attempt to deal with these pricing problems through government policy and industry control. Scarce items may be rationed or prices may be artificially manipulated, but the price of central control may be inefficient organizations that lack the discipline of markets. Moreover, it is not unusual for black markets to emerge in centrally planned economies despite the best efforts of governments to control all allocation of goods and services.

The extent of government control has an important effect on the types of organizations that exist and how those organizations are managed. Central planning often dictates the specific form of organizations as well as how those organizations will be managed. One problem many former communist countries faced as they moved from centrally planned economies to market economies was that they lacked financial institutions such as banks, brokerage firms, and equity markets. In market economies owners and managers decide on the specific characteristics of organizations.[26] Even in the relatively free market environments of North America, western Europe, and Japan, government still exerts significant control over the economy. Political debate in the United States typically focuses on how much control over business and the economy the federal government should exercise.[27]

The nature of the economic system is not the only aspect of the economic sector that is important to organizations. The general condition of the economy also has great impact. Economic conditions refer to a wide array of factors including the unemployment rate, inflation rate, currency stability, currency exchange rates, capital availability, interest rates, cost of labor, and population demographics (i.e., age, sex, and education levels of the populace). These factors affect many aspects of organizational existence, including the competitive advantages firms may enjoy in certain economies, the cost of doing business, and the stability of the business environment.

Like every other element of an organization's environment, the economic sector is constantly changing. We have already noted the movement toward market-based economic systems in the former communist countries of eastern Europe. More subtle changes in economic conditions can also have profound effects. The German economy, renowned for its robustness, has experienced some difficulty since the early 1990s as a result of reunification. Unemployment rates increased to levels unknown since World War II. Tight monetary and fiscal policies helped to drive up the value of German currency, making German products expensive in the United States. Some companies, such as BMW and Mercedes Benz, have relocated manufacturing outside Germany while others have attempted to purchase U.S. companies.[28] From the early 1990s through the turn of the century, the once-mighty Japanese economy has stalled badly. Banks and the government have even resorted to interest-free loans to stimulate the economy, but little progress has been made. By contrast, the economies of France, Spain, and Ireland, once saddled with double-digit unemployment, have recently shown signs of significant growth and robustness.

Part of the change in the economic sector is that economics has become more of a global issue and less restricted to local or national economies. Products that were traditionally developed and manufactured in the United States, such as steel, motor vehicles, electronics, and heavy equipment, are now made in many other locales. Many companies operate in multiple locations throughout the world. Sometimes products are developed in one nation, manufactured in another, and sold in still a third location. General Motors, Ford, Volkswagen, Honda, and Toyota, for example, manufacture and sell cars throughout the world and are affected by economic conditions in each of the countries where they operate. Ratification of NAFTA and the WTO, along with the EU's move to a single currency (among 11 members) and unrestricted trade among members, increase the importance of global economies. Although local economies are still important—just ask retailers in a market where a large employer has laid off thousands of workers—businesses cannot ignore global economic conditions.

Technology Sector

The term *technology* has a very specific meaning in organization theory. The term refers to *specific skills, knowledge, tools, and abilities necessary to complete a job*.[29] This includes making and delivering a product or service. (This conceptualization of technology should be clearly differentiated from the development of new high-tech consumer products, what we refer to as product innovations.) We explore this concept in greater detail in Chapter 6.

For now, it is important to understand that all organizations use technology to do their work. Given the common use of the word, we may typically think only about things such as computers and automation, but technology is a much broader concept and also refers to such diverse factors as whether work is done by individuals or by groups, the level of training or skill needed to complete a task, and the number of different tasks people in an organization or work unit perform.

Technology is relevant to the discussion of external environment because the environment is a significant source of technological innovations—new ways for members of organizations to do their jobs. To be able to compete successfully, organizations must have access to technological improvements that potentially provide greater efficiency, superior quality, or products or services that would otherwise not be possible.[30] A roofer using conventional hammer and nail technology to put shingles on a house would have great difficulty competing against one using a pneumatic staple gun and staples. The latter tool allows the roofer to work several times faster. Kmart has struggled to compete effectively with Wal-Mart because of the latter's superior inventory control system that allows it to track inventory levels and monitor shipments.[31] Levi's has had some success with customization through computerized fitting systems that allow for custom manufactured jeans. These examples emphasize how new equipment can change the way work is performed and provide competitive advantages.

Technological innovations may also involve how people interact to carry out their jobs.[32] One of the most startling innovations at GM's Saturn plant was *not* the equipment but the team approach that was used to assemble cars—something very different from the techniques used at typical GM assembly lines.[33]

Economics plays a critical role in technological decisions. As noted earlier in this chapter in the discussion of the industry sector, factors such as capital requirements and economies of scale can be deterrents to entry into an industry. Such industries as automobile manufacturing and steel production require extensive investments in part because of the technology used. However, one of the dramatic changes in some industries is that new technologies—new approaches to assembling cars and new methods for smelting iron ore—produce new, lower economies of scale.[34]

Managers must scan the environment and investigate new technologies to find the best methods for transforming inputs into outputs. Failure to do so eventually results in inefficiencies and an inability to compete successfully.

Human Resources Sector

Recall that a key part of the definition of an organization is that it is made up of people. Organizations must go outside their boundaries to obtain these human inputs. The nature of the organization determines to a large extent the kinds and amounts of abilities that are required of potential workers. The human resources sector is the source of these human inputs.

There is more to the human resources sector than just the mere availability of labor. Levels of training and education, local wage and benefit standards, presence or absence of labor unions, and prevailing worker values or attitudes are a few examples of human resources sector variables that organizations must consider in their human resources policies and their decisions on where to locate. Earlier, it was mentioned that Honda's decision to locate its American auto and motorcycle assembly facilities was largely motivated by the cost of labor and local worker values.[35] Other key factors that motivate firms to locate in specific places are the average level of education of the populace and the availability of educational facilities. Businesses that depend on innovations and new technology seek to locate where the workforce is highly educated.[36] In the United States, the Raleigh/Durham, North Carolina, area ranked first, largely because of the proximity of three major research universities: the University of North Carolina–Chapel Hill, Duke University, and North Carolina State University. In fact, as organizations move toward broadening worker responsibilities, downsizing, and greater automation of routine tasks, worker knowledge and education are becoming more important factors in decisions concerning human resources.

Several human resources trends are worth noting and demonstrate the critical nature of this sector. First, with the trend toward downsizing and a leaner, more flexible workforce, many organizations are beginning to hire more part-time, temporary, or contract workers.[37] These workers can be used during periods of peak demand or for the completion of specific, specialized tasks. When demand slackens or when special needs cease, temporary, part-time, or contract workers are released. While such arrangements may reduce an organization's overhead (these workers receive only minimal benefits), they may also result in less stability and reduced worker commitment. Second, as organizations become leaner and flatter, they are requiring workers to become more flexible, perform more and different tasks, and take greater responsibility.[38] This trend, as noted earlier, requires that workers be better educated, but it may also mean that workers suffer greater on-the-job stress. This may come about as full-time workers work longer hours while worrying about downsizing, restructuring, and their job security. These trends to leaner and flatter organizations also frequently create situations in which managers know less about specific technical problems than their subordinates. This demands that managers learn new skills in managing highly trained technical and professional workers. Third, trends toward the globalization of organizations suggest that managers will frequently face situations in which they manage workers from different cultural backgrounds than their own. At ABB Asea Brown Boveri, Swedish managers sometimes face the difficult human resources task of managing workers from different backgrounds who speak different languages and have different values. Additionally, changing trade and immigration laws that increase companies' access to new markets will likely make the labor market more complex. Obviously, managers must consider carefully the human resources sector when making a wide range of strategic decisions about their firms' future.

Physical Resources Sector

The physical resources sector of the environment contains all the physical resources an organization needs to operate. A prime feature is those raw materials that serve as inputs to an organization. For example, the steel, plastic, rubber, electronic components, paint, and so forth that a car manufacturer needs to build cars are part of the physical resources sector. Wide fluctuations in the cost and availability of crude oil have caused problems in a broad cross section of businesses either directly involved in oil exploration and refining or indirectly involved as consumers of crude oil. The degree to which critical resources are concentrated in the hands of a few suppliers can be a critical factor in the success or failure of organizations attempting to acquire those resources. Concentration of resources gives suppliers significant bargaining leverage.

The physical conditions an organization faces are also a critical part of the resource sector. These may include climatic conditions and geography. In the highly competitive fast food industry, a prime factor in the success of a restaurant is geographic location. Yet, in that mature industry, the number of prime locations still available to newcomers is rather limited.[39] New firms must either manage with less advantageous locations or find ways to compensate for their inferior sites. Subway manages with strip mall or other high-traffic locations. Rally's hamburger chain has prospered using small parcels of land that are not in high demand.

Natural disasters, such as earthquakes or fires, and diseases can cause significant problems for many organizations. In the late 1980s, early 1990s, and again in 2001 we have seen severe floods threaten the midwestern United States. In recent years European agriculture has been devastated by mad cow disease and foot-and-mouth disease. Nearly every year we read of earthquakes reducing some metropolitan center to rubble. These events pose serious threats to the viability of organizations affected.

Some aspects of the physical environment, such as climate and physical disasters, are unpredictable and/or uncontrollable. Other aspects, such as the supply of raw materials, are somewhat more amenable to control. Nonetheless, it is critical that managers monitor the physical environment and attempt to manage or at least respond to developing conditions. It is also important that managers have disaster plans in place to cope with such unpredictable natural disasters as hurricanes, earthquakes, tornados, floods, and other events. The 1995 earthquake in Kobe, Japan, a key shipping terminus, caused innumerable problems for companies in Japan depending on the transshipment of supplies. Local businesses as well as imports and exports were seriously disrupted by this disaster.[40]

Consumer and Client Sector

The systems model of organizations, introduced in Chapter 1, showed that organizations acquire resources (both human and physical) from the environment, internally transform those resources through the use of technology, and then try to dispose of those resources in the external environment. Essentially, the organization is concerned with converting resources into products or services that are desired by consumers or clients. Marketplace success depends on careful analysis and a thorough understanding of market conditions.

It is imperative for managers to identify characteristics of the consumer and client market that an organization serves. In the previous chapter, we noted how Southwest Airlines had succeeded by filling a different niche from the one targeted by traditional airlines. They identified a group of potential customers who were interested in discount fares and no-frills service that the large airlines were not serving. Southwest also identified particular locations that were underserved by the major airlines. These strategies are all aimed at managing the consumer and client sector.

Organizations must also be aware of the potential power of buyers. Buyers who are the largest or most significant customers of an organization can exercise significant control, much like the resource suppliers mentioned earlier. For example, Wal-Mart can influence its supplier firms because of the large volume of business it does. Wal-Mart can win special pricing concessions, better service, or even special products. Sears has also done this in many areas and has been especially successful selling private label Kenmore washing machines and dryers produced for them by Whirlpool.

Organizations must continue to be aware of changing consumers' and clients' preferences in order to serve those needs. The survival of an organization that fails to stay abreast of its marketplace is likely to be precarious. In Chapter 5 we more systematically examine a wide array of techniques that can be used in some or all sectors of the environment.

Sectors of the Environment: A Recapitulation

Each of the eight sectors of the environment—industry, culture, legal and political, economic, technology, human resources, physical resources, consumer and client—can have a profound impact on an organization. However, each organization—even similar organizations in the same industry—has a unique environment. Clearly, the more similar the organizations are, the more likely they are to share similar environmental elements. These eight sectors make up the ***general environment***. The configuration of sectors and elements within sectors that are most important to a given organization make up that organization's ***task environment***. There is more to the environment, however, than the sectors. We turn our attention now to painting a more dynamic view of environments.

ENVIRONMENTAL COMPLEXITY, CHANGE, AND MUNIFICENCE

The environment creates problems for organizations because it is a source of uncertainty and constraints. ***Uncertainty*** arises because organizations face difficulty finding information and because situations change unpredictably. Two factors, ***environmental complexity*** and ***environmental change,*** contribute to uncertainty. Limitations or constraints also arise because of the limited capacity of the environment to support organizations. The term ***munificence*** refers to the availability of resources or the environment's capacity to support organizations.[41]

Environmental Complexity

Environmental complexity refers to the *number* and *relatedness* of environmental elements that affect an organization. Some organizations are directly affected by only a few environmental sectors, or elements within those sectors, and the elements and sectors are closely related. An environment characterized by a few related elements or sectors is defined as *simple.* Organizations that must interact with many sectors, or elements within those sectors, in which the elements or sectors are unrelated face a *complex* environment.[42]

Two examples illustrate differences in environmental complexity. A company like Mrs. Fields Homemade Cookies may face a relatively simple environment, especially compared with an aircraft company or an automaker. Mrs. Fields requires only a few physical resources—baking ingredients and store equipment. Human resource demands are not great; industry competition, while increasing, is not a major problem; clearly, consumer demand must be present; and the impact of the economy would be two-fold—the availability of capital to finance expansion and general consumer confidence. The net result is a fairly simple environment. By contrast, a company like Boeing faces a complex environment. Nearly every sector is important, and each contains multiple elements to which Boeing must respond. For example, the legal and political sector affects Boeing because the government, through the military, is one of Boeing's largest customers. The government also affects Boeing through its regulation of the airline industry and through restrictions on trade with foreign countries. Moreover, things like economic conditions, international trade, environmental regulations, and oil costs are more likely to have an impact on Boeing than on Mrs. Fields. The point is that Boeing has a complex environment and must attend to far more of its environment than a company such as Mrs. Fields. Complexity means that organizations must gather more information about their environments. Greater complexity raises the amount of information that is required to successfully manage.

Environmental Change

By now it should be obvious that environmental conditions that affect organizations change. Economic conditions change: Interest rates fluctuate; employment levels change; consumer confidence moves; and government economic policies are modified. New technologies are introduced in many industries. Consumer preferences are fluid. Styles that were popular just a few years ago are now regarded as in poor taste. New competitors may enter an industry. All of these changes create **turbulence**.[43] Like complexity, environmental change or turbulence means that managers have to pay close attention to the environment and gather much information. Strategies that worked in the past may not fit the changing conditions. Old technologies may no longer be efficient and competitive. Organizations and their managers must be flexible and responsive to changing conditions. When an organization faces a calm or placid environment, one characterized by little change, yesterday's methods or plans are acceptable and tried-and-proven strategies suffice. The organization does not need to carefully monitor the environment and gain new information because things probably have not changed much since the last time the environment was monitored.

Computer companies live in a rapidly changing environment. Technology, competition, software, and customer preference all change and change rapidly. Firms dealing in this industry must not only constantly monitor these changing conditions, they must also try to forecast and predict future conditions and develop strategies to cope. They must respond quickly—speed may be the most important factor in coping.

Munificence

We have repeatedly mentioned that the implication of an open systems view of organizations is that organizations must turn to the environment for resources. However, the environment is not an infinite store of resources. Some resources are abundant while others are quite scarce. **Environmental munificence** takes into consideration that abundance or scarcity of resources presents opportunities or places constraints on organizations.[44] More specifically, munificence refers to the capacity of the environment to

TABLE 4-2 Environmental Characteristics

Environmental Dimensions	Description
Environmental Complexity:	The *number* and *relatedness* of environmental elements that affect an organization
Environmental Change:	The *amount* and *speed* with which elements of the environment change (turbulence)
Munificence:	The abundance of resources present in an organization's environment

support organizations. Munificence may be applied to the availability of financial support, access to prime locations, presence of key human resources, or possession of critical physical resources. The earlier example of competition for scarce prime restaurant locations in the fast food industry is an example of an environment that would be low in munificence for new firms entering the business. In general, low munificence makes success for organizations far more difficult. Think how difficult it would be to get into the diamond mining industry. DeBeers of South Africa controls 65 percent of the diamond supply and the next largest firm controls the world's largest diamond mine, located in Australia. Table 4-2 summarizes these environmental conditions.

Contemporary Environments

Even though we presented the environment sector by sector, in reality, organizations face the entire environment. Some parts may be more important or salient than others, and this may even change over time. The trend in environmental conditions in recent years has definitely been toward increasing environmental turbulence. Alvin Toffler's classic, *Future Shock,* stands as witness to the unprecedented change with its all-encompassing impact on virtually every institution in society. In business many writers have argued quite convincingly that *all businesses* are facing increasingly complex and turbulent environments.[45] Management has a new and challenging responsibility—to monitor environmental conditions and to develop and implement effective strategies for dealing with those conditions. Organizations must also learn. More effective adaptation requires that organizations learn better. A key point of the contingency framework introduced in Chapter 1 is that different conditions in the organizational context—and environment is part of that context—require different ways of organizing and managing. Much of the focus in both academic organizational theory and popular management literature has been on how organizations should respond. Chapter 5 takes up the issue of specific methods or strategies for managing environments.

SUMMARY

All organizations exist within a larger environmental context. That larger environmental context is composed of eight sectors, and each of those sectors has an international or global component. Although all organizations exist in a general environment, each organization faces a unique environmental domain that is specific to that firm.

The industry sector contains the set of similar and competing firms. In addition to the extent of competition within an industry, the sector also involves the barriers to new entrants in an industry. Students of organizations should realize that these industry concepts—competition and barriers to entry—can be applied to all types of organizations, including public, private, profit, and nonprofit.

Culture, composed of the values, norms, artifacts, and accepted behavior patterns in a society, affects the way the organizations operate. One must recognize that cultures vary widely, and they place differing demands or constraints on organizations. We will return to the idea of culture later in the text to examine specific organizational cultures.

The effects on organizations of the legal and political sector are pervasive. Laws, regulations, policies, tax levees, tariffs, trade agreements—the list of legal and political elements of the environment is nearly endless. As organizations face global environments, the traditional boundaries of legal and political influence are reduced. Now organizations must confront a vast array of legal and political factors.

We noted that the economic sector is closely tied to the legal and political sector. Much of the activity in the economic sector is linked to government policy and action. Once again, this could refer to local, regional, national, and foreign government action. The economic sector consists of the type of economic system that an organization must confront, as well as the general economic conditions.

Organizations use technology to convert inputs into outputs. The environment is a source of new technologies that may make work easier or more efficient, or simply make some task possible.

The notion of an organization as an open system means, by definition, that organizations must go outside their boundaries to acquire resources. Two critical resource sectors that organizations must manage are human resources and physical resources. The human resources sector contains the set of human characteristics firms may need while the physical resources sector contains the specific resources and general physical conditions that firms face.

The final sector of the environment is the customer and client sector. Without customers or clients no organization would last long. The consumers are the ultimate arbiters of an organization's success. Organizations must identify and respond to customer and client demands.

Finally, the concepts of environmental complexity, change, and munificence are useful in characterizing the uncertainty and resource availability present in a given environmental domain. The trend today is toward increasingly uncertain environments and decreasing munificence. For organizations to succeed in these uncertain and scarce environments they must monitor and manage environmental conditions, and that is the focus of Chapter 5.

Questions for Discussion

1. Describe fully the environment that a typical local business (e.g., fast food, pizza, computer retail, bank) might face, and explain why it is important for managers to be aware of that environment.
2. Why is it important to view organizations as open systems?
3. Describe typical barriers to entry that a business like the one you chose in question one might face.
4. It may be obvious how government actions can constrain or put limits on businesses. How can government create opportunities for businesses?
5. This chapter focuses on the global environment. It was stated that even small, local businesses can be affected by global environmental conditions. Discuss how this may be so.
6. Give some examples of how conditions in the physical environment may affect businesses.

7. Describe the environmental factors (both positive and negative) that affect your university. What sectors of the environment appear to be most important?
8. Select an event in the recent world, national, and/or local news, and analyze its environmental impact on business.

References

1. R. L. Daft, *Organization Theory and Design,* 4th ed. (St. Paul, MN: West, 1992); Richard H. Hall, *Organizations: Structures, Processes, and Outcomes* (Upper Saddle River, NJ: Prentice Hall, 1991).
2. Gene Bylinsky, "Catalytica: How to Leapfrog the Giants," *Fortune* (October 18, 1993): 80.
3. Gregory G. Dess and Donald W. Beard, "Dimensions of Organizational Task Environments," *Administrative Science Quarterly* 29 (1984): 52–73; Mark P. Sharfman and James W. Dean, Jr., "Conceptualizing and Measuring the Organizational Environment: A Multidimensional Approach," *Journal of Management* 17 (1991): 681–700.
4. Michael E. Porter, *Competitive Strategy: Techniques for Analyzing Industries and Competitors* (New York: The Free Press, 1980).
5. Richard A. Melcher, "How Goliaths Can Act like Davids," *Business Week* (Special Enterprise Issue, 1993): 192–201; James B. Treece, "Sometimes, You Still Gotta Have Size," *Business Week* (Special Enterprise Issue, 1993): 200–201.
6. J. Brittain and J. Freeman, "Organizational Proliferation and Density Dependent Selection," *Organizational Life Cycles* (San Francisco: Jossey-Bass, 1980), 291–338.
7. G. Burns, "Bye-bye to Fat Times," *Business Week* (January 9, 1995): 89.
8. Based on Donald G. McNeil, Jr., "Selling Cheap 'Generic' Drugs, India's Copycats Irk Industry," *The New York Times on the Web* (www.nytimes.qpass. com/qpass-archives?), December 1, 2000.
9. Timothy K. Smith, "Why Air Travel Doesn't Work," *Fortune* (April 3, 1995), 43–56.
10. Harrison M. Trice and Janice Beyer, *The Cultures of Work Organizations* (Upper Saddle River, NJ: Prentice Hall, 1993), xiii.
11. Daniel Benjamin, "Some Germans Pin Hopes on Service Jobs," *The Wall Street Journal* (November 10, 1993), A18.
12. E. Updike, "The Land of the Rising Eyebrow," *Business Week* (March 27, 1995): 8.
13. W. Jack Duncan, *Organizational Behavior* (Boston: Houghton Mifflin, 1978), 177–82.
14. Paul Hotheinz, "Yes, You Can Win in Eastern Europe," *Fortune* (May 16, 1994): 110–12.
15. Peter Behr, "Honda Is Rolling Success Off Its Ohio Assembly Line," *Washington Post* (May 3, 1987), H1, H2.
16. Stewart Toy, Mark Maremont, and Ronald Grover, "An American in Paris: Can Disney Work Its Magic in Europe," *Business Week* (March 12, 1990): 60–64; Julie Solomon, "Mickey's Trip to Trouble," *Newsweek* (February 14, 1994): 34–39.
17. D. Katz, *Just Do It* (New York: Random House, 1994).
18. Alex Taylor III, "The Auto Industry Meets the New Economy," *Fortune* (September 5, 1994): 52–60.
19. "Drugs—Manufacturing Jobs in Puerto Rico," *Monthly Labor Review* (March 1995): 19.
20. D. Harbrecht, "What Has NAFTA Wrought? Plenty of TRADE," *Business Week* (November 21, 1994): 48–49.
21. www.lanic.utexas.edu/cswht/tradeindex, April 6, 2001.
22. Associated Press, *The New York Times,* May 7, 2001, C-1.
23. www.europa.eu.int/index_en.htm, April 6, 2001.
24. D. Harbrecht, "How Business CAN Manage the Backlash," *Business Week* (December 5, 1994): 37.
25. World Trade Organization, www.wto.org/english/ thewto_e/whatis_e/whatis_e.htm.
26. H. Mintzberg, "Managerial Work: Analysis from Observation," *Management Science* 18, no. 2 (1971): 97–110.
27. L. Walczak, R. S. Dunham, H. Gleckman, and S. B. Garland, "The Conservative Agenda," *Business Week* (November 21, 1994): 26–34.
28. P. Dwyer, K. Lowry Miller, and R. Neff, "Suddenly, It's Time to Buy American," *Business Week* (March 27, 1995): 58.
29. C. Perrow, "A Framework for the Comparative Analysis of Organizations," *American Sociological Review* 32 (1967): 194–208; J. D. Thompson, *Organizations in Action* (New York: McGraw-Hill, 1967); D. Gerwin, "Relationships Between Structure and Technology," *Handbook of Organizational Design,* vol. 2 (New York: Oxford University Press, 1981), 3–38.
30. Lowell W. Steele, *Managing Technology* (New York: McGraw-Hill, 1989); Eric Von Hippel, *The Sources of Innovation* (New York: Oxford University Press, 1988).

31. Christina Duff, "Blue-Light Blues: K-Mart's Dowdy Stores Get a Snazzy Face Lift, but Problems Linger," *The Wall Street Journal* (November 5, 1993), 1–6.
32. See Thompson in note 29.
33. W. J. Cook, "Ringing in Saturn," *U.S. News & World Report* (October 22, 1990): 51–54.
34. See note 2.
35. See note 15.
36. Kenneth Labich, "The Best Cities for Knowledge Workers," *Fortune* (November 15, 1993): 50–78.
37. Otis Port, "The Responsive Factory," *Business Week* (Special Enterprise Issue, 1993): 48–53; Christopher Farrell, "A Wellspring of Innovation," *Business Week* (Special Enterprise Issue, 1993): 56–62; Michael Hammer and James Champy, *Reengineering the Corporation: A Manifesto for Business Revolution* (New York: Harper Business, 1993).
38. Thomas A. Stewart, "Reengineering: The Hot New Managing Tool," *Fortune* (August 23, 1993): 40–48; Joseph Weber, "A Big Company That Works," *Business Week* (May 4, 1992): 124–32.
39. See note 7.
40. M. Magee, "Japanese Quake Sends Ruin Through Business," *San Francisco Chronicle* (February 6, 1995), D1. Suein L. Hwang, "Healthy Eating, Premium Private Labels Take a Bite Out of Nabisco's Cookie Sales," *The Wall Street Journal* (July 13, 1992), B1–B3.
41. See Dess and Beard in note 3; H. Aldrich, *Organizations and Environments* (Upper Saddle River, NJ: Prentice Hall, 1979); F. E. Emery and E. L. Trist, "The Causal Texture of Organizational Environments," *Human Relations* 18, no. 1 (1965): 21–32.
42. See Aldrich in note 41; see Emery and Trist in note 41.
43. See Aldrich in note 41; see Dess and Beard in note 3; see Emery and Trist in note 41.
44. See Dess and Beard in note 3.
45. Tom Peters, *Thriving on Chaos* (New York: Alfred A. Knopf, 1988); *Fortune* (Special Issue: "The Tough New Consumer: Demanding More and Getting It," Autumn/Winter 1993); *Business Week* (Special Issue: "Reinventing America: Meeting the New Challenges of a Global Economy," 1992); John W. Verity, "Deconstructing the Computer Industry," *Business Week* (November 23, 1992): 90–100.

Is a Budweiser by Any Other Name Still a Budweiser?*

"'What are we going to drink?' ask the Americans in a *Budweiser Budvar* commercial. 'Surely not our American Budweiser again?'"[1]

To North Americans the name Budweiser is inextricably linked to the American company Anheuser-Busch, the world's largest brewery. However, the story of the Budweiser name and its implications on international trade are more complicated than one might expect. A little history lesson may help untangle the situation.

Bohemia, today part of the Czech Republic, has a long and illustrious history of brewing fine beer. In 1265, King Premysl Otaker II founded the city of Ceske Budejovice at the confluence of the Vltava and Malse rivers. Because even at that time the region was known for brewing fine beers, the king granted the town leaders brewing privileges. In the mid-sixteenth century the king, who later became Emperor Ferdinand I, gave the city a special award for its beer. The beers of Ceske Budejovice have continued to gain great favor among royalty and beer connoisseurs, and have won numerous awards worldwide. However, since 1939, the major brewer in Ceske Budejovice has been unable to sell its beer under its traditional name in the Americas, from Panama north. Since 1872, that beer has been called "Budweiser Budvar," drawing on the German name of the city, "Budweis." (Many residents of Bohemia are of German heritage and speak German.)

In 1872 two businessmen from St. Louis, of German descent, began exporting Budweiser Beer from Budejovice. They retained the Budweiser name because of its association with the high-quality Czech product. In 1878, the name Budweiser Lager Bier was registered in the United States as a trademark and in 1891 the name was sold by the two Americans to Anheuser-Busch; the company began production and distribution of beer with the Budweiser name. In 1911 Anheuser-Busch and the Czech company Eesky akciovy pivovar (the precursor to Budweiser-Budvar) reached agreement to allow Anheuser-Busch to use the Budweiser name but without the word "original" on the label. The agreement involved payment of damages to Budweiser-Budvar, and the Czech company retained the right to sell products throughout the world with the Budweiser name.

Conflict over the Budweiser name decreased during Prohibition in the United States. However, in the 1930s, the Czech company registered the trademark and successfully exported "Imported Original Bohemian Budvar Beer from Budweiser City." Beginning in 1938, at the same time that Nazi Germany began its occupation of Czechoslovakia, Anheuser-Busch began pressuring Budweiser-Budvar to relinquish use of all variations of the Budweiser name in markets outside of Europe. In the 1970s, Budweiser-Budvar won several trademark cases in individual European markets including Greece, Finland, and Sweden. To this day, the Czech company Budweiser-Budvar (now known in the United States as BBNP) cannot use Bud, Budweiser, Budvar, Budweis, or any similar name on its labels outside of Europe. They cannot even give more than minor attention to the city of origin of the beer.

Since the fall of the "iron curtain" in central and eastern Europe, Budweiser-Budvar has been trying to crack the North American market. The company faced the critical problem of how to market their beer in this market and capitalize on its long history of quality and excellence without reference to its original name. While the overall U.S. beer market in recent years has been flat, the area that has had some growth is premium brews, including imports.

The solution to the problem was the name "Czechvar." After a 62-year absence, BBNP has begun limited distribution and sale of its famous product in selected states (California, Florida, New York, Illinois, Massachusetts, Georgia, and North Carolina) under the Czechvar name. According to the company's advertising, Czechvar is a European beer from the Czech Republic, which is slightly sweet and full-bodied, with the taste of hops. Whether Czechvar provides much of a challenge to Anheuser-Busch remains to be seen. ∎

[*]This case is based on information from a Budweiser-Budvar advertisement, the Budweiser-Budvar Web site (www.budvar.cz), and the Czechvar Web site (www.czechvar.com).
[1]From a Budweiser Budvar advertisement.

QUESTIONS FOR DISCUSSION

1. What were the primary environmental threats that the Czech company faced in the late 1800s and early 1900s? Did those threats change in the latter part of the twentieth century?

2. As BBNP enters the U.S. market with Czechvar, what are likely to be the most significant environmental threats?

3. If you were a manager at Anheuser-Busch, would you see Czechvar as a major environmental threat? If not, what would be the biggest threats facing a company like Anheuser-Busch?

CHAPTER

Managing the Environment

5

CASE: MANAGING THE CROWDED SKIES[*]

If you have checked the video monitors in most large international airports, and even many regional airports, you may have noticed something very intriguing. Many flights have multiple flight numbers, each associated with a different airline. For example, two flights each day leave Cincinnati, Ohio, for Paris, France. Each of those flights has two flight numbers, one for Delta Airlines and one for Air France. The first flight leaves Cincinnati at 6:50 P.M. and is designated as Delta flight 44 and as Air France flight 8885. The plane and flight crew are from Delta. The second flight leaves Cincinnati at 9:15 P.M. and is designated as Delta flight 8701 and Air France flight 381. The plane and flight crew are from Air France. A passenger on either flight could be flying on a Delta or an Air France ticket.

When you get to the Charles de Gaulle Airport in Paris, the scene gets even more confusing. All of the Air France flights have Air France numbers, Delta numbers, and Continental Airlines numbers. If you scan the monitors, you will see a similar scenario for other airlines. British Airways (BA) flights will have BA numbers, American Airlines numbers, and others. United Airlines shares numbers with Lufthansa, Air Canada, Scandinavian Airlines (SAS), and others. What you are witnessing is an attempt by the airlines to manage a very complex and changing air travel environment.

DEREGULATION

Before 1978, the airline industry was heavily regulated by national governments and international treaties. Routes, fares, and airport gates were carefully controlled to limit competition. In the United States, the government regulated routes, gate space, and fares. International flights were regulated by the 1944 Chicago Convention and the subsequent formation of the International Civil Aviation Organization (ICAO) and International Air Transportation Association (IATA). International flights were primarily handled by "national flag carriers." Most international flights from the United States were on TWA, Pan American Airlines, or carriers from the destination countries (e.g., Air France for France or British Overseas Airways for the United Kingdom). Within the United States, United Airlines and American Airlines served most parts of the country and the remaining carriers were primarily regional. Eastern Airlines served the east coast; Piedmont served the southeast; Northwest served the midwest and west coast;

---

[*]This case is based on material from the following sources: Nigel Evans, "Collaborative Strategy: An Analysis of the Changing World of International Airline Alliances," *Tourism Management,* 22 (2001): 229–243; Daniel Chan, "The Development of the Airline Industry from 1978 to 1998: A Strategic Global Overview." *Journal of Management Development,* 19 (2000): 489–514. Delta Web site: www.delta.com/ home_url/dal_stats_facts/index.jsp, June 11, 2001.

North Central served the upper midwest; and so on. The rationale for this regulation and segmentation of the market was much the same as existed in utility and telecommunications business: avoidance of what was viewed as destructive competition that would threaten safety and quality. On the international front, regulation was often aimed at protecting domestic airlines as part of protecting national security.

The situation began to change with passage of the U.S. Airline Deregulation Act of 1978. One of the most widely publicized changes that the act brought about was the elimination of government price regulation. Deregulation of international routes has progressed since 1978. In 1998 the European Union agreed to deregulation within the EU that closely parallels U.S. deregulation. However, most countries still have regulations that limit the extent to which foreign companies can own domestic airlines. For example, in the United States, foreign ownership of a U.S. airline is limited to 49 percent (and only 25 percent of voting shares). The ownership limitations are driven largely by nationalism—the belief that a country's security (and pride) is best served by domestic (sometimes government) ownership.

The rationale for domestic and international deregulation was the belief that competition and market forces would produce lower fares and better service for consumers. It was also believed that market forces would result in greater efficiency in the allocation of routes and gates. What most industry watchers did not expect was the flurry of failures (e.g., Eastern Airlines, Pan American, People Express), mergers and acquisitions (e.g., U.S. Air and Piedmont, Northwest and North Central), and alliances (e.g., Star Alliance, Oneworld, Sky Team). It is this last area that has produced the confusing array of flight numbers for any given flight that we see in most airports.

DELTA'S ALLIANCES

As the third largest U.S. airline, Delta Airlines faces a constant struggle to compete with United Airlines and American Airlines. Delta has been able to dominate the Atlanta Hartsfield Airport, one of the busiest in the world, and two of its other hubs (Salt Lake City and Cincinnati), but its presence in the lucrative and busy east coast, west coast, and international markets has been limited. To increase its scope, Delta has joined forces with several airlines to form an intricate web of alliances and partnerships.

In the United States Delta began to expand its reach through the Delta Connection. This alliance joined Delta to several regional carriers that served small markets. Atlantic Coast Jet (AC Jet) fed passengers from several small markets on the east coast to Delta flights in Boston, New York, and other major markets. This link bolstered Delta's position in both the small markets and on Delta's existing routes. SkyWest provided a link for small markets in the west to Delta's Salt Lake City hub. Atlantic Southeast Airlines (ASA) and Comair served the midwest, south, and southeast, providing links to Atlanta and Cincinnati. (Both ASA and Comair were acquired by Delta.)

Delta's Sky Team Alliance extends the company's international scope to Europe, Mexico, and Asia through Alliances with Aero Mexico, Air France, CSA Czech Airlines, and Korean Air. Delta can feed domestic U.S. passengers to their own international flights or to those of their partners. Similarly, passengers flying partners' international flights can be fed to Delta flights in the United States.

The key to the Delta Connection and Sky Team Alliance is code sharing. Partners will provide space on their flights and allow multiple flight numbers. Thus, the Delta flight from Cincinnati to Paris carries both Delta and Air France numbers, as does the

Air France flight. Similarly, flights from Dallas/Fort Worth to Mexico City would carry a Delta number and an Aero Mexico number. Customers can fly on a Delta or Air France ticket from Cincinnati to Paris and on a Delta or Aero Mexico ticket from Dallas/Fort Worth to Mexico City, and the price of the ticket on the same flight may vary depending on which airline is selling the ticket. The plane the passenger flies may be Delta or one of the Alliance or Connection partners'. Additionally, once passengers get to Paris or Mexico City, they can seamlessly link to the partner's flights to other destinations. So you fly from Cincinnati to Toulouse, France, on a Delta ticket, on flights with Delta numbers. The plane to Paris could be Delta or Air France and the plane from Paris to Toulouse would be Air France. Since Air France serves destinations throughout the world, the Delta customer could connect to destinations such as Vienna, Prague, or Moscow, to name just a few.

Further expanding Delta's reach is their list of Worldwide Partners: Aeropostal, Air Jamaica, Austrian Airlines, China Southern, Malaysia Airlines, Royal Moroc, Singapore Airlines, South African Airlines, TransBrasil, and United Airlines. These partners provide Delta customers with frequent flier mileage credit or award tickets and some provide code sharing to Delta reservationists or travel agents.

For Delta, these alliances and partnerships allow them to expand their reach and provide a steady flow of customers to their flights. The expansion is much less expensive than entering new markets with entirely their own equipment and personnel. Delta does not necessarily need to provide ticket agents or gate personnel in each of its international locations. For example, in Paris, Delta passengers and planes are serviced by Air France ground personnel. Similarly, in Cincinnati, Air France planes are serviced by Delta ground personnel. Moreover, even with worldwide deregulation of the airline industry, Delta would still find regulatory, economic, and cultural barriers to entering some markets outside the United States. It simply may not be possible or economically feasible for Delta to acquire routes and gate space in all markets it would like to reach. However, with the alliance, Delta can share risks, gain economies of scale and scope, learn from the experience of partners, and gain access to resources that would be beyond their reach if they had to "go it alone" in each new market. Delta can serve all the flight needs (and gain a portion of the revenue) of a passenger from the United States trying to reach some large or small market throughout the world.

The case shows how firms attempt to control a complex and changing global environment. Strategic alliances (with or without cross holdings of equity) are relatively flexible and inexpensive ways to gain some control of the external environment. In this chapter we will read about several techniques that organizations can use to try to control the environment. As you read this chapter, keep in mind the importance of trying first to understand the environment and then trying to manage it. The environment must be constantly monitored or scanned if an organization is to stay in alignment. It is the external environment that provides the inputs and absorbs the outputs that are the lifeblood to long-term survival. However, as we discussed in Chapter 4, the environment is complex and constantly changing. It may be difficult for any firm to stay ahead of the game. Some indications of this volatility are Delta's previous failed alliances with Swiss Air and Sabena and its labor difficulties with its Comair division.

MANAGING THE ENVIRONMENT

We take for granted that organizational leaders can adapt their organizations to meet environmental demands and even change the very environment that they face. These assumptions are at the foundation of a strategic perspective on organizations—managers formulate strategies and conduct their organizations to maximize the organization's "fit" with the environmental conditions the organization faces. We assume that when managers discover new and different environmental conditions, they take action to change the organization to better match the environment or, in some instances, change the environmental conditions to better fit their organization's strengths. Contained within this view of the organizational world are the assumptions that managers can and will obtain valid and reliable information about the environment; that organizations are flexible and can be made to respond to the environmental conditions; and that managers can knowingly and meaningfully manipulate the environment to create conditions that are advantageous to their organization.

Our primary focus in this chapter is on how managers try to accomplish these tasks. First, we examine how managers come to know their environment. What can managers do to gather information? What are the obstacles to gathering information? What happens to that information? Second, we explore how organizations adapt or respond to environmental conditions. Once managers learn about the environmental conditions, what kinds of changes can reduce uncertainty and make the organization more effective? The third step is to understand how managers can take actions that actually change the environmental conditions to make them more amenable to the organization's strengths.

There can be little doubt that organizations do each of the three things mentioned above: gather information about the environment, adapt to the environment, and change the environment. Increasingly, however, some organizational theorists are challenging these fundamental assumptions that managers can *meaningfully* and *significantly* adapt to or change the environment. We conclude this chapter by introducing the rather controversial organizational perspective called ***population ecology*** that asserts that managers are more or less powerless to knowingly and meaningfully change organizations or the environment. Fundamental to this view is the belief that environments are so complex and unpredictable that managers can never know enough or anticipate conditions appropriately to meaningfully adapt either the organization or the environment.

KNOWING THE ENVIRONMENT

The open systems view of organizations highlights the critical nature of the environment. The environment is the source of ***opportunities*** for an organization in the form of necessary resources and markets; and ***threats*** in the form of uncertainty, dependency, and scarcity. Organizations learn about these external conditions through ***boundary spanning*** and ***environmental scanning*** activities.

Boundary spanning activities are those functions that require members of the organization to spend all or part of their time interacting with people and organizations outside the boundaries of their own organization.[1] Boundary spanning units aid the organization in adjusting to the conditions that exist in the environment. The boundary spanning activities serve two general functions: (1) They gather information and provide feedback about the environment to the organization, and (2) they represent the organization to the outside world. Let us look at the first of these two functions. For example, sales or service representatives who visit customers can be an important source of information not only about the customers' needs, but also about competitors. Customers and competitors represent only two parts of the environment, albeit important ones. Purchasing, sales, human resources, finance, government relations, public relations, investor relations, advertising, and countless other departments may encounter important information through interactions with suppliers, bankers, investors, government, and the general public—people and organizations outside their own boundaries. Figure 5-1 depicts the positions that boundary spanning units occupy with respect to the organization and its environment.

It is important to keep in mind that boundary spanning activities are not restricted to those individuals or units whose roles are explicitly designed for boundary spanning. Chief executive officers of major corporations or other types of organizations often fulfill the role of boundary spanner. When Lee Iacocca led Chrysler Corporation through difficult periods in the 1980s, he played a highly visible and prominent role interacting with government, bankers, investors, and even customers. Other CEOs have played similar high visibility roles either conveying information about their companies or gathering information. Examples include Bill Gates who authored a syndicated newspaper column and a book, and Jim Cook of Boston Brewing (Samuel Adams) who has been prominently featured in that company's advertising. When the CEO appears before stockholders or analysts to report on the firm's past performance and future direction, he or she is acting as a boundary spanner. When a university dean or president appears before the community or the state legislature, he or she is acting as a boundary spanner. Indeed, CEOs, presidents, and deans are often selected because of their connections to the external environment, prestige, or status. These figurehead and liaison roles are often among the most important roles of organizational leaders.[2]

As shown in Exhibit 5-1, the CEO or president of an organization sometimes plays a critical boundary spanning role in representing the organization to the external environment. In the example given the president attempts damage control—minimizing the harm done—when a serious environmental threat occurs. The president tries to reestablish the university's legitimacy and positive image in the community.

FIGURE 5-1   Boundary Spanning Units and the Environment

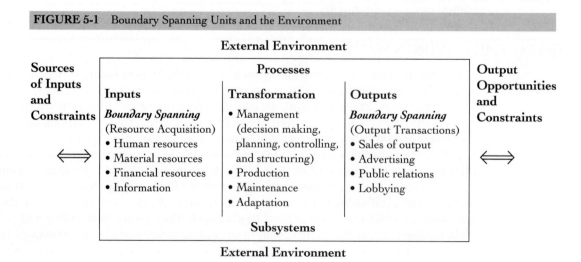

External Environment

Sources of Inputs and Constraints	Processes			Output Opportunities and Constraints
	Inputs	**Transformation**	**Outputs**	
	Boundary Spanning (Resource Acquisition)	• Management (decision making, planning, controlling, and structuring)	*Boundary Spanning* (Output Transactions)	
⟺	• Human resources • Material resources • Financial resources • Information	• Production • Maintenance • Adaptation	• Sales of output • Advertising • Public relations • Lobbying	⟺

Subsystems

External Environment

EXHIBIT 5-1

The President Attempts Damage Control

Since development of the first atomic bomb during World War II, the U.S. government has been interested in determining the effects of radiation exposure on humans. Recently, the public has learned of questionable ethical behavior by the federal government, public institutions, and medical researchers. It appears that the federal government directly and indirectly conducted radiation exposure experiments on humans, even though a growing body of knowledge at the time suggested that exposure could lead to serious illness and death.

One such experiment was conducted in the late 1960s and early 1970s at a large midwestern university hospital. Terminal cancer patients were exposed to large doses of full-body radiation. The purpose of the experiment was ostensibly to provide the Department of Defense with data on the effects of radiation exposure. Numerous questions about the ethics and wisdom of this experiment were raised at the time of the study, but in the midst of the Cold War, critics were silenced. Nearly all patients in the experiment died shortly after exposure, but it is unclear whether they died from their illness or from radiation.

Nearly 25 years after the experiments, the public has learned the lurid details. Questions have been raised about whether patients were given full information, whether they gave informed consent to participate, and whether the experimenter conducted the study in an ethical and scientifically sound fashion. Surviving family members, legislators, doctors, researchers, and the general public were outraged and demanded a full accounting of what happened. Some families threatened to sue the university and the researchers.

One can imagine the public relations nightmare that this scenario presents. Initially, the university attempted to deal with this crisis in a conventional fashion. Hospital administrators and the university public relations office issued press releases and set up a hot line to respond to questions. Still, the community was not satisfied and thought the university was stonewalling. Finally, the university president went on TV news programs and met with community leaders to assure everyone that the university was doing its best to get to the bottom of this mess. The belief was that the prestige and legitimacy of the president would calm fears and appease an angry public. This may, however, be a case of too little, too late.

Boundary spanning may also be conducted by units that are not within the organization's boundaries at all. For example, a law firm, employment agency, or advertising firms may gather environmental information or represent an organization's interests to outsiders.

Environmental Scanning

Information gathering may be a primary, explicit role or a secondary, implicit role for individuals in organizations. These are the boundary spanning roles referred to above. In addition to collecting information through boundary spanning, organizations must process this information. ***Environmental scanning*** is a particular type of boundary spanning concerned with collecting and processing information, and assessing or projecting change in various sectors of the environment.[3] The central functions of environmental scanning activities are to gather and interpret important environmental information and to introduce the results of analyses into the organization's strategic planning process. The goal of scanning is to help the organization reduce the amount of environmental uncertainty it faces.

As organizations face increasingly complex and uncertain environments, they create more numerous and specialized boundary spanning units and they engage in more scanning activity. Organizations often examine changes in demographics, competition, technology, customer needs and requirements, regulations, and a variety of other environmental forces. Information gained from scanning is used to make projections about likely conditions the organization will encounter and to aid in planning the future direction of the organization. Scanning data are the input for product development, advertising, personnel planning, production scheduling, and myriad other functions. For example, market research can yield information about changing consumer demographics, emerging buying patterns, and dying markets. Studies of local labor markets may help the personnel department anticipate labor shortages and increasing labor costs.

Research evidence suggests that, in general, the most important sectors to monitor, in the eyes of top management, are the market sector, the economic sector, and the sociocultural sector.[4] Clearly, in some industries other sectors of the environment may be equally or more important than these three sectors. For example, product innovations would clearly be important to monitor in the computer and electronics industry, and regulatory changes and supplier prices are likely to be critical factors to examine in health care–related businesses. The task facing managers is how to focus the organization's limited scanning resources in environments that are complex and uncertain. No organization can hope to cover everything. Although the specific answer to the question of what to monitor may differ from one setting to another, we can generalize that organizations that scan more of their environment and do so more often are likely to perform better than organizations that ignore the changing conditions in their environment.[5] Additionally, organizations that are facing increasingly uncertain and complex environments will create organizational designs that include more specialized units to engage in boundary spanning and scanning.[6] Thus, organizations attempt to manage environmental complexity with structural complexity.

Some scanning activities involve closely monitoring the actions of competitors. Retailers may use comparison shoppers to monitor competitors' pricing. Manufacturers may engage in reverse engineering (disassembling products to understand how they are engineered, designed, and constructed and how they can be duplicated), and some companies even use spying to gain critical information. Exhibit 5-2 provides some examples of corporate spying activity. Many lawsuits have been fought in the computer industry over reverse engineering and cloning of products.

Even with sophisticated scanning and product development, we are all aware of product flops and other ill-conceived attempts to manage the environment. Ford's infamous Edsel was the result of intensive market research; yet it is the epitome of a flop. The company surveyed car buyers in the earlier and mid-1950s to determine features that buyers valued the most. The Edsel was supposed to include all these features. However, the result in this case was an example of the whole being less than the sum of its parts. The car was poorly designed, and its eclectic collection of features was not pleasing to car buyers. More recently, the Beech Starship, a radically innovative general aviation aircraft, represents a similar failure.[7] The plane was such a radical departure from standard aircraft that potential buyers were scared away.

EXHIBIT 5-2

Corporate Cloak and Dagger: Scanning of Another Sort[8]

Now that the Cold War is over, you may think that spying is a thing of the past. But that is not at all the case—especially in the corporate world. It is estimated that U.S. businesses lose as much as $20 to $30 billion a year as a result of spying by domestic and foreign competitors. Some executives and political leaders have taken these threats as the impetus for clandestine warfare against competitors. Consider the following examples.

- The FBI arrested two Koreans who allegedly purchased blueprints of a new Dow Chemical polymer plant in Texas.

- Mitsubishi and Hitachi officials were arrested in the early 1980s for purchasing IBM trade secrets.

- A unit of the French government, the Direction Générale de la Sécurité Exterieure (DGSE), actively engages in surveillance. French students in the United States and French workers in European divisions of foreign companies have been used to ferret out trade secrets. French engineers visiting the United States posed as French government officials in an effort to acquire radar-evading stealth technology. French diplomats rummaged through the garbage of a U.S. computer industry executive, searching for secrets that could aid French manufacturers.

- The Japanese Ministry of International Trade and Industry (MITI) coordinates the country's largely legal information gathering that includes monitoring foreign competitors throughout the world and seeking industries ripe for Japanese challenge.

- U.S. firms doing business in the former East Bloc communist countries must be concerned that the military intelligence agencies of those countries are now turning their attention to industrial spying. Many former agents are now for hire as freelancers and use many of the same wiretapping and photo reconnaissance techniques of the Cold War for business customers.

- Domestic competitors are not beneath spying on each other. Agents working for Avon Cosmetics were caught rummaging through dumpsters at Mary Kay. Spies have posed as students, university researchers, and journalists all in an effort to pry trade secrets from competitors.

- Perhaps one of the most widely used techniques in high technology fields is reverse engineering. Firms purchase competitors' products and take them apart to uncover engineering and design secrets. This is common practice among chip manufactures, computer makers, and software developers. Intel has encoded computer chips with cryptic messages such as "steal the best" to discourage copycats.

It's not all illegal and it's not all cloak and dagger, but corporate spying is pervasive and is a critical, costly threat that must be taken seriously.

BOUNDARY PERMEABILITY, RESILIENCE, AND MAINTENANCE

The message is that boundary spanning and environmental scanning are critically important functions if an organization hopes to be responsive to its environment. Failure to respond to the environment will result in organizational decline and, eventually, failure. An organization must, however, strike a balance in boundary spanning and scanning. The concepts of boundary *permeability*, *resilience*, and *maintenance* are useful in understanding the nature of the balance that an organization must maintain.

Permeability refers to the extent to which the organization facilitates the inward and outward flow of information. Which information and how much information does top management need to make decisions? Which information and how much information should management release to the outside world? These are critical questions that management must address and that affect the permeability of the organization's boundaries. The answer to this question depends in part on the uncertainty of the environment the organization faces. Increasing levels of uncertainty call for increasing permeability.

If the organization fails to monitor and screen incoming information, there is the danger that the organization as a whole may be overwhelmed by information, some of which may be irrelevant. For example, the U.S. Commerce Department produces extensive reports on the economy, labor market, consumer demand, weather conditions, and a multitude of other environmental sectors that *could* affect a business. A critical management task is to determine how much of this information is relevant and filter out the remainder. Failure to make such a determination could result in a flood of information that could easily overwhelm even a very large firm. The proliferation of databases and Internet search engines has made information management crucial. Often the problem is not one of insufficient information. Rather the problem is determining the quality of the information available and which information is most relevant. Similarly, some individuals in organizations play the role of **gatekeepers**. They restrict access to managers by filtering out information they deem to be irrelevant and unnecessary while forwarding information that is important and useful. For example, secretaries and administrative assistants often screen incoming information so that their bosses are not overwhelmed with trivial data. These activities are likely to involve screening mail, phone calls, and potential visitors.

Some parts of the organization may need to be protected or **buffered** from information.[9] For example, the production department of a computer company may need information on consumer demand to aid in production scheduling, but additional information about environmental conditions may be irrelevant and may even adversely affect production. Management should buffer the production department from information that could cause undue concern or even raise uncertainty.

Resilience refers to the degree to which boundary spanning units respond to changes in the mission and goals of the organization, as well as changes in the environment. Suppose a company decides to change its goals by pursuing a new market niche. Such a shift necessitates the collection of new information relevant to that new market niche and dissemination of new information to people and organizations in the environment. Resilience refers to the ability of boundary spanning units to shift and change in ways that allow them to collect the appropriate information.

The Cadillac Division of GM provides both negative and positive examples of resilience. In the mid-1970s and early 1980s the luxury car market was undergoing extensive change. Small sports and luxury imports like BMW, Audi, Volvo, and Saab were carving out a new entry-level luxury niche. Cadillac had enough resilience in its boundary spanning units to recognize the market changes and to realize that the change was consistent with the division's mission as a luxury car manufacturer. Cadillac Division of General Motors marketed the Cimarron, a new type of car aimed at the new market niche. This small, entry-level Cadillac was supposed to compete with the early upscale imports. Unfortunately, the Cimarron was unsuccessful, and auto industry critics point to the Cadillac Division's unfamiliarity with its import competition and with the potential customers as factors in this failure. The car was small and had many of the luxury appointments typical of Cadillac products, but it lacked the refinements characteristic of the import competitors. It was also a different type of car from the ones that typical Cadillac customers would consider. In other words, Cadillac's boundary spanning departments—marketing, product development, and dealer relations—had enough resilience to recognize changing conditions and new opportunities, but lacked the ability to convert the information into appropriate actions.

In the 1990s, Cadillac tried again, with greater success this time, to deal with the import threat. This time, Cadillac focused on the upper end of the market, a niche that was more familiar to management. The Seville STS was aimed at the luxury sport coupe and sport sedan market. The result was a car that has successfully competed with the large BMW, Mercedes, Lexus, and Infinity cars.[10] However, Cadillac continues to struggle in its attempts at the entry level of the luxury market, an area still out of its expertise. The company's Catera, based on a European Opel design, failed to live up to expectations.

The blame for failure or credit for success cannot all be placed on the boundary spanning units. The concept of resilience depends, to a great extent, on a smooth and close relationship between top management setting the new goals and mission and the boundary spanning units that are responsible for collecting and disseminating new information. Boundary spanners must be aware that the goals or environmental conditions have changed and that new and different information must be sought. In the Cadillac example boundary spanners recognized that environmental changes had taken place. Consumers were shifting to a different type of product, but boundary spanners and top management failed to recognize exactly the specific nature of the market changes that had taken place. In order for boundary spanning units to respond effectively—to be both permeable to information and to be resilient to change—it is necessary to monitor and maintain these units.

Maintenance is especially important in boundary spanning units. Because boundary spanners oftentimes operate outside the organization's boundaries, these people and departments must be carefully managed. A typical boundary spanning role, such as that of a sales representative, requires that the role occupant leave the organization in order to carry out his or her job. When the person leaves the organization, especially when departures are often and extensive, that person may lose some contact with the organization's mission or goals. Boundary spanners may also be influenced by people outside the organization and either fail to properly represent their organization or fail to acquire appropriate and relevant information. The term *going native* is used to refer to situations in which people in boundary spanning roles take on characteristics of their customer or target organization rather than their own organization.[11] This is a particular problem for drug enforcement agents, corrections officers, and others in law enforcement, but it can also happen in more typical business organizations among sales and service personnel who spend extensive amounts of time with customers. Careful monitoring and periods of resocialization (i.e., retraining and refamiliarization with organizational goals) are necessary to counter this tendency.

Maintenance of boundary spanning units requires that they maintain or periodically reestablish links to decision-authority centers (e.g., top management) in the organization. This is important so that boundary spanners can renew their commitment to the organization, learn about new goals and priorities, and identify appropriate areas of the environment to scan. Maintenance of boundary spanners may take place in periodic meetings for which field representatives return to headquarters, share information they have acquired, and learn about new directions the organization may be pursuing.[12]

ENVIRONMENTAL UNCERTAINTY AND DEPENDENCE

As noted in Chapter 4, organizations can potentially encounter uncertainty or problems from three aspects of the environment: (1) complexity—the number of sectors or elements of the environment relevant to an organization; (2) change—the extent or speed with which elements in the environment undergo change; and (3) munificence—the availability of critical resources in the environment.

The net result of a complex and changing environment is uncertainty. The more environmental elements a firm needs to monitor, the more likely it is that the environment will push the organization's limited capacity to monitor. Because of the increasing demands on an organization's monitoring abilities, complexity can cause uncertainty. Similarly, the more and the faster the environment changes, the more a firm needs to closely watch the environment and take actions to adapt to changed conditions. Once again, because every organization has only a limited capacity to monitor the environment, increasing levels of change will cause uncertainty. Organizations must take some actions to manage environmental uncertainty.

Munificence creates a somewhat different problem and different type of uncertainty. Clearly, all organizations must acquire critical resources. When resources are abundant, acquisition is not much of a problem. When resources are scarce, the potential exists for an organization to become dependent upon one or a few suppliers.[13] Scarcity and the resulting dependence create problems for an organization. The firm's ability to act independently and decisively may become restricted. A firm that is dependent on the pricing and availability of supplies cannot freely and independently set production schedules, arrange shipping and receiving, or set its own pricing. As scarcity increases, dependence increases. As dependence increases, a firm's autonomy decreases. Its ability to independently and freely design and implement strategy is jeopardized. Organizations, in general, will take actions to either entirely avoid dependencies—which is often impossible—or they will take actions to manage dependent relationships.

Dependence also occurs when power is asymmetrically distributed between organizations. This is apparent in buyer-supplier relationships. Wal-Mart, for example, has grown so large in the market that it has enormous power relative to supplier companies. Suppliers, even large ones, have become dependent on Wal-Mart's business. To lose Wal-Mart as an account would be devastating to most firms. As a consequence, Wal-Mart is able to exercise its power to achieve lower prices and better terms from suppliers.

The following sections describe strategies and techniques that organizations use to adapt to or reduce uncertainty and avoid or manage dependencies. These strategies and techniques are incomplete or imperfect. Organizations will always face some uncertainty and some dependence on others. Additionally, these strategies and techniques are not necessarily mutually exclusive. Organizations will typically use several techniques or strategies in concert.

ADAPTING TO THE ENVIRONMENT

Gathering information about the environment is merely the first step toward successfully managing it, which requires that an organization take further action. Boundary spanners have scanned the environment and detected some conditions for which the organization may be unprepared, or they may anticipate new conditions for which the current organization is ill suited. To better manage these new or anticipated conditions, management may choose to change or adapt the organization. In this section we examine the variety of ways in which the organization can adapt to meet these new or anticipated changes. It is important to remember that environmental adaptation refers to strategies that focus on the organization's attempts to change in response to the environment. One must keep in mind that there are many ways the organization can change, and more than one method of adaptation may be successful—but not all methods of change or adaptation are equally appropriate. Moreover, as we discuss at greater length in Chapter 13, change itself can cause problems for an organization.

Forecasting and Strategic Planning

Strategic management deals with the future. Scanning the environment is perhaps most important as an ingredient to forecast the future. Any strategic plan is only as good as the forecasts that predict the future. To the extent that predictions are accurate, the building blocks for plans and decisions will be solidly constructed. A complete discussion of forecasting is beyond the scope of this book. The following brief discussion describes two popular methods of forecasting: trend analysis and scenario analysis.

Most forecasts are based on a ***trend analysis***. Trend analysis uses historic data to determine future conditions. For example, a hardware-home center may examine sales of snow shovels and snowblowers over the past five years. It uses those trends, along with weather trends and long-range weather forecasts, to predict future snow shovel and snowblower sales. Some trends are predictable. Trends may be straight lines representing steady growth, no change, or decline; or trends may be curvilinear cycles. Snowblower sales may have decreased gradually over recent years because of the combination of warm winters and environmental concerns. By analyzing this trend, the retailer can predict that sales will probably continue to decline. Trends may also be cyclical. The retailer may find that snow equipment sales are tied closely to weather trends. An examination of weather trends may suggest cycles of bad winters. Thus, the retailer may forecast greater demand because the region is due for a bad winter. Some trends or cycles can be punctuated by unpredictable events. Unpredictable cycles make forecasting and planning difficult. The winter of 1993–94 was one of the most severe on record in the East and Midwest. Record cold temperatures combined with unrelenting snow and ice storms. However, winters in the East and Midwest were rather mild in the late 1990s. No amount of scanning and forecasting could have predicted those weather conditions and the resulting demand for snow removal equipment. As a result, retailers and local government agencies may be caught without adequate inventories of snow removal equipment or with oversupplies.

Not all trends are as unpredictable as weather. Population or demographic trends are comparatively rather predictable. Business forecasters follow closely the tastes and trends among baby boomers, busters, and Generation X members to discern changing tastes, work habits, and living conditions. Phenomena like the boom in minivan, sport utility vehicle, and truck sales; movements toward self-employment; and growth in aging-related industries can be traced to population trends.[14]

Scenario forecasting is a method that presents alternative trends or events and attaches probabilities to those alternatives. The hardware–home center retailer could project the likelihood of a mild winter, an average winter, and a severe winter. A payoff matrix can be constructed for each scenario, and planners can make decisions based on these expected outcomes. Table 5-1 provides an example of scenario forecasting and contingency planning based on the scenarios.

Forecasting presents managers with a bit of a paradox in trying to adapt to environments. The most accurate forecasts can be constructed in a simple and stable environment. When environments become increasingly complex and increasingly unstable, forecasting becomes increasingly difficult, time-consuming, and inaccurate. The paradox exists because forecasting is not particularly important when the environment

TABLE 5-1   Scenario Forecasting and Contingency Planning

Scenario	Probability	Plan	Financial Benefit a. if correct b. if incorrect
1. Mild winter	30%	Small inventory	a. $5,000 b. −$5,000
2. Average winter	65%	Average inventory	a. $10,000 b. −$2,000
3. Severe winter	5%	Large inventory	a. $30,000 b. −$20,000

is simple and stable. What works today should work tomorrow. Forecasting becomes a *potentially* important tool when the environment is complex and unstable—when management needs new ways to deal with the environment—but the forecast may not be accurate or useful. However, in extreme uncertainty, forecasting and planning may be difficult and costly to accomplish successfully *because* of the uncertainty, and the results of the forecasting may be inaccurate and unreliable.

Withdrawal: Protecting the Organizational Core

Organizations may adapt a strategy of sealing themselves off from portions of the environment. The key to this strategy is developing means for keeping the environment from interfering with the organization's core operations.[15] Temporarily, withdrawal or taking a defensive posture may protect an organization from some environmental uncertainty. In the long run, withdrawal, especially if carried to an extreme, will place an organization out of "sync" with its environment and will likely damage the organization. How can an organization be successful if its products or services are inconsistent with the diverse demands and pressures of the environment?

Organizations typically accomplish this insulation from environmental uncertainty by focusing on narrow, specialized, and/or stable portions of the environment. For example, early in the development of the personal computer market, Compaq Computer was able to defend itself from some of the environmental uncertainty in its industry by concentrating its efforts only on a narrow market segment—premium-priced portable computers. Similarly, Apple Computer focused early attention on educational computing, a niche that was less crowded and more stable than business computing. As a result, Compaq and Apple were able to avoid some of the environmental uncertainty that befell companies such as IBM and Digital Equipment Company. However, this strategy backfired for Apple because the majority of growth has been in the business market.

It is not only in the market or industry sectors that organizations attempt to avoid uncertainty through partial or complete withdrawal. **Buffering,** as noted earlier, can be used to protect parts of the organization against environmental uncertainty. Purchasing, marketing, and customer service departments are examples of units that buffer the core of the organization from uncertainty. For example, the purchasing department can protect operations from shortages or seasonal fluctuations of supplies through stockpiling. Customer service protects operations from uncertainty resulting from customer demands or complaints.

It should be obvious that protecting operations from these sources of uncertainty may be counterproductive in the long run. Ignoring or insulating oneself from environmental uncertainty will likely just delay the inevitable. How else will the operations department know about supply problems or customer dissatisfaction unless it is exposed to that uncertainty? Many new management techniques, such as total quality management and just-in-time inventory control, require that managers of most or all departments be exposed to environmental uncertainty and that they respond to it.[16] This occurs because these methods provide a strong focus on the customers and suppliers, and require that people in the organization work together as teams, thus sharing experiences and exposure.

Differentiation and Integration

The very reason for the existence of organizations is that they can perform tasks more effectively and efficiently than individuals working alone. We noted in Chapter 2 that organizations can use differentiation (horizontal, vertical, and spatial) to divide the overall task to be accomplished into subtasks and assign those tasks to departments or individuals throughout the organization. This specialization allows the organization to perform more efficiently and with greater expertise. As the environment presents the organization with greater and greater complexity and uncertainty, the organization can respond with greater differentiation.[17] The greater specialization that differentiation yields brings specific expertise to bear on problems but requires integrator mechanisms to ensure coordination of effort.

Many reasons may be used to justify a horizontally differentiated or complex organization, but the present focus is on the environment. A basic principle of organization theory is that organizations should be structured to best meet the demands of their environment. A key to managing environmental complexity is to create an organization that is structurally complex. Horizontal differentiation is one way to achieve that complexity.

If an organization faces a complex environment characterized by many important and relevant environmental sectors, it should have a structure that reflects that environmental complexity. If an organization faces numerous potential legal woes, it should create a department to deal with those problems. If a firm has entered many market niches, it will need a marketing department (or, perhaps, marketing departments) that is large enough and diverse enough to manage those many niches, conduct market research, and design selling strategies. Organizations facing complex environments should also create more numerous boundary spanning roles to link and coordinate with sources of uncertainty in the environment. The idea is that the organization will create departments or positions in the organization to deal with specific areas of environmental uncertainty. The more complex the environment is, the more complex the organization should be, with more departments and more positions.

The case of vertical differentiation and environmental conditions is less clear-cut. As we learned in Chapter 2, high vertical complexity means that an organization has many layers of hierarchy and individuals at any given level of the hierarchy have only narrow decision-making authority or responsibility. As one moves up the hierarchy, each subsequent level of the organization should be associated with increasingly important decisions.

The problem with increasing levels of vertical complexity or differentiation is that decisions tend to get pushed up the hierarchy because individuals or departments do not want to take responsibility for possible problems. Pushing decisions up the hierarchy slows down decision-making and response time to environmental crises. The current thinking is that organizations should match environmental uncertainty with decentralized decision making and *less* vertical complexity. This allows the organization to push decisions down to those departments or individuals who encounter the sources of complexity and uncertainty.

Organizations may use ***spatial differentiation*** to respond to an environment that is geographically or regionally fragmented. For example, regional differences in consumer tastes, worker training and skills, or conditions in the physical environment may present problems for an organization. To manage these varied conditions, the organization creates departments or divisions based on location or region. For example, beverage companies often create local and regional distribution units so that they can respond to local and regional differences in consumer preferences.

Increasing amounts of differentiation necessitated by an uncertain and resource-starved environment place increasing importance on integration mechanisms. The key to integration is selecting mechanisms that are consistent with the environment. Although mechanisms such as formalization and standardization may play some role, organizations should seek methods, such as professionalism and decentralization, that promote flexibility. Additionally, informal mechanisms, such as liaison roles, integrator roles, and team leaders, are important in linking diverse departments together so that an organization can create a unified response to the environment.

Structuring for the Environment

In Chapter 1 it was noted that modern contingency perspectives on organizations take exception to the one-best-way view of organizing and suggest instead that structure must match the organizational context. Environment is one of these contextual factors. In the early 1960s two British researchers, Tom Burns and G. M. Stalker, described two polar examples of organizations that fit different environmental conditions.[18] In Chapter 2 we introduced the mechanistic and organic organizations as prototypical structures. The ***mechanistic*** organization, characterized by a strict centralized hierarchy of decision-authority, heavy reliance on rules, narrowly divided labor and specialized tasks, and emphasis on vertical (upward and downward) communication, is best suited for a stable and simple environment.[19]

The ***organic*** organization, with its characteristic decentralization of decision-authority, few rules, broad integrative tasks, and emphasis on horizontal communication, is suited for unstable and complex environments. Organizations facing shifting environments with many relevant sectors find that an organic structure permits greater coordination (similar to the integrator mechanisms mentioned earlier) because of lower levels of specialization and greater horizontal communication and quicker response to problems because of decentralization. Organic structures also allow for flexibility in responding to new conditions because they are less constrained by rules.[20]

The choice between a mechanistic or organic structure is the essence of the ***contingency framework*** introduced in Chapter 1. Neither structure is necessarily better than the other. Rather, it is important that managers recognize and understand the environment they face and select the *appropriate* organizational structure for that environment. These characteristics are summarized in Exhibit 2.10 of Chapter 2. In general, mechanistic organizations are best suited for stable, simple environments, and organic organizations are best suited for complex and unstable environmental conditions.

In Chapter 4 we noted that contemporary environments are becoming increasingly complex and unstable. The revolution in information and communication technology coupled with globalization make the business environment uncertain. Thus, it is not surprising that more and more organizations are adopting organic structures. Downsizing and flattening organizations remove much mechanistic hierarchy. Reducing the number of job descriptions, as most U.S. automakers have done, eliminates the narrow specialization of mechanistic organizations and replaces those jobs with broadly defined jobs that require many skills. Does this mean that the mechanistic organization is an antique? Probably not. Mechanistic organizations may be less common today, but there are still environments in which they can operate efficiently and effectively.

Imitation

The previous section suggested that managers scan the environment and select designs that are appropriate to the conditions they detect. An alternative viewpoint is that managers do not scan the environment just for sources of environmental uncertainty to address, but that they also seek examples of successful organizations, operating in similar environments, to imitate.[21] The rationale for imitation is both pragmatic and defensive. From a practical standpoint, an organization struggling to manage in a highly uncertain environment may borrow the strategies or structures of successful competitors just because the competitors were successful. Managers also imitate other successful firms to protect themselves from accusations of managerial incompetence. If a poorly performing company fails to imitate successful firms in its industry, management may be accused of not exercising *due diligence* (i.e., exercising prudence and good business judgment).[22] The result of imitative behavior is that organizations within an industry tend to look more similar than different.

An example of a management imitative strategy is the widespread adoption of total quality management (TQM) techniques in many industries. Many U.S. manufacturing companies, particularly in automobile-related areas, were unable to successfully compete in the 1980s and early 1990s with Japanese manufacturers. Although American and Japanese firms differ in many ways, many U.S. companies focused on the various quality-enhancing programs that companies like Toyota used. Now TQM programs are a common feature in many U.S. companies, particularly those competing in the auto industry.[23] One interesting feature of TQM helps to perpetuate imitative behavior. This process, called *benchmarking*, is the search among competitors and others for the *best practices* that will lead to superior quality and performance.[24] The process of searching for the best practices among competitors and firms in other industries leads directly to imitative behavior.

Additional forces motivate managers to imitate successful organizations rather than initiating novel responses to the environment. Investors and others who have a stake in a company are unlikely to want management to engage in behavior, develop strategies, or create designs that are radically different from the standards set by other successful companies. Radical deviations would be viewed as risky. Stockholders investing in a company and bankers lending money are likely to be risk averse and may insist that a firm adopt behaviors, strategies, and designs that are consistent with those practiced by the most successful firms in the industry.[25]

CONTROLLING THE ENVIRONMENT

Strategies for adapting to the environment assume that an organization is more or less a passive recipient of the environment. The organization can change or adapt to fit environmental conditions. Now we advance a step further in managing the environment by actively manipulating the environment itself. The strategies presented in this section assume that an organization can through its actions change the environment. Two general categories of actions, described below, are typically used to control environments: niche or domain selection and interorganizational linkage strategies or, as they are often referred to, strategic alliances.

Niche or Domain Selection

When we study a given organization at a specific point in time, we often take for granted that an organization's top management actively selects, and sometimes changes, the environmental niche in which the company operates. As a particular portion of the environment becomes too complex, unstable, or resource starved, a firm may choose to exit that market and search for an environment that is simple, stable, and munificent. These changes can be realized through internal product development, acquisition of other companies, or in the case of exiting a domain, divestiture of a division or product line.

In the latter part of the twentieth century the tobacco industry was characterized by extensive uncertainty and resource scarcity. Problems for the industry began in the 1960s with the emergence of evidence suggesting a link between cigarette smoking and health problems. The subsequent Surgeon-General's report outlining the risks associated with smoking provided justification for the banning of televised cigarette commercials and attaching warning labels to cigarette packages. In the years following the Surgeon-General's report, the tobacco industry has had to face mounting scientific evidence documenting the various tobacco-related health risks, vigilant antismoking public relations and lobbying activities, rising public awareness of smoking-related problems, restrictions on smoking, increased taxation, numerous legal battles over liability, and threats of further restrictions on all these fronts. One strategy that tobacco companies have used to deal with the uncertain and resource-scarce environment is to enter new domains. Nearly every tobacco company has diversified into domains unrelated to tobacco, including food products and assorted consumer goods. Perhaps the best example of this strategy is Philip Morris, maker of Marlboro—the largest selling cigarette in the world—which is now the largest diversified food products company in the United States.[26] The Philip Morris food division includes Kraft General Foods. The company also owns Miller Brewing.

In the extreme, a company may entirely abandon a market niche or enter a new domain when the existing domain becomes too uncertain or the supply of resources becomes too scarce. For example, Motorola is a highly successful developer and manufacturer of computer chips, telecommunications equipment, and other electronic components. However, early in the company's history its core business was manufacturing radios and televisions, neither of which it produces today. Similarly, as noted in Chapter 2, General Electric abandoned its small appliance and television businesses in the 1980s when the company's top management determined that they could no longer be competitive in those markets. In each of these cases companies adjusted niches to avoid uncertainty and resource scarcity. By contrast, when companies find munificent environments and acceptable levels of uncertainty, they may enter new niches or domains as Honda, Toyota, and Nissan did in the late 1980s when they created luxury car divisions. This was a niche that each of the companies had previously avoided, but the combination of consumer demands, sparse competition, reduced regulatory pressure, and available capital provided the necessary inducements to enter the niche.

Linkage Strategies

Organizations can use a wide array of strategic alliances to link with other players in the environment to actively control uncertainty and scarce resources.[27] As we noted in Chapter 4, uncertainty and resource constraints arise because other organizations or people in the environment place demands on an organization and because an organization becomes dependent on others in the environment. Every organization must go outside its boundaries to acquire some key resources. When members venture outside the boundaries, the organization becomes dependent on others and must deal with uncertainty. Moreover, these demands and dependencies shift and change over time, sometimes in an unpredictable manner. Linkage strategies are ways of connecting an organization with a source of certainty or with a controller of resources so that uncertainty is reduced and resources are more accessible. Figure 5-2 identifies conditions that foster the formation of various types of interorganizational linkage strategies. The strategies, described in the following paragraphs, can be used to control uncertainty and resources in one or more of the environmental sectors that a given organization faces.

Agreements, Norms, and Contracts   Perhaps the simplest mechanisms that an organization can use to control uncertainty and guarantee the supply of critical resources are informal agreements or norms. Over a period of time and with repeated interactions several organizations may develop helping relationships based on *reciprocity* and *mutual benefit*. One organization agrees to do something to help another, not necessarily with the belief that there will be an immediate payback. Later on, however, the helping organization may seek a favor from the former recipient of a favor. For example, a firm may agree to purchase a key raw material, such as coal, from only one supplier for a specified period of time provided that the supplier guarantees delivery dates and quantity even in periods of shortages. When coal is in short supply the supplier is obliged to deliver, but the supplier may also demand that the purchaser buy coal, perhaps at a high price, even in periods of abundance. Sometimes these informal agreements involve swaps of knowledge, information, or expertise. In the United States organizations must exercise caution in these agreements, particularly those between wholesalers and retailers, to avoid violation of the Robinson-Patman Act, which outlaws certain types of agreements that may reduce competitiveness. The act prohibits agreements whereby a retailer agrees not to carry a product from a

FIGURE 5-2   Conditions That Foster Interorganizational Linkage Strategies

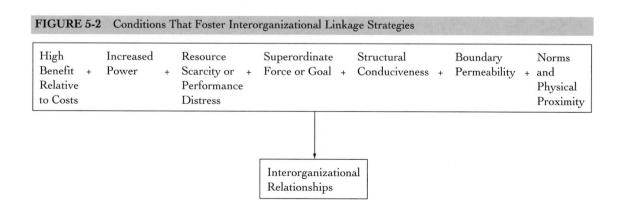

supplier's competitor or requires a retailer to purchase one undesired product in order to purchase a product the retailer really wants. These rules are often circumvented through informal agreements, although such agreements may also prove to be illegal.

Clearly, not all informal agreements are attempts to violate (either in spirit or principle) rules or laws. Other informal agreements may involve barter or resource sharing. The main problem with informal norms or agreements is that they only work in situations in which there are repeated interactions with partners and the partners can be trusted to act fairly.

Contracts or formal agreements make official and document interactions among organizations. For example, oil refiners purchase contracts with oil drillers or shippers to guarantee price, quantity, quality, and delivery of crude oil. The contract removes uncertainty about the supplier's behavior and ensures the refiner access to a critical resource. That same contract also removes uncertainty in the marketplace for the seller. The seller does not need to be as concerned about the unpredictability of demand for its product. Contracts or agreements can be used to guarantee the supply of labor, consulting work, construction, shipping, advertising, and nearly every facet of organizational existence.

Although contracts or agreements can be used to control many sorts of uncertainty and resource scarcity, problems are inherent in their use. First, contracts and agreements are expensive and time-consuming to write. A legal department or outside legal counsel must research and prepare documents. When the environmental conditions are complex and unstable, it is difficult to write contracts or agreements that adequately cover all possible situations and remove all uncertainty. When resources become exceedingly scarce, a contract or agreement may not adequately protect an organization. For example, if the current price of crude oil far exceeds the price specified in a contract, the contract may not prevent the supplier from noncompliance. Finally, contracts and agreements must be monitored. An organization must observe the behavior of a contract partner for compliance. Monitoring is costly, and when the contract is complex or extensive, it may be difficult to monitor. Although contracts are widely used, they are imperfect mechanisms for controlling environments.

Joint Ventures   Sometimes organizations form a strategic alliance for a specific purpose or project. A joint venture is a specific strategy in which two or more organizations join together, pool resources, and spread risk to accomplish a goal that is mutually beneficial. A large number of joint ventures have been formed (and, in some cases, disbanded) in recent years. For example, General Motors joined with Toyota to produce small cars at a joint venture in California, called New United Motors Incorporated (NUMI). General Motors got access to Toyota's expertise in manufacturing small cars while Toyota established an American manufacturing presence, prior to the company's larger investment in Kentucky where it now makes the Camry, Avalon, and the company's minivan. That early move also helped partially diffuse some initial resentment against Japanese imports. In many communities hospitals form joint ventures to purchase expensive equipment and provide costly diagnostic and treatment services. Such moves spread costs and risk among participants. In some cases no single hospital could efficiently operate the equipment. One of the largest construction jobs in history, the building of the Alaskan pipeline, was done by a joint venture consortium called Alyeska, formed by a group of oil companies. No single company possessed the skills or resources necessary to accomplish this job alone. Procter & Gamble Co. and Coca-Cola Co. are joining forces to improve marketing of beverages and snack foods. Despite the fact that the Coca-

Cola name is arguably one of the most recognized brands in the world, the company has stumbled trying to expand its market, especially in the juice market. Similarly, P&G has had only limited success with its Sunny Delight juice and its Pringles snack foods. The hope is that by joining forces in a global venture, the companies can achieve greater growth than either could alone. The joint venture will market and distribute approximately 40 beverage and snack food products throughout the world. By linking brands such as Minute Maid, Sunny Delight, Fruitopia, Hi-C, Pringles, and Eagle Snacks and by sharing marketing and distribution, the companies hope to gain market share that has up to now been unattainable.[28]

In each case, the joint venture was formed to manage environmental uncertainty. Organizations joined together to share information, expertise, resources, and risk. However, by forming a joint venture, the joined organizations must now deal with each other's unpredictability and idiosyncratic behavior. In a joint venture no one party exercises complete control over the others. Thus, this strategy may be suited for only removing some uncertainty and resource scarcity, but it will not completely eliminate those problems.

Mergers and Acquisitions   Mergers and acquisitions occur when two or more organizations become one. In a ***merger*** two or more companies join together to form a new third company. For example, Daimler-Benz and Chrysler joined forces as a merger of equals. However, the reality has been something short of true equality. Daimler has dominated the management of the merged companies. In an ***acquisition*** one company purchases another. The acquiring company becomes a parent company, and the acquired company may become a subsidiary, branch, or division. As noted in the introductory case, Delta acquired Comair, a regional airline that served the midwest, south and parts of the east coast. Comair became a division of Delta that included Atlantic Southwest Airlines. Sometimes the acquired company is fully absorbed within the acquiring company; sometimes it becomes a division or subsidiary of the acquiring company. As we will explore later, joining the cultures of two companies, whether through merger, acquisition, or joint venture, can be difficult. Many of the problems that have plagued Daimler-Chrysler are the result of two very different company cultures.

Mergers and acquisitions can be used to control several sources of uncertainty, including competitive uncertainty within an industry, market uncertainty within a niche, supplier uncertainty, and customer uncertainty. When an organization acquires or merges with a supplier, distributor, or customer, it is called ***vertical integration***.* The organization is bringing within its boundary functions or operations that were formerly carried on outside the boundary. Vertical integration can be either ***backward*** to suppliers or ***forward*** to users, distributors, or customers. Figure 5-3 describes the ***value-added chain*** of activities that an organization may require and the types of vertical integration that can take place.

When an organization merges or acquires competitor firms, it is called ***horizontal integration***. In the United States the banking industry has been the site of several horizontal mergers during the 1980s and early 1990s. For example, North Carolina National Bank (NCNB) was a regional bank that primarily served the state of North

---

*Recall that in Chapter 2 we introduced the concepts of structural integration and differentiation. At that time we noted that the term *integration* was used in two distinctly different ways in the field of organization theory. Here we introduce the second use of the term. Integration in the current context refers to a business's entry into another area of business through mergers, acquisitions, or the creation of a new business.

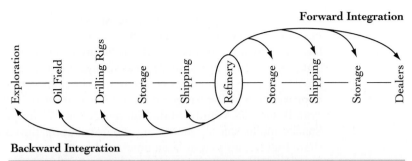

FIGURE 5-3 Integration and the Value-Added Chain for a Petroleum Refinery

Carolina until the mid-1980s. Since that time, NCNB has gone through many mergers and acquisitions, the latest with Bank of America (the new corporate name). The resulting bank serves 21 states and the District of Columbia and has 4,500 banking centers, the most of any U.S. bank. Such moves are usually motivated by the desire to increase economies of scale, improve the efficiencies of operations, gain larger market share, and reduce competition. Horizontal mergers or acquisitions can also occur outside a firm's primary market or industry. This is called ***diversification***. Some diversification is into related areas. For example Delta Airlines' acquisition of Comair, a regional short-haul airline that serves small markets not served by Delta's main routes, feeds passengers to Delta flights. Other diversification may be into unrelated areas. Philip Morris, a tobacco company, diversified by acquisitions into food and consumer goods to reduce risks resulting from the 1964 Surgeon-General's report on smoking and health, the subsequent ban on television advertising, the required warning labels, and the resulting public concern over smoking. Philip Morris now includes Miller Brewing, Kraft General Foods, and other nontobacco businesses. That move exemplifies unrelated diversification and its attempt to diminish the effects of uncertainty in tobacco by spreading risk to other market sectors.

Companies merge or acquire other companies for many reasons:

- Growth and enhanced power and competitive status in the market
- Enhancement of economies of scale, efficiencies, and profitability
- Improved access to supplies of critical resources
- Reduction of environmental uncertainty
- Risk management

Space does not permit us to explain the legal, economic, political, and financial forces affecting mergers and acquisitions. Table 5-2 summarizes some of the terminology used in this field. It is important to note that mergers and acquisitions are complex phenomena that have important organizational and environmental ramifications. Often these forces go beyond one organization's attempts to control its environment. Some critics argue that the flurry of acquisitions and buyouts of the mid-1980s were motivated by greed and avarice rather than attempts at environmental control and efficiency. Nonetheless, our focus here is on management of the environment. Indications are that the forces that push companies toward mergers and acquisitions still exist in the environment and that organizations will continue to view these as viable alternatives for managing environmental uncertainty and resource constraints. One of the issues that we have thus far ignored is the difficult task of integrating for-

---
EXHIBIT 5-3

Profile of a Failed Acquisition: Novell and WordPerfect[29]

The software industry of the 1980s was full of gritty rags-to-riches stories of young entrepreneurs, lucky and creative "techies," and others who struck it rich by producing innovative software packages that fit the burgeoning business and personal computer industry and consumer demands. The adventures of Bill Gates and his tremendous success at Microsoft are well known. Perhaps less well documented, but more illustrative of the new problems and opportunities confronting software companies, is the cautionary tale of WordPerfect.

WordPerfect was the brainchild of two former Brigham Young University employees, Bruce Bastian, a former marching band director, and Alan Ashton, a former computer science professor. The company they formed experienced dramatic growth after they developed an easy-to-use word processing program. But the market has changed radically since the late 1970s when Bastian and Ashton started. Technology changes quickly. Consumers and business users are becoming more sophisticated and demanding. And competition has increased. On top of these issues is the shadow that Microsoft casts over the industry. As the developer of the leading operating system (DOS) and of Windows, Microsoft has built-in advantages over competitors in producing application software that works more easily and efficiently in the DOS and Windows environment. All software that is to run on DOS- and Windows-based computers must be designed to be compatible with DOS and Windows. However, since DOS and Windows are the properties of Microsoft, independent competitive developers such as Novell and WordPerfect are dependent on Microsoft. Thus, when Microsoft developed Windows '95, it had a distinct advantage over these competitors in creating and supplying application software such as networks, word processing, and spreadsheets. Microsoft is also able to bundle together application software when selling DOS and Windows to computer makers and consumers. Because of its power and success with DOS and Windows, Microsoft can bring applications to market faster and price them more aggressively.

To combat the power of Microsoft, Novell acquired WordPerfect. Novell hoped to capitalize on the apparent synergies of the two companies. Both companies realized that they could not successfully compete on their own. Unfortunately, even the union of Novell and WordPerfect was not enough to counter Microsoft's dominance. Novell eventually sold WordPerfect to Corel, and that company has struggled to survive.

---

merly separate organizations into one. At this point it is sufficient to say that merely because a firm merges with or acquires another does not guarantee that it will be better able to control the environment. The merged organization or acquired firm must be successfully integrated and structured to fit the environment.

A variation on vertical integration that has gained much attention recently is the ***virtual organization***, also called the network organization.[30] Through a series of agreements, contracts, and other arrangements, an organization achieves relationships with other organizations that provide many of the advantages of vertical integration without the economic costs and reduced flexibility that true vertical integration involves. Athletic footwear companies, such as Nike, form alliances with several manufacturers who make shoes. Nike designs, distributes, and markets shoes, but it does not manufacture them. Instead, Nike (and many of its competitors) relies on a network of independent manufacturers throughout Asia to make the shoes. These relationships may involve partial ownership by the parent company, but the relationships remain in place

TABLE 5-2	Merger and Acquisition Terminology
Term	**Description**
Leveraged buyout	Acquisition of a company with little money down and a large amount of debt financed by a lending institution; the debt to be paid back from earnings of the acquired company
Hostile takeover	Acquiring a company against its will
Greenmail	The buying back of stock involved in a hostile takeover, often at a premium price not offered to all shareholders, so the target company can regain control
Golden parachute	A large salary benefit in the form of severance or termination pay guaranteed to a top executive of the acquired company by the acquiring company, should the acquiring company eventually decide to terminate the executive
Poison pill	Taking on a large load of debt or some other obligation by a company to make it less attractive to a hostile takeover bid
Shark repellents	Actions to strengthen management's control to avoid a hostile takeover. Example: issuing a new class of stock with greater voting rights than the stock widely held by outsiders
Junk bonds	Low-rated (i.e., high-risk) corporate debt used to finance mergers and acquisitions that have high interest rates compared to the rates for more secure (less risky) bonds
Pac-man	A company that is a target of a hostile takeover taking the offensive and becoming the acquirer of the previous pursuer
White knight	A friendly company summoned by a company that is the target of a hostile takeover in hopes that the friendly company will out-bid the hostile pursuer

only as long as the parent company and supplier companies find it profitable. The same parent company may have other temporary alliances in other areas, such as shipping and marketing. The hallmarks of the virtual organization are its temporary nature and partial integration into the parent company. We return to this subject in Chapter 8.

Boards of Directors   The primary function of a board of directors (or, in the case of nonprofit or voluntary organizations, a board of trustees) is to act as a *fiduciary* for owners by helping manage or govern an organization. (A fiduciary attempts to protect the interests of stockholders.) The board functions to oversee management's actions and make recommendations to or direct management. Beyond these specific tasks, boards often carry out other jobs that link an organization to its environment and help reduce uncertainty and resource constraints. To understand these linkage functions it is necessary to understand two specific types of board members.

Boards are typically composed of both ***insiders*** and ***outsiders***. Inside directors are individuals who are also officers or employees of the organization. For example, it is common for the president or chief executive officer (or both officers of a firm) to be insider members of the board of directors. Outsiders can come from just about anywhere. Typical categories of outsiders include bankers or venture capitalists, retired executives, executives from other businesses, consultants, academics, retired politicians or military personnel, or religious leaders. These outsiders may be chosen for their expertise, their access to scarce resources, or their links to critical outside communities or constituents. A number of large corporations have bowed to investor pressure and included more outsiders in leadership positions on boards. A controversial issue with regard to boards of directors is whether one person should be both the chief executive officer—a management position—and chairman of the board of directors—the chief representative of the investors. The argument in favor of combining the positions is that the CEO is the person with the most knowledge of the firm. In theory, he or she should be concerned about maintaining investor value. However, in practice many CEOs pursue actions that are in their own best interests that may not be in the best interest of the investors.[31]

Many researchers in the fields of organizaton theory, strategy, and organizational economics have studied the issue of competing management and shareholder interests under the heading of *organizational governance,* yet there is no definitive agreement on the wisdom of combining the roles of CEO and chairman of the board. Nonetheless, shareholder activists and institutional investors (e.g., large pension funds and mutual funds) have called for governance reforms that would separate these two roles.

Two other terms used to describe board of director linkages are ***interlocking directorates*** and ***cooptation***. ***Interlocking directorates*** form when one or more individuals serve on two or more boards of directors. This is done for two reasons: (1) to facilitate interorganizational communication and coordination and (2) to increase organizational effectiveness through sharing of expertise and resources.[32] For example, it is common for supplier and buyer organizations to have members on each other's board of directors. It is also common for banks and large users of capital to exchange board members. In the automobile industry boards of directors often include executives from large banks that do business with the auto company and executives from supplier companies. Although board of director interlocks are common, the practice in the United States is discouraged and monitored by the antitrust division of the Justice Department.

Cooptation takes place when an organization tries to influence representatives of specific sectors of the environment. The belief is that as key outsiders gain familiarity and understanding with the conditions, opportunities, and problems that an organization faces, these outside representatives will become more receptive to the organization. For example, in the aftermath of urban riots in the late 1960s and early 1970s, many organizations tried to improve race relations and influence key African-American community leaders by including them on the firms' boards of directors. When Chrysler began having serious financial difficulties in the early 1980s, it became clear to management that one key to reducing costs and improving operations was to change the company's relationship with its union laborers. One step to accomplishing this task was to include Douglas Fraser, then the United Auto Workers Union president, on Chrysler's board where other board members could attempt to influence him into more favorable treatment of the company. Through his work on Chrysler's board, Fraser came to understand that the union's failure to compromise on certain demands could result in the company's failure.[33] It is important to note that influence and cooptation are two-way streets. Outsider members of boards can also influence management to change in ways that are consistent with the outsiders' demands. Such was the hope when John Smale, an outsider and former CEO of Procter & Gamble, became chairman of the board at GM.

Management Recruiting   Many firms have hired managers from other firms, often competitors in the same industry, as a means of gaining key skills, knowledge, and connections. For many years the auto companies raided each other's top management ranks to build their own knowledge and skill base. The practice has also been common in the computer software and hardware industries, where many skills are in short supply. To maintain the confidentiality of corporate information, many firms institute non-compete agreements that prevent employees from moving to competing for a specified period of time.

Associations In the United States the federal government has, through antitrust laws, attempted to control the amount of cooperation and coordination among competitors within an industry. However, firms are often able to work together to control uncertainty and resource availability through ***trade associations*** and other types of cooperative groupings. Trade associations can reduce some competitive uncertainty by setting industrywide technical standards so that products of various manufacturers are compatible. Perhaps the most pervasive and far-reaching activity of trade associations is lobbying government. Trade associations can leverage the strength of an entire industry to influence the legislative process at any level of government to receive more favorable treatment for their industry through ***lobbying*** activities. During negotiations over the North American Free Trade Agreement (NAFTA) and the General Agreement on Tariffs and Trade (GATT), several trade associations vigorously lobbied the federal government. For example, the U.S. textile industry sought greater protection from imports while the auto industry sought the tax-free exchange of parts and finished vehicles between the United States, Canada, and Mexico. Although any CEO can (and many do) individually lobby government agencies and representatives, the strength of trade or industry associations in this area is undeniable. It is no coincidence that nearly every major trade association has some office or representation in Washington, D.C.

Other forms of association can be important in garnering scarce resources for member organizations. In several industries it is common practice for potential competitors to group together into formal or informal buying groups, marketing groups, and cooperatives. In several agricultural product markets formal cooperatives play key roles in sales and distribution. Sunkist, Sunsweet, Blue Diamond, and Ocean Spray are well known trade names of cooperative marketing organizations. These companies are wholly owned by the citrus, dried fruit, nut, and cranberry producers, respectively. In the hardware and building supply business, retailers have removed some supply uncertainties by either joining buying groups like Pro and Trustworthy or by joining distribution cooperatives like Ace, True Value, or HWI (described in Exhibit 5-4). In each case the cooperative or buying group is a mechanism to remove some uncertainty in input or output markets. In the retail pharmacy business the National Association of Chain Drug Stores (NACDS) has formed a cooperative network to help members compete with large managed care systems such as PCS Health Systems, which sells prescription drugs under contract for insurance plans and employers. NACDS uses the leverage created by pooling the buying power of its member retail pharmacies to obtain pricing from pharmaceutical companies comparable to that obtained by the large managed care providers.[34]

Advertising and Public Relations Most of the linkage mechanisms described thus far involve links to specific organizations or groups of people. One method for linking with the general public is through advertising and public relations activities. Firms use advertising and public relations to influence the public perception of the organization, to differentiate the company from competitors, and to focus the firm on a specific market niche. For example, Anheuser-Busch spends extensively on advertising and public relations focused on alcohol education subjects, such as safe drinking ("Know when to say when"), drunk driving (designated drivers), and underage drinking as well as conventional advertising intended to sell specific products. These efforts attempt to

---

EXHIBIT 5-4

Anatomy of a Distribution Cooperative

One problem many small businesses face is a lack of power when negotiating with suppliers or buyers. For example, a traditional neighborhood hardware store would have great difficulty competing with Lowe's, Wal-Mart, Home Depot, or other large retailers in part because of the power that these large retailers have to negotiate favorable prices from suppliers. Home Depot may buy as many as 50 or 100 of a specific model of lawn mower for just one of its many stores while a neighborhood store may buy only 10 or 20 lawn mowers in total. Not surprisingly, Home Depot can obtain more favorable pricing and terms of payment from the lawn mower manufacturer than the neighborhood retailer can receive.

Small businesses in some industries have developed a powerful mechanism to compete and receive favorable treatment from manufacturers and suppliers. In the retail hardware–home center industry, retailers have formed distribution cooperatives. These cooperatives, the largest distributors in the industry, are among the 100 largest service companies in the United States and their trade names are widely recognized among shoppers: ACE, True Value (Cotter Company), and HWI. The companies are *cooperatively* owned by retailers, meaning that the distributors are not profit-making businesses. Nearly all excess revenues are returned to the customer-owners (i.e., the retailers). The combined buying power of the thousands of member businesses, along with the nonprofit nature of these companies, results in merchandise costs for the retail members that are close to the prices that large retailers pay for their goods. The cooperatives have nearly as much leverage in bargaining with manufacturers as do their large competitors.

Cooperatives also provide retailers with advertising, expertise, counseling, and other support services that help the retailers successfully compete against giant "category killers" and mass merchandisers. The cooperative tie between buyer and seller helps retailers control much uncertainty in their environment.

---

blunt public criticism of the brewing industry. Similarly, the tobacco industry has mounted a vigorous campaign aimed at protecting smokers' rights in the face of increasing attacks from government and antismoking groups. At the same time, the tobacco companies are required to participate in advertising campaigns aimed at discouraging minors from starting to smoke. Many companies contribute to public television and radio to enhance their public image. In each case these companies are using advertising and public relations to reduce uncertainty and increase munificence. From an environmental control standpoint, advertising and public relations are both used to increase a firm's visibility, create or modify its image, and identify or solidify its niche.

SUMMARY

Thus far this chapter has reviewed first how organizations come to know about the environment through scanning and boundary spanning and then how organizations can adapt to or change the environment that they face through a wide variety of activities. Organizations can match the environment with the appropriate level of structural complexity, plan and forecast for the future, withdraw from or avoid uncertain environments, carefully select munificent niches, imitate other successful organizations, or employ one or more linkage strategies to form relationships with other organizations.

These activities are not necessarily mutually exclusive. Organizations can and do use several strategies together to manage environmental uncertainty and resource scarcity. In fact, scanning the environment and forecasting may be critical ingredients that fuel other methods of environmental adaptation or control. Scanning and forecasting may drive the selection of supplier relationships, organizational restructuring, or advertising campaigns. Moreover, management may apply certain of these strategies to specific departments or divisions while using a different set of strategies in other areas. A manufacturing department may be buffered from the environmental uncertainty that affects many other departments. Buyers may rely on contracts, while top management uses board interlocks to control uncertainty. The important issue that these strategies raise is *how* to adapt to or control the environment. Not all strategies are equally suitable for all organizations or all environmental conditions. The key task is to determine the most suitable set of strategies for the organization and the environment. This is key to a contingency framework. In general, more uncertain and resource-starved environments may require more aggressive and proactive adaptation and control strategies.

Postscript

This contingency framework, however, leaves unanswered two critical questions. First, how aggressive should an organization be in attempting to adapt and control environments? In discussions of buyer-supplier relationships and board of director interlocks we broached the legal issues related to manipulation of the environment. In the section below we further investigate the relationship between environmental conditions and ***illegal activity***. In the final section we address a controversial theoretical issue: What are the consequences of management's attempts to adapt to and control environments? Some organizational theorists suggest that managers may select responses to environmental conditions, but their ability to *successfully* adapt and control is highly questionable. The final section of the chapter presents this controversial view under the heading of ***population ecology***.

Illegal Activity   It must be clear at the onset that we are not advocating that organizations skirt the law to deal with scarcity or uncertainty in the environment. However, the reality is that as organizations face increasingly difficult environments, the likelihood increases that they will resort to illegal activity to control the environment.[35] Markets characterized by much competitive uncertainty may encourage managers to offer kickbacks, bribes, or other illegal inducements for favorable treatment. Firms have at times paid bribes to various foreign government officials in order to win contracts, gain favorable treatment, or simply expedite imports through customs. Where potentially large markets exist, firms may illegally cooperate to fix prices or agree to not compete so as to reduce competitive pressures. For example, several large dairy companies illegally cooperated to divide the school lunch market because they believed competition would simply drive down profits and hurt all the companies. As a result, school districts throughout Ohio and Kentucky overpaid for milk. Several companies have already admitted guilt and are paying steep fines as well as reimbursing the affected school districts for damages. Collusion, bribery, price fixing, and other forms of illegal activity may reduce some uncertainty, but the risk of detection and subsequent damage to the firm may be considerable. The Foreign Corrupt Practices Act now makes it a crime for a U.S. company to break U.S. laws in conducting business in foreign countries—even if those acts are not illegal in the foreign country. These represent only a few of the potential illegal activities that firms do conduct.

Population Ecology   The population ecology view of organizations is largely adopted from the study of animal ecology and evolution. The focus is on ***organizational forms***, which are broadly defined to include ***unique configurations of structure***, ***ownership***, ***boundaries***, and ***goals***. This viewpoint applies the Darwinian notion of natural selection and survival of the fittest to organizations—those organizational forms that are the most efficient and that fit best with the prevailing environmental conditions will persist.[36] The problem, in light of the preceding discussion of adapting and controlling environments, is that population ecology is unconcerned with the forces that make an organization more efficient and a better fit with the environment. Population ecologists refer to ***variations*** among firms. Variations may be planned, or they may be unintentional, random, or accidental. Variations include differences or changes in structure, ownership, boundaries, or goals of the organization—many of the very characteristics that we discussed earlier in this chapter as means for responding to or controlling the environment. Additionally, some population ecologists maintain that the environment, even for the simplest of organizations, is so complex and dynamic that it is impossible for managers to know all there is to know and to anticipate critical changes. Any sector of the environment may produce unanticipated conditions that threaten the very existence of an organizational form.

It is the environment that *selects* those forms of organizations that best fit, regardless of whether change was intentional or accidental. One must keep in mind that the population ecology definition of *organizational form* is not identical to the conventional understanding of *organization* or *form*. Traditional full-service gas stations may be disappearing as an organizational form (i.e., a cluster of goals, structure, boundaries, and ownership), but the remaining gas stations may be owned and operated by the same groups that formerly ran the full-service gas stations. It is the full-service form that is disappearing—not the specific organization. Finally, organizational forms that are successful fits with the environment are *retained*. Ironically, retention is fostered by forces that support stability and replication or imitation of a form. Those very factors that support retention are, in fact, the same forces that work against frequent organizational change and adaptation. Thus, frequent restructuring and changing may be destabilizing and result in failure, according to population ecologists.

This is merely a brief, thumbnail sketch of population ecology. The subject has been the focus of much research, writing, and misunderstanding among organizational theorists. The interested reader should consult the references listed at the end of this chapter. The important point is that this view presents an interesting, deterministic image of organizations that contrasts with the proactive strategic view of management adapting to and controlling environments that we have presented in this chapter. Some scholars have argued that the population ecology may be relevant for ***populations of organizations*** (all organizations of a similar type occupying the same niche) but not for individual organizations. Others have argued that the population view may be accurate for the long term, but they question whether this view fits the short-run changes and adaptation. Nonetheless, mounting research evidence suggests that the population ecology perspective has at least some value in predicting or explaining the emergence and disappearance of organizational forms.

Questions for Discussion

1. Is it more difficult for today's managers to cope with the external environment than it was for managers of, say, 20 years ago? Why?
2. Distinguish between boundary spanning and environmental scanning. Should these activities be the sole responsibility of management? Explain.
3. Interview a manager in your locality, and see what he or she knows about the topic of managing the environment. If this manager does not know a great deal (in your opinion), what would you tell him or her to stress the significance of this topic? What strategies for managing or controlling the environment would you suggest that the manager use?
4. What do permeability, resilience, and maintenance have to do with environmental management?
5. "I never waste time forecasting and making strategy. I just react to conditions of the moment." React to this quote from a CEO of a successful manufacturer of consumer health care products.
6. How can structure be used in the management of the environment? Give an example.
7. What is a linkage strategy, and how can one be used to help an organization deal with its environment?
8. What effect(s) do you think the signing of the North American Free Trade Agreement (NAFTA) and the General Agreement on Tariffs and Trade (GATT) will have on the agricultural combines located in southern Texas? Suggest how they might deal with this legislation's effect on their environment.
9. Define *population ecology*. Do you agree with this concept? Why or why not? Pick an example of a type of organization that you think is unlikely to survive. Why? What does population ecology say about the role of top management and strategic planning?

References

1. J. Stacey Adams, "The Structure and Dynamics of Behavior in Organizational Boundary Roles," in *Handbook of Industrial and Organizational Psychology*, ed. by M. D. Dunnette (Chicago: Rand McNally, 1976), 1175–99.
2. Henry Mintzberg, *The Nature of Managerial Work* (Upper Saddle River, NJ: Prentice Hall, 1980).
3. Andrew C. Boynton, Lawrence M. Gales, and Richard S. Blackburn, "Managerial Search Activity: The Impact of Perceived Role Uncertainty and Role Threat," *Journal of Management* 19 (1993): 725–47; Mary J. Culnan, "Environmental Scanning: The Effects of Task Complexity and Source Accessibility on Information Gathering Behaviors," *Decision Sciences* 14 (1983): 194–206; Richard L. Daft, J. Sormunen, and D. Parks, "Chief Executive Scanning, Environmental Characteristics, and Company Performance: An Empirical Study," *Strategic Management Journal* 9 (1988): 123–39; Liam Fahey and William R. King, "Environmental Scanning for Corporate Planning," *Business Horizons* 63 (August

1977): 61–71; A. Keflas and P. Schoderbek, "Scanning the Business Environment," *Decision Sciences* 4 (1973): 63–74.
4. See Daft, Sormunen, and Parks in note 3; Sumantra Ghoshal and Seok Ki Kim, "Building Effective Intelligence Systems for Competitive Advantage," *Sloan Management Review* 49 (1986): 53.
5. See Daft, Sormunen, and Parks in note 3.
6. R. T. Lenz and J. L. Engledow, "Environmental Analysis Units and Strategic Decision-Making: A Field Study of Selected Leading-Edge Corporations," *Strategic Management Journal* 7 (1988): 69–89.
7. Alan Farnham, "It's a Bird! It's a Plane! It's a Flop!" *Fortune* (May 2, 1994): 108–110.
8. Based on the following articles: Roderick P. Deighen, "Welcome to Cold War II," *Chief Executive* (January/February 1993): 42–46; Norm Alster, "The Valley of the Spies," *Forbes* (October 26, 1992): 200–204; Stephen A. Carlton, "Industrial Espionage: Reality of the Information Age," *Research Technology Management* (November/December 1992): 18–24.

9. James D. Thompson, *Organizations in Action* (New York: McGraw-Hill, 1967).

10. C. Van Tune, "Class Action: BMW 540i versus Cadillac STS," *Motor Trend* 45, no. 12 (1993): 46–52; S. Mitani, "Elite Eights," *Road & Track* (March 1995): 96–107.

11. See note 1; R. H. Miles and W. Perreault, "Organizational Role Conflict: Its Antecedents and Consequences," *Organizational Behavior and Human Performance* 17 (1976): 19–44.

12. Richard H. Hall, *Organizations: Structures, Processes, and Outcomes* (Upper Saddle River, NJ: Prentice Hall, 1991).

13. Jeffery Pfeffer and Gerald R. Salancik, *The External Control of Organizations: A Resource Dependence Perspective* (New York: Harper & Row, 1978).

14. L. Zinn, J. Berry, K. Murphy, S. Jones, M. Benedetti, and A. Z. Cuneo, "Teens: Here Comes the Biggest Wave Yet," *Business Week* (April 11, 1994): 76–86; J. Treece, S. Anderson, G. Sandler, and K. Murphy, "Why We Love Trucks," *Business Week* (December 5, 1994): 70–80; K. Labich, "Kissing Off Corporate America," *Fortune* (February 20, 1995): 44–52.

15. See Thompson in note 9; Raymond E. Miles and Charles C. Snow, *Organizational Strategy, Structure and Process* (New York: McGraw-Hill, 1978).

16. James W. Dean, Jr., and James R. Evans, *Total Quality: Management, Organization and Strategy* (St. Paul, MN: West Publishing, 1994).

17. P. R. Lawrence and J. W. Lorsch, *Organization and Environment* (Boston: Harvard Business School, 1967).

18. T. Burns and G. M. Stalker, *The Management of Innovation* (London: Tavistock Institute, 1961).

19. D. S. Pugh, D. J. Hickson, and C. R. Hinings, "An Empirical Taxonomy of Structures of Work Organizations," *Administrative Science Quarterly* (1969): 115–26.

20. See note 18; see note 19.

21. W. Richard Scott, *Organizations: Rational, Natural and Open Systems,* 3rd ed. (Upper Saddle River, NJ: Prentice Hall, 1992); John W. Meyer and Brian Rowan, "Institutionalized Organizations: Formal Structure as a Myth and Ceremony," *American Journal of Sociology* 83 (1977): 340–63; Christine Oliver, "Strategic Responses to Institutional Processes," *Academy of Management Review* 16 (1991): 145–79; Paul J. DiMaggio and Walter W. Powell, eds., *The New Institutionalism in Organizational Analysis* (Chicago: University of Chicago Press, 1991).

22. Commerce Clearing House Business Law Editors, *Responsibilities of Corporate Officers and Directors Under Federal Securities Laws* (Chicago: Commerce Clearing House, 1993), 14.

23. See note 16.

24. Ibid.

25. See DiMaggio and Powell in note 21; see Oliver in note 21; L. G. Zucker, ed., *Institutional Patterns and Organizations: Culture and Environment* (Cambridge, MA: Ballinger, 1988); P. S. Tolbert and L. G. Zucker, "Institutional Sources of Change in the Formal Structure of Organizations: The Diffusion of Civil Service Reform, 1880–1935," *Administrative Science Quarterly* 28 (1983): 22–39.

26. "The *Fortune* 500," *Fortune* (April 19, 1993): 173–284.

27. J. C. Jarillo, "On Strategic Networks," *Strategic Management Journal* 9 (1988): 31–41; R. R. Kamath and J. K. Liker, "A Second Look at Japanese Product Development," *Harvard Business Review* (November–December 1994): 154–58.

28. Randy Tucker, "P&G, Coca-Cola Join Drinks, Snack Foods," *Cincinnati Enquirer* (www.Cincinnati Enquirer.com/archive), February 22, 2001.

29. Based on G. Pascal Zachary, "Consolidation Sweeps the Software Industry; Small Firms Imperiled," *The Wall Street Journal* (March 23, 1994), A1–A8.

30. John A. Byrne, "The Virtual Corporation: The Company of the Future Will Be the Ultimate in Adaptability," *Business Week* (February 8, 1993): 98–102; Hans B. Thorelli, "Networks: Between Markets and Hierarchies," *Strategic Management Journal* 7 (1986): 37–51; O. E. Williamson, "Comparative Economic Organization: The Analysis of Discrete Structural Alternatives," *Administrative Science Quarterly* 36 (1991): 269–96.

31. C. W. L. Hill and S. A. Snell, "Effects of Ownership Structure and Control on Corporate Productivity," *Academy of Management Journal* 32 (1989): 25–46; E. Fama and M. Jensen, "Separation of Ownership and Control," *Journal of Law and Economics* 26 (1983): 301–25.

32. See note 13; B. D. Baysinger and R. E. Hoskisson, "The Composition of Boards of Directors and Strategic Control: Effects on Corporate Strategy," *The Academy of Management Review* 15 (1990): 72–87; E. Fama and M. Jensen, "Separation of Ownership and Control," *Journal of Law and Economics* 26 (1983): 301–25; J. Pfeffer, "Size and Composition of Corporate Boards of Directors: The Organization and Its Environment," *Administrative Science Quarterly* 17 (1972): 218–29.

33. See note 13.

34. Elyse Tanouye, "Pharmacy Trade Group Creates Firm to Compete for Prescription-Drug Plans," *The Wall Street Journal* (April 11, 1994), 3–4.

35. B. M. Staw and E. Szwajkowski, "The Scarcity–Munificence Component of Organizational Environments and the Commission of Illegal Acts," *Administrative Science Quarterly* 20 (1975): 345–54; see note 13.

36. H. Aldrich, *Organizations and Environments* (Upper Saddle River, NJ: Prentice Hall, 1979); G. Carrol, "Organizational Ecology," *Annual Review of Sociology* 10 (1984): 71–93; M. T. Hannan and J. Freeman, "The Population Ecology of Organizations," *American Journal of Sociology* 82 (1977): 929–64.

CASE

*Brand Management**

Consumer goods giant Procter & Gamble (P&G) wrote the book on brand management over 70 years ago. The system that P&G developed gives one person the primary responsibility for managing a particular product line. While some of those responsibilities are focused on the internal operations related to producing and shipping the product, the majority of the role is focused on boundary spanning activity: dealing with people and organizations outside the company's boundaries. The brand manager may need to coordinate with Wal-Mart, Target, or other large retailers; develop a marketing strategy that includes market research, meetings with advertising agencies, organizing focus groups, or meeting with consumer groups; and working with the company's sales organizations to ensure that sales representative provide the best information to distributors and retailers, and that they gather relevant information in the marketplace.

The management of the Dryel brand provides a good example of some of the responsibilities of a brand manager. Dryel is a novel product: a do-it-yourself dry-cleaning product that consumers use in their dryers. The brand manager, Noel Geoffroy, and her staff meet weekly with a team of people in finance, product development, and packaging. However, perhaps most important for this new product are their meetings with sales staff and their advertising agency. These people provide current information on how the product is being received in the marketplace. Additionally, Ms. Geoffroy has traveled to many of the nearly 300 shopping mall demonstrations of the product. Because of the nature of this product, P&G had to install clothes dryers at the malls for demonstrations.

The experience with the dryers led to a key marketing idea. Ms. Geoffroy convinced Whirlpool, Maytag, and General Electric to put a Dryel cycle on their dryers. To gain cooperation from the appliance manufacturers requires the boundary spanner to reach beyond the P&G boundaries to other organizations.

Geoffroy's contact with consumers also gave her insights into product extensions. Early in 2001 the company rolled out a new "whisper-fresh" scent in response to consumer demands.

In 2001 P&G had approximately 156 U.S. brand managers. The brand manager has to be deeply committed to his or her product line. They have to eat, sleep, and breathe that brand, says Bob Wheling, P&G global marketing officer. The brand management system has aspects of religious fanaticism at the company. And the religion has paid off in many areas with strong brands like Sunny Delight, Tide, Ivory, Huggies, and Pert. ∎

*This case is based in part on Cliff Peale, "Branded for Success," *The Cincinnati Enquirer,* (May 20, 2001), A-1, A-16.

QUESTIONS FOR DISCUSSION

1. How is the brand manager's job related to managing the environment?
2. What are the key boundary spanning functions that the brand manager fulfills?
3. What types of skills do you think a brand manager should have?

4. Think of a typical consumer product that you frequently use. Design a brand manager job for that product. What would be the important sources of information that you would need to gather? With what types of organizations would you need to interact?

C H A P T E R

Organizational Technology

6

CASE: DON'T FORGET YOUR (E-)TICKET

Work in nearly every organization field has been affected to some extent by computerization and the Internet. Computer-aided design (CAD) and computer-aided manufacturing (CAM) have revolutionized design and production technologies. For example, Boeing's 777 generation of aircraft benefited from a design system that virtually eliminated traditional blueprints. Design information became more easily available within the company and to suppliers. Several automobile manufacturers have used CAD systems to accelerate the time-to-market for new car models. Manufacturers in a host of industries have introduced greater flexibility and customization to manufacturing through CAM systems and flexible manufacturing. And although the years 2000 and 2001 saw the failure of many Internet businesses, the trend toward e-commerce is likely to be irreversible.

The airline industry provides an interesting study in how these developments are changing the nature of work. It is now possible to check on flight availability, prices, and special deals from all major airlines, either through the company Web sites or through travel services like Travelocity.com, Expedia.com, Orbitz.com, travel consolidators such as Cheaptickets.com, or auctions such as Bestbuy.com. Depending on your destination, you may be given an "e-ticket" or your boarding pass may be issued by e-mail. Several of the airline Web sites and all of the travel services allow you to complete your travel arrangements by making reservations for rental cars, hotels, and other necessities. Several of the airline Web sites allow you to pick your seats online. Most sites allow you to check your frequent flier accounts and even use your accumulated miles to get a ticket. It is no longer necessary to call or visit an airline ticket agent or travel agent. In fact, several airlines provide incentives such as discounts or extra frequent flier miles for online purchases. If you have no luggage to check, it is now possible that the first human contact you will have is when you check in at the gate for departure.

The move to e-tickets—no physical ticket is actually issued—has significant work process implications. The airline no longer needs as many people or machines to print and issue tickets. Tickets no longer need to be mailed to customers (although some airlines still send an itinerary and receipt). Along with the ticketing efficiencies that the system creates, there's an added benefit for both customers and the airlines. E-tickets eliminate lost tickets—you can't lose what you don't have. In the days before e-tickets, airlines would charge customers as much as $75 to replace lost or stolen tickets. Replacing lost tickets involved substantial costs to the airlines. Ticket agents had to verify reservations, complete paperwork to track the lost ticket, and issue a new ticket. Moreover, customers often complained about what they saw as excessive fees for replacing lost tickets. The potential benefits to the airlines are so significant that some airlines have added a service charge of $10 for paper tickets to encourage customers to use e-tickets. That's quite a turnaround from charging $75 for a lost ticket.

We typically imagine that computers and automation will change work through robotics, artificial intelligence, and other "futuristic" enhancements to work. While those sorts of changes have taken place, many of the far-reaching and revolutionary changes in the nature of work affect more seemingly mundane processes like sales and ticket writing. Still, these technological innovations bring about important changes to work and organizations. Think, for example, of the kinds of skills that an airline or travel agency now needs to sell and process tickets compared to the old days of telephone or person-to-person selling. The companies now need computer technicians, programmers, Web designers, and e-business experts. These types of tasks require different training, skills, and knowledge from those needed by the telephone operator or ticket agent. Efficiencies are gained with these new work processes but not without significant changes to the nature of work.

Now, the next time you are on the way to the airport, you may not have to worry about whether you remembered to grab the ticket on the kitchen counter.

Technology, by its very definition, affects how we carry out our work. The work of writing and selling airline tickets has gone through dramatic change as the result of widely available and inexpensive computer technology. The successes of the changes in airline ticketing demonstrate the interplay of technology, work processes, and the environment. Not only have the changes in technology affected work in the airline industry, they have also altered the traditional structure of the travel industry. Although these developments may produce greater efficiency for the airlines and new options for customers, traditional sources of revenue for travel agents are disappearing.

As you read this chapter, keep in mind that technology is both more and less than computers, robotics, and the Internet. The skills, knowledge, information, and tools we use to perform our work are key contingency factors that we must consider when determining how we organize.

ORGANIZATIONAL TECHNOLOGY

Technology has a profound impact on organizations. Like goals, environment, and organizational size, variations in the types of technology that organizations use require different methods of management and different types of organizational structure. In this chapter we begin by examining the basic construct—what is technology—and then explore the ways in which organizations must structure to manage their technology.

In fields as diverse as organization theory, organization behavior, management, operations, economics, ergonomics, and industrial engineering, researchers and practitioners have searched for better tools and methods for performing work in organizations. The eighteenth-century economist Adam Smith wrote in *The Wealth of Nations* (1776) that the manufacturing efficiency of a simple pin factory could be dramatically increased through division of labor (*specialization*) and better machines. In the early twentieth century, the writings of Frederick W. Taylor and the Scientific Management School advocated improved efficiency through a similar pattern of specialization and better use of tools and people. Both of these early works, although separated by over 100 years, essentially dealt with the same topics—technology and its relationship to structure.

We briefly introduced the concept of technology in Chapter 1 as part of the discussion of the contingency framework. We again touched on the concept in Chapter 4 when we identified the technology sector of the environment as an important part of the environmental domain. In this chapter we explore some of the effects that technology has on organizations. All organizations employ technology—ways of carrying out jobs or tasks. In fact, there are several ways of looking at technology, and organizations typically have multiple technologies.

Because the term *technology* has a current, everyday meaning, its use and meaning in the context of organization theory may at first seem somewhat confusing. Such terms as *high tech* and *low tech* that grace our everyday language are not useful in organization theory. These terms may in fact mislead us about the nature of work. The essential questions that should guide our thinking about technology are these:

1. How does the organization get its work done?
2. How can management properly control that technology?

These questions are embedded in the larger and more central question of what technology is. That is where our journey begins.

WHAT IS TECHNOLOGY?

Definitions of *technology* vary widely among organizational writers.[1] One reason for the diversity of definitions of *technology* is that technology researchers have focused on different aspects or levels of the organization (e.g., the whole organization, departments or work units within the organization, or the relationships among individuals, groups, or departments). Additionally, some researchers have focused on inputs or materials used in tasks. Others have examined the operations used to transform inputs or materials into outputs. And still others suggest that the knowledge or information needed to complete tasks is an indicator of technology. Synthesizing these varied approaches, we define technology in the following way. First, **technology is the term used to refer to the work performed by an organization.**[2] Second, and more specifically, technology refers to the **knowledge, tools, machines, information, skills, and materials used to complete tasks within organizations, as well as the nature of the outputs of the organization.**

DEFINITION

Technology is the term used to refer to the work performed by an organization. Technology refers to the knowledge, tools, machines, information, skills, and materials used to complete tasks within organizations, as well as the nature of the outputs of the organization.

This definition implies that technology incorporates the idea of the *way* an organization uses resources to produce products and services. In other words, technology deals with the *throughputs* or *transformation processes* in our systems model, with the application of knowledge, skills, and tools to problems or tasks. Technology deals with how people in an organization carry out their tasks to produce the products and services of the organization. Technology, however, applies to more than just those tasks directly involved with the transformation process. It also deals with how products and services are distributed, the supporting activities necessary to bring services and products to market, and every other activity within an organization. Some versions of technology can be used to describe the nature of any task or job within an organization.

For example, we can envision the technology used in a typical automobile assembly line. Certain tasks are performed that use machinery, worker knowledge, and worker skills to produce large numbers of nearly identical automobiles. Machinery must be placed in an appropriate configuration to enhance coordination among workers. Various raw materials, semifinished goods, and products are needed at specific times in the appropriate quantity and quality. People with the necessary knowledge and skills to operate the machines and handle the raw materials must be present. All of these factors make up the technology of automobile manufacturing. But in addition to these people and tasks, people in other departments of an auto manufacturing facility (e.g., marketing, accounting, human resources, and clerical staff) also have specific technologies associated with their tasks. The market researcher uses people's opinions or perceptions as raw materials. He or she must have knowledge of market research, statistics, computers, and an array of other areas in order to do the job. Thus, every job or task in an organization involves some conceptualization of technology. Not only does each of these operations involve technology, but technology also comes into play when we consider the coordination of all of these activities so that the organization works smoothly. Although some writers on technology look strictly at the production-transformation process, we are interested more broadly in the technology of any organizational task. We are interested in the methods as well as the machinery. Some writers refer only to machinery, but methods also define the technology.

One might ask why technology is associated with structure. The *technology imperative* argues that technology drives structure.[3] In other words, the technology used in an organization causes an organization to structure or organize in a certain way. The decision about the type of technology an organization uses dictates the most appropriate structure. Compare the structure of an automobile assembly plant with that of a university or a hospital. In an auto plant people are organized around process. But even this organizing may vary. The transformation process in a conventional assembly line auto plant is different from the team-based assembly used by General Motors in the Saturn factory. The structuring of the Saturn plant is also different from that in conventional auto assembly plants. In a university, people are organized around disciplines or subjects (e.g., marketing department, management department). In a hospital, people are structured around procedures performed. By organizing around technology, organizations often achieve better coordination and reduce uncertainty because work procedures, methods, and machinery become the basis for setting up internal relationships and policies. Structure is necessary to reduce uncertainty and aid in information gathering; coordinate efforts across groups, work units or departments; and direct people. A key question faced by both organizational researchers and managers is how to structure an organization in the evolving North American and western European economies dominated by services and e-business.

Viewpoints on technology abound. Thus, placing each perspective in a readily understandable framework is not easy. The simplifying framework that we apply is to examine the various **levels of technology**. Organizational or **core technology** concepts are used to characterize the whole organization, and these views are examined in the following section. Although core technology is a useful idea for making broad generalizations about an organization, it may not capture the complexity and diversity of the organization's tasks. To understand this complexity and diversity we focus on smaller

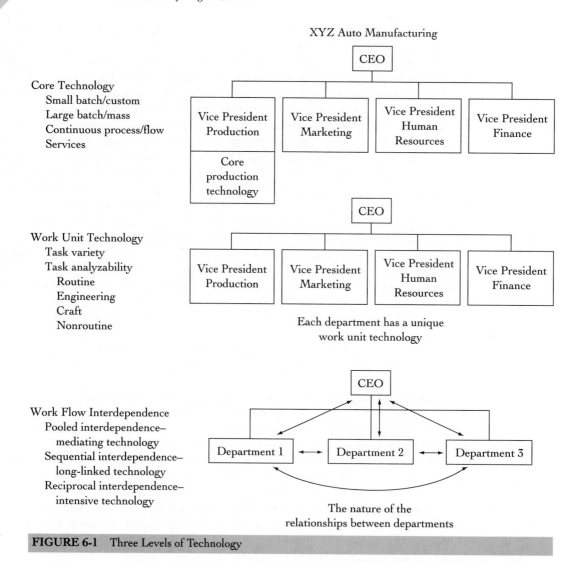

FIGURE 6-1 Three Levels of Technology

portions of the organization—***work unit*** or ***departmental technology***. However, work units or departments typically do not work in isolation. For an organization to accomplish its goals, work units or departments must coordinate and work together. Thus, our final level of focus is on the ***interdependent relationships*** that result from the flow of work among departments or work units because of the technology used to carry out the organization's tasks. Figure 6-1 illustrates these three levels of technology.

ORGANIZATION-LEVEL TECHNOLOGY: THE TECHNICAL CORE

One of the first systematic studies of the relationship between technology and organization was completed by British sociologist Joan Woodward in the early 1950s.[4] Woodward intended only to study organizational and administrative aspects of British manufacturing firms. However, her study of the administrative structure of these firms failed to confirm the conventional management thinking at that time. Rather than finding one ideal form of organization, Woodward found wide variations in an array of structural components of organizations, including the amount of direct versus indirect labor, the number of levels in the hierarchy, and the spans of supervisory control. It was only after Woodward's research team began looking at technology that they discovered the relationship between technology and structure. The result was a three-category scheme for classifying organization-level technology.[5]

Unit or Small Batch

Production runs consist of only a few units at a time, such as those found in a specialty job shop. Production is often customized to the specific needs of individual customers, which makes stockpiling finished goods impractical. Production requires significant direct labor (labor intensity). Examples include a custom tailor shop where garments are made to specific customer measurements and preferences, a machine toolmaker that designs tools to the needs and requirements of manufacturers, or an aircraft jet engine maker that makes small quantities of different engines, each of which may be modified for specific applications.

Mass or Large Batch

Many units of the same or similar products are produced at one time in long production runs. Production involves both moderate mechanization (capital intensity) and moderate amounts of direct labor (labor intensity), is more or less undifferentiated, and can be inventoried or stockpiled for future sale or use. Examples include assembly line production of automobiles, personal computers, and most clothing manufacturing.

Continuous Process or Flow

Production runs continuously with infrequent start-ups or shutdowns. Start-ups, breakdowns, or shutdowns can be dangerous, costly, and time-consuming. Production is the most highly mechanized (high capital intensity) and standardized. Output is highly uniform, and the process often has a flowlike quality. This process involves little direct labor. Examples include petrochemical refineries, breweries, and electric power generation.

CORE TECHNOLOGY AND STRUCTURE

In addition to providing a system of classifying organizational core technologies, Woodward also identified a ***contingency relationship*** between technology and structure. Her research showed that no single organizational structure best fit all organizations. Instead, she noted that structure varied with technology in the following fashion:

1. ***Unit or Small Batch***—Organic (flexible and adaptable): moderate size span of control, highly skilled workforce, low degree of formalization, low degree of specialization, and decentralized decision making
2. ***Mass or Large Batch***—Mechanistic-bureaucratic (stable and somewhat rigid): large size span of control, low level of workforce skill, high degree of formalization, high degree of specialization, and centralized decision making
3. ***Continuous Process or Flow***—Organic (flexible and adaptable): small span of control, highly skilled workforce (professionalized), low degree of formalization, low degree of specialization, and decentralized decision making.

Woodward's classification scheme has been useful in the development of a contingency framework for examining organization structure. Her work was the first to clearly document that there was not one best way to structure or manage an organization. Recently, work by Hull and Collins[6] expanded on Woodward's framework by adding a fourth core technology that subdivides small batch or unit technology into two categories. ***Traditional small batch technology*** includes operations that are low in knowledge complexity such as custom tailoring or dressmaking, while ***technical batch technology***, such as the manufacturing of jet aircraft engines or aerospace components, requires high knowledge complexity. Table 6-1 presents Hull and Collins's elaboration of Woodward's core manufacturing technology framework. The main structural implications of Hull and Collins's view of small batch technology are that traditional small batch technology requires skilled craftspeople in a simple organic structure, and there is little opportunity for automation or computerization. Technical batch technology requires highly skilled professional workers in an organic-profession ***adhocracy*** and presents greater opportunities for automation and computerization. An adhocracy is a highly flexible structure that can be altered or changed as needed. Hull and Collins have improved upon Woodward's typology by recognizing the diversity of technologies and their effects on the organization.

The types of core manufacturing technologies that Woodward and Hull and Collins present represent prototypes. Some core technologies may involve combinations or aspects of all these types. Parts of steel and sheet glass production are flow technology, yet the end products are discrete pieces much like large batch or mass technology. Moreover, this body of research is not without shortcomings. Woodward largely ignored the confounding effects of organizational size on technology. Studies of core technology resulted in a ***technology imperative***—that technology should be the princi-

TABLE 6-1   Revision of Woodward's Typology of Production Systems with Structure and Innovative Activity

Knowledge Complexity		Scale of Operations	
	Technical Batch		**Continuous Process**
High	Example: aerospace electronics		Example: petrochemical plant
	Capital equipment: computer controlled, general purpose		Capital equipment: automated, sometimes computer controlled; integrated
	Human resources: professional and technical experts, skilled and semiskilled operatives		Human resources: skilled operatives, large percentage of engineers
	Structure: organic-professional adhocracy		Structure: mixed, professional bureaucracy
	Innovative activity: high R&D and innovation		Innovative activity: medium-high R&D and innovation
	Traditional Batch		**Mass Production**
Low	Example: dressmaking, printing		Example: carburetor assembly
	Capital equipment: nonautomated, general purpose		Capital equipment: automated, repeat-cycle, sequential
	Human resources: skilled or unskilled operatives		Human resources: semiskilled operatives, small proportion research and engineering
	Structure: traditional-craft, simple structure		Structure: mechanistic-bureaucratic, machine bureaucracy
	Innovative activity: low R&D and innovation		Innovative activity: low-medium R&D and innovation
	Small	**Scale of Operations**	Large

Source: Frank M. Hull and Paul D. Collins, "High-Technology Batch Production Systems: Woodward's Missing Type," *Academy of Management Journal* 30, no. 4 (December 1987): 788.

pal factor in determination of the appropriate structure. Yet, as we noted early in the text, an organization's strategy will play a key role in selection of an appropriate core technology and, hence, an appropriate structure. Moreover, as we noted in the previous chapter, the organization's size also plays a crucial role in determining an appropriate structure.

A number of other relevant issues must be examined. First, these works focus solely on manufacturing and ignore technology employed in the increasingly large and important service sector of the economy. Second, innovations in technology, such as computer-integrated manufacturing (CIM), flexible manufacturing, computer-aided design (CAD)/computer-aided manufacturing (CAM), and various group or team approaches to manufacturing, challenge some of the conventional wisdom of Woodward's framework. Third, this approach to technology is useful only for classifying core (whole organization) technology. It does not deal with the varied technologies used by people in other parts of the organization but not involved with the technical core. We will examine all three of these issues. We first examine the technology of service organizations.

SERVICE AS A CORE TECHNOLOGY

In recent years, increasing attention has been focused on the service sector of the economy. Some writers suggest that the future strength and job growth in the U.S. economy will be in the service sector. Regardless of the future, the reality today is that services constitute a major segment of the organizational landscape. Thus, it is important to understand how and why service technology differs from manufacturing technology. Definitions of *service* typically allude to the *intangible* nature of the output. That is, in the extreme, **services are intangible offerings of value that do not have a physical form and are provided to a customer or client**. Teaching, medical services, legal services, banking, insurance, restaurants, and retail stores are a few examples. In reality, however, a continuum or range of technologies exists from pure services involving no tangible output (e.g., legal services, insurance, education, and transportation) to pure manufacturing technologies such as those discussed earlier in this chapter.[7] In the midrange are technologies that involve both services and manufacturing (e.g., restaurants, banks, and retail stores). Figure 6-2 provides examples of the full range of core technologies.

FIGURE 6-2   Service Technology

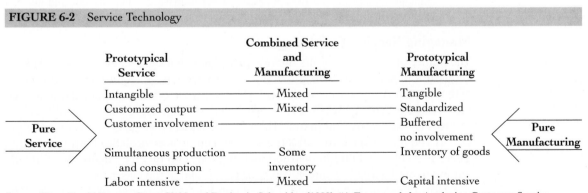

Source: From David Bowen, Caren Siehl, and Benjamin Schneider (1989), "A Framework for Analyzing Customer Service Orientations in Manufacturing," *Academy of Management Review* 14 (1989): 75–95.

The differences between service and manufacturing technologies can best be seen by examining the extreme or prototypical cases on five dimensions: tangibility, standardization, customer participation, timing, and labor intensity.

1. **Tangibility.** Tangibility refers to the concreteness or abstractness of output. As one moves from pure manufacturing technology to pure service technology, the degree of *intangibility* increases, so that with pure services there is no tangible or concrete output. Compare manufacturing an automobile to servicing one. Manufacturing an automobile involves a clearly identifiable tangible output—the car. Servicing an automobile involves some tangible output—new oil, filters, and spark plugs—but the primary output of interest to the customer is a car that runs better than it did prior to servicing. The intangibility of this output creates uncertainty for both the organization providing the service and the consumer. Because there is no concrete, tangible output, judgments about the quality and appropriateness of the output are more subjective and debatable than is typically the case with tangible outputs.

2. **Standardization.** Services tend to be less standardized and more tailored to customer needs than do manufacturing technologies. Although we noted that small batch or unit technology tends to emphasize customization, a key difference with services is that customization takes place at the point of sale or exchange. Even with mass customization, the customer and the processes are separated. However, the move toward mass customization has eroded the degree of standardization in many manufacturing technologies. Compare auto manufacturing to counseling services. Although there are standard guidelines for counseling, how it is delivered depends very much on characteristics of the individual receiving the counseling.

3. **Customer Participation.** Services directly involve the customer in the production process. This is a boundary issue. In manufacturing technology the core technology is protected or buffered from customers. The production and exchange of a service requires that the customer enter into the technical core of the organization. This lack of buffering increases the potential for uncertainty. Compare making a movie to viewing one. In the latter case, the service can only be rendered in the presence of the consumers. Making the movie does not require direct customer participation.

4. **Timing.** Services require *simultaneous production* and *consumption*. Producer and consumer must be present for production to take place. Production of services requires customers to consume the output. Unlike manufacturing technology, services cannot be inventoried or stockpiled for later consumption. Even small batch manufacturing technologies do not require the immediate presence of customers. Outputs of small batch technology can be held for later consumption. Compare manufacturing a computer to a software development class. The computer can be manufactured and then stored in inventory for later consumption. A class cannot be stored. Production takes place only when students are present.

5. **Labor Intensity.** Services tend to be more labor intensive than manufacturing technologies. Services require that workers interact directly with customers. Conversely, manufacturing technologies tend to be more capital intensive. Compare the mix of labor and machinery necessary to make a car with the labor intensity to service one.

Managing Service Technology

The nature of services presents the organization with a significant challenge. The characteristics of service organizations noted earlier create a technology that is fraught with uncertainty and unpredictability.[8] The results are often ambiguous; timing is critical; boundaries are highly permeable; work defies a high degree of standardization; and services are not easily automated. Think of the typical college class. What is the product? If you miss a class, you miss the service. Timing is critical. Students come and go. There is great variability in instructional methods and quality. Finally, it is difficult to automate the instruction and learning process found in the classroom.

How does one manage under these conditions? Research by the Aston Group from the University of Aston in Birmingham, England, provides some preliminary answers to this question.[9] They developed a scale for classifying both service and manufacturing technologies that was based on the following three factors:

1. **Automation of equipment:** the extent to which machinery and equipment is *self-operated* (i.e., automated) versus the extent to which work must be performed directly by workers
2. **Work flow rigidity:** degree of flexibility in both human skills and machinery capabilities
3. **Specificity of evaluation:** the degree to which work flow can be measured quantitatively as opposed to the need for subjective evaluation

The Aston researchers combined these factors into a general measure called ***work flow integration***, which provides a fundamental basis for classifying organizations. Organizations with technologies that scored high on work flow integration were characterized by high levels of automation, greater rigidity of work, and more precise measures of operations (e.g., auto assembly plants or refineries). Low scores indicated the opposite—low work flow integration—difficulty automating tasks, greater flexibility of work, and ambiguous or unclear measures of operations (e.g., college teaching, legal practice, or medicine). Not surprisingly, services score low on work flow integration.

The Aston research suggested that increasing levels of work flow integration should be matched with increasingly bureaucratic or mechanistic structures. Low levels of work flow integration, on the other hand, require more organic organizational structures. Thus, service organizations should be managed with organic structures that include low formalization, low specialization, and decentralization. Additional research suggests that service organizations can adapt to their conditions through geographical dispersion—locating facilities close to customers—another form of decentralization.[10] This strategy is being tried in Florida and several other states in health, welfare, and human services departments. Regional district offices are being established close to clients, and the power of the headquarters office in the Florida state capital is being reduced. The belief is that those employees closest to the customers can deal best with local problems and idiosyncracies.

RECENT ADVANCEMENTS IN MANUFACTURING TECHNOLOGY

Technology is not static. Organizations develop new methods of production internally or acquire new technology from the external environment. For example, advanced manufacturing technology (AMT) includes an array of computer-based production systems, such as computer-aided design and manufacturing (CAD/CAM), robotics, flexible manufacturing systems, and fully computer-integrated manufacturing (CIM). These techniques are being implemented in the automobile and paper industries, to name just two examples. Other types of advances in the production core technology of organizations rely on changes in the people aspect of production. For example, ***group*** or ***team approaches*** emphasize a high degree of coordination among production team or group members who may be responsible for an entire manufacturing process, where previously individuals had responsibility for small, isolated tasks.[11] GM adopted this approach in designing and operating the Saturn Division. Group and team approaches highlight the interdependent nature of many operations in organizations. Accomplishment of tasks often requires skills, knowledge, and expertise from diverse functional areas. Including people from different areas or disciplines in a group or on a team facilitates coordination. Group and team approaches to production have had significant impact on traditional large batch or mass core technologies such as autos, steel, rubber, and electronics.

Common to all the AMT approaches is an extensive reliance on computers and information technology to support the production process.[12] Although debate still exists over the full range of implications of AMT, a few consequences are clear. Each of these techniques increases the automation of tasks, thus reducing the number of people required to produce the same amount of output as under traditional large batch techniques. In many cases, these technologies have increased manufacturing flexibility. Assembly processes that once supported production of only a single type of output can, through AMT, support numerous variations in outputs. For example, AMT can be used to produce several car models on a single assembly line. Computer controls ensure that the correct parts and components are routed to the appropriate location at the right time. Much of the individual decision-making responsibility in the production process is taken over by computers. AMT reduces the amount of direct labor involved in production, and although some production tasks may now require *less* skill because of computerization, the new jobs required to program, operate, and monitor AMT require greater levels of skill and professionalism. Thus, AMT resembles a combination of technical small batch and continuous process technologies. Using AMT, the Ford Chicago Heights, Illinois, stamping plant can change dies in a matter of hours. It used to take several days.

Research shows that these technologies are associated with greater decentralization in decision making—much like small batch and continuous process technologies—but increased formalization.[13] Decentralization is necessary and possible because operators now have greater access to information because of computer-based information and they have the professionalism to execute decisions. That same computer-based system, however, also supports and requires greater formalization. Greater formalization is possible because more information is available to convey and support rules, and greater formalization may be necessary to counterbalance the risk and uncertainty resulting from decentralization. In other words, computers allow us to gather and use more information to make policy, which is used to coordinate decentralized units.

Group- or team-based approaches to production emphasize a movement away from the narrow specialization present in traditional large batch or mass production technologies. Instead, production teams include members with a broad range of skills necessary for the entire production process. The belief is that this holistic cooperative approach to production results in greater flexibility, increased coordination, better quality, and more innovativeness. The net result is that group or team production processes make traditional large batch operations function more like traditional or technical small batch production. Such approaches require a greater range of skills on the part of team members. They must now be able to communicate effectively, solve problems, monitor quality, perform calculations, and implement solutions. The philosophy behind using groups must also be congruent with the local management and culture, as the discussion in the following box suggests.

CORE TECHNOLOGY: A SUMMARY

Woodward's study of manufacturing firms represents the first attempt to classify the core technology of organizations and to determine the relationship between technology and structure. The primary criterion used in Woodward's scheme is *technical complexity,* or the degree to which the core operation can be automated. Subsequent studies have broadened the scope of the framework to cover other technologies besides the three described by Woodward. Absent from this framework is service technology.

EXHIBIT 6-1

Groups in the United States and Japan[14]

The use of teams or groups in manufacturing has become quite popular in the United States in recent years following successes in Japan and Sweden. However, the record of success in the implementation of group- or team-oriented manufacturing in the United States has been rather uneven. One suggested reason for the mixed record for team and group production in this country is that groups and teams, as they have been used in Japan and Sweden, run counter to basic American work philosophy. In particular, U.S. and Japanese cultures differ in five critical areas that affect groups and teams.

1. *Individualism and collectivism:* American culture and American business glorify individual creativity and industry. Success is dependent on the skills, knowledge, and motivation of individuals. By contrast, Japanese culture emphasizes membership, unity, and harmony. In Japan, to single out an individual team member for praise is typically viewed as inappropriate. Group or team approaches to management and production would appear to be a natural outgrowth of Japanese culture whereas American culture may inhibit harmony and cohesiveness.

2. *Conflict and conformity:* A natural extension of the emphasis on harmony mentioned above is that Japanese culture emphasizes conflict avoidance. Group harmony and conformity are key elements of the culture. American culture emphasizes individuality and independence. Conflict is a natural outgrowth of this situation. Again, American culture may inhibit group- or team-oriented approaches while Japanese culture aids in their use.

3. *Power:* Japanese workers tend to be more respectful of the power and authority of managers than do American workers. Thus, status hierarchies are likely to develop within Japanese groups. American groups are more likely to emphasize democratic or egalitarian approaches to management. As a result, American teams or groups may have greater difficulty achieving cohesiveness and consensus.

4. *Time orientation:* U.S. culture tends to emphasize the present and reward fast results. Conversely, Japanese culture places greater emphasis on the past (tradition) and the future. The result is an acceptance of slower and more incremental change. This approach to investing in capital and infrastructure is referred to as *patient capital.*

5. *Homogeneity and heterogeneity:* Much has been made of Japan's homogeneous culture. The country is dominated by one cultural, racial, and ethnic group. By contrast, the United States has a heterogeneous culture that is highlighted by racial, cultural, ethnic, and religious diversity. In fact, recent trends in this nation have been in the direction of emphasizing diversity. The result is that it is more difficult to use collectivism, cohesion, and commonality of purpose in American groups or teams compared with those in Japan.

Three factors are key to successfully using groups or teams in the American cultural setting. First, managers should value and encourage dissent. Differences and disagreement can be valuable tools in producing creative solutions. Second, managers should encourage fluid and shifting group or team membership. In this way groups or teams are more likely to reflect the shifting and changing nature of U.S. culture. Overemphasis on stability and cohesiveness runs contrary to U.S. culture and may inhibit group functioning. Finally, groups must be empowered to make decisions. For team or group approaches to be successful, the group or team must be given the power and authority to implement its decisions or suggestions. Forcing groups to go through the organizational hierarchy removes much of the rationale (and motivation) for using groups.

The key point is that group or team approaches to organizational tasks may be useful and effective ways of altering technology, but management must make certain that the approach is consistent with the large culture and philosophy in which the groups or teams are embedded.

Approaches to service technology have progressed on two fronts. First, some researchers have attempted to determine the characteristics of service that distinguish it from manufacturing technology. These characteristics include output tangibility, degree of standardization, timing of production, consumption, and labor intensity. However, the more closely one looks at services, the more one realizes that similarities exist between some aspects of services and the core manufacturing technologies. Moreover, services vary by degrees. Some organizations, such as insurance companies, have pure service technologies in which outputs lack tangibility, are consumed as they are produced, and involve extensive direct labor. Others, such as fast food restaurants, involve some tangible output, permit extensive standardization, can be stockpiled, and can be partially automated. The second approach to services (and technology in general) identifies general characteristics of technology that apply to both manufacturing and services. Although the two approaches look at technology in different ways, they are compatible.

Advances in manufacturing technology have partly changed the way we view technologies—particularly traditional large batch and mass technology. AMT and group or team approaches remind us that the organizational world is not static. While AMT may fit with Hull and Collins's view of technical batch technology, it is not consistent in all respects with the Aston Group's work. Contrary to the Aston Group's conclusion, increased automation under AMT increases rather than decreases flexibility.[15] Thinking and theorizing on issues such as technology must be revisited and modified periodically.

The modern multiproduct, multidivisional corporation may have several core technologies. A company like Procter & Gamble has large batch technologies and flow technologies, and is even getting into small batch technologies in some of its specialty divisions. Moreover, the organizational core is not the only place where technology is relevant. Organizations employ many technologies, as we can see if we look at how people throughout the organization contribute to organizational goals and objectives. Our attention now turns to describing work unit or departmental technology.

WORK UNIT OR DEPARTMENTAL TECHNOLOGY

Technology is a concept that can be used not only to characterize an entire organization, but also to describe work throughout the organization. The framework developed by Charles Perrow[16] and elaborated by Richard Daft and his colleagues[17] is useful for understanding not only an organization's predominant technology, but also the varied technologies that exist in departments and work units throughout organizations. Clearly, the nature of work in departments such as marketing, human resources management, accounting, and production differs. The work unit or departmental view of technology explicitly examines these differences. According to this framework, technology is defined along two dimensions of work: ***exceptions*** or ***variety*** * and ***analyzability.***

Originally, Perrow described task exceptions as the number of exceptions to standard procedures, unexpected or novel events, or variations in inputs or raw materials

---

*Although Perrow used the term *exceptions* in his original work on work unit technology, the term *variety* has gained wide usage in the organization theory field. We regard the terms as essentially analogous in the context of work unit or departmental technology. To avoid confusion, we will use *variety* to refer to this dimension.

encountered during the performance of tasks. Recently, the concept has been broadened to include *task variety.* Thus, tasks that are characterized by many exceptions to standard operating procedures, that involve the performance of a large number of different or unrelated tasks, that may involve numerous novel or unexpected events, or that may use many different kinds of raw materials are defined as high in variety. By contrast, jobs that must closely follow standard operating procedures, that involve the performance of a small number of different or closely related tasks, that rarely involve novel or unexpected events, or that use a limited number of raw materials are defined as low-variety tasks. The degree of variety present in jobs is associated with the degree of flexibility that a department or work unit has in carrying out its operations. Low-variety technologies permit little flexibility; high-variety technologies permit greater flexibility.

An example of a low-variety work unit would be the team responsible for the operation of a typical chain carryout pizza outlet. The number of different tasks that people perform might include taking phone orders, managing delivery people, making pizzas, waiting on customers, and stocking the supplies. Employees would normally follow a set of standard operating procedures that describes telephone manners, guidelines for supervision, specific recipes for pizzas, and quotas for stocking supplies. Exceptions could be tightly limited by requiring that customers order only those items specifically listed on the menu. In general, fast food restaurants carefully manage jobs to maintain low variety. This makes managing such jobs relatively straightforward.

By contrast, the marketing department at the corporate headquarters for a pizza chain will likely be characterized by high variety. The number of different types of tasks that people perform could vary widely and include such things as market research, advertising, new product development, packaging, public relations, and other related activities. Within each of these areas, individual jobs may vary greatly and the number of exceptions or novel events would likely be relatively large. Managing the corporate marketing department would be more difficult and would require greater flexibility.

The second work unit or departmental technology dimension is ***problem analyzability***. One explanation of analyzability is the ease or difficulty encountered in searching for information to solve problems or complete tasks. Tasks that are characterized by readily available information that is easily obtained are designated as high-analyzability tasks. Tasks that are characterized by unavailable information or information that is difficult to obtain are designated as low-analyzability tasks. High-analyzability tasks are ones where information can be easily obtained to solve problems or perform tasks. Low-analyzability tasks are typically uncertain, ambiguous, and complex. Low-analyzability tasks are difficult to solve and require problem solvers to use judgment, instincts, intuition, and experience, rather than programmed solutions, to solve these problems.

Returning to the pizza company example, the job of the work unit responsible for the store operation is generally a high-analyzability task. Readily available information guides employees in the conduct of their tasks. Menus and recipes guide the food preparation tasks. Store manuals inform employees of general policies and procedures for day-to-day operations. By contrast, the strategic planners at corporate headquarters encounter a low-analyzability task. To plan the company's direction for the next few years, they need to know about a wide range of events in the future: general economic conditions, consumer preferences, competition, labor availability, government regulations, and so on. Moreover, the planners need to know how to evaluate this information and combine it to develop a plan. These tasks are characterized by information that is difficult to identify, obtain, and manipulate into a coherent and useful strategic plan. The planners will likely rely on their extensive experience, good judgment, and instincts or intuition to guide them.

Using the two dimensions of variety (exceptions) and analyzability, Perrow developed a four-category taxonomy of work unit or departmental technology as shown in Table 6-2. The categories are routine, engineering, craft, and nonroutine. Routine technologies deal with few exceptions or low-variety and highly analyzable tasks—the employees at the pizza store. Engineering technologies have many exceptions or high variety, but the tasks are still highly analyzable. The accounting department at corporate headquarters would be an example. Although the accountants may perform many different tasks or encounter numerous exceptions, solving these task problems is facilitated by information or techniques that are easily available. Craft technologies deal with little variety or few exceptions, but problems are difficult to analyze. An example would be the packaging designers responsible for creating new packaging for microwave pizzas. Although they have only a few tasks to perform in packaging design, it is difficult to acquire information and to know what information is important (i.e., what packaging works best in microwaves; what packaging is easiest to handle, ship, and stock; and what packaging is most attractive to customers). Finally, nonroutine technologies combine high variety or many exceptions with low analyzability. Our strategic planners must perform many different tasks; they may encounter many exceptions, and the information they need is not clearly defined or readily available.

Much like the relationship between Woodward's core technology and organizational structure, Perrow's research suggests the need to adopt appropriate structure for departments or work units. Structure defines how work is supervised and coordinated to ensure that tasks are completed in a timely and efficient manner.

Table 6-3 elaborates the contingent relationship between work unit or departmental technology and the appropriate departmental structure.[18] As departments move away from routine technology toward nonroutine technology, they require increasingly organic structure to operate efficiently. Selecting inappropriate structures for specific technologies results in departments or work units that perform suboptimally. A second important point to emphasize is that a given organization may have examples of each of these four types of technology. At the departmental level, an organization may have a variety of structures. Such conditions may make the overall management of the organization difficult—each unit is structured differently. It is difficult to establish overall corporate policy that applies to each unit. In the next section we examine how organizations must coordinate interactions that arise from these variations in technology.

TABLE 6-2 Work Unit or Departmental Technology: Sample Departments from a Pizza Chain

Variety (Exceptions)

Few	Many
Craft Packaging development, test chefs	**Nonroutine** Corporate strategic planners, product development
Routine Store managers, clerical	**Engineering** Accounting, legal

TABLE 6-3   Work Unit or Departmental Technology and Structure

Craft Technology	Nonroutine Technology
Mostly Organic Structure:	Organic Structure:
Moderate formalization	Low formalization
Moderate centralization	Low centralization
Experienced workers, moderate specialization	Highly trained and experienced workers, generalists
Moderate span of supervisory control	Small span of supervisory control
Requires horizontal communication	Requires extensive horizontal communication
Examples: Designers, advertising	Examples: Strategic planners, top management

Routine Technology	Engineering Technology
Mechanistic Structure:	Mostly Mechanistic Structure:
High formalization	Moderate formalization
High centralization	Moderate centralization
Low skill, narrow specialization	Formal training, moderate specialization
Wide span of supervisory control	Moderate span of supervisory control
Requires little vertical communication	Requires vertical and horizontal communication
Examples: Maintenance, clerical	Examples: Accounting, legal research

Source: Based on Richard L. Daft, *Organization Theory and Design* (St. Paul, MN: West Publishing, 1992), 130.

WORK FLOW AND TECHNOLOGICAL INTERDEPENDENCE

James Thompson developed a technology framework, elaborated by others, that focuses on the nature of *interdependence* and *coordination* among departments or work units that results from the technology.[19] Thompson's view acknowledges that various parts of an organization must come together and interact for the organization as a whole to accomplish its goals. Technologies in organizations vary in how much they require or depend on individuals or departments to interact with one another in order to complete tasks. Technologies with low interdependence require little interaction and coordination; those with high interdependence require comparatively high levels of interaction or coordination. ***Thus, the essential questions about technological interdependence are these: (1) How much is one unit or department dependent on another to complete work? (2) What is the nature of that interdependence? (3) How can we achieve the necessary coordination?***

Thompson identified three types of technologies that result in three different levels of interdependence. These three technologies and the resulting interdependence are best managed by different methods of coordination. A description of each follows.

Mediating Technology

This technology brings together individuals, departments, or organizations with complementary needs. For example, banks bring together borrowers and lenders, real estate agencies bring together home buyers and home sellers, and employment agencies bring together potential workers and employers. In each case some part of the organization (or individuals in the organization) mediates between the organization and the external environment. The bank example above illustrates mediating technology. Branch offices of a bank interact with customers. In carrying out their jobs, personnel in a branch office may not be particularly dependent on the bank's central office. Questions or problems that may arise during the conduct of business can usually be answered by following standard procedures, obeying rules, or consulting policy manuals. Standardization of jobs can create consistency across units of the organization. Thus, horizontal communication between units at the same level (i.e., other branch offices) does not need to be extensive. In general, communication needs are low, and it is not necessary to locate departments or units (in this case, branch banks) close together. However, the performance of the bank as a whole is dependent on the performance of each individual branch. This type of interdependence is called ***pooled interdependence*** because the organization's technological output is the pooled total of all units (i.e., the branch banks). Little coordination among branch offices, units, or departments is necessary.

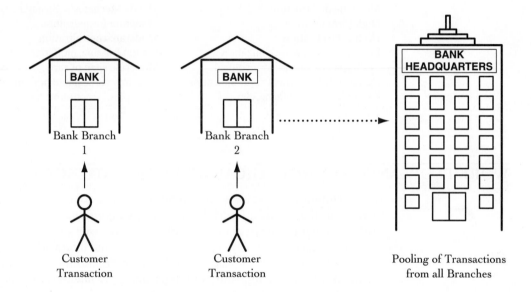

Bank Branch 1 — Customer Transaction

Bank Branch 2 — Customer Transaction

BANK HEADQUARTERS — Pooling of Transactions from all Branches

Long-Linked Technology

The typical assembly line operation exemplifies long-linked technology. Operations within the organization proceed in a serial or stepwise fashion. One step must be completed after another in a specific order, much like links in a chain. Each department must be able to anticipate inputs from the unit occupying the prior position in the chain, and each unit must be able to schedule the disposition of its output. For example, on an automobile assembly line the group responsible for installing the engine on the chassis is dependent upon the group that delivers nearly completed engines to the assembly line. The next group that attaches controls and wiring on the engine must wait for the installers to complete their job. The result is ***sequential interdependence*** because of the required sequencing of tasks.

Long-linked technology and sequential interdependence can be coordinated by locating interdependent individuals, departments, or units close together or adjacent to one another; by allowing for communication and feedback between interdependent individuals, departments, or units; and by using schedules or plans.

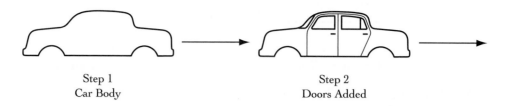

Step 1
Car Body

Step 2
Doors Added

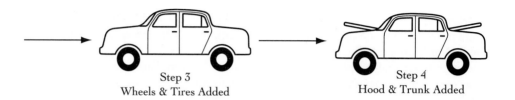

Step 3
Wheels & Tires Added

Step 4
Hood & Trunk Added

Intensive Technology

The third form of technology that Thompson describes involves situations in which the outputs of one individual, unit, or department become the inputs of another individual, unit, or department. Typically, a variety of different skills, techniques, and methods is brought together for a specific time period to accomplish a specific purpose that may involve several products and services. For example, the intensive care unit of a hospital requires that doctors, nurses, X-ray technicians, inhalation therapists, dietitians, and other specialists interact extensively to deliver treatment to a patient.

The nature of the interdependence that results from intensive technology is what Thompson called ***reciprocal interdependence***. In the example of the intensive care unit, the doctors' work may create inputs for the X-ray technician and a radiologist. The work of the X-ray technician and radiologist then may become inputs for the doctors. Similar reciprocal relationships are likely between other members of the intensive care team, such as nurses, physicians, dietitians, and physical therapists. Coordination of intensive technology and reciprocal interdependence can be achieved by locating individuals, departments, or units close together so that communication is facilitated. Communication is critical to the *mutual adjustment* of individuals or groups. Mutual adjustment means that individuals or groups are able to understand and adjust to the conditions or needs of others. Reciprocal interdependence can also be managed through teamwork and through frequent face-to-face meetings.

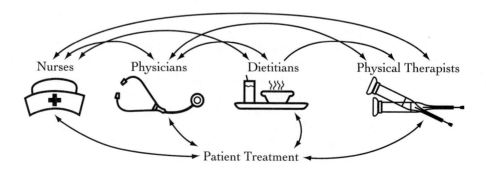

EXHIBIT 6-2

Intensive Technology and Reciprocal Interdependence[20]

Dell Computer is the number 1 direct marketer of PCs. The bulk of its sales are through online or telephone orders. By tracing a typical order from the time Dell receives it until the finished product is shipped to the customer we can clearly identify examples of mediating technology and sequential technology. Shifting our focus to Dell's top management team provides an example of intensive technology.

Mediating Technology. When a customer places an order with Dell Computer, that order is received and processed by one of several sales representatives. This individual mediates between the customer and Dell Computer. The representative enters the order on the computer but does not need to interact with other Dell employees to carry out his or her job. The sales representative's actions are guided by rules and the specific computer-based order entry system the company uses. The sum total productivity of the sales department is the pooled output of all the sales representatives.

Sequential Technology. After checking the customer's credit, an order sheet is created that contains all the components to be included in the customer's computer and an order identification number. This order is sent to the assembly area where the computer is produced in a stepwise or sequential fashion. At each station along an assembly line different components, such as the specific type of processor, Video card, DRAM, hard drive, and CDROM, DVD, or other devices are built into the computer. Each task must be completed according to an orderly sequence of steps. Skipping a step or failure to complete a step results in a defective machine. The final steps include loading the software, testing the computer, packing it, and shipping it to the customer. Production schedules, the layout of the assembly facility, and the order sheet help to coordinate these activities.

Intensive Technology. At the same time that the order is being processed, top management is studying the market and planning for the future. This planning may involve gathering past sales and financial performance data, economic data, and market research data; examining the results of ongoing research and development activities; surveying the competition; negotiating with suppliers or potential partners; meeting with investors and investment analysts; and numerous other similar activities. Extensive interaction is required among members of the top management team. This may involve both planned and unplanned meetings, face-to-face and telephone conversations, and other exchanges of information. Information flows in many different directions. Coordination or agreement on the strategic direction of the firm is achieved through these interactions.

Thompson's framework is one that can be used to examine any type of organization, and, while it can be used to characterize the technology and interdependence of an entire organization, it is most useful as a model of the social interactions necessary for individuals, departments, or work units to coordinate their work efforts to accomplish the organization's mission. This model of technology and interdependence does not just give suggestions about structure in the ways that we have come to think about structure (i.e., formalization, standardization, centralization, etc.). Rather, Thompson addresses mechanisms necessary to coordinate departments or units. He addresses how interdependent departments work together. We have also examined issues such as the location of interdependent departments and the amount of communication necessitated by the interdependence. Table 6-4 summarizes Thompson's work flow interdependence framework and the suggested means for managing interdependence.

TABLE 6-4	Thompson's Work Flow Technology and Interdependence Framework			
Type of Technology	**Nature of Interdependence**	**Methods for Coordination**	**Communication Requirements**	**Physical Location Requirements**
Intensive	Reciprocal: high interdependence	Teamwork, meetings, face-to-face conversations, mutual adjustment	High need for horizontal communication	Locate units close together or allow for exchange of personnel across departments
Long-Linked	Sequential: moderate interdependence	Planning, work schedules, scheduled meetings, verbal feedback	Moderate communication needs; horizontal communication with adjacent work units; vertical communication for oversight	Locate units with adjacent functions close together; other units can be dispersed
Mediating	Pooled: low interdependence	Rules, policies, and procedures; work standardization	Low communication needs; mostly vertical	Low need to locate units close together

Source: Based on Richard L. Daft, *Organization Theory and Design* (St. Paul, MN: West Publishing, 1992) and Andrew H. Van de Ven, Andre Delbecq, and Richard Koenig, "Determinants of Communication Modes Within Organizations," *American Sociological Review* (1976): 41.

TASK DESIGN AND TECHNOLOGY: SOCIOTECHNICAL SYSTEMS

The use of a particular technology in an organization results in a particular set of tasks. These tasks are then grouped together into a particular set of jobs. A job is a grouping of tasks within a prescribed unit or department. A job encompasses a set of duties, functions, and responsibilities. Secretary, supervisor, engineer, electrician, sales clerk, and vice president are all examples of jobs.

In this section we do not provide a complete overview of task and job design; that is a more appropriate subject for books on organizational behavior, work motivation, or human resources management. Our objective is briefly to examine how technology affects the way tasks and jobs are designed. The most traditional approach is to *fit people to jobs.* A second approach is to *fit jobs to people.* A third view, *the sociotechnical perspective,* takes the middle ground and *considers both the person and the technology simultaneously.*[21]

Fitting People to Jobs: The Traditional Industrial Ethic

In fitting people to jobs, a technology that is best from the standpoint of productivity and economic efficiency is employed. This results in a set of jobs to be filled. People are then selected and trained so that they can perform the jobs. People are viewed almost as an extension of the machine. The job is regarded as nearly inflexible as determined by the technology, and the person is seen as flexible enough to be fit to the job. This is the traditional manner in which jobs have been designed as a country industrializes. It is conducive to job specialization and assembly line–type operations.

Unfortunately, human beings are not infinitely malleable. Some people or groups cannot adapt to some task conditions. For example, in the 1970s General Motors opened a new highly automated factory in Lordstown, Ohio. However, in designing the plant GM did not take into consideration the needs of workers to communicate as part of their jobs. The new automated equipment created unnatural barriers to worker interaction. Although there were many factors that caused significant productivity and morale problems, the emphasis on technical solutions without consideration of human consequences added to Lordstown's poor performance. GM sought to avoid this problem when it designed the Saturn plant with the help of work teams that would operate the facility. Other examples include repetitive motion problems among clerical workers who perform the same limited set of tasks many times each day and back problems among workers doing heavy lifting. In general, the low rate of successful adoption of new technologies is likely to be because many organizations fail to adapt organizational and work practices (i.e., people) to the requirements of new technologies.[22]

Fitting Jobs to People: The Postindustrial Society

In fitting jobs to people, the capabilities of an available labor force take precedence over the technology to be employed. The skills, abilities, and aspirations of the available labor force are first analyzed, and a technology is adopted that results in jobs consistent with the available skills and abilities. The job is viewed as flexible and the person, with his or her complement of skills, abilities, and aspirations, is viewed as rather rigid and unbending. This view of jobs and workers has spawned a movement toward job redesign (creating jobs with a greater variety of tasks that tap into the diversity of workers' skills and interests) and job enrichment (creating jobs with greater variety and with more responsibilities). The idea is to create jobs that are more challenging and inherently more motivating because they better fit the abilities, needs, and desires of workers.

Although much debate persists about the merits of job redesign and job enrichment, the argument is made that jobs of the future should be designed to tap the higher skills, abilities, and aspirations of a developed workforce. Unchallenging, routine jobs should be done by machines, robots, and computers. People in a postindustrial society should be left to do the challenging jobs, especially those involved with service aspects of the economy. On the other hand, evidence suggests that some people prefer highly structured jobs with little responsibility—what many people regard as routine, unchallenging jobs. Moreover, years of research fail to support the notion that a satisfied workforce is necessarily more productive.[23] Thus, job redesign and job enrichment may not always be the answer to the person- or technology-fit question or to improving organizational performance.[24] The sociotechnical approach suggests that the set of relationships between individual, organization, task, and technology may be more complex.

Sociotechnical Systems: A Middle Ground?

Sociotechnical systems is an approach that explicitly considers both the people (socio) and the technology (technical) aspects of jobs simultaneously. This explicit recognition of each factor considers each as equally occurring and important within a holistic systems framework. The whole person is considered, and the range of factors that impinge on the human-machine interface is explicitly considered.[25]

The sociotechnical approach has its roots in the study of group dynamics (the study of human behavior in group settings) and ergonomics (the study of how tools and equipment can be adapted to human use). A basic assumption of this approach is that technology cannot be fully understood in an organization apart from its relationship to people. The design of tools, equipment, and even the entire manufacturing process must consider various human aspects, including the strength, durability, range of motion of the human body, and ability to socially interact in the conduct of one's job. Simultaneously, the design must also take into consideration the degree to which humans can adapt to the job requirements through learning, conditioning, and experience.

The sociotechnical approach is not a panacea for increased productivity or worker satisfaction. Earlier in this chapter we briefly mentioned several technology innovations under the heading Advanced Manufacturing Technologies that are beginning to prove fruitful. Tremendous advances in computer and communications technology are also beginning to change the very nature of work. Shoshanna Zuboff suggests that the changes in the workplace that will eventually be realized as the result of computerization are likely to equal those brought by mechanization during the Industrial Revolution.[26] She describes the great transformation that computerization has brought to the paper industry. Computerized paper mills differ greatly from traditional mills. Few workers walk through the hot, smelly plant. Dials, gauges, and levers on machines have been replaced by computerized sensing nodes, and people work at computer terminals in air-conditioned comfort. One of the most difficult adjustments people had to make was believing what the computer screen told them. Initially, they would run out to the factory floor to verify what was on the screen. Gradually, they began to trust the computer and ceased running out to the machine to "see it with their own eyes."

SUMMARY

Technology is a major factor in the contingency model of organizations. (Although each perspective was initially created to totally capture organizational technology, recent views regard core technology, work unit or departmental technology, and work flow interdependence as addressing different aspects of technology.) We present the reader with a three-level framework for understanding technology: Woodward's core technology describes the central technology of the whole organization; Perrow's work unit or departmental technology describes the variety of technologies that may exist in the diverse collection of departments and work units throughout the organization; and Thompson's work flow interdependence describes the technological relationships that exist among work units or departments that need to interact for the organization to accomplish its overall mission. We have also explored recent views on service technologies.

In addition to describing these various levels of technology, we explored the contingency relationships. Technology may be interesting in and of itself; however, it is of particular interest to organizational theorists and managers because of the specific demands it places on the organization. Thus, we examined the structural and managerial requirements that each type of technology presents to the organization. Our goal (and management's goal) should be to understand the need to match or fit organizations to their technology.

Finally, we briefly investigated the person–technology relationship. The current organizational wisdom is that management must simultaneously understand the demands that technology places on the individual and that the individual places on the technology. The sociotechnical approach suggests that ignoring either the technological aspects of the job or the social aspects of the job may result in suboptimal performance for the organization.

Questions for Discussion

1. The *technological imperative* suggests that technology drives structure. What does this mean? Why and how does technology drive structure?
2. Why do you suspect that the subject of technology has come to occupy so much attention in the popular management literature as well as in management practice?

3. In which industry do you see the most dramatic technological advances in the next 10 years? Which characteristics of that industry invite such advances?

4. How can one distinguish between service and manufacturing technologies? Why is it important to make this distinction?

5. "Most large organizations employ not one technology, but many technologies." Do you agree with this statement? If not, why not? If so, what are the implications for organization theory and management practice?

6. Think of a typical online business like Amazon.com. How would you use the organizational technology constructs (core, work unit, and interdependence) to describe the work?

References

1. R. C. Ford, B. R. Armandi, and C. P. Heaton, *Organization Theory: An Integrative Approach* (New York: Harper & Row, 1988).

2. W. Richard Scott, *Organizations: Rational, Natural and Open Systems,* 3rd ed. (Upper Saddle River, NJ: Prentice Hall, 1992).

3. Charles Perrow, *Complex Organizations: A Critical Essay,* 3rd ed. (New York: Random House, 1986).

4. Joan Woodward, *Industrial Organization: Theory and Practice* (London: Oxford University Press, 1965).

5. Joan Woodward, *Management and Technology* (London: Her Majesty's Stationery Office, 1958).

6. Frank M. Hull and Paul D. Collins, "High-Technology Batch Production Systems: Woodward's Missing Type," *Academy of Management Journal* 30 (1987): 788.

7. D. E. Bowen, C. Siehl, and B. Schneider, "A Framework for Analyzing Customer Service Orientations in Manufacturing," *Academy of Management Review* 14 (1989): 75–95.

8. R. B. Chase and D. A. Tansik, "The Customer Contact Model for Organizational Design," *Management Science* 29 (1983): 1037–50.

9. D. Hickson, D. Pugh, and D. C. Pheysey, "Operations Technology and Organizational Structure: An Empirical Reappraisal," *Administrative Science Quarterly* 14 (1969): 378–97.

10. See note 8; G. B. Northcraft and R. Chase, "Managing Service Demand at the Point of Delivery," *Academy of Management Review* 10 (1985): 66–75.

11. A. Nahavandi and E. Aranda, "Restructuring Teams for the Re-Engineered Organization," *Academy of Management Executive* 8, no. 4 (1994): 58–68.

12. J. W. Dean, Jr., S. J. Yoon, and G. I. Susman, "Advanced Manufacturing Technology and Organizational Structure: Empowerment or Subordination," *Organization Science* 3 (1992): 203–29; C. A. Beatty and J. R. M. Gordon, "Advanced Manufacturing Technology: Making It Happen," *Business Quarterly* (Spring 1990): 46–53.

13. See Dean, Yoon, and Susman in note 12.

14. Based on article in note 11.

15. See Dean, Yoon, and Susman in note 12.

16. C. A. Perrow, "A Framework for the Comparative Analysis of Organizations," *American Sociological Review* (April 1967): 194–208.

17. M. Withey, R. L. Daft, and W. C. Cooper, "Measures of Perrow's Work Unit Technology: An Empirical Assessment and a New Scale," *Academy of Management Journal* 25 (1983): 45–63; R. L. Daft and N. Macintosh, "A New Approach to Design and Use of Management Information," *California Management Review* 21 (1978): 82–92.

18. R. Daft, *Organization Theory and Design* (St. Paul, MN: West Publishing, 1992); Christopher Gresov, "Exploring Fit and Misfit in Multiple Contingencies," *Administrative Science Quarterly* 34 (1989): 431–53; Jerald Hage and Michael Aiken, "Routine Technology, Social Structure, and Organizational Goals," *Administrative Science Quarterly* 14 (1969): 368–79; Lawrence G. Hrebiniak, "Job Technologies, Supervision, and Work Group Structure," *Administrative Science Quarterly* 19 (1974): 395–410; Michael Tushman, "Work Characteristics and Subunit Communication Structure: A Contingency Analysis," *Administrative Science Quarterly* 24 (1979): 82–98.

19. James Thompson, *Organizations in Action* (New York: McGraw-Hill, 1967); A. H. Van de Ven, A. L. Delbecq, and R. Koenig, Jr., "Determinants of Coordination Modes Within Organizations," *American Sociological Review* 41 (April 1976): 322–38.

20. Stephanie Losee, "Mr. Cozzette Buys a Computer," *Fortune* (April 18, 1994): 113–16.

21. William Passmore, Carol E. Francis, and Jeffery Haldeman, "Sociotechnical Systems: A North American Reflection on the Empirical Studies of the '70s," *Human Relations* 35 (1982): 179–204; Eric Trist and K. Banforth, "Some Social and Psychological Consequences of the Long Wall

Method of Coal-Getting," *Human Relations* (1951): 3–38.

22. A. B. Shani, "Advanced Manufacturing Systems and Organizational Choice: Sociotechnical Systems Approach," *California Management Review* 34, no. 4 (1992): 91–111.

23. Cynthia D. Fisher, "On the Dubious Wisdom of Expecting Job Satisfaction to Correlate with Performance," *Academy of Management Review* 5 (1980) 607–12.

24. Louis Davis, "The Design of Jobs," *Industrial Relations* (October 1966): 21–45; J. Richard Hackman, "Work Design," from *Motivation and Work Behavior,* 5th ed., ed. by Richard M. Steers and Lyman W. Porter (New York: McGraw-Hill, 1991), 418–44.

25. Kenneth R. Brousseau, "Toward a Dynamic Model of Job-Person Relationships: Findings, Research Questions, and Implications for Work Systems Design," *Academy of Management Review* 8 (1983): 33–45; see Passmore, Francis, and Haldeman in note 21; see Trist and Banforth in note 21; see note 22.

26. Shoshanna Zuboff, *In the Age of the Smart Machine* (New York: Basic Books, 1988).

Technology and Education

Many people might not think of teaching and technology together, but nearly every aspect of the educational process has undergone a technological revolution. The changes are exemplified and perhaps most extreme in higher education where we have everything from computer-based electronic classrooms, to online office hours for professors, to online text delivery, and even entire online universities.

At one level, new work processes have been combined with traditional lecture, discussion, and seminar processes in an attempt to be more efficient and cater to different learning styles. Laptop computers, presentation graphics software, and computer projectors have replaced chalk, blackboards, and overhead projectors. Taken a step further, systems such as Blackboard (a Web-based platform for "course management") allow professors to distribute materials, administer exams, communicate using e-mail, hold online chats or office hours, and post messages. Most textbook publishers now include Web sites for students and professors that include learning aids, support materials, updated information, and Web links. Some of these publisher sites are even linked to Blackboard. There are electronic Web-based publishers such as Atomicdog.com, who along with textbook writers, are developing new e-textbooks (e.g., www.atomicdogpublishing.com) Many databases and search engines are also available to help students and professors find materials relevant to classes. Although teaching and learning have never been restricted to the classroom, the boundaries of the teaching task and the nature of the work itself are changing dramatically.

An additional change in the boundaries results from the electronic classroom and real-time, online course broadcasts. Video courses have been around for many years; however, the scope and sophistication of those courses has evolved. In the late 1960s, it was not uncommon at large state universities for big, popular courses to be broadcast from one classroom to several remote sites on campus. Courses were also videotaped for broadcast at later times. These early uses of broadcast technology did not involve

two-way communication between the broadcast site and the remote location. That is quite a contrast to the current technology that allows for multiple sites to link together and engage in a real-time dialog. For example, a course on the North American Free Trade Agreement could be hosted simultaneously by faculty at universities in the United States, Mexico, and Canada. Experts and students from each location could engage in a dialog. Questions from the U.S. university could be directed to students or faculty at Canadian and Mexican schools. The potential to enrich the learning experience is tremendous.

Finally (at least for now), the online university (e.g., www.online.phoenix.edu) represents the most radical departure in the delivery of university education. The University of Phoenix Online, the largest private university in the United States, is an online university in which the traditional classroom is replaced by the Internet. Lectures and course materials are delivered through the Internet. Students can take classes at any time and anywhere they can link to the Internet. Assignments and tests are conducted online. Students can interact with other students through chat rooms and with professors by e-mail. Clearly, the boundaries of the traditional university have been changed.

But what has also changed is the nature of the work of teaching. The typical professor must be proficient in the use of a whole array of technology, or he or she must have a technical support staff. It is no longer enough to have mastery of the content material and to be a scintillating lecturer. Professors must now know something about broadcast technology. Lecturing in a classroom is a different process from transmitting a course to remote locations and interacting with students and professors at those sites. Professors must have advanced knowledge of computer and Internet technology in order to develop course materials and communicate with students. To efficiently deliver courses in the global, computerized Internet world requires a different set of skills and knowledge (technology, culture, communications, and language) from those the traditional classroom required.

Not all of these changes in pedagogy are regarded as universally appropriate or effective. Some are even rather controversial. Nonetheless, they are changing dramatically the skills, knowledge, information, and tools necessary to teach at the university level. The hope is that these changes in education technology will make education more efficient, effective, and fitting for a wider array of potential students. ■

QUESTIONS FOR DISCUSSION

1. Use one of the models of technology presented in the chapter to describe how the work process of teaching has changed.
2. Have the technology changes for the typical professor made her or his job more or less routine? Why?
3. Given the nature of the technology used at a school like the University of Phoenix Online, would a different structure be required to manage it efficiently compared to your university?

CHAPTER

Organizational Size, Growth, and Life Cycles

7

CASE: A PENNY FOR YOUR THOUGHTS*

JCPenney is one of the largest and oldest retailers in the United States with more than 1,140 stores in all 50 states, Puerto Rico, and Mexico, and 49 Renner department stores in Brazil. Although other venerable retailers who started out as catalog merchants have abandoned that line of business (e.g., Sears), JCPenney still operates its catalog business. In fact, today it is the largest general merchandise catalog merchant. The company also operates nearly 2,600 Eckerd Drugstores in the Sunbelt, southeast, and northeast parts of the United States. Until June of 2001, the company also operated a direct marketing service that sold life, health, accident, disability, and credit insurance in the United States, Canada, Australia, and the United Kingdom. While this portrait of Penney may seem bright, their situation, like that of most of their competitors, is precarious.

JCPenney began business as the Golden Rule Store in Kemmerer, Wyoming, in 1902. From the beginning, Penney has always focused on customers, employees, and the community. Penney tries to provide value to customers by selling quality merchandise at fair prices. Employees are treated as "participants" who should share in the company's good fortune. And the company is committed to the communities it serves. John Cash Penney, the company's founder, emphasized fairness in the treatment of employees and customers and giving back to the community as part of "The Golden Rule" that became "The Penney Way."

Relying on price, value, and house brands, the company carved out a niche in the U.S. retail shopping market as a strong competitor to Sears and other department stores and general merchandise retailers. But like many of its aging rivals, Penney stumbled in the 1970s and 1980s. The company failed to see threats from discount retailers such as Kmart and Wal-Mart or from the specialty retailers like Circuit City, Best Buy, Home Depot, and The Gap, Old Navy, and others. At the same time, the company failed to recognize opportunities outside its traditional markets in the United States. Wal-Mart and Home Depot began ambitious expansion programs in Mexico and South America in the early 1990s, and several competitors had moved strongly into

---

*This case is based on material from an article by Bob Ortega, "Penney Pushes Abroad in Unusually Big Way as It Pursues Growth," *The Wall Street Journal* (February 1, 1994), A1 and A6, and from the JCPenney Web site: www.jcpenney.net, accessed June 25, 2001.

Europe. Penney, according to its own executives, was slow to recognize the vast opportunities outside of its traditional markets.

In the mid-1990s Penny began a program of expanding outside the United States. The company's first stop was Mexico where it embarked on a two-pronged approach: entering into private label agreements to sell its products in stores other than JCPenney outlets and to eventually open its own stores. The North American Free Trade Agreement was a key catalyst to Penney's entering the Mexican market. The company pursued similar strategies in South America, Europe, and Asia—beginning with licensing agreements to enter markets with the intention of opening their own stores. This strategy has been complemented by the company's traditional catalog business, which it continues to operate in several markets throughout the world and by acquisitions. For example, it acquired the Renner department store chain in Brazil that has grown to 49 stores.

Penney's thinking in the mid-1990s was that it must enter untapped markets to grow and compete. However, growth in the global marketplace is fraught with many risks, as Penney managers learned. Currency exchange rate fluctuations, political instabilities, and cultural barriers were relatively new challenges for the company. For example, plans to build hypermarkets in Belgium were met head-on by fierce opposition from what would be zoning boards in this country. These boards, loaded with local merchants, saw Penney as a threat to their existence. The alternative for Penney was small, crowded, expensive downtown locations. Penney also encountered problems with strict labor laws in Europe. As many American firms learn, laying off employees in Europe can be a difficult and expensive proposition. As a result, the company departed from Belgium, taking a $16 million loss.

At the same time that Penney moved into the international market, it began upgrading its images as a "middle-brow" retailer. However, its attempts to move upscale with merchandise from Liz Claiborne Inc., Estee Lauder, Elizabeth Arden, and others ran into difficulty. Those suppliers did not think that the Penney image was a good fit for them. In the late 1990s the company struggled to compete. Its market share continued a downward slide, as was the case for many department store retailers. The stock price sank to new lows and in 2000 traded below $10 per share. As a result, the company initiated a turnaround campaign. The board hired Allen Questrom, former CEO of Federated Department Stores, who had many years of experience in retailing and had led Federated out of bankruptcy. The company returned to its roots, enhancing and promoting its own brands, and supplementing those where possible with compatible national brands. The company has also begun to refocus on fundamentals and its traditional customer base in the United States: working and middle-class families earning $30,000 to $80,000 per year. In June of 2001, the company announced the sale of its direct marketing division that sold insurance. This would provide needed financial resources and allow the company to focus more squarely on the retail business. By the middle of June 2001, the stock had risen to over $25 per share and was viewed by analysts as one of the top turnarounds of the past year.

One thing has remained consistent during all the peaks and troughs that company has gone through, and that is its adherence to its core values of providing value to customers, fair treatment to employees, and commitment to the community.

This case shows a typical pattern of growth, stagnation, and attempts at reinvigoration of an organization. Penney's desires for growth and competitive advantage took it into the realm of global business. Managing the complexities of global business, however, takes considerable resources and expertise. Moreover, the need for coordination and control can be affected by foreign political, economic, and cultural forces. Even though some of Penney's early international ventures were unsuccessful, it has learned from the experiences and has not entirely abandoned international operations. It has been successful in Mexico and Brazil. The company has, however, learned that it needs to stay focused on its core competencies and make certain that it has the knowledge and resources to compete effectively.

In this chapter we explore the related issues of organizational size, growth, and life cycles. The Penney experience, to some extent, is a product of each of these forces. Growth is an ongoing need of organizations. Penney's domestic opportunities were few and competition in its mature industry was intense; thus they turned to the international market. Participation in the international market requires substantial resources that are likely to be more available to a large firm such as Penney. Yet even Penney stumbled. The pattern of growth, stagnation, and attempts to change and refocus are characteristic of the life cycles that many organizations experience. We examine each of these areas in this chapter.

ORGANIZATIONAL SIZE, GROWTH, AND LIFE CYCLES

Perhaps one of the most obvious features of organizations that casual observers recognize is organizational size. This attention to organizational size is furthered by the number of leading business periodicals that list the largest and fastest growing firms across a number of different categories (e.g., the *Business Week* 100, the *Fortune* 500 largest companies, or the *Inc.* 100 largest privately held businesses). The size of business organizations is not the only thing in which the public is interested or about which it is concerned. Concerns about organizational size extend beyond business organizations. In academic institutions we constantly hear arguments about the comparative value of large versus small universities and colleges. Perhaps most notably, politicians, journalists, and the public debate the supposed evils of big government.

By the amount of attention and the volume of the concerns about "bigness," one would think that there is universal agreement as to what constitutes a large or small organization and the relative value of size. That, however, is not the case. As we begin to see, many methods can be used for measuring size. We will also discover that size (and its companion, growth) may be a mixed blessing to an organization. Some organizations may be particularly adept at managing their large size while others may struggle under the weight. Moreover, we will see that in some industries large size is a necessity for economies of scale and competitive purposes.

By tackling the issues of organizational growth and size, we indirectly open the door to the dynamic nature of organizations. In particular, we confront the notions of ***negative entropy***, ***growth***, and ***organizational life cycles***. Inherent in these discussions is the idea that organizations are not static or stagnant entities. They grow, shrink, and otherwise change over time. In this chapter we examine the life cycle perspective on organizational change—that organizations change sequentially over time as a function of their growing size, changing conditions, and organizational maturation. These sequential changes differ from the planned organizational change that is the focus of Chapter 13. Planned organizational change is change that management intentionally undertakes to improve conditions in the organization. The changes associated with shifting life cycles may overlap to some extent with planned organizational change, but that is not necessarily the case. Some life cycle changes are the result of evolutionary changes in the organization, while some of the changes are the result of the organization's attempt to deal with crises that it faces as it progresses through the various stages of the life cycle. We reserve a more detailed discussion of those planned changes for Chapter 13. For this chapter, our focus is on size, growth, and life cycles.

With increasing size comes complexity. As an organization grows, its operations and structure invariably become more difficult to manage. A manager's challenge thus becomes the task of balancing the advantages of size with the demands of complexity.

WHAT IS ORGANIZATIONAL SIZE?

One may think that the definition of organizational size is rather simple and straightforward. However, by now you probably realize that little in organizational life is simple and straightforward. There are in fact many ways to measure the size of an organization. The particular measure that is picked to assess the size of an organization should be related to *why* one is asking about size.

If you are interested in an organization's role in its industry or in the economy in general, you may want to focus on financial and market measures such as the firm's asset value, revenues, or market share. For example, *Fortune* magazine's ranking of the 500 largest global firms is based on firm sales revenue. The listing also includes rankings of profits and asset value. Note in Tables 7-1–7-3 that the largest firms in sales revenue may lag in other categories. General Motors, the largest firm in 1999 in terms of sales, ranks 14th in profits, and 11th in number of employees. General Electric has the largest profits in the world and Sinopec (China's petroleum refiner) employs the largest number of people.

If we are studying a particular industry, we may also want to know the *relative* size of a firm compared with others in the industry. In that case, measures such as *market*

TABLE 7-1   *Fortune* 10 Largest Firms (sales revenue rank) in the World — 1999

Company	Sales $ millions	Profits $ millions	Employees
1. General Motors	176,558	6,002.0 (14)	388,000 (11)
2. Wal-Mart	166,809	5,377.0 (19)	1,140,00 (19)
3. Exxon-Mobil	163,881	8,159.0 (9)	106,00 -
4. Ford Motor	162,558	7,237.0 (12)	364,550 (13)
5. Daimler-Chrysler (Germany)	159,985.7	6,129.0 (13)	466,938 (8)
6. Mitsui (Japan)	118,522.2	320.5 -	38,454 -
7. Mitsubishi (Japan)	117,765	233.7 -	42,050 -
8. Toyota Motors (Japan)	115,670	3,653.4 (39)	214,631 (38)
9. General Electric	111,630	10,717 (1)	340,000 (15)
10. Itochu (Japan)	109,068.9	−792.8 -	5,306 -

Source: www.Fortune.com, accessed June 25, 2001.

TABLE 7-2   *Fortune* Global 500 Most Profitable Firms—1999

Company	Profits $ million	*Fortune* Global 500 Revenue Rank
1. General Electric	10,717	9
2. Citigroup	9,867	18
3. Royal Dutch/Shell Group UK/Netherlands	8,584	11
4. SBC Group	8,159	42
5. Exxon-Mobil	7,910	3

Source: www.Fortune.com, accessed June 25, 2001.

share and *concentration ratios* become important indicators of size. We may want to know the number of firms in the industry, the relative market share of the largest firms, and the rate of market growth. Market measures may also be useful for nonbusiness organizations. For example, universities are often described by the number of students enrolled—a measure of market share. Hospital size may be measured by the number of patients served or the number of patient beds. Hotels and motels typically use the number of rooms as indicator of size.

Another set of market-oriented measures of size addresses the number of markets in which a firm operates. One may be interested in the number (and diversity) of products and markets that a company serves. The number of different markets a firm captures has implications for the way the firm is managed, the way it allocates resources, and its potential for growth. For example, Coca-Cola and Pepsi compete vigorously for entry into new markets in such emerging economies as China, India, eastern Europe, and the former Soviet republics. Much of Coca-Cola's growth in recent years is because it has been better positioned than Pepsi to enter these new markets.[1] In addition to the number of markets in which the firm sells, we may also want to examine the location of various facilities. A company with manufacturing and distribution facilities scattered throughout the world presents different organizational problems and opportunities from those of a firm that concentrates its operations in one location.

Concentration ratios, mentioned briefly in Chapter 2, indicate the degree to which an industry is concentrated in the hands of a few giants or dispersed among many smaller firms. Typically, industries are described according to three-firm or five-firm concentration ratios: the percentage of the market dominated by the top three or five

TABLE 7-3   *Fortune* Global 500 Largest Employers—1999

Company	Number of Employees	*Fortune* Global 500 Revenue Rank
1. Sinopec (China)	1,172,200	58
2. State Power Corp. (China)	1,149,306	83
3. Wal-Mart	1,140,000	2
4. United States Postal Service	905,766	26
5. Industrial & Commercial Bank of China	549,038	208

Source: www.Fortune.com, accessed June 25, 2001.

EXHIBIT 7-1

Sometimes a Large Pizza with Everything Doesn't Amount to Much

We all recognize the major national chains in the pizza industry: Pizza Hut, Domino's, and Little Caesar's are the three largest. All three are large by any standard measure of size. These three companies have battled heatedly over market share in the pizza business and have spent millions of dollars on advertising. Pizza Hut and Little Caesar's have experienced modest increases in market share in recent years. Domino's has lost market share. The top three firms, however, still do not dominate the pizza market. Look at your local *Yellow Pages* under the Pizza heading, and see how many independent small businesses crowd the market. For example, in the Greater Cincinnati, Ohio, *Yellow Pages*, 71 other pizza restaurants crowd the pages. Most of these are small single-location operations or local and regional chains. A few firms, such as Papa John's and Donatos, are attempting to penetrate the national market. This suggests that large size may not be a critical feature in the success of a pizza restaurant, and large size may not confer great competitive advantage at the local level. On the other hand, most of the international expansion in the pizza business is through the efforts of these large firms. Few small operations could afford to effectively compete in the international markets.

firms, respectively. Before the import boom of the 1970s, the Big Three U.S. auto companies (GM, Ford, and Chrysler) accounted for nearly 80 percent of the domestic U.S. auto market. GM alone accounted for over 50 percent of U.S. car sales. This suggests that in the 1970s these were large firms compared to foreign competitors and that domestic firms dominated the industry. By contrast, in 1994 the same three firms account for about 74 percent of the U.S. automobile market. While these firms are still big (note their positions at the top of the *Fortune* 500 list), the industry changes suggest that other large firms have entered the market as challengers and that factors leading to success in the industry may have changed. For example, Toyota's share of the U.S. market has been as high as 8.1 percent in the 1990s.

Financial and market measures are important indicators of size, but they represent only a partial picture. A comparison of the number one and number three firms in the *Fortune* 500 list suggests the importance of exploring other aspects of size. General Electric is only ninth in sales revenues, but ranks first in profits. The U.S. Postal Service is twenty-sixth in revenues and the second largest employer in the United States, but profitability is not even an appropriate measure for this quasi-government agency. Differences in size of labor forces are largely the result of the technology and industry. Labor-intensive businesses such as retailing (e.g., Wal-Mart) require large numbers of workers. Mass production technologies such as automobile manufacturing also require high levels of direct labor and tend to have large workforces. By contrast, firms that use continuous flow technology (e.g., petroleum refining) use relatively less labor. However, you may notice that the largest employer in the world, Sinopec, is a Chinese petroleum refiner. Their reliance on a large labor force may be related to the relatively low cost of labor in China, as well as the scope of the firm.

This section began with the question, What is organizational size? Like so many other issues in organization theory, the answer depends on why one is asking the question. If we are interested in size because we want to design control systems to manage people in the organization—a key objective of applied organizational theory—we would likely focus on the number of people in the organization. Although all of the previously mentioned measures of size are used in the organizational literature, measuring the number of employees is one of the most commonly used.[2] If we are interested in market share, then sales revenues would provide an important basis of comparison. If our interest is in financial performance, then profits would be an important measure of size.

This section has presented some of the most widely used measures of size, all of which are useful in answering the question, How large is an organization? One must be careful to select a measure that is consistent with the reason for asking the question. Because organization theory is most specifically interested in the management, coordination, and organization of people in the organization, people-oriented measures of size are of particular interest.

WHERE ORGANIZATIONS TEND TO GROW FIRST

In order to place the beginning of growth in perspective, let us follow the case of someone who starts an automobile repair shop. The person who begins such a business usually possesses the skills required to work on cars. Although this person may have a wide range of skills and expertise, he or she may not possess the skills necessary to manage the entire operation, particularly as the business begins to prosper and grow.

When repairs are done, they must be properly recorded; invoices must be prepared; taxes must be computed and paid; inventories of parts and supplies must be maintained; and as employees are needed to deal with the increasing demand for repair services, they must be hired, trained, managed, and compensated. These are just a few of the tasks associated with running the business that require different skills from those necessary to repair automobiles.

In the beginning when the business is small, these activities might be simple and undemanding on the owner-mechanic. As the business experiences success and begins to grow, however, these activities require increasing time and greater expertise. With increasing business the owner usually finds that he or she is unable to carry out all these support tasks, as well as perform the repair work itself. With the increasing demands of a larger business, it is now time for some specialization and delegation of responsibilities. Where in the past the owner-mechanic did a little bit of everything, it is now appropriate to bring in someone with specialized bookkeeping or accounting skills to take care of the financial management of the business; then someone to answer the phone and schedule appointments; someone to take people to their workplace while the car is being fixed; someone who specializes in transmission repairs; and so on.

Success can also bring about the need for other specialized support activities including marketing to plan advertising strategies and personnel to hire, train, promote, and, if necessary, fire employees. Growth may also require operational specialization. Mechanics with special expertise on particular models of cars (e.g., domestic, Japanese, German) or specific types of repairs (e.g., transmissions, mufflers, or brakes) may improve the efficiency and effectiveness of the business.

In short, as the business grows, the owner (and the organization) is faced with the need for the specialized knowledge required to support the main operations and the need to coordinate activities among the growing number of people in the organization. Thus, the effects of success and growth can be seen on task differentiation (increasingly narrow specialization) and on increasing emphasis on support functions (e.g., clerical, accounting, and marketing functions) not directly involved in the core operation of automobile repair.[3]

WHY GROW? THE MIXED BLESSING OF LARGE ORGANIZATIONAL SIZE

Organizational researchers have long been intrigued by organizational growth. Debate has focused on such issues as whether growth is inevitable or intentional and on the consequences of growth.[4] Earlier, many organizational theorists thought that growth was inevitable—a consequence of *the open systems view and negative entropy.* One interpretation of the open systems perspective is that organizations must continue to import resources from the environment to grow and change in order to avoid a state of *entropy* (i.e., decline and collapse of the system). More recently, perhaps in the shadow of the widespread downsizing of organizations, theorists have suggested that growth is more likely an intentional action pursued by owners and managers. Clearly, organizations can continue to prosper in the face of downsizing—perhaps because of downsizing. On the other hand, the by-product of growth, large size, has certain undeniable advantages. Thus, if growth is an intentional and advantageous action, it is important to examine the reasons for and consequences of growing larger.

Growth, Competitive Advantage, and Survival

Management may pursue a strategy of growth to give an organization a better competitive position in its industry. Growth can be achieved from strategies directed at expanding production and sales, entering new markets, mergers, acquisitions, and other linkage strategies. As we noted in Chapter 4, these strategies can increase an organization's power to control its environment. Greater power in the environment provides strong motivation to pursue growth.

Large organizations can exert significant power over suppliers, buyers, regulators, and nearly every facet of the environment. While government agencies may have little or no interest in supporting a failing small business, it was politically and economically unwise for the U.S. government to abandon Chrysler (prior to its merger with Daimler-Benz) during its financial troubles in the early 1980s. Chrysler's large size gave it significant clout when dealing with the government and creditors. No politician wanted to be held responsible for the tremendous loss of jobs and the general economic instability that would have resulted if Chrysler had failed. Similarly, large firms, because of their market power, are often able to pressure suppliers for special treatment. Large health insurance companies that provide prescription insurance and the U.S. government through Medicare and Medicaid put pressure on doctors and pharmacies to substitute generic drugs and older, but equally effective, drugs for the latest products of the pharmaceutical companies. For example, insurers may request that doctors substitute older allergy drugs for Claritin or Allegra in order to reduce costs. Because of the size of the insurers and the government, they can exert great pressure on the drug companies. To counteract that pressure, the drug companies resorted to directly advertising to patients in the United States (although several countries forbid this practice). In the appliance business, large chain stores such as Circuit City are able to get manufacturers to make special models of appliances with model numbers and features that are unique to that chain. A customer trying to comparison shop will have difficulty comparing brand-name products because each large chain will have its own model numbers. Thus, products may be similar but not identical. Small firms are unable to obtain such special treatment from suppliers and are thus likely to feel more competitive pressure. Look at how Wal-Mart has driven out the smaller hardware stores, drugstores, and other small businesses in the various towns it has entered. Wal-Mart's size gives it discount buying power with manufacturers and allows it to offer greater variety at a lower cost compared to small family-owned businesses.

The notion that "big is good" has been most clearly illustrated by ***economies of scale***. The economies of scale argument states that the larger the organization is, the more goods or services it can produce at a lower fixed cost per unit—up to a certain point. This idea applies not only to production, but also to marketing, research and development, and sales efforts as well. For example, mergers in the banking and financial services industry (e.g., Chase Manhattan and Chemical Bank; Nations Bank, Boatman's National, and Bank America; and the merger of First Union and Wachovia) have dramatically changed the industry. The combination of assets allows the merged companies to cut the number of branch banks, cut service personnel, and consolidate many operations that are duplicated in the two banks. The result should be more efficient operations. Similarly, Disney's acquisition of Capital Cities/ABC will give the company unparalleled access to network television outlets and cable television. The acquisition, combined with Disney's presence in television and theatrical film production, theme parks, and a variety of related entertainment businesses, makes the company a formidable force in the industry.[5]

An important limitation on the economies of scale argument is that there is a point of diminishing returns at which increasing size no longer brings about lower costs—and may even raise costs of doing business. Recently, questions have been raised about how large an organization needs to be to achieve economies of scale.

It has been suggested that because of technological and environmental changes, smaller organizations can achieve the economies of scale formerly reserved for large organizations. An example can be seen in the steel industry. Through the 1960s the model organization in the steel industry was large with many large mills that operated in a near-continuous fashion. Giants, such as U.S. Steel (now USX) and LTV, dominated the industry. During the 1970s and 1980s, the large traditional U.S. steel mills went through a period of serious decline because of their inability to compete with Japanese and European manufacturers. Many U.S. mills closed. Now because of changing technology in the production of steel, changes in the supply of raw materials (availability of recycled scrap), and changes in market demand, it is economically feasible to run minimills such as Nucor or Birmingham Steel. The old mills used huge coal- or gas-fired blast furnaces. The new mills use electric furnaces and are much smaller—Birmingham had sales of $344 million in 1989 compared to $7.6 billion for LTV. They operate more like small batch technology, producing specialty steel on demand.[6] The economies of scale for steel production have been lowered, and small firms can now compete.

Despite eroding economies of scale in some industries, there are still situations or conditions in which large size gives organizations clear advantages. Theodore Levitt of Harvard University, quoted in *Business Week,* succinctly stated the case for bigness:

> *Some things can only be done by large organizations. Who's going to be the general contractor to go to the moon or build a massive pipeline in Alaska? If you had to commit money for a project that takes five years to complete, like building a plant, would you turn it over to a small company? Some things inherently require scale.*[7]

For example, businesses that require large capital investments (e.g., automobile manufacturing or oil refining), extensive distribution networks (e.g., beer and soft drinks), large marketing budgets (e.g., athletic footware, consumer products), or intensive research and development activities (e.g., pharmaceuticals and semiconductor technology) still benefit from large size.[8] It would be difficult for small organizations to compete with the capital facilities of GM or Exxon-Mobil, the distribution networks of Anheuser-Busch or Coca-Cola, the market power of Nike or Procter & Gamble, or the R&D budgets of Merck or Intel.[9] It has been argued that as large companies learn to be more flexible and to subcontract out more actual manufacturing, they will continue to dominate as an organizational form well into the century.[10] Still, the trends toward downsizing and reengineering suggest that small size may provide organizations with certain advantages in some industries.

WHAT HAPPENS WHEN ORGANIZATION SIZE INCREASES: LIFE CYCLES

Much the way people change as they grow and mature, organizations experience different passages or stages as they move through periods of growth. Organizations emerge, prosper, grow, stagnate, decline, and sometimes die. However, the human maturation process is tightly constrained by human genetics and biology. We all emerge as newborn infants, and those who survive become, by turns, toddlers, children, adolescents, teens, young adults, and onward toward our eventual death. Accidents or disease can stop the progress at any time, but each stage of human development is marked by well-defined physiological, emotional, and cognitive developments.

Organizations differ from humans in a few respects as will become clearer as the stages of development are described in the following sections. One important difference is that not all organizations emerge in the same way. Our auto repair business may be the prototype for birth—an entrepreneurial venture started by some individual with an idea and a willingness to take a risk. However, some businesses emerge as more or less fully formed large operations. For example, Lexmark was a "new" business when it was formally established in 1991. This was not, by any stretch of the imagination, a new entrepreneurial venture such as the auto repair business described earlier. Yet, this spin-off of IBM—Lexmark is the former printer and typewriter division of IBM—is a new company.[11] A spin-off company faces problems of its own that are different from those of an entrepreneurial venture. Most important, it must establish an identity that is separate from its former parent company. But this type of organization does not suffer the same *liability of newness* that plagues start-up new ventures.

A second critical difference between organizations and humans is that organizations can "backtrack." Old, mature organizations can recapture some of their youth through reorganization, downsizing, and other forms of organizational change. Unfortunately we humans are quite limited in the degree to which we can recapture our youth. Certainly, we can change our lifestyle, exercise and change our diets, embark on new careers, and make many other changes, but the fountain of youth is still illusive. Organizations can, albeit not without difficulty, recapture characteristics of earlier phases of the life cycle. We introduce the ideas of organizational change and renewal as strategies for dealing with the stagnation of the elaboration stage. We return to those issues in Chapter 13 in which we discuss organizational change in greater detail.

Generally speaking, the trend is for organizations to become *more formalized* and *more complex* as their size increases and they mature. Recall that formalization refers to the rules, policies, and regulations used to govern people in the organization, and complexity refers to three aspects of division of labor: horizontal division of tasks, vertical (or hierarchical) division of responsibility, and spatial separation of departments or divisions.[12]

Formalization and complexity are the direct result of the need to divide the increased work in the organization and the desire to achieve greater specialization. There comes a point, as described earlier in the auto repair business example, when one person (or even a few people) can no longer do all the jobs that must be done to make the organization work effectively and efficiently. The addition of people usually means that the organization becomes more formal and structured. Rules and policies are implemented to guide people so that their efforts are consistent with the organization's goals, to achieve coordination among people and tasks, and to avoid waste and inefficiency. People's jobs become more narrowly defined and more specialized — horizontal differentiation. Work becomes more segmented. Administrative layers must eventually be added to supervise and coordinate activities across the growing number of departments and to control the behaviors of the increasingly large workforce — vertical differentiation. Early in its existence, the few employees of the auto repair business may have been generalists — each one did a little of everything. As the company grew and prospered, it became increasingly formal and differentiated. The business may eventually add new repair locations throughout its expanding market. This contributes to spatial dispersion. Should management become more ambitious and decide to open facilities in other countries, this would vastly increase the spatial dispersion and resulting complexity.

In the following sections we examine the typical pattern of stages through which an organization passes. See Table 7-4 for a summary of organizational life cycles. Although much has been written on organizational growth and life cycles, the field has not yet reached universal agreement on the stages and processes. We provide an integration of three perspectives.[13]

Organizational Birth

In this stage, primary focus is on the entrepreneur's attempts to invent or develop a new product or service, create a new technology for producing a product or service, or simply to improve upon existing products, services, or technologies. The entrepreneur sees an opportunity — an available niche and the necessary resources — and attempts to fill that niche. Often the organization has not yet been officially created and may not be recognizable as an organization. Henry Mintzberg has used the term *adhocracy* to describe the organization at this stage.[14] The organization is informal; structure is created, implemented, or changed as needed and often in response to rapid growth and expansion — hence, the name adhocracy. The structure that is present tends to be highly organic. Leadership and control are vested in the owner entrepreneur; some theorists refer to this as the ***entrepreneurial stage.***[15] Entrepreneurs spend much of their time in unscheduled meetings and touring facilities.[16] This differs somewhat from the pattern of activities engaged in by managers of more firmly established firms. In fact, the

TABLE 7-4 Organizational Life Cycles		
Stage	**Characteristics**	**Challenge**
1. Birth — entrepreneurial	Rapid growth, liability of newness	Survival
2. Emergent structure — collectivity	Continued growth, balance, stability, and flexibility	Delegation of responsibility, professional management
3. Formal organization — formalization	Slow growth, formal organization, beginning of bureaucracy	Balancing needs for coordination and control with needs for flexibility and responsiveness
4. Dinosaurs and turnarounds — elaboration	Slow growth or stagnation, large and complex; highly bureaucratic	Restructuring; reinventing, downsizing

hands-on leadership and heavy involvement of founders is in many respects a substitute for formal structure. This is the situation that exists in the early years of many organizations. The loose informal atmosphere in the early days at companies like Ben & Jerry's, Apple Computers, and many of the dot.com Internet companies of the 1990s, and the prominent role that the founders played initially are indicative of the entrepreneurial stage.

The critical task that organizations face in this first stage of development is survival. Although statistics on new business failures vary widely, a majority—between 60 percent and 75 percent—of new business ventures fail within the first six years.[17] They fail for many reasons: Lack of adequate capital, inexperience, poorly conceived ideas, and hostile environments are just a few. The meteoric rise and fall of many Internet businesses in the late 1990s and 2000 clearly illustrate the range of problems faced by new firms. The term **liability of newness** has been used to describe the nearly overwhelming odds against success for new businesses.[18] New organizations face the daunting task of establishing legitimacy, creating or discovering new knowledge, learning new roles, training new employees, and developing new markets.[19]

To survive, the organization must bring in management knowledge and business leadership to begin creating some permanence to the organization. Typically, the entrepreneurial founders turn over the day-to-day management of the organization to someone with business and leadership skills. This is not always an easy transition for founders. It is often difficult for founders to place their *baby* in the hands of a virtual stranger. Steve Jobs and Steve Wozniak, cofounders of Apple, experienced just that problem and eventually had to leave the company after outside professional managers arrived. Exhibit 7-2 describes the problems John Walker, founder of the software maker Autodesk, experienced as the company grew and required outside management expertise.

Emergent Structure

The odds against an organization's surviving the entrepreneurial stage are steep. If the venture solves the financial, market, and managerial problems of its birth, it will need two characteristics of a formal organization. Mike Lawrence at Thrifty in Chapter 1 and John Walker at Autodesk each realized that they could no longer do a little bit of everything to run their organizations. As the firm grows, management must provide leadership, establish clear goals, differentiate departments, divide labor, delegate responsibilities, and develop a hierarchy. This stage, referred to as the **collectivity stage**, represents the emergence of structure with some degree of stability.[20] Although the organization is beginning to be formally structured, it still retains an air of informality and flexibility. Members are likely to rely on shared values, commitment, and informal communication means to accomplish the organization's goals.[21] New and fast growing companies like Starbucks, Amazon.com, Southwest Airlines, and many of the surviving dot.com Internet firms place as high a value on shared values and commitment to the organization as they do on technical skills. Southwest Airlines's extensive interviewing process is focused specifically on values and commitment. The company believes that it is easier to train for the desired skills than it is to develop values and commitment. The shared values and commitment make communication easier and increase the likelihood that organizational members will all pursue the same objectives.

The critical tasks that the organization faces at this point are balancing the needs for some formal structure with the needs to continue growing and adapting to external conditions. Additionally, the top management team that has been brought in to run the former entrepreneurial venture must successfully delegate responsibilities to

---

EXHIBIT 7-2

The Strange Case of Autodesk[22]

Autodesk is hardly a household name even though it is among the largest firms in the crowded PC software market. Autodesk's lack of recognition is due in part to its market—inexpensive computer-aided design (CAD) software for engineers. That market lacks the high-consumer visibility of word processing or spreadsheets. However, another reason for Autodesk's obscurity is the behavior of its founder, John Walker.

Walker is a brilliant software engineer who has an uncanny knack for identifying industry trends. Walker's skill in refining and marketing low-cost CAD software for use on PCs is without question. As a result, Autodesk has grown rapidly, with sales increasing tenfold in its second year and increasing by a magnitude of 10 over the next 4 years. Over the years Walker has played many roles in the company, including writing press releases and ad copy, working trade shows, and offering philosophical pronouncements.

However, Autodesk's growth has not been without problems. One person can't do everything, and Walker notes, "I'm an engineer. I'm a programmer. I'm a technologist. I have no interest in running a large U.S. public company."[23]

In 1986, Walker turned over management responsibility to Alvar Green, the firm's chief financial officer. But this relationship was an uneasy and contentious one. The real power in the company still remained with Walker and his programmers. These eccentric freethinkers often quarreled among themselves and severely attacked managers through highly critical electronic mail messages. They held Green, who had essentially no background in computers, in low regard. The proverbial straw that forced Green out of the company was a scathing 44-page letter from Walker that attacked Green's management philosophy and strategic direction of Autodesk.

The critical question Autodesk faced was whether any manager could succeed in reigning in the creative and idiosyncratic nature of Autodesk, which was its source of early success, while preserving the financial stability. Enter Carol Bartz, a former executive with Sun Microsystems. Thus far, Bartz's combination of tough management and experience in the computer industry has helped her and Autodesk succeed. Walker has promised to support her and let her manage. Perhaps Autodesk can now move past the entrepreneurial phase and continue to prosper in the competitive software industry.

---

lower-level employees. Otherwise, decision making and problem solving will quickly overwhelm top management, and lower-level employees will become frustrated or leave the organization.

The Formal Organization

Over time and with ongoing but slower growth, an organization continues its march toward formalized structure and bureaucracy. The slower growth creates an environment of greater stability and predictability than that which existed in previous stages. The *formalization stage* is marked by greater reliance on traditional bureaucratic mechanisms of control: rules are implemented; tasks become more narrowly specialized; domains of responsibility become more clearly articulated; hierarchy and formal communication channels become institutionalized.[24] Mintzberg notes that organizations often expand into new markets or begin to operate in new locations at this stage.[25] To hold the organization together it may be necessary to create a more elaborate and complex divisional structure with divisions representing markets, products, or

---

EXHIBIT 7-3

The Weight (or Wait?) of Bureaucracy

The stories are legendary and, unfortunately, all too common at large bureaucratic organizations. A customer makes an unusual request—a custom product, individualized service, special shipping instructions, or maybe an unusual installation. The technical staff low in the organizational hierarchy knows that the customer's request can be met, but it may require the cooperation of several departments unaccustomed to working together, or it may mean bending a few rules. However, the bureaucratic organization works by rules and standard procedures. Special requests often mean exceptions to rules and standard procedures. When bureaucracies become burdensome, it may take a long time to coordinate across departments or to get permission to bend the rules. Many forms or reports must be completed to document the unusual request. Often requests for variances from standard operating procedures must travel up many layers of the hierarchy. Weeks may pass before action is taken. The customer may get impatient; employees may get frustrated; competitors may intervene; and a sale is lost. This is the weight (or wait) of bureaucracy. Try registering for a course at your university after the registration period ends or try taking a class for which you lack prerequisites. How easily does your school respond to such out-of-the-ordinary requests? Or even try something as simple as ordering a nonstandard item at a fast food restaurant like McDonald's.

Growing organizations must balance the need for control and consistency in their operations—hallmarks of bureaucracies—with the need for flexibility and timely responsiveness. Weber developed the notion of a bureaucracy as an efficient and effective organization, but too much of a good thing may cripple an organization.

---

geographical regions. Managers will spend the majority of their time in scheduled meetings and performing desk work.[26] This contrasts with the earlier emphasis on the unscheduled meetings and touring of facilities of the entrepreneurial stage.

Organizations must balance the greater need for structure at this stage with the continuing need to remain flexible and responsive to changing environmental conditions. Examples abound of companies such as Sears, IBM, and General Motors that created exceedingly complex and bureaucratic structures to deal with a multitude of products, markets, and operations. However, overreliance on complex formal structure and bureaucratic mechanism may result in inefficiencies and unresponsiveness to internal and external conditions. The organization fails to respond in a timely fashion to changing conditions in the environment, and employees become stifled by bureaucracy.

"Dinosaurs" and Turnarounds

The organizational landscape is populated by many well-recognized behemoths. We need only to look at the *Fortune* 500 list of largest firms (www.Fortune.com) for U.S. and international examples. Many of these organizations have reached the point at which bureaucratic controls no longer work. Rules and policies become too numerous and cumbersome. Because of their size and complexity, bureaucratic controls designed for one part or division of the organization often are inappropriate for other parts or divisions. To deal with the complex multidimensional organization, managers write more rules and more complex rules. Thus, the rules themselves inhibit control and communication rather than enhance them. People spend increasing time learning the rules, petitioning for exceptions to the rules, monitoring and enforcing the rules, or devising schemes to skirt the rules.

This stage has been labeled the ***elaboration stage*** by some authors because of the need to elaborate on bureaucratic mechanisms.[27] Often organizations at this point in development utilize teamwork and the self-management by shared values and norms to replace bureaucratic rules and procedures. Managers of organizations at the elaboration stage often speak of reinventing their firm, delayering, downsizing, reengineering, or in other ways restructuring the organization to better fit its environment and its internal conditions.[28] The changes necessary to avoid decline at this phase often also involve changes in goals, people, and technology. Change may include restructuring, reengineering work processes, and rethinking the basic nature of the organization.[29] ***Restructuring*** refers to reconfiguring organizational units or departments. The organization may subdivide into smaller units and rely on control mechanisms other than bureaucracy. At this stage, organizations often institute complex structural solutions including multidivisional structures or matrix structures. In effect, the single large organization is trying to act like many smaller organizations. Changing the structure is typically an important element to maintaining or restoring a thriving organization. One need only look at the top *Fortune* 500 companies to see the prevalence of change efforts among large corporations. General Motors, Ford, IBM, Xerox, General Electric, and Procter & Gamble have each instituted major organizational restructuring to increase efficiency, improve communication, and enhance responsiveness to environmental conditions. And these organizational restructurings do not include the massive changes brought about by mergers and acquisitions at firms such as Bank America, Exxon-Mobil, Daimler-Chrysler, and others. These structures are discussed in greater detail in Chapter 8, but for now it is important to note that structurally defined lines of communication and responsibility reduce some of the need for bureaucracy. ***Reengineering*** refers to reconfiguring the work process. This may involve restructuring, but it also involves altering technology. ***Rethinking*** refers to a reevaluation of the organization: its identity (what the organization is and what it stands for), its purpose (who the organization benefits), its values or philosophy, and its methods or capabilities (how the organization achieves its purpose and identity).[30]

Another important feature of the late-phase organization is the nature of its workforce. Studies on workforces are referred to as ***organizational demography***.[31] Demographers try to characterize an organization's workers with respect to such factors as age, gender, work experience, skills, training, and education level. These average worker characteristics can be used to make judgments about the potential productivity and commitment of workers, and the need for training. Older workers and workers with longer experience at one organization are more likely to stay on the job and be committed to the organization, thus reducing costly turnover. However, younger workers and workers who have been on a specific job for a short period of time may bring into the organization more training and current knowledge. Unfortunately, they may lack the commitment of the older workers and thus may be more likely to leave after only a short stay.

Demographers have also noted that greater uniformity of workers (i.e., greater similarity in age, training, skills, etc.) may aid social interactions in the organization, thus facilitating task coordination and control. The assumption here is that workers who share a similar background are more likely to hold similar values. Having employees who share similar values should improve the communication necessary to coordinate and control tasks and is likely to reduce conflict.

One must be careful in interpreting these findings. This does not necessarily mean that uniformity in the workforce is good and diversity is bad. Although it may be true that uniformity makes communication and coordination easier, too much similarity or uniformity may lead the organization to stifling conformity and a lack of creativity. Demographic diversity may, however, produce conflict. An example of this conflict can be seen in organizations that have downsized by using early retirement. Older workers who remain in the organization often lose their cohort group and are at odds with their new, younger bosses or managers.[32] Younger bosses or managers sometimes fail to respect the experience and history of their older coworkers and subordinates. Much of the miscommunication is based on the different values of the different groups of workers and the stereotypes and biases that sometimes result from those value differences. But even this conflict and miscommunication can be constructive in moving the organization forward. Diversity, conflict, and discussion can help an organization realize new and creative directions.

Organizational Decline

Decline is not a separate stage of organizational development; rather, it is the negative outcome of an organization's failure to effectively resolve the respective crises of each stage. Definitions of decline focus on the ***organization's inability or reduced capacity to cope with its environment.***[33] For example, the organization may be unable to adapt to changing consumer demands, changing markets for raw materials, changing regulatory constraints from government agencies, or changing labor market conditions. Bankruptcy (either Chapter XI reorganization or Chapter VII liquidation of the Federal Bankruptcy Code) are obvious indicators of decline, but organizations may be in distress well before they are legally labeled as such by the bankruptcy designation.[34]

Typically, the failure of an organization is not a swift fall. The failure is likely to be a slow, agonizing retreat, described as a downward spiral[35] that has its own set of characteristic stages.[36] By its very nature, decline is a difficult process to reverse.[37] As a firm's fortunes begin to decline, it may face difficulty attracting a wide array of resources. Investors generally shy away from a declining firm. Employees who are able to leave—sometimes the best and brightest workers—leave for greener pastures. The organization is left with a less skilled and demoralized workforce. Suppliers, fearful about the financial instability of the declining firm, may be reluctant to service the firm. These problems typically plunge the declining organization farther down the road of decline, and thus, the downward spiral continues.

The five stages of decline are characterized by five distinct sets of organizational actions described in Table 7-5. During the first four stages the organization can take corrective actions to reverse the trends. The final stage of decline is the point of no return, and the organization eventually ceases to exist. Chapter 13 provides a more comprehensive examination of strategies that organizations use to avoid or reverse decline.

ADVANTAGES OF SMALL SIZE: A TREND FOR THE FUTURE

As noted earlier in this chapter, organizations pursue growth and the resulting large size for many reasons. Until recently, the prevailing wisdom was that bigger is better. However, the discussion of organizational life cycles and the tendencies of large organizations to become increasingly bureaucratic suggest that there may be some problems associated with managing large organizations: increasing administrative

TABLE 7-5 Stages of Organizational Decline		
Stages	**Decline-Related Actions**	**Attempts to Reverse Decline**
1. Blinded	Failure to detect environmental pressure	Gather information
2. Inaction	Failure to decide on corrective actions; misinterpretation of information; noticeable decline in performance	Prompt action
3. Faulty Action	Faulty decision and/or faulty implementation of solutions; steepening decline	Corrective action
4. Crisis	Given faulty action in a hostile environment: last chance for reversal	Major restructuring or reorganization
	Given a favorable environment: slow decline unless corrective actions are taken	
5. Dissolution	Given a hostile environment: quick demise	No choices
	Given a favorable environment: slow decline	

Source: Adopted from W. Weitzel and E. Jonsson, "Decline in Organizations: A Literature Integration and Extension," *Administrative Science Quarterly* 34 (1989): 97–102.

overhead, increasing red tape, slowness to respond, difficulty coordinating among disparate units of the organization, lack of responsiveness to employee and customer needs, difficulty communicating, and more. Countering the bigger-is-better philosophy is a growing movement toward thinking small.[38]

Thinking small does not necessarily mean that companies want to reduce financial or market performance indicators such as revenues, market share, or profits. Rather, thinking small may mean many different things: downsizing the human resources component of the organization (i.e., doing more with fewer people); splitting an organization into several smaller divisions that run more or less autonomously; selling off unprofitable divisions or divisions that do not mesh well with a firm's core business; or changing the structure and culture of the organization so that people behave more like employees in small businesses.[39] Each of these strategies is briefly described below. We return to each of them periodically throughout the text because they are also related to topics such as organizational change (Chapter 13), design (Chapter 8), control (Chapter 9), and culture (Chapter 10).

Downsizing

One result of the progression through the life cycle model is development of a significant administrative staff whose purpose is to service the organization. The administrative staff becomes responsible for fulfilling the requirements of a bureaucracy—documentation of actions, completion of paperwork, and supervision of workers. Coincidental with the previous trend is the increasingly narrow specialization of jobs.

At the auto repair shop described earlier in the chapter, the founder was originally responsible for all varieties of repairs: brakes, mufflers, transmissions, fuel injection systems, ignition systems, and so forth. As the business grew, it became apparent that some economies and efficiencies could be gained by specialization. Brake and muffler repairs did not require great training or skill to perform, while fuel injection and ignition repairs were quite complex and required significant amounts of skill and training. Specialization ensured that adequately trained (i.e., specialized) employees performed the appropriate tasks. In a perfect world, this sort of specialization may work. Unfortunately, the repair traffic at the shop was unpredictable. Some days all of the repairs were brake and muffler jobs; other days were all fuel injection problems. On any given day some part of the workforce might be idle because there was no demand for their expertise.

One solution to this problem was to downsize—eliminate some of the employees—and broadly train the remaining employees in all facets of auto repair. Additionally, the remaining employees could work in teams with one member more expert in brake and muffler work and the other more expert in fuel injection and ignition work. As a team, their strengths would complement each other and, because they are more broadly trained, they would lack the weaknesses of the former system. Similar sorts of teamwork and broadening of jobs could be accomplished in other areas of the organization.

Under the old system, the shop relied extensively on supervisors to assign work and to ensure its satisfactory completion. The brake and muffler repair division supervisor would assign repair jobs, make certain that employees were making timely progress toward completing the job, and inspect work to ensure that it was properly completed. The supervisor, however, did not perform any actual repairs. After downsizing, the supervisor's job was eliminated. Under the new system, the repair teams were responsible for monitoring and guaranteeing their own work. In addition to downsizing, other changes in design, control, and culture were necessary to make the new system work.

Redesign

As the auto repair business grew larger and as the structure grew more complex and bureaucratic, the firm started losing its personal feel. In the early days, the founder knew all the customers or quickly learned about them. The founder also knew all the employees and considered them friends. But as the company grew, the founder was no longer able to know each customer or employee. As CEO, the founder's responsibilities were also more specialized—setting the strategic direction of the firm and meeting with investors, bankers, and suppliers. In fact, this trend was duplicated throughout the organization's top management. There was a feeling that managers had lost touch with the day-to-day operation of the business. The solution, made possible in part by downsizing, is to redesign the formerly bureaucratic organization into a flatter, more organic organization. The redesigned firm would need fewer layers of hierarchy because people were now supervising their own work, and coordination would be easier because people were working in teams.

Another step in redesigning (and downsizing) may be the elimination of certain divisions. As the auto repair business grew, the management decided to integrate backward in the auto parts distribution business. The belief was that by buying an auto parts wholesale company the auto repair business would have a more dependable and cheaper source of parts. This purchase also involved some diversification. The firm began selling auto parts to other repair shops. Management soon learned that the skills and expertise necessary to run the parts business were different from those necessary to run the auto repair business. After a few years of losing money, management decided to sell the parts business so that they could focus on their core business—auto repair.

Management could have made a different decision concerning the parts business. If they had thought there was still potential to profitably operate the parts business independently of the repair business, they could have spun it off as a separate autonomous unit of the company. It would have had its own management team and it would have operated nearly independently of the repair business. The result of the spin-off would have been that both remaining businesses would have operated more like small companies. These are called ***strategic business units (SBUs)*** to reflect the autonomy of each division. Companies such as General Electric (www.ge.com/business.htm) and Johnson & Johnson (www.johnsonandjohnson.com) operate many of their divisions in this fashion. For example, Johnson & Johnson has over 190 business units around the world that operate as small independent companies.

Virtual Organization

More and more, organizations are subcontracting out much of their work in order to achieve the advantages of smaller size and flexibility. It is possible that an organization could contract out so much of its work that it becomes a shell or umbrella organization. This is sometimes referred to as a ***virtual organization***. We discuss this in more detail in subsequent chapters. Its relevance here is that the virtual organization allows the firm to concentrate on those business areas for which it is best suited and contract with outsiders for everything else.

An example of a virtual organization is Nike. Nike is primarily a product design and marketing company. Nearly all of its products are manufactured by contractor firms in Asia and elsewhere. Nike's core competence is identifying or creating new market niches, designing products, and developing marketing strategies. Their shoes are made by independent firms in the People's Republic of China (PRC) and elsewhere in southeast Asia by independent firms. Its garments are made by contractors around the world. The value to Nike is that the company does not have to invest in capital assets. As production costs change, Nike can find new, lower-cost providers in other parts of the world. This, in fact, has been their strategy. Early in Nike's history, its shoes were made by Japanese and then Korean firms. As the labor costs in each of those countries escalated, Nike abandoned the Japanese and Korean manufacturers for Taiwanese and PRC firms. When Nike decided to enter the golf ball market, they contracted with a firm already in the business to produce the balls rather than spending their assets to build a factory. Nike's strategy differed from that of the golf equipment company Callaway that built its own plant when it entered the golf ball market.

One value of the virtual organization is that a company is able to adapt quickly as conditions change. Many movie production and construction companies are run as virtual organizations. When a company gets a new contract or starts a new project, it is able to contract for the necessary labor, assets, and expertise. For example, under the old studio system in Hollywood, film studios had long-term, multifilm contracts with actors, directors, producers, camera and sound crew, editors, and a host of others. Many film production companies today will contract for this labor for each new project. When the contract or project ends, the firm ends its relationship with the other firms. If the next contract or project calls for similar skills and expertise, the company may return to former providers. If the new job calls for different qualities, the firm has no commitment to the former providers and is free to develop new relationships. In the film industry, the trend toward virtual film production companies has spawned many specialty firms such as Industrial Light and Sound, which specializes in special effects, and Pixar, which specializes in animation.

Coordination and Control: Changing the Culture

Culture, the principal focus of Chapter 10, embodies the basic philosophy and values of an organization. Without going into a detailed discussion of culture, it is important now only to note that large organizations can act much like small ones by changing their culture—their basic values and philosophy. To some extent, changing the culture is an extension of the rethinking mentioned earlier. Instead of valuing largeness, hierarchy, authority, and power, the large firm can shift its values and philosophy to mirror small firms—think small. The dominant values become entrepreneurship, risk taking, closeness to customers, decentralized authority, individual responsibility, and other similar values that contribute to innovativeness and responsiveness.[40] In many industries that are heavily dependent on new technological developments, new information, and new skills or training, the old hierarchical bureaucratic system no longer works. Employees low in the organization may possess more information about how to solve the problems and accomplish the goals of the organization than do top managers. Thus, hierarchical bureaucratic control over employees will not be efficient and effective. Instead, the organization must rely on clearly communicating its basic values and attracting employees who share those values—an approach called ***clan control***.[41]

The transformation from large organization to a small-thinking, small-acting large organization is not easy. None of the changes is easy to accomplish. One need only follow the recent experiences of General Motors and IBM as they try to downsize and redesign to see the great difficulty in reversing years of bureaucratic largeness and excess. It is still difficult for employees to adopt the values and philosophy of small firms. But there are success stories. We have already mentioned GE and Johnson & Johnson as successful large businesses that act much like smaller firms.[42] Other large firms that face the test of acting small include Microsoft, Xerox, and General Motors. In fact, nearly every firm on the *Fortune* 500 is already facing this problem or soon will.

SUMMARY

Organizations, if they are successful, can generally expect to grow and change over time. The growth can be measured by a number of indicators, such as market share, profits, revenues, geographical dispersion, number of products, or number of employees. The appropriateness of a given measure depends upon one's intended purpose. All these measures can play an important role in organization theory; however, our primary emphasis is on the number of people in the organization.

Growth can occur in nearly any portion of the organization, but it commonly appears first in the administrative or support staff. As the organization grows, it tends to become more specialized and differentiated. Technical support staff multiplies, and supervisors are added. Eventually, this leads to an increasingly complex and bureaucratic organization.

Growth and the resulting large size are associated with several competitive advantages. Large size may produce economies of scale, market power, political power, and other desirable outcomes. In some industries, large size is a requirement for a firm to be competitive. However, we also noted that large size is not always a clear advantage. Large size may burden an organization with inflexibility, rigidity, bureaucracy, and lethargy.

We presented a life cycle model that is useful in describing the general trend of development that organizations typically follow. Unlike human models of development, organizations do not necessarily start with the conventional entrepreneurial birth. Some, like spin-offs, start farther along the developmental path. Also, unlike humans, organization can revitalize themselves and return to earlier phases of development through various change efforts.

At any stage of development an organization can slip down the path to decline. Decline itself has a series of unique stages with specific problems and potential solutions. Unfortunately, the organization that repeatedly fails to turn itself around continues the downward spiral of decline.

The concluding section of this chapter suggests a trend toward acting like a small business. Many organizations have undertaken downsizing, restructuring, and culture changes in an attempt to capture the entrepreneurial spirit and management style of small firms.

Questions for Discussion

1. Must all organizations either grow or die? Explain.
2. What would you suggest to be the best measure of a university's growth? Would this be the same if you were to measure the growth of a local high school? Explain.
3. What would you expect to be the big differences between a large and a small organization?
4. For a growing small business, why do you think growth begins in the support areas?
5. How are size and complexity related? Explain.
6. This chapter describes five stages of organizational decline. Using an organization with which you are familiar, see where they fit it now. What actions (if any) can the organization take to prevent its dissolution? Who is responsible for taking these actions?
7. Is growth always good? Why might you as the president or chancellor deliberately try to keep your company or university from growing?
8. What can happen to the culture of a growing organization? A declining one?
9. How is the downsizing trend related to growth? Why is downsizing undertaken? Is it usually permanent?

References

1. Nathaniel C. Nash, "Coke's Great Romanian Adventure," *The New York Times* (February 26, 1995): 10 (Sect. 3).
2. J. D. Ford and J. W. Slocum, Jr., "Size, Technology, Environment and Structure of Organizations," *Academy of Management Review* 2 (1977): 561–75.
3. John Child and Roger Mansfield, "Technology, Size and Organizational Structure," *Sociology* 6 (1972): 369–93.
4. J. Pfeffer and G. R. Salancik, *The External Control of Organizations: A Resource Dependence Perspective* (New York: Harper & Row, 1978): 131–39; W. Richard Scott, *Organizations: Rational, Natural, and Open Systems*, 3rd ed. (Upper Saddle River, NJ: Prentice Hall, 1992): 82–85.
5. M. J. Mandel, "Land of the Giants," *Business Week* (September 11,1995): 34–35; K. Holland, "Wow! That's Some Bank," *Business Week* (September 11, 1995): 36–39.
6. John A. Byrne, "Why a Big Steelmaker Is Mimicking the Minimills," *Business Week* (March 27, 1989): 92.
7. John A. Byrne, "Is Your Company Too Big?" *Business Week* (March 27, 1989): 85–90.
8. Richard A. Melcher, "How Goliaths Can Act Like Davids," *Business Week* (1993 special Enterprise issue): 192–201.
9. Ibid.
10. Bennett Harrison, *Lean and Mean: The Changing Landscape of Corporate Power in the Age of Flexibility* (New York: Basic Books, 1994).
11. Paul B. Carroll, "Culture Shock: Story of an IBM Unit That Split Off Shows Difficulties of Change," *The Wall Street Journal* (July 23, 1992): 1.
12. Richard H. Hall, *Organizations: Structure, Processes, & Outcomes* (Upper Saddle River, NJ: Prentice Hall, 1992).
13. Henry Mintzberg, *The Structuring of Organizations* (Upper Saddle River, NJ: Prentice Hall, 1979);

Robert K. Kazanjian, "Relation of Dominant Problems to Stages of Growth in Technology-Based New Ventures," *Academy of Management Journal* 31 (1988): 257–79; Robert E. Quinn and Kim Cameron, "Organizational Life Cycles and Shifting Criteria of Effectiveness: Some Preliminary Evidence," *Management Science* 29 (1983): 33–51; K. S. Cameron and D. A. Whetten, "Models of the Organizational Life Cycle: Applications to Higher Education," *Review of Higher Education* 6 (1983): 269–99.

14. See Mintzberg in note 13.

15. See Quinn and Cameron in note 13.

16. S. Dunphy, "An Ethnographic Study Comparing the Nature of Managerial Work to the Nature of Entrepreneurial Work," *Journal of Business & Entrepreneurship* 8, no. 2 (1993): 37–44.

17. Justin G. Longnecker, Carlos W. Moore, and J. William Petty, *Small Business Management: An Entrepreneurial Emphasis* (Cincinnati, OH: South Western Publishing, 1994).

18. Arthur L. Stinchcombe, "Social Structure and Organizations," in *Handbook of Organizations*, James G. March, ed. (Chicago: Rand McNally, 1965): 142–93.

19. See Scott in note 4.

20. See Quinn and Cameron in note 13.

21. R. L. Daft, *Organization Theory and Design*, 4th ed. (St. Paul, MN: West Publishing, 1992): 164.

22. G. P. Zachary, "Theocracy of Hackers' Rules Autodesk Inc., a Strangely Run Firm," *The Wall Street Journal* (May 28, 1992): A1.

23. Ibid, p. 1.

24. See Quinn and Cameron in note 13.

25. See Mintzberg in note 13.

26. See note 16.

27. See Quinn and Cameron in note 13.

28. Thomas A. Stewart, "Re-Engineering: The Hot New Managing Tool," *Fortune* 128, no. 4 (August 23, 1993): 40–48; Michael Hammer and James Champy, *Reengineering the Corporation: A Manifesto for Business Revolution* (New York: Harper Business, 1993); Noel M. Tichy, "Revolutionize Your Company," *Fortune* 128, no. 15 (1993): 114–18.

29. R. W. Keidel, "Rethinking Organizational Design," *Academy of Management Executive* 8, no. 4, (1994): 12–28.

30. See note 29.

31. R. Ely, "The Power of Demography: Women's Social Constructions of Gender Identity at Work," *Academy of Management Journal* 38 (1995): 589–634; A. Lomi, "The Population Ecology of Organizational Founding: Location, Dependence, and Unobserved Heterogeneity," *Administrative Science Quarterly* 40 (1995): 111–44.

32. Sue Shellenbarger and Carol Hymowitz, "Over the Hill: As Population Ages, Older Workers Clash with Younger Bosses," *The Wall Street Journal* (June 13, 1994): A1–A8.

33. W. Weitzel and E. Jonsson, "Decline in Organizations: A Literature Integration and Extension," *Administrative Science Quarterly* 34 (1989): 91–109.

34. L. M. Gales and I. F. Kesner, "An Analysis of Board of Director Size and Composition in Bankrupt Organizations," *Journal of Business Research* 30 (1994): 271–82.

35. D. C. Hambrick and R. A. D'Aveni, "Large Corporate Failures as Downward Spirals," *Administrative Science Quarterly* 33 (1988): 1–23.

36. See note 33; D. A. Whetten, "Organizational Growth and Decline Processes," *Annual Review of Sociology* 13 (1987): 335–58.

37. R. I. Sutton and A. L. Callahan, "The Stigma of Bankruptcy: Spoiled Organizational Image and Its Management," *Academy of Management Journal* 30 (1987): 405–36; see note 35.

38. E. F. Schumacher, *Small Is Beautiful; Economics as if People Mattered* (New York: Harper & Row, 1973).

39. See note 8.

40. See note 8.

41. William G. Ouchi, "Markets, Bureaucracies and Clans," *Administrative Science Quarterly* 25 (1980): 129–41.

42. See note 8.

*Fading Memories**

It's the dream of nearly every entrepreneur: Come up with a simple idea that quickly captures the market. Legends of successful entrepreneurs are filled with rags-to-riches stories of individuals who plunked down their life savings to start a business out of a basement, garage, or storefront and went on to great success. Names such as Ford Motor Company, Apple Computers, and Performance Cycle are examples of such entrepreneurial ventures that grew from humble beginnings to later catch fire and win significant market share in their respective markets. Harvey Harris had similar dreams for his company, Grandmother Calendar Co.

The idea behind Grandmother Calendar was quite simple. Harris marketed elaborately customized calendars that featured personalized artwork and photographs supplied by the customer. Calendars could include detailed collages, birth certificates, traffic tickets, and other official documents that were scanned into the finished product. Special dates in the body of the calendar could also be personalized. Harris offered his high quality product at a starting price of $20, about $5 less than the closest competitive product, although special features added to the price.

Greeting card retailers, gift shops, drugstores, and even discounters such as Kmart sold the Grandmother Calendar mail order kit to hopeful customers. The kit included instructions for the calendar layout and for designation of special dates. Customers would complete the instructions, enclose photos, drawings, or documents they wanted included on the calendar and send these materials to the Grandmother Calendar headquarters in Oklahoma City.

When a calendar order was received at the Grandmother Calendar plant, photos, artwork, and documents were scanned into a computer, arranged, and edited to meet the customer's request. At the same time, information about special dates, such as anniversaries and birthdays, was entered into the computer. To produce the calendar, graphic images and information were electronically merged. The calendar was then printed, spiral-bound, and mailed to the customer.

The idea was really quite simple, and the technology was not terribly difficult to manage . . . at least under normal circumstances it was not too difficult. The problem was too much success, too fast. One retailer, Paragon Gifts, sold nearly 25,000 kits in six months. This was three times more sales than Harris had anticipated. As the Christmas holiday season approached, orders flooded in faster than they could be processed. To deal with the influx of orders, Harris added some new state-of-the-art equipment and he pushed employees to speed up production, but it was a case of too little, too late. At the height of the Christmas season, the 300-calendar-per-day production lagged far behind the incoming order rate of 1,000 per day. Thousands of orders went unfilled.

The press of orders spelled the beginning of a disaster. Equipment started to break down from overuse and workers began to make mistakes. The quality of those calendars that did get made suffered from poor color reproduction and spelling errors. Retailers selling the calendar kits were unaware of problems and kept selling to unsuspecting customers. This further fueled the backlog. Keep in mind the time-sensitive nature of this market and product. Calendars, especially customized ones like these, are gift items and keyed to the holiday season and the new year. Sales lost in December are not likely to be made up in January, and dissatisfied customers are unlikely to be patient.

By December, it was clear to Harris that he had serious problems. The company wrote to customers trying to reassure them that they would get their calendars but not in time for Christmas. Late in December, paychecks to many of Grandmother's employees bounced. Finally, in early January, the company shut down entirely—not from a lack of customers, but from an inability to meet customer demand.

In the aftermath, retailers who sold the Grandmother Calendar packets were trying to make certain that photos, documents, and other materials were returned to customers. Most customers received refunds of the base charge of $20, but charges over $20 paid for special features were not refunded. Creditors and suppliers are sifting through Grandmother's remains for anything of value to cover their claims. The state attorney general's office is also investigating Grandmother's failure.

What went wrong at the Grandmother Calendar Co.? At some level, Harris was a victim of his own success. He clearly had a good idea, a good product (at least before the rush of orders came in), and a good market niche. However, Harris lacked the management and organizational skills necessary to manage this venture. He did not plan for this level of success. Grandmother was undercapitalized. The company lacked the resources to add enough equipment and enough people to serve the avalanche of orders. Harris admitted, "I made mistakes . . . I'm not an attorney. I'm not an accountant . . . (I) did not track receivables, payables, and funding. I should have made, well, better decisions." One former employee discussing the demise of Grandmother alluded to the fact that it was just a small company. ■

*Based on an article by Louise Lee, "Picture This! A Firm Failing from Too Much Success," *The Wall Street Journal* (March 17, 1995): B1, B6.

QUESTIONS FOR DISCUSSION

1. At what life cycle stage was the Grandmother Calendar Co.? What evidence suggests that the company was at that stage?
2. Could Harris have avoided the eventual failure of his company? What should he have done to avoid failure?
3. Do you agree with the former employee's judgment that the company's problems were the result of its small size? Why? Why not?

PART III

Managing the Organizational Context

We began this text by introducing the contingency framework—no one method of organizing or managing is inherently superior. Rather, the best way to organize or manage depends on the context an organization confronts. In Part Two, we identified in considerable detail the nature of the organizational context: the goals, environment, technology, and size of an organization. These conditions are likely to vary considerably from one organization to another—even for different organizations within a single industry.

Part Three explores the ways in which organizations can respond to these diverse conditions. In Chapter 8, we examine organizational design as a strategic response to the organizational context. In that chapter, we first focus attention on how people are grouped together in departments or divisions. Functional groups place people together based on the nature of the tasks they perform. For example, people performing marketing-related tasks are grouped into a marketing department. An alternative way to group is on the basis of output. We explore three distinct types of output groupings: products or service, markets or customers, and geography. Functional and output grouping can be combined in designs such as the matrix and hybrid forms. Each type of design has specific strengths and weaknesses that match particular contextual conditions.

Chapter 8 also introduces recent trends in design. Many organizations are adopting looser affiliations, such as the virtual organization and the federal organization. In addition, several distinctly national organizational forms have emerged. We present two of these from Asia: the Japanese keiretsu and the Korean chaebol.

Design is not the only mechanism for managing the context of an organization. Chapter 9 introduces the concept of governance as it has developed in the organizational economics field. Two theoretical frameworks, agency theory and transaction cost economics, deal with the ways owners and managers of firms handle the critical problems of governing. Agency theory addresses the methods owners use to manage the contractual relationship with their managers. Transaction cost economics delves into the problem of managing transactions for goods and services both within the firm's boundaries and across them.

The governance mechanisms described in Chapter 9 are a stepping-stone to the broader concept of organizational culture. Culture, discussed in Chapter 10, is the collection of attributes that make organizations distinct and different. Think, for example, of organizations such as Kmart and Wal-Mart. These two retailing giants are in the same industry, yet they are very different. Part of what distinguishes them is the different values, norms, and beliefs of the key people in these two companies. Culture plays a crucial role in an organization's response to its context.

CHAPTER

Patterns of Strategic Organizational Design

8

CASE: AGENCY.COM*

Agency.com was founded in 1995 at the start of the Internet revolution as an Internet Web building company by Chan Suh, CEO. As of 2001, it had over 1,000 employees in eight countries. Forty percent of the company is owned by Omnicom Group, an international holding company.

The firm's mission is "to empower people and organizations to gain competitive advantage by creating powerful interactive relationships." Their vision is "to be a global leader in understanding, inventing and delivering on the promise of the future." To accomplish this mission and vision, the firm provides interactive strategy, branding, technology, and marketing services that help firms grow their interactive business, empower knowledge sharing, and drive marketing initiatives. Their services cover all digital channels—Web, mobile, and interactive television.

The firm's specific services include the following:

Brand strategy and extension

Customer response management

E-commerce and transaction systems

Enterprise Portals and extranets

Interactive marketing and advertising

Interactive television and broadband

M-business

Multiple digital channels

Strategic consulting

Technology assessment and implementation

The firm's client list includes Coca-Cola, British Airways, Compaq, Nike, Sprint, Texaco, and other major *Fortune* 500 companies.

The firm's organizational structure is depicted in Figure 8-1. The structure is rather lean, with few upper-level managers. Note that a regional or geographic basis for differentiation is used to reflect the location of major client groups. As in many Internet companies, the creative nature of the business is reflected in the job titles of several of the top-level managers.

The structure is nonpyramidal. It reflects a goal of the company—to have a flexible structure that is able to focus quickly on changing customer needs. Because technology changes rapidly in this industry and the industry is still in the embryonic growth stage, the firm needs a structure that is quickly adaptable. The firm emphasizes that its structure is the antithesis of bureaucracy. Lower-level employees are heavily empowered to

---

*Material for this case is taken from the www.agency.com Web site accesssed June 2001 and an interview, June 4, 2001, with Craig Mathe, project director with the company.

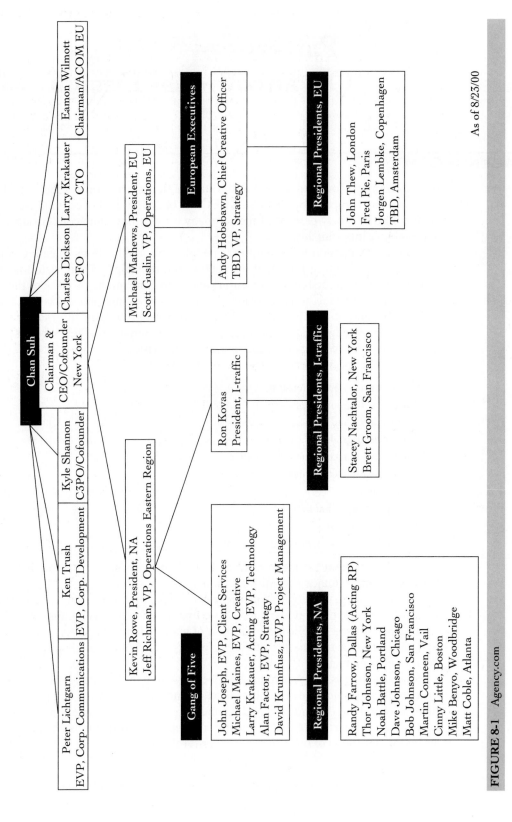

FIGURE 8-1 Agency.com

As of 8/23/00

Chan Suh
Chairman & CEO/Cofounder
New York

| Peter Lichtgarn EVP, Corp. Communications | Ken Trush EVP, Corp. Development | Kyle Shannon C3PO/Cofounder | Charles Dickson CFO | Larry Krakauer CTO | Eamon Wilmott Chairman/ACOM EU |

Kevin Rowe, President, NA
Jeff Richman, VP, Operations Eastern Region

Michael Mathews, President, EU
Scott Guslin, VP, Operations, EU

Ron Kovas
President, I-traffic

Gang of Five

John Joseph, EVP, Client Services
Michael Maines, EVP, Creative
Larry Krakauer, Acting EVP, Technology
Alan Factor, EVP, Strategy
David Krunnfusz, EVP, Project Management

European Executives

Andy Hobsbawn, Chief Creative Officer
TBD, VP, Strategy

Regional Presidents, NA

Randy Farrow, Dallas (Acting RP)
Thor Johnson, New York
Noah Battle, Portland
Dave Johnson, Chicago
Bob Johnson, San Francisco
Martin Conneen, Vail
Cinny Little, Boston
Mike Benyo, Woodbridge
Matt Coble, Atlanta

Regional Presidents, I-traffic

Stacey Nachtalor, New York
Brett Groom, San Francisco

Regional Presidents, EU

John Thew, London
Fred Pie, Paris
Jorgen Lembke, Copenhagen
TBD, Amsterdam

194

make decisions and respond to customer needs quickly without having to get clearance "from the top." People are rewarded strictly on performance and not seniority. The team concept is heavily emphasized. People are hired for their creativity, adaptability, and teamwork skills.

> Agency.com exemplifies a relatively new trend in organizational structure — the flatter, responsive structure instead of the traditional pyramid structure so often used in companies.

When one thinks of the design of organizations in U.S. industry, the pyramid comes to mind. Like the pyramids in Egypt, they have a broad base that tapers to a sharp point at the top. That is, most members are at the bottom of the organization, "governed" by a decreasing number of managers as one shifts focus toward the top. The essence of such a design is centralization with a few managers making most, if not all, the company's critical decisions.

These designs stress control, place little emphasis on subordinate development, and emphasize effectiveness over empowerment. They reflect the values that U.S. managers have traditionally placed high on their decision agenda.

But there is a move today to change the design of organizations—a move aimed at stressing opposite values. Decentralization, involvement, and personnel development are believed to be better means to achieve the essential aim of all organizations— coordination and customer satisfaction. Although there are perhaps many driving forces for this movement, cultural change has produced a workforce that almost demands involvement in the life of the organization.

This new organization form is horizontal rather than vertical in its basic shape. It reflects the elimination of layers of management and the granting of more responsibility to employees. The focus is on the customer as opposed to loyalty to a particular functional grouping.

Organizing around process stresses that attention be given to customer satisfaction and product development from a holistic perspective rather than a focus on individual functions, such as product planning and statistical control. It is, in short, a type of organization-culture revolution, a revolution that is unsettling, to say the least, for traditional managers schooled in the culture of the pyramid organization.

The move to the horizontal organization has so far been concentrated at the lower levels where teams of employees work together on the entire process needed to get the product to the customer. In other words, the customer is the overarching focus for the teams' efforts. The benefits attained from this beginning, however, are expected to find their way to the top.

The few managers who traditionally guided the pyramid will perhaps be replaced by teams of managers who will operate much like employees in the lower ranks. This means that decision making will be the responsibility of a group of managers, all of whom are focused on the customers' needs and expectations of the product or service the organization provides.

This horizontal organization form seems well adapted to both small and large organizations as well as old and new companies. For example, Astra/Merck Group, a new stand-alone company set up to market anti-ulcer and high blood pressure drugs licensed from Sweden's Astra, is built around a half dozen market-oriented processes instead of following a more traditional functional design. Modicon, Inc., a company that makes automation control equipment, sees product development as a process that involves a team of 15 managers rather than considering it as an engineering function.

Eastman Chemical Company, a spin-off of Eastman Kodak Company, is built around self-directed work teams instead of the senior vice presidents who would otherwise be in charge. Kodak sees this as the most dramatic change in the 70 years it has been in business. The company even views its organization chart as an "organization pizza," with a lot of "pepperoni" sitting on it in place of the usual boxes and lines of the pyramidal design. American Telephone & Telegraph, DuPont, General Electric, Motorola, and Xerox have also employed the horizontal structure, to some degree at least.

Basically built on managing laterally rather than vertically, the horizontal structure is based on seven principles or concepts:

1. Organize around process, not task.
2. Flatten the hierarchy.
3. Use teams to manage everything.
4. Let customers drive performance.
5. Reward team performance.
6. Maximize supplier–customer contact.
7. Inform and train all employees.

Note, however, that companies have not abandoned the pyramid altogether. There still appears to be a need for specialists, especially in finance and in manufacturing as well. Even if the horizontal form is beginning to find its way into corporate organization structure, it will probably not completely replace the vertical, functional structure, at least in the foreseeable future. The firm that will finally evolve will probably be a hybrid in which managers manage process and teamwork.

In any event, both theorists and practitioners are beginning to craft what will likely replace the "ancient pyramids" of organization design. For the student of organization theory, this is a move well worth watching.

This introduction brings attention to a developing movement in the design of organizations that could revolutionize not only the way structures are built but also the ways of thinking and working in them. This chapter describes some of these developments with which today's student should be familiar. Keep these examples in mind as you study the chapter material and see whether they change the way you think about organizations and how they might be shaped to better suit their reason for existence—customer satisfaction.

PATTERNS OF STRATEGIC ORGANIZATIONAL DESIGN

In Chapter 2, we introduced the subjects of structure and design. The focus was primarily on structural differentiation and integration—that is, how finely or broadly to segment tasks and how to coordinate those same tasks. We discussed how structural characteristics tend to cluster into identifiable organizational prototypes: the mechanistic organization (machine bureaucracy) and the organic organization. In this chapter, our focus shifts to the related issue of design configuration—how tasks and people are grouped together in the organization. We examine specific organizational forms.

In our strategic systems approach to organizations, organizational design is part of the transformation process in the input-output analysis. Proper design should facilitate the acquisition and use of inputs, management of the transformation process (i.e., the technology), and disposal of outputs. In short, good design should lead to organizational efficiency and effectiveness. Although good design may not be sufficient to provide for efficiency and effectiveness, it is clearly a key factor.

Essentially, design involves strategic decisions about the grouping of individuals or tasks into work units, departments, or divisions of the organization. An organization faces a basic dilemma with regard to design. The very reason an organization exists is so that people working together can accomplish more than people working individually. Synergy is achieved through specialization (differentiation) so that people become proficient in specific areas. That is how differentiation is reflected in the organization's design. But the more the organization differentiates, the more difficulty it has in coordinating effort. In Chapter 2, we discussed mechanisms that can bring about some integration. The design of the organization can also play a critical role in integration. In making decisions about the appropriate design for an organization, top management seeks to find the configuration that permits the optimal mix of differentiation and integration while allowing the organization to adapt to its surroundings.

Like the world in which organizations are embedded, the tasks and decisions concerning appropriate designs are becoming complex. As we have noted repeatedly, the advent of inexpensive, high-speed computing and telecommunications technology has radically changed the world of organizations. Not only have these technologies made more information available cheaper and faster, but they have also, in effect, made the world smaller. These technologies have had dramatic impact on the emergence of new organizational designs that make use of the technologies as coordination mechanisms.

We begin by discussing bases for grouping work and designing organizations. These bases for grouping lead to two basic design configurations—the functional and product or market organizations—and to two combination design configurations—the hybrid and the matrix organizations. We conclude by examining recent design trends brought about by the joint pressures of information technologies and globalization.

BASES FOR ORGANIZATION DESIGN

The essential question one asks when making decisions about grouping workers and forming departments or divisions is this: Should workers be grouped together based on what they do (tasks and equipment) or based on the outcomes they hope to achieve (products, services, or markets)? There are specific advantages and disadvantages to both configurations. Grouping workers together according to the nature of the work (tasks and equipment) is called functional grouping; grouping according to outcomes is called product or market grouping. These two principles for grouping result in two fundamentally different designs.

Functional Grouping

In functional grouping, work done by the organization is classified into the primary functional components that need to be carried out for the organization to operate. People are grouped together on the basis of the functions they perform and the equipment they use. Functions such as production, marketing, finance, accounting, personnel, or human resources management often serve as broad categories for differentiation.

The following examples show different ways functional grouping can be achieved. In a personnel or human resources division, positions could be further subdivided into units such as compensation, benefits, recruiting, and training. Each of these subfunctions requires specialized knowledge, skills, and information to accomplish the personnel or human resources function. Workers in each subunit of the personnel or human resources department perform essentially the same or similar tasks using the same skills, knowledge, and equipment. Similarly, in a manufacturing setting, workers who use the same equipment or skills may be grouped together. For example, workers in an auto plant may be grouped into units such as assemblers, painting technicians, and welders. These groupings are based both on the functional skills the workers possess (e.g., knowledge of welding) and the equipment they use (e.g., welding equipment).

The general principle of functional grouping is that workers in each unit would be performing the same or similar tasks or activities, using the same equipment, or possessing the same sets of skills and knowledge. No single department bears full responsibility for the organization's outputs. Figure 8-2 illustrates a functional manufacturing organization.

The functional organization has a characteristic set of strengths or advantages. First, by grouping people together on the basis of functions, skills, or knowledge an organization is likely to develop a high degree of functional expertise, and individual department members will be able to develop highly refined functional skills. Moreover, communication within a functional department is facilitated by a common knowledge and language base. Functional areas often develop jargon that aids communication among experts but may also keep outsiders in the dark. For example, the personnel or human resources department would be able to enhance its collective human resources skills through the synergies of working together. Employees in the department could develop specific human resources expertise (e.g., compensation) while being exposed to the full range of human resources functions. This aspect of functional grouping is also important in career development as it enables newly hired employees to more easily develop functional skills and training. The career path from new human resources assistant to human resources vice president is clearly defined. Second, functional departments are more likely than other types of groupings to enhance economies of scale. By grouping together people who share information, skills, equipment, and facilities, the organization is able to carry out its assigned function more efficiently. When existing departments, such as product and market, are combined, the result is often redundant functions and facilities that reduce economies of scale. When the overlap is eliminated, however, the resulting functional expertise and economies of scale can lead to a highly efficient department with high levels of technical competence.

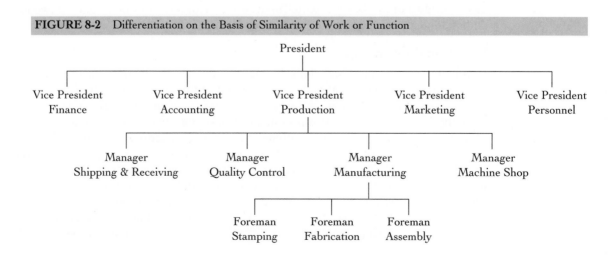

FIGURE 8-2   Differentiation on the Basis of Similarity of Work or Function

Certain weaknesses are also associated with the functional design and, as we see shortly, limit its usefulness to specific conditions. First among these weaknesses is the difficulty of coordinating across functional lines. All the factors that make communication within the functional areas easier—common tasks, knowledge, language, and training—are likely to inhibit communication between different functional departments. Cross-functional coordination is critical because the overall tasks and goals of the organization are rarely functional. Thus, a second weakness of the functional design is that it is likely to produce a functional view of the organization. A classic study of managers' perceptions of the organization suggested that managers viewed as most important the functions of their specific departments.[1] The problem is that organizational goals and objectives are rarely stated in terms of functions. For example, the goals of an automobile manufacturer are likely to be to produce and sell the best cars, not to have the best human resources department. Achievement of the company's goal requires extensive cross-functional coordination, which may be difficult when functional departments think narrowly.

Poor coordination and the narrow, functional view of the organization may lead to further difficulties in managing the company. Because many of the problems and decisions the organization faces involve several different functional areas, decision making must be pushed up the organizational hierarchy to top management. This results in slower decision making. Information must wind its way up through each functional department to the point where managers have an overview of the organization. In addition to slowing decision making, this may overload top managers with trivial decisions. One final weakness of the functional form is that it is likely to inhibit innovation. New products, services, and processes typically require an integrative, cross-functional view of the organization especially when they must be developed quickly, as is usually the case these days. Functional grouping makes integrative, cross-functional thinking difficult.

These combined strengths and weaknesses limit the applicability of the functional organization. This design is best suited for small- or medium-size organizations with a single product or a few closely related products. This structure helps functional departments focus on a common overall organizational goal. Because of the difficulties with decision making, functional organizations are best for low-uncertainty (stable and simple) environments, those with low-interdependence, routine technologies.

Some of these limitations of functional organizations can be overcome through structural mechanisms described in Chapter 2. Cross-functional coordination can be attained through horizontal linking techniques such as liaison roles, integrator roles, and horizontal information systems. Cross-functional teams or task forces can also be used on an ad hoc basis to deal with cross-functional coordination. Heavy reliance on these means of coordination may signal the need to restructure the organization.

Output Grouping: Products, Markets, and Geography

Grouping can also be based on outputs. Three types of output groupings are products (or services) produced, markets served, or geographical regions served.* Differentiation is based on output, and the resulting designs are characterized by departments

---

*Geographical groupings could also be used in functional organizations, especially if the availability of specific skills or facilities were limited to specific locations. For example, inexpensive or skilled labor may be more readily available in an identifiable country or region. Thus, production facilities would be located in those regions. Rail lines or deep water ports may be necessary for the location of certain shipping facilities. Still, however, the primary rationale for grouping is function.

or divisions dedicated to specific products, services, customer groups, or geographic regions of customers. Departments or divisions are essentially semiautonomous organizations with people and positions representing all functional areas. Figure 8-3 illustrates each of the three output-based designs.

In large, multiproduct, geographically dispersed, multimarket organizations, grouping by output has become increasingly common. The classic example of product-based grouping was General Motors with its Chevrolet, Pontiac, Oldsmobile, Buick, Cadillac, and GMC Truck and Coach divisions. Each product group was essentially a self-contained division. Chevrolet, for example, had its own design, production, marketing, human resources, and accounting departments. Procter & Gamble, the consumer products giant, also used a product-based design for many years. Divisions included Tide, Crest, and Oil of Olay. Many companies involved in defense contracting or other areas of government contracting have specific divisions assigned to different markets. Some computer hardware and software companies have specific federal government divisions. Johnson & Johnson is an example of an organization that uses both product and market differentiation simultaneously. Different divisions produce and sell baby products, over-the-counter medicines, surgical supplies, and other of the company's myriad products. These divisions, which are semiautonomous units, represent both different products and different groups of customers. Increasingly, as businesses become more global in their reach, they are adopting divisional designs based on geography. Ford Motor Company, which in the past was mainly a product design (Ford, Lincoln-Mercury, Ford Tractor, Ford Aerospace), is moving to a geographical design with North American, European, South American, and Asian divisions.

The primary advantage of these output-oriented designs is that they focus attention and effort on the specific requirements of the product and customers. The departments or divisions are multifunctional groups that work together, allowing business functions to more easily and effectively coordinate. Thus, they are a good match for nonroutine, high-interdependence technologies. Because the design is more product- and customer-oriented, adaptability to new product designs, product requirements, customer demands, or market conditions is easier than in a functionally designed organization with more than a single product, market, or region. Because these divisions are largely self-contained, decision making can be decentralized, relieving the burden on top management and aiding in responsiveness to changing environmental conditions. Thus, the design is particularly well suited for uncertain environments. These designs also provide a method for placing responsibility for efficiency and profitability at the divisional level. If a product, market, or region is underperforming, identifying and tracing the responsibility is easier.

Although there are numerous advantages to the product, market, and geographical forms of output designs, there are also disadvantages. Although functional designs may create functionally biased views of the organization, output-based designs can create product, market, or geographic biases. This can, for example, lead to conflict between product groups. Some internal competition may be useful in forcing divisions to become more efficient; however, extensive competition may jeopardize the viability of the entire company. Additionally, dividing a company into many divisional units may reduce the potential for economies of scale. A product, market, or geographical organization typically must duplicate many functions and facilities to meet each division's needs. This lack of economies of scale can be reflected in such things as inefficient use of facilities and suboptimal use of human resources. Because each division may need marketing expertise, for example, it is likely that no single marketing department will grow large enough to develop the economies of scale and level of aggregate

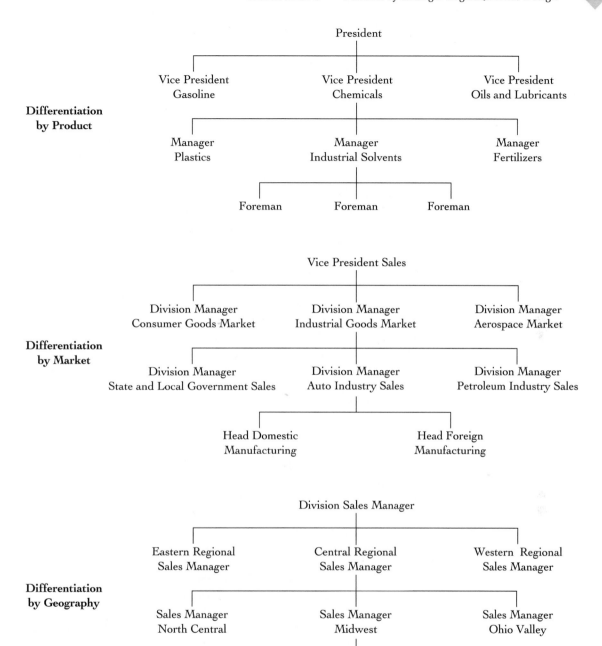

Differentiation by Product

President

Vice President
Gasoline

Vice President
Chemicals

Vice President
Oils and Lubricants

Manager
Plastics

Manager
Industrial Solvents

Manager
Fertilizers

Foreman   Foreman   Foreman

Differentiation by Market

Vice President Sales

Division Manager
Consumer Goods Market

Division Manager
Industrial Goods Market

Division Manager
Aerospace Market

Division Manager
State and Local Government Sales

Division Manager
Auto Industry Sales

Division Manager
Petroleum Industry Sales

Head Domestic
Manufacturing

Head Foreign
Manufacturing

Differentiation by Geography

Division Sales Manager

Eastern Regional
Sales Manager

Central Regional
Sales Manager

Western Regional
Sales Manager

Sales Manager
North Central

Sales Manager
Midwest

Sales Manager
Ohio Valley

Milwaukee Office
Sales Manager

Detroit Office
Sales Manager

Chicago Office
Sales Manager

FIGURE 8-3   Output-Based Designs

competence that a single marketing department for the entire organization would achieve. The organization must weigh the comparative advantages of specialization for a specific division versus the efficiencies offered through economies of scale.

A divisional design based on products, markets, or geography may also reduce the company's ability to share information and resources across divisions. We noted that cross-functional coordination is often a problem in functional organizations. Coordination across different products, markets, or regions can be problematic in the output-oriented organization. Some lack of sharing may be the result of internal competition, but much of it may be simply the result of ignorance and poor communications.

Some of these disadvantages are reflected in a number of recent restructurings. For example, GM and Procter & Gamble have altered their former product-based groupings to improve efficiency and cross-product coordination. We can see how problems associated with output-based designs can become dysfunctional by examining General Motors' operations in the early and mid-1980s. Because of a lack of coordination among different product divisions, in addition to loose controls at the top management level in corporate headquarters, GM suffered greatly in the marketplace as customers became disenchanted and confused by the various GM products.

Although the various car lines were targeted at different market segments, they were nearly indistinguishable in appearance. Yet, GM failed to achieve any economies of scale through shared functions or facilities. In many respects GM was in a worst-case situation. It operated with a product structure that was intended to yield distinctive products, but the products lacked uniqueness. At the same time, GM's efficiency suffered because of the duplication of functions and facilities. Chrysler and Ford were able to exploit GM's inefficiencies and the market's confusion about GM's offerings. As a result GM has been moving away from its traditional product-oriented design, a change that has been difficult and time consuming.

Combining Function and Output: Hybrid and Matrix Designs

A careful examination of most large organizations shows that some combination of functional grouping and output grouping is typically used. Outside of single-product organizations, it is increasingly uncommon to find strict functional designs. Similarly, divisionalized organizations using some form of output grouping are discovering that maintaining some functional units to serve all divisions is often the most efficient and effective path. Some organizations, particularly those in areas that demand both technical precision and responsiveness to market conditions, have decided that it is important to differentiate and integrate across both functional and output areas. The result is that many organizations are creating designs that incorporate elements of both functional groupings and output groupings. Two such prototypical designs are the hybrid design and the matrix design.

Hybrid Organizations   A careful examination of typical large, multiproduct organizations shows some combination of all the forms of groupings discussed thus far. Few organizations maintain strict output-oriented divisional designs without retaining some centralized functional areas. Figure 8-4 illustrates the hybrid organizational design, which combines both functional and output groupings (product, market, and/or geographical). The rationale for this mixed form of grouping is that certain functional areas may not vary across the organization or may require a comparatively large size to operate efficiently. These areas are contained within functional departments. At the same time, it may be important for other areas of the organization to be tailored to meet specific product, market, or geographical requirements. Thus, the organization may want to create product,

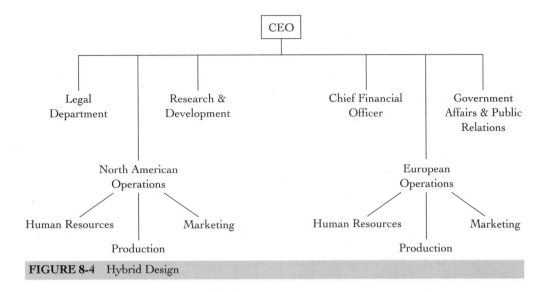

FIGURE 8-4   Hybrid Design

market, or regional divisions with self-contained production, marketing, and human resources activities. A critical decision the organization must make is determining which areas to maintain as functional units and which to assign to products, markets, or regions.

It is common, for example, for a large organization to maintain a single functional legal department to serve the legal needs of all divisions or departments of the organization. This is because of the cost associated with maintaining a legal department—economies of scale can be achieved by a centralized functional legal department—and the opportunity a single department provides for developing high levels of technical sophistication. It is also becoming increasingly important to maintain a functional information systems department that serves the entire company so that diverse and geographically scattered departments or divisions can be linked together. Otherwise, individual departments or divisions may adopt hardware and software that are not compatible with computer systems in the rest of the company and find themselves cut them off from communication with the larger organization. However, in an area such as information systems it is important that specific needs and requirements of departments and divisions be taken into consideration when adopting a companywide standard. Failure to do so may mean that some parts of the organization are using equipment or techniques poorly suited to their tasks.

A large, hybrid, multiproduct, multimarket organization operating in widely dispersed regions will still be able to retain separate cross-functional divisions to deal with distinctive products, markets, or regions. This allows the organization to respond to the specific conditions in diverse environments and to utilize an array of technologies that have different design requirements.

In most respects, the hybrid design retains most advantages of both the functional design and the output design. The organization achieves economies of scale and expertise in functional areas while maintaining responsiveness to product, market, or regional differences in other areas. Thus, the hybrid is well suited to both environmental and technological uncertainty. Simultaneously, the presence of a core headquarters organization in the functions allows for the necessary coordination.

The most significant problem faced by hybrid organizations is that the functional headquarters operation may become distant and detached from divisional units. There is a tendency for a lack of shared vision between divisions and functional units. Great care must be exercised to maintain links between the divisions and headquarters. Nonetheless, the hybrid is a highly desirable form with advantages that appear to outweigh the disadvantages for many large organizations.

Matrix Organizations A design that became increasingly common in high tech organizations of the 1970s and 1980s is the matrix design.[2] Figure 8-5 shows an array of matrix organizations. The essence of the matrix is the joint existence of functional (vertical or column) groupings and output (horizontal or row) groupings that overlap. The output groupings may be products, projects, or programs. The functional managers and product, project, or program managers are also referred to as matrix managers. Functional resources are allocated among the products, projects, or programs on the basis of need. Projects may go through a development cycle in which the functional expertise of various areas is needed at different times. People with different functional skills can be moved from one project to another as each project progresses. Similarly, product managers may have varied functional needs based on such things as production cycles, product changes, or seasonal marketing campaigns. For example, a marketing expert assigned to a particular product group may be temporarily moved to another product as specific needs develop. Similar types of moves can be made across program groups. The allocation process points out one of the conditions for which matrix organizations are well suited. Matrix organizations work well when functional resources are in short supply.

The rationale behind the matrix design is that it is uniquely suited to respond to two sets of competing demands. First, the organization, through its project, product, or program managers, can be responsive to environmental conditions. Second, at the same time, the organization, through its functional managers, provides high levels of scarce functional expertise. Some observers claim that for the matrix design to work effectively, the organization must face nearly equal demands for responsiveness to the environment (e.g., markets) and for functional precision or expertise. Without these nearly equal pressures to balance the power of the vertical and horizontal axes, one side will dominate and the organization will lose effectiveness. A responsibility of top management is to maintain the balance and mediate among the horizontal and vertical matrix bosses.

A second key feature of the matrix design is that it violates a basic principle of management—unity of command. In typical designs each worker is responsible to one, and only one, boss. In a matrix design, a portion of the workforce called two-boss managers must be responsive to two bosses: a functional boss and a product, project, or program boss. This arrangement is often called a dual-authority structure.[3] Not everyone in the matrix organization has two bosses; only the two-boss manager must deal with two bosses. He or she must implement actions that take into consideration functional and output-oriented demands. It is also the two-boss manager who may suffer the stress over potentially conflicting demands placed on him or her by the matrix bosses.

The chief advantage of the matrix organization is allowing the proper technical advice, expertise, and other functional resources to be present at the proper location and at the desired time. The matrix design is flexible. Thus, the matrix may be appropriate when the external environment is complex and changing. It allows for changes in shifting emphasis on product, projects, or programs as needs or conditions dictate.

A second advantage is that the organization can be simultaneously responsive to the demands for functional expertise and precision and the demands of the marketplace for varied and specialized outputs. The combination of a functional focus and an output focus in the matrix permits greater coordination around specific problems or tasks. For this reason the matrix design tends to be well suited to tasks that are nonroutine and highly interdependent. That is why the design is often used in organizations that specialize in research and development or high-tech areas.

Because of the competing functional and product, project, or program dimensions of the matrix, potential for conflict is inherent in the design, and that is a chief disadvantage. The dual-functional and output-oriented pressures that must exist for

FIGURE 8-5 Matrix Designs

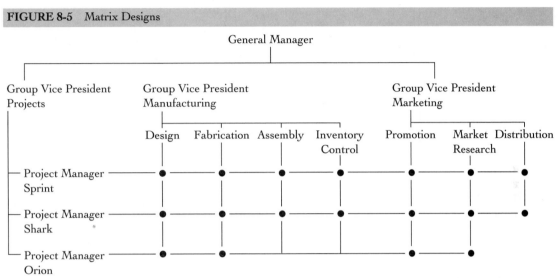

Project Matrix Structure

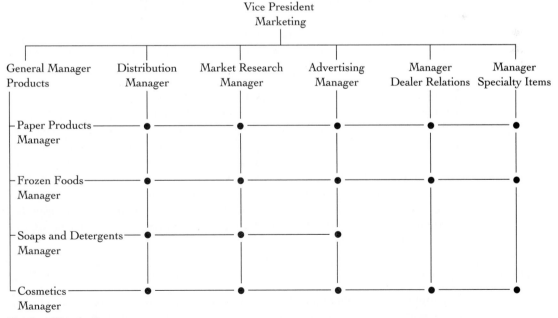

Product Matrix Structure

(continued)

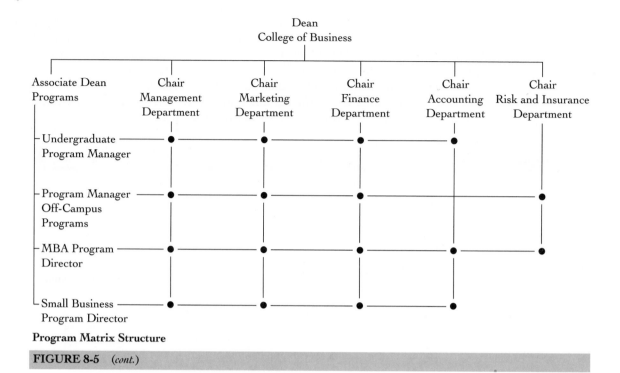

Program Matrix Structure

FIGURE 8-5 *(cont.)*

a matrix to work also require extensive cooperation and the ability of managers to handle conflict. The design requires managers to be skilled negotiators, able to mediate between conflicting parties. Additionally, the matrix design places the two-boss manager at the nexus of these conflicting functional and output demands. The people who occupy these roles must be able to manage the stress of potentially conflicting role demands from two bosses. Moreover, because the two-boss managers may be periodically moved from projects, products, or programs, they must also be able to deal with the role stress and traumas that frequent relocation entails (e.g., breaking and forming work and friendship groups, forming new supervisor-subordinate relationships, and possibly even relocating their families).

Finally, a potential paradox is inherent in the matrix design. We noted that the design is particularly well suited to complex, changing environments, but it may be problematic when swift responses are required. The potential for conflict, the need for frequent meetings, and the extensive negotiation and mediation required to manage functional and product demands are cornerstones of the matrix design and may slow responses to the environment. Thus, when rapid responses are of paramount importance, the matrix may not be the best design. However, when the speed of response must be balanced with a high-quality or high-precision response, a matrix may be appropriate.

ORGANIZATIONS FOR THE TWENTY-FIRST CENTURY: EVOLVING DESIGNS

The four designs discussed so far are prototypes that organizations have modeled for many years. Recently, many organizational leaders and theorists have come to realize that the conditions facing organizations have changed dramatically. The chapters on environment and technology have already alluded to these changing conditions. Three related sets of changes are presenting managers and theorists with new challenges in designing organizations. First, inexpensive, fast, and pervasive computer and tele-communications technology (information technology) has dramatically changed the way people work. These technological changes have made information more readily available to more people. They have permitted extensive automation and, in some areas, reduced the direct human component in tasks. Moreover, these technologies have made communication easier. Information technologies are directly involved in the other two areas of change: task technology and globalization. Information technologies have been important factors in many of the advanced manufacturing techniques, such as flexible manufacturing, customization, and just-in-time inventory and production. Finally, the advent of advanced information technologies has made the world marketplace more accessible to more organizations. These conditions both require and allow organizations to adopt new design configurations.

Before describing these contemporary designs, a note of caution is in order. If you visit any substantial bookstore you will see an extensive collection of books (not including conventional textbooks) that deal with issues related to organization design. There is no shortage of writers suggesting new twists on design. There is, however, considerable overlap in what most of these authors propose. On the one hand, that consistency is comforting—it suggests that there is some order to the universe of organizations. On the other hand, many of these authors use different labels to identify their new design configurations. Thus, the reader should be aware that several different terms are used to describe the same or similar organizational forms.

The Virtual Organization

The label that has won widespread use in both the popular and academic literature is the virtual organization.[4] At the heart of the virtual organization is a core organization that carries out some critical functions to which the organization is particularly well suited. Functions outside this core area of competence may be performed by tempo-rary or contract workers, or farmed out to other organizations with which the core organization has formed alliances or affiliations. The core organization maintains these relationships only as long as they are productive and beneficial. In many respects the virtual organization is an extension of the interorganizational external control strategies discussed in Chapter 5. Two other terms used to describe similar designs are sham-rock[5] and network organizations.[6]

A good example of a virtual organization is Nike, the athletic footware and apparel marketer.[7] Nike's core competencies are product development, marketing, and distribution. In its history, the company has done very little manufacturing of its products. Those products can be produced more efficiently through a vast set of sup-plier companies throughout Asia and elsewhere that specialize in shoe or apparel manu-facturing. This arrangement allows Nike to avoid much of the capital cost of investing in production facilities while at the same time giving the company flexibility. Should a particular type of product lose favor in the marketplace, Nike can move out of its alliance with the producer. Such a move would avoid the costs of either selling or retooling a manufacturing facility that Nike owned. The major advantage is that Nike can concentrate on the things it does best: designing, marketing, and distributing its products. Nike has mastered the art of selling its products through prominent person-alities such as Michael Jordan, Charles Barkley, and Bo Jackson.

The downside to the virtual organization is that the core organization has less control than in a conventional organization. Monitoring and controlling supplier companies as well as contract or temporary employees outside the core may be more difficult than it would be if these functions were carried on inside the organization's boundaries by regular employees. An organization must balance its need for control with its need for specialization and flexibility. Another criticism of the virtual organization is of a broader nature. Some critics have claimed that these new organizations are, in effect, hollow organizations.[8] They concentrate their efforts on high-skill technical and professional work. Productive labor often takes place elsewhere, typically in the developing economies of other nations. The fear is that organizations (and nations) that do not actually produce things will lose their economic clout and skills to producer companies (and nations).

Even short of these competitiveness issues, there are other social and economic concerns.[9] First, the core work of the virtual organization requires increasingly higher levels of education. Some critics question whether current educational systems are capable of producing the requisite education levels among the pool of employees. Second, the entire nature of jobs will change. Because the virtual organization requires a cadre of temporary and part-time workers, future workers will move between more jobs and often hold several jobs simultaneously. Third, there is fear that the organizational stratification of workers into "core" and "others" will result in further economic stratification of society. All these issues are critical and will need to be answered as the virtual organization gains increasingly wide use in the workplace.

The Federal Organization

A second design that has become widely used in various forms is what Charles Handy has labeled the federal organization.[10] This design is, in many respects, an extension of the product-based divisional design. It is characterized by a small central organization that provides overall leadership and planning and a number of loosely affiliated subsidiaries. Although the central organization provides tight financial control over the subsidiaries, the subsidiaries maintain extensive freedom and flexibility in the general conduct of business.

Johnson & Johnson provides a good example of the federal design.[11] This company is well known to consumers for Band-Aid brand products and Johnson's baby products, all produced by the Johnson & Johnson Consumer Products division. Other divisions include McNeil Consumer Products, maker of Tylenol; Ethicon surgical products; and Ortho Pharmaceutical, a prescription drug company. In fact, Johnson & Johnson is made up of 166 separately operating units that are, in most respects, independent companies. Interestingly, although the notion of a federal organization may be new to the organization theory lexicon, Johnson & Johnson's founder Robert Wood Johnson created an organization of small, decentralized units in the 1930s because he believed that this design would promote accountability and market responsiveness.[12] Those same ideals are still central to the federal design. Johnson & Johnson's success with the federal design is mirrored by General Electric, Formosa Plastics, and the Swedish-Swiss conglomerate Asea Brown Boveri (ABB).

Two distinctly Asian versions of the federal organization are the Japanese keiretsu and the Korean chaebol. Although the nature of each of these designs and of firm ownership is different, the keiretsu and the chaebol are similar in that they involve large numbers of affiliated organizations that are rather loosely tied together through cross ownership.

Keiretsu   The keiretsu are major families or groups of independent organizations and were considered to be the key to Japan's post–World War II redevelopment and economic success.[13] Prior to World War II, Japan's economic and political system was dominated by the zaibatsu. The zaibatsu were extremely powerful family-centered holding companies. A small number of large zaibatsu dominated the Japanese economy. Equally as important, the zaibatsu's power extended beyond business to government and politics. Many zaibatsu leaders played leading roles in government. Some critics claim that the zaibatsu's drive for market expansion and domination was a key factor in Japan's imperialistic tendencies leading up to World War II. At the conclusion of World War II, the United States occupation forces in Japan broke up the zaibatsu, but certain of the former zaibatsu companies regained some economic clout as the industrial groupings we now know as keiretsu.

At the core of the keiretsu are major banks and trading companies. These core companies act very much like holding companies do in the United States. The member companies are independent entities tied together through cross holding of shares, overlapping boards of directors, and formal or informal agreements. The largest keiretsu were previously known as the Big Six; however, since the economic troubles of Asia in the late 1990s, there are now only four major keiretsu. They are, in order of size, Mizuho, Sumitomo-Mitsui, Sanwa-Tokai, and Mitsubishi.

In the early 1990s, each of the Big Six had larger revenues than either General Motors or Exxon. This did not hold true, however, for the four remaining keiretsu in 2000.[14] Figure 8-6 depicts the member companies of the Mitsui group in 1991. Since that time, the Mitsui group has grown and become even more complex.[15]

In addition to the formal ties that bind member companies together, top executives of the affiliated companies often interact extensively in social and business settings. For example, Mitsubishi, the largest keiretsu, grew out of a post–World War II organization known as Kinyo Kai, or Friday Conference. Kinyo Kai developed as a forum to discuss the postwar reindustrialization of Japan. Today, the conference is a mechanism through which the presidents of most important member companies to discuss policy issues that affect the keiretsu.[16] Thus, the core companies may even play a role in strategy development for member firms.

The value of the keiretsu to member firms is that they work together cooperatively to ensure each other's viability and competitiveness. For example, Toyota is a member of two keiretsu that also include a wide array of supplier companies critical to its just-in-time production and inventory control systems, banks that supply debt to finance operations, advertising firms that market Toyota products, and shipping companies that transport those products. Toyota has an ownership stake in many of these companies, and the companies often have small ownership stakes in Toyota. Unlike most Japanese companies, Toyota has continued with this strategy into the new millennium and continues to benefit from it.[17] Joint ownership holdings provide a basis for cooperation among these companies. Regardless of ownership, however, managers realize that it is in everyone's best interest to work together. When Toyota, for example, requests a design change in certain electronic components, the supplier knows that creating better parts in a timely fashion at a competitive cost and with extremely high quality will improve not only Toyota, but also the supplier firm.

The keiretsu is not a perfect solution or the only solution to interfirm coordination. Sony, for example, is essentially independent of the keiretsu system. Moreover, the economic uncertainty that has persisted in Japan from the mid-1990s has caused several problems for the tightly linked keiretsu companies resulting in the merger or collapse of many of them.[18] The tight links between suppliers and manufacturers has proven to be inefficient and too rigid during times that call for flexibility and cost cutting. Nonetheless, the keiretsu have provided tremendous clout to the Japanese economy.

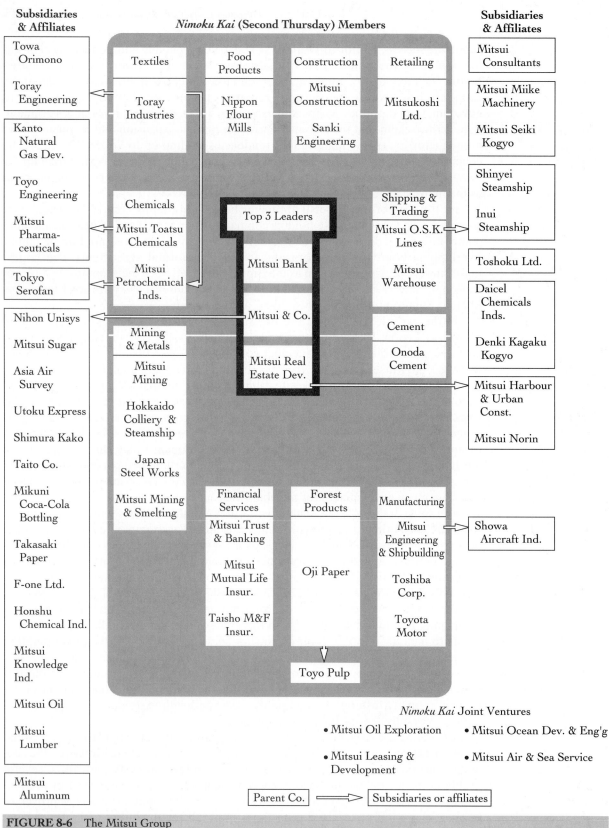

FIGURE 8-6 The Mitsui Group

Source: Adapted from Max Eli, *Japan Inc.* (Chicago: Probus Publishing & Company, 1991): 25.

Chaebol   The Korean chaebol, formed with the cooperation and support of government, are largely family-based collections of businesses. The collection of companies is typically large and diverse. Cross ownership and long-standing family ties are at the core of the chaebol.[19] Its basis in family ownership is similar to the zaibatsu in Japan. However, in Japan the pre–World War II zaibatsu played a controlling role in government. The role is reversed for the chaebol. Its continued operation depends on government support and acceptance.

The chaebol system is characterized by six distinctive features.

1. **Family controlled and managed:** Large numbers of leaders of divisions and subsidiaries who are family members.
2. **Paternalistic leadership:** One central leader with near-absolute authority; separation between the CEO and the lower divisions of the organization; a fatherlike figure; concern for welfare of employees.
3. **Centralized planning and control:** Centralized oversight of the diverse holdings; centralized decision making.
4. **Entrepreneurial orientation:** High value placed on ambition, clear vision, and political skills.
5. **Close ties with government:** Success dependent on cultivating strong links to people with political power; extensive government financial support; many former government workers employed to help manage relationships with government; government leads and business follows.
6. **Strong ties to schools:** Going to the "right" school (both high school and college) an important element to success.

The four largest chaebol are well-recognized names in the world marketplace: Hyundai, Samsung, LG (formerly Lucky-Goldstar), and SK.[20] Although some of the names may be familiar to consumers, the wide diversity of products affiliated with each company may not be apparent. In recent years, chaebols have shifted to a more division-oriented structure.[21] The diverse divisions that comprise the Samsung chaebol produce food products, aircraft engine parts, computer chips, consumer electronics, and many other products and services. Table 8-1 lists the four largest chaebol and their array of products. Table 8-2 lists the companies under the key divisions within the Samsung chaebol.

The large chaebol accounted for over 60 percent of Korea's GNP in the 1980s, and links with government have made the chaebol companies potent economic and political forces. The companies were able to manage competition, avoid organized labor, and

TABLE 8-1 Four Largest South Korean Chaebol	
Company	**Products/Services**
Hyundai	Construction services, automobiles, shipbuilding, electronics, heavy equipment, semiconductors, shipping, and group tours
Samsung	Electronics, semiconductors, food products, coal, chemicals, minerals, metals, ships, large machinery, and insurance
LG	Electronics, semiconductors, telecommunications, oil, fashion, shopping centers, chemicals, trading, and financial services
SK	Energy production and distribution, films, fibers, petrochemicals, telecommunications, engineering and construction, international trade and finance

Source: From Laxmi Nakarmi and Robert Neff, "Korea's Powerhouses Under Siege," *Business Week* (November 20, 1989): 52; additional information retrieved May 2001 from the World Wide Web: www.hyundai.com; www.samsungcorp.com; www.lgicorp.com; and www.sk.com.

obtain favorable government treatment because of the government's desire to foster economic growth. Although some of the chaebol's power has eroded through the 1990s, these companies still represent potent forces in the world marketplace.[22]

These brief descriptions of the keiretsu and the chaebol give a glimpse of these Asian organizational forms. Although they are similar, important differences distinguish the two. The keiretsu firms are more loosely tied together than those in the chaebol. Control is more centralized in the Korean chaebol than in the Japanese keiretsu. Keiretsu managers are more likely to have more extensive professional training and credentials than are the Korean managers. We also noted the important role the government plays in the chaebol. In Japan, the keiretsu and the government interact more as political peers.[23]

There is much more of importance about both forms that is beyond the scope of this text. The purpose here is only to show that both are variations on the federal form of organization. Both involve collections of semiautonomous organizations that work together for extraordinary market and political power, and both are products of the national cultures in which they are embedded.

CHARACTERISTICS OF EFFECTIVE STRUCTURES

Up to now, this chapter has described various ways of grouping work in organizations to create specific design configurations. What we have not yet addressed, however, are the characteristics of an effective design.

We must point out at the outset that there is no one right design that is best for all organizations.[24] There are designs that are more appropriate for a particular organization, given the circumstances it faces. A federal design may work for Johnson & Johnson, but it may prove disastrous for a firm that seeks synergies from its diverse product groups. Major determinants of the most appropriate designs are the environmental conditions the firm faces, the technology (or technologies) that the firm uses, the firm's strategic goals or objectives, its size and point in the organizational life cycle, and finally its culture—an area we will explore in Chapter 10.

Regardless of these circumstances, all organization designs should have certain characteristics if they are to be effective. These are efficient operation, encouragement of innovation, flexibility and adaptiveness, facilitation of individual performance and development, facilitation of coordination and communication, and facilitation of strategy formulation, implementation, and achievement.

Efficiency

An organization's design should encourage the efficient pursuit of the organization's goals. Efficiency, doing things right, is a critical factor for the survival and success of an organization, and the appropriateness of the organization's design is among the key factors.[25] One need only look at struggling organizations of the late 1980s and early 1990s such as IBM, Kmart, and General Motors. In each case, among the first actions these companies took to restore efficient operation was to implement a new design. It is not only struggling firms that modify their designs to enhance efficiency. Many firms change design configurations to eliminate duplication, improve responsiveness, and achieve economies of scale. Efficient design should provide a skeleton or network of task differentiation and integration for the allocation and utilization of an organization's resources.

TABLE 8-2   The Samsung Chaebol: Principal Business Areas and Descriptions

Company	Description
Trading Co.	
Samsung Corporation	Import-Export, natural resources
Electronics	
Samsung Electronics Co., Ltd.	TVs, VCRs, audio equipment, appliances
Samsung SDI Co., Ltd.	Digital communications, technology licensing, Internet purchasing services
Samsung Electro-Mechanics	Mobile communications components, computer components and peripherals, audio and video components, Internet and network products, passive components and circuit boards.
Samsung Corning Co., Ltd.	TV glass products
Samsung SDS Co., Ltd.	Computer consulting and support services, database and network centers, computer software
Heavy Industry and Chemicals	
Samsung General Chemicals Co., Ltd.	Polyolefins, resin compounds, basic petrochemicals
Samsung Petrochemical Co., Ltd.	PTA (purified terephthalic acid)
Samsung Fine Chemicals Co., Ltd.	Chemicals, paints, pharmaceuticals
Samsung-BP Chemicals Co., Ltd.	Acetic acid, VAM (vinyl acetate monomer), hydrogen
Samsung Heavy Industries Co., Ltd.	Shipbuilding, structural steel, digital control systems, waste and water treatment facilities, tank systems, engineering and construction
Precision Instruments	
Samsung Techwin Co., Ltd.	Defense systems, engine and turbo machinery, semiconductor systems, optics and digital imaging, aviation

Banking and Insurance
Samsung Life Insurance Co., Ltd.; Samsung Fire & Marine Insurance Co., Ltd.; Samsung Card Co., Ltd.; Samsung Securities Co., Ltd.; Samsung Capital Co., Ltd.; Samsung Investment Trust Management Co., Ltd.; Samsung Venture Investment Co.

Miscellaneous Products and Services
Samsung Engineering Co., Ltd.; Cheil Industries Inc.; Unitel Co. Ltd.; Samsung Everland Inc.; Shilla Hotels and Resorts Co., Ltd.; Cheil Communications Inc.; S1 Corporation; Samsung Lions; Samsung Medical Center; Samsung Biomedical Institute; Samsung Economic Research Institute; Samsung Human Resources Development Institute; Samsung Advanced Institute of Technology; Samsung Foundation of Culture; Samsung Welfare Foundation; The Ho-Am Foundation; Samsung Press Foundation; The Ho-Am Art Museum

Source: Based on R. Steers, Yoo Keun Shin, and Gerardo R. Ungson, *The Chaebol: Korea's New Industrial Might* (New York: Harper & Row, 1989); additional information accessed May 2001 from the World Wide Web: www.samsungcorp.com/companies.html.

Innovation

Even organizations in static, simple environments need innovation—the ability to generate more effective and efficient ways of operating and new products or services to offer. Design should encourage innovation by providing the pooling of resources and the necessary communication for innovation to take place. This important concept is discussed further in Chapter 13.

Campbell's Soup had an image as a stodgy, old-fashioned company. Its performance into the mid-1980s was lackluster. The company had become slow and inefficient. Change was clearly needed if the company was to remain viable and competitive into the twenty-first century. The company instituted a number of operational and technological changes to improve the efficiency of its operation. However, to implement these changes, it was also necessary to reconfigure the company into a combined geographic and product-oriented design. Organizing in this manner facilitated the communication necessary to coordinate new technologies.[26]

Organizations facing dynamic, complex environments require even more innovation if the organization is to stay in tune with and respond to its environment. Design should thus facilitate scanning of the environment, boundary spanning, and innovation. In these environments, designs that keep the organization in close contact with elements of the environment are critical to survival. Links between the environment and top decision makers who formulate and implement strategy are critical.

Flexibility and Adaptiveness

All organizations need to be flexible and adaptive. Fewer and fewer industrial environments can be characterized as stable and simple because the ability to change and respond to new environmental conditions is critical to survival. It is not only necessary to innovate in areas of operations and products or services, but the organization itself, as the Campbell's example suggests, must also be in a position to change itself and respond. An effective design must balance the needs for consistency and predictability with the needs for flexibility and responsiveness.

Designs can facilitate flexibility and adaptiveness in two ways. First, the design and supporting structure can act as a conduit to transmit information from boundary spanners and environmental scanners to top decision makers, allowing management to formulate and implement new strategies, including redesigning the organization. Second, the design itself can create units, departments, or divisions close to the environment that can respond. For example, in matrix organizations resources can be moved around as needed in response to changing conditions. This can happen without much involvement of top management.

Facilitation of Individual Performance and Development

Probably the most common complaint about organizational designs made by organization members is that instead of facilitating performance, they often block effective performance and stifle the individual. Although many of these complaints are directed at bureaucratic structures, the design configuration itself may also be a problem. Functional designs may pigeonhole people into narrowly defined functional tasks. Some functional departments, such as human resources or information systems, may, in some firms, be organizational backwaters far from the action because these functions are not directly involved in producing output. People in these departments may become alienated. More recently, progressive organizations have begun realizing the importance of these support services. On the other hand, output-oriented and federal designs may hinder personnel movement among divisions, which may stifle advancement within the organization.

Whatever the design, it should offer the individual the opportunity to perform at his or her highest level of ability in areas of interest and competence. The design should encourage employees to grow on the job by learning new skills and accepting increasing responsibilities as they become more experienced. The design should provide a clear career path or ladder of organization jobs or positions and a system whereby employees can get necessary training to qualify them for higher level jobs.

Facilitation of Coordination and Communication

At the core of structuring and designing organizations is the effective execution of tasks. Leaders should differentiate tasks, group employees together, and then integrate their work so that the work of the organization can be conducted in a nearly smooth and seamless manner. Key to that smooth and seamless operation is the design configuration that management selects. Managers must ask several questions. Should work be organized around functional expertise, outputs, or both? How big must units be to achieve economies of scale? How much interaction do units, divisions, or departments need? The appropriate design will then facilitate coordination and communication where it is most needed. Note, however, that merely picking a design that fits is not enough. In Chapter 2, we discussed a number of structural and nonstructural mechanisms that play important roles in integration. These must be present along with the appropriate design if coordination and communication are to be achieved.

Facilitation of Strategy Formulation and Implementation

The relationship between strategy and structure, or design, has been the focus of extensive investigation in the organizational literature. Structure and design are key factors in the development of strategies as well as key outcomes of the strategy formulation process. Appropriate design and structure of the organization are essential to the scanning of environments by boundary spanners and the transmission of information to top management. This information is fundamental in the formulation of strategy. Whether these units are functional may depend on a multitude of factors, but it is critical that the appropriate information be transmitted to top management.

The organization may be strategically redesigned as a result of the information transmitted to top management. Organizations may move from functional groupings to some other design configuration as they grow and develop new products or services. Matrix designs may be adopted as organizations face increasing pressure for quality and responsiveness to customer demands. Federal or virtual organizations may alter their collection of affiliations as they enter new or exit old markets. The point is that strategy and design are tightly linked. As organizations adopt new strategies, they may need to modify their designs. Different design configurations may make available different information and resources that may result in shifting strategies. Designs may again need to be realigned with strategy.

SUMMARY

The basis for designing an organization is the grouping of workers into departments, work units, or divisions. At its simplest level, two different approaches can be used for grouping: by function (i.e., people's tasks, knowledge, skills, training, or equipment) or output (i.e., products, services, markets, or geographic regions). These two approaches to grouping lead to basic design configurations: functional and output oriented (i.e., product, market, or geographic).

The two basic design configurations can also be combined to form two additional designs. The hybrid design allows the organization to retain some functional departments serving the entire organization while creating output-oriented departments or divisions for most areas of the organization. The matrix simultaneously uses both functional and output groupings to create an organization with dual lines of authority and responsibility. The matrix creates some unique conditions and problems for organizations. Matrix bosses must head the functional and output dimensions of the design, and two-boss managers must balance the demands of both sets of matrix bosses. This configuration violates one of the basic principles of organizations—unity of command.

The virtual organization and the federal organization are two contemporary variations on organizational design made possible by telecommunications and computer technologies. The loose network of cooperating organizational units in the virtual organization create unprecedented flexibility and adaptiveness. The federal organization is, in many respects, an elaboration of the product-based, output-oriented organization. The federal organization, with its diverse collection of affiliated, semiautonomous organizations, allows large organizations to act like small ones. As was the case with the virtual organization, the federal design is well suited to a complex, changing environment.

The keiretsu and the chaebol represent two Asian variations on the federal organization. Although there are some similarities between these two forms—large sets of cooperating and interacting firms—they are as distinctively different as the two countries in which they are found. The keiretsu is characterized by cross ownership among numbers of cooperating but independent firms. The chaebol is a collection of diverse companies with some common family ownership ties and a strong, centralized leadership.

Finally, we examined the design-effectiveness relationship. The key points are that (1) no one design is best for all organizations and (2) the appropriate design depends on the conditions the organization faces. The most appropriate design allows the organization to pursue its goals in an effective and efficient manner. This, of course, assumes that the organization's goals are appropriate!

Questions for Discussion

1. How has the technological "explosion" affected organizational design?
2. One common form of differentiation results in what is termed functional grouping. Name and describe a corporation that has such an organization design. What do you see as the cause(s) or reasons for employing this type of design?
3. Describe and show possible uses for the three types of output groupings.
4. Under what conditions would a hybrid design work best? Explain.
5. Under what conditions would a matrix design work best? What basic principle of management does the matrix design violate? Explain. Does this present problems or unusual challenges in managing a matrix organization?
6. Describe the virtual organization design. Is this a new concept in design or a new label for an old one? Explain.
7. How can you explain the use of the Japanese keiretsu and the Korean chaebol? Would they work in the United States? Explain.
8. How can you tell whether a company has a good organization design?

References

1. D. C. Dearborn and H. A. Simon, "Selective Perception: A Note on the Departmental Identification of Executives," *Sociometry* 21 (1958): 140–44; M. J. Wallen, G. R. Huber, and W. H. Glick, "Functional Background as a Determinant of Executives' Selective Perception," *Academy of Management Journal* 38 (1995): 943–74.

2. Jay Galbraith, "Designing Matrix Organizations," *Business Horizons* (February 1971): 29–40; Stanley M. Davis and Paul R. Lawrence, *Matrix* (Reading, MA: Addison-Wesley, 1977).

3. Richard L. Daft, *Organization Theory and Design*, 4th ed. (St. Paul, MN: West Publishing, 1992).

4. William H. Davidow and Michael S. Malone, *The Virtual Corporation: Structuring and Revitalizing the Corporation for the 21st Century* (New York: Harper-Collins, 1992); Maggie Biggs, "Tomorrow's Workforce," *Infoworld* (September 18, 2000): S59–S61; W. Bridges, "The End of the Job," *Fortune* 130 (September 9, 1994): 62–74; Paula Dwyer, "Tearing Up Today's Organizational Chart," *Business Week* (November 18, 1974): 80–90.

5. Charles Handy, *The Age of Unreason* (Boston: Harvard Business School Press, 1989).

6. Jay R. Galbraith and Robert K. Kazanjian, "Strategy, Technology, and Emerging Organizational Forms," in *Futures of Organizations*, ed. by Jerald Hage (Lexington, MA: Lexington Books, 1988); David Limerick and Bert Cunnington, *Managing the New Organization: A Blueprint for Networks and Strategic Alliances* (San Francisco: Jossey-Bass, 1993).

7. Donald Katz, *Just Do It!* (New York: Random House, 1994).

8. See note 7; see note 5.

9. See note 5.

10. See note 5.

11. Joseph Weber, "A Big Company That Works," *Business Week* (May 4, 1992): 124–32; Johnson & Johnson homepage, Retrieved May 2001from the World Wide Web: www.jnj.com/home.html.

12. See note 11.

13. Max Eli, *Japan Inc.: Global Strategies of Japanese Trading Corporations* (Chicago: Probus Publishing, 1991).

14. See note 13; "Regrouping," *The Economist* (November 25, 2000); "Keiretsu Watch," taken from Autumn 2000 Japan Company Handbook, retrieved May 2001 from the World Wide Web: www.efn.org/~dredmond/keirwtch.html; Global 500: The World's Largest Corporations (July 24, 2000), retrieved May 2001 from the World Wide Web: www.fortune.com/.

15. "Major Subsidiaries and Associated Companies," Mitsui & Co., Ltd., retrieved May 2001 from the World Wide Web: www.mitsui.co.jp/tkabz/english/corp/index.htm.

16. See note 13.

17. Stephanie Strom, "In Japan, an Established Company Is Transformed," *The New York Times* (December 18, 2000): C19.

18. T. Arakawa, "Keiretsu Walls Cracking as Auto Industry Feels the Squeeze," *Tokyo Business Today* 61, no. 4 (April 1993): 14–15; Naohisa Ishida, "Merge-or-Submerge Fever Spreads as Keiretsu Die Out," *The Daily Yomiuri* (December 21, 1999): 9.

19. Benjamin Gomes-Casseres, "State and Markets in Korea," Harvard Business School (Boston: President and Fellows of Harvard College, case 9-387-181, 1987); Richard Steers, Yoo Keun Shin, and Gerardo R. Ungson, *The Chaebol: Korea's New Industrial Might* (New York: Harper & Row, 1989).

20. Laxmi Nakarmi and Robert Neff, "Korea's Powerhouses Are Under Siege," *Business Week* (November 20, 1989): 52–55; "Economic Power Concentrated on Four Chaebols More Than Ever," *Korea Economic Weekly* (April 24, 2000).

21. Yeon-Hak Kim and Nigel Campbell, "Strategic Control in Korean MNCs," *Management International Review* 35 (1995): 95–108.

22. See note 20.

23. See R. Steers, Yoo Keun Shin, and G. R. Ungson in note 19.

24. Y. K. Shetty and Howard M. Carlisle, "A Contingency Model of Organization Design," *California Management Review* 15 (Fall 1972): 38–45.

25. J. Pfeffer and G. Salancik, *The External Control of Organizations* (New York: Harper & Row, 1978).

26. B. Saporito, "Campbell Soup Gets Piping Hot," *Fortune* 124 (September 9, 1991): 142–48.

*Virtual Growth Continues to "Grow" Thanks to Outsourcing**

Virtual Growth, based in New York City, is no ordinary financial and accounting company! Founder and CEO, Stephen King, has brought this 5-year-old company into a world of Internet-powered outsourcers. King claims that technology made it possible for him to start a business that wouldn't have been feasible 10 years ago.

He realized that the Internet provided a vehicle through which the company could provide accounting services for clients anywhere. King designed software to simplify data entries and allow access to employees who were not in the accounting department. With Virtual Growth's financial services, an employee can file expense reports online from any location. At headquarters, his or her supervisor can authorize these reports, and auditors can also access the information from yet another location. Virtual Growth serves as an example of outsourcing financial services. King's accountants are not located at headquarters in New York but in South Carolina where the office space is far less expensive.

Virtual Growth attempts to remove the toil of "crunching the numbers" for their clients, which are small companies and startups. The firm takes control of nearly all their clients' financial activities ranging from payrolls to taxes to supplier procurements. It also revamps and simplifies routines relating to financial and accounting practices. Clients not only save themselves from the hassle of performing these services in-house but they also save 30 percent to 40 percent of the cost of the services if they were done in-house. As King notes, "You can't afford a senior accountant when you're a 15-person company. We're the next best solution."

Customers such as Rob Lindo are pleased to outsource their accounting services to Virtual Growth. Lindo is president and CEO of Providio, a Web-development company out of Boston. Because of the services provided by Virtual Growth, Providio financial information can be easily accessed on the Internet.

While it was more common a couple of years ago for a company to outsource computing and data services, the trend has shifted to business processes, such as Virtual Growth's financial and accounting services. When a company outsources a business process, the duties and accountability associated with that process are transferred to a "supplier." In spite of the current downward slope in the economy, this movement toward increased outsourcing continues.

Virtual Growth looks forward to a very bright future. Researchers project that the worldwide market for financing and accounting services will triple in revenue by 2004. Furthermore, while information technology outsourcing has decreased with the current economic decline, experts anticipate that business process outsourcing will continue to grow. However, the greatest reason for confidence may be that Virtual Growth provides an Internet-driven service.

There is continued growth among application service providers (ASPs) who lease software on the Web. ASPs are an appealing and economical way to keep information technology within the formal boundaries of an organization. A new ASP can develop to fulfill almost any need. Sam Kellet developed an ASP called eAttorney to help law firms recruit new law school graduates whose abilities match the needs of the firm. After scanning the market, King found that there was a need for accounting software offerings for smaller and mid-size companies. Thanks to the Internet, Virtual Growth can supply financial services to smaller companies, which, because of limited earning potential, wouldn't have attracted such suppliers in the past.

Some experts speculate that the outsourcing trend is unaffected by variations and patterns in the economy. The *Outsourcing Index 2000* reported that the economy grew at only 25 percent of the rate of growth in outsourcing. According to Peter Bendor-Samuel, publisher of *The Outsourcing Journal*, companies seek to outsource in time of economic prosperity in order to put more of their product on the market quickly when they lack the resources to do so. However, when the economy is in decline, companies seek ways to save money, and outsourcing provides these companies with ways to do so. In times of tighter budgets, a company with a business need that can be addressed at a lower cost by a supplier makes the obvious decision to outsource.

As the economy continues to fluctuate in the future, outsourcing companies such as Virtual Growth will continue to flourish by providing its clients with the "cheaper alternative" to needed services and products. ∎

*This case is based on the following sources: Doug Garr, "Inside Outsourcing," *Fortune/CNET Technology Review* (Summer 2001): 85–86, 88; the Outsourcing Institute and Dun & Bradstreet, "Outsourcing Index 2000: Strategic Insights into U.S. Outsourcing," accessed June 15, 2001, www.Dun&Bradstreet.com.

CHAPTER

Organizational Governance and Control

9

CASE: FIRE UP THE GRILL*

The backyard barbecue is almost as American as apple pie. The image of a barbecue has been one of messy charcoal grills, noxious smoke, and, of course, the dreaded cleanup afterward. But the Thermos Company is attempting to change all that.

Long known for its Thermos vaccuum bottle that keeps liquids either hot or cold (how does it know which it should do?), the company is also becoming a major player in the cookout grill business. Until recently, a competitor to such well-known brands as Sunbeam, CharBroil, and Weber, Thermos had seen its annual $225 million annual sales volume as "medium rare" in a one-billion-a-year market. Clearly, a new product was needed if Thermos was to "relight" its business.

To do this, CEO Monte Peterson decided to change the traditional organization structure with its concentration on product to a teamwork pattern based on the consumer. Peterson believes that the market is experiencing a consumer revolution not unlike that which faced Henry Ford. An enlightened consumer simply is not seduced by slick packaging and glitzy ad campaigns. Instead, if a company is to sell its product successfully, it simply must build and market one that is sharply focused on what the consumer wants, not on one that is the most cost-effective or is best engineered from the manufacturer's point of view.

Peterson believes that innovation based on consumer needs is the key to winning in this new marketplace. And so he put together a different kind of organization to bring out Thermos's Thermal Electric Grill, which he hopes will capture some 20 percent of the market in the next few years. This product development team had the unreserved commitment from top management and followed a strict deadline schedule, keys to success in the product development field.

Eric Olson of the University of Colorado's College of Business cautions, however, that product teams are not necessarily the answer to all development ventures. He found in his research of 45 projects at 12 or so *Fortune* 500 companies that teamwork was not best for product modification (like new handles or shapes). The forming of teams for these types of modifications simply proved too cumbersome and took too much time to assemble. The result was that competitors often were in the market perhaps before teams could even be put together. But product modification was not what Thermos needed; it needed a brand new grill. So Peterson set out to build his "clan" organization.

The "Lifestyle" team, as it was called, was made up of six Thermos middle managers from functional fields such as engineering, finance, manufacturing, and marketing. But it was not to be a function-based group. It was to design a totally new grill that

---

*This case is based on the following article: Brian Dumaine, "Payoff from the New Management," *Fortune* (December 13, 1993): 103–104, 108, 110.

was to be just what the "customer ordered." The team was assigned the task of actually going into the field to find precisely what people looked for in their grills and to develop a product that met those needs.

To complete the "Lifestyle" team, Thermos enlisted outside help from suppliers and consultants. In this connection, Fitch, Inc., an industrial design firm, provided 10 members to help in the design of the new electric grill. It is important to know that this group began with no assumptions about what the product should look like, but rather got involved in the total strategy necessary to bring it to market.

There was no designated leader for the team who would serve as the final decision maker. Instead, the member whose area of expertise was needed would lead the clan. So marketing experts and R&D specialists took their turns as leader as the situation demanded. And the design of the new product was to be the sole focus of the group effort. Peterson made this move in recognition of the fact that all too often, in his opinion, team efforts failed because they were working on too many projects at the same time.

As its first task in designing the new grill, the field research unit took to the road. Traveling all across the country, they interviewed people while they were barbecuing and even videotaped some sessions for later review. They found out that many women were the chief cook instead of the stereotypical man clad in his apron and chef's hat. Rusty, dirty grills were found to be incompatible with the many new decks being built. Condo living and environmental regulations were big factors for people with cramped space who couldn't use smoke-belching charcoal grills.

Armed with field information, the team returned to its Schaumburg, Illinois, headquarters to share it with the rest of the group. After these meetings the team built a working model and a plastic dummy that they took to retailers and customers to get feedback needed for final production specifications.

While the research team was in the field, the engineering group was busy doing computer runs in an effort to improve electric grill technology so that any new ideas found in the field could be incorporated into the new product. The result of these efforts was a product of Thermos's core—vacuum technology. Conventional electric grills did not get hot enough to provide the searing characteristic of barbecuing. So engineers designed a domed vacuum hood that would keep the heat inside the grill in the same way the Thermos bottle held heat. It even left the sear marks associated with barbecuing!

The product was not to be just another electric grill. It had to be seen not only as functionally different, but also as one that had features to suit the areas where it would be used. Tripod legs, a larger storage table, and a way to keep utensils out of the way of the cook were all features added as a result of talks with consumers and retailers. Manufacturing would not have known about these requirements until much later in the overall production process if it had not been for the clan approach of product design that was Peterson's brainchild.

When the final product was ready for its ultimate test, Thermos gave 100 grills to its employees with instructions to "treat them ugly." Peterson thought this was a better way to find out about the grill's acceptance than to learn about its problems from Kmart or Target customers. That would have simply been too late. Finally, Thermos loaded grills on the back of a U-Haul truck and took them to trade association conventions where they were demonstrated to potential buyers. They were now ready for market.

This new clan approach to product development has yielded what Thermos hopes will be a way to ratchet-up its market share—a new product that doesn't require its user to "fire up the grill."

This case illustrates how the Thermos Company abandoned traditional top-down structural arrangements in favor of a type of "clan" pattern to bring out its new product, the Thermal Electric Grill. This interdisciplinary-team concept replaced bureaucracy with flexible groups who determined leaders based on situation-specific expertise rather than on the chain of command. As a result, innovation and customer satisfaction were achieved.

This chapter explains the concepts of organizational control and governance. Two economic approaches to organization provide the framework for discussing several mechanisms for control. We look at contracting, boards of directors, markets, bureaucracy, and clans as ways of gaining control.

ORGANIZATIONAL GOVERNANCE AND CONTROL

In the first chapter of this text, we presented a definition of organizations that highlighted four key features: organizations are social entities made up of people; organizations are goal directed; organizations are structured; and organizations are open systems with identifiable boundaries. Several important issues are assumed within this definition that now need to be discussed explicitly. These issues come under the heading of organizational governance and control. Specifically, this chapter investigates the mechanisms that organizations use to get members to perform desired tasks that help the organization achieve its goals.

Recall that our definition emphasized that organizations are made up of people. When an organization assembles a collection of people, one problem that managers may encounter is how to ensure that this diverse group of people is engaged in activities that contribute to the achievement of organizational goals. How do owners create control systems that maximize the effectiveness and efficiency of the organization? How do owners make certain that employees do not loaf on the job, steal, or in other ways engage in counterproductive behaviors? Or, in the case of Thermos, how does an organization ensure high-quality inputs from employees? The discussions of structure and design provided some answers to this question; however, in this chapter we examine additional mechanisms for control.

AGENCY THEORY AND TRANSACTION COST ECONOMICS

Much of our discussion in this chapter is based on a segment of organization theory called organizational economics.[1] Organizational economics is actually made up of distinct theories, of which the two major branches are *agency theory*[2] and *transaction cost economics*.[3] Although these two theoretical perspectives are not identical, there is some overlap in both how they view the organization and how they view governance.

The field of organizational economics has developed a language and vocabulary of its own that may seem to the reader a bit unusual and obscure. However, because the field attaches rather specific meaning to these terms, we have tried to both remain faithful to that language and vocabulary and to clearly define terms.

Agency theory regards the organization (or firm, as is often preferred) as a series of contractual relationships between owners and workers.[4] Potential owners invest in firms to increase their wealth. This ownership may be through stock ownership in a publicly traded company or through direct ownership (e.g., proprietorship or partnership). Owners, also called ***principals***, contract with managers and employees, also called ***agents***, to produce goods and services. Because of a variety of factors, including basic human nature and the uncertain nature of some tasks, managers and other employees may engage in activities that are not conducive to owner wealth maximization. Instead, these behaviors may be directed at satisfying the particular goals and objectives of managers and employees. These counterproductive activities produce ***agency costs***. Contracts, agreements that specify the exact duties and obligations of employees, are fashioned to guarantee that the agents perform as required. Those contracts must be written and monitored, all of which requires time and resources. In subsequent sections, we discuss why, according to agency theory, contracts are necessary and the types of contracts that owners can use to safeguard their interests.

Transaction cost theorists view the organization as a series of transactions.[5] Transactions are exchanges of goods and services among individuals and organizations. The firm has transactions with suppliers, with labor, or with customers. Some of these transactions take place within the organization, and some take place across the organization's boundaries. Because of the varying degrees of uncertainty that exist in transactions, the people and organizations involved experience ***transaction costs*** in executing transactions. Some transaction costs, such as brokerage fees, service charges, and points on loans, are explicit. Other transaction costs, such as monitoring the performance of transaction partners, are implicit in a transaction. Transaction costs are an indicator of inefficiency in a transaction. The greater the transaction costs to a firm, the less efficient the transaction and the less wealth available to owners. Thus, owners of a firm seek the lowest possible transaction costs. In subsequent sections we investigate the sources of these costs and the governance mechanisms that are used to control transaction costs.

Although there are important differences between these two theoretical perspectives, most of the differences are relevant to researchers and theoreticians. The important similarity between these two perspectives is that they both deal with how owners of a firm attempt to ensure that employees, suppliers, or contractors conduct themselves in ways that aid the organization in the achievement of its goals and objectives. According to both perspectives, owners should seek organizational arrangements that maximize economic efficiency; that is, those arrangements with the lowest agency costs or transaction costs. As a consequence of this emphasis on wealth enhancement through efficiency, agency theory and transaction costs economics are often labeled as *economic efficiency* views of organizations.[6] Both theoretical perspectives discuss ***governance*** mechanisms that can be used to ensure goal-directed behaviors, to control behaviors inside the firm, and to control the behaviors of transaction partners outside the firm. Thus, we group agency theory and transaction cost economics together.

THE NATURE OF THE PROBLEM OF ORGANIZING

Chapters 1 and 2 presented a somewhat traditional view of organizations and organizing. Organizations are created to accomplish some commonly held goal and organizations are structured—that is, tasks are divided vertically and horizontally among the people in the organization—in ways consistent with those goals, the organization's technology, its environment, and its size. Economic perspectives on organizations take a rather specific view concerning organizations and organizing. ***Owners*** of organizations create organizations as a means for accomplishing their rather specific goal—wealth maximization. Owners must make decisions about how to best achieve this goal of wealth maximization. To organizational economists, this question—how owners can maximize wealth—is central to how the firm should be organized.

Agency theory is primarily directed at the relationship between ***principals (owners)*** and ***agents (employees)***. Thus, agency theory focuses on the structuring of the relationship between owners and employees ***(principal-agent relationships)***. Agency theory examines the appropriate types of contracts and monitoring to ensure that owners can control the behavior of employees and reduce agency costs. Basic points are summarized in Table 9-1.

Transaction cost economics focuses on the question of how to maximize the efficiency of transactions. Transaction cost theory attempts to determine the ***efficient boundaries of the firm***.[7] That essentially means whether transactions should take place within the organization's boundaries, be conducted across the boundaries, or be housed within some sort of hybrid arrangement.[8] For example, is it more efficient (i.e., lower transaction costs) for a company to buy critical supplies or components from an outside supplier firm or should the company produce those supplies or components internally? Basic points of the transaction cost perspective are summarized in Table 9-2.

The problem an owner faces is that all forms of organizing have associated with them certain ***transaction*** or ***agency costs***. Organizational economists use the term *cost* to refer to a wide range of problems that owners must remedy in order to create an organization that allows for wealth maximization. These costs are described in the following sections.

Bounded Rationality

We have already examined the concept of bounded rationality elsewhere. Recall that bounded rationality means that humans (e.g., managers and owners) are limited in their ability to process information.[9] Another way of thinking about this is that owners and managers always face some uncertainty in transactions or contract relationships because they are unable to process all available information. They may lack time, attention, or ability to effectively gather and use the information needed. The situations owners face may be inherently complex and uncertain. Owners may be unable to process all potentially available information about managers; managers may likewise be unable to process all information about employees, suppliers, or customers. Additionally, because of uncertainty, some information may just not be available at any cost. Thus, a goal of organizing is to create an organization or some set of governance mechanisms that reduces as much as possible the uncertainty, that maximizes the available information, and that reduces the impact of bounded rationality.

Opportunism

Economic theorists assume that human beings operate on the bases of self-interest,[10] that individuals attempt to maximize their positive outcomes and minimize their efforts or inputs. This results in a critical problem for organizations—a lack of goal

---

TABLE 9-1   Basic Points of Agency Theory

Organizations—series of contractual relationships between agents and principals
Principals—owners (shareholders) of a firm
Agents—people hired by the owners to run the firm (managers and workers)
Agency Costs—costs associated with monitoring agent behavior and enforcing contracts
Goal—efficient arrangement (lowest agency costs) of agent-principal relationships

EXHIBIT 9-1

Shareholder Rights

Recently, shareholders of U.S. firms have demanded a greater say in the way many firms are run. This activism on the part of shareholders has been driven by many factors, but two issues stand out. First, top managers of several large firms, many of whom own only small numbers of shares in their firms, have taken actions to further their own goals at the expense of shareholders. This is the classic agent-principal problem. The second governance problem results when there are two classes of shares in a firm, each with different voting rights. This second problem is not too common in the United States but is often found in parts of Europe.

MANAGERS VERSUS OWNERS

Many U.S. firms combine the roles of chief executive officer (CEO) and chairman of the board. The CEO is the top manager (agent) of the firm. His or her responsibility is to serve the owners by setting strategy and implementing that strategy in a way that maximizes the owners' return on their investment. The chairman of the board of directors (BOD) is the primary representative of the shareholders. His or her responsibility (referred to as a *fiduciary responsibility*) is to make sure that the management runs the business in a legal manner and acts in the best interests of shareholders. One part of the BOD's responsibilities is to hire, monitor, reward, and discipline the top management, including the CEO.

When the roles of CEO and chairman of the board are separated, the system, in principle, should work. The CEO will operate the company in a sound and efficient manner. The chairman and the BOD will oversee the operation and reward or discipline top management depending on the performance of the firm. Even when the roles of CEO and chairman are separated, the system does not always work as expected. Often, the chairman and other BOD members are nominated by top management. Additionally, the CEO typically selects compensation consultants who make recommendations to the BOD about top management compensation. Since the compensation consultants are recommended by the CEO, they are unlikely to make recommendations that are unfavorable. Moreover, BODs are often reluctant to harshly discipline underperforming managers for fear of alienating existing and future managers.

The situation gets even more problematic when the CEO is also the chairman of the board. Any objectivity in evaluating top management is likely to be lost when the two roles are combined. How likely is a CEO to discipline or remove himself or herself in the event of poor performance? Instead, when the roles are combined, top managers often engage in behavior that is likely to entrench them in their management position.

In the mid-1990s, the largest single shareholder of General Motors was CALPERS (the California Public Employees Retirement System). CALPERS was distressed by the poor performance of GM stock at the time. During that time, one person, Jack Smith, served as both CEO and chairman of the board. CALPERS representatives felt that the CEO was responsible for the poor performance, but they were unable to influence the chairman or CEO (the same person!) or the BOD, since the chairman/ CEO had stacked the board with people friendly to him. CALPERS threatened to unload its shares (approximately 15 percent of all GM shares), which would further depress the stock, if the chairman did not step down. After extensive pressure from outside investors, he did eventually step down and was replaced by an outsider (no connection to GM), the retired CEO of Procter & Gamble, John Smale.

(continued)

(continued)

SECOND CLASS SHAREHOLDERS

Consider the following scenario. You own 500,000 shares in a leading company, an amount equal to the holdings of one of the founders of that company. However, your shares are designated as Class B shares and you have only 100,000 votes for your shares. The founder's shares are Class A shares and have somewhat different values, but each share supposedly represents an equal portion of the firm. Sounds unfair, doesn't it?

This situation evolved for different reasons in different types of organizations. Consider Ford Motor Company. The two classes of shares evolved to protect the interests of the Ford family. Even though the family owned a small minority share of the firm in the 1940s and 1950s, holders of Class B shares could not oust Ford family members from top management positions, even when the company was on the verge of bankruptcy. Top management was protecting the interests of the Ford family.

A similar situation exists at the New York Times Co., but the motivation is different. The founding families of the *New York Times* wanted to ensure the journalistic independence and integrity of the newspaper in the face of potentially hostile owners driven solely by profit motives. Thus, the Sulzberger and Ochs families continue to hold Class A shares, which have greater voting rights than shares held by the general investing public. Whether this system protects the newspaper is open to question. However, other newspapers that do not have this system have taken many actions viewed by journalists as controversial in an effort to increase profits.

TABLE 9-2   Basic Points of Transaction Cost Perspective
Organization—series of transactions, some within the organization, some across the organization's boundaries
Transaction—exchange of goods and services among groups within the organization or across organizational boundaries
Transaction Costs—explicit fees or costs associated with a transaction; implicit costs of monitoring and controlling a transaction
Goal—to determine the most efficient arrangement of transactions—whether transactions should take place inside the organization or across organizational boundaries; seek lowest possible transaction costs

consensus. Owners, managers, and lower-level employees often operate under different assumptions about what is important to the organization and what is important to the individual. The goal of owners is the economically efficient operation of their firm and minimization of risk. Such a situation should lead to wealth maximization. Employees, according to organizational economic theorists, seek to minimize their work and maximize their rewards.

Economic theorists suggest that agents (i.e., managers and workers) do not perform in the manner in which they agreed because they value leisure more than hard work. Agents *shirk* their responsibilities and duties. This problem is referred to as **_moral hazard_**—workers will not put forth the agreed-upon effort.[11] Also, agents are likely to misrepresent themselves by claiming skills, knowledge, achievements, or other advantages that owners cannot easily verify. This condition is known as **_adverse selection_**.[12]

For example, suppose you were enrolled in a large lecture class of 250 students and you agreed as part of the class to attend every class meeting. However, it is spring term and the weather is nice, so you skip class—even though you agreed (contracted) to attend class. You have *shirked* your responsibility. When the professor entered into a contract with you to attend class, she was faced with the problem of *moral hazard*—that you might not obey the contract. You realized that in a class of 250 students it might be difficult for the professor to monitor attendance. In entering into this contract, you portrayed yourself as an honest and dependable individual. The professor had no way of easily verifying that image of you. Consequently, the professor was faced with the problem of adverse selection. Thus, an objective of organizing and creating governance mechanisms is to reduce the opportunities for people to behave opportunistically.

Information Asymmetry

Information related to exchanges or transactions is not evenly distributed among participants.[13] One participant is likely to have more information than another. For example, a department or division may mislead or withhold information from top management about performance or conditions in that department or division to enhance how it is perceived. This is possible in large, complex organizations because it may be difficult to monitor the department or division. In Chapter 11, we present a brief example of just such behavior in an automobile company division.

Agency theory has used this concept to explain the opportunism and moral hazard problem. Agents (employees) are likely to have certain information about their own behavior and shortcomings that is not readily available to principals (owners). If the owners knew of these shortcomings, they would either terminate the relationship or, at a minimum, pay the agents less. Principals (owners) attempt to reduce information asymmetry by carefully monitoring and constructing contracts and by using other governance mechanisms discussed later in this chapter. Some critics of agency theory note that agency theorists emphasize information asymmetry favoring agents and contributing to opportunism. These critics suggest that principals (owners) may also possess information advantages and exhibit opportunism toward agents (employees).[14]

According to transaction cost theorists, the problem of information asymmetry is, in part, what motivates key decisions about whether to conduct certain tasks (i.e., transactions) within the boundaries of the organization (i.e., internalized) or outside the boundaries through contracts with suppliers and contractors. If management believes that potential outside suppliers and contractors have considerably more information and knowledge about issues related to a specific transaction, management may fear that the outsiders may cheat the firm through misrepresentation. Under such conditions, management may regard the cost of such a transaction—fear and uncertainty about the supplier's conduct along with the costs of gathering information and monitoring the supplier's conduct—as too high. Under those conditions, the firm's management may decide that internalizing the operation is more efficient.

A university may rely on outside contractors to perform cleaning and maintenance tasks, for example. The rationale for hiring outsiders to perform this work is that these companies specialize in cleaning and maintenance tasks. Moreover, the university administration would not have to deal with the capital costs of upkeep for cleaning and maintenance equipment or the management and supervision of these workers. A typical agreement would require that cleaning and maintenance be performed after hours. However, it may be difficult, particularly in a large university, to completely monitor

EXHIBIT 9-2

Human Nature: An Alternative View[15]

The view of human nature painted by organizational economics, especially agency theory, is rather bleak—humans are motivated by self-interest. Whether you call it self-interest or opportunism, the result is the same. Agents will do virtually anything, including misrepresentation (adverse selection) and shirking responsibilities (moral hazard), in order to extract the best possible outcomes from principals.

Organizational theorist Charles Perrow believes this economic view is, at best, an oversimplification and, at worst, downright wrong. He identifies several problems with the economic view of the world of organizations.

First, the agency theory view of interactions between agents and principals suggests that agents are the problem. Information asymmetries favor agents in their interactions with principals. It is equally probable that principals can misrepresent themselves to agents. Agents do not always know the true value of their work to principals. Internal and external labor markets are imperfect mechanisms for valuing work. Thus, the problem of adverse selection can work both ways, but agency theory only considers agent misrepresentation. Exploitation of workers by owners is more than just an abstract possibility.

Second, Perrow notes that the opportunism, shirking, and laziness associated with the moral hazard problem may be overstated. Our work interactions often go well beyond the simplified idea of a contract between owners and workers. It is possible that employees do not have to be coerced, that they willingly take on responsibilities, and that they are capable of honest and charitable acts. Not everything we do is done simply for economic reward. Agency theory assumes that self-interest is human nature; yet, much that people do is either neutral or is directed toward improving the conditions of others. Perrow warns that agency theory in its extreme may even be dangerous. He notes that it creates a lens through which we view much that goes on. We are likely to attribute our good fortune to hard work and misfortune to laziness or avarice. Often luck or circumstances come into play, and we may make faulty assumptions about the causes of people's behaviors. Moreover, viewing an organization as merely a collection of contracts oversimplifies the richness of organizations.

the performance of the outside contractor. Thus, the contractor may withhold information and misrepresent the quality and extent of the cleaning tasks performed. Other problems might involve damage to the buildings and theft. If the cost of monitoring and enforcing the agreement with the contractor grows too large, the university may decide that it will be better off (i.e., the transaction is less costly) if the task is internalized. This, of course, means that the university now has to create a cleaning and maintenance department, hire workers and supervisors, and invest in the appropriate equipment and supplies. However, the university is assuming that monitoring and disciplining the performance of internalized cleaning crews who are university employees will be easier than monitoring and disciplining the contractor.

Asset Specificity

Any organization has to invest in some specific assets necessary to achieve its goals. The degree to which these assets are fixed and specific (versus flexible and general) is referred to as asset specificity.[16] A high degree of asset specificity means that an organization may lack flexibility. It may be locked into certain relationships with outside suppliers, or it may have difficulty changing internal tasks and relationships.

For example, a manufacturing company that invests heavily in customized milling and grinding equipment may find it difficult to change the nature of tasks in the milling and grinding department. The machinery—specific assets—restricts flexibility. That same investment may also make it costly for the company to turn to an outside company to perform milling and grinding work, even if conditions change and the outside company can do the work more efficiently. Thus, the decision to invest (or not invest) in specific assets has implications for how the organization governs its relationship with employees and other firms.

Let us return to the earlier example of the cleaning crews at the university. Suppose the university, rather than hiring outside contractors for cleaning and maintenance, invests in cleaning equipment, employees to perform the cleaning, facilities to house the equipment, and supervisory staff. By making these investments, the university has created some asset specificity. Once these investments are made, it may be costly, difficult, or impossible to switch these assets to other uses. The cleaning equipment cannot be used for other tasks; the personnel may be limited in the tasks they can perform (e.g., they cannot teach organization theory); and the new facility may be difficult to convert to other uses. Thus, once these investments are made, the costs of switching to other options for cleaning are increased. In this way asset specificity adds to transaction costs.

Small Numbers

Another transaction problem that organizations may face is having only a small number of potential trading partners (i.e., an oligopoly).[17] For example, Aldila, a maker of graphite composite golf club shafts, was the primary supplier to Callaway Golf, a premier club maker. Aldila sold nearly two-thirds of its production to Callaway and Callaway depended on Aldila for a majority of its shafts.[18] Early in this relationship there were only a few other companies manufacturing high-quality graphite golf club shafts. This situation illustrates small numbers trading relationships for both Callaway and Aldila. In this case, each company is highly dependent on the other, although it is not necessary for both partners to be so dependent that a small numbers trading problem exists. Aldila has the potential to sell its product to many other golf club manufacturers. Callaway, until recently, had only a few other potential suppliers of shafts.

The problem with small numbers is that an organization can be more easily exploited by a trading partner. Knowing that Callaway depended on Aldila for a reliable supply of shafts, Aldila could exploit the situation and raise the transaction costs for Callaway. For example, it could have forced Callaway to pay more, buy in larger quantities, or agree to less favorable terms, although there is no evidence that Aldila acted in this way. Callaway eventually decided to reduce its dependence on Aldila by seeking other suppliers. By expanding its supplier base, Callaway lessens its dependence on any one supplier and reduces the small numbers problem. It could also have decided to **internalize** (i.e., vertically integrate) either by acquiring a graphite shaft maker or by starting its own operation. That action would have required a significant investment in specific assets, and as we just noted, asset specificity creates other transaction costs that could be a problem for Callaway.

Table 9-3 summarizes this discussion of costs. In general, firms seek ways of organizing that reduce all of these **transaction** or **agency costs**. Transaction and agency costs are sources of inefficiency. They detract from owners' goals of wealth maximization. In the

TABLE 9-3 Sources of Agency and Transaction Costs

- **Bounded rationality**—Humans (e.g., managers and owners) are limited in their ability to process information.
- **Opportunism**—Human beings operate on the basis of self-interest resulting in problems of moral hazard and adverse selection.
- **Information asymmetry**—Information related to exchanges or transactions is not evenly distributed among participants.
- **Asset specificity**—Degree of investment that are in specific fixed assets that cannot easily be used for other purposes.
- **Small numbers**—Organizations are faced with only a small number of potential trading partners (an oligopoly).

following section we examine mechanisms that are used to control transaction and agency costs.

MECHANISMS FOR ORGANIZATIONAL GOVERNANCE

In the previous section we noted considerable overlap between the two economic perspectives. That was true with respect to identifying costs and inefficiencies. However, the overlap and similarity between agency cost and transaction cost perspectives are less when it comes to remedies. This is, in part, because of the differences in the organizational phenomenon upon which they focus. Nonetheless, there are still similarities. Both economic perspectives, using the organization as a mechanism to support exchanges, address exchanges between owner and employee and exchanges between the organization and its environment. Organizational economics seeks governance mechanisms or organizational arrangements that reduce the costs of these exchanges.[19] Agency theory emphasizes legal aspects of control—contracts and legally designated governing bodies. The transaction cost perspective emphasizes the designation of efficient boundaries for an organization—which operations should take place inside the organization and which should take place outside.

Contracting and Monitoring to Reduce Agency Costs

According to agency theory, problems are the result of goal differences between principals (owners) and agents (employees).[20] Principals seek to maximize wealth through the efficient operation of the firm. Agents seek to maximize their share of wealth in relation to the effort they put forth on the job (i.e., maximize pay and benefits while minimizing effort). Therein lies the first part of the problem: Owners seek maximal effort from employees at minimal cost (i.e., efficiency) while employees seek to minimize effort and maximize remuneration (i.e., pay and benefits).

Owners attempt to protect their interests by creating contracts that obligate either employee behavior (i.e., *behavioral contracts*) or employee performance (i.e., *outcome-based contracts*).[21] Behavioral contracts are contracts that specify that employees engage in specific activities.

For example, behavioral contracts may specify employee work hours and tasks to be performed. Employee compensation would be based on behavior—being at work during prescribed hours and performing required tasks. Behavioral contracts are used when the desired outcomes are unclear or difficult to measure, when tasks are fairly routine, and when the extent of goal conflict between owners and employees is not great.[22]

Outcome-based or performance contracts tie compensation and rewards to measurable outcomes. Piece-rate production, commissions, and pay-for-performance are all examples of outcome-based contracts. For example, in some leading corporations chief executive pay and bonuses are based on the company's overall performance. Compensation may be tied to the company's stock price, sales growth, or profits. Another example of an outcome-based contract is the sales commission paid to a salesperson. Outcome-based contracts are used when there are large differences in goals between owners and agents, when behavior on the job is difficult to monitor, and when outcomes are easily measured.[23]

Boards of Directors and Control

Boards of directors potentially play an important role in the control and governance of a company. Boards are charged with the responsibilities of advising, counseling, and critically listening to reports by management; assessing firm performance; acting on designated board tasks; and suggesting means for improving the organization.[24] Stockholders select a board of directors that is supposed to represent stockholder interests in an organization. The board is charged with the *fiduciary responsibility* (i.e., legal trusteeship) of safeguarding the stockholders' investments in the company. The board of directors plays the role of intermediary between the officers of the company and the stockholders.

Boards are usually composed of two sets of representatives: insiders, who are officers, former officers, or relatives of officers of the firm, and outsiders, who may be stockholders but lack any other formal work relationship to the company (i.e., they are not employees, former employees, or relatives of employees of the company). Outsiders are supposed to be objective observers of the organization as well as potential sources of knowledge, skills, expertise, and information. Ideally, it is the outside board members who monitor and provide oversight for the organization. Inside board members can provide insight and expertise into the specific operational issues associated with running the company. Overall the board of directors should play the following key roles:

- Establish policies and objectives of the firm
- Elect, monitor, advise, evaluate and compensate the corporate officers, and approve their actions
- Protect the value of the corporate assets
- Monitor, approve, and report on the financial condition of the firm, including required reports to stockholders and regulators
- Delegate selected board powers to others, as necessary
- Ensure that the corporate charter and by-laws are enforced and are revised, as necessary
- Maintain the integrity of the board.[25]

In theory, the board of directors should provide an important system of checks and balances against opportunistic behavior by management. However, practice and reality sometimes do not coincide. Often the board of directors lacks objectivity and independence. As the following executive pay example in Exhibit 9-3 suggests, some board members are beholden to the top management of the firm. One problem is that many of the potential directors are selected by management and usually run for election to the board unopposed. Stockholders are left with only limited choices to fill board positions. The result is that boards are often packed with friends and business acquaintances of the firm's top management. This situation is made more precarious when the

---

EXHIBIT 9-3

Pay-for-Performance?

It is really a very simple idea—pay people on the basis of their performance.[26] Many organizations manage to do just that with lower- and mid-level employees. Some companies pay lower-level production workers based on their productivity. This is referred to as piece-rate compensation. The employee gets paid for each piece produced. Produce more widgets; get paid more. Produce fewer widgets; get paid less. Salespeople paid commissions on sales are also receiving performance-based compensations. Sell more cars; get paid more. Sell fewer cars; get paid less.

The idea, although imperfect, is consistent with the idea of outcome-based contracting. Workers contract to perform certain tasks—produce widgets or sell cars—and receive compensation. The compensation system becomes a governance mechanism for the control of performance desired by the firm's owners. The system requires that outcomes or performance be easily measured.

But compensation of top managers, a place where pay-for-performance seems logical, is exactly where it is most problematic.[27] Top managers, particularly chief executive officers (CEOs), are responsible for the overall performance of the firm. For owners (shareholders), that performance is probably best indicated by the firm's stock value. The problem is that CEO pay typically bears little relationship to the firm's stock performance. Moreover, determining the value of a CEO's complete compensation package, which typically includes bonuses, stock grants, options, and other "rewards" in addition to base salary, is often quite difficult. It's clear that when companies do well and stock value increases, CEO compensation rises. What's not as clear is what happens when a company's value doesn't rise as fast as the industry average, or when the value falls. A few examples illustrate the point.

Fortune magazine used to run annual surveys of executive compensation. *Fortune* reported in 1993 Travelers, Inc. CEO, Sanford Weill, received the highest total compensation package among *Fortune* 500 firms, worth $45.7 million. That huge compensation package may be justified by the 30 percent annual rate of return for shareholders over the past 5 years. But that return on investment for shareholders ranked only 11th among the top 200 firms. In fact, among companies with the 200 highest paid CEOs, International Game Technology had the highest annual rate of return for shareholders (88.5 percent) in the past 5 years. Yet, CEO John J. Russell's compensation package of $4.4 million was only 55th on the list of highest paid CEOs in the United States.[28] These *levels* of compensation and performance also deal with the *increases* in compensation and performance.

In a 1991 *Fortune* survey, compensation expert Graef Crystal developed a model for realistically valuing executive compensation packages and for determining the match between the compensation the CEO received and what should have been received, based on the company's performance.[29] Eighty-six out of 200 CEOs received more than Crystal's model predicted they should receive. The top 23 compensation packages exceeded the predicted amounts of compensation by over 100 percent! The top-paid CEO in the 1991 survey was Time Warner CEO Steven Ross, whose compensation ($35.1 million) exceeded the model by over 1,000 percent. Number two was Reebok's Paul Fireman, whose compensation ($20.8 million) was 960 percent over what the model predicted. Clearly, there were many CEOs whose salaries fell below the levels predicted by Crystal's model.

Why is compensation imperfect as a governance mechanism? Crystal points to several factors. First is the problem of *information asymmetry*.[30] The group responsible for setting CEO compensation is the compensation committee of the board of directors. This committee is considered to be lowest in prestige of the various board committees, which may mean that compensation committee members are not particularly committed to their task. Additionally, the committee is made up of outsiders, board members who are not officers, retired officers, or relatives of officers of the firm. This is supposed to give

(continued)

them independence, but they often lack key information in making compensation decisions. As a result, the CEO can selectively provide information to the committee that enhances his or her positive performance and downplays negative performance. Second, CEOs typically hire compensation consultants to craft and present generous compensation packages to the board of directors. Although the compensation expert is hired by the CEO, he or she is really under contract to the organization. This presents problems of objectivity and loyalty. Does the consultant develop a package that is best for the company (i.e., owners and principals) or best for the CEO (agent)? The consultant's arcane presentation of compensation information to the committee may also go well beyond the limited expertise of committee members. Third, outside board members are often selected by and beholden to the CEO. Thus, CEOs often select people on whom they can count to rubber-stamp generous compensation packages. These factors can result in CEO compensation packages that are overly generous and unrelated to the company's performance.

It is interesting to note that Time-Warner (now AOL Time-Warner) stopped publishing Crystal's studies. While the company never confirmed its reasons for that action, many critics speculate that the negative attention given to many firms and their CEOs was a factor. (See www.bloomberg.com for articles by Graef Crystal on compensation.)

chairman of the board of directors is also the chief executive officer—the top management position in the firm. Other members often have their own agenda that is not consistent with that of either management or owners of the firm. And sometimes boards of directors lack the skills and expertise to monitor and act in ways that improve the control and performance of the firm.[31] The net result is that, in the best case scenario, an independent and intelligent board can provide some control over management. In the worst-case scenario, boards may become merely a rubber stamp for top management or they may even be completely inept at controlling top management.

Markets as Disciplinary Forces

Important sources of control that are exerted on a firm are the disciplinary force of markets.[32] This means that various markets, such as the stock market, labor market, and debt market, can provide feedback about a company's performance. This feedback pressures the company's management to perform better.

The following example illustrates how markets discipline managers. Games Incorporated (GI) is a maker of electronic games. The company is traded on the stock market, and many investors own shares in the company. GI's management embarked on an aggressive campaign to expand its market and invested large amounts of money in research, facilities development, and new personnel. At the beginning of the year, the company's stock traded at $10 per share. When the company announced this new strategy, the share price went up to $13. Investors were indicating their approval of the aggressive new strategy. However, at the end of the year management announced that sales were disappointingly low, and investors tried to unload shares in GI. The share price dropped to $7. Investors signaled their disapproval of management's performance. In an extreme case, owners who thought the firm had been mismanaged could try to force management out (i.e., fire them) or a potential owner could try to take over the firm by buying all the shares. The new owner of the firm would be indicating that he or she thought that the firm had potential to do better under different ownership and management.

Labor markets and debt markets can provide similar forms of discipline on managers. Successful managers should find that they are in demand in the labor market. Other firms may attempt to woo them away from their companies. However, after the expansion plans at GI backfired, it was unlikely that GI executives would be in high demand by other firms. Thus, the labor market, the potential to move among different firms, and the ability to demand higher salaries provide an incentive to perform. If prior to GI's recent expansion plan the company had performed well, it would probably not have had difficulty borrowing money. Borrowing money puts pressure on a company to become more efficient because the firm now has to pay off debt. After GI's poor performance, the debt market will discipline the company by lowering the company's credit rating and forcing it to pay higher interest.[33] In the extreme, the debt market can discipline a company that is performing poorly by forcing it into bankruptcy.

TRANSACTION COSTS AND THE EFFICIENT BOUNDARIES OF THE FIRM

According to the transaction cost economic perspective on organizations, a critical choice that a firm faces is the determination of efficient boundaries of the organization. This phrase means that firm owners must make decisions about which activities should take place within the boundaries of the firm and which activities should be done outside the firm's boundaries. When transactions take place outside a firm's boundaries, the firm must monitor the marketplace in search of trustworthy, reliable providers of key resources. This is referred to as *market control*. When markets fail, when these transactions are too costly or difficult to monitor, the firm will internalize the transaction. Once internalized, management has two options for controlling the transactions: *bureaucratic control* and *clan control*.

Market Control

Early in the history of Ford Motor Company, the company purchased steel from the major steel producers. At various times during the automobile production cycle, buyers would conduct transactions with steel producers to buy quantities of steel. This type of transaction is often referred to as a market transaction or market control. The company would seek bids from competing steel companies to supply specific quantities and qualities of steel.

Market control relies on prices and competition in external markets to control transaction-related costs. With many suppliers and many buyers of steel, there should be extensive (nearly perfect) competition among sellers for customers. To attract customers, sellers of steel are forced through price competition to offer fair market value. Sellers would be unable to extract high prices because of competition. Some other seller is always willing to undercut a competitor's high price until the market reaches equilibrium. With nearly perfect competition, buyers and sellers all know the fair market price. Market control should work to produce efficient transactions as long as sufficient numbers of sellers and buyers are present in the marketplace to produce nearly perfect competition and as long as sufficient knowledge or information is present so that buyers can safeguard against seller opportunism. So, for example, Ford Motor Company needed to be able to judge accurately the quality of steel the sellers were offering. If the buyer is unable to make this type of judgment, then market controls may fail. It is also important to note that when two companies are engaged in repeated transactions over a long period of time, there is strong motivation for the supplier firm to honestly represent its goods. Otherwise, once the buyer firm learns of the deceptions or misrepresentations, it will discontinue transactions.

Market control can also be used inside a firm when an individual, department, or division has outputs that can be easily measured with respect to their price. In many respects, the outcome-based contracts mentioned earlier are examples of market control. The firm rewards performance and bids for the continuation of that performance on a market basis. Internal and external labor markets exist to fix the price of specific types of labor. However, it is difficult to price many support services and basic functions such as information systems support and accounting, but some organizations are using external bidding in the marketplace to force greater internal efficiency and control. Additionally, market control can be used to monitor the performance of divisions or departments, especially self-contained product divisions where there is a measurable outcome that can be priced in the marketplace. For example, earlier in the book we noted General Electric's drive to be number one or number two in everything it does. The company used the external marketplace to evaluate the performance of various divisions.[34] GE determined that the performance of the television and small appliance divisions was unsatisfactory and thus decided to sell those divisions. Prior to the time of the sale, the market pressure on these divisions acted to control and direct performance. Division executives knew that their performance would be judged against that of marketplace competitors.

Bureaucratic Control

Let us return to Ford Motor Company. In 1919, Henry Ford determined that he did not want his company to be at the mercy of large steel companies. Perhaps he feared that the few large steel companies would exploit Ford's dependence on steel and raise prices. Ford may also have worried that the steel companies would pass off inferior goods. Or perhaps the steel makers would be insensitive to Ford's specific needs. As a result of the increasing dependence on steel, Ford built the large River Rouge industrial complex that included a steel foundry where Ford processed its own steel.[35] In sum, Ford decided that the transaction costs of dealing with the large steel companies were too high; thus, he vertically integrated into the steel business. He defined the efficient boundaries of his firm so that they included steel making. This internalization of a transaction is also referred to as hierarchical or bureaucratic control.[36]

Bureaucratic control means that control of a particular transaction is done through the organization's hierarchy or bureaucracy. Recall that a bureaucracy emphasizes narrow specialization; limited areas of decision responsibility; and the extensive use of rules, policies, and procedures. Thus, when Ford Motor Company internalized steel production, the operation was controlled by the narrowly skilled specialization of employees; referral of problems up the organizational hierarchy; and application of rules, policies, and procedures. Control mechanisms often include such things as comprehensive job descriptions and performance appraisal systems, statistical or numerical control systems to monitor and control production, budgeting and accounting systems to monitor financial performance, and work rules or procedural guidelines for the conduct of tasks.[37] As you can see, bureaucratic control is similar in many respects to the behavioral contracting of agency theory. Through the use of bureaucratic control mechanisms, Ford could attempt to ensure that steel was more efficiently produced for its operations than if the company had relied on outside firms to supply steel. By directly monitoring employees and applying rules, hierarchy, and specialization, Ford could remove many of the problems of dealing with an imperfect market and external firms for steel.

Clan Control

In both Chapters 2 and 8 we mentioned that bureaucracies can become inefficient. This is especially true when the organization faces uncertainty from the environment and the technology. Rule creation, monitoring, and enforcement require personnel, time, and money. With the creation of rules and layers of hierarchy for monitoring and enforcing rules, the organization becomes inflexible and unable to meet changing conditions. Organizational efficiency can suffer.

The organic organizational structure was proposed as an alternative to bureaucratic structure. Jobs and responsibilities are broadened; hierarchy is reduced; and decision making is pushed down to lower levels of the organization. We did not, however, discuss in detail in those earlier chapters how the organization can achieve control in the organic organization. For control in the organic organization we turn to ***clan control***.

Clan control utilizes the shared norms, values, and beliefs of organizational members to ensure that people pursue common goals and objectives.[38] At the root of these shared norms, values, and beliefs is the organization's culture, which gives them expression through cultural mechanisms such as stories and myths about the organization, symbols, traditions, and ceremonies. We discuss these in greater detail in Chapter 10. For now, note that these commonly held norms, values, and beliefs, as expressed through the culture, operate to produce goal consensus and commitment to the organization.

Clan control can be implemented through the careful screening, selection, or training of employees. For example, some organizations only hire graduates of specific colleges or universities with particular degrees because the employer believes that the college or university, along with the academic discipline, instills a particular set of values or beliefs in employees. Other organizations rely on internal training, sometimes coupled with specific initiation rites to produce shared norms, values, and beliefs. The armed forces provide good examples of this approach. The combination of uniforms, boot camp, and training provides recruits with a common vision and shared identity. The armed forces combine clan control with a heavy dose of bureaucratic control. Clearly, significant numbers of rules and official procedures are also used to achieve goals in the armed forces. Fraternities, sororities, social organizations, and religious institutions use clan control. Businesses are relying more on clan control, particularly as they downsize, eliminate layers of hierarchy, and reengineer.

When members of the organization share values, norms, and beliefs and when they are committed to the commonly held goals of the organization, it is less likely that opportunism will be a problem. Employees come to realize that their well-being and the well-being of the organization are intimately linked. If opportunism is not present, then information asymmetry is less of a problem. Employees use information and knowledge in pursuit of the shared goals of the organization. Clearly, clan control does not eliminate all transaction costs, but it does reduce problems of opportunism.

One area in which Ford Motor Company successfully emphasized shared values was in its "Quality is Job #1" campaign. Like GM and Chrysler, Ford was plagued in the 1970s and early 1980s with low-quality products compared with those of Japanese and European competitors. In the mid-1980s, Ford instituted the "Quality is Job #1" campaign with signs placed prominently throughout factories and advertisements featuring the slogan. Workers were trained in techniques to improve quality, and quality circles were instituted to get worker insights on how the company could change procedures to increase quality. In short, quality became a shared value among Ford employees. That shared value, a foundation of clan control, became a mechanism for controlling employee behavior. Workers would monitor their own work and that of fellow workers to ensure quality. Some aspects of bureaucratic control (rules) and market controls (customer demands for higher quality) were present, but shared values were a key factor.

Similarly, in the introductory case on the Thermos Company, clan control was used to achieve teamwork. Because both Ford and Thermos were facing new and uncertain conditions, it was important that they assemble autonomous work groups that could make decisions and enact policies that dealt with the environment and technology. Reliance on bureaucracy could have been cumbersome and might have produced inefficiencies and delays. The belief is that the organization can count on team members to perform in appropriate ways because they share the basic values, norms, and beliefs of the organization. At Ford, workers shared the value that quality was critical to the success of the company and were thus committed to quality improvement. At Thermos, team members shared the basic commitment to product innovation and cross-disciplinary cooperation.

SUMMARY

This chapter has introduced organizational economics as a vehicle for describing organizational control. In particular, two theoretical frameworks have been presented. Agency theory focuses on the relationships between owners (principals) and employees (agents). Transaction costs focus on decisions about the organization's boundaries—whether certain operations should be conducted within the organization or outside its boundaries. The objective of both perspectives is to describe *efficient forms of organizing.*

Owners and managers run into problems in their quest for efficiency. These problems, also called agency costs or transaction costs, include bounded rationality, opportunism, information asymmetry, asset specificity, and small numbers of exchange partners. The objective of owners is to maximize efficiency by reducing these sources of transaction and agency costs.

Transaction and agency costs can be reduced through the use of appropriate governance mechanisms. Agency theory emphasizes legal aspects of control through behavioral and outcome-based contracting or through boards of directors. Through the use of markets, bureaucracies, or clans as control mechanisms, transaction cost theory describes the conditions under which transactions should be internalized or conducted by external suppliers. Markets, bureaucracies, and clans represent different governance mechanisms for controlling transactions.

Questions for Discussion

1. According to agency theory, how would you describe basic human nature? How does this basic human nature contribute to agency costs?
2. How do behavior contracts and outcome-based contracts differ? Describe the situations in which each would apply.
3. Transaction cost economics focuses on determining the efficient boundaries of the firm. What does this mean? According to transaction cost theory, what is the central decision that firms face?
4. What are the sources of transaction and agency costs that affect transactions and agent-principal relations?

5. Compare and contrast bureaucratic control and clan control. Under what conditions would you use each?
6. Charles Perrow voiced concern about the dangers of economic theories of organizations, particularly agency theory. What are his concerns? Do you think he is justified? Why? Why not?

References

1. A. A. Berle, and G. C. Means, *The Modern Corporation and Private Property* (New York: Macmillan, 1932); R. Coase, "The Nature of the Firm," *Economica* 4 (1937): 386–405; E. Fama, "Agency Problems and the Theory of the Firm," *Journal of Political Economy* 88 (1980): 288–307; O. E. Williamson, *The Economics of Discretionary Behavior: Managerial Objectives in a Theory of the Firm* (Upper Saddle River, NJ: Prentice Hall, 1964).
2. See Fama in note 1; M. Jensen, and W. Meckling, "Theory of the Firm: Managerial Behavior, Agency Costs, and Ownership," *Journal of Financial Economics* 3 (1976): 305–60; K. M. Eisenhardt, "Agency Theory: An Assessment and Review," *Academy of Management Review* 14 (1989): 57–74.
3. See Williamson in note 1; O. E. Williamson, "Comparative Economic Organization: The Analysis of Discrete Structural Alternatives," *Administrative Science Quarterly* 36 (1991): 269–96.
4. B. M. Oviatt, "Agency and Transaction Cost Perspectives on the Manager-Shareholder Relationship: Incentives for Congruent Interests," *Academy of Management Review* 13 (1988): 214–25.
5. See Williamson in note 1.
6. W. S. Hesterly, J. Liebeskind, and T. R. Zenger, "Organizational Economics: An Impending Revolution in Organization Theory?" *Academy of Management Review* 15 (1990): 402–20.
7. O. E. Williamson, "The Economics of Organization: The Transaction Cost Approach," *American Journal of Sociology* 87 (1981): 548–77.
8. See Williamson (1991) in note 3.
9. Herbert A. Simon, *Administrative Behavior*, 3rd ed. (New York: The Free Press, 1976); G. R. Jones and C. W. L. Hill, "Transaction Cost Analysis of Strategy-Structure Choice," *Strategic Management Journal* 9 (1976): 159–72; see Eisenhardt in note 2.
10. Ibid.
11. See Eisenhardt in note 2.
12. Ibid.
13. Ibid; see Jones and Hill in note 9.
14. C. Perrow, *Complex Organizations*, 3rd ed. (New York: Random House, 1986).
15. This discussion is based on Chapter 7 of *Complex Organizations*, see note 14.
16. See Jones and Hill in note 9.
17. Ibid.
18. Michael Gonzalez, "Stock Prices Rally to End Mixed After Sell-Off Tied to Mexico Aid," *The Wall Street Journal* (January 24, 1995), C2.
19. See note 6.
20. See Eisenhardt in note 2.
21. Ibid.
22. Ibid.
23. Ibid.
24. J. K. Louden, *The Director* (New York: American Management Association, 1982).
25. R. S. Chaganti, V. Mahajan, and S. Sharma, "Corporate Board Size, Composition, and Corporate Failures in Retailing Industry," *Journal of Management Studies* 22 (1985): 400–17; Conference Board, *Corporate Directorship Practices, Studies in Business Policy* (New York: Conference Board, 1967).
26. Thomas Rollins, "Pay for Performance: Is It Worth the Trouble?" *Personnel Administrator* (May 1988): 42–46; Charles Cumming, "Linking Pay to Performance," *Personnel Administrator* (May 1988): 47–52.
27. Graef S. Crystal, "Why CEO Compensation Is So High," *California Management Review* 34 (Fall 1991): 9–29.
28. Brian Dumaine, "A Knockout Year for CEO Pay," *Fortune* 130, no. 2 (July 25, 1994): 94–103.
29. Graef S. Crystal, "How Much CEOs Really Make," *Fortune* 127 (June 17, 1991): 72–80.
30. See note 27.
31. Myles L. Mace, *Directors: Myth and Reality* (Boston, MA: Harvard Business School Press, 1971); Murray L. Weidenbaum, "Battle of the Boardroom: Controlling the Future Corporation," *Business and Society Review* 58 (1986): 10–12.
32. O. E. Williamson, Corporate Finance and Governance," *The Journal of Finance* 43 (1988): 567–91; see Jones and Hill in note 9; Rita D. Kosnik, "Greenmail: A Study of Board Performance in Corporate Governance," *Administrative Science Quarterly* 32 (1987): 163–85.
33. See Williamson in note 32.
34. Stratford Sherman, "A Master Class in Radical Change," *Fortune* (December 13, 1993): 82–90; Tim

Smart, "Jack Welch on the Art of Thinking Small," *Business Week* (Special Enterprise Issue, 1993): 212–15.

35. P. Collier and D. Horowitz, *The Fords: An American Epic* (New York: Summit Books, 1987).

36. W. G. Ouchi, "Markets, Bureaucracies and Clans," *Administrative Science Quarterly* 25 (1980): 129–41.

37. R. L. Daft and N. B. Macintosh, "The Nature and Use of Formal Control Systems for Management Control and Strategy Implementation," *Journal of Management* 10 (1984): 43–66; see note 36.

38. See note 36.

CASE

Sweet Tooth*

For anyone who has ever had a sweet tooth, Mars has tried to have the answer for this craving. With a rich mix of brand names such as Snickers, Milky Way, and M&Ms, the Mars Company seemed to have a corner on the candy market. But lately the sugar coating is melting.

Ownership of the privately held company is vested in the hands of John, Forrest, Jr., and Jacqueline, children of Forrest Mars, Sr. Mars is a closely held and private company. Because its stock is not publicly traded, the usual performance information found in annual reports and other documents supplied to investors is not available for Mars. That which is available, however, tells of a company yielding market share to its competition (e.g., Hershey, Nestlè, and Cadbury Schweppes), both on the domestic and foreign fronts. But its $13 billion estimated annual sales still make it a potent player in the confectionery, pet food, and food-vending businesses.

The lack of innovation in new product development has resulted in no new "big-sale" items. Marketing and sales arms of the company simply have not kept pace with Mars's fanatic quest for quality control. In spite of this condition, competitors are worried because, as they argue, Mars simply doesn't play by everyone else's rules. They're unpredictable, and they don't seem to be too worried about market share loss. They even seem to ignore the situation.

Instead of worrying about losing its domestic market, Mars seems bent on pursuing its global expansion strategy at full speed. Is this tack a visionary move or one based on virtually ignoring environmental information? Whatever the answer, Mars isn't saying, following its veil-of-secrecy stance.

Inside Mars, there is an air of everyone for himself or herself, and it seems everyone is afraid of John and Forrest, Jr., who run the company. Forrest, Jr., is known for his fiery temper and for seeming to enjoy publicly upbraiding Mars's managers. This atmosphere invites filtering information to the point of withholding. This secrecy has probably contributed

to Mars's present condition. Managers can be loath to share information that is either likely to help a fellow manager about to absorb an upbraiding from Forrest, Jr., or to share ideas. If they prove wrong, such ideas could get their "genius" into trouble.

The brothers seem to genuinely enjoy running the company. They are a kind of contradiction, of a sort, when it comes to money, however. They are willing to pay far-above-average salaries and yet demand economy rental cars and make use of discount coupons at hotels when they are on the road. This disdain for fancy spending was doubtlessly handed down from Forrest, Sr., known for his penchant for simplicity and economy.

At corporate headquarters in McLean, Virginia, perks are frowned on, and in operating headquarters in Hackettstown, New Jersey, open offices are the norm. There, there are no private offices, and desks are arranged in an open area divided into zones, from Zone Five for brand managers to Zones One and Two for senior executives. Salaries are posted for all to see, and not from the vantage point of a private dining room, which does not exist. There are no reserved parking spaces either.

This approach to management (a combination of secretiveness, openness, and frugality) has worked from the beginning, but it appears to be faltering now. The best answer to the question, Why? seems to be that the Mars brothers have simply ignored the company's changing environment.

The candy business has seen major mergers and consolidations, exemplified by Philip Morris, Nestlè, and Cadbury Schweppes acquiring smaller companies and then outdoing Mars on the advertising front as well. New products have come from these new organizations. Hershey has been active on its own in this regard with its introduction of new Hugs, Nutrageous, and Nuggets. While all this was happening, Mars simply sat back and watched while it lost significant market share to Hershey.

Mars paid little attention to similar occurrences in the European market where Philip Morris and Cadbury bought companies to consolidate their positions in that market. Result? Mars has seen its share of the German market, for example, fall from 30 percent to 20 percent in just the last 3 years.

Mars has not handled changes occurring in its distribution chain well either. Supermarkets and discount stores have realigned and restructured. Many have centralized and concentrated their buying. At the same time Mars has aggressively pursued a strategy of cost cutting. The result is that Mars has not been able to supply the product necessary to meet the orders it takes. Even though special committees have been established to deal with the problem, success so far has been elusive. The company's policy of asset exhaustion has caused sales to exceed production capacity. The policy is especially worrisome because managers know their pay is directly tied to asset-utilization rates. This policy also means that production facilities may be straining to fulfill orders. In the long run, this may mean equipment breakdowns and further delays.

Special discounts to retailers were abruptly canceled, and these price breaks represent a sizeable portion of retail profits. This lack of sensitivity has caused many to turn to Hershey, which has shown far more flexibility in promotional spending.

The Mars organization doesn't reward risk taking and independent thinking—seemingly necessary conditions for success in the global market that Mars seeks to serve. The company truly believes in global marketing—one market, one product, one message—for what it sees as a homogeneous environment. It has found, however, that the same market program for Spain did not work for England. Same-color labels for all of its Whiskas cat food products did not appeal to all European cat owners.

Mars's venture into "scientific" health food for dogs failed when it was introduced in supermarkets. Mars later learned that buyers bought this type of food in pet stores or vets' offices.

In view of this series of ill-founded decisions, it is no wonder that there is concern about whether the Mars brothers have the ability to lead the company into a bright future. With a history of "chewing up" executive talent, lacking innovation, ignoring the environment, and displaying irritating personalities, could it be that Mars's ability to satisfy our sweet tooth might be turning sour? ∎

*This case is based on the following article: Bill Saporito, "The Eclipse of Mars," *Fortune* (November 28, 1994): 82–84, 86, 90, 92.

QUESTIONS FOR DISCUSSION

1. How would you describe the methods of governance and control that the Mars brothers have used to run their company?

2. Mars is a privately held company (stock is not traded on any market). How would this affect the control of management's behavior and performance? How else could Mars use markets to discipline management?

3. Could clan control be used at Mars? How could the company adopt a clan control philosophy of management?

4. If you were brought in as a consultant to Mars, what would you recommend that the company do with respect to control in order to achieve better performance?

PART IV

Organizational Processes

Organizations are not static entities. They develop, grow, act, and change. We have already begun the process of investigating this dynamic nature of organizations under such topic headings as organizational growth and life cycles, adapting to environmental change, and altering technology. In these final four chapters, we directly examine the dynamic nature of organizational processes.

Chapter 10 introduces the concept of organizational culture. As you look around the landscape of organizations, one of the first things that will strike you is that organizations, even those in the same industry, all look different. The differences go beyond simple appearances and affect the fundamental values, norms, beliefs, expectations, and behaviors of members. Chapter 10 explores how cultures emerge, the impact they have on the organization, how they change, and how they should fit with the basic strategic focus of the organization.

Many business and organizational experts maintain that we are living in an information society today. Among organizational theorists, there are those who view organizations as essentially information processors. True, information is critical and crucial to the functioning of organizations. But information is often only an intermediate stop in the journey to a decision. The process of decision making is ubiquitous in organizations. With the flattening and decentralizing of organizations, more and more members are involved in decision making, as we discuss in Chapter 11.

As outsiders, we sometimes watch organizations do strange and unexpected things. Perhaps a company introduces a new product of dubious merit, for example, a car design that seems to appeal to no particular market. Sometimes a firm fires a person for no apparent reason—at least no apparent reason to outsiders. In Chapter 12 we explore power within organizations and the political nature of organizations. Organizations are not simple machines, but, as we noted in Chapter 1, they are made up of people—people from diverse backgrounds, with different skills, knowledge, goals, and expectations. The result is that organizations do not always act in a rational and predictable manner.

Finally, Chapter 13 formally introduces the notions of organizational innovation, change, and renaissance. Implicitly, we have discussed these topics throughout the book. A hallmark of our strategic perspective is that we have suggested how managers can use knowledge of organizations to bring about desired changes. In Chapter 13, we specifically examine a variety of perspectives on how to change organizations. Additionally, we speculate about the nature of organizations of the twenty-first century and how knowledge of organizations will help managers.

C H A P T E R

10

Organizational Culture

CASE: PUT ON YOUR MAKEUP*

For many women, putting on makeup is an integral part of getting dressed. Few users probably think about what is involved in getting the products to them. For Mary Kay Cosmetics, Inc., every aspect of selling products is intimately tied to the company's culture.

Mary Kay Ash, chairwoman emeritus until her death in 2001, began her career in cosmetics as a young saleswoman for Stanley Home Products, a company that sold cleaners and brushes directly to customers. After failing in 1937 to receive the annual prize for the best sales record in the company, she vowed to gain the prize the following year. Ash's recognition as the top seller at Stanley in 1938 was the beginning of her success and enthusiasm for direct selling.

Ash worked for other direct selling companies and even went into an early "retirement" before deciding in 1963 to start her own company. While she was still employed at Stanley Home Products, Ash learned of a family of particularly effective skin-care products. She invested $5,000 to purchase formulas to begin what is now arguably the most successful direct sales organization in the world—Mary Kay Cosmetics, Inc. The company's sales force numbers approximately 300,000, and many of them share Mary Kay Ash's enthusiasm for selling. That, according to Ash and many analysts, is critical to the company's success. Thus, a key factor in understanding Mary Kay Cosmetics' success is understanding how the company maintains, motivates, and nurtures that enthusiasm for selling.

Cornerstones in the Mary Kay culture are symbols and ceremonies of recognition. Annually, the company holds "The Seminar" at the Dallas headquarters. Beauty consultants (Mary Kay representatives are not merely salespeople) gladly pay their own registration fees and all expenses to be at the "greatest sales party in the United States." At The Seminar consultants learn about products and selling techniques, but the central focus is on the recognition ceremonies where sales performance is publicly rewarded. Nearly every level of performance is in some way recognized with pins and trophies, but the fiercest competition is for the top prize—a pink Cadillac—the symbol that says "You've made it in the company."

To make the sales that are the bases for these recognitions, consultants buy from Mary Kay Cosmetics a basic starter kit for about $100. The mark-up on these basic items is 100 percent. Consultants then call a few friends and hold a Mary Kay Party where they sell items and recruit their own sales force. Income for consultants is unlimited, but real increases in income and promotions typically depend on increasing one's sales force. At the top of the promotion ladder, a national sales director for Mary Kay can earn in excess of $200,000 annually.

---

*Based on Alan Farnham, "Mary Kay's Lessons in Leadership," *Fortune* (September 20, 1993): 68–77.

Emotional and symbolic rewards are perhaps as important as monetary rewards to the consultants, and Mary Kay bestowed them generously. At the annual seminar, color-coded badges, emblems, and even suits are unmistakable symbols of how well their wearers did in the past year. Lapel pins read "$25,000" or a diamond bracelet proclaims "$1,000,000." Many successful consultants were invited to join Ms. Ash on trips.

Shot through all of these rewards for success was the sincerity of Mary Kay Ash. Mary Kay was an icon for the success of direct selling. Moreover, she had the uncanny ability to make her consultants really feel that they were a vital part of a truly successful organization. Her genuine caring for the consultants was further reinforced by her remembering birthdays, children's illnesses, and other individual events or circumstances. The recognition of performance and recognition of the individual are critical to Mary Kay's effective motivational effort and to sustaining the Mary Kay culture. Cynicism has no part to play at Mary Kay Cosmetics.

Another critical feature of the Mary Kay culture was the values she espoused. Ash believed in putting God first, family second, and career third. She stressed this message repeatedly to consultants and to their husbands. Because most Mary Kay consultants are women, the traditional support role falls to their husbands. Mary Kay encouraged her "daughters," as she referred to her consultants, to show their appreciation to their supportive spouses.

Mary Kay created a culture that is the primary vehicle for instilling her strongly held beliefs and values into each consultant and to make each one feel that she is a genuine member of the Mary Kay family. The result is a highly successful company with a cadre of successful and committed consultants who help a lot of women "put on their makeup." With the death of Mary Kay Ash in 2001, the company will be challenged to replace her charismatic leadership that has been an integral part of the culture.

Culture is the key to understanding an organization like Mary Kay Cosmetics. It is the strong set of norms, beliefs, and values of the organization's members along with the stories, myths, symbols, and celebrations that distinguish Mary Kay. Culture is the glue that binds the sales force to the company. Culture gives the company a sense of mission and a distinctiveness. It is key to motivating the consultants, and it is an integral part of the success of Mary Kay Cosmetics.

While every organization has a distinctive culture, not every one is as strong and deep as Mary Kay Cosmetics'. Additionally, culture does not always play the positive role it does at Mary Kay. Some organizations are stifled by cultures that inhibit flexibility, responsiveness, and change.

This chapter presents the key elements of culture and describes how those elements create a sense of purpose and distinctiveness. As you read this chapter, keep in mind that culture is a holistic, overarching phenomenon. Culture is the sum of all parts of an organization—and then some. This is unlike many of the discrete characteristics of organizations that we have examined thus far. Culture, particularly strong culture, plays a critical role in all aspects of organizational life.

ORGANIZATIONAL CULTURE

Since the dawn of human social systems, culture has existed to help people deal with the uncertainty and ambiguity of their existence. Culture develops naturally when groups of humans come together. Members of formal organizations face uncertainties and ambiguities much like those that exist in the larger social system. Thus, it is not surprising that organizations develop distinctive cultures as part of the mechanism for managing the environment.[1] Despite the central nature of culture to human endeavors, exploration of organizational culture is a recent phenomenon. Beginning in the late 1970s, organizational scholars and others realized that culture plays a large part in determining a wide variety of behaviors, attitudes, and beliefs related to work and the workplace. Two important popular books, *Theory Z* by William Ouchi and *In Search of Excellence* by Thomas Peters and Robert Waterman, Jr., marked a heightened awareness of the potential importance of culture among managers, academic researchers, and the general public.[2] Culture appears to develop in organizations much as it does in other types of human groupings and draws from the culture of the large community in which it is embedded. We are beginning to better understand its impact in work organizations.[3]

This chapter presents a multifaceted view of organizational culture. First, culture is defined. We then examine four different perspectives on the formation of culture. Because of the newness and complexity of the concept of organizational culture, the field has not yet arrived at one consistent and widely held set of views about it. After exploring these four perspectives on culture formation, we begin to examine characteristics of culture. After identifying these characteristics, we take the logical next step of describing how to audit organizational culture. Finally, inherent in the discussion of culture is the idea that culture plays a role in an organization's performance. Thus, auditing culture may be an important step to adjusting, adapting, or changing it to better fit an organization's strategic position. The chapter concludes with a discussion of the link between culture and strategy.

CULTURE DEFINED

Scientists from the fields of anthropology and sociology have been studying culture for many years. Still they are quick to note that culture is an abstract and complex concept; thus, many definitions of culture exist. The same is true even with a narrowed focus on **organizational culture**. Most definitions of organizational culture, however, contain some common elements. Most definitions note that culture exists at two levels in organizations: the *observable* traces or indicators of the culture (also referred to as *symbols*) and the *unobservable* forces present in the organization.[4] Observable traces may include physical characteristics of the organization such as architecture, artwork, dress patterns, language, stories, myths, behavior, formal rules, rituals, ceremonies, and appearance.[5] But these physical traces are not the culture itself. They are symbolic indicators of the unobservable characteristics of culture—the norms, beliefs, assumptions, ideology, values, and shared perceptions held by members of the organization.[6] Organizational culture, as one set of scholars has defined it, is a set of broad, tacitly understood rules that tell employees what to do under a wide variety of unimaginable circumstances.[7] It is the "patterns or configurations of these interpretations" of the observable characteristics that make up the culture,[8] the taken-for-granted and shared meanings, beliefs, and assumptions that people in the organization use to cope with problems, adapt to external conditions, and develop internal integration.[9] Thus, culture is a force that orients and directs the behavior of individual organizational members so that there is consistency and predictability within the organization.[10]

DEFINITION

Organizational culture is a two-level construct that includes both observable and unobservable characteristics of the organization. At the observable level, culture includes many aspects of the organization such as architecture, dress, behavior patterns, rules, stories, myths, language, and ceremonies. At the unobservable level culture is composed of the shared values, norms, beliefs, and assumptions of organizational members. Culture is the pattern or configuration of these two levels of characteristics that orients or directs organizational members to manage problems and their surroundings.

For example, in the United States, because the basic values and beliefs that underlie our form of national government are contained in our Constitution, it can be thought of as a reflection or product of our national culture. Many companies have credos or codes of beliefs that similarly reflect their organizational culture. Such documents are at least one indicator of culture.

For example, we discussed JC Penney in the introduction to Chapter 7. The company's credo dates back to the founder, James Cash Penney, who promoted it in 1908.

EXHIBIT 10-1

JC Penney's Credo

THE PENNEY IDEA

- To serve the public, as nearly as we can, to its complete satisfaction.
- To expect for the service we render a fair remuneration and not all the profit the traffic will bear.
- To do all in our power to pack the customer's dollar full of value, quality and satisfaction.
- To continue to train ourselves and our associates so that the service we give will be more and more intelligently performed.
- To improve constantly the human factor in our business.
- To reward men and women in our organization through participation in what the business produces.
- To test our every policy, method and act in this wise: "Does it square with what is right and just?"

Source: From www.jcpenney.net/company/history/history.htm, accessed July 1, 2001.

THE FORMATION OF CULTURE

Culture is not static. Organizational cultures emerge and change as the organization itself changes. Several organizational scholars have written on the formation of organizational culture, each offering somewhat different views on the subject. The perspectives of four leading scholars—Edgar Schein, Christian Scholz, Charles Fombrun, and Meryl Louis—on the formation of organizational culture are presented in the following sections.

Schein's Stages of Culture Formation

People form groups seeking to satisfy needs. They bring goals, values, and even hopes to the group process and endeavor to find ways in which they can achieve what they want. Schein suggests that groups progress through a series of stages that affect culture. Throughout the stages of group development, maintenance and continuation of the group depend on its finding ways to preserve the shared values and norms that hold it together.[11]

According to Schein, the first stage of cultural development revolves around issues of dependency and authority. The question of who will lead the group (or organization) is the focal point. The group looks for someone to give it direction. The type of person who is selected to lead is indicative of many values and norms of the group or organization. Leader characteristics such as age, training, background, gender, and experience may all be important in the formation of the culture. The group or organization must grapple with issues of who they want to lead them and how they want to be led. Some issues that may surface are these: He's too inexperienced to be president; no outsider can understand this business. Both these statements point out issues that surface in this first step of cultural development.

Historically, initial leaders and founders have had great impact on the future culture of their organizations. The JC Penney Company still reflects its founder's beliefs about customer satisfaction and fairness. The "Penney Way" codifies James Cash Penney's beliefs and values about how to conduct business. Henry Ford's ideas about building cars and treating workers influenced (both positively and negatively) the Ford Motor Company long after he died.

Schein's second stage of cultural development involves the "confrontation of intimacy, role differentiation, [and] peer relationship issues."[12] Successful first efforts to deal with the authority issue (first stage) are likely to produce a sense of success and good feelings about membership that are likely to carry over for an extended period of time. Early success can often motivate employees to give greater commitment and effort to the organization. This can be exemplified by NASA's early success at putting Neil Armstrong on the moon or the experience of winning athletic teams. The cultures of Notre Dame's football program, the Boston Celtics and Chicago Bulls professional basketball teams, the Montreal Canadiens hockey team, or the Dallas Cowboys and San Francisco 49ers professional football teams owe much to early success, even long after that success has faded. Each of these organizations has developed unique strong cultures around winning traditions: the divine blessing of Notre Dame, the Celtic mystique, the other-worldliness of the Michael Jordan–led Bulls, the business approach to football of the Cowboys, and the finesse of the 49ers.

During the third stage of cultural development, creativity and stability issues must be confronted. The group or organization begins to cope with the innovative approaches that brought its initial success as that innovation and creativity come into conflict with the needs for order and stability. Although creative and innovative forces may be critical factors in the formation of an organization, those same forces can disrupt the order of the organization.

This clash is typical of many entrepreneurial firms. For example, Steve Jobs, the cofounder of Apple Computers, was a creative, energetic, and visionary manager. Under his leadership the company became a highly successful start-up with unique products. In many respects, Apple Computers defined the concept of personal computing. However, early in the history of Apple, the company had difficulty reining in the creative and innovative spirit. As a consequence, the company had difficulty establishing order and stability. This was most noticeable in the company's haphazard approach to early product development and its inability to successfully market its products to large business users.

Apple owners and managers finally determined that they would need to introduce a skilled business manager to bring about the order and stability the firm needed to grow and prosper. John Sculley, a former Pepsico executive, was eventually hired to provide the professional managerial skills that were deemed necessary for Apple. It would be nice and simple if the Apple story ended here with a successful and prosperous company, but that is not the case. The arrival of Sculley caused great turmoil. His managerial style and philosophy clashed with those of Steve Jobs and many of the early Apple people. Much turnover and tumult followed over the company's need to develop a somewhat more bureaucratic management system, and many managers, including Jobs, eventually left the company. Although Sculley was able to forge a more stable and orderly organization, his tenure at Apple was rocky because of the challenge to the old Apple way of doing things, and he stepped down in 1994. After several leaders failed to provide inspiration and direction, Steve Jobs finally returned to lead Apple. In the late 1990s the company struggled to regain its early position as an innovative leader in personal computing. As the company's market share hovered around 5 percent, analysts questioned whether Apple can survive.

Finally, the organization or group matures only to encounter a confrontation of survival and growth issues. The organization or group learns whether it is flexible and adaptable to changing conditions in the surrounding environment or whether its very survival will be questioned.

The airline industry has been characterized by dramatic upheaval over the past several years due in part to deregulation. Some companies have successfully dealt with survival and growth issues and have made various adjustments to their cultures. Southwest Airlines has developed a unique culture that delivers relaxed, casual, inexpensive transportation to business and recreational travelers. The culture is based on a high degree of employee involvement. After several brushes with failure, Continental Airlines appears to be surviving because of its emphasis on customer service.

In the early 1980s, Lee Iacocca almost single-handedly saved Chrysler Corporation from bankruptcy by leading a major cultural change. The old Chrysler culture was characterized by aversion to risk, pessimism, one-way (top-down) communication, and the insularity of different Chrysler subunits. Chrysler's culture underwent a massive transformation under Iacocca's leadership. The company became aggressive in pursuing government support, new markets, products, and technology; a new optimism pervaded management and production workers; the organization became more streamlined with emphasis on two-way communications (i.e., production workers became important sources of new ideas); and cooperation among subunits became standard procedure.

Since Daimler-Benz merged with Chrysler to become Daimler-Chrysler, the companies face a new cultural challenge—integrating the two disparate cultures of Daimler-Benz and Chrysler. These companies had very different histories, different values, and different symbols; they are the products of different national cultures. Although both Daimler and Chrysler trace their origins to the early days of the automobile industry, Daimler has always been a prestige leader with emphasis on engineering quality. By contrast, Chrysler has occupied a mid-price market niche, and while the company has been known for engineering innovations, it has not had an enduring reputation for quality. Moreover, Daimler was a quintessential German company and Chrysler was a typical American company. The combined company faces the task of trying to integrate these two very different cultures—no easy task.

The stages of cultural development represent changed goals, values, and focus of the organization. The underlying question throughout these stages of development is whether the organization can forge the kind of culture that is needed to survive. This is true even when members are not necessarily aware of attempts to form and change the culture. Table 10-1 summarizes Schein's four stages of cultural development.

Scholz's Typology of Culture Formation

Christian Scholz views organizational culture as a complex phenomenon.[13] He argues that culture develops along three dimensions: an evolutionary dimension, an internal dimension, and an external dimension. These three dimensions make up his typology.

The ***evolutionary dimension*** of cultural formation is somewhat similar to Schein's view: culture develops over time in a series of stages. Scholz proposes that a nascent culture is already in place and that subsequent stages are the result of how the organization responds to challenges to the culture. He outlines five evolutionary stages: (1) the stable stage during which no change is contemplated; (2) the reactive stage during which minimal change is accepted; (3) the anticipating stage when incremental changes are accepted; (4) the exploring stage during which large amounts of change are possible; and (5) the creative stage when continuous change is possible. According to Scholz, not all organizations follow this sequence, nor is any one stage regarded as better than another.

TABLE 10-1   Schein: Culture Formation in Groups

Stage	Dominant Assumption	Group Focus
1. Dependency/ authority confrontation	A leader will guide the group to its maximum benefit.	Leadership selection
2. Confrontation of intimacy, role differentiation, peer relationship issues	The group is successful and the members like each other.	Normative consensus; harmony
3. Creativity/stability issue	The group can be innovative and stable at once.	Team continuity and accomplishment
4. Survival/growth issues	The group has endured and so must be "right."	Group's attention: status quo/resistance to change

Source: Adapted from Edgar H. Schein, *Organizational Culture and Leadership* (San Francisco: Jossey-Bass, 1985): 191.

The focus of the ***internal dimension*** of culture is on particular internal conditions operating within the organization that affect the culture. For example, an organization that uses standardized production processes would create conditions for a culture that is constant and process oriented. The result is a *consistency culture* that places high value on standard procedures and consistent outputs.[14] McDonald's attention to consistent appearance of restaurants and consistent content and preparation of foods is a classic example of the consistency culture. On the other hand, a professional organization with employees possessing varied skills and high levels of professional expertise is likely to foster development of a culture that emphasizes individualism and professionalism. This type of culture is referred to as a *clan* or *involvement culture.* Employees' values and commitment to the organization are central.[15] Southwest Airlines, profiled in Chapter 3, is a clear example of an involvement or clan culture. Shared values are the mechanism that the company uses to create predictability of behavior.

External environmental conditions are the forces that constitute the ***external dimension*** of culture. External conditions and how organizational members perceive and respond to those conditions play a critical role in the development of the culture. A company facing a complex and dynamic environment is likely to develop a culture that values flexibility, innovativeness, and risk taking. The external focus can be manifested in two different ways: as an *adaptability culture* directed at innovations or other attempts to change in response to the environment, or as a *mission culture* with a focus on meeting customer needs.[16] Southwest Airlines and JC Penney have elements of a mission culture; 3M, with its long tradition of research and development, is an example of an adaptability culture focused on innovation. Conversely, an organization facing a simple and stable environment is likely to adapt a culture that features conservatism, risk aversion, and bureaucracy.

Scholz's model of cultural development is somewhat more complex than Schein's. He views organizational culture as arising from these three diverse sets of pressures: time, internal characteristics of the organization, and external conditions in the environment.

Fombrun's Levels of Culture

Charles Fombrun has described the development of culture through forces at three major levels: societal, industrial, and organizational. According to Fombrun's view, organizational culture is a product of the broader culture in which organizations are embedded. Understanding the interplay between societal and industry levels of culture with characteristics of the organization is vital for an accurate analysis of culture and for guidance on how to modify culture.[17]

At the ***societal level*** culture represents the values, attitudes, and meanings that members bring to the organization. This may be influenced by such social forces as the educational system, political system, economic conditions, and the social structure of the larger society. The organization operates within this general cultural atmosphere. These conditions may influence the strategies, mission, objectives, norms, and practices in the organization in subtle but real ways. A company's strategy, products, and advertisements must be consistent with the community culture if the organization wishes to maintain legitimacy and approval.

For example, Cincinnati, Ohio, is regarded as a culturally conservative community. Movies, art exhibits, and music that raise no objection in East Coast or West Coast communities sometimes offend local sensibilities. A local rock radio station, with a tendency toward wacky advertising, offended many in the community with a recent campaign. Billboards featured the heads of two male on-air morning personalities on bodies of naked pregnant women. The billboard text referred to morning sickness. While the campaign was consistent with the station's bizarre sense of humor and its off-the-wall morning show, some people in the city found the billboards so offensive that they withdrew advertising, wrote complaints, and stopped listening to the station. The station eventually withdrew the advertising. The societal level is often an ethical, legal, and social guide to conducting business in a community.

The essence of the ***industrial level*** of culture is best realized by considering the similarities of cultures within and differences in cultures between industries. Often there are dominant values or beliefs of an organization that are espoused by a majority of organizations within an industry. Over time industries develop styles that have a remarkable influence on such things as decision making, political stances, member lifestyles, and even dress codes. For example, the banking industry has had a unique and prevalent way of doing business. At one time banks were concerned almost exclusively with efficiency, cost control, and basic standard service. Until the late 1960s many banks had limited business hours (i.e., "bankers' hours"), staying open only from 9:00 A.M. to 3:00 P.M. with some additional late hours on Fridays. Extended weekday hours, Saturday banking, and ATMs are fairly recent phenomena in the industry, but once a few banks experimented with extended hours, most others joined in. Now banking is characterized by more extensive services, more aggressive marketing, and a customer-oriented focus. Nonetheless, the industry is still characterized as conservative and formal. Managers dress conservatively, avoid risk, and generally advocate fiscal and social conservatism.

Compare banking with the industrial culture present in the entertainment business (i.e., television, recording, and films). The dominant values are for more casual or flamboyant dress, high-risk behavior, and fiscal and social radicalism.

Louis's Multiple Cultures

Up to this point in the discussion we have treated organizational culture as monolithic—that is, an organization has a *single* culture. Cultural researcher Meryl Louis suggests that organizations, especially large, complex ones, often develop different cultures at different sites or ***loci*** within the organization.[18] Thus, unique cultures (perhaps *subcultures* is a better term) may develop around different levels in the organization or within different divisions or departments. Conditions, problems, or personnel at different loci can produce pressures for different cultures within the organization. Moreover, loci outside the organization may also produce conditions for different cultures. For example, in southern California many firms hire large numbers of Hispanic and Asian workers. These workers bring in values, beliefs, and norms derived from their neighborhood ethnic cultures. Another example where the cultural locus is outside the firm is legal departments. Legal departments in firms as diverse as Ford and Exxon may have similar departmental cultures because of the shared values, norms, and beliefs of attorneys.

INTERNATIONAL CULTURAL CONSIDERATIONS

The previous views on culture should reinforce the idea that organizational cultures do not develop independently of national cultures. Nations tend to exhibit certain characteristics (values, norms, practices, beliefs, and standards) that are collectively created over long periods of time. These characteristics become ingrained in human nature. A culture, for example, develops a common language and ways of thinking that consciously and subconsciously direct activities performed by members of the culture. Geert Hofstede surveyed people from around the world concerning their work-related values.[19] Table 10-2 summarizes Hofstede's dimensions of culture. In societies high in individualism, individual achievment or accomplishments are expected, celebrated, and rewarded. For example, the United States, which is moderately high in individualism, has a long history of celebrating individual entrepreneurial success. People like Ted Turner, Bill Gates, Donald Trump, and Henry Ford are given much of the credit for the success of their companies. Compensation systems in this country are typically based on rewarding individual contributions and individual successes. In collectivist cultures, the team, group, family, or nation is more important than the individual. Individuals are seldom singled out for commendation. In fact, in a collectivist culture it may be inappropriate to praise an individual. Rewards and recognition go to the team. Compensation is more likely to be based on equality (all team members receiving the same level of reward).

Uncertainty avoidance refers to how comfortable a society is with uncertainty and ambiguity and the mechanisms the society creates for dealing with uncertainty. Countries that are low in uncertainty avoidance are comfortable with uncertainty and ambiguity. Thus, they are more likely to embrace innovations and unusual situations or behaviors. For example, New Zealand, which is very low in uncertainty avoidance, has

TABLE 10-2 Hofstede's Dimensions of National Culture	
Cultural Dimension	**Description**
Individualism–Collectivism	Degree to which individuals are expected to act individually (without regard to the welfare of others) or to act out of consideration for the well-being of others in a family, group, team, organization, or country.
Uncertainty Avoidance	How society copes with uncertainty; how comfortable people are with uncertainty. In low uncertainty avoidance cultures, people embrace innovation and are more tolerant of unusual or eccentric behaviors.
Power Distance	Degree of social and economic stratification in the society. Societies with high power distance tolerate greater inequities in the distribution of wealth, power, prestige, and status. Societies with low power distance tend to suppress inequities in wealth, power, prestige, and status.
Masculinity–Femininity (Assertiveness)	Masculine cultures maintain clearly separated gender roles. Men are expected to be assertive and women are expected to be nurturing. Greater emphasis is placed on work, careers, and wealth acquisition. In feminine cultures gender roles are less distinct and clearly defined. Feminine cultures place more emphasis on relationship, physical environment, and service to the community or family.
Time Orientation (Confusion Dynamism)	Some cultures tend to be highly focused on the present and on short-term horizons; others (particularly Oriental societies) tend to be focused on long-term horizons and history.

Source: G. Hofstede, *Culture's Consequences: International Differences in Work-Related Values* (Beverly Hills, CA: Sage, 1980); M. J. Hatch, *Organization Theory* (New York: Oxford University Press, 1997), 206–10; N. J. Adler, *International Dimensions of Organizational Behavior* (Cincinnati, OH: South-Western Publishing, 1997), 57–58.

far fewer personal liability rules and laws than most countries. New Zealanders are comfortable with the uncertainty that results from personal risks. Southern European countries such as France, Spain, Portugal, and Greece are characterized by strong uncertainty avoidance. In France, heavy reliance on rules and laws attempts to remove some uncertainty from daily life. In Spain, Portugal, and Greece, it is the role of religion to reduce uncertainty. Differences in uncertainty avoidance are typically reflected in the acceptance or avoidance of business risks and the degree to which organizations rely on rules to guide behaviors.

In masculine societies, particular jobs or tasks are specific to men or women and it is difficult or unacceptable for men to fill women's roles or women to fill men's roles. Many Islamic societies are examples of high masculinity cultures. Women are forbidden to enter many occupations and their access to education is restricted. In addition, masculine cultures are characterized by more aggressive or assertive behavior, a focus on work, careers, and accumulation of wealth. Feminine cultures, by comparison, have less differentiation of gender roles. One is more likely to find women in technical and professional jobs in feminine cultures such as Scandinavian countries than in masculine cultures. Feminine cultures are also more focused on personal relationships and physical comfort and well-being.

The rags-to-riches stories that are part of American mythology are an indication of relatively low power distance that exists in the United States. A person from the lowest levels of society can rise to greatness in business, politics, sports, or any other domain. The quintessential American dream is that a child born in a log cabin can become president. Countries characterized by low power distance also tend to have tax systems that redistribute wealth. The people who earn the most are taxed at significantly higher rates than lower wage earners. Northern European and Scandinavian countries are low in power distance and tend to levy high taxes. On the other hand, those same countries tend to redistribute wealth through extensive social welfare systems that provide medical care, unemployment insurance, and pensions for everyone. In high power distance countries, position in the hierarchy, family social status, and wealth are important. For example, in France family status (old money) and the school one attended are very important to careers in business, politics, and government service. You must attend the "right" schools to qualify for top jobs.

Hofstede's initial work on national cultures did not include the time dimension. It was not until he and colleague Michael Bond replicated his early studies in Asia that important differences in how cultures treat time became apparent. In some cultures the focus is primarily on the present and short periods into the future. Time is linear and timeliness is important. Traditions and history are less critical. The United States would fit this view of time. After all, time is money! In many Asian societies, particularly those with a Confucian influence, history and tradition are important. Time may be viewed less as a linear relationship. Patience and age are virtues.[20] Thus, in the United States, performance appraisals are typically conducted formally on an annual basis and we need laws to protect aging workers against discrimination. In Japan and China, performance appraisals are likely to be much less frequent and less formal. The elderly are revered for their age, wisdom, and experience. History and tradition are more important than the present.[21]

In recent years, much discussion has focused on the national and organizational cultural differences that distinguish Japanese and American organizations. To fully understand Japanese management, it is important to understand the national culture in which Japanese firms are embedded.[22] Several important characteristics of Japan and Japanese culture contribute to the unique Japanese management culture. First, history

TABLE 10-3 Contrasting Japanese and American Organizational Cultures	
Japanese Culture	**American Culture**
Emphasis on collectivism and groups	Emphasis on individualism
Emphasis on family and respect for authority	Emphasis on individual and youth
Emphasis on cooperation and harmony	Emphasis on competition, conflict, confrontation, and differences
Emphasis on patience, long-term results	Emphasis on immediacy, short-term results
Emphasis on humility and austerity	Emphasis on self-promotion and material wealth

Source: Adapted from Harrison M. Trice and Janice M. Beyer, *The Cultures of Work Organizations* (Upper Saddle River, NJ: Prentice Hall, 1993), 54, 342.

and geography contribute to Japan's emphasis on protecting its borders from foreigners. Japan was essentially closed to foreigners until late in the nineteenth century. This, in turn, has contributed to the homogeneity of the Japanese population and their fear and mistrust of foreigners. Japanese culture is, to a large extent, based on Confucianism and Buddhism. By contrast, American culture is a product of largely open borders and heterogeneity. The Protestant ethic plays a central role in American culture, but the United States was settled by diverse immigrant groups who often brought with them their unique ethnic and national cultures. Thus, we often speak of Italian-Americans, German-Americans, Mexican-Americans, and Asian-Americans. The different national histories and cultural paths of Japan and the United States have produced distinct national organizational cultures. Table 10-3 highlights the differences between these two cultures.

Organizations develop cultures within the context of their national cultures. An organization is, above all, a citizen of a particular country, and the country's dominant norms, standards, styles, and beliefs set the parameters in which an organization's culture develops. Problems likely arise when organizations develop cultures that are not congruent with societal cultures. Also, organizations are increasingly multicultural. Many large multinational firms blend the cultures of the various national cultures in which they are embedded.

THICK AND THIN CULTURES

Organizational culture is the result of a complex interplay of forces. If the forces that contribute to the development of an organizational culture are favorable, an organization may develop a culture that is widely and broadly held by members and that strongly unifies members as they pursue organizational goals. The thickness or thinness of the culture is a measure of its strength.[23] Organizational culture is said to be *thick* if it is widespread and accepted throughout the organization. Organizational members subscribe to a shared set of beliefs, values, and norms. A *thin* culture is one that is not widely held and does not enjoy acceptance throughout the organization. The organization lacks a core of commonly held beliefs, norms, and values. Employees may find it difficult to identify with such a company or to even identify its core goals and values.

An example of a thick culture is Ford Motor Company. All employees carry a 3-by-5-inch plastic card that lists the company's creed, the company's basic values. The message is a simple reminder of Ford's culture: At Ford the quality of the products and services is an extension of the employees.[24] This value is reinforced with banners and through the example of quality circles. Ford has tried to extend this culture of quality and service to its dealers with a President's Award based on service rather than on sales. In the introductory case on Mary Kay Cosmetics we saw that award ceremonies can be powerful mechanisms for spreading the culture. Company creeds and award systems are just two mechanisms for spreading a culture. Later in this chapter we explore several others.

When a company is successful in widely and broadly spreading its values, like Ford's message about quality and service, it is more likely to develop a thick culture. A thick culture is a strong tie that binds the total organizational system together. A thick culture can help organizations channel energy into productive and predictable behaviors and responses that help the organization manage ambiguity and uncertainty. For example, customers and clients, as we noted in Chapters 4 and 5, can be important sources of uncertainty. One part of that uncertainty is how those customers and clients respond to boundary spanners—for example, sales and service representatives. To manage this uncertainty, many companies develop formal and informal dress codes for their sales and service people.

Perhaps one of the most widely recognized codes was the unofficial dress code at IBM. For many years, it was nearly universal that IBM employees, especially those who dealt with customers, dressed in conservative dark suits, white shirts, and muted ties.[25] Customers could gain some reassurance from the appearance of IBM personnel— these were knowledgeable, official representatives of IBM. Such reassurance may have been particularly important for mainframe computer customers who were spending millions of dollars on IBM systems. The movement away from mainframe computing and the increasing emphasis on innovation and creativity in the information technology business is pressuring IBM to adopt a more relaxed culture with more casual dress.

CULTURAL INDICATORS AND MANIFESTATIONS

Early in this chapter we noted that culture exists on two levels: the unobserved but implied values, norms, and beliefs of the organization and the observable indicators of those values, norms, and beliefs. We turn our attention now to those observable indicators and manifestations of culture. Often it is through the study of these observable indicators and manifestations of the culture that we learn of the underlying values, norms, and beliefs. For the members of an organization, the physical manifestations of culture provide "sense-making" mechanisms by which members try to gain some common perception and understanding of events and circumstances.[26] The following sections explore these physical manifestations of culture.

Rites, Rituals, and Ceremonies

Rites, rituals, and ceremonies (sometimes called *ceremonials*) are public social events that mark the passage of some event or milestone. Rites and rituals celebrate discrete individual events, while ceremonies combine several rites or rituals into a single event.[27] Typical types of rites, rituals, and ceremonies include those that celebrate entry into the organization (orientation, boot camp, or induction ceremonies); transitions (promotions); renewal and enhancement (annual meetings, Christmas parties, picnics); degradation (firings and layoffs); or parting (retirement parties, farewell parties). Some rites and rituals may be highly planned, rehearsed, and formal to the extent that they are defined and described in company documents. Others may be spontaneous, unplanned events. Ceremonies tend to be more elaborate, planned activities much like the Mary Kay Seminars mentioned in the introductory case.

Ceremonies, rites, and rituals hold the group together. In fact, many ceremonies, rites, and rituals require that the members of the organization come together to conduct them. Religious meetings, graduations, recognition events, homecomings, annual meetings, and Christmas parties are examples of events that require the organization's members to come together in order to carry them out. These events are manifestations of the beliefs and values, and the perceptions and understandings of the organization—for example, Mary Kay's rewards for selling and the valuing of family. A small entrepreneurial banking firm provides a less formalized example of rituals. The bank's founder gathers employees together every day or two for informal meetings in which he dispenses his views on banking. These events provide a basis for making sense of the environment and give the organization a sense of continuity and stability that binds members together.

Symbols and Slogans

Firms spend considerable time and effort developing means of ready recognition of the organization and its products. "We deliver for you" is a slogan used by the U.S. Postal Service to share with the consumer the organization's desire to provide timely, convenient, dependable service. UPS uses the company's brown uniforms and brown trucks to provide employees and customers with a common vision of the company and to convey the image of efficiency. Wal-Mart uses the word "*Always*" in conjunction with advertising and in-store displays to convey to customers and employees the company's dedication to consistent low prices and quality service. Delta Airlines has used slogans extensively to transmit to employees and consumers the company's customer-oriented values. The slogans have included "We love to fly and it shows" and, more recently, "You'll love the way we fly."

The Disney Company, especially its theme park division, has an especially strong and rich culture. Slogans and symbols play important roles in sustaining that culture. In particular, Disneyland is labeled by Disney people as "The Happiest Place on Earth" where "everyone is a child at heart."[28] Symbols such as the ever-present mouse ears, the multitude of Disney animation characters, and the fantasy recreations in park locations (e.g., Fantasyland, Frontierland, Tomorrowland) and rides (e.g., Small World, Pirates of the Caribbean) reinforce the Disney values of youth, fun, and fantasy.

Logos and trademarks also indicate cultural values and beliefs. Sometimes these logos may simply be unique, readily identifiable markers of a company's products and services. The three-pointed star of Mercedes-Benz (a unit of Daimler-Chrysler) is a widely recognized symbol of high-quality, luxury autos. Perhaps one of the most widely recognized sets of corporate symbols are those associated with Coca Cola—the red disk, the script logo, and the "wave."

Nike has developed a thick culture with many symbols. One of the primary symbols of that culture is the "swoosh" emblazoned on shoes, hats, and clothing. In the 1970s, the "swoosh" became identified in the minds of employees and consumers with a youthful, innovative, free-spirited company that led a national craze in fitness.[29] The "swoosh" was thought to embody the antiestablishment and antitraditional business values of the company's founder, Phil Knight. The "swoosh" became such an important identifying logo that many Nike field representatives tattooed the symbol on various parts of their anatomy as a sign of their commitment to Nike.

Language

One of the marks of a group is its tendency to develop a language or jargon of its own. The language serves as shorthand to members and as a barrier to nonmembers. Members of the organization can quickly and easily discern the meaning of particular words or phrases that are unknown to outsiders. Members develop an organizational vocabulary, and members use it in their daily contacts with each other. Professional groups and technical professions develop sophisticated jargon as can be seen among doctors, lawyers, and computer hardware and software specialists.

A strong culture may not necessarily be a positive factor. At one accounting firm, partners used a particularly derogatory term to refer to clients.[30] The term served two purposes. First, everyone in the firm knew that the term meant *client*. Outsiders would be less clear about the meaning. Second, it conveyed to employees the firm's rather negative value toward its clients—clients were a source of problems with which the firm must deal.

Nike, with its thick culture, developed the label *Ekin* (Nike spelled backward) for its special breed of technical field representatives.[31] The Ekins are those highly committed employees noted earlier who often tattoo the Nike "swoosh" on their bodies. As described by one Ekin, they are hard-working, passionate, committed representatives who bring information about the latest Nike innovations to retailers and customers. Their passion for Nike is matched by their passion for fitness and athletics. Many are former collegiate and professional athletes. Thus, the term *Ekin* takes on an important role in conveying the values and beliefs of Nike about free spirit, sport, fun, passion, and innovation. Nike has used the "Just Do It" slogan to generate a similar level of commitment and identification in the consumer marketplace.

Disney theme parks have evolved a colorful language that is a critical element of the company's culture.[32] Language is used to reinforce the ideas that Disney theme parks are theatrical performances and that good wholesome fun is the main attraction. Some examples of the Disney lexicon are these:

- Disney theme parks are referred to as "parks," not "amusement parks"
- Park visitors are referred to as "guests," never "customers"
- Employees at Disney parks are called "cast members"
- Cast members do not wear "uniforms"; instead, they have "wardrobes" and "costumes"
- Cast members work on "attractions," rather than "rides"
- "Security hosts," not police, investigate "incidents," but Disney parks do not have "accidents"

Not all of the language examples at Disney parks are officially approved.[33] "Cast members" have developed their own slang that may not further the official Disney culture but is, nonetheless, an important part of the Disney culture. For example, lower-status "cast members" are called "peanut pushers" and "soda jerks." Problem "guests" may acquire the label of "duck" or "duffess." And even "cast members" who become too imbued with the Disney culture are not immune from negative labeling. These gung-ho followers are called "Disnoids."

Myths and Stories

Groups and organizations develop a history of operations and events over time in the form of myths and stories that is handed down from one generation to another. Mary Kay Ash's rise from a sales representative at Stanley Home Products to the head of a multibillion dollar cosmetics company is a story that inspires many of the legion of sales associates at Mary Kay Cosmetics. Similar myths and stories of leaders, founders, and innovators serve to motivate and lead people through adversity and uncertainty.

A classic example of the strength and pervasiveness of a myth is the image that Lee Iacocca built during his years leading Chrysler out of chaos and financial crisis in the early 1980s.[34] Iacocca took over a deeply troubled company in 1979. Chrysler trailed GM and Ford in nearly every category imaginable: cost, product quality, innovativeness, service, and customer appeal. Iacocca, who had been fired from Ford Motor Company in a political squabble with Henry Ford II, did have a track record of success. In the 1960s, Iacocca was instrumental in the development and marketing of the Ford Mustang and the Cobra sports/racing cars. While Iacocca clearly did play a key role in the turnaround at Chrysler in the early- to mid-1980s, he did not do it singlehandedly. Many people inside and outside the company played important roles in reversing Chrysler's declining fortunes. However, the myth that prevails in many circles is that Lee Iacocca personally and singlehandedly pulled Chrysler out of its decline.

Although myths and stories typically involve elements of truth, they often get distorted or exaggerated over time. Mary Kay Ash's rise to success took many years and much hard work. Iacocca's success at Chrysler was due in part to his skill and expertise, but was also the result of hard work by many others behind the scenes. These myths and stories play a part in guiding members about the appropriate and expected behaviors. Mary Kay's story of her rise to prominence glorifies the commitment to hard work and the value of enhancing personal beauty. Lee Iacocca's story also documents the value of hard work, but also emphasizes hardball politicking, showmanship, and risk taking.

Physical Environment

People work in organizations that have a concrete physical presence. Organizations have buildings, factories, and grounds. Buildings and factories have ornamentation such as artwork, furniture, and other adornments. The specific architecture often affects the process of work and may give evidence of the culture or contribute to the development of culture. Often the physical grounds include parking lots, gardens, and outdoor recreation areas. These conditions may also be important elements of culture. In general, physical structure, symbols, artifacts, and other stimuli are an integral part of an organization's culture. The physical environment is composed of three basic elements: physical structures, physical stimuli, and symbolic artifacts.[35]

Physical Structure Consider, for example, a basic aspect of the physical layout or design of a building. Layout or design determines the size and location of various offices. This can give important evidence about culture. The design of buildings and one's location in them can have a profound effect on attitudes and behavior. To some extent, buildings are designed to meet certain functional needs—to determine what can be done in the buildings and how successfully or easily it can be done. Consider the following examples.

Levi Strauss's corporate culture is characterized by openness, friendliness, flexibility, and innovation. In the 1970s, the company moved to a new headquarters building in San Francisco. The building, a high-rise glass tower, was not amenable to the Levi Strauss culture. Headquarters' offices were scattered throughout several floors; offices were closed in; and there were few open areas where workers could congregate. Such a physical environment may be a good match for a highly bureaucratic culture, but it was a poor match for the open, flexible culture of Levi Strauss. In 1982, Levi Strauss built a new headquarters' facility that matched its culture of openness and flexibility. The new facility featured a set of four-story buildings around a central, open courtyard. Offices were open, interconnected, and faced the courtyard.

At Nike, founder and chief executive Phil Knight has a large, well-appointed private office that is far off the beaten path. Few employees ever see the inside of Knight's private office. Instead, most Nike executives interact with Knight in an outer office. This office configuration perpetuates the mystery and mystique that surround Knight. On the other hand, Nike's headquarter facilities in Beaverton, Oregon, are much like an exclusive college campus with tasteful architecture, elaborate sports and recreational facilities, extensive sports-related artwork, and other artifacts that contribute to the unique Nike culture that emphasizes innovation, creativity, fun, athleticism, competition, and hard work.[36]

The executive offices at Ford Motor Company are on the top floors of Ford's World Headquarters (the "glass house") in Dearborn, Michigan. The layout of the headquarters is hierarchical with higher-level departments located on upper-level floors of the building. This configuration replicates the hierarchical culture of Ford. During Henry Ford II's presidency at Ford, his executive office suite on the top floor of the "glass house" included a private dining room (with a personal chef for Ford). Few people other than top Ford Motor executives ever had the privilege of entering this dining room. This contributed to a culture of privilege for top management and a separation of top management from lower-level employees that was characteristic of the company during Henry Ford II's leadership.[37] It will be interesting to see if this architecture continues to match Ford Motor's needs as the auto industry undergoes extensive change and Ford strives for a more participative culture.

These examples show the effects that physical structures can have on people in organizations. Friendships can be made or broken; communication can be facilitated or inhibited; work can flow smoothly or encounter barriers because of the physical layout of organizations. Thus, the physical structure of organizations can play a crucial role in the development and support of a culture.

Physical Stimuli   The second aspect of the physical environment is the physical stimuli present in the organization. These are parts of the physical environment that gradually come into members' awareness. Examples include such things as mail deliveries, time clocks, and telephone calls. The physical stimuli are often distractions to routines. For example, employees may become aware of patterns of mail delivery and structure their work around those deliveries. Employees may stop work in anticipation of mail deliveries. Much of the folklore of organizational life focuses on friendships or information exchanges around the office watercooler. These physical stimuli have a great deal of influence on culture.

Symbolic Artifacts   Finally, we must consider symbolic artifacts—"aspects of the physical setting that individually and collectively guide (our) interpretation of the social setting."[38] These things give us cues and clues about the culture. Spartan surroundings, like those characteristic of many Japanese corporate headquarters, convey an image of efficiency; the opulence of the Ford Motor chief executive suite during Henry Ford II's reign gave an image of privilege and social stratification. The presence or absence of corporate jets, executive parking spaces, executive dining rooms, and expensive artwork and furnishings can contribute to the specific culture of an organization. For example, think about the meaning conveyed by a company that provides convenient, covered parking for top executives, but relegates lower-level employees to open parking lots that stretch for acres around an office complex. Or

TABLE 10-4 Cultural Manifestations*

Manifestation	Description
Rite	Relatively elaborate, dramatic, planned sets of activities that consolidate various forms of cultural expressions into one event, which is carried out through social interactions, usually for the benefit of an audience.
Ceremonial	A system of several rites connected with a single occasion or event.
Ritual	A standardized, detailed set of techniques and behaviors that manage anxieties, but seldom produce intended, technical consequences of practical importance.
Myth	A dramatic narrative of imagined events, usually used to explain origins or transformations. Also, an unquestioned belief about the practical benefits of certain techniques and behaviors that is not supported by demonstrated fact.
Saga	A historical narrative describing the unique accomplishments of a group and its leaders.
Legend	A handed-down narrative of some wonderful event that is based in history but has been embellished with fictional details.
Story	A narrative based on true events—often a combination of truth and fiction.
Folktale	A completely fictional narrative.
Symbol	Any object, act, event, quality, or relation that serves as a vehicle for conveying meaning.
Language	A particular form or manner in which members of a group use vocal sounds and written signs to convey meanings to each other.
Gesture	Movements of parts of the body used to express meanings.
Physical setting	Those things that surround people physically and provide them with immediate sensory stimuli as they carry out culturally expressive activities.
Artifact	Material objects manufactured by people to facilitate culturally expressive activities.

*Our discussion of cultural manifestations is a representative sampling rather than an exhaustive treatment of Trice and Beyer's list.

Source: Harrison M. Trice and Janice M. Beyer, "Studying Organizational Culture Through Rites and Ceremonials," *Academy of Management Review* 9, no. 4 (October 1984): 655.

think of the image that Nike conveys to employees and visitors to its headquarters who encounter extensive displays of art depicting sports and sports celebrities.

From this discussion of cultural manifestations, one can see that they are both a result of culture and a reflection of culture. They are an integral part of organizational culture and must be considered along with the other, more abstract, components of culture. Table 10-4 presents a comprehensive list and description of cultural manifestations.

EFFECTS OF CULTURE ON ORGANIZATIONS

In our earlier discussion of thick and thin cultures, we briefly mentioned how cultures can affect organization. We now expand that theme by examining five specific aspects of culture's effect on organizations: direction, pervasiveness, strength, flexibility, and commitment.[39]

Direction refers to the way culture affects goal attainment. Culture can help push an organization toward its goals or away from them. It can either be consistent with organizational goals (a positive force) or it can be inconsistent with goals (a negative force). For example, if a firm's culture fosters a "not-invented-here" attitude toward innovation, the firm will be reluctant to go outside its boundaries for innovations. This attitude breeds a belief that any innovation not invented or developed inside the organization cannot be any good. Such a culture may be an important factor in directing the organization to maintain an active research and development division, but it also directs the firm away from potentially valuable outside innovations. The company may periodically reinvent the wheel; that is, it may spend valuable time and resources developing innovations that are already available outside the firm.

The degree to which members share a culture is an indication of its ***pervasiveness.*** Cultures like those at Nike and Mary Kay Cosmetics are pervasive. Adherence to the basic tenets of those cultures is widespread among members. Widespread adoption of the basic culture is key to a thick culture, while thin cultures are not pervasive.

Strength of culture refers to its impact on members. Some religious sects and political organizations have what amounts to a compelling force over their members. Take the case of the Japanese religious sect that commanded highly educated followers to engage in urban terrorism, releasing lethal nerve gas in the Tokyo subway system. We can even find strong cultures, albeit somewhat weaker than the above example, among businesses. Recall the earlier example of the Ekins at Nike who tattooed the "swoosh" emblem on their bodies. Such behavior is indicative of a strong culture.

Flexibility in a culture indicates that it is adaptable to changing conditions. Organizations, particularly those that face changing and complex environments, must retain flexibility to accommodate. Evidence of flexibility (or inflexibility) can be seen in how organizations respond in times of crisis. Several techniques can be used to establish flexibility.[40]

One method is to establish a senior management position that is responsible for questioning proposed actions and questioning the status quo in general. This person should have considerable experience with the organization so that he or she has legitimacy in the organization and can see situations from a total organizational perspective.

A second strategy is to recruit outsiders to fill positions on governing boards and management. Outsiders can bring a fresh perspective to organizational problems and can help the organization avoid the "not-invented-here" syndrome. When IBM began to suffer serious erosion to its position in the computer industry, its initial responses were indicative of an inflexible culture. The company responded with some cost cutting, but it maintained its same conservative culture—reliance on mainframe computers, promotion from within, and risk-aversive behavior in everything from employee appearance and dress to how the company produced and marketed its computers. More recently with the arrival of Louis Gerstner as CEO, IBM has shown signs of developing a more flexible, adaptive culture. The hiring of Gerstner itself, a man who was an IBM outsider, was symbolic of the breakdown of the old culture. Outsiders, particularly on boards of directors, can also serve as boundary spanners to the environment. One cautionary note related to the recruitment of outsiders for executive positions is that it may lower morale in the organization. Some managers may feel that they have been passed over.

Finally, flexibility can be enhanced throughout the organization by cross training and frequent job reassignments. With cross training, workers learn many different jobs. This tends to reduce the narrow provincial view that often accompanies a narrow, functional job focus. Frequent reassignments help familiarize employees with the total organization and can help reduce divisional alliances that may not be in the best interest of the total organization. Flexibility is an important factor in the integration of culture and strategy.

The culture of an organization also has impact on the degree of ***commitment*** shown by its members. Commitment is a condition in which members of a group give their efforts, abilities, and loyalties to the organization and its pursuit of its goals in return for satisfaction. In other words, the culture creates conditions in the organization whereby members are either willing or not willing to commit themselves to the pursuit of the organization's goals in exchange for some general state of satisfaction. A strong culture can enhance the likelihood that members will display a high degree of commitment.

Culture aids the attainment of member commitment by laying out the mission and the values to be observed in pursuit of that mission. Culture may also aid by spelling out to the member the value of the organization to the individual. By committing to an organization, the member is choosing one set of options over those offered by committing to other organizations.[41] Commitment is a type of emotional (and perhaps financial) investment in the organization.

Several factors, including salary and the physical environment, can reinforce employee commitment to the organization. Being accepted as a member of a desirable group gives an individual a strong incentive to adopt the culture as a way of life. Recall the earlier example of the Ekins and Nike. Similar examples can be found in college fraternities and sororities. Willingness to adopt an organization's rituals and way of life is essential to acculturation. Over time, the individual feels a sense of identity with the group and is even willing to make sacrifices for it. This, in turn, leads to a deeper sense of commitment. Thus, one of the prime requirements for, or conditions of, commitment is the sense of identification with the organization that culture provides.

CULTURE AND COMPETITIVE ADVANTAGE

From a strategic standpoint, a strong thick culture can even become a source of competitive advantage.[42] Competitive advantage is a means by which one company can achieve superior performance relative to another competitor organization. Because culture is a powerful influence on behavior, a culture that stimulates productive behaviors that contribute to company success can be a powerful determinant of long-term firm success. Three conditions must be met before culture can guide success over the long haul. First, the culture must be valuable. The culture must facilitate high sales, low costs, high margins, or some other outcomes that are conducive to adding financial value to the firm. Second, the culture must be rare. Characteristics of the culture must not be commonly found among other competing companies' cultures within the industry. If all companies possess the same cultural characteristics, one specific firm cannot gain competitive advantage from those characteristics. Third, imitation of the culture must be difficult and imperfect. Other firms should be unable to build or imitate the culture perfectly and thus gain the same competitive advantages. If other firms can easily imitate the culture, its value as a source of competitive advantage dwindles. However, the advantages of strong and thick cultures may be fleeting. One only needs to look back at Peters and Waterman's *In Search of Excellence*[43] to see that many companies the authors identified as "excellent" are no longer in business, have been acquired by competitors, or are struggling. Note also that modifying or changing cultures effectively is difficult.

In the following two sections, we turn our attention to the process of cultural change. It is first necessary to assess culture through a culture audit. This helps to establish the current state of the culture. We then look at the specific process of changing culture.

THE CULTURE AUDIT

Just as companies conduct financial and managerial audits, they should also put their culture under the microscope. The purpose of such investigations is to ensure that the organization's culture fits with the organization's other characteristics (e.g., goals or mission, structure, people, processes). A culture that fits should have a net positive effect on the organization and its mission.

Two key reasons for recent interest in culture are the increasingly turbulent environment in which organizations currently exist and the increasing attention given to the methods of non–U.S. companies—particularly the attention to Japanese management.[44] As a result, awareness of culture's role in organizational life has increased. At the same time, managers, organizational scholars, and journalists have begun to study organizational cultures in other countries to identify cultural advantages.

The Informal Culture Audit

Culture seems to creep into assumptions that organization members make every day about all manner of organizational issues. Over time, the culture becomes almost second nature, a normative consensus like wearing a tie, getting to work on time, or answering the phone. Only when changes occur do members of the organization become conscious of the values, assumptions, and norms that form the foundation of the culture.[45]

Role changes are prime causes for attention to culture. When we enter new situations, we attempt to see whether our old culture fits. Think, for example, about your first days in college. We try to learn about the accepted ways of doing things in our new environment; we examine dress codes and language. We try hard to discern the pecking order and jargon so that we are not so awkward as to stand out in the crowd.

The acculturation process involves both the newcomer's attempt to learn and adopt the prevailing culture and the old-timer's attempt to mold the newcomer to the culture. This process is often formally addressed by orientation programs aimed at teaching new members the official culture. However, there is also an informal culture that must be learned. As we noted in the chapter on organizational politics, how things get done and how people behave is often different from what is written in the official documents of the organization.

Conflict among different subcultures within an organization may also call attention of members to the culture of the organization. Variations in culture within an organization are common across functional or product groupings. For example, it is not unusual to see somewhat different values and norms among a company's engineering and operations groups compared with those in marketing or human resources. Value and norm differences may affect such seemingly trivial things as dress or such important issues as organizational priorities.

How top managers behave also causes members to monitor culture. What top executives say and do goes far to show the organization's culture. When IBM spun off its printer business into a separate independent business, Lexmark, top management at Lexmark took great pains to establish a culture that was unique and separate from the old IBM culture.[46] In particular, top management wanted to establish a more casual work environment. To do this, they relaxed the old norms for dress that existed at IBM with Friday dress-down days. On Fridays even top managers wore open-neck sports shirts with no ties. At IBM the norm for reports for corporate strategy sessions was for managers to have extensively prepared presentations with many graphs and overhead slides. This often inhibited the free exchange of new ideas and critical evaluation of projects. Lexmark tried to change this by insisting that managers reduce the use of overhead slides. Top management's attention to these behaviors caused others in the organization to pay attention to culture.

A culture audit, then, is a look at values, beliefs, norms, behaviors, and other aspects of culture. It consists of monitoring, evaluating, and perhaps changing various components of culture. Audits show the extent to which both the formal and informal rules of the organization operate.

Culture audits can be conducted by asking questions aimed at finding out how members feel and think about the organization and their places in it. As an exercise, you can do the same for your college or university. What are the key values? What do people believe? How do students behave? How do faculty behave? These and other questions can be quite revealing in showing the underlying culture of your institution.

The Formal Culture Audit

The audit outlined in the previous section describes an informal process that may be appropriate for an individual in an organization. The individual can gain great insight into an organization's culture, and individual managers may even be able to take actions to facilitate the fit between the culture and individual employees. But what if top management (or others in the organization) suspect that there may be problems with the culture? What if management is contemplating changing the culture? The simple observational process of an informal audit is not likely to be rigorous enough. Management should turn to a *formal culture audit* to gain a comprehensive picture of the culture.

The formal process of learning about a culture is difficult, and no single method is without problems.[47] Managers may themselves attempt to assess the culture through structured observations and data collection. After all, managers are likely to have access to more data about their organization than outsiders. However, insiders may be too close to the culture of their organization to accurately and objectively assess that culture. Thus, organizations often turn to outside consultants to work with insiders in conducting an audit.

Insider Audit An audit may involve the use of surveys or questionnaires to gain information about employee behaviors, beliefs, values, and norms. Although surveys and questionnaires can sometimes provide useful information about culture, most experts discourage their use. The belief is that the resulting behaviors, beliefs, values, and norms identified by these methods are likely to be superficial and perhaps even biased (i.e., not accurate). Experts recommend that the culture be examined through systematic and "intensive group discussions to bring cultural substance to the surface."[48] This process can be used to develop a list of the various characteristics of the culture. The listed characteristics can then be analyzed for evidence of underlying beliefs, values, and norms. Once a tentative sketch of the culture is developed, it can then be validated with further observations of the organization.

Outsider Audit An outside consultant can often provide a different perspective on the culture of an organization.[49] Edgar Schein, whose 4-stage model of culture we introduced earlier, has developed the 10-step process for auditing culture that is described here.[50]

1. *Entry and focus on surprises.* The outside consultant enters the organization and begins to "feel" its culture and watch for surprises—that is, responses to things that are unexpected.

2. *Systematic observation and checking.* Consultant attempts to verify that "surprises" really are surprises.

3. *Locate motivated insider.* Outsider would probably have a difficult time analyzing culture without some key insider to provide insights. It is important to find a key insider with access to important information who is also motivated to assist in the audit process.

4. *Revealing surprises, puzzlement, and hunches.* Outsider reveals to members of organization his or her initial assessments in order to get reactions about their appropriateness and accuracy.

5. *Joint exploration to find explanations.* Consultant uses feedback to modify or change the initial assessment presented in number 4 above. Consultant and insiders attempt to fit observations with the assumption about culture in an attempt to explain behaviors.

6. *Formalizing hypotheses.* Consultant and insiders collaborate to form statements about the culture based on data and observations. These hypotheses become a model of the culture.

7. *Systematic checking and consolidation.* Consultant gathers additional observations, surveys, questionnaires, interviews, and other data to verify the hypothesized culture.

8. *Deriving cultural assumptions.* Once hypotheses are validated, the evaluator derives cultural assumptions and sees how the assumptions affect member behaviors and beliefs.

9. *Perpetual recalibration.* The model is fine tuned to fit it to the actual underlying assumptions that are present in the culture. Caution must be exercised in this process because some members of the organization may be unaware of the underlying assumptions that guide their behaviors or they may be reluctant to admit those assumptions.

10. *Formal written description.* Consultant reduces the model to a written description to see whether a true description can be found. If the data are accurate and the logic used to develop the model is sound, then the written description should be possible; otherwise, a coherent written description may be impossible. Finally, the written description must be periodically updated and modified to keep pace with changes in the organization.

The process outlined above is just one audit method. Others are also available, but most share many of the features of Schein's system. This formal audit can be useful because it provides order and direction to the process. Management can use this systematic process to better understand and strategically adjust the organization's culture.

A note of caution is in order. Culture, by its very nature, is an elusive aspect of organizations. The second level of culture, the underlying norms, values, beliefs, and assumptions, are latent — we can never directly observe them. As a result, we must infer them from other observable aspects of the organization. The inference process we use for moving from the observable to the latent characteristics may be subject to error and bias. Thus, the resulting description of an organization's culture may be imperfect and inaccurate. Nonetheless, a systematic and rigorous audit should provide useful information in the strategic management of an organization.

CULTURE CHANGE

Cultures of organizations are, by nature, dynamic. That is, they naturally change and evolve in response to changes in the organization, the members of the organization, and its environment. However, when we specifically refer to **culture change**, we are focusing on *planned change of a more substantial and extensive nature.*[51] Management of an organization includes the idea that managers can change a culture, or parts of a culture, to be more consistent with the organization's strategic objectives. As we noted above, the audit is a key component to systematic cultural change.

Management can use two basic approaches to the task of culture change: top-down change and bottom-up change. With **top-down change**, top management plays the lead role in changing the culture. The culture may be changed by "decrees" that different norms of behavior are to be observed. For example, management at Ford Motor Company could decree that "Quality is Job #1," indicating to employees that new values, expectations, and behaviors should be observed with regard to quality. Top management can also attempt to change the culture through leadership and example. For example, a company's leadership may advocate new norms and behaviors toward customers. To indicate the company's sincerity, top management could visit key customers. This shows both members of the organization and customers that the company is serious about being customer oriented. Lexmark, a former IBM division that is now an independent company, has had great difficulty trying to shed the old IBM culture. One technique the company used was that top management served as a model for the new norms, values, and behaviors that were to be part of the Lexmark culture. This included such things as top managers dressing more casually and holding more informal meetings.

The major advantage of top-down change is that it can be implemented quickly. One particular strategy that is often used to bring about top-down change is through a change in the top management team. Bringing in new leaders often involves an implicit attempt to change the culture. One problem with top-down culture change, however, is that the changes may not be consistent with the values and norms of lower-level members of the organization. This may produce resentment and resistance, and may produce changes that are not long lasting.

With *bottom-up* or participative approaches to change, organizational members are involved in the change process. This type of change may be slower, but it is likely to be longer lasting because employees are involved with and committed to the change.

AT&T provides a classic example of bottom-up change.[52] The breakup of AT&T in the early 1980s into the regional telephone companies (the so-called Baby Bells) and the AT&T Company that provides long-distance service and research and technical support presented AT&T management with a unique opportunity to create a new corporate culture. Under the old monopolistic system AT&T had grown bureaucratic, unresponsive, and insular. With the breakup of AT&T and the development of long-distance competition, the company's management realized that change was needed. Management conducted surveys of several thousand employees, gathered recommendations from 20 key managers, and employed a management consultant to get an independent perspective. Changing the culture has taken nearly a decade, but the result has been a culture that emphasizes openness, customer focus, teamwork, and flexibility. No longer was AT&T lethargic, unresponsive, and bureaucratic. Now, AT&T will again have to deal with culture change as it breaks off some business units into separate companies.

In reality, the changes at AT&T involve both top-down and bottom-up approaches. Key top managers have changed since the breakup, and they have led by example. But they have also consulted with and involved many lower-level employees. A combination of approaches is likely to lead to more consistent and long-lasting culture change.

CULTURE AND STRATEGY

Because of its crucial role in organization performance, the relationship between culture and strategy must be examined. The formulation and pursuit of a strategy involves the allocation of an organization's resources (including human resources) and attention to a specific set of long-term purposes. The beliefs, values, norms, and philosophy

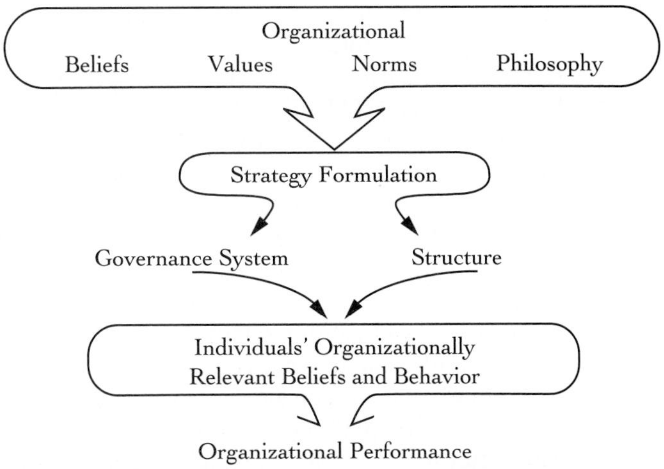

FIGURE 10-1   The Relationship of Culture to Strategy

Source: From Stanley M. Davis, *Managing Corporate Culture* (Cambridge, MA: Ballinger, 1984), 6. Copyright 1984 by The Human Resource Planning Society. Reprinted with permission from Ballinger Publishing Company.

of top management should guide the strategy formulation. These might include such fundamental beliefs as being an innovation leader or price leader in a particular market, the fair and equitable treatment of employees and customers, and doing no harm to the environment. The formulation of that strategy then sets a context or agenda for organizational action. Individuals' beliefs are the rules, norms, values, and assumptions that members observe when engaging in behaviors directed at the fulfillment of the strategy. These beliefs may include work rules; norms about interactions with peers, subordinates, or superiors; and expectations about how to interact with customers. Thus, managing the culture and strategy so that they are consistent and congruent is a key managerial task. As can be seen in Figure 10-1, culture and strategy interact with other aspects of the organization to produce performance.[53]

Taking our strategic systems view of organizations, culture is both an input that guides the strategy formulation and implementation process and part of the throughput process. Culture provides guidelines for strategy formulation and implementation, and culture provides a context for the organization to pursue the strategy. Thus, there must be congruency between culture, strategy, and organization.

SUMMARY

This chapter has explored the role of culture in the overall scheme of organization theory and demonstrated how organizations must know and manage their cultures for long-term survival. Culture is a complex and multifaceted concept that has a major influence on organizational life that includes two levels: observable and unobservable characteristics of the organization. The observable level includes many characteristics such as architecture, dress, behavior patterns, rules, stories, myths, language, and ceremonies. The unobservable level of culture is composed of the shared values, norms, beliefs, and assumptions of organizational members. Culture is the pattern or configuration of these two levels of characteristics that orients or directs organizational members to manage problems and their surroundings.

We presented four views on organizational culture. Schein's view of culture emphasizes the stagelike evolution of culture over time. Scholz also describes an evolution of culture but includes focus on internal and external attributes of culture. Fombrun argues that we must consider the different levels of culture and how society and the firm's industry have profound impact on the organization's culture. Fombrun reminds us that organizations are themselves embedded in larger cultural entities—communities and nations. Finally, Louis's emphasis is on the location of cultural genesis. Different elements of a culture, and even different subcultures, can emerge in different parts of the organization or can even come from outside the organization.

Not all organizational cultures are equally powerful in affecting the members. Thick cultures are ones in which the cultural forces are spread widely and deeply throughout the organization. As a result, the culture becomes a core of organizational life. A thin culture is one that does not spread so deeply and widely throughout the organization. As a result, the culture is not central to everyday organizational life.

Related to the concepts of thick and thin culture are three characteristics: direction, strength, and pervasiveness. Culture can direct behavior toward or away from organizational goals. Pervasive cultures are ones that are shared by nearly all members of the organization. A strong culture is one that has significant force or control over the behaviors of members.

One can study culture by looking at such observable features as ceremonies, rituals, symbols, slogans, myths, stories, and language. The physical environment of the organization, including offices, buildings, grounds, artwork, and other physical traces, can also give insight into an organization's culture. At the root of these observable features are the norms, beliefs, values, assumptions, and expectations that guide behaviors.

A key to managing an organization's culture is the cultural audit. The purpose of a formal audit is to ensure congruence or agreement between the culture and the *other* parts of an organization—its strategy, design, structure, tasks, and people.

When a culture is no longer congruent with other aspects of an organization, it can be changed. Top-down change focuses first on changes in top-management values, beliefs, norms, expectations, and behaviors. It may even involve a change in top-management personnel. Bottom-up change begins with input from all levels of employees, including those lowest in the organizational hierarchy. Both types can be critical to successful cultural change.

Culture and strategic management of the organization are closely tied together. Adjustments in one often signal the need for changes in the other. Our strategic systems approach emphasizes the need for alignment between culture and all other aspects of the organization.

Questions for Discussion

1. Under what conditions would a thick culture be desirable? Undesirable?
2. Under what conditions would a thin culture be desirable? Undesirable?
3. How would you describe the culture of your college or university? Identify key observable features of the culture. What are the basic underlying values, beliefs, norms, and expectations that are part of the culture? Is it a thick or thin culture? Why?

4. Is your college or university's culture congruent with the other key characteristics of the organization? Strategy? Structure? Design? Tasks? People?
5. Devise a plan for changing either a part or all of your college or university's culture or that of a business with which you are familiar. Use both top-down and bottom-up approaches.

References

1. Harrison M. Trice and Janice M. Beyer, *The Cultures of Work Organizations* (Upper Saddle River, NJ: Prentice Hall, 1993).
2. See note 1, page 29.
3. Ralph H. Kilmann, Mary J. Saxton, and Roy Serpa, "Issues in Understanding and Changing Culture," *California Management Review* 27, no. 2 (Winter 1987): 92–93.
4. See note 1; J. Steven Ott, *The Organizational Culture Perspective* (Pacific Grove, CA: Brooks/Cole Pub., 1989).
5. Joanne Martin, *Cultures in Organizations: Three Perspectives* (New York: Oxford University Press, 1992); Maryan S. Schall, "A Communication-Rules Approach to Organizational Culture," *Administrative Science Quarterly* 28 (1983): 557–58; Andrew Pettigrew, "On Studying Organizational Cultures," *Administrative Science Quarterly* 24 (1979): 572; Edgar H. Schein, *Organizational Culture and Leadership* (San Francisco: Jossey-Bass, 1985).
6. Ibid; Sonja A. Sackman, "Cultures and Subcultures: An Analysis of Organizational Knowledge," *Administrative Science Quarterly* 37, no. 1 (1992): 140–61.
7. Colin Camerer and Ari Vepsalainen, "The Economic Efficiency of Corporate Culture," *Strategic Management Journal* 9 (1988): 115–26.
8. See Martin, page 3, in note 5.
9. See Schein in note 5; see Sackman in note 6; Alan L. Wilkins and William G. Ouchi, "Efficient Cultures: Exploring the Relationship Between Culture and Organizational Performance," *Administrative Science Quarterly* 28 (1983): 468–69.
10. See note 1, pages 1–2.
11. Edgar Schein, "The Role of the Founder in Creating Organizational Culture," *Organizational Dynamics* 13 (1983): 13–28; see Schein in note 5.
12. See Schein, pages 163–65, in note 5.
13. Christian Scholz, "Corporate Culture and Strategy— The Problem of Strategic Fit," *Long Range Planning* 26, no. 4 (August 1987): 79–85.
14. D. R. Dennison and A. K. Mishra, "Toward a Theory of Organizational Culture and Effectiveness," *Organizational Science* 6 (1995), 204–23; R. L. Daft, *Organizational Theory and Design*, 7th ed.

(Cincinnati, OH: South-Western Publishing, 2000): 319–21.
15. Ibid.
16. Ibid.
17. Charles Fombrun, "Corporate Culture, Environment, and Strategy," *Human Resources Management* 22 (1983): 139–52.
18. Meryl R. Louis, "An Investigator's Guide to Workplace Culture," in *Organizational Culture*, ed. by Peter Frost, Larry F. Moore, Meryl R. Louis, Craig C. Lundberg, and Joanne Martin (Beverly Hills, CA: Sage Publications, 1985): 73–98.
19. L. M. Gales and C. Barzantny, *The Cultural Boundedness of Organizational Behavior Constructs: The Case of Procedural and Distributive Justice* (Paris: XI Congrès de l' AGRH, November 2000).
20. R. D. Lewis, *When Cultures Collide* (London: Nicholas Brealey Publishing, 1999).
21. Geert Hofstede, *Culture's Consequences: International Differences in Work-related Values* (Beverly Hills, CA: Sage, 1980).
22. See note 1, pages 340–50.
23. See note 13, page 81.
24. Arthur Flax, "Ford Brings Its Culture to Its Dealers," *Automotive News* (March 12, 1986): 1.
25. Jenny C. McCune, "Who Are Those People in Blue Suits," *Management Review* 80 (September 1991): 16–19.
26. Gareth Morgan, Peter J. Frost, and Louis Pondy, "Organizational Symbolism," in *Organizational Symbolism*, ed. by Louis Pondy, Peter J. Frost, Gareth Morgan, and Thomas C. Dandridge (Greenwich, CT: JAI Press, 1983): 3–39.
27. Harrison M. Trice and Janice M. Beyer, "Studying Organizational Cultures Through Rites and Ceremonials," *Academy of Management Review* 9 (1984): 653–69; see Martin, page 44, in note 5.
28. John Van Maanen, "The Smile Factory: Work at Disneyland," in *Reframing Organizational Culture*, ed. by Peter J. Frost, et al. (Newbury Park, CA: Sage, 1990): 58–76.
29. Donald Katz, *Just Do It* (New York: Random House, 1994).
30. See Ott, page 28, in note 4.
31. See Ott, pages 86–87, in note 4.

32. See note 23.

33. Ibid.

34. See note 1, pages 271–72; Lee Iacocca, *Iacocca: An Autobiography* (New York: Bantam, 1984).

35. Tim R. V. Davis, "The Influence of the Physical Environment in Offices," *Academy of Management Review* 9 (1984): 271–83.

36. See note 29.

37. Peter Collier and David Horowitz, *The Fords: An American Epic* (New York: Summit Books, 1987).

38. See note 35, page 276.

39. See note 3, pages 88–89; Jay W. Lorsch, "Managing Culture: The Invisible Barrier to Strategic Change," *California Management Review* 26 (Winter 1986): 105–109; see Pettigrew, page 578, in note 5.

40. See Lorsch in note 39.

41. See Pettigrew, page 578, in note 5.

42. Jay B. Barney, "Organizational Culture: Can It Be a Source of Sustained Competitive Advantage?" *Academy of Management Review* 11 (1986): 656–65.

43. Thomas J. Peters and Robert H. Waterman, *In Search of Excellence* (New York: Harper & Row, 1982).

44. Alan L. Wilkins, "The Culture Audit: A Tool for Understanding Organizations," *Organizational Dynamics* 12 (Autumn 1983): 24–25; William G. Ouchi, *Theory Z: How American Business Can Meet the Japanese Challenge* (Reading, MA: Addison-Wesley, 1982).

45. See Wilkins, pages 34–36, in note 44.

46. Paul B. Carroll, "Story of an IBM Unit That Split Off Shows Difficulties of Change," *The Wall Street Journal* (July 23, 1992): A1.

47. See note 1, pages 360–61.

48. Ibid, page 361.

49. Ibid, page 362.

50. See Schein, pages 114–19, in note 5.

51. This definition of culture change is based on the one used by Harrison M. Trice and Janice M. Beyer in note 1, page 395.

52. W. Brooke Tunstall, "The Breaking Up of the Bell System: A Case Study in Cultural Transformation," *California Management Review* 26 (Winter 1986): 110–24; David Kirkpatrick, "Could AT&T Rule the World?" *Fortune* (May 17, 1993): 11.

53. David Nadler and Michael Tushman, *Strategic Organizational Design: Concepts, Tools, and Processes* (Glenview, IL: Scott, Foresman, 1988).

The Americanization of Siemens[*]

Siemens (http://siemens.com) is one of those huge diversified global firms that many people outside of Europe don't recognize, despite the firm's aggressive $25 million television advertising campaign in the Americas and the fact that 27 percent of their revenues come from North and South America and that nearly 20 percent of its employees are in the United States (just short of the 24 percent in Germany). The company competes directly with such global giants as General Electric and Asea Brown Boveri (ABB) in the production of automation, telecommunications, power, and transportation systems. It produces semiconductors, automotive electrical components, medical imaging equipment, and even lightbulbs under the Westinghouse and Osram Sylvania names. The company has production, distribution, and support service throughout the world. Yet despite its global presence, until recently the company was regarded as a typical German firm.

In the past, the values that drove Siemens were innovation, engineering excellence, and contribution to the German social welfare system through maintaining high levels of employment. Siemens prided itself on its 154-year history of technical innovations. The firm began as a telegraph company and created the first long-distance telegraph lines in Europe, established the first Indo-European line between Calcutta and Berlin, and laid a transatlantic line in 1874. Many of the early developments in medical imaging came from Siemens, including the first electron microscope. The company has been a leader in development of rail transport and electric lighting. Nonetheless, in recent years it had not been known for stellar financial performance, at least in the eyes of stockholders. The company was driven by engineering processes rather than profits. Profit margins in several of its core businesses were a fraction of those obtained by its competitors. For example, in the mid-1990s GE earned margins of 18 percent in the power generation business compared to 0.7 percent for Siemens. The company was inefficient and had excess human resources.

The transformation at Siemens in the past 5 years has been dramatic. While the company has not abandoned its German heritage, it has Americanized many processes. First, the company has begun to focus on shareholder value, a necessity in global markets where it competes with GE not only for customers, but also for investors. In the past 3 years income has gone up by 150 percent and share prices have increased threefold.

To compete with GE and others in their diverse industries, Siemens had to become more efficient. Siemens has followed the American practice of downsizing, no easy task in Germany and much of Europe. Laws in Germany and elsewhere in western Europe require firms to pay generous severance pay when releasing employees. Between 1995 and 1998 the company cut nearly 13,000 employees at a cost of $3.2 billion dollars. The move was also unpopular because of the rising unemployment in Germany resulting from reunification. Siemens has also pursued the typical American strategy of shedding unprofitable businesses and acquiring new ones, many in the United States, that fit the company's portfolio of businesses. The clear objective is enhancing shareholder value.

Siemens has even Americanized some of its internal operations. For a company operating in 193 countries, language could present a monumental barrier. Like many other global firms, Siemens has adopted English as the common language of the company. The firm has also adopted U.S. accounting practices that emphasize profits, compared to German practices that emphasize tax savings. Additionally, Siemens is following the American practice of providing shareholders with quarterly financial results on a business unit basis.

In the area of compensation, Siemens has initiated performance-related bonuses and stock options for top executives. The practice is rare in German firms and stock options are heavily taxed. However, the change in compensation is consistent with Siemens's new values of emphasizing shareholder value. In the words of Gerhard Schulmeyer, chief executive for the company's U.S. unit, "We've gone from basically an employment company to being a shareholder-value company. In other words, we've Amercanized."[†]

Perhaps the clearest indication of the Americanization of Siemens is the change in the company's Washington, D.C., office. In the past, the primary function of the office was to gather political and eco-nomic data to send back to corporate headquarters. The company has replaced many of the research analysts with bona fide lobbyists, taking an active role trying to influence government policy. How much more American can you get! It remains to be seen how deep and lasting these changes will be and whether Siemens will retain any of its distinctly German culture. ∎

*Based on Claudia H. Deutsch "German Heritage, Americanized Future," *New York Times* (March 27, 2001), C-1 and C-19; http://siemens.com, accessed July 1, 2001.
[†]Deutsch, p. C-19

QUESTIONS FOR DISCUSSION

1. What were the key German values that Siemens displayed?
2. What are the American values that Siemens has adopted?
3. Using Hofstede's framework, where would you place Germany with regard to uncertainty avoidance? Why? How is that changing as the firm Americanizes?

Information and Organizational Decision Making

11

CASE: MIDWEST CITY UNIVERSITY REBUILDS ITS STADIUM*

Midwest City University (MCU) is a large (approximately 32,000 students), state-supported urban university serving the southern part of a midwestern industrial and agricultural state. MCU has several outstanding programs, including medicine, music and performing arts, engineering, and architecture. However, MCU has rarely rated anywhere near outstanding in intercollegiate football. Among the university's sports teams, football was always in the shadows of MCU's successful basketball program. Winning seasons had been a rarity in recent years. In the 10 years prior to the opening of the rebuilt stadium (1983 to 1992), the team had a combined record of 32-76-2. The best season was 5-6.

Nonetheless, in the late 1980s, the university spent nearly $10 million to refurbish the on-campus stadium. The president attempted to justify this decision by noting that the continuation of a competitive intercollegiate athletic program had to include football and that the football program could not recruit potential players or attract opponents without a first-class facility on campus. The stadium was essentially useless in its current state of disrepair, and the county had threatened to condemn it. If the university wanted to continue playing football, it either had to move games five miles away to a downtown stadium used by the local NFL team or rebuild the campus stadium. Although some groups such as the board of trustees and alumni supported the decision to rebuild, many others questioned the wisdom of this project.

Some background may help to put the stadium renovation decision in context. The late 1980s were a difficult time for many state universities, and MCU was typical in this regard. MCU faced the dual threats of declining enrollments and declining levels of state financial support. From 1988 to 1994, the state support for MCU was cut by nearly 25 percent. Declining enrollments meant that tuition revenues were also falling. In general, the university was experiencing serious budget constraints.

Despite the rather dire financial conditions and protests from faculty members and others, the administration decided in the late 1980s to embark on a major stadium renovation. Funding for the stadium project was done in an unconventional manner. Typically, building funds are taken from a separate capital funds budget. The stadium project, however, was funded by a combination of bonds underwritten by the general operating budget and some funds actually taken from the general operating budget. The general operating budget is typically reserved for the day-to-day operation of the university—to pay faculty and staff salaries and to pay general operating expenses. Drawing on general funds increases the cost of running the university and reduces the funds available for educational programs and salaries. Needless to say, the funding decision was controversial and unpopular in some quarters.

---

*Although the name of this university has been changed, the events portrayed in this case are real.

During this same period the administration, through the president and provost, made draconian cuts in support services, staffing levels, and resources. Many vacant faculty positions were not filled with new faculty. A significant number of clerical workers, custodians, and other support staff were cut. Simultaneously, several union contracts expired and bitter, divisive negotiations dragged on. At one point, the faculty held a referendum resulting in a vote of no confidence in the president. Many faculty pointed to the stadium project as a major reason for their dissatisfaction with the president. It was not just the spending that bothered faculty members. Many professors objected to what they saw as a rather heavy-handed decision process that ignored any role for faculty input on the stadium project. To the dismay of the faculty, the MCU board of trustees ignored the referendum and gave the president a resounding vote of confidence. Not long after this vote, contract negotiations between the faculty and the university broke off and a strike was called. The stadium project was just one of many issues.

The strike was short-lived, with faculty winning only a few concessions from the administration. The local media portrayed the faculty as petty, whiny, and out of touch with the economic and educational reality of the state. At no point was there any mention in the media of the stadium spending. Shortly after, the faculty agreed to a new contract with minimal raises (average of 2 percent per year for 3 years). The president was rewarded by the board of trustees with a 3-year contract extension and a significant raise (an average of over 10 percent per year).

In 1993, MCU's football fortunes took a turn for the better. The team, playing in its renovated stadium, had its first winning season in over 10 years (8-3) and was mentioned as a possible bowl participant. Attendance at games was up. The athletic department had begun to receive increased recognition. New sources of revenue were being developed.

It would be nice if the story ended here with a vastly improved football program that added recognition and revenue to the university. Unfortunately, intercollegiate football, like organizational life in general, is filled with turbulence and uncertainty. After the 1993 season, the head coach left for a better job—the offer coming in recognition of his accomplishment in turning around a perennially losing team. The team also lost a core group of 17 starting seniors, and because of the loss of their head coach, the team had a poor recruiting year. The team finished the 1994 season with a 2-8-1 record. Faculty and others in the university community were once again questioning the wisdom of spending large sums of money on a football stadium.

Information processing and decision making are critical events in organizations. Some theorists suggest that information processing and decision making are at the root of all organizational activity. We normally think of decision making as an orderly, rational process—and sometimes it is, but not always. In this chapter we first look at information as the raw material that feeds the decision-making process, and we then look at three models of decision making. The first two of these are models that suggest a rational or bounded rational approach to decision making. Decision makers identify problems and attempt, in an orderly fashion, to find solutions to problems. These two models differ in the degree of rationality present. The second model, bounded rationality, suggests reasons why rationality in decision making is bounded or constrained. Finally, we examine garbage can decision making, a situation such as that at MCU where even the pretense of rationality vanishes.

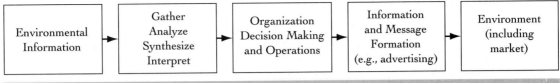

FIGURE 11-1   Information Flows from and to the Environment

As discussed in earlier chapters, the organization must develop a linkage system to keep it in tune with its external environment. Following the establishment of such systems, the organization is in the posture of gathering and processing information in order to make proper organizational choices. This chapter examines the value of such information and describes its characteristics.

In this chapter, we describe the information process from a generic point of view. We briefly describe the management of the information process and show how information is related to decision making. We discuss the tremendous impact that high-tech information systems can have on organizational structures, processes, and relationships.

Organizations are basically information processors. They gather, analyze, synthesize, and interpret information from their environment for their own uses and for return to the environment. They use this information to make choices or decisions about what the organization does and does not do and how it does it. In short, information and the knowledge it represents are the lifeblood of the organization. No organization can exist for long if it does not have valid and reliable information on which to base its decisions and operations. Using our systems approach, we can depict the information flow through the organization as seen in Figure 11-1.

THE VALUE OF INFORMATION

Information is valuable to the organization only if it is useful in decision making and operations. The more useful the information, the more valuable it is. General Motors is certainly more interested in consumer auto preferences than it is in consumer satisfaction with toothpaste.

There are seven primary characteristics of information that make it valuable to the organization: *relevance, quality, richness, quantity, timeliness, accessibility,* and *symbolism.* Let's look at each of these.

Relevance of Information

The more relevant the information to the core technology of the organization, the more valuable it is.[1] Two of the key information challenges faced by the organization are deciding what environmental information is relevant and to whom in the organization the information is relevant. By using the concepts of domain and task environment, the organization decides which aspects of the environment are relevant for scanning purposes. A decision is made on scanner or sensor placement and function in order to avoid both taking in too much data, resulting in information overload, and tracking inappropriate aspects of the environment.

In addition, linking scanners or sensors to proper decision-authority centers ensures that environmental information is provided to the decision center where action can be taken, as shown in Figure 11-2. For example, the personnel unit needs to

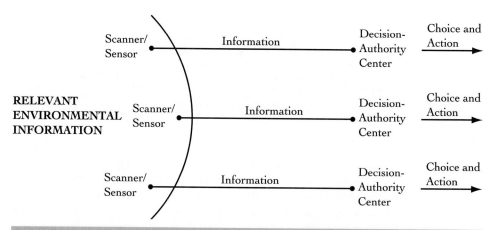

FIGURE 11-2   Information Links the Environment with the Decision-Authority Center

know labor market availability figures and the purchasing manager needs to know raw material prices, not vice versa.

The most relevant information the organization needs is information required to make strategic decisions. Strategic decisions are those major decisions that affect the long-term direction of the organization. Decisions to build a new plant, develop a new product, or enter a new market with an existing product are examples of strategic decisions.

Strategic decisions made without the proper information can often lead to organizational disaster. For example, Bank of America Corporation was one of the world's most successful banking organizations until its decline in the middle and late 1980s. Although analysts attributed numerous reasons for this organization's problems, one cannot deny that Bank of America made many significant strategic decisions without first having adequate information. The bank lent heavily to Third World countries without having enough qualified credit specialists to obtain and report back vital information about these countries' abilities to repay the loans. In addition, A. W. (Tom) Clausen, president of Bank of America from 1970 to 1980, neglected to hire enough auditors so that control information about the bank's myriad operations, particularly loan repayments, could be relayed to top-level Bank of America officials. Clausen and his successor, Samuel Armacost, were also criticized for not investing quickly enough in computers and telecommunications equipment. Indeed, until the end of 1984, Bank of America had *40 different* computer networks that it used for different purposes.[2] Thus, while its competitors had already installed and were using powerful, integrated systems for obtaining and synthesizing information, Bank of America still had to rely on separate systems for functions such as branch teller operations, automated teller operations, mortgage banking, U.S. commercial operations, Asian commercial operations, and so on. Bank America even continued to invest in "oil patch" real estate after the U.S. oil industry went into recession in the mid-1980s. In short, Bank of America's failure to design, implement, and use a system for obtaining relevant and timely information for both day-to-day operations and strategic decision making was most definitely one of the causes behind this banking organization's crisis in the early 1990s. The vulnerability that resulted may have been an important factor in the bank's acquisition by Nations Bank (although the merged banks continue to use the Bank of America name).

Quality of Information

The quality of information refers to its accuracy. Does the information accurately represent reality? The more accurate the information, the higher its quality and the more confident organizations can be when using it to make decisions.[3] The cost of information generally increases as the quality desired becomes higher. However, this cost must be balanced against the cost of having and acting on erroneous information. If General Motors believed the market wanted sporty, high-performance cars and designed cars to meet this objective, a grave mistake would be made if, in reality, the market wanted large, luxury sedans.

Type I and Type II Errors   Two essential types of errors can be committed with information quality. The first, ***Type I error***, occurs when the organization accepts as *true* a piece of information that is actually *false* (e.g., believing that people want to buy expensive home computers when they do not). A ***Type II error*** occurs when the organization accepts as *false* something that is actually *true* (e.g., believing that the purchase of home videorecorders has peaked, thus leaving the market, only to realize 2 years later that sales continue to increase). In both cases organizations act on faulty information and make poor decisions.

"Unk-unks," "unknown-unknowns," are especially problematic. With an unk-unk, the organization does not know something but does not realize that it *should* know it. A known-unknown, on the other hand, reflects that even though the organization does not know something, at least it realizes it should know it.[4] This concept came from the early days of the space program. Envision this: A rocket is sitting on the launch pad. The countdown begins. The button is pushed. A powerful explosion immediately occurs, and the rocket disintegrates in a ball of fire on the pad. The engineers and scientists are puzzled as to what happened. As they read through their data printouts and examine the wreckage, they realize that the fuel pressure in a second-stage secondary fuel line became excessive, causing the line to break and the rocket to explode. They did not measure this pressure at the time of launch because they did not believe it to be important.

However, prior to the launching of a similar rocket, they install a sensor to measure the pressure on the secondary fuel line. As the countdown proceeds, they are reading their telemetry and they notice that they are not receiving a readout from the secondary fuel line. They then make a very important decision—they do *not* push the button for launch.

In both cases—the first one, in which the rocket exploded, and the second one, in which the launch was aborted—the engineers did not know the pressure in the secondary fuel line. But in the second case, they realized it was an important fact so they did not push the button. They had turned an unknown-unknown into a known-unknown, which resulted in their taking an entirely different course of action.

Thus, organizations face a conundrum: They must seek information to reduce uncertainty, but unk-unks are uncertainties about which the organization is unaware. An organization cannot seek information to solve uncertainties that are not known to the members. Although there are no solutions to unk-unks, organizations must scan the environment widely and broadly to discover potential problems as well as sources of information.[5] It is a reality of organizational life that uncertainty, both of the known and unknown varieties, will always be present.

Information Richness

Two related aspects of information that have received considerable attention are ***information richness*** and ***information quantity*** (or amount).[6] Information quantity is discussed in the next section. Information richness refers to the "carrying capacity" of a particular method of conveying information.[7] Methods that convey great meaning are defined as ***rich*** while those that convey less meaning are ***lean***.

Perhaps the best way to explain richness is by example. You could convey the same basic message to your boss using several different communication media: reports, memos, letters, telephone calls, or face-to-face meetings. Although the basic message in each interaction—say, for example, that sales of a new product are exceeding expectations by 25 percent—is the same, the richness of the potential information that is conveyed differs.

Written forms of communication are viewed as lean communication media. The written report may be useful for conveying a large quantity of specific, precise, numerical data. You could give a precise accounting, production, or sales report of the new product's performance using computer printouts, spreadsheets, graphs, and other similar mechanisms for reporting the data. However, written reports tend to be lengthy (hence, they often include an executive summary), and they provide only for one-way communication. Reports do not include mechanisms for querying the data or for feedback. Reports take time to write, which may reduce the timeliness of the information, another related and important dimension of information. You may choose to send a memo summarizing the sales situation. This increases the richness slightly by condensing the information and addressing it to a specific target individual, but feedback is still slow. Additionally, both reports and memos lack an extensive visual component that may be important to you in judging the accuracy and confidence that you (the reporter) have in the information. Your boss's perception of the person behind the report or memo may be important to his or her assessment of that information.

Spoken communications, by phone or voice mail, add new dimensions of richness to efforts to convey information—the sound of the sender's voice. Information about the speaker's tone of voice can provide the recipient with some information about the sender's confidence in the information. A live telephone conversation allows the boss to ask you to "get to the point" so that he or she does not have to waste valuable time filtering through marginally relevant information to get to the heart of the issues at hand. A live telephone conversation also allows the receiver to query the sender. The boss may ask you about your confidence in the information, or he or she may ask about some issues that you may not have thought to put in your initial report: Will the sales trend continue and are competitors entering the market? Still, telephone and voice mail information lack the visual component that may provide other important information.

The richest form of information is that given by face-to-face communication. The recipient gets the verbal message and voice cues mentioned earlier as well as visual cues. Visual cues may be important sources of nonverbal information about both the speaker and the issues. Figure 11-3 illustrates the relationship between communication medium and information richness.

Researchers have found important relationships between information richness and the types of tasks being carried out,[8] position in the organizational hierarchy,[9] and the type of control system used in the organization.[10]

Recall from Chapter 6 that one dimension of work unit or departmental technology is task analyzability, which is defined as either task programmability or ease or difficulty of obtaining information. Organizational members need increasingly rich infor-

FIGURE 11.3   Information Richness and Communication Medium

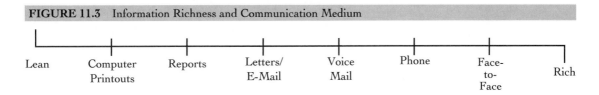

Lean — Computer Printouts — Reports — Letters/E-Mail — Voice Mail — Phone — Face-to-Face — Rich

mation as tasks become lower in analyzability. Low analyzability tasks require rich information, particularly because of the availability of feedback and the multiple information cues that are characteristic of rich information sources.

For much the same reason, as you move up the organizational hierarchy you find that individuals need increasingly rich information. Top management jobs are generally characterized as nonroutine. As such, they require rich information to deal with the low analyzability and ambiguity typical of those roles. Much of the information that top managers receive is highly processed and highly condensed. For example, technical reports often include executive summaries—condensed versions of the report that are often only one or two pages long and simply summarize main points.

Finally, as we noted in Chapter 9, organizations differ in the types of control systems that are used to direct and control employee behavior. Market control systems emphasize measurable outcomes. Thus, information requirements are modest. All that is needed is to record individual performance levels (e.g., sales, production). The information required is primarily lean numeric information. Bureaucratic control with its reliance on rules and its emphasis on documentation and recordkeeping also requires mostly lean information, but a large amount of it. Clan control systems rely on shared values and norms to control employee behavior. To learn about the norms and values of employees and to convey the norms and values of the organization, the organization must make extensive use of rich information.

Quantity of Information

Organizations walk a tightrope with respect to quantity of information. Enough information is needed to make an informed decision, but too much information causes information overload. When information overload occurs, decision–authority centers often ignore *all* the information provided. They reason, Who has time to wade through that thick report and find the information I need in my job?

Consequently, organizations must constantly monitor the linkage between scanners or sensors and decision–authority centers to ensure that the right quantity of information is provided. There is a tendency today to provide too much information, most of it irrelevant. The computer is a wonderful machine for generating printout after printout. Without careful monitoring, organizations can drown in a sea of computer printouts.

All too often, a situation is created as shown in Figure 11-4. In this figure the three boxes (information a manager receives, information a manager wants, and information a manager needs) overlap in a relatively small shaded area. A large portion of the information that a manager needs (Box 3) is not even recognized by the manager (Box 2). This is a good example of an unknown-unknown to the manager.

Assumptions   Some organizations are slow to make decisions because they think they need more information. In effect, they study an issue to death. Organizations never have perfect and complete information. In fact, Simon states that managers operate

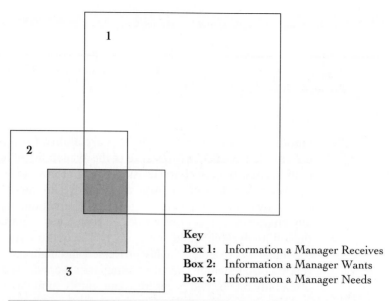

Key
Box 1: Information a Manager Receives
Box 2: Information a Manager Wants
Box 3: Information a Manager Needs

FIGURE 11-4 Information Needs of a Manager

Source: Sumantra Ghoshal and Seok Ki Kim, "Building Effective Intelligence Systems for Competitive Advantage," *Sloan Management Review* 49 (Fall 1986): 57. Reprinted by permission of the publisher. Copyright 1986 by the Sloan Management Review Association. All rights reserved.

under *bounded rationality*,[11] a concept first encountered in our discussion of goals. Bounded rationality means that even though managers intend to be rational in their organizational activities, they can act rationally only to a point.

Several factors contribute to bounded rationality. First, as we noted, decision makers never get perfect information. Even in the simplest of decisions, decision makers experience at least some uncertainty. Also, despite the fact that we live in an information age in which large quantities of information are readily and cheaply available, human beings have limited cognitive capacity or ability to handle all of the information available. Moreover, the personal biases and emotions of decision makers affect judgments. Thus, more information is not always the key to quality decision making. We return to these issues later in this chapter when we look at different models of organizational decision making.

Organizations must make assumptions about pieces of information they know they need but do not have. They must fill in the gaps, as shown in Figure 11-5. These assumptions must be reasonable. That is, they must be based on the information available. For example, if an organization decides to introduce a new product related to fitness, such as a home exercise machine, assumptions about the future of the fitness trend, health, home exercise, and so on should be based on what it knows is occurring now and what it can reasonably project for the future.

Organizations also must know about information they need to make assumptions about. There are two key issues involved here. First, they must realize their known-unknowns. (No assumptions will be made about unk-unks because the organization does not know it needs the information.) For example, if the primary factor that determines the success of walk-in emergency facilities is future population density average over either age or income, then when a health-care organization is making an expan-

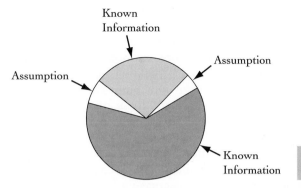

FIGURE 11-5   Assumptions Fill in the Information Gaps

sion decision, it needs to make an assumption about future population density. It does this only if it knows population density is the key factor. Ignoring population density and making assumptions about future age or income patterns would be incorrect in this case.

Second, the cost of information increases geometrically as the organization tries to gather more information about a particular issue, as shown in Figure 11-6. This occurs because the organization usually has some information about an issue readily available in regular reports or on file. However, as the need for more information on the subject expands, the organization may need to begin gathering new reports and gathering new data. It may be able to use secondary data sources, such as census data on markets, or it may need to conduct a special market survey, which is quite expensive. The organization must always balance the cost of this new additional information with its benefit.

Timeliness of Information

There is a time value to information. Knowing after the fact that a given stock has doubled in value is not as useful as knowing of this potential prior to its actually doubling in value. Being able to know immediately the actions of a competitor is much more valuable than learning of these actions 6 months after they occur. Most information the organization uses is historical. Data are collected on customer buying patterns, inventory turnover, sales, assets, and so on, and these data reflect what *has* occurred. Accounting data are all historical. The usefulness of these data increases the more recent they are. A company is more interested in quarterly sales reports for the past year than in reports from 2 years ago.[12] Speed is a major factor for using information,

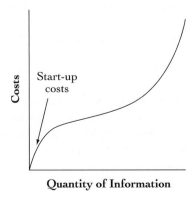

FIGURE 11-6   Information-Gathering Costs Increase Geometrically

and one of the major contributions of the computer is the speed it affords for information access and utilization.

Historical data can be used to project future trends. Through trend line analysis and other forecasting techniques, organizations attempt to project historical data into the future. This is fine as long as the conditions that shaped the historical data are similar to those that will shape future data. Forecasters were predicting oil prices would rise to $50 to $55 per barrel in the early 1980s, only to see the price drop below $20 per barrel in 1986. The assumptions about world oil usage, oil supply, and the power of OPEC were all flawed. In the aftermath of Desert Storm, embargoes against Iraq, shifting alliances in the Middle East, and cracks in OPEC solidarity, the price of oil became increasingly unpredictable. The U.S. energy supply became a critical issue in the 2000 presidential election. Decreasing fuel efficiency of U.S. automobiles and trucks, increasing consumption, and other problems pushed crude oil prices as high as $35 per barrel in early 2001. Predictions were once again made of prices in the $50 per barrel range ($3.00 or more per gallon of gasoline). By early summer of 2001 prices had once more retreated to $25 per barrel.

The key factor in timeliness is the need to obtain information soon enough to take or not to take action. In 1986, had the crew of the space shuttle *Challenger* known of the fuel leak in the right solid rocket booster during lift-off, they might have been able to jettison the craft from its rockets and fuel tank and escape the horrible explosion that occurred.

No one ever knows the future with certainty, and hindsight is always illuminating. We can all be Monday morning quarterbacks. Organizations should learn from their mistakes and try to obtain information in such a way that they do not repeat the same mistakes in the future. If it takes several hours for the results of a quality-control check to get to the production superintendent, a whole production run may need to be stopped if poor quality greatly exceeds tolerance levels. If a company continues to push a computer product that has become obsolete because it is unaware that a competitor has introduced a markedly better and less expensive product, much sales effort, time, and money that could be better spent elsewhere will have been wasted. If an organization does not have the proper information to develop a new product to meet or beat the competition, it might find itself out of business. There is a tremendous *opportunity cost* for doing the wrong thing at the wrong time. That cost is the action that *could have* been taken but was not. It is the cost of a lost opportunity.

Accessibility of Information

In order for information to be valuable to the organization's decision makers, it must be accessible. In other words, it must be available and relatively easy to obtain. Research has indicated that the accessibility of information, rather than its quality, might be a more important determinant of a manager's preference for information sources.[13]

Ideally, managers would select information from those sources perceived to offer the highest value (i.e., relevancy, accuracy, quantity, and timeliness). However, in practice, the less-qualified, more easily accessible information sources might be used more frequently by managers. Indeed, managers indicate that they chose information sources because of their accessibility even though the information obtained from such sources might be of a quality inferior to that obtained from less accessible sources.

Managers choose information based on accessibility for several reasons. First, managers incur both social and economic costs in searching for valuable information that might not be readily available. Because of organizational pressures on managers to produce results, the more accessible sources of information are likely to be used. Second, the structure of the organization can restrict access to higher-quality, more valued information sources. Think of a situation in which an organization's marketing managers need technical information that is readily available only to the firm's production managers. Third, organizational incentive systems can reward members for seeking information from a particular source while punishing them for seeking information from other sources. For example, in some organizations employees are forbidden to rely on certain types of information. Finally, information in organizations is often incomplete, vague, and subject to various interpretations; therefore, managers may come to rely on those sources used over a period of time that are considered both trustworthy and readily accessible. For example, coworkers can be considered by some managers to be very trustworthy and accessible sources of information. Thus, the student of organization theory should be aware that accessibility is a key factor in determining information value, even to the point that it might outweigh other factors, particularly relevance and quality.

Fast, powerful, low-cost computers and Internet connections have dramatically increased accessibility of information. The increased accessibility has reemphasized the importance of judging the quality and accuracy of information. Because of the ease of posting information on the Internet, we are often exposed to information of questionable quality and accuracy. In the late 1990s and early 2000s, the Internet has witnessed several scams in which seemingly objective news sources posted inaccurate and misleading data. In the worst of these situations, those posting the information were perpetrating frauds for personal gain.

Symbolic Value of Information

Finally, information has a *symbolic value.*[14] That is, the mere fact that a manager has access to or receives information may confer status or prestige on that person, even if the person does not use or need the information. For example, a middle manager may receive revised quarterly budget estimates that usually go only to the very top-level managers in the organization. Even though the mid-level manager does not need or use this information, the mere fact that he or she receives it has value to the person because it confers a status associated only with those holding high-level positions in the organization.

The authors have also noticed that the value of a strategic plan for some managers is that it is leatherbound with gold inlay and placed on the corner of the desk for display, *not* that it is actually used. The same phenomenon is also observed with the purchase of expensive coffee-table books that are never read but are used for display purposes.

Consequently, including certain people in the "information loop" has a symbolic value, even though the actual information is of little use to them. The design and management of an information system should recognize this value aspect of information.

The concepts of relevance, quality, richness, quantity, timeliness, accessibility, and symbolism of information all give information value. Organizations should manage their information in a way that enhances these attributes, at the same time realizing the costs associated with doing so. The next section discusses how this can be accomplished.

SYSTEMS FOR MANAGING INFORMATION

Information consists of a series of both stocks and flows, as shown in Figure 11-7. Information moves between the organization and its environment, and within the organization as well. It also moves from one unit to the next within the organization.[15] However, information is also stored in the environment and organization for later use. The system of gathering, reporting, analyzing, accepting, storing, retrieving, and using information in the organization is the *information system*. This system must be managed by the organization just as its production, marketing, or accounting systems must be managed.[16] Let us briefly look at the information process and then at some ways organizations manage it.

The Information Process

The information process is shown in Figure 11-8.

Gathering Information   Gathering involves obtaining necessary information from both outside and inside the organization. This information may come from *primary* data sources such as personal interviews or conversations, observation, or mailed questionnaires, or it may come from *secondary* sources such as census data, industry reports, or reports generated by the organization for other purposes.

The issues of *validity* and *reliability* are key factors when information is gathered. Because information is sometimes gathered through questionnaires, tests, or interviews, the validity and reliability of information-gathering devices become critical.

Suppose, for example, that the organization tests its job applicants for manual dexterity. The test would need to have high levels of validity and reliability if it were to be truly useful to the organization in screening applicants. Let us assume that manual dexterity is, indeed, a job requirement. The test would be *valid* if it actually measured what it claims to measure. In this case the test would need to measure the applicant's ability and skill in using hands and fingers to do a manual task of some sort. The test would be *reliable* if it produced consistent measurements over time, that is, if applicants were retested the following day or several days thereafter, and the same results were obtained. Whenever gathering information using some measuring device such as a

FIGURE 11-7   Stocks and Flows of Information

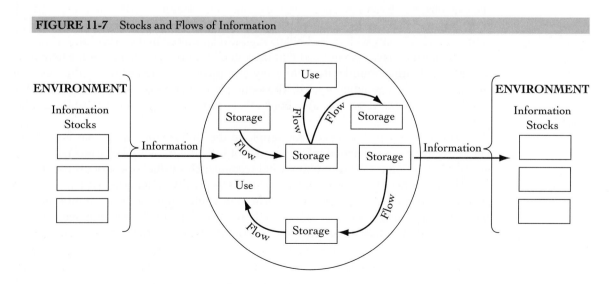

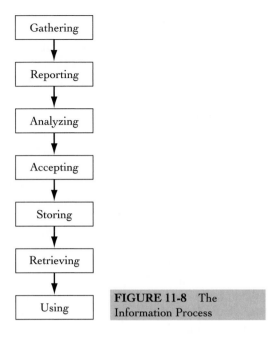

FIGURE 11-8 The Information Process

questionnaire or test, one should be very concerned with assessing the validity and reliability of the device or instrument.

Let us revisit the issue of test relevance. If the job in the example cited does not require manual dexterity, then testing for it obtains an irrelevant piece of information about the job applicant. If this information is used in selecting and hiring decisions, the quality of the decisions is severely affected. A random drawing might as well be used. This situation unfortunately exemplifies an all-too-common situation in information gathering in organizations—information is gathered for one purpose but is used for a different, inappropriate purpose. For example, some organizations may gather information on employees' ages in order to plan retirement programs, only to use the information to discriminate against older employees. Such discrimination is illegal.

The purpose of gathering information should be clearly spelled out and understood by all involved. Checks should be made periodically to ensure that the information is being gathered for the purposes intended.

Reporting Information   Making sure that the information is reported or communicated to the right person or unit is extremely important. For environmental information, this means it must eventually be received by the decision–authority center. For internally generated information, it means that the information is sent to a unit or person for decision and operations purposes.

The problem here, of course, involves information coordination. Organizations must address the question of how to get information to proper units fast enough so that the right hand knows what the left hand is doing. Information reporting is critical for coordination. Of course, modern computer systems have enabled some organizations to ensure that the right information is reported to the right person within a matter of minutes, even seconds.

The importance of this step in the information process can be seen by the following example. If the production unit implements a new process requiring a different skill, the personnel unit needs to know this in order to design a training program and to begin using that skill as a criterion in the selection process. If marketing undertakes a heavy sales and promotional campaign, production needs to know this in advance so that it can produce enough product to avoid extended delivery delays; purchasing needs to order enough raw materials and semifinished goods; personnel may need to hire more people; and so on. The point is, very often a decision in one unit of an organization affects many others, and this information must be reported or communicated to these other units.

Analyzing Information   This step answers the question, What does the information mean? Often staff groups in an organization are responsible for performing detailed analyses of information for line managers. The key issue of analysis is to balance the need for it with any bias that may occur. Any time information is analyzed, there is a potential for bias. The person who analyzes the information may interpret it in such a way that personal bias intentionally or unintentionally enters the analysis. Important points may be omitted and minor points emphasized. Politicians often claim to be quoted out of context by the news media.

The problem of bias is exacerbated if the information is analyzed at each stage as it passes through the organization. Each time it is analyzed, it is reinterpreted. One ends up with a message at the end much like one receives at the end of the line when children play telephone-pass-it-on.

Therefore, the organization needs to provide guidelines for those analyzing information. Sometimes standard reporting forms help—such as those frequently used for sales, production, or budget reports. In addition, people may be required to include original data as appendices. Care must also be taken to ensure that the information is not needlessly transferred to a unit for analysis when additional analysis is not useful.

Again, we cannot overestimate the importance of computer technology concerning the analysis of information. Executive information systems permit organizations' top-level managers to manipulate and analyze data in a multitude of ways. And the software that permits such manipulation and analysis is available not only in the executive suite. Lower-level employees with basic computer literacy and access are now able to obtain, manipulate, and analyze information as never before.

Accepting Information   Information is useless unless it is accepted by those to whom it is sent. Just because it is sent to an organizational unit does not mean it is received and accepted. There needs to be a follow-up of some sort (e.g., a phone call, return initial sheet, and so on) to indicate something was received.

Acceptance does not mean agreement. Acceptance means that the unit has received the information and should have read it. The individuals in the unit may or may not agree with the information.

Storing Information   Sometimes the information can be acted on immediately, but often it is stored. This may simply mean placing it in a pile on some executive's desk, or it may mean storing it in a file or on computer disk or tape. The key factors in storing are cost, timeliness, and access. Any time an organization stores information, it costs something. Not only are personnel costs involved with the actual storage procedure, but there are also equipment costs (e.g., computer, filing cabinet) and access costs, the costs of not having the information readily available. It costs something not to have the data when needed and to retrieve them. Of course, the computer has substantially reduced the need for storage space and thus its cost.

Retrieving Information   How accessible is the information? Again computers have made information much more accessible than ever before. As we have already seen, online capability allows executives to retrieve information from desktop terminals or personal computers. This has greatly expanded managers' access to information. Although this is generally viewed as good, it can cause problems if managers retrieve data and information out of their job area and attempt to tell others how to run their operations.[17]

The retrieval decision is actually made at the time the information is stored. At that point the ease and time of retrieval should be considered as factors in information storage. Information would not be stored in boxes in some faraway warehouse if the organization expected to retrieve it soon.

Using Information   Information should be gathered only if it is to be used. Too often, organizations gather information because someone determined that "it would be nice to have—you never know what might come up." This contributes to irrelevant information and information overload. There should be a purpose and a goal for every piece of information. In other words, the expected use of the information should be clearly formulated *before* it is gathered.

This characteristic of information is called *user-based.* The users of the information should have the most significant say-so as to what information is to be gathered and how it is to be reported. This helps to ensure that the information is *user-friendly,* that is, the users find the information easy to use. Although this seems obvious to many people, it has not often occurred in the past. Rather, the person or unit gathering the information or the unit analyzing and storing it (e.g., the computer unit) often would determine the quality, form, and purpose of the information. The end user would have little say-so.

Frequently, this situation is particularly bad with budgetary information. Managers in an organization that the authors have worked with receive computer printouts of budgetary expenditures that are difficult to read and interpret. These printouts usually arrive several weeks late as well. When both the budget staff and computer people were asked for a different form depicting the information in a different way on a more frequent basis, the response was that "the system was not set up to do that." Consequently, no changes were made, and the managers continue to keep their budgets using pen and paper, or on their own PCs, while the computer printouts end up unused in a filing cabinet.

An *information audit* is a useful tool for determining if and how information is actually being used. An information audit reviews reports, memos, printouts, and so on to determine how they are generated, where they go, and how they are used. The goal is to streamline information flow and reporting procedures as well as to ensure that information being collected is being used as intended. It also attempts to determine whether there are information needs not being satisfied and whether it would be cost effective to satisfy them.

MANAGING THE INFORMATION PROCESS

The organization should be concerned with managing information just as it manages its other resources—people, money, materials, plant, and so on. To do this, organizations must design a *management information system* (MIS). An MIS is a formalized system of making available to management timely, accurate, and relevant information for decision making.[18] It implies that the organization has established a formal system to ensure that the right information is available at the right time for the right managers so they can make the best possible decisions.

An organization has basically two options in managing information: It can either increase information-processing capacity or it can decrease it. Computer information systems are popular because they increase capacity in an organization. Because organizations face ever-increasing requirements for information, not only from the macro environment but from the micro (i.e., internal) environment as well, computers have become not only popular but essential for information management purposes.

Characteristics of an Effective MIS*

An effective MIS has several characteristics. First, the information should be *user-based.* It should fulfill the needs of the user for effective decision making. Second, it should be *timely, accurate,* and *relevant.* Third, it should be *tied to a computer* for ease of analysis, storage, and access. Fourth, it should be *cost effective.* The process, as well as the information carried, should justify itself in terms of benefits. Fifth, the MIS should be a *system of systems.*† The accounting system, marketing information system, inventory control system, and so on should be viewed as a total system of information to be integrated and coordinated in order to minimize overlaps, duplicate reports, and separate systems for data gathering. Finally, the system should be *managed.* An organizational unit should be vested with the authority to manage the system and to act in a staff support capacity to line managers.

One of the main challenges facing an MIS department and its managers is to ensure that the information it provides truly benefits the entire organization, that is, that the information has value both to the organization as a whole and to various subunits within the organization. The importance of information systems in organizations is highlighted by the creation in many organizations of a top management position designated chief information officer (CIO). This position has charge of developing and implementing the firm's information strategy and linking it to the overall strategy. Some firms such as Ragoual Corporation have created information policy boards (IPB) that bring together representatives from all areas of the firm to set policy and direction for MIS.[19]

INFORMATION AND THE DECISION-MAKING PROCESS

Information is the raw material that feeds decision making at all levels in the organization. To understand the role of information better, it is useful to digress briefly and examine decision making. Theorists have developed three models of decision making, and information plays important but different roles in each of these models. Table 11-1 summarizes key points of these three models.

Rational Decision Making

Economists have long used simplifying assumptions about human economic choices to model human behavior. One result of these simplifying assumptions is the ***rational*** or ***economic model of decision making.*** The model assumes that decision makers gather perfect information available at no cost, use perfect rationality, and arrive at *utility-*

---

*We have used the term *MIS* or *management information system* to refer specifically to the reporting and control system the managers use to carry out their jobs. Terminology is constantly evolving and many experts in the field now prefer the term *IT* or *information technology* to refer to the broad array of hardware and software used throughout the organization.
†Ralph Stair, *Principles of Information Systems: A Managerial Approach* (Boston: Boyd & Frazer, 1992).

TABLE 11-1 Decision-Making Models			
Model	**Assumptions**	**Decision Processes**	**Decision Outcomes**
Rational/ Economic	1. Perfect information at no cost. 2. Perfect rationality.	Stepwise; linear. Begin with problem identification; end with solution implementation.	Utility. Maximization.
Bounded Rationality	1. Imperfect information—uncertainty—and information costs. 2. Power and personal preferences affect decisions. 3. Decision makers face cognitive limitations.	Decision makers attempt to act in a stepwise, linear rational fashion, but rationality is bounded or constrained.	Satisficing.
Garbage Can	1. Multiple, ambiguous and conflicting goals. 2. Means for achieving goals not well understood (ambiguous technology). 3. Fluid participation of members in decision making.	Nonlinear process; no clear beginning or ending points; decision process can start at any point.	Solutions where there are no problems. Problems that go unsolved. Some problems get solved.

maximizing decision outcomes. A utility-maximizing outcome is one that provides the decision maker with the best possible set of outcomes.[20]

For example, a retail grocery business may try to use this approach to deal with the problem of the optimal inventory levels of various products to stock on the shelves. The process would start with ***problem recognition*** or ***identification***: The store must stock the right amount of inventory. Too much inventory results in storage and opportunity costs—the money tied up in inventory cannot be used for other things; too little inventory results in lost sales. The next step would be for managers to ***determine the desired outcomes***: Managers must determine the appropriate levels of inventory. Once the problem has been identified and the desired outcome has been determined, managers must ***collect data*** about the underlying causes of the gap between the desired state and the current state: Why is the firm unable to achieve utility maximizing inventory levels? In the case of inventory levels, two obvious problems would be unpredictability in supply and unpredictability in demand for goods. Clearly, many other issues may affect supply and demand: weather conditions, competition, new products, changing consumer habits, and so on. Once the decision makers have collected data, they ***develop alternative solutions*** to the problem. Managers may, for example, develop expert systems to monitor inventory levels and automatically place orders as needed. The marketing department may conduct consumer surveys and focus groups to track consumers and develop a model of consumer preference to guide inventory control. The purchasing department may suggest a variety of purchasing strategies and strategic relationships with suppliers to guarantee pricing and supply of inventory. Once these solutions are developed, management ***assesses*** the alternatives for the one solution or set of solutions that provide a utility-maximizing outcome. The final step is to ***implement*** the decision.[21]

Fundamental to this stepwise process are the assumptions that (1) managers will obtain perfect, unbiased information, (2) managers will use this information to act in a perfectly rational manner, and (3) managers will select the utility-maximizing outcome. The decision process is linear in nature (an identifiable beginning and end) and rational. However, a close look at the inventory control problem suggests that although perfect rationality may be a desirable state, it is likely to be unattainable. Any number of problems are likely to make rationality bounded or constrained. Decision makers may be unaware of certain consumer trends. The purchasing department may be unable to forecast the financial well-being of certain suppliers. Unpredictable weather conditions may affect the availability of certain goods. On top of problems of uncertainty, differences of opinion among different departments involved may affect decision premises and information availability. The information systems department may believe that the bulk of resources should go toward the development of a highly sophisticated computer system and software to monitor and control flows of inventory. The marketing department may believe that the key to better inventory control is enhancing the firm's ability to predict consumer preference. Thus, they believe that the bulk of resources should be spent on surveys, focus groups, and development of a computer model of consumer preference. As we see in Chapter 12, these sorts of differences are not unusual. For now, it is important to note that such differences further constrain the organization's ability to act in a truly rational fashion. Instead, we are most likely to witness bounded rationality.

Bounded Rational Decision Making

One way to think about the decision-making process in organizations is to recognize the difference between how the organization would like to make decisions—using perfect rationality—versus how an organization actually makes decisions—using bounded rationality. The organization members' best intentions may be to make rational decisions, but the real-life conditions place boundaries or constraints on their ability to act rationally.

Earlier in this chapter, we identified factors that contribute to bounded rationality. In summary, decision makers face uncertainty, and perfect information is not available. Information searches cost money and take valuable time. Often, decisions need to be made quickly, precluding a comprehensive information search. Decision makers have cognitive limits; they may not be able to process all available information. Individuals or departments may have biases or preferences for certain information and certain types of solutions, regardless of whether the outcomes are utility maximizing. Decision makers may ignore information and rely instead on intuition or gut instincts.[22]

The result of bounded rational decision making is *satisficing*. A satisficing outcome is one that is of lesser quality than a utility maximizing outcome. Typically, a satisficing outcome is the first outcome that meets some minimum level of acceptability. It may be a compromise between different departments, although it need not be. It may be the outcome preferred by the most powerful department, even though a solution suggested by a less powerful group may be better.

In the earlier example of the inventory control problem, the marketing department may be the dominant and most powerful department in the organization. It may influence the decision process in such a way that most of the resources are devoted to surveys, focus groups, and decision modeling of consumer preference. Some smaller amount of resources may be used to develop a computerized inventory control system, and nearly no resources may be devoted to developing better relations with suppliers. The results may produce a system that improves inventory control but is far from utility maximizing.

Most decisions in organizations exhibit at least some degree of bounded rationality. As we see in Chapter 12, the complexity of the decisions, the degree of uncertainty present, and the decentralization of power in an organization contribute to bounded rationality. In some specific types of organizations and with some specific types of problems, the norms of rationality present in bounded rationality vanish. In the following section we explore decision making in which linearity and rationality are no longer present.

Garbage Can Decision Making

Perhaps you've been involved in or witnessed a decision that completely defied common sense. It may be that ***garbage can decision making*** was at work.[23] The stepwise decision-making process that is the hallmark of rational decision making and, to a somewhat lesser extent, of bounded rationality, is no longer present. In fact, solutions may precede the identification of problems, or no problem may even exist. Decisions may be made that do not solve problems, and those problems may continue. Sometimes some problems eventually get solved, although any thought of utility maximizing should be abandoned.

Rational decision making and bounded rationality were presented as decision-making models for individual decisions. The problems of bounded rationality are exacerbated by the necessity for organizations to make many decisions. The garbage can model, unlike the first two models, is an attempt to characterize the complexity of organizations faced with multiple decisions.

Garbage can decision making gets its name from the colorful way in which researchers portrayed the process. Think of peering into a garbage can and seeing problems, solutions, information, participants swirling around in a random fashion. Decision makers can enter the decision process at any point. The "decision" may start with a solution in search of a problem. The following example will shed some light on garbage can decision making.

This case presents many key elements of garbage can decision making. Specific organizational conditions must be present; those conditions lead to a nonlinear decision process; and the results may vary greatly. These points are summarized here.[24]

The Organization   The goals and objectives of the organization are ambiguous, conflicting, and poorly articulated. Many problems exist simultaneously. These conditions may lead organizational members to pursue different sets of problems and set different priorities. One characteristic of garbage can decision making is that many decisions are being made simultaneously. In educational institutions like the university in the example, it is common for multiple and conflicting goals to exist and for some of the goals to be ambiguous. For example, it is unclear how a new sports and convocation center will further teaching or research goals.

A second organizational characteristic is that the means for accomplishing the organization's goals are ambiguous or poorly understood. Essentially, this means that the organization's technology is characterized by great uncertainty. For example, what means or technology does the university in the example use to increase the quality of teaching and research or to increase the prestige of the school? Building the center may add to visibility of athletic teams, but even that is questionable. The school would still need to recruit and train a highly skilled group of potential players. And as we saw, the center reduced the university's prestige among the local community members who were unhappy about increased traffic.

EXHIBIT 11-1

The Sports and Convocation Center

The president of the 12,000-student private urban university sat at his desk pondering the offer—$12 million to build a new multipurpose center on campus. The only conditions of the offer were that the money be spent for a multipurpose center and that the center bear the name of the donor. That should be no problem, the president thought.

Over the next few weeks the president began to put the wheels in motion. The public relations department put out a news release announcing the donation and the tentative plans for a new multipurpose sports and convocation center. An architectural firm was hired to draw up plans, and a handpicked committee of faculty, staff, board of trustee members, and others was assembled to guide the process.

Two months after the donation, the architect presented plans to the president. The president, the donor, and the board of trustees accepted the plan and hired a construction company to begin building the center.

As the center neared completion, a number of problems rocked the university. First, the donor received extensive negative publicity in the national press because of his involvement in highly publicized criminal activities. The wealthy donor had made his millions not in the oil business, but as an international arms merchant, selling weapons to just about any government or political group that could come up with hard currency. Some of the weapons that he sold were U.S. made, and their sale in foreign markets was prohibited. Questions were raised about the propriety of an academic institution being associated with a suspected criminal, especially one associated with terrorism and unsavory political groups. Second, several prominent faculty members suggested that the university had lost sight of its educational mission. Many classroom buildings were in disrepair; educational facilities were hopelessly out-of-date; student fees had to be raised to offset cost overruns for the sports and convocation center; and faculty, whose salaries lagged behind national averages, had not received raises in several years. The final problem was that once the center opened, the local community, one of the wealthiest in the city, complained vigorously about the increased auto traffic, noise, drinking, and rowdy behavior on nights of basketball games and concerts.

Shortly after the center opened, a faculty leader at an all-university meeting asked the president a critical question: How did the university end up with this center? The president then tried to reconstruct the decision process. He noted that the old athletic and special event facilities were in terrible condition. Basketball games and graduation programs had not been held on campus since the mid-1960s. The last three basketball coaches complained that they could not recruit top-notch prospects because of the horrendous facilities. Students and physical education faculty members had voiced concern about inadequate facilities for physical education classes, intramural sports, and recreational use.

The donor presented a potential solution to these problems. The president went on to note that he had sought input from his committee, but that most members failed to respond. When asked about the other problems on campus, the president merely deflected the questions and said that there were many problems on campus and in higher education today, but those were not the problems that this donor wanted solved. Faculty and students were displeased with the president's answers to their question. But as the meeting broke up, it was clear to those in attendance that they were stuck with the new sports and convocation center.

In retrospect, the center has become a focal point of campus activity. The athletic facilities receive heavy student and faculty use. Users boast about the high quality and comprehensiveness of the sports center. The center also houses the new student bookstore and a convenience store, both of which are very popular with students and faculty. Basketball, graduation, and concerts are back on campus for the first time since the mid-1960s. Still, other problems persist. Many classroom facilities need maintenance and upgrading. Computer facilities are several years behind the current technology. Faculty have received modest raises in the past 3 years, but they still lag behind those at comparable schools. Most significantly, the university has a new president who has tried to build bridges to all the important stakeholder groups: students, alumni, faculty, local residents, business, and government. Whether he will be able to solve all of the problems of the university is still uncertain.

The third organizational characteristic is referred to as *fluid participation.* In organizations in which garbage can decision making is likely to take place, participants move in and out of the decision process frequently. This fluidity in participation may be because of employee turnover or because employee commitment to the decision and time for decision making is limited. In the example, several different groups of people were involved in the decision process at different times with little consistency over time.

In general, this organizational situation has been labeled **organizational anarchy**.[25] The organization is highly organic and may be going through a period of rapid change. These conditions do not fit all organizations, but they may be found temporarily in many organizations. When these conditions are present, we are likely to find the type of decision making described in the next section.

The Decision Process   Whereas rational and bounded rational decision making are linear, stepwise processes, garbage can decision making is nonlinear. It can start and stop at any point. Four different streams of the decision process weave in and out in a nearly random fashion. These four streams are problems, solutions, organizational participants, and choice opportunities.

As noted in earlier decision models, problems are identified gaps between where an organization wants to be and where it is. The same is true in the case of garbage can decision making, but problems sometimes do not precede solutions and solutions may not solve problems. In fact, problems may be invented to fit solutions as in the case of the sports and convocation center. As this suggests, the sequence of problem identification leading to solutions may be reversed. Some problems may be solved, but they may not be the most important and pressing problems. Some problems continue to go unsolved.

We noted previously that the participation of organizational members in the decision process is fluid. This fluidity affects the decision process by creating inconsistency. Different participants are likely to see the set of potential problems and solutions in a different light and set different priorities. For example, the university faculty in the earlier case may have seen the solution to lagging prestige as recruiting better faculty and students. Or they may have seen an entirely different problem. Shifting decision-making participation makes it difficult to reach any consensus or common ground.

Recall from the case that this "decision event" began with an opportunity—the donor pledged money for a center. In this example, the decision process began with an opportunity. It may also be that a choice opportunity is lacking. Thus, an organization can identify a problem and a potential solution but cannot implement that solution because the appropriate set of problems, solutions, and participants is not present.

The consequences of garbage can decision making are that solutions are sometimes enacted where no problems exist. The sports and convocation center was a solution to a problem that had not yet been identified. It may also be that problems continue even after a solution has been implemented. The sports and convocation center did not increase the prestige of the university and did not improve the quality of sports teams appreciably. At the same time, other problems continued with no solutions in sight. Classroom buildings were still in disrepair, and faculty salaries still lagged behind national averages. However, even in a garbage can situation, some problems do get solved. The sports and convocation center did provide a much needed facility for recreational sports, concerts, and university events.

It is important to note that garbage can decision making is not a desired state of affairs. The chaotic and random nature of decision making is not likely to lead to high-quality decision outcomes. The garbage can model is a *descriptive model*. It describes conditions and consequences that are likely to occur in certain organizational settings. No organization intends to make garbage can decisions. Thus, the garbage can model is *not* something that one would prescribe or suggest for an organization.

INFORMATION TECHNOLOGY AND THE MODERN ORGANIZATION

Given the rapidly changing information technology, it is difficult and foolish to make specific suggestions about changes in organizations. The proliferation of fast, inexpensive, and comprehensive information technology is revolutionizing organizations and work life.

The changes currently going on in organizations as a result of the introduction and use of information technology are as profound as those brought about by the Industrial Revolution two centuries ago. Indeed, the changes in jobs and organizational structures will be radical, and organizations are only beginning to experience the effects that these "smart machines" are causing.[26]

The advent of fiber optics, microwave and satellite communications, and numerous other innovations facilitate the linking of buyers and suppliers, workers at all levels, and even competitors. These innovations are at the core of the new organization with its flatter hierarchy, its flexible workforce, and its global network. The problems facing organizations in the twenty-first century are determining which information is critical, judging the quality of information, and determining who should get the information. From an organizational standpoint, the problem is determining the appropriate structure to facilitate information management.[27]

In addition, traditional status and power relationships based on hierarchy might crumble should certain trends continue. Computerization undermines traditional forms of authority and breaks down barriers between job categories and functions.[28] Thus, being part of the *network* can become more important than having a certain position in the hierarchy.[29] Knowledge is power, so the saying goes, and many people in modern organizations are gaining power to an unprecedented degree because of their access to vitally important information.

Finally, before we leave this subject, the reader should note that information technology, by being able to enhance the speed and amount of information transferred, can allow for greater control and coordination down and across organizational units. Conversely, information technology can also lead to greater decentralization and flexibility. Top-level managers' use of executive information systems often permits these executives to delegate more authority to their subordinate managers because the former have a means to check more easily on company operations. Like many other facets of organization theory, a manager's particular philosophy has a great deal to do with how power and authority are delegated and dispersed throughout the organization.

SUMMARY

Information is the lifeblood of the organization. It links the organization to its environment, and it is the oil that lubricates the internal operations. Consequently, information must be managed just as any other valuable resource is managed.

Information has several key characteristics that are important for managers to understand and recognize. These include the relevance, quality, richness, quantity, timeliness, and accessibility of information. Additionally, information, or access to information, has symbolic value in organizations. Sometimes people collect information simply because that is what is expected in the organizations. Sometimes control of information, as we see in the next chapter, becomes a symbol of power.

Regardless of the stage of information evolution of a particular organization, the information process remains basically the same. Information is gathered, reported, analyzed, accepted, stored, retrieved, and used. The system of information management must ensure that the right quantity, quality, timeliness, and relevance of internal and external information is provided to decision-authority centers.

Information is a key input in the decision-making process. When making decisions, managers in organizations try to behave in a systematic, rational fashion. However, because of a variety of factors, decision makers face bounded rationality. These conditions include the complexity of most organizational problems, the uncertainty of technology and the environment, the limitations on human cognitive processes, individual emotions, and individual preference. Under conditions of bounded rationality, decision makers attempt to act rationally, but they are bounded or constrained in the ability to do so. Under some rare conditions even bounded rationality is absent from organizational decision processes. Garbage can decision making is likely to occur when organizations have multiple goals that may be ambiguous or conflicting, when the technology is unclear, and when participation of organizational members in the decision process is fluid. With garbage can decision making, even the pretense of rationality is gone.

Finally, we are beginning to see evidence that the introduction of information technology is having an impact on structures and processes in organizations. Information technologies are permitting organizations to become more flexible and more organic. Forms like the virtual organization discussed in Chapter 8 would not be possible without advanced information technology. The interplay between information, information technologies, and organizational design is key to the strategic success of organizations.

Questions for Discussion

1. Why is information important for an organization?
2. What is bounded rationality? Why does it often happen in business decisions?
3. What are the key characteristics of information?
4. What is the relationship between information richness and task technology? Explain why you think the relationship is that way.
5. What are the key assumptions of the rational economic decision-making model? Are they reasonable assumptions in the typical organizational context?
6. Why does bounded rationality plague most organizational decisions? What is the consequence of bounded rationality on decisions?
7. Under what kinds of conditions are we likely to see garbage can decision making? Describe a situation or organization in which you think garbage can decision making is likely.
8. Think of an example of an organization that has recently automated its information technology. What effects did this have on the administrative hierarchy and processes in the organization?

References

1. James O. Hicks, Jr., *Management Information Systems: A User Perspective* (St. Paul, MN: West, 1984): 12.

2. Jonathan P. Levine, "Bank of America Rushes into the Information Age," *Business Week* (April 15, 1985): 110–12.

3. John G. Burch, Jr., and Felix R. Strater, *Information Systems: Theory and Practice*, 2d ed. (New York: John Wiley & Sons, 1979): 16–17.

4. J. W. Dean, Jr., and M. P. Sharfman, "Procedural Rationality in the Strategic Decision-Making Process," *Journal of Management Studies* 30 (1993): 587–610; L. M. Gales and D. Mansour-Cole, "User Involvement in Innovation Projects: Toward an Information Processing Model," *Journal of Engineering Technology Management*, 12 (1995): 77–109.

5. See Dean and Scharfman in note 4.

6. R. L. Daft and R. H. Lengel, "Information Richness: A New Approach to Managerial Behavior and Organizational Design," in *Research in Organizational Behavior*, vol. 9 (Greenwich, CT: JAI Press, 1984): 191–233; R. L. Daft and R. H. Lengel, "Organizational Information Requirements, Media Richness and Structural Design," *Management Science* 32 (1986): 554–71.

7. See Daft and Lengel in note 6; see Gales and Mansour-Cole in note 4.

8. See Daft and Lengel in note 6; see Gales and Mansour-Cole in note 4.

9. H. Mintzberg, *The Nature of Managerial Work* (New York: Harper-Row, 1973); R. L. Daft, J. Sormunen, and D. Parks, "Chief Executive Scanning, Environmental Characteristics, and Company Performance: An Empirical Study," *Strategic Management Journal* 9 (1988): 123–39.

10. W. G. Ouchi, "A Conceptual Framework for the Design of Organizational Control Mechanisms," *Management Science* 25 (1979): 833–48; W. G. Ouchi, "Markets, Bureaucracies, and Clans," *Administrative Science Quarterly* 25 (1980): 129–41.

11. Herbert A. Simon, *Administrative Behavior*, 2d ed. (New York: Macmillan, 1957).

12. See note 1.

13. Charles A. O'Reilly III, "Variations in Decision-Makers' Use of Information Sources: The Impact of Quality and Accessibility of Information," *Academy of Management Journal* 25, no. 4 (December 1982): 756–71; A. C. Boynton, L. M. Gales, and R. S. Blackburn, "Managerial Search Activity: The Impact of Perceived Role Uncertainty and Role Threat," *Journal of Management* 19 (1993): 725–47.

14. M. S. Feldman and J. G. March, "Information in Organizations as Signal and Symbol," *Administrative Science Quarterly* 26, no. 2 (June 1981): 171–76.

15. Don Matthews, *The Design of Management Information Systems* (New York: Petrocelli/Charter, 1976): 42–49.

16. Henry C. Lucas, Jr., *Information Systems: Concepts for Management* (New York: McGraw-Hill, 1967), 7–13.

17. Peter F. Drucker, "Playing in the Information-Based Orchestra," *The Wall Street Journal* (June 4, 1985): 32.

18. James A. E. Stoner and Charles Wankel, *Management*, 3d ed. (Upper Saddle River, NJ: Prentice Hall, 1986): 622.

19. John P. Murray, "Developing an Information Center at Rayovac," *Data Management* (January 1983): 20–25.

20. J. G. March, "Bounded Rationality, Ambiguity, and the Engineering of Choice," *The Bell Journal of Economics* 9 (1978); H. A. Simon, *The New Science of Management Decision* (Upper Saddle River, NJ: Prentice Hall, 1960); H. A. Simon, "A Behavioral Model of Rational Choice," *The Quarterly Journal of Economics* (February 1955): 99–118.

21. Danny Samson, *Managerial Decision Making* (Homewood, IL: Richard D. Irwin, 1988).

22. See note 11; James G. March and Herbert A. Simon, *Organizations* (New York: John Wiley & Sons, 1958); Richard M. Cyert and James G. March, *A Behavioral Theory of the Firm* (Upper Saddle River, NJ: Prentice Hall, 1963).

23. Michael D. Cohen, James G. March, and Johan P. Olsen, "A Garbage Can Model of Organizational Choice," *Administrative Science Quarterly* 17 (1972): 1–25.

24. Ibid.

25. Ibid.

26. Shoshanna Zuboff, *In the Age of the Smart Machine* (New York: Basic Books, 1988).

27. Curtis Bill Pepper, "Fast Forward," *Business Monthly* (February 1989): 26–27; John Child, "Information Technology, Organization, and the Response to Strategic Challenges," *California Management Review* 30, no. 1 (Fall 1987): 48; Thomas J. Peters and Robert H. Waterman, *In Search of Excellence* (New York: Harper & Row, 1982); see Child in note 32.

28. See note 30.

29. Gareth Morgan, *Riding the Waves of Change: Developing Managerial Competencies for a Turbulent World* (San Francisco: Jossey-Bass, 1988).

Trusting Your Instincts — The Story of Katharine Graham and Rise of The Washington Post*

On July 17, 2001, Katharine Graham, the former publisher, CEO, and chairman of the board of The Washington Post Co. died as the result of injuries suffered from a fall. In the aftermath of Mrs. Graham's death many people learned of her extraordinary rise to power and control in the intersecting worlds of newspaper publishing and politics. Mrs. Graham "transformed *The Washington Post* from a mediocre newspaper into an American institution."[1] At the heart of the transformation of the *Post* were three critical decisions.

Katharine Graham's rise to prominence in the newspaper business is not the typical story of hard work, grit, and determination. It is much more than that. Graham's father, Eugene Meyer, a financier and high-ranking political appointee, purchased *The Washington Post* in 1933 at a bankruptcy auction for $825,000. The paper had a paltry circulation of 50,000 and lost a million dollars per year.

Although Graham did spend time in the newspaper business working at *The San Francisco News* and *The Washington Post*, the job of running the paper eventually fell on her husband, attorney Philip Graham. Philip Graham laid the groundwork for bringing financial and journalistic viability to the *Post*. He engineered the acquisition of a competing *Times-Herald*, *Newsweek*, and other D.C. media properties. Under Philip Graham, the *Post* challenged Senator Joseph McCarthy, the notorious leader of the anticommunist witch-hunt of the early 1950s. But Graham's stewardship of the *Post* was plagued by mental instability and he committed suicide in 1963.

The 46-year-old widow was thrown into the fray of dealing with her husband's death and running the *Post*. Although Katharine Graham had not been involved in the day-to-day operations of the paper, she did have "ink in her veins." Her father and husband had both been deeply involved in the business and she had many contacts with leading journalists. After a shaky beginning and some missteps in the first 2 years, Graham made a decision that would have lasting impact on the paper. She hired

Newsweek's Washington bureau chief, Ben Bradlee, to be the *Post*'s deputy managing editor and then quickly elevated him to the position of executive editor. This decision is one that is hard to put in quantifiable terms. Bradlee was successful at *Newsweek*, but running a daily newspaper is much different from being responsible for one office of a weekly news magazine. Gut instincts and emotional comfort are typically the important factors in this type of decision. Graham had no way of knowing at the time she hired Bradlee that he would be a decisive leader who would impart a new style to the *Post*. Under Bradlee's leadership, the paper moved dramatically into investigative reporting and developed a brash and innovative style.

The second critical decision came in 1971 at the height of the Vietnam conflict. *The New York Times* had begun publishing the Pentagon Papers, a behind-the-scenes view of the convoluted and often contradictory decision process that guided U.S. military and political policy in Vietnam. Shortly after the *Times* began publishing the Pentagon Papers, a federal judge, concerned about military security, issued a restraining order that prevented the *Times* from continuing their publication. This was the first time that a U.S. newspaper had been subject to a prior restraint order on publishing a story.

Shortly after the *Times* was restrained from publishing the Pentagon Papers, *The Washington Post* obtained its own copy. The decision of whether to publish the papers was left to Graham, the president and publisher of the *Post*. In the tradition of investigative reporting and muckraking, the journalists at the *Post* advocated publishing the papers. The *Post*'s attorneys were more cautious, fearing that the courts would close down the paper and its other media properties. Graham stated: "Frightened and tense, I took a big gulp and said, 'Go ahead, go ahead. Let's go. Let's publish.'" Graham's decision was later vindicated by the Supreme Court's decision against prior restraint. Graham's decision also moved the *Post* into the upper echelon of newspapers. People began speaking of *The New York*

Times and *The Washington Post* together. The *Post* was then seen as a national newspaper of record. This decision too was one fraught with uncertainty and emotion. The outcome was not at all clear at the time of the decision. Even the degree of risk was not clear.

Not long after the Pentagon Papers decision, Graham was faced with a third crucial decision that would eventually put the *Post* at the forefront of a national crisis. In the middle of 1972, investigative reporters at the *Post* tied a break-in at the Democratic National Committee office in the Watergate complex to the Nixon White House. Under Graham's somewhat reluctant leadership, the *Post* doggedly pursued the story directly to the Oval Office, President Nixon, and his immediate advisers. Graham did not back down in the face of pressure and intimidation from the White House. What began as a story of simple burglary eventually brought down the Nixon presidency and landed many of his aides in jail.

In 1972 there was no way to know that the Watergate reporting would lead to a Pulitzer Prize in 1973. The initial story certainly didn't have the hallmarks of a national scandal. Had it not been for a plea-bargaining deal that led to discovery of the White House recording systems and the infamous tapes, the story might never have amounted to much. Instead, the story reaffirmed the *Post*'s position as a journalistic leader.

The story of Katharine Graham is a remarkable testament to decision making under uncertainty. Graham's decisions were critical to the future of *The Washington Post,* but they were not the cold, calculating, quantitative decisions that we typically associate with business decisions. The reality is that, more often than not, the decisions that business leaders face are like those that Katharine Graham faced. Emotions and gut instincts were at the center of each of these decisions. Values, both organizational and personal, constrained the options. While financial implications were not ignored, they were not necessarily the critical criteria. ∎

---

*Based on Marilyn Berger, "Katharine Graham of Washington Post Dies at 84," *New York Times* (Wednesday, July 18, 2001), A-1 and C-18.
[1]Ibid., A-1.

QUESTIONS FOR DISCUSSION

1. Use the decision-making models to assess each of Graham's three decisions? Were they rational, bounded rational, or garbage can? Why?

2. Is there something unique about the newspaper business that might produce the kinds of decisions that Graham made?

CHAPTER

Power and Politics: Organizations as Political Entities

12

CASE: ORGANIZATIONAL POLITICS ON THE SMALL SCREEN*

It's happened again. That new television show that debuted last fall has been canceled. It was the only thing that you and your friends watched, and the critics even agreed that the show was one of the few bright spots in the TV season. What gives? Are you really that much out of the mainstream? Perhaps, but the answer is really more complicated.

It's the middle of the spring and the television season has moved into reruns and mid-year replacements for programs that flopped in the previous fall. It's also the time of year when network executives are assessing the past season's shows for the coming season. In a perfectly rational world (at least according to economic rationality) the process of assessing the past year's performance should not be too difficult. The size of the audience, or "share," is thought by many to be the critical factor. Audience share is largely what determines advertising revenues. And advertising revenues are the life-blood of TV shows.

Shows like *E.R.*, *Friends*, and *Seinfeld* enjoy long runs because they garner large audience share. Advertisers pay more for ad space during those shows. So it stands to reason that the inverse should also be true: Shows with small audience share, that don't generate sizable ad revenues, are likely to be canceled. But the relationship is not that simple.

Sometimes a weak show is kept on a network because the show's creators have other strong shows with the network or have a history of successful programs. Network executives fear alienating these successful producers and are likely to give them more latitude around audience share. Take, for example, the now popular series on CBS, *Everybody Loves Raymond.* The show's share numbers in its first season (1996–1997) were weak, but the show remained on the network largely because one of the producers was Worldwide Pants, David Letterman's production company. According to the *New York Times*, "Internal politics have always stamped renewal decisions. . . . CBS did not want to offend the network's late-night star if possible."[1] Now the show is one of CBS's strongest sitcoms.

Sometimes politics can sustain a weak show that, based on simple economic rationality, should be terminated. NBC maintained the show *Veronica's Closet* for two seasons even though the show clearly was not gaining sufficient audience share. Network executives feared angering the show's creators, who were also responsible for *Friends*, one of the highest ranked shows on TV.

---

*This case is based largely on Bernard Weinraub, "For TV's Vulnerable Shows, It's Fear-and-Lobbying Season," *New York Times* (May 1, 2001), B1 and B7.
[1]Ibid, B-1.

Apparently there is much more at work than audience share (and ad revenues) in selecting which shows live, which shows die, and which new shows light our TV tubes. Network executives must also judge "potential"—how likely a struggling or new show is to eventually gain satisfactory ratings. Given the large number of programs that fail each season, judging potential ranks right up there with reading tea leaves as a science. It seems clear that "other factors" besides audience share enter into the judgments. As is clear from the examples of *Everybody Loves Raymond* and *Veronica's Closet,* these other factors largely have to do with the power of the shows' creators. Competition and scheduling complicate the decision process: what shows do competing networks put up against your favorite show and what shows precede or follow your show. These factors can have unpredictable impact on a given program.

And now the decision process has become even more uncertain due to two new breeds of TV shows: high stakes quiz shows like *Who Wants to Be a Millionaire* and reality shows like *Survivor.* These have been quite successful and are considerably less expensive to produce than hour-long dramas or sitcoms. Yet it is not clear at this time how much staying power these new types of shows will have. Imitators have flooded the networks and in some cases the networks have possibly given viewers too much of a good thing.

In the end, the decisions about which shows to cancel, which shows to renew, and which new shows to add is a judgment call plagued by uncertainty, unpredictability, emotions, and, oh yes, some economics.

This brief look at decision making in the entertainment industry demonstrates many of the typical conditions that result in the exercise of power and political behavior in organizations. Decision makers are faced with uncertainty. Emotions and personal preferences enter the picture. Groups of individuals form coalitions or relationships based on similar desires or preferences. The outcome is that decisions are made not solely on the basis of economic optimization. Instead, the results are "satisficing" decisions—decisions that meet minimum criteria for acceptability. More often than not, this is the nature of decision making in organizations.

This chapter explores the concepts of power, authority, and politics in organizations. We are moving from consideration of organizations as rational entities with consistent, coherent, shared goals to situations in which organizations are faced with meeting the diverse and often conflicting objectives of many stakeholders.

POWER AND POLITICS: ORGANIZATIONS AS POLITICAL ENTITIES

Beginning in Chapter 1 and continuing through the early parts of this book, we have regarded organizations as intentional and purposeful. That is, we have assumed that organizations are intentionally structured and designed to accomplish specific, organizationally determined goals and objectives. Elsewhere, we have introduced the strategic contingency framework that suggests that managers will structure and design a company to ***best fit*** the context (i.e., goals, environment, technology, size, and culture) it faces. Implicit in the definition of organizations and in the contingency framework is the notion of ***rationality***. We assumed that rational managers would act in ways to maximize the efficiency and effectiveness of the organization; that managers would do what is best for the collective good of the organization.

As we progressed through our study of organizations, we encountered some chinks in this rational view of organizations. In Chapter 3 we discovered that organizational goals and objectives may be incongruent, ambiguous, or otherwise problematic. Furthermore, it was noted that judging organizational effectiveness was itself problematic. Chapter 11 pointed out the human limitations brought about by **bounded rationality.** By now it should become clear that organizations do not always behave rationally.

In this chapter we explore in greater detail power and the political nature of organizations. We investigate authority—the rational basis of power. One way to think about the rational side of an organization is to think about what an organization *should do*. Authority is based on what individuals should be doing according to the official, formal dictates of the organization. However, we will see that not all power is associated with authority and the official, formal dictates of the organization. Instead, individuals throughout the organization can derive power from many different sources that are unrelated to authority. Often this power allows individuals to pursue goals and objectives other than those that are officially documented. Understanding the divergent nature of power in organizations leads us to a **political perspective** on organizations. Rather than discussing what organizations *should do,* the political perspective addresses what organizations *actually do.*

This is not a case of organizations being either rational or political. Every organization has a political side, some more so than others. Understanding the distribution of power and the political nature of organizations is critical to understanding the actions (or inactions) of organizations. We begin this examination with an overview of authority— the rational basis of power.

THE NATURE OF POWER AND AUTHORITY

This section of the chapter examines the component parts of power and authority and how they fit together to provide the influence a decision maker needs to make choices that are accepted and implemented.

Authority

The word *authority* probably brings to mind a picture of a parent scolding a child or of a sergeant giving a command to the troops. One person gives a command or issues an order in an attempt to elicit some form of desired behavior from another person or group of people. Clearly, the president of a university or the CEO of a corporation has authority to issue directives.

What happens when a superior issues an order or gives a command? First, the superior makes the decision or choice; this requires the *right* to do so. In other words, the superior must be given approval or sanction to make decisions in the name of the organization, and this requires some form of recognition by the organization itself. In the case of formal business organizations, this approval ultimately comes from the owners who have the right to direct the use of their property. Recall the discussion in Chapter 9 of governance and the problems associated with the relationship between owners and managers. The positive outcome of successfully solving the governance problems between owners and managers is that owners grant to managers the authority to make decisions and give orders or commands. The rights of owners, in turn, are based on the legal system and social norms that grant to property owners the right to use private property in such ways that its use does not infringe upon the rights of others.[1] In essence, the right of a manager to make decisions and to issue orders, instructions, and so on comes from ownership and property rights.

Directing the behavior of others is based on two "subrights": (1) the right to decide and (2) the right to issue appropriate implementing instructions or directions. Without the right to decide, no manager could be a successful planner, and without the right to issue orders and instructions, the manager's plans would be worthless because there could be no assurance of the implementation of the plans. Thus, authority is fundamental to every organization because the nature of managerial responsibility involves decision making and influence. This fact of organizational life was clearly recognized in Weber's bureaucratic model of organizations. The hierarchical division of labor and the accompanying scalar principle defined levels of authority and decision-making responsibility.

The essence of authority is rights. These rights are determined (ideally, at least) by obligations. The obligation (responsibility) should determine the nature of the right (authority), and these should be equal or in balance. As we noted in Chapter 9, the fundamental role and responsibility of management is to protect and enhance the wealth of owners. This management obligation is the source of management's authority to run the organization. A manager accepts the responsibility to use organization resources effectively and efficiently and to guide others in pursuit of the organization's goals and objectives. Critical to the management of the organization is the determination of how much and what type of authority managers must have if they are to adequately discharge their responsibilities.

Two points emerge from this discussion. First, authority is a right determined by an obligation, and second, authority is solely associated with the formal organization that has formal sanction or approval from society. This latter point becomes important when we discuss power, which may be independent of the formal organization.

We can define *authority* as ***the rationally based formal right to make decisions and influence behavior to implement decisions based on formal organizational relationships.*** The organization must be a formal one and officially recognize the organizational relationship between owners, managers, and subordinates if authority is to be granted. Influence attempts that fall outside of these formally recognized parameters involve the exercise of power.

Foundations of Authority

Authority is the mainspring of influence in the formal, rational organization. It has its roots in the official recognition of the organization by society at large. From a rational perspective, it is a prime mover for guiding the organization and its various membership groups toward their objectives. Several forms of authority are discussed in the sections below and are summarized in Table 12-1. Additionally, the discussion treats the components and uses of authority to demonstrate how this force affects organizational behavior.

Managerial Authority Managers of formal organizations are responsible for acquiring, deploying, and controlling resources needed to accomplish objectives. To do this, managers must have the right to make and enforce necessary decisions. This right is termed *authority* and is possessed by all who hold managerial positions. Managerial authority is composed of the right to choose among alternatives and the right to enforce those choices, based on official position. Without both of these components, no manager can successfully carry out responsibilities. This is true because managers by being so designated are charged with the responsibility to make decisions and ensure that they are carried out.

TABLE 12-1	Foundations of Authority	
Type	**Meaning**	**Example**
Managerial	Right to make and enforce decisions	Decision to direct a subordinate's behavior
Staff	Right to make suggestions and recommendations	Study recommending a change in job descriptions
Situational	Right to make binding decisions within a very restricted area or scope	Accountant deciding proper accounting methods
Operative	Right to work without undue supervision	Tool and die maker rejecting poor raw material

You will recall from our discussion of bureaucracies in Chapters 2 and 7 that authority is rationally allocated according to position and responsibility in the organizational hierarchy. As one moves up the hierarchy, position authority becomes broader and greater. The manager's responsibility should be a determining factor in deciding the amount and type of authority that an individual is granted. This balance between responsibility and authority is in keeping with the ***principle of parity of authority and responsibility***, a long-recognized guide to building and maintaining a rationally sound organizational structure. The principle simply states that it is desirable to maintain balance between authority and responsibility in order to avoid the dysfunctional situation in which managers are given responsibility for some actions but no authority to carry them out effectively. This also avoids the situation in which a manager's authority exceeds his or her responsibility. Individuals should possess authority and use it to enforce the decisions and actions needed to carry out their responsibilities for the accomplishment of organizational objectives.

Staff Authority   Every day, members of an organization make suggestions and recommendations about the solutions to various problems, procedural changes, or other improvements. Each time this happens, staff authority is being exercised. Even though we normally associated this type of authority with staff experts or professionals (e.g., attorney, information systems specialist), it is actually possessed by every member of the organization.

Everyone in an organization has the right to recommend, to suggest, to advise, and to attempt to exert influence to gain acceptance for ideas.[2] Individual job expertise is the basis of many popular management techniques including total quality management, suggestion boxes, employee empowerment, and the simultaneous flattening and decentralizing of organizations. The assumption is that individuals should know best how to carry out their jobs and that staff experts should know the most about their specific specialty.

One possibly confusing aspect of the use of staff authority is that subordinates sometimes elect to not use their staff authority for one reason or another. Sometimes superiors discourage their subordinates from using it, perhaps because exercising staff authority may contradict or diminish the supervisor's managerial authority. Whether or not the individual exercises staff authority, it is still possessed by all organizational members.

Situational Authority   Situational authority is a type of hybrid authority that contains elements of both managerial and staff authority. Generally, it is delegated to a staff expert by a manager. The staff expert is restricted rather specifically in the areas in which the authority can be exercised.

Recall that staff authority embodies the right to make suggestions and recommendations and managerial authority is the right to make and enforce decisions. Situational authority may begin as staff authority. For example, an accountant may make recommendations about changing specific accounting procedures. A manager may then delegate authority to the accountant to enact changes in the accounting system as the accountant sees fit. This authority normally resides with the manager but has been delegated to the accountant. However, the accountant's authority to make changes is limited to changes in the accounting system. He or she has no authority to make changes in other systems; thus, the authority is situational.

Operative Authority   All members of an organization have some authority to make certain decisions about how, in what order, and with which tools they will carry out their tasks. The right to work without undue supervision is also commonly considered to apply to all members. These rights, taken collectively, are operative authority.[3]

Operative authority is made up of two basic rights: the right to carry out responsibilities of the job and the right to determine, within reason, how and when it will be done. Whether one is a manager, a technician, or an unskilled laborer, one has these minimum rights. Without them, it would not be possible to plan and carry out one's personal responsibility.

Authority provides the formal, official, and rational basis for the distribution of power in organizations. One problem with the concept of authority is that in many organizations, especially those that are decentralized and where lower-level employees are empowered, the hierarchical lines of authority are blurred. Different divisions may end up engaging in strategies that conflict with each other either through internal competition for scarce resources or through competition in the marketplace.

In the following sections we investigate power. The reader should be cautioned that authority and power are not analogous. Authority is but one source of power. Individuals acquire and exercise power that is derived from sources unrelated to formal authority. We will see in the concluding sections of the chapter that these sources of power, which are unrelated to formal authority, are in part what gives rise to the political nature of organizations.

Power

Power is the ability (potential or actual) to impose one's will on others;[4] it is the ability of one person to affect the behavior of someone else in a desired way. This ability can be based on a number of factors at both the individual level and the organizational level. Some of these factors include knowledge, authority, information, personality, and resource control. In subsequent sections we systematically investigate these varied sources of power.

Authority is simply power that the organization formally sanctions or recognizes. Power, on the other hand, is influence that does not necessarily depend on formal organizational recognition. Power may exist within or outside the bounds of formal organizational relationships. In other words, power is a larger concept than authority and, indeed, subsumes authority as a formal power relationship.

An example will clarify the difference between power and authority. Consider the situation in which a supervisor issues directions to subordinates that require them to carry out a normal work task. These directions are considered by both supervisor and subordinate to be legitimate or official. The supervisor in this instance can be said to be using power in the form of position authority, which is derived from his or her role as a manager and which was delegated to him or her by superiors in order to accomplish certain organizational goals.

Now assume that the supervisor directs a subordinate to do a personal errand for him or her. This errand is clearly outside the official job description for the subordinate and the relationship between the supervisor and subordinate. This command cannot be founded in the official authority vested in the supervisor. Rather, this attempt to use power is not based on the formal organization. If the subordinate performs the errand, the influence attempt is successful, and we can say that the supervisor has power over the subordinate.

In this example, there is a dependency relationship between the supervisor and the subordinate. Even though this relationship is not based on formal job relationships, the subordinate may feel compelled to carry out the requested errand because he or she depends on the supervisor for various rewards. Formal relationships often have a kind of carryover effect into informal relationships. This can be particularly troublesome when supervisor requests border on sexual harassment or demands to violate ethical codes.

The extent to which an individual can exercise power can be viewed as a function of the dependency relationship that exists between parties. If person B depends on A (for knowledge, income resources, and so forth), then A is in a position to exercise influence or power over B. The more dependent that B is on A, other things being equal, the more power A can exercise over B.

One thing that may not be obvious is that power may not necessarily be consistent with the organizational hierarchy. In the rational, bureaucratic view of organization, power should increase as one moves up the hierarchy. However, when one fully understands the nature of power and dependency in organizations, it should become clear that power (separate from authority) may be independent of position and level in the organization. Two perspectives on power are presented in the next sections. The first focuses exclusively on individual bases of power in the organization, while the second explores how individuals, groups, or departments gain power through dependency relationships.

The French and Raven Power Typology

The classic work by J. R. P. French and B. Raven lists and describes various bases of power found within organizations.[5] The French and Raven power typology provides insight into sources and potency of power in organizations. A summary of these sources is presented in Table 12-2.

Rational or Legal Power   Rational or legal power stems from one person's acceptance that its exercise by another person agrees with some set of rules or protocol considered legitimate by both parties. The legitimacy of this power, in fact, provides an alternative name for this base of power—legitimate power. Rational or legal power typically results from the type of position one holds and from the position in the organizational hierarchy that one occupies. A police officer has the power to give tickets and arrest people because of the societal rules and protocol that assign that responsibility. Supervisors have rational or legal power over subordinates because of the power vested in their respective positions.

The conditions of legitimacy are a function of the culture that is instrumental in helping define societal norms. For instance, in countries of the Far East it is considered legitimate for the older members of a group to be shown more deference (and thus be given more power) than younger members. In other cultures that may not be the case.

TABLE 12-2   The French and Raven Power Typology

Type	Meaning	Example
Rational/legal	Accepted as legitimate by those involved	Obeying commands of police officer
Reward	Granting of benefits to others	Working hard for a promotion or recommendation
Coercive	Punishing others	Disciplinary action of a three-day suspension
Referent	Identification with person in a power position	Hero worship
Charismatic	Dynamic personality	Religious leaders
Expert	Extensive knowledge or high-level skill	Computer programmer

Other factors may override age and be more potent sources of power, as can be seen when power is traceable to knowledge, ability, or some other factor.

Reward Power   Power that comes from one's ability to control and dispense benefits to others is termed *reward power*.[6] The controller of benefits has the ability to shape the behavior of others by the simple act of dispensing or withholding these benefits.

The strength of reward power is primarily determined by two major forces: the size of the reward and the belief that it will, in fact, be dispensed. In other words, A's reward power over B increases as the size of the benefit increases. Other things being equal, a larger reward gives the person granting that reward greater power over the recipient than a smaller reward.

A supervisor who has control over subordinate pay raises or bonuses gains not only the legitimate power of his or her position but also has power over subordinates because of his or her ability to grant or withhold raises or bonuses. The larger the pay raise or bonus, the more power the supervisor has to get subordinates to perform tasks that they otherwise might not perform.

In the use of reward power it is also important that the person controlling the rewards has some means for determining whether the requested task has been completed. While this may seem rather obvious, the actual process of performance appraisal is often not easy and is prone to inaccuracy and distortion. This is particularly the case with jobs or tasks characterized by uncertainty or ambiguity.

Coercive Power   The ability to coerce or punish another person is a strong foundation of power or influence.[7] This base of power often provides strong motivation and can, in many ways, be viewed as the reverse of reward power. Where reward power relies on the dispensing of rewards for its strength, coercive power depends on the meting out of punishment for its effectiveness. On many professional sports teams players who show up late for training camp or miss or show up late for practices are typically fined. Depending on the frequency and extent of the transgression, the player may be fined a few hundred dollars to several thousand dollars. In many organizations poor performers may lose specific benefits or perquisites. For example, a sales representative whose sales decline may be moved to a less desirable territory or lose access to a company car. Continued poor performance may result in demotion. Of course, the ultimate in coercive power is the threat of firing.

Although the punishment that results from the exercise of coercive power may result in the cessation of undesirable behaviors or the performance of desired behaviors, it may also produce undesirable side effects. First, the targeted person may shift goals and behavior to doing as little as possible while avoiding punishment. Thus, the undesirable behavior may be eliminated, but the targeted person is still only a marginal contributor to the organization. Second, the person on the receiving end of coercive power is likely to feel estranged from the person using that power. The estrangement may be manifested in resentment, feelings of victimization, and possibly the desire to retaliate. This sense of resentment and latent frustration can have serious dysfunctional consequences in a relationship, especially if it is unresolved over a period of time.

The effectiveness of coercive power depends on the nature of punishment, its perceived impact, the probability that it will be used, and the measurement of desired behaviors. If punishment is not defined by the targeted person as punishing, if it is seen as relatively mild, or if the likelihood that it will be used is slight, coercive power is made less potent. For example, professional hockey games were, for many years, plagued by fighting—a behavior deemed inappropriate by the National Hockey League (NHL). The NHL tried to eliminate fighting through a combination of penalties, fines, and suspensions. Initial efforts were unsuccessful because the penalties were only mildly punishing and the likelihood of the league's assessing fines or suspensions was low. The effort to cut fighting became successful only after the NHL decided to increase the severity of penalties and increase the certainty that players engaged in fights would receive stiff fines and suspensions. The coercive power was used by the NHL to enforce its formal authority as a governing body. Still, many incidents in which star players have been injured as a result of fighting and other violence have raised questions about the relationship between the severity of the acts and the degree of punishment assessed.

Referent Power   Referent power can be defined as the power A has over B because B identifies with A.[8] This sense of identification makes A capable of influencing B's behavior even though neither A nor B may be aware of the sense of identification.

This type of power can be illustrated in the case of hero worship. Star athletes are worshiped by aspiring youngsters who see that their own abilities can be enhanced by emulating the star's behavior. The controversy over athletes as role models exists because of the referent power star athletes possess. Because most people at one time or another have known this feeling of identification with success, this is a common and powerful foundation of influence.

Kirk Cottrell, the founder of Island Water Sports, a Florida surf shop chain, has this type of power with young people. "I watch this guy with young people, and believe me, it's uncanny," stated Nancy Lyman, a friend and former classmate of this young entrepreneur, who succinctly stated the case of hero worship of Cottrell by young surfers and employees.[9] People with referent power are often able to get their admirers to follow and commit to the organization in ways unavailable to other individuals.

People with whom others identify might not be aware of their own referent power. This makes tracing power relationships difficult. Secret admiration of successful people is an example. Such relationships would be difficult to identify and analyze even though they are undoubtedly common and have tremendous impact on interpersonal relationships.

Charismatic Power   Influence or power based on one's personality can be defined as charismatic power. There are those who have an almost undefinable magnetic quality about their personalities that attracts others to follow them.[10] Some would argue that Hitler had this type of influence in pre–World War II Germany. Gandhi's power in India was due in part to his charisma. In the United States John F. Kennedy was said to have been a charismatic leader.

Those who possess charisma find it relatively easy to influence their followers. One dimension of charismatic power that helps explain its potency is that charismatic leaders also help their followers attain personal goals. By following such a leader, the followers can realize their own objectives even though they might primarily be serving the leader's purposes.

Within the business world a few leaders stand out because of their charismatic power. Former Chrysler CEO Lee Iacocca clearly had charisma that extended beyond the boundaries of the Chrysler Corporation. In the early 1980s, when the company was on the verge of bankruptcy, Iacocca was able to influence the federal government to guarantee loans to Chrysler. He convinced the United Auto Workers union to make several contract concessions so that the company could reduce its costs of production. Finally, Iacocca appeared in print, radio, and television advertisements promoting Chrysler products.[11] Phil Knight, one of the cofounders of Nike, has provided his company with a similar type of personal leadership.[12]

No special effort is required to exercise charismatic power. Charismatic personalities, both positive and negative ones, often retain their power to influence even long after they have left office or died. Such power is potent and a formidable influence in organizations. Followers of charismatic leaders follow because of the compelling nature of the leader's persona.

Expert Power There are those who wield power because of their knowledge or special skills. They are respected for this knowledge or skill, irrespective of their position in the organization. Those who admire this expertise or who need it to solve problems are willing to subordinate themselves in return for the expert's assistance. For example, a scientist, an information systems specialist, or a technician may exert power beyond that typically associated with their position because of the expertise they possess. Academic degrees, professional certification, or other forms of official documentation are often associated with expert power. For example, consider labels such as MBA, MD, CPA, CFP (certified financial planner), CLU (certified life underwriter).

This base of power is important and unique because it is independent of the organizational hierarchy. People low in the organization can exercise power based on expertise. One consequence of the pervasive downsizing taking place today is that more and more expertise is accumulating low in the organization. Expert power, as we will note shortly, is similar to the dependency-based view of power. The more specialized and the more scarce the specific expertise one possesses, the more power one can exert.

The power typology discussed above helps identify and clarify some sources of power in and around organizations. Thus far, the focus has been on individual power. Often power resides not in individuals, but in departments or units of an organization. To understand departmental and unit power, it is necessary to understand dependencies and critical contingencies within organizations.

Dependency, Critical Contingencies, and Power

As we noted above, power can come from many sources, but these sources at some level revolve around dependency. When individuals, departments, or organizations become dependent upon other individuals, departments, or organizations, the dependent party loses power. Similarly, individuals, departments, or organizations that can solve problems—critical or strategic contingencies—for other individuals, departments, or organizations gain power. The abilities to create dependencies or solve critical or strategic contingencies are among the most important determinants of power.[13] Although some dependency relationships and some ability to solve critical problems of the organization are associated with the formal organizational hierarchy, this need not be the case. In fact, one interesting consequence of this view of power is that some individuals lower in an organization (lower-order participants) can obtain power that would seem inconsistent with their position.

Power Through Control of Resources   Every organization must have resources to convert into products or services. Without a sufficient amount and proper distribution of such resources, the organization will soon cease to exist. The control over resources thus has important power implications both inside the organization and among organizations. In Chapter 5 we addressed the issue of how organizations avoid or manage dependencies through either vertical integration or through structuring their relationships with suppliers. In this section, we focus on the internal power dependency relationships that may develop in organizations.

In general, individuals or departments who control critical or scarce resources within an organization can wield tremendous power.[14] Resources that are in short supply and resources that are central to the organization's continued success are sources of power. Individuals who or departments that possess or allocate these resources to others have great ability to influence the organization.

Think about your own university or college. Which departments on campus seem to possess the greatest power to influence the direction of the university? Typically, those departments that enjoy the greatest power are the ones that control critical resources. These days, two critical resources on most campuses are money and highly qualified students. Departments with greater access to these two key resources should be able to exert significant influence. For example, on many campuses departments that are able to acquire outside grants or funding from the federal government, businesses, foundations, private individuals, or other sources gain power to influence decisions about hiring and development of facilities. Similarly, if a university, as many are, faces a shrinking population of potential students, a department that maintains high enrollments should gain some power to influence decisions.

Power Through Solving Critical or Strategic Contingencies   Broadly speaking, we may regard information, knowledge, and special skills as types of resources in an organization. Uncertainty or lack of knowledge creates the potential for power dependency relationships. Those individuals who or departments that solve key problems facing an organization or reduce uncertainty are likely to gain power as a result. For example, in many organizations the maintenance or physical plant department is not regarded as having much power. However, a machinery breakdown or a power system failure will remind an organization quickly of the critical role that the maintenance or physical plant department plays in the organization. Solving these problems may give the department significant power to influence future decisions about machinery or plant facilities.

In general, the more pervasive the threats or uncertainty are to the organization, the more power will result to those who can manage the threats and uncertainty. If, for example, environmental threats are felt by the entire organization and one particular department has the ability to solve those environmental threats, then that department will gain power. Because of the widespread potential for litigation that many organizations face, legal departments, with their specialized knowledge and ability to deal with the legal environment, often have extraordinary power over many key aspects of organizations. The legal department often gives final approval on product designs, packaging, labeling, contracts, policies, and public relations communications, to name just a few areas. The human resources function gained significant power in U.S. firms in the late 1990s. As the U.S. economy approached the level of functional full employment (unemployment below 4 percent), recruiting potential employees and retaining existing employees—functions of the human resources department—became critical to success.

Substitutability The ability to solve critical problems or supply scarce resources for an organization clearly provides a basis of power. However, when the organization can somehow substitute for those skills, expertise, or resources, individuals or departments lose power.[15] As many organizations move toward downsizing and network (or virtual) organizations, they begin to contract out many functions that they once viewed as critical in-house activities. For example, many organizations use outside suppliers of marketing, legal, human resources, accounting, and even engineering expertise.[16] Reliance on outsiders will likely diminish the power of insiders who once carried out those functions. This is one reason the United Auto Workers union has fought so vigorously against outsourcing in the auto industry. In shifting to outsiders for solutions to critical organizational problems, the organization may have reduced insider power, but the organization now becomes more dependent on outside contractors. Organizations face key questions about trade-offs between powerful internal coalitions or dependencies on external suppliers. The decision over internal supply versus external supply is a critical one, and the power dependency is but one of the key issues top management must face.

Power and Location in the Organization How often have you tried to get the "ear" of some key decision maker, whether to voice a complaint, ask a question, or obtain permission to carry out some action? And how often have you been frustrated by some secretary or assistant who bars your access to that key decision maker? This scenario is fairly common in organizations. People in positions such as secretary or administrative assistant often knowingly or unknowingly exercise power because of their proximity to holders of legitimate position power and because they control access to that person. People in these roles can control the flow of information and people to their superiors. They can make appointments; set the calendar; control the agenda for meetings; and screen incoming communications.[17] In a sense, these people occupy the role of **gate keeper**, and they control a scarce resource.

One's position in an organization's network can also be a source of power. This concept is referred to as ***network centrality***. The power that a manager derives from network centrality is the power of information—the power of being well informed. A manager who has contacts throughout the organization may gain power because he or she knows what is going on in far-flung corners of the organization and has the ability to get a broader view of the organization. This can become useful in forming coalitions within the organization.[18]

Power and Position in the Organization Earlier in this chapter, we noted that one source of power was a person's position in the organization. This base of power was referred to as the rational or legal (or legitimate) position power that is associated with one's position in the organizational hierarchy. In general, a person's power in the organization is related to his or her rank within the hierarchy—the higher up one resides, the more power one has. This is consistent with the bureaucratic and rational view of organizations. However, many changes that have taken place in the latter part of the twentieth century have eroded some of that rational or legal basis of power. As a consequence, middle managers and even employees lower in the organization's hierarchy have gained power to influence an organization's direction and actions.

The extensive downsizing at many organizations and the increasing reliance on new, sophisticated information technologies have given rise to more power for individuals

---

EXHIBIT 12-1

Purchasing Automobile Components

An automobile is an extremely complex product, made up of many subassemblies. Some subassemblies are made internally, and others are made by outside suppliers. When a new car is designed, the design team typically gives various groups design parameters and asks them to design such components as steering systems, suspension systems, interiors, and even engines and engine control systems. The designs of many of these component systems are themselves very complex. The result is that the design team (the rational or legal authority) may be unable to evaluate the quality of component systems.

At one of the Big Three U.S. car companies, the design team for a new car model provided detailed information on steering and suspension requirements to the division that produced those components. The Steering and Suspension Division (SSD) was to bid on the job (i.e., create a design) and was to also seek external bids on the design. SSD was given this responsibility because it had more knowledge and expertise in steering and suspension design than any other group in the company—despite the fact that the head of SSD was lower in the organization than the head of the design team. Thus, SSD could control the flow of information to outside firms bidding on the steering and suspension system, and it would evaluate the incoming bids. SSD could further influence the process by controlling the flow of information back to the design team because the design team members lacked the knowledge, information, or expertise to make appropriate judgments.

As you will see in the continuation of this story, this situation is ripe for political intrigue.

---

lower in the organizational hierarchy. Downsizing has created scarcity of expertise in some organizations. It is likely that fewer people will possess specialized skills and knowledge, and it is likely that these people will not be top managers.[19] These conditions should yield power. These lower-level individuals can control the flow of information to top management, which, in turn, can affect the decision premises of top managers.

Several factors can contribute to the power of lower-level members of organizations. First, when individuals are indispensable because of skills, knowledge, or information they possess, they gain power. Additionally, the longer an individual is in an organization, the more likely he or she is to have access to sources of power: critical information, people important to the organization, or instrumentalities—aspects of the physical plant of the organization or its resources.[20]

Another important source of power for lower-level organizational members is the power vacuum created when there is a leadership transition, particularly if the new leader is from outside the organization. Under such conditions new leaders often become highly dependent on lower-level staff assistants for guidance navigating around their new organizational home. This problem may be particularly acute in large, complex organizations. Some new leaders try to counter this tendency by bringing in their own staff of assistants.

Finally, the rules of the organization can themselves be used as a source of power for lower-level employees.[21] No organization can successfully survive an exact enforcement of all its rules. By simply following the rules, lower-level employees can be quite powerful, and the more important their tasks are to the organization, the more powerful they can be. For example, in the transportation industry drivers, pilots, shipping clerks, baggage handlers, and others can exert extensive influence by insisting on following rules to a T. Sometimes such actions can be used to change archaic rules or to force other changes or actions.

HOW TO ASSESS POWER

Because power permeates the organization and all its members are, in some way, affected by it, it is important to find some means to measure or assess it—even if such assessments are informal. If people are able to assess power, they can more easily find their place in the power structure. The following sections identify several indicators of power.[22]

Power Determinants as Indicators of Power

To measure power by its determinants requires a judgment about how much of a particular type or basis of power a person or department possesses. Determinants (sources or origins) of power are *indirect* measures of power that a given person or department has at a particular time.

An example of the determinants of power as a measure of power should help. When people have expert power, it means that they have special expertise or knowledge about a given field; their power originates from this expertise. If they appear to have considerable in-depth knowledge, we may tend to assign disproportionate power to them. The more fields in which they effectively demonstrate expert power, the more powerful they can be as employees.

Employees, of course, can behave in a way that creates the impression that they have more power than they actually do by using double-talk and by appearing sure of their positions. Only experience with a given employee can reveal whether that power is based on legitimate expert power (or on some other basis).[23]

Power Consequences

Another means of assessing power is to determine the effects or consequences of the decisions made by various actors. A look at who makes the significant organizational decisions gives a good indication of who has the most power in the organization. It is important, however, to distinguish between who *makes* the decisions and who *announces* them. For example, the president of a corporation might announce a merger plan that was actually the work of a close adviser. A dean might announce a plan to allocate the school's budget that could really be the work of a staff assistant.

Those actors called on to make the decisions that cause the most severe consequences or alter the behavior of the most important actors are those whose power can be measured by the consequences of its use. Consider, for example, the various magnitudes of the following decisions: mergers, building new plants, introducing new products, allocating the budget to departments, and hiring new employees. Although there are countless other types of decisions, the point is that a hierarchy of power consequences exists. That hierarchy varies from one organization to another and may vary over time within any given organization.

Power Symbols

Those who have power often like to display the trappings of that power. This may include such things as larger offices, more luxurious office furnishings, more expensive company cars, reserved parking spaces, access to special dining or recreational facilities, or even the manner of dress. In one organization managers could discern power by counting ceiling tiles in their offices. Larger offices, which were associated with greater power, had more ceiling tiles. One manager could boast of an office with 20 ceiling tiles, a clear indication that she had more power than colleagues in offices with only 15 tiles, even though the difference in office size was a mere 24 square feet. Often the type of furnishing is a symbol of power. In some organizations, such things as wooden desks (rather than metal), upholstered furniture, and couches are symbols of power.

Even though symbols signify power, it is impossible to generalize their applicability. In some organizations and in some cultures, spartan conditions (e.g., small offices, modest furnishings) may be a form of reverse symbolism. For example, some organizations avoid special treatment for managers. They forgo executive dining rooms and parking spaces. They insist that managers share in moves toward efficiency by using small offices and driving modest cars. Such avoidance of perquisites is common among Japanese organizations.

Representational Indicators of Power

Membership on influential boards and committees or participation in critical teams or task forces can be indicative of an individual's power.[24] If a midlevel manager is the head of a special team or task force, this may be an indication of the individual's popularity with top management and of his or her ability to influence the organization. Every organization has key jobs or positions that are associated with possession of power. The title (executive vice president) or function (budget officer) of the position are sometimes good indicators of power.[25]

There appears to be no overall best way to assess power. One measure may be best in one circumstance while another measure may be best suited for a different set of circumstances. We simply describe these indicators and suggest that individuals be aware of the multidimensional nature of power in organizations.

THE USE OF POWER IN ORGANIZATIONS

We have discussed a number of concepts relating to organizational power as well as the power of individuals within organizations. Power is a complex, ever-changing force in any group. It can arise from a number of sources and be possessed to some extent by all members. Basically, though, power is used to alter events and circumstances to fit the holder's preferences. This is true whether we are concerned with organizational or individual power.

One requirement for the effective use of power is effort: Some energy, and perhaps ingenuity, must be exerted to have influence. Power vacuums (opportunities to gain resources or solve critical problems) exist in all groups and organizations; it remains for someone to spend the energy to fill the vacuum.

Some functional areas make the effort to fill a power vacuum quite worthwhile. Organizations rely on information about their financial health, and so an enterprising member of the budget department has an opportunity to store up this valuable resource. The budget officer can, for instance, devise an allocation system known only to himself or herself so that no one else can gain access to needed information without permission. This, of course, can cause problems for the organization, but it nonetheless makes the budget officer powerful. This condition can easily permit the budget officer to make *unauthorized* budgets that contradict the organization's intent.

Similarly, how the budget officer decides to report budget data can affect the perceptions of how well specific departments are doing. For example, in a nonprofit professional association (e.g., legal association, medical association, accountants association), the budget officer can affect judgments about the effectiveness of the publications department by choosing to emphasize either the cost of publications or the revenues generated. Typically, nonprofit professional associations provide publications to members as a service. A portion of membership dues is used to offset the cost of publications. Advertising revenues can be used to reduce the cost to members for this service. If the budget manager wants to emphasize the positive contributions of the publications department, he or she could emphasize the increasing revenues that publications generate, which reduce the real costs to members. If the budget manager wishes to shed a less favorable light on publications, he or she could emphasize the increasing cost of publications while deemphasizing or ignoring revenues generated.

Clearly, the control of information flows in an organization can be a tremendous source of power. People who and departments that control information can quickly develop a multitude of "friends" seeking favors. A position such as budget officer or information systems manager can be key to the allocation or diversion of resources.[26]

Coalitions of members are potent forces in an organization. Because we are all part of many different organizations, we have probably observed and even participated in various coalitions. Every organization seems to have an "in" group (those in favor in the organization) and an "out" group (those who are out of favor in the organization). Regardless of the type of organization, there typically appears to be a relatively small "in" group that determines what happens. Consider your college or business school. It is likely that one group (perhaps a department or a program group) has more power than other groups. Perhaps because of the popularity of a particular major, the research productivity of a group of faculty, or faculty success obtaining grants or outside funding, a group may become powerful and influential in affecting the policies and strategic direction of the college or school. This power may be separate from the formal or official power structure of the organization, or the power may reside in top management. The power resides in these ***dominant coalitions*** because the group holds extensive power and authority, and as a result, they become influential to the decision-making process.

DEFINITION

Dominant coalition: group holding extensive power and authority that may be separate from formal power; key group of decision makers with extensive influence.

THE STICKINESS OF POWER

One interesting characteristic of power is that those who hold power are reluctant to relinquish it. As a consequence, transitions of power in organizations are not smooth and seamless. Rather, transition of power is characterized by stickiness—power holders try to retain as much power as long as they can. This can produce conflict, challenge, and confrontation over power transitions.

A group or coalition that obtains power because it can solve key problems facing an organization may try to retain power by redefining all future problems in ways that fit the group's particular competence. For example, in the late 1950s and early 1960s stylists and marketers were dominant coalitions in the automobile industry. Style and marketing sold cars; thus, those groups that possessed knowledge and competence to solve styling and marketing problems gained great power. This distribution of power was fine when the external environment demanded that the automobile companies market cars based on styling.

In the late 1960s, the environment began to shift. Several factors converged to drastically change the automobile marketplace. Small, inexpensive imports began to penetrate the market at the same time baby boomers were becoming first-time car buyers. The ecology movement and the counterculture of the late 1960s and early 1970s emphasized living simply and efficiently. The final blow to the big-car mentality of the earlier generation was rising gasoline prices brought about by the embargoes and boycotts of the mid-1970s. Unfortunately for the U.S. automobile companies, the dominant coalitions tried to retain their powerful positions by redefining these problems as styling and marketing problems. Essentially, the coalitions were saying, "This is merely a marketing and styling problem that we can solve with our expertise." For example, Ford tried to deal with foreign competition by marketing existing products "dressed up" to look more like the imported competition. Many earlier attempts at fuel efficiency and pollution control were based mainly on appearance, rather than substance. No one successfully challenged the assumptions and proposed solutions of the stylists and marketers because of the past successes of these groups.

When these early, feeble attempts based on marketing and styling failed to deal with the changed environment, power finally shifted. New coalitions that possessed the unique skills, knowledge, and resources to deal with the changed environment began to emerge as power centers. However, the transition was far from smooth. It lagged far behind the environmental changes and was characterized by conflict and confrontation. This stickiness in the transition of power is characteristic of the unwillingness of power holders to give up their source of power. As the U.S. automobile industry entered the twenty-first century, new groups were poised to gain power. As companies like Ford encountered liability problems due to product failure, lawyers gained power. As the industry became increasingly global in its focus, experts in international business gained power.

Power is a dynamic force used by many organization members for many purposes. A snapshot of the power structure is not adequate—we need a high-speed, full-length motion picture of it in order to appreciate it as a part of organizational life, composed as it is of all those activities that characterize the members' efforts to use power for their benefit.

POWER AND POLITICS

Earlier in the chapter, we examined authority relationships and power in organizations. Here, we examine the relationship that power has to political forces within the organization. Our focus is on how the political processes at work in the organization affect organizational actions.

We have already laid the groundwork in previous chapters and in the earlier sections of this chapter for explaining and understanding organizational politics. In Chapter 3 we noted that organizational goals are often characterized by ambiguity and conflict. Lack of agreement about the legitimate goals of the organization leads to the formation of coalitions intent on pursuing their own views of goals. Additionally, when we examined organizational effectiveness, we noted that different constituents, both internal and external to the organization, had different perceptions of what constituted an effective organization. One of the primary messages of Chapters 4 through 6 was that organizations faced varying degrees of uncertainty from the environment and from the technologies used by the organization. Structure, design, control systems, and information can resolve some uncertainty, but, as pointed out in Chapter 11, individuals and organizations face the constraints of bounded rationality when trying to reduce uncertainty and solve the organization's problems. It is these conditions that give rise to power—power that is often unrelated to the official hierarchy of the organization. It is also these conditions that give rise to the political nature of organizations.

Most of us spend much of our lives in organizations of one form or another. But how many of us have stopped to ponder who really governs these organizations? We do not necessarily mean who holds the top management or administrative position because, as we've noted, those are not always the people in control.

Earlier, we asked you to think about who has power in your university or college. Think again about your school. Can you identify the different constituencies that exercise control over that institution? Is it the president, the deans, the provost or vice president, the faculty, the alumni or the students, the governing board or the state government if your school is public? To pose such questions is to indicate the difficulty in finding clear answers. For at the same time, we could say that no one group or person mentioned above has complete control of your college or university. This lack of clarity over control arises because of the political nature of organizations.

The alumni exert influence on the course and direction of your college or university through promising or withholding financial and moral support. At MCU in the introductory case of Chapter 11, the alumni were key to supporting the stadium project. The governing board exerted pressure through issuing and enforcing rules. In the case of a state institution the state government influences the direction of the school through legislation and financial support. The president, vice presidents, provost, and other administrators make decisions and offer directives. Yet, two things are important to understand the political nature of organizations. First, each of these groups may be pursuing very different, sometimes conflicting, goals for the institution. Second, in addition to these formal influence wielders, there exist myriad groups and individuals attempting to informally influence the direction of the organization.

These informal and unofficial power sources are able to influence the organization because of the multiple, and perhaps conflicting, goals that exist. Because the goals may be unclear or ambiguous, it may be difficult to clearly determine the effectiveness of the organization. The appropriate technology for accomplishing these goals may be unclear, and even if the type of technology is obvious, the technology may itself be characterized by uncertainty. Achieving the goals may be made more difficult and uncertain because of environmental turbulence and complexity. Furthermore, as the environment changes, the appropriateness of some goals may be drawn into question. Finally, our decision makers, both those formally recognized by the organization and those who informally and unofficially try to influence the decision process, are prone to bounded rationality. Their judgments are affected by a lack of information, personal biases, self-interest, emotions, and faulty reasoning. All these factors together produce conditions ripe for organizational politicking.

Politics Defined

These examples indicate the necessity for a clear definition of politics in organizations. Jeffery Pfeffer has suggested the following definition:

DEFINITION

Organizational politics involves those activities taken within organizations to acquire, develop, and use power and other resources to obtain one's preferred outcomes in a situation in which there is uncertainty or [a lack of consensus] about choices.[27]

According to this definition, issues can be resolved through both the formal and informal use of power. The important factor that defines an action as political is that power is used in pursuit of one's own preferred outcomes. These may or may not coincide with the official organizationally preferred outcomes.

The Rational and Political Nature of Organizations: A Summary

Following Pfeffer, we have identified four organizational characteristics that differentiate the political and rational perspectives of organizations. They are summarized here.[28]

Goals   As we have already noted, the political view of organizations is premised on the multiple and conflicting goals that typically exist in organizations. This situation allows for the formation of coalitions around different sets of goals. For example, in colleges and universities there is often a lack of agreement about the relative importance and priorities that should be assigned to teaching and research. Different coalitions with differing priorities form around these goals. If the organization were entirely rational, there would be consensus—perfect agreement—on the nature and priority of the goals.

Power   In a sense we have already documented the differences between the rational and political views of power. The rational view of power follows the bureaucratic authority structure of the organization. Power increases as one moves up the organizational hierarchy. One's power is derived from one's official position. Thus, the bulk of power in the organization is centralized and in the hands of top management. However, the political view of power is based not just on position. Power also results from control of resources and information, and from possession of specific skills or knowledge necessary to solve key strategic contingencies. Thus, the political view indicates that power is likely to be diffused throughout the organization and decentralized. As problems and conditions shift, the political power structure also shifts.

Uncertainty and Information   It should be clear by now that organizations face uncertainty from many sources. Two views of organizations differ on the extent of this uncertainty and on the degree to which searching for information will resolve uncertainty. The rational view suggests that organizations face only low to moderate uncertainty and that uncertainty can be overcome by searching for information. From a political perspective, organizational uncertainty is problematic. Uncertainty may be extensive and not easily reduced by an information search. Sometimes it is not clear what information should be sought. And because of the power associated with information, groups or coalitions may withhold or distort information in an effort to maximize self-interest.

Decision Making　The rational view of decision making is as we described in Chapter 11—rational-economic decision making. Decision making follows a stepwise process beginning with problem identification and ending with solution implementation and evaluation. All necessary information is available, and the utility-maximizing outcome is obvious. Moreover, how desired outcomes are to be achieved is clearly agreed upon. But as we noted in Chapter 11, perfect information and perfect rationality are infrequently the case. In the political organization, decision making is characterized by bounded rationality. Groups or coalitions pursue self-interest. Conflicts may result, and negotiation will be a necessary part of the decision-making process. Methods appropriate for achieving these outcomes are unclear, and coalitions may disagree about how they should be attained. The outcome will be satisficing, and some groups will retain or increase power while others lose power.

Recall the earlier example of the Steering and Suspension Division (SSD) and the problem of selecting a steering and suspension system for a new car. We noted that this division had extensive power because of its ability to transmit or withhold information and because of its specialized skills and knowledge relative to a critical organizational problem. The description below illustrates organizational politics in action.

The question is not whether or not an organization is political. All organizations display some aspects of political behavior. The degree to which political behavior is present or dominates an organization depends on a number of factors that include size, complexity, uncertainty, an organization's life cycle stage and structure, to name just a few.

The larger and more complex the organization, the more likely it is that politics plays a prominent role.[29] This is clearly illustrated in the example of the car maker and the Steering and Suspension Division. Size and complexity contributed to the political environment. The situation with SSD was also characterized by both technological and environmental uncertainty, conditions that contribute to political activities in an organization.

The four-stage view of organizational life cycles that was presented in Chapter 7 provides a foundation for examining shifting power bases and political action in organizations.[30] Essentially, during the first two stages of the organizational life cycle, most political activity emanates from the founder as he or she tries to influence and control different cadres of subordinates. Political activity is minimized by centralized control held by the founder. In the third stage, the increasingly bureaucratic nature of the organization results in diffusion of skills, resources, information, and power. As a result, coalitions form and struggle for control. In the fourth stage when the organization may be spiraling downward, coalitions that gained power in the third stage may exert themselves and try to shift the primary strategic focus of the organization. Politics often turns to outright conflicts over the very nature and future of the organization.

This life cycle framework raises an important and interesting point about political behavior in organizations. The reader may conclude that political behavior is not good or healthy in organizations. That is not necessarily or always the case. Political behavior and the conflict that it often produces can be useful in bringing forth new and divergent ideas. Coalitions may question the organizational orthodoxy. For example, in the introductory case to Chapter 11 the university may be better off in the long run to have a viable football program. A highly visible athletic program may bring positive publicity and revenues to the university. SSD's behavior may be seen as a short-run effort to save

EXHIBIT 12-2

Politics and the Steering and Suspension Division

The Steering and Suspension Division was given responsibility to design an advanced steering and suspension system for a luxury sedan. At the same time, SSD was to seek bids from outside vendors to design and build the same steering and suspension system. While the division that would ultimately build the car gave SSD general design and performance requirements for the system, it was up to SSD to set specific technical requirements and to judge the performance of any system that was submitted for bidding.

SSD held a unique position. The division had knowledge and skills about steering and suspension systems that the car-building division did not have. It could also convey and withhold critical data to outside developers that would either facilitate or inhibit design and production. SSD could maximize the likelihood that its own design would be selected by withholding or distorting information that it passed on to the car-building division.

Eventually, several firms and SSD bid on the steering and suspension job. Even to an objective observer, it was not entirely clear which design was superior. What was clear was that the SSD design was not the least expensive. However, in passing information to the car division, SSD highlighted the positive qualities of its own design and downplayed the negative qualities. At the same time, SSD emphasized (perhaps, even distorted) the negative characteristics of competitors' designs while giving little attention to any positive characteristics.

SSD's actions could, at best, be described as self-serving. To understand why SSD acted in the way it did, one must look at goals, power, uncertainty, and the decision process. SSD's goals were to preserve jobs within the division even if its steering and suspension system was more expensive or less technically sophisticated. To give the new steering and suspension system to an outside vendor would mean a loss of jobs for SSD. SSD was willing to suboptimize on cost and quality to save jobs.

The company had decentralized power by placing expertise and information control in individual divisions. SSD had power because of its expertise in steering and suspension systems and because of its control of information flows to supplier firms and to the car division.

The company faced uncertainty in the design of cars because of the high degree of complexity in the tasks and technology used to make them. The company faced additional uncertainty because of the external environment. The competence and reliability of supplier firms were questionable. Customer demands for advanced steering and suspension systems was uncertain. Finally, the actions of competitors were unpredictable. As a consequence, the company and the car-building division faced high levels of uncertainty. Collecting more information may not have addressed this uncertainty, especially when some information collection was placed in the hands of SSD.

The decision process for selecting a steering and suspension design was fragmented. Perfect information did not exist, and the decision needed to be made in a limited time frame. Coalitions played key roles and struggled over local goals rather than the larger organizational goal. The result was a satisficing decision—an acceptable, but not utility-maximizing, steering and suspension system. The steering and suspension system provided some, but not all, of the technical and performance characteristics that were desired, and the cost was higher than desired. Design and production employees in SSD retained their jobs.

jobs. However, in the long run, keeping the steering and suspension development and production internal may help the company retain certain critical personnel and expertise. It may also allow the company to protect sensitive technology from competitors. Thus, the political nature of organizations is neither all bad nor all good; it is merely the way things are in organizations.

SUMMARY

Because they are the prime means of influence in both formal and informal organizations, authority and power are critical aspects of organizational existence. Authority is the formal and official right to decide and act in the formal organization. Power, on the other hand, is the ability to exert influence over others that may or may not be consistent with the official organization.

When considering the formal authority structure of organizations, four types of authority were considered: managerial, staff, situational, and operative. These four types of authority constitute the formal rights of organizational members and provide the legitimate basis of power.

Power was examined at the individual and organizational level. First, a typology of individual power within organizations identified six bases of power: rational or legal, reward, coercive, referent, charismatic, and expert power. The focus then shifted to power that results from dependency relationships, control of information, control of resources, and the ability to solve key problems within the organization. Power of this sort is not necessarily distributed according to the official, formal authority structure of the organization. Individuals and coalitions at nearly any level in organizations can hold and exercise power.

Because of the decentralized nature of power, the lack of goal consensus, and the uncertainty organizations face, political behavior is a fact of life in organizations. Political behavior involves those actions aimed at acquiring and using power to gain individually preferred outcomes. Although political behavior in organizations is ubiquitous, the degree of political action is related to such things as the size and complexity of the organization and the stage of the organizational life cycle. Finally, we noted that political behavior is not necessarily negative. Although political behavior may be associated with suboptimizing, the conflict and negotiating associated with political behavior may also help an organization reorient itself.

Questions for Discussion

1. Define the term *authority* and discuss the bases of authority. How does authority differ from power?
2. "Power is not necessarily consistent with the official organizational hierarchy." Do you agree with this statement? Explain.
3. Apply the French and Raven power typology to an organization with which you are familiar. Describe how the people can derive power from each of the bases.
4. Now take the same organization as described in Question 3 and show how people, departments, or subunits can gain power through control of resources, through centrality, and through solving key problems or contingencies.
5. How does substitutability affect power and its use?
6. Show how Pfeffer's concept of politics helps you understand the way organizations behave. Give an example of the political nature of an organization.

References

1. B. J. Hodge and H. J. Johnson, *Management and Organizational Behavior* (New York: John Wiley & Sons, 1970), 38–40; also based on Weber's notions of power in bureaucracies; M. Weber, *The Theory of Social and Economic Organization* (New York: Free Press, 1947).

2. See Hodge and Johnson in note 1.

3. See Hodge and Johnson, pages 145–47, in note 1.

4. R. A. Dahl, "The Concept of Power," *Behavioral Science* 2 (1957): 210–15; R. M. Emerson, "Power-Dependence Relations," *American Sociological Review* 27 (1962): 31–41; D. Mechanic, "Sources of Power of Lower-Level Participants in Complex Organizations," *Administrative Science Quarterly* 7 (1962): 349–64; H. Joseph Reitz, *Behavior in Organizations* (Homewood, IL: Richard D. Irwin, 1977): 463–64.

5. J. R. P. French and B. Raven, "The Bases of Social Power," in *Studies in Social Power*, ed. by D. Cartwright (Ann Arbor, MI: Institute for Social Research, 1959): 150–67; J. S. Adams and A. K. Romney, "The Determinants of Authority Interactions," in *Values and Groups*, ed. by N. F. Washburne (New York: Pergamon Press, 1962): 227–56.

6. B. Raven, "The Bases of Social Power," in *Current Studies in Social Psychology*, ed. by I. D. Steiner and M. Fishbein (New York: Holt, Rinehart, and Winston, 1965): 374.

7. B. Raven, "Legitimate Power, Coercive Power, and Observability in Social Influence," *Sociometry* 21 (1958): 83–97.

8. See French and Raven, page 162, in note 5; Walter Nord, "Development in the Study of Power," in *Concepts and Controversy* in *Organization Behavior* (Pacific Palisades, CA: Goodyear, 1976): 437–38.

9. David Bailey, "Kirk Cottrell: Riding the Crest of a Retailing Wave," *Florida Trend* (May 1987): 38.

10. W. Jack Duncan, *Organizational Behavior* (Boston: Houghton Mifflin, 1978): 313.

11. Lee A. Iacocca with W. Novak, *Iacocca: An Autobiography* (New York: Bantam, 1984).

12. Donald Katz, *Just Do It* (New York: Random House, 1994).

13. D. J. Hickson, C. R. Hinings, C. A. Lee, R. E. Schneck, and J. M. Pennings, "A Strategic Contingencies Theory of Intraorganizational Power," *Administrative Science Quarterly* 16 (1971): 216–29; Jeffery Pfeffer, *Power in Organizations* (Marshfield, MA: Pitman, 1981); Jeffery Pfeffer and Gerald Salancik, *The External Control of Organizations* (New York: Harper & Row, 1978).

14. Jeffery Pfeffer and Gerald Salancik, "Organizational Decision Making as a Political Process: The Case of a University Budget," *Administrative Science Quarterly* 19 (1974): 135–51; see Pfeffer in Note 13.

15. Rosabeth M. Kanter, "Power Failure in Management Circuits," *Harvard Business Review* (July–August 1979): 65–75.

16. Amanda Bennett, "Growing Small: Big Firms Continue to Trim Their Staffs, 2-Tier Setup Emerges," *The Wall Street Journal*, no. 12 (May 4, 1987): A1.

17. A. M. Pettigrew, "Information Control as a Power Resource," *Sociology* 6 (1972): 187–204.

18. W. Graham Astley and Paramjit S. Sachdeva, "Structural Sources of Intraorganizational Power: A Theoretical Synthesis," *Academy of Management Review* 9 (1984): 104–13.

19. See Mechanic in note 4.

20. Ibid.

21. Ibid, pages 362–64.

22. See Pfeffer in note 13.

23. V. L. Huber, "The Sources, Uses, and Conservation of Managerial Power," *Personnel* 58, no. 4 (1981): 62.

24. See Pfeffer in note 13.

25. Henry Mintzberg, *Power In and Around Organizations* (Upper Saddle River, NJ: Prentice Hall, 1983): 68.

26. A. B. Wildavsky, "Budgeting as a Political Process," in *International Encyclopedia of the Social Sciences*, vol 2, ed. by D. C. Sills (New York: Cromwell, Collier, Macmillan, 1968): 191–93.

27. See Pfeffer, page 7, in note 13.

28. See Pfeffer in note 13. This is based on Pfeffer's discussion on page 31.

29. Don R. Beeman and Thomas W. Sharkey, "The Use and Abuse of Corporate Politics," *Business Horizons* (March–April 1987): 26–30.

30. Barbara Gray and Sonny S. Ariss, "Politics and Strategic Change Across Organizational Life Cycles," *Academy of Management Review* 10 (1985): 707–23.

*The Politics of Education**

When you think of politics and colleges or universities, you may think of them in the traditional sense of the term: social and political causes or movements such as racial justice, pro- or antiwar movements, environmental movements, and many other causes across the political spectrum. While these political and social movements are interesting and an important part of the intellectual dialogue that is part of higher education, there is another type of politics that is less obvious but no less important—organizational politics. How a college or university allocates resources, recognizes sources of power, and deals with its various constituents is critical to its very existence. To understand the shifting political fortunes in academia, it is useful to look at a typical university.

Midwest City University (MCU) is a nearly 200-year-old, large, urban, state university enrolling approximately 30,000 students on three campuses in and around a major midwest city. MCU is the second largest university in the state, has undergraduate, master's, and doctoral programs, and is classified as a "research" university. It has schools of medicine, nursing, law, business, education, engineering, arts and sciences, art and architecture, and a music conservatory. In addition to the main campus programs, MCU has three "access colleges" that admit students to two-year associate degree programs or allow students to begin pursuit of a bachelor's degree and transfer to the main campus. If you were to look at the organizational chart for the university or to read the titles and job descriptions of the people who work there, you would get only a small and inaccurate picture of power and political behavior in this organization.

FOLLOW THE MONEY

As is the case in nearly every organization, money talks. MCU is a state university, so the state legislature is its primary source of funding. The legislature allocates money to the university that the president then distributes along with tuition revenue to the various schools or colleges. Most of these funds are based on enrollment. Specific dollar amounts are allocated according to how many students are enrolled in specific programs. During periods of economic growth, the state may give special funds to a particular school, college, or program, but most of the discretionary money (money that is not specifically targeted for teaching) comes from grants, fundraising or endowments. The schools or colleges that can raise discretionary money have relatively more power than those who are unable to do so. Thus, a medical school or engineering school that is able to successfully land government research grants can build laboratories, supplement faculty salaries, pay for graduate assistants or support staff, and purchase other perquisites unavailable to other schools or colleges.

Some schools or colleges may become the favorite of the local donors who may be alumni or may just have an appreciation for the objectives of that unit. At MCU both of these scenarios are present. For many years the school of engineering has successfully competed for several large grants from government agencies including the Department of Defense, the National Science Foundation, the Environmental Protection Agency, and the Department of Transportation. A quick review of the school of engineering will indicate that they have the most up-to-date computer equipment and the most lavish lab facilities. But they are not alone. The conservatory (school of music and performing arts) has a wealthy local patron of the arts who has donated large sums of money to build a state-of-the-art performance center and has endowed several professorships. While the school of engineering and the conservatory have an embarrassment of riches, several colleges or schools at MCU struggle with facilities that are out of date, bursting at the seams to handle students, and badly in need of repair.

Clearly, the distribution of resources around the university is uneven, but the relationship between money and power is more complex. It is the old game of the "rich get richer." Units that have money use that money as a source of political power and leverage to influence the overall direction of MCU. The dean of the school of engineering can use his success in receiving grants to pressure the university president to allocate resources to his school to support grant activity. In fact, many grants require the recipient to match the grant with funds from the university. Thus, when the school of engineering received a $5 million grant from the National Aeronautics and Space Administration (NASA), the dean was able to leverage the grant to get additional money from the university.

A GOOD REPUTATION IS EVERYTHING

Discretionary money gained through grants and donations is not the only currency of the realm at MCU. In the past 20 years, rankings of colleges and universities, and of the particular schools or colleges within universities, has become a high-stakes game. Publications such as *US News & World Report, Business Week,* and others rank undergraduate programs, business schools, law schools, engineering schools, medical schools, and many other special programs. The fortunes of a university or school can rise or fall on these rankings, despite the fact that they are controversial and imperfect tools. It is not unusual to hear of a school or university that aspires to break into the ranks of the "top 10," "top 25," or "selective" schools. The fact of the matter is that very little movement occurs among ranked schools. Sure, a number 1 business school may slip to number 3, or an unranked school may bump number 49 or 50 from the rankings, but it is highly unlikely that an unranked school will suddenly move into the top 10 or even top 25 in its field.

At MCU much discussion is directed at rankings of various departments, schools, or colleges. For example, the school of engineering dean boasted in the past that his school was a top 25 school, although no published ranking listed it as such. A few engineering departments did, however, gain recognition as top 25 in their respective fields. About 5 years ago the law school emerged for the first time on a published list of the top 50 law schools. Since that time, the law school has teetered precariously at number 48 or 49 on the list. The most clear-cut rankings success is the conservatory, which is typically ranked among the top 5 nationally. Each of these ranked

schools or programs is able to use that ranking to get special treatment from the university president. The rankings are valuable to the president when he goes to the state legislature and asks for additional support. They are an implicit, albeit imperfect, measure of quality.

STAKEHOLDERS

MCU must deal with many external stakeholders who have a variety of sources of power and can influence the direction of the university. Perhaps the most obvious stakeholders are the students. They will attempt to influence the university to provide programs, services, and an environment that they deem to be favorable. Like consumers of any products or services, they will vote with their dollars and their feet. A university that fails to provide the quality of educational programs students seek will see its enrollments decline. Today, student services has become as important, if not more so, as academic quality. Attracting and retaining students has become a business. The care and feeding of students is no longer an afterthought. Universities are now providing dormitories that cater to student tastes and a broad array of food service options. Many universities are spending millions of dollars on student fitness centers and other amenities such as cable TV and Internet connections in dorms. Because of the increasingly intense competition for enrollment, today, students are able to exert collective pressure on universities.

MCU had a long history of bureaucratic neglect of students. Students complained that they could not get answers to questions about fees, student aid, dorm assignments, or other critical aspects of student life. Students complained about misinformation, delays, mistakes, and rude or uncaring administrators. The perception on campus was that administrators just did not care about student well-being. In the mid-1990s, MCU went through a period of declining enrollment, particularly among undergraduate students. Some colleges or schools lost as much as 20 percent of their students. The impact was almost immediate. MCU embarked on a "Quality of Student Life" campaign. Surveys of students were produced. Workshops were given for administrators. Student-focused total quality programs were implemented. Perhaps the most dramatic outcome was the targeting of over $60 million for a student center complex that will house a new student union, stores, and fitness center.

But students are not the only important stakeholders who influence the direction of the university. Like many other states, the state where MCU is located has suffered significant economic deterioration since 2000. Tax revenues have declined, thus budgets for all of the state universities have declined. Unfortunately for MCU, the president has not endeared himself to the state legislators. Some of the president's past actions and statements were regarded as controversial or not in line with the party in control. As result, compared to the other state universities, the legislature was less generous to MCU in recent budget allocations.

The local business community is another important stakeholder for MCU. Many graduates of MCU stay in the area and seek employment with local companies. As a consequence, two of the largest employers in the area have had extraordinary influence on the university. One of the firms is extensively involved in technology-related areas. The firm used extensive pressure, threats to move operations from the area, and promises of donations to get MCU to build a computer technology and automation training and research center. The other firm achieved its objective in more subtle ways. It encouraged the school of business to develop a center for consumer research by offering research grants to faculty, offering scholarships to students, and providing funds for computer equipment.

Many other stakeholders influence the directions that MCU pursues, but one can't ignore the faculty. Just like students, the market for top faculty has become intensely competitive. In fields like medicine, economics, business, and law, MCU has to deal with both academic competitors and non-academic job markets. Thus, salaries for new professors from the top universities in fields such as economics and business can easily be in six figures. Professors in those highly competitive fields are making demands for amenities that were unheard of a few years ago. Some highly sought-after professors will demand limited teaching responsibilities, selected classes, personal secretaries, and other perquisites. Like most other state universities, MCU is unable to successfully attract star professors. In another example of the "rich getting richer," most of these stars move between a few top private and public universities. At MCU the exceptions are the medical school and the conservatory. Because of their respective reputations and the presence of endowments, those schools have been able to compete at the top of their markets.

CONCLUSION

Power in organizations is not necessarily distributed equally within the hierarchy. At MCU, the power of the deans of schools and colleges varies widely. Those who are able to bring in money, enhance reputations, or recruit stars have much greater ability to influence the direction of the university than their colleagues with little access to money, reputation, or stars. But when assessing power and influence, one must also look outside the boundaries of the organization and study the stakeholders. At MCU the state legislature, local businesses, students, and faculty are key stakeholders who have exerted substantial influence. As universities move into the information and technology age, it will be interesting to see how these events change the power structure. ■

*This case is based on a composite of several universities where the author has taught or been a student.

QUESTIONS FOR DISCUSSION

1. Which academic units at your school have the most power? The least power? Why? How does that compare with MCU?
2. At many universities the sports programs (e.g., football, basketball) have power. Which team has the most power at your school? Why? How does the program's power compare with the power of academic units?
3. Who are the key external stakeholders at your school? What are their sources of power? How does that compare with MCU?

CHAPTER

Innovation, Strategic Change, and Organizational Learning

CASE: TEACHING A 132-YEAR-OLD DOG NEW TRICKS*

Graybar is not part of the "new economy," at least not directly. However, the 132-year-old maker of electrical switches, connectors, and cables must keep in step with its customers, many of whom are part of the "new economy." The Internet and the telecommunications revolution have created strong demand for Graybar's core products, but in 1997 the company was having difficulty meeting the demand. The problems at Graybar were a culture and structure that no longer fit the fast pace of the "new economy."

In 1869, inventor Elisha Gray and entrepreneur Enos Barton founded Gray and Barton; in 1872, it became the Western Electric Company, supplier of components to Western Union. With the invention of the telephone, Western Electric became the exclusive supplier of telephone equipment to the Bell system and also managed a thriving nontelephone electrical distribution business. In 1925 the latter business was spun off as a separate company—the Graybar Electric Company. In 1929 the employees purchased Graybar from Western Electric, and the company has been employee owned ever since.

Graybar developed a very conservative and traditional culture befitting a company that dates back to the early days of the telegraph business. Even today, it is not uncommon for executives to spend their entire career with the company. Men in the company still wear white shirts and ties, a far cry from the informality and breeziness of Internet companies. The culture resulted in risk aversion and slow decision making, a bad mix in the fast-paced Internet environment where things are measured in nanoseconds.

The culture and history were further reflected in the company's design. Graybar had developed a highly decentralized system of 231 independent local distribution centers. Local managers stocked only those items for which they believed there was sufficient demand. Unfortunately, the company had difficulty keeping all 231 distribution centers stocked with adequate inventory. Local distributors who were out of stock would turn to other distribution centers for the missing items. The result was that orders took as long as a week to fill and were often shipped to customers from several warehouses with several invoices. Clearly, customers were not pleased with the inefficiencies.

Change has not been easy for Graybar. The long rich history of success made the company resistant to change. The cost of changing the structure was high, both in terms of the financial investment and the potential threats to the company's culture. The price tag for the change was $144 million over 4 years, an amount equal to 2 years' income. But the changes also threatened a culture built on employee ownership and managerial independence in decision making. Local managers were concerned that the newly centralized distribution system would cut into their sales commissions.

---

*This case is based largely on Faith Keenan and Timothy J. Mullaney, "Clicking at Graybar," *Business Week* (June 18, 2001), 132–134.

The solution, which might seem counterintuitive, was to recentralize the distribution to 16 large warehouses to support the local distributors. One might think that a system of decentralized distribution centers would allow the company to closely monitor local customers and respond in a timely fashion. However, the system of 231 distributors was spread too thin. Individual distributors lacked adequate capacity to meet customer demands. Turning to other distributors to fill in gaps was too time-consuming. The goal was to build economies of scale in warehousing. It was more efficient for 16 warehouses to stock larger numbers of items and in larger quantities than for 231 distributors to do so. With large warehouses, orders could be filled more rapidly with fewer out-of-stock items. The rationale is much the same as that employed by "big box" stores like Home Depot.

The restructuring of Graybar's distribution system did result in reductions in local inventory for distributors, and the central warehouse system was better able to accommodate customer needs. Now the main issue that Graybar faces is dealing with the weak telecommunications sector. In the first quarter of 2001, sales were up by only 2 percent. However, management is confident that the company is well positioned for growth, and they expect the company's 2004 revenues to exceed those of 2000 by 50 percent. The new structure has the speed and capacity to respond to the rapid changes in the telecommunications industry.

Throughout this book we have emphasized that organizations are open systems. Any firm is open to many threats and opportunities in its environment. Typically, a firm fails to respond to conditions in the environment.

Organizational changes, learning, and innovation can help reverse declining performance. In this final chapter, we discuss how organizations face the difficult, demanding, and critical task of changing. Nothing in the universe of organizations is static, and organizations themselves must change to match changing conditions. To remain static in the face of a changing world is to invite decline and eventual failure. Change merely for the sake of change or change that is not carefully planned can also invite failure. Change must be carefully planned, and that is the focus of this chapter.

We devote attention to the process of organizational renewal through a variety of approaches to planned organizational change. In particular, we explore a number of techniques, including reengineering and Total Quality Management, aimed at making organizations more responsive to their environments. Finally, we introduce the concept of the learning organization, a concept that embodies the notion of ongoing, continuous change.

THE CONCEPT OF CHANGE

The twenty-first century is a period of unprecedented change in organizations. The popular business press constantly documents organizational restructuring, reengineering, downsizing, and other assorted changes. Even during the robust economy of the late 1990s, many large companies were shedding jobs at an incredible pace. The economic slowdown in 2000–2001 has hastened the pace. Terms such as *downsizing* and *rightsizing* may suggest a one-time fix, but many experts view this as an ongoing process for organizations of the future.[1] But the features in the popular press beg the question: What is organizational change? Can we specify a definition that is broad enough to encompass the wide range of manipulations to organizations about which we read?

Change is simply the alteration of the status quo. In a technical sense it occurs continuously; no moment is exactly like the one that preceded it. For practical purposes, however, we are interested in significant, planned changes to the organizational system: changes to input and output relationships, changes to the technology or transformation processes, changes to structure or design, changes to coordination mechanisms, changes to people and roles in the organization, changes to culture, or basically, changes to any of the aspects of organizations that we discussed in the previous 12 chapters of this book. The forces for change are everywhere; they can be found within the organization itself and they can be found in the external environment.

Language and terminology add some confusion to the discussion of organizational change. The focus of this chapter is on *planned change;* that is, change that is intentional and guided by individuals within (or hired by) the organization. Often, discussion of change includes the term *innovation.* The definition of *innovation* is nearly identical with the definition of *change* given earlier: "a departure from existing practices or technologies [representing] a significant departure from the state of the art at the time it appears."[2] *Innovation* is often used to identify changes in technology (i.e., process innovations) and new products (i.e., product innovations), but the term also is used to refer to changes in administrative practice and in the organizational structure and design. Thus, to differentiate between change and innovation is fruitless. Rather, types of changes are clearly specified in the following discussion—for example, structural change, process innovation, and new product development.

THE DILEMMA OF ORGANIZATIONAL CHANGE

Organizations face a dilemma with respect to planned change. On the one hand, organizations desire change in order to remain competitive, to adopt more effective and efficient means of operation, and to remain in harmony with their environments. On the other hand, organizations often resist change because of their desire for relative stability and predictability.[3] Organizations must have stable outputs, predictable costs, and protection of their financial integrity. One group of writers on organizational change have noted that "successful organizations have an inherent drive toward stability and increasing rigidity."[4] However, this stability and rigidity may prevent an organization from learning about its environment and adapting to changing conditions. A key question thus becomes, Can the organization meet the needs for change and responsiveness while maintaining enough stability to prevent disruption of operations? The organization must find its place along the following continua:

Stability _____	*Rapid change*
Predictability _____	*Unpredictability*
Staleness _____	*Innovation*
Familiarity _____	*Unfamiliarity*
Boredom _____	*Energy*
Certainty _____	*Uncertainty*
Atrophy _____	*New strength*

An organization that maintains the status quo may find that it has a great deal of stability and familiarity, but it may also find that the status quo generates staleness, boredom, and atrophy. Change can bring new challenges, new markets, and new technology, but it can also be a source of instability, uncertainty, and unpredictability. Finding the proper point on these continua to balance the desirable and undesirable consequences of change is a critical challenge for managers. In the study of new product and process innovations, researchers typically distinguish between incremental (minor) innovations or changes to existing conditions and, at the other extreme, radical (major) innovations or changes.[5] Choosing the right point is not an easy task, and there is no one right answer for all organizations. Such factors as the nature of the organization's environment, the people in the organization, and the existing culture, to name only a few, have differential impact on how much change an organization needs and on how an organization manages change.

THE CHANGE PROCESS

The process of changing an organization may be a complex and drawn-out affair that involves many people, large amounts of organizational resources, and lots of time. Nonetheless, in many respects, organizational change is much like the processes associated with any generic decision process (see Chapter 11). As we see in Figure 13-1, the first step in the process is recognition of a need for change, recognition that a gap exists between the organization's current state of affairs and its desired state of affairs. Management may recognize changes in the external environment such as new laws, new competitors, new products, new technological advances, or other sorts of relevant change. Or management may recognize internal conditions that are undesirable. In either case, members of the organization recognize a gap between the current organizational conditions and the desired conditions. Those desired conditions could include greater profitability, greater efficiency, new products, new markets, new operations, or other changed conditions.

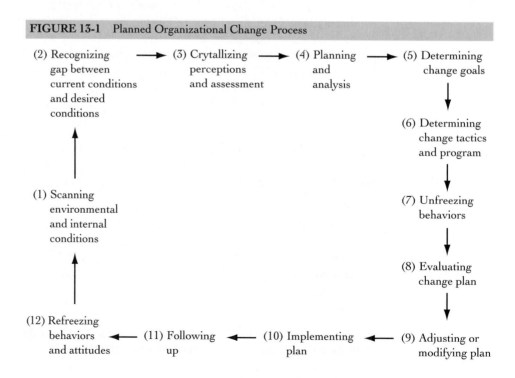

FIGURE 13-1 Planned Organizational Change Process

(2) Recognizing gap between current conditions and desired conditions → (3) Crytallizing perceptions and assessment → (4) Planning and analysis → (5) Determining change goals

(1) Scanning environmental and internal conditions

(5) Determining change goals → (6) Determining change tactics and program → (7) Unfreezing behaviors → (8) Evaluating change plan

(12) Refreezing behaviors and attitudes ← (11) Following up ← (10) Implementing plan ← (9) Adjusting or modifying plan

This gap between what is and what is desired becomes the impetus for change. People recognize the gap and decide that something should be done about it. If the change process proceeds in a planned fashion, the process will follow a series of specific steps. Following recognition that a problem exists, managers perceive and assess the types of changes that they think are necessary, the degree of change needed, and the speed of change required to narrow the gap. However, because of bounded rationality and the culture of the organization, the nature of problem identification and the assessment of the nature of change are likely to be biased and perhaps incomplete. How does management view change? Do they find it threatening? Do they see it as a nuisance or a challenge? How much experience does management have with change? Is the culture one that is receptive to change? All of these questions come to bear as managers attempt to assess the extent and type of change that may be performed.

It is at the planning and analysis stage that management decides how it will deal with change. This is the first step for management in designing a specific change strategy. Managers (or whoever makes up the change team) determine the parts of the organization in need of change. For example, a company may determine that it needs to improve efficiency (i.e., a gap in performance) and that this can be achieved by improving operations. At this point management often determines (either formally or informally) the scope and direction of change, whether change efforts are to be actively encouraged, redirected, amplified, ignored, or even prevented. Thus, some managers may focus attention on ways to improve efficiency (e.g., decrease labor costs, decrease waste, improve maintenance to reduce downtime). Other managers may take this efficiency mandate as license to make many other types of changes that are only peripherally related to efficiency. Still other managers may try to thwart any changes because they fear the impact the changes might have on their jobs, power, and prestige in the organization.

Once the nature of the change has been identified, it is necessary to specify the goals of the change effort. The problem may be inefficiency, but management must specify the goals of change. For example, an automaker may specify a decline in direct labor costs of 10 percent or a steel company may desire a reduction in waste material of 5 percent. The goals should be specific and verifiable. Goal specification is critical because without clear objectives it is hard to know what to change and whether the change effort has been successful.

At this point, management still has not determined the specific change tactics or program to be used to accomplish the goals. That is the next step. The organization needs to develop the specific strategies that will achieve the goals.[6] If the goal is to reduce direct labor costs by 10 percent, management now needs to identify how this is to be achieved. The company could reduce the labor force and demand that existing workers work harder, faster, and smarter. The company could also adopt new technology (e.g., robotics, work teams) that increases productivity (i.e., a decrease of direct labor costs). Management may also note that workers take a long time to make cars because of the large number of parts involved or options available on the product. Thus, another type of change could be a redesign of the product itself (e.g., fewer parts and fewer options) that would make it easier to produce. For any given problem or gap there are likely to be many change strategies that could prove useful—individually or in combination.

Once the change program has been determined, the organization must focus on implementation. Implementing change means that people are likely to be affected and that changes in employee behaviors will be required. Change frequently involves unlearning old ways of doing things and learning new ways to do them. This step is the unlearning or unfreezing step. Attempts must be made to ensure that employees approach change with open minds. As part of this step, the organization needs to be sure that employees have certain information:

- What is being changed
- Why change is needed
- What will be expected of them
- What will be the benefits for them
- What disadvantages or problems might crop up and how they will be handled
- What behavior changes will be needed in programs, tasks, and activities

As we stated at the beginning of the chapter, the mid-1990s were characterized by radical changes in organizations. One such type of change has been the extensive downsizing at many organizations. In the past, layoffs were largely the result of downturns in the business cycle. The latest round of downsizing, however, appears to be different. Many prosperous companies (as well as those that are underperforming) are shedding workers. A variety of complex and often interactive forces, including worldwide competition, deregulation, new technologies, and demanding stakeholders, have resulted in these changes.

The success of downsizing strategies has been mixed at best.[7] However, results of several studies suggest that when the above-listed points are followed, it is more likely that remaining employees will respond favorably to downsizing. In particular, when employees know what to expect, why it is happening, and what impact it is likely to have on them, they are more likely to respond positively to the change.

Employee receptivity to organizational change of any sort is never a sure bet. However, one way to increase the likelihood that employees will accept and embrace change is to have them participate in planning and carrying out the change strategy. Employees could help to identify gaps and potential solutions. They could also be involved in the actual implementation of the potential change strategy. This participation should occur in an open, nonthreatening, and supportive environment. It is not unusual for employees to oppose change because they feel threatened by it or do not fully understand it. Managers can to some extent overcome these concerns through employee participation.[8]

Change efforts do not end with implementation. Once changes have been implemented, the organization must assess the changes to determine whether they have solved the problems that motivated the change in the first place. Although this may seem to be an obvious and necessary step, it is one that is sometimes missing from change strategies. Fear may keep managers from evaluating change strategies—fear that they may not have been successful. However, assessment can lead to modifications and adjustments that eventually produce successful changes in the organization. Given the complexity of organizations and the disruptive nature of change, it is likely that any change strategy needs at least some fine-tuning, and maybe even major adjustments.

The formal change process ends with refreezing of behaviors and attitudes. The new behaviors and attitudes that have been brought about by the change strategy need to become part of the institutional fabric of the organization. Through official policies such as work rules, compensation systems, and training, and through unofficial means such as the culture (e.g., language, symbols, and stories), the organization must establish the new behaviors and attitudes as the ones that are desired and appropriate. An organization that has downsized and flattened its administrative hierarchy needs to establish new rules and norms for communication between layers of the organization.

Perhaps the organization has set guidelines for lower-level employees to take new responsibilities for making decisions. The organization must create an internal environment to support these new behaviors. One company that delayered failed to set new communication norms and found that lower-level employees, who were supposedly empowered to make decisions, were still asking for permission because that was the way things used to work.

An organization that wants to avoid major problems and subsequent radical change should continue to monitor change efforts long after they have been implemented and adjusted. Continuous monitoring may bring problems to the forefront before they are serious and require radical or extensive change.

INITIATING CHANGE

Not all change is initiated at the same pace. Change can be slow and deliberate or it can be quick and radical. Up to this point our focus has been on formally planned change. But change may also emerge through an unplanned and unforeseen process. We briefly review these avenues of change.

Planned incremental change is change that is evolutionary rather than revolutionary. For example, suppose an organization decides to institute a new human resources system. A human resources system involves many facets of organizational life including recruiting, training, performance evaluation, compensation, promotions, and benefits. To change all these components at one time may severely disrupt the organization. A planned incremental change strategy would approach changing the human resources system one piece at a time. The process might begin with a change in the performance appraisal system. Even that change may be phased in one department or one division at a time.

The value of this approach is that disruptions to the organization would be limited and the organization would be able to evaluate the new performance appraisal system in a limited setting. Thus, if problems developed, it might be easier and less costly to correct them on a small-scale introduction rather than if the change had been made in the entire organization.

Hewlett-Packard, the computer technology company, used incremental changes in new product innovations to keep the company competitive in the rapidly changing computer industry. The company's domination of the printer market has been due in no small part to its attitude toward change and innovation. The company has avoided a crisis mentality and has continually revamped and modified its products.[9]

Radical change, sometimes referred to as framebreaking change, is brought about by major changes in the business strategy.[10] Changing strategy typically requires a change in structure, people, and organizational processes. Researchers suggest that organizations often go through long periods of stability and then face a brief period of fundamental change in the industry that requires the organization to undergo radical, framebreaking change.[11] For example, Kmart went through the period from the 1960s through the mid-1980s without undergoing much significant change. However, the challenges presented by Wal-Mart and various "category killer" stores like Toys "R" Us and Home Depot forced Kmart to alter its basic business strategy. Kmart has attempted to change nearly every aspect of its business. It has sold several divisions and has closed many unprofitable units. It has revamped and refurbished stores, and has attempted to upgrade its image as a discount retailer. In an attempt to regain its position in the market place, Kmart reinstituted the "Blue Light Special," a staple of the 1960s and 1970s. All of these strategic shifts were accompanied by organizational changes. Since the early 1990s Kmart has made several changes in top management. As the company shed business units such as Borders Books and Office Depot, the company consolidated management. In spite of all its efforts to manage change and its consequences successfully, however, Kmart was forced to declare bankruptcy in 2002.

Although major framebreaking changes may seem to be rare events, they are a little deceptive. What managers and consultants find is that even incremental changes often have a chain reaction in an organization. It is not unusual to find that subtle changes in one area necessitate changes in another area, and so on. Jack Welch, former chairman of the board at General Electric, notes that change strategies often underestimate the impact and scope of the effects on the organization.[12] Thus, what sometimes begins as minor fine-tuning or adjustment to the organization ends up being more akin to radical change.

Unplanned change is change that just happens or emerges. Strategy and practice in the organization emerge in the course of business as a stream of actions and decisions.[13] As we have noted throughout this text, organizations are dynamic and changing entities. The environments in which they are embedded are also constantly changing. Thus, it is reasonable to assume that change takes place in organizations regardless of whether it is guided by management. Organizations do not just wander aimlessly; they change and respond to events in their environment, often with only minimal conscious planning by management. Recall the discussion in Chapter 7 on the sequence of natural changes through which organizations progress as part of normal organizational life cycles. These, too, constitute unplanned changes.

TYPES OF ORGANIZATIONAL CHANGE

Perhaps the greatest challenge facing modern organizations is the need to identify appropriate areas to change, to nurture those changes, and to maintain change in various aspects of the organization. We have at various times throughout this text discussed the variety of forces, particularly those emanating from the environment, that demand adaptation and change from the organization. We have also implicitly, and occasionally explicitly (see Chapter 5), described aspects of the organization and its context that can be changed. Nonetheless, it is useful at this point to list the broad categories of organizational change and innovation that are possible. The following six sections identify and briefly describe discrete aspects of an organization that can be changed. Although we treat these as discrete parts of the organization, it is important to reiterate that change in one area often necessitates change in other areas.

Goals and Strategy

Most types of planned organizational change involve some modification of organizational goals and strategy. Some planned changes may emerge from lower levels of the organization in response to local problems or conditions. Although these changes may not be motivated by changing corporate-level goals or strategy, they are most likely to be driven by local department or work unit goals.

Typically, changing the goals and strategy are but the starting point for changing other aspects of the organization. Goals for new products would likely require research and development, new production, and perhaps new personnel and new structures. Improving financial performance could involve such changes as increased efficiency (i.e., less waste, greater productivity), improved marketing, less overhead, or other sorts of changes. A goal of improving quality could involve changes in virtually all aspects of the organization, from the skills and training of personnel to the culture of the organization. The point is that most large-scale planned organizational changes begin with new or modified goals and strategy, but changing the goals and strategy is just a preliminary step to further organizational change.

People

This text began with a definition of organizations that emphasized the human social nature of organizations—that, first and foremost, organizations are made up of people. Thus, it makes sense that one element of the organization that we can change is the people who make up the organization.

One of the more pervasive forms of change that has affected organizations around the world has been downsizing. Although there are typically structural aspects to downsizing (the elimination of layers of bureaucracy, merging of departments or divisions, etc.), the most obvious aspect of downsizing is that the organization eliminates people. Management must decide on rules and strategy for determining who will be cut from the organization as well as on the procedures for actually eliminating personnel. Eliminating the wrong people from the organization can be costly. Critical skills and knowledge may be lost, as was the case at General Motors. In some cases, firms that have downsized have belatedly realized that they cut the wrong people and have faced the embarrassing task of rehiring released workers.[14]

How the organization releases the eliminated workers can have profound impact on not only those who lose jobs, but also on those employees who remain on the job.[15] Keys to successful downsizing include keeping employees informed of possible job elimination, providing a fair and just system for eliminating jobs, helping to place departing workers in new jobs, allowing departing workers to retain self-esteem and dignity, and using cultural ceremonies and rites to manage feelings and attitudes of remaining workers. Creating a supportive work environment can be an important step in smoothing the difficult process of laying off workers.

Several other people changes are also available to the organization. The organization can recruit new employees with particular skills or background. For example, with the increasing emphasis on international business, many organizations are seeking potential employees fluent in several languages and familiar with diverse national cultures. The emphasis on computerization and automation has forced many organizations to seek employees with higher levels of education and with specific computer training. However, recruiting is not the only way to obtain these or other specialized skills. Many firms use extensive and ongoing on-the-job training and development to ensure that employee skills and knowledge are current and relevant.

Products and Services

We noted in Chapter 5 that one mechanism for managing environmental uncertainty was to develop new products or services. New products and services may allow a company to enter new market niches that are less crowded and less competitive. Some industries and firms are dedicated to new product and service innovation. For example, the financial health of many large pharmaceutical companies is based on their ability to generate new patented products. Once a patent expires, the company is exposed to generic drug makers who do not bear the research and development costs and who can produce generic versions of drugs at considerably lower prices. However, even before a patent expires, a drug company may face competition from another firm making a similar, more effective, or cheaper product. Thus, pharmaceutical companies must spend considerable resources and time developing new products.[16]

It is not just the pharmaceutical industry that lives and dies with new products and services. Much of the computer hardware and software industry and the consumer electronics industry is driven by product and service innovations. The relative advantage of a computer maker may be the result of bigger and faster processors and memory, better customer service, or new technical twists. However, it is important to recognize that the ultimate success of product and service innovations is low. Only 31 percent of product innovations ever make it to the marketplace, and among those that do, only 56 percent are still there 5 years later. The most astounding statistic is that only 12 percent of new products are ever financially successful (i.e., producing a positive return on investment).[17] One need only look at the marketplace for examples of product and service flops.[18] In the early 1980s, Xerox marketed an innovative and powerful workstation that was far ahead of available computer technology. But poor timing and high price doomed the 8010 Star. Shortly after the Xerox product hit the market, IBM introduced the comparatively low-cost PC. Apple's entry into the PDA market, the Newton, was similarly ill-timed and ill-conceived. The product was expensive and unreliable. Thus, while some industries like computers, consumer electronics, movies, pharmaceuticals, and toys depend on new products for their lifeblood, the success rate across industries is quite low.

There are no guarantees to success in product or service innovation, but a number of studies have identified several features that are likely to increase the probability of success.[19] These are summarized in Table 13-1 and include (1) close involvement with potential customers and identification of customer needs; (2) products or services that are consistent with the strategy and skill base of the organization; (3) creativity and scientific or technical expertise necessary for product or service development and production; (4) entrepreneurial skills to sell the innovation in the organization and to market it outside; (5) appropriate organizational structure to develop, produce, and market the innovation; (6) project manager to oversee and coordinate development, production, and marketing; and (7) an innovation *champion*—a person who can advocate and represent a product or service innovation to top management.

Technology

In an attempt to increase productivity and flexibility in manufacturing, many firms are changing their technologies. Several trends in technology come under the broad heading of *advanced manufacturing technology* or AMT.[20] Most of these involve the use of computers and advanced communication technology. Some examples include computer-aided manufacturing (CAM), computer-aided design (CAD), material

---

TABLE 13-1 Keys to Product and Service Innovation Success

1. Identification of customer needs and customer involvement
2. Consistency with organizational strategy and skill base
3. Creativity and scientific or technical expertise
4. Entrepreneurship; sell the innovation to top management and customers
5. Structure congruent with the innovation
6. Project manager to oversee and coordinate development, production, and marketing
7. Champion to advocate and represent a product or service innovation to top management

requirements planning, flexible manufacturing systems and cells (FMS or FMC), robotics and numerical control, automated materials handling, and computer-integrated manufacturing. A comprehensive discussion of these technological changes is beyond the scope of this text, but each is briefly described in Table 13-2.

Some technology changes, such as computerization or robotics, do not involve specific technical advances but rely instead on changing the deployment of people or arrangement of tasks. One approach that has gained widespread application in manufacturing and service settings is the movement to *cross-functional teams*. For example, a manufacturer may assemble a team of individuals with a broad range of skills to produce a product rather than using functional departments to conduct narrow tasks. The advantages of cross-functional teams are better integration and coordination of work and greater flexibility. With cross-functional teams, workers with different skills, knowledge, and perspectives are in closer contact and can exchange ideas or discuss problems more easily. In cross-functional teams, members are more likely to learn diverse skills in addition to the ones they bring to the team. This allows for flexibility in work arrangements. Finally, cross-functional teams are more likely to take a holistic view of the manufacturing or service process because the team is involved in the total process rather than just some narrow portion.

The General Motors Saturn Division adopted cross-functional teams as a way to assemble cars. In a traditional General Motors assembly plant, workers have narrow skills and narrowly defined jobs.[21] For example, a worker may be responsible for just attaching the driver's side front door to a car. He or she would take a preassembled door panel that had the door handle, lock, and latching mechanisms already installed. This worker's only task would be to attach the door to the car body by bolting the hinge to the door opening. At most, he or she would also be responsible for completing connections for lights, warning bells, and electric locks and windows. The old way of thinking was that this worker could become expert at attaching doors to the car. Workers could easily be trained for this job. Therefore, workers who were absent or

---

TABLE 13-2   Examples of Advanced Manufacturing Technologies

Computer-Aided Manufacturing (CAM): Technologies that involve the computerization of various aspects of the manufacturing or production process, including numerical control (use of coded instructions to run machinery) and robotics (use of computer-controlled devices or manipulators to perform specific tasks in the manufacturing process).

Flexible Manufacturing Systems or Flexible Manufacturing Cells: Two or more machines teamed together to perform cutting or forming operations along with automated materials handling. Arrangements of machines and machine pathways can be altered or changed on relatively short notice to produce varied outcomes.

Computer-Aided Design (CAD): Use of computer and computer database to create or modify product designs and engineering data. Often paired with CAM to produce CAD/CAM, in which design and production systems are closely linked and design information is used in machine control.

Material Requirements Planning: Computer-based inventory and production scheduling system used to ensure timely supply of parts for production system. This may be used as an integral part of a just-in-time (JIT) inventory control system.

Computer-Integrated Manufacturing: Combination of two or more of the above individual advances under the control of a central computer system.

who performed poorly could easily be replaced. The new view of work is that this type of job is boring, demotivating, and dehumanizing. At Saturn, an assembly team would work together closely on all parts of the car body assembly. A team would follow a car throughout most of the assembly process.

The rationale behind the team approach is that through teamwork the company can produce a better product and produce it more efficiently.[22] Workers are taught to be more highly motivated by the broad range of tasks they perform and by identification with a completed final product. Cross-functional teams permit better communication among workers (but workers are also required to possess better communication skills) so that coordination of tasks is handled more easily and efficiently. Workers working as a team may discover a better process for assembling door panels and attaching them to the cars. Because the workers work together as a team on the entire assembly process, it is more likely that they will see and understand the larger nature of the job. Rather than seeing his or her job as attaching doors to a car, a worker is more likely to see his or her job as being part of the work of a team that builds the entire car. The results are greater quality and efficiency.[23]

Cross-functional teams are not just for manufacturing. Many service companies from banks to insurance companies to health care providers have turned to cross-functional teams as a way to improve the quality of work and the quality of work life. Like any other management practice, cross-functional teams are not without costs and are not the answer to every organizational problem. The teamwork required to make cross-functional teams work smoothly requires an educated workforce and workers who are skilled at communications, negotiations, and conflict resolution. Because workers are working together closely and because the organization's authority structure is typically decentralized with teams, there is a greater potential for conflicts and disagreements. Additionally, for some tasks, the efficiencies and expertise gained by the old-style specialization may outweigh the benefits of teams. Finally, the use of teams (cross functional or otherwise) must fit with the prevailing culture of the organization.[24] Merely using teams because other organizations successfully use them is certainly no guarantee of success.

Process mapping is an attempt to change the technology by streamlining the process.[25] Process mapping involves describing the sequences of operations, tasks, machines, tools, people, and supplies involved in completing a process. For example, General Electric has used process mapping in its Evendale, Ohio, jet engine manufacturing facility to schematically describe all the steps involved in manufacturing a jet engine. The task of mapping is complex. GE took more than one month to map the production of just one jet engine. The paperwork for this task was so extensive that it wrapped around an entire conference room.[26] When the mapping is successfully completed, managers can see wasted or inefficient steps and bottlenecks in the process. The mapping then becomes a diagnostic tool for rearranging a production process to operate more smoothly.

With any of these changes in technology, it is important to keep in mind that the technology must be congruent with other aspects of the organization.[27] For example, implementation of advanced manufacturing technology (AMT) may require additional training for personnel and extensive capital expenditures on computer systems. Technology changes may require changes in the organizational design and structure as well as the culture. One problem encountered by many firms moving to cross-functional teams is that recognition, rewards, compensation, and other aspects of the culture are geared toward the individual rather than the team. This situation makes teamwork difficult to maintain.

Organizational Development

Even before many organizations began moving in the direction of teamwork and group approaches to work, organizations faced the problem of getting people from diverse backgrounds with different needs and talents to work together. Extensive team-oriented approaches to work make working together even more important. Two additional trends in organizations today make working together both more important and more problematic: Organizational membership is becoming increasingly diverse with more women, minorities, and foreign-born workers on the job, and organizations are becoming increasingly international in focus and in operation. These trends place increasing pressure on the social aspects of organizing: being able to communicate effectively, understand the different needs and backgrounds of fellow workers, and either reach agreement or constructively disagree.

Organizational development (OD) is the area of organizational change that aims at improving the social functioning of organizations. OD is a subgroup of organizational change strategies that uses knowledge of the behavioral sciences for planned interventions in organizational processes with the goal of increasing organizational health and effectiveness.[28] Although OD change efforts could conceivably address any aspect of an organization, these approaches have typically focused on improving and facilitating interactions among people in organizations. Thus, the focus has been on such things as attitudes about trust, cooperation, acceptance, and tolerance. The goals of OD have been to improve communication among workers, to develop norms of trust and acceptance, and to move toward collaboration and consensus.[29]

Several techniques can be used individually or as part of a larger change plan. A first step in OD intervention is often a diagnostic survey of worker attitudes about jobs, supervision, and the general quality of work life that is used to identify problem areas. *Survey feedback* to organizational members can be used to initiate further change plans. Feedback may provide a basis for managers to improve their management and leadership skills.[30] Results of survey feedback may also be used by a consultant to guide *process consultation*, interventions in which a consultant would observe actual organizational processes (group meetings, teamwork, and other work events).[31] As a result of observing these processes, consultants would provide feedback on ways to improve communications, leadership, decision making, and conflict management. Consultants may also intervene with *team building* activities that deal with methods for improving communication and understanding among team or group members. As we noted above in our discussion of cross-functional teams, team approaches change the basic nature of technology (how we do the job), but they also depend on new and different interpersonal skills. Without attention to the development of these skills, team-based work is not likely to be successful. These same techniques that are used within specific groups or teams in an organization can also be used across many groups, departments, or units of an organization. A current trend in OD is *diversity training* as shown in Exhibit 13-1.

Structure and Design Change

In Chapters 2 and 8 we identified a number of current trends in organizational structure and design: downsizing, flattening or delayering, and decentralizing. Essentially, structural changes involve changes in division of labor and coordination—changes in differentiation. Changes in design involve changes in grouping of jobs, tasks, or output. We also identified two new organizational forms—the virtual organization and the

---

EXHIBIT 13-1

Organizational Development: Diversity Training[32]

One type of OD intervention that many organizations are using today is diversity training. Organizations have become increasingly diverse, with more women; racial, ethnic, and religious minorities; foreign nationals; and others whose lifestyles, beliefs, or behaviors are out of the mainstream. Accommodating this diversity has not always been easy. Many large organizations face increasing managerial and even legal challenges because of sexual or racial harassment, discrimination, or other forms of perceived unfair treatment. Some problems may result from ignorance, but others are the result of ingrained dislike, misunderstanding, or even hatred. Often the first step in combating these problems is diversity training. The belief is that understanding breeds tolerance and acceptance, that tolerance and acceptance should lead to improved working conditions, and that all these forces will lead to a more productive organization.

Large numbers of companies, both large and small, have seen the benefits of diversity training. Not only does training improve individuals' understanding of their coworkers' differences, but it is also a springboard to more creative problem solving. Companies as different as Ford Motor, Rohm & Haas, Corestates Financial, and IBM have found that diverse work teams are likely to see problems and opportunities differently from the way homogeneous teams see them. These teams may be the source of novel solutions to critical problems.

The news on diversity training, however, is not all positive. News reports have highlighted some unscrupulous methods used by overambitious trainers. Some reports have highlighted the experiences of white males who have been *forced* to confront real or imagined racism or sexism. Force simply does not work. Real understanding and acceptance requires a supportive and trusting environment.

---

federal organization.[33] The reader should refer to those chapters that provide a more detailed discussion of these types of change. According to many popular management books and articles, the conventional wisdom is that most organizations are (or should be) moving in the direction of becoming flatter, more decentralized, and connected or networked to other organizations (e.g., suppliers, customers, regulators, and even competitors).[34]

As is the case with any of the other changes mentioned thus far, altering the structure and design of an organization is an ambitious undertaking. We have at various points in the text discussed the great difficulty experienced by many large organizations attempting to restructure. Changes in structure and design must be carefully managed to be congruent with other aspects of the organization—in particular, people, technology, goals, and culture. For example, downsizing and decentralization often mean that workers need new skills and need to learn new decision-making processes. The organization's culture must also support the newly found autonomy and initiative of workers.

Managers and others involved in changing structure and design must be aware of the informal side of the organization. The informal structure may remain unaltered and may be counter to the changes made to formal structure and design. This is where careful attention to the people and culture of the organization is particularly important. Thus, as we noted at the beginning of this chapter, change in one aspect of an organization often necessitates change in other aspects.

Culture Change

Changing an organization's culture is an extensive and ambitious undertaking. At the deeper level of culture, we are talking about a change in the norms, values, beliefs, and expectations in the organization. Moreover, this type of change typically involves changes in all the areas previously mentioned: people, goals, technology, teams, structure, and design. Rather than restate the issues surrounding cultural change (the interested reader can refer to Chapter 10), we offer the following description of total quality management; it should give the reader a sense of perspective on the all-encompassing nature of cultural change.

During the decade of the 1970s, many U.S. companies suffered market share declines at the hands of Japanese companies. One major reason for this was the perceived lack of quality of U.S. goods. U.S. automakers were hit especially hard. Not all the declines resulted from Japanese competition, however. Such companies as Sears, and Kmart suffered setbacks from Wal-Mart, Target, and Nordstrom. The last three retailers were seen as providing superior quality service. As managers and management scholars began to study Sears and other companies with similar problems of poor performance, they discovered that poor quality was a significant problem.

Early approaches to the quality problem included several different techniques: quality circles, participative decision making, and decentralized decision making. Although some of these techniques produced some improvements in quality, the results were often limited in scope and duration. Critics pointed out that these approaches were frequently piecemeal and directed only at small segments of the organization, especially production. When investigators looked more closely at the Japanese experience with quality, they found that in such companies as Toyota, the whole organization focused on quality.

Several models of total quality management (TQM) have guided management practice, but the two perspectives that have received the most attention are those of Deming and Juran.[35] The following are common elements of the Deming and Juran approaches to quality.[36]

First, the organization must ***focus on the customer and create total customer satisfaction.*** Many companies have stated an emphasis on customer satisfaction, but what differs in the TQM approach is that the customer, not the company, defines satisfaction. This means that organizations must get to know their customers better. This means listening to customers and seeking customer input during the design phase of products or services. It is important to note that TQM gives broad meaning to the term *customer.* Customers may be inside the organization. For example, at an automobile manufacturer the assembly plant is a customer of both internal and external parts suppliers.

Empowerment is a second feature of TQM. Empowerment incorporates the ideas of participative management, delegation, and the granting of real power to lower-level employees to make and enforce decisions. For example, production workers at Ford can stop the assembly line if they see problems. They do not need to get permission or authorization from a supervisor. The idea behind empowerment is to give responsibility to people who are involved with the work process.

Third, TQM embodies the concept of ***team-based management***. Like the earlier Saturn example, TQM takes teamwork beyond mere cooperation. Work is organized around teams rather than individuals. Teams are empowered to make most decisions, and managers serve as coaches or facilitators rather than as bosses or supervisors. As we noted in describing Saturn's use of teams, a result of the team approach is team identification with outputs. A team assembling a whole car is more likely to identify with the output than an individual who attaches a few bolts. Team-based management goes beyond the performance of tasks. The organization must be committed to team-based organizing and team-based compensation.

Continuous improvement and measurement is the fourth key to TQM. Three component processes make up continuous improvement and measurement: measurement and tracking of critical success factors, use of statistical process control, and benchmarking best practices. Error rates, output, waste, delays, customer satisfaction, manufacturing tolerances, and other important data must be measured and tracked on a consistent basis. Results of the measurement should be posted so that people know what is going on. Sometimes posting these data is enough to motivate people to pay attention to quality. Monitoring can also provide keys to improving quality. Scientific sampling is conducted during the production process so that problems or errors can be detected and fixed during the process rather than waiting until the end. The point is that changes add quality that can and should be made at any time.

Benchmarking involves identifying a competitor or another company in a similar industry that is doing something particularly well, studying that process, and then trying to emulate that process in your organization. For example, a university identified the registrar's office as a significant problem area. Students complained about the cost, delays, and errors in getting transcripts sent to employers or other schools. The registrar surveyed several universities to find registrars' offices that were particularly good at serving student needs. A team from the university visited the exemplary registrar's office to study the processes used and adapt them to their office. Surprisingly, even in the competitive business environment, companies are often willing to share best practices.

Finally, TQM entails ***open communication*** and ***feedback***. Neither communication nor feedback is a new concept. Both have been discussed extensively under other organizational change headings. However, at the heart of TQM is the idea that people must feel free to broach sensitive subjects related to quality. Communication must be up, down, and across the organization, as must the commitment to TQM. Departments that are customers to other departments within the organization must feel free to communicate their needs and satisfaction.

TQM represents a culture change for organizations adopting it because it involves changing the core values, norms, beliefs, and expectations in the organization. (It also frequently involves other forms of change: employee skills, work teams, and structure.) The first aspect of the new norms, values, beliefs, and expectations involves the concept of quality itself. The organization must embrace a customer-defined idea of quality. Although the old saw "the customer is always right" is time-honored, the notion of customer-defined quality takes that idea a few steps further. This devotion to quality means that the organization must do anything and everything it can to satisfy customers—even when those customers are members of the same organization. A second part of the new norms, values, beliefs, and expectations is directed at the notion of power in the organization. TQM upsets the typical expectation that power should be hierarchical. A third change, one that is often difficult in the rugged individualism of American culture, is the team approach. The organization must shift its thinking from the glorification of individuals to the glorification of teams. Another shift in beliefs is the change to measuring ongoing processes to detect errors, waste, and problems rather than measuring after processes are completed. This often goes against such traditions as production cycles and model years. Finally, honest, open communication and feedback may violate past norms of discretion, professional deference, and hierarchy.

For TQM to work, everyone must understand that the process encompasses nearly all aspects of the organization. This is not a one-time, one-shot deal. It is a continuous and ongoing process.

ORGANIZATIONAL LEARNING

Most approaches to organizational change attempt to fix or change portions of the organization. Even attempts to change the culture may only modify components of the organization—changing values, norms, beliefs, and expectations. It is true that some of these changes can be quite radical and may result in more efficient and effective organizations. ***Organizational learning*** offers a different perspective on change and organization that addresses the fundamental nature of an organization. The organizational learning perspective is an attempt to create an organization that is able to continually monitor the environment and adapt to changing conditions.

The organizational learning framework proposes that organizations, much like people, have memory and can learn. Clearly organizations are made up of people who think and learn, but the organizational learning framework goes a step further. Organizational memory and learning are more than just the aggregate of individual memory and learning. Organizations have a memory of what works and what does not work, as well as a rich history of past events. This memory is stored in a variety of forms including documents, policies, procedures, reports, products, databases, and most important, in the minds of employees of the organization—sometimes referred to as human capital. The fact that people carry around a great deal of know-how in their minds, often in the form of tacit knowledge, is underappreciated by most managers. This fact sometimes becomes evident when organizations undergo downsizing and release employees with key tacit knowledge relevant to the organization.

Several organizational authorities have written extensively about what constitutes organizational learning. We have synthesized these into the following five attributes of a learning organization.[37] First, a learning organization develops systematic approaches to problem solving, developing an understanding of what works and what does not work, learning from experience, and learning from the best practices of others. Second, in a learning organization people must override past mental models. This is sometimes referred to as "thinking outside the box." People must become accustomed to trying new things, experimenting. Third, people in the learning organization must develop personal mastery, including developing skills to be open with others. Like many of the approaches to organizational change that we mentioned earlier, communication is key to learning. That communication is critical to the fourth characteristic of a learning organization—transferring and disseminating new knowledge quickly and effectively throughout the organization. Knowledge, information, and skills should not be hoarded or hidden from other members of the organization. Finally, the learning organization should use the learning process and the transfer of information to develop and pursue a shared vision. Table 13-3 summarizes characteristics of the learning organization.

Peter Senge, one of the principal advocates of organizational learning, maintains that learning organizations derive competitive advantage from constant learning. Becoming a learning organization involves a transformation in thinking. Members can no longer think that any one person has all the answers. Senge further notes, "People working together with integrity and authenticity and collective intelligence are profoundly more effective as a business than people living together on politics, game playing, and narrow self-interest."[38]

TABLE 13-3   The Learning Organization
1. Develop systematic approaches to problem solving to understand what works and what does not work in the organization.
2. Develop the ability to "think outside the box"; override old, outmoded ways of thinking.
3. Develop personal mastery of skills.
4. Transfer and disseminate knowledge and information throughout the organization.
5. Develop a shared vision of the organization's world.

In the 1990s, the Lincoln-Mercury Division of Ford Motor Company adopted an organizational learning approach.[39] Application of organizational learning to the development of the new Lincoln Continental demonstrated impressive results. The development team saved over $65 million budgeted for fixing engineering glitches by opening up the development process. Because of open communication, sharing of ideas, transfer of knowledge, and other learning tools, the team identified nearly three times as many potential problems early in development when fixing and modifying the design was easier and less costly. The development team was able to resolve conflicting systems problems (e.g., air-conditioning, headlights, power seats) without the bickering that typically accompanied such problems.

Adopting an organizational learning approach was not without cost for the Lincoln Continental project. The approach collided with the engineering-dominated culture at Ford and created massive chaos. Despite the success of the Continental project, the project manager, Fred Simon, was passed over for a promotion and eventually retired. Thus, although the Lincoln-Mercury Division may have adopted an organizational learning framework, the approach has not yet diffused throughout Ford.

FACILITATING CHANGE

Now that we have explored a variety of approaches to organizational change, we need to consider those factors or conditions that pave the way for change. Researchers and practitioners have identified conditions that make change strategies more likely to be successful. The list of characteristics presented below assumes that the change plan has been clearly developed and documented. This should include a time line for implementation and goals or benchmarks for performance.

Top Management Support

For any change strategy to be successful it must garner the support of top management. Without that support, it is likely the lower-level managers will view the change strategy with suspicion. Moreover, it may be risky for managers to pursue actions that lack top-management support. Recall the experience of the Lincoln Continental project manager who adopted an organizational learning strategy that was inconsistent with the general culture at Ford.

Structural Support

The ***ambidextrous organization*** possesses both organic and mechanistic structural characteristics.[40] Organic characteristics are necessary for the flexibility and creativity required to generate new ideas. Product development teams, research and development departments, or teams and task forces devoted to developing change strategies are given organic characteristics. However, change strategies that effectively diffuse through the organization and become institutionalized (i.e., part of the daily fabric of the organization) require some degree of formalization, standardization, and centralization—all mechanistic characteristics. Although some organizations may simultaneously possess ambidexterity, other organizations achieve similar results by switching from organic to mechanistic as they go through the process of first developing a change strategy and then implementing it. One way of achieving this ambidextrous nature on a temporary basis is through the use of teams or task forces with specific responsibility for developing and implementing the changes.

Champions

We already noted in discussion of innovations the role of a champion to oversee the project and to fight for it with others in the organization. A champion is an enthusiastic supporter of a proposed change. A champion can be critical to the successful development and implementation of any type of change strategy. The champion can answer questions, remove roadblocks, and persuade those who resist.

Communications

Change does not occur in a vacuum. People need to be informed about the nature of proposed change and how that change is likely to affect them.[41] Resistance, confusion, and anger can be minimized with clear and timely communication about the nature and impact of proposed changes. These communications can include meetings, videos, documents, and briefing sessions.

Resources

Although there are stories of organizations successfully pulling off changes or innovations with very limited resources,[42] these are the exception rather than the rule. Change is risky for an organization, and underfinancing a change strategy merely increases the risk. If an organization is going to expose itself to the risk and uncertainty associated with change, it should provide adequate resources, including personnel, equipment, facilities, consultants, and money.

Resources are a two-edged sword, however. Often an organization in need of change lacks a generous supply of resources. On the other hand, we discussed the notion of *slack resources* earlier in the text. Slack may provide a cushion for experimenting and taking risks. However, an abundance of resources may also lull an organization into complacency, and it may fail to perceive the need for change.[43]

SUMMARY

We began this chapter by noting that change is simply the alteration of the status quo. That simple statement belies the complexity and difficulty associated with changing organizations. In this chapter we have described various characteristics of change, mapped the change process, described a wide array of types of change, and discussed ways to facilitate change. Along the journey through this material and throughout the text as a whole, we have repeatedly noted that change is endemic to organizations. That is, whether planned or unplanned, radical or incremental, change is experienced by organizations as a result of their being open systems. At the same time, forces exist in the organization that attempt to maintain stability and to fight against change.

Moreover, we have noted that change typically has a ripple effect—changing one aspect of an organization often necessitates (or even causes) change to other parts of the organization.

The primary focus of this chapter was on planned organizational change—those changes that are intentional and formally planned. The normal progression through organizational life cycles and the natural political activities in organizations also produce unplanned and unintended change.

Planned changes vary on the continuum between incremental changes that involve minor modifications or adjustments to radical or framebreaking changes. As change strategies become increasingly more radical, they become riskier and typically are more difficult to implement.

We noted that the previous 12 chapters provide an outline for the types of changes that organizations can adopt. The first type of change we identified was changing the organization's goals and strategies. These changes may include identification of new markets, new products, new internal practices, or new guidelines for employee conduct. People in the organization can be changed in several ways. Examples include recruiting new employees, training existing employees, and changing compensation or benefit plans to alter motivation. Organizations often implement change through new products and services; however, the success of new product and service strategies is quite low. Many organizations are adopting new technologies as part of change strategies. These include an array of advanced manufacturing technologies (AMT), team approaches to tasks, and refining existing technologies through process mapping. One of the oldest types of change strategies is the assortment of techniques that come under the heading of organizational development. These techniques focus on the social nature of organizations and attempt to change people's attitudes and behaviors toward other people in the organization. Techniques include survey feedback, process consultation, and team building. Structural and design changes are attempts to alter the division of labor and bases for grouping people together in the organization. Organizations are moving in the direction of flatter, decentralized, networked structures and designs. In discussing cultural change, we introduced total quality management (TQM) as an example of a total system change in an organization that involves a basic shift in the values, norms, beliefs, and expectations that are at the foundation of the organization. Finally, we introduced organizational learning, not as a change strategy, but as a different way of thinking about an organization. The learning organization is really an organization that should be flexible and responsive enough to undergo continuous change.

The last section of this chapter identified five aspects of organizations that can facilitate the change process. These include top-management support, an ambidextrous structure, change champions, communication of intent, and the availability of resources. Although these factors will likely facilitate change, there is no guarantee that changes will be accepted or will result in the desired outcomes.

Throughout this text, and especially in this final chapter, we have focused attention on the changing nature of organizations. The information technology revolution (inexpensive computing and telecommunications devices) has laid the groundwork for the emergence of new types of organization. We are seeing the emergence of the virtual organization and the federal organization we discussed in Chapter 8. This will probably be only the beginning of the changed nature of organizations as we head into the twenty-first century. The very nature of jobs and careers is changing radically. Regardless of what form new organizations take, this text should provide you with the bases for understanding organizations and organization theory.

Questions for Discussion

1. What is change? What parts of an organization are affected by change?
2. How can change be managed?
3. What is the difference between incremental and radical change? Why is this an important distinction?
4. Why and how does change pose a dilemma to organizations? What do you think are the likely consequences for an organization that does not change? Why?
5. Why do you think that many change efforts fail or fall short of their objectives?
6. Select one type of change that you think would be appropriate for your college or university. Design a brief plan for introducing this change, including diagnosis of the problem(s) it is intended to solve.
7. Some critics of organizational change have suggested that most of these change efforts (e.g., TQM, reengineering, organizational learning) are just fads. Based on what you have learned in this text, why do you think organizations often "jump on the bandwagon" for the newest fad?
8. What is meant by organizational learning? What is new and different about this concept compared with other change strategies?

References

1. Louis S. Richman, "When Will the Layoffs End?" *Fortune* (September 20, 1993): 54–56.
2. Richard H. Hall, *Organizations: Structures, Processes, and Outcomes*, 5th ed. (Upper Saddle River, NJ: Prentice Hall, 1991), 193.
3. Bill McKelvey and Howard Aldrich, "Populations, Natural Selection, and Applied Organizational Science," *Administrative Science Quarterly* 28 (1983): 101–28.
4. Michael L. Tushman, Charles O'Reilly, and David Nadler, *The Management of Organizations* (New York: Harper & Row, 1989), 461.
5. Lawrence Gales, Pamela Tierney, and Andrew Boynton, "The Nature of Information Ties and Development of Technology: An Integration of Information Processing and the Strength of Weak Ties," in *Advances in Global High-Technology Management*, vol. 5, Part B, ed. by L. Gomez-Mejia and M. Lawless (Greenwich, CT: JAI Press, 1995), 3–29; Lawrence Gales, Pamela Porter, and Dina Mansour-Cole, "Innovation Project Technology, Information Processing and Performance: A Test of the Daft and Lengel Conceptualization," *Journal of Engineering Technology Management* 9 (1992): 303–38.
6. Peter Pae, "Big Company Tactics Spur Turnaround at Small Firm," *The Wall Street Journal* (August 15, 1989), B1.
7. J. Brockner, "The Effects of Work Layoffs on Survivors: Research, Theory and Practice," in *Research in Organizational Behavior*, vol. 10, ed. by B. M. Staw and L. L. Cummings (Greenwich, CT: JAI Press, 1988), 213–55; D. Mansour-Cole and L. Gales, "Work Groups and Transition Events: Understanding the Effects of Commitment, Cohesion and Climate on Employee Justice Perceptions" (paper presented at the Academy of Management Meetings, Vancouver, B.C., Canada, 1995).
8. Paul Hersey and Kenneth Blanchard, "Change and the Use of Power: The Management of Change, Part I," *Training and Development Journal* 26 (1972), 6–10; David Nadler, "Concepts for the Management of Organizational Change" in *The Management of Organizations*, ed. by M. Tushman, C. O'Reilly, and D. Nadler (New York: Harper & Row, 1989), 490–504.
9. Stephen H. Wildstrom, "Laptops for the Desktop," *Business Week* (July 3, 1995): 18; Stephen H. Wildstrom, "Tony Printer for the Home," *Business Week* (May 15, 1995): 24.
10. M. Tushman, W. Newman, and E. Romanelli, "Convergence and Upheaval: Managing the Unsteady Pace of Organization Evolution," *California Management Review* (1986): 29.
11. E. Romanelli and M. Tushman, "Organizational Transformation as Punctuated Equilibrium: An Empirical Test," *Academy of Management Journal* 37 (1994): 1141–66.
12. Sherman Stratford, "A Master Class in Radical Change," *Fortune* (December 13, 1993): 82–90.
13. H. Mintzberg, "The Pitfalls of Strategic Planning," *California Management Review* (Fall 1993): 32–47; R. Moss Kanter, B. Stein, and T. Jick, *The Challenge of*

Organizational Change: How Companies Experience It and How Leaders Guide It (New York: Free Press, 1992).

14. K. Kerwin, "Rumble in Buick City," *Business Week* (October 1, 1994): 42–43; K. Kerwin, "Fixing G.M.: Pages from a Radical Repair Manual," *Business Week* (November 16, 1992): 46.

15. See Brockner in note 7; See Mansour-Cole and Gales in note 7; R. Sutton, K. M. Eisenhardt, and J. V. Jucker, "Managing Organizational Decline: Lessons from Atari," *Organizational Dynamics* 14 (Spring 1986): 17–29; D. C. Feldman and C. Leana, "Managing Layoffs: Experience at the *Challenger* Disaster Site and the Pittsburgh Steel Mills," *Organizational Dynamics* (Summer 1989): 52–64; R. L. Daft, *Organization Theory and Design*, 4th ed. (Saint Paul, MN: West Publishing, 1992): 473–74.

16. Julia Flynn, "That Burning Sensation at Glaxo," *Business Week* (October 3, 1994): 76–78.

17. Christopher Power, "Flops," *Business Week* (August 16, 1993): 76–82; Edwin Mansfield, J. Rapaport, J. Schnee, S. Wagner, and M. Hamburger, *Research and Innovation in Modern Corporations* (New York: Norton, 1993).

18. H. Fersko-Weiss, "The High-Tech Hall of Shame: Products We Have Known and (not quite) Loved," *High Tech Marketing* 63 (July 1987): 36–41; S. Wilkinson, "Boom and Bust in Toyland," *Working Women* (September 1988): 110–12, 222–23.

19. See Gales, Porter, and Mansour-Cole in note 5; Eric von Hippel, *The Sources of Innovation* (New York: Oxford University Press, 1988); Lowell W. Steele, *Managing Technology* (New York: McGraw-Hill, 1989); F. Axel Johne and Patricia Snelson, "Success Factors in Product Innovation: A Selective Review of the Literature," *Journal of Product Innovation Management* 5, (1988): 114–28; Modesto A. Maidique and B. J. Zirger, "A Study of Success and Failure in Product Innovation: The Case of the U.S. Electronics Industry," *IEEE Transactions in Engineering Management* 31 (1984): 192–203; see Daft in note 15.

20. Donald Gerwin and Harvey Kolodny, *Management of Advanced Manufacturing Technology* (New York: John Wiley & Sons, Inc., 1992); James W. Dean, Jr., and Gerald I. Sussman, "Organizing for Manufacturing," *Harvard Business Review* (January/February 1989): 28–36.

21. William J. Cook, "Ringing in Saturn," *US News & World Report* (October 22, 1990): 51–54.

22. Stephanie Overman, "Saturn Teams Working and Profiting," *HRMagazine* (March 1995): 72–74; David Woodruff, "At Saturn What Workers Want Is . . . Fewer Defects," *Business Week* (Special Industry/Technology Issue, December 2, 1992): 117–18.

23. David Woodruff, "Where Employees Are Management: Commitment Equals Empowerment at Saturn," *Business Week* (Special Industry/Technology Issue, December 2, 1992): 66.

24. Amanda Sinclair, "The Tyranny of a Team Ideology," *Organization Studies* 13 (1992): 611–26.

25. D. Keith Denton, "Process Mapping Trims Cycle Time," *HRMagazine* (February 1995): 56–61; Thomas Stewart, "GE Keeps Those Ideas Coming," *Fortune* (August 12, 1991): 41–49.

26. See Stewart, p. 48, in note 25.

27. See Dean, Jr., and Sussman in note 20.

28. Richard Beckhard, *Organizational Development* (Reading, MA: Addison-Wesley, 1969), 9–14; Wendel L. French and Cecil Bell, *Organizational Development: Behavioral Science Interventions for Organizational Improvement* (Upper Saddle River, NJ: Prentice Hall, 1995).

29. Don Bryant, "Action Research and Planned Change," in *Managing Organizational Change*, ed. by Roy McLennan (Upper Saddle River, NJ: Prentice Hall, 1989): 146–47.

30. James Smither, "An Examination of the Effects of an Upward Feedback Program over Time," *Personnel Psychology* (1995): 1–34.

31. E. Schein, *Process Consultation: Its Role in Organizational Development* (Reading, MA: Addision-Wesley, 1969).

32. Based on the following articles: Shari Caudron, "Diversity Ignites Effective Work Teams," *Personnel Journal* 73 (September 1994): 154–63; Andrew Martin, "Man Charges Harassment at Sensitivity Training," *Chicago Tribune* (September 8, 1994), C1; Daniel Howes, "More Firms Investing in Diversity Training," *Detroit News* (May 19, 1994), E1; Melissa Lee, "Diversity Training Brings Unity to Small Company," *The Wall Street Journal* (September 2, 1993), B2.

33. Charles Handy, *The Age of Unreason* (Boston, MA: Harvard Business School Press, 1989); Thomas A. Stewart, "The Search for the Organization of Tomorrow," *Fortune* (May 18, 1992): 92–98.

34. For example: Rosabeth Moss Kanter, *When Giants Learn to Dance* (New York: Simon & Schuster, 1989); Tom Peters, *Thriving on Chaos* (New York: Alfred A. Knopf, 1988); William H. Davidow and Michael S. Malone, *The Virtual Corporation: Structuring and Revitalizing for the 21st Century* (New York: HarperCollins, 1992); Michael Hammer and James Champy, *Engineering the Corporation: A Manifesto for Business Revolution* (New York: Harper Business, 1993).

35. R. Aguayo, *Dr. Deming: The American Who Taught the Japanese About Quality* (New York: Simon & Schuster, 1990); J. M. Juran, *Juran on Quality by Design* (New York: The Free Press, 1992).

36. See Aguayo in note 35; See Juran in note 35; James W. Dean, Jr., and James R. Evans, *Total Quality: Management, Organization, and Strategy* (St. Paul, MN: West Publishing, 1994).

37. Peter Senge, *The Fifth Discipline: The Art and Practice of the Learning Organization* (New York: Doubleday Currency, 1990); Henry P. Sims and Dennis A. Gioia, Jr., *The Thinking Organization* (San Francisco: Jossey-Bass, 1986); David A. Garvin, "Building a Learning Organization," *Harvard Business Review* 71 (1993): 78–91; Brian Dumaine, "Mr. Learning Organization," *Fortune* (October 17, 1994): 147–57.

38. See Dumaine in note 37.

39. Ibid.

40. Robert Duncan, "The Ambidextrous Organization: Designing Dual Structures for Innovation," in *The Management of Organizations*, vol. 1, ed. by Ralph Kilmann, Louis Pondy, and Dennis Slevin (New York: North-Holland, 1976), 167–88; Edward F. McDonough III and Richard Leifer, "Using Simultaneous Structures to Cope with Uncertainty," *Academy of Management Journal* 26 (1983): 727–35; see Daft, pp. 271–72, in note 15.

41. See Nadler in note 8.

42. Tracy Kidder, *The Soul of a New Machine* (Boston: Little, Brown, 1981).

43. Faribouz Damanpour, "The Adoption of Technological, Administrative, and Ancillary Innovations: Impact of Organizational Factors," *Journal of Management* 13 (1987): 676–78.

Saving the Family Legacy at Motorola*

CEO Chris Galvin is the third family member to run Motorola since his grandfather Paul Galvin founded the company (then called Galvin Manufacturing) in 1928. The company was a high-tech darling of the 1980s and was recognized with the Malcolm Baldrige Quality Award in 1988. However, the company once known for innovative, high-quality products stumbled badly in the mid-1990s and has yet to recover. A look at the situation and some of the missteps that Galvin has taken illustrate the difficulty in changing a large, complex organization.

There was a time when Motorola was considered a leader in the development of radio and telecommunication devices. The company had been a successful innovator in radios, cellular phones, chip design, and many other related fields. In the company's early days, it was a leader in car radios. It has made its mark with innovative two-way radio systems, micro chips (including codeveloping the Power PC, G-3, and G-4 for Apple) and cellular phones. But by the middle of the 1990s, the company was beginning to have difficulty competing. Nokia, Intel, Palm, Texas Instrument, and others have taken large chunks of Motorola's market in an increasingly difficult and competitive environment. For example, the company's share of the cellular phone market has shrunk to 13 percent, compared to Nokia's 35 percent. Granted, the entire cellular phone business went through a major decline beginning in late 2000, but only Lucent Technologies has slipped more than Motorola.

To make matters worse, under Galvin's leadership the company has made some bad product decisions, the worst of which was sticking with the ill-fated Iridium satellite telecommunications venture. The system was supposed to make telephone communication possible from virtually any point in the world without the development of costly ground-based infrastructure. However, the system was cumbersome and expensive, with phones costing $1,500. The company has also been slow to innovate in the digital communications and microprocessor arenas. A newly designed cellular phone, labeled the Shark, missed in the important European market. The phone was oddly shaped, large, and too heavy. Many other new products have also not been well received in the marketplace. The result has been devastating to shareholder value. In a little over a year, from May 2000 to July 2001, the company's stock lost 72 percent of its value.

It is hard to pin all of Motorola's problems on any one factor. The entire telecommunications industry has struggled since the middle of 2000, but Motorola's problems do seem more profound than those of other firms in the industry. Some critics have pointed to leadership as a problem. Galvin's style is ponderous, to the point that some people think he is indecisive. For example, he took several years to find a leader for the company's largest unit, the wireless phone business. Galvin has also been criticized for being too much of a "hands-off" manager, often trusting assistants to make the correct decisions and then failing to monitor their performance. He was slow to react to the poorly performing cellular phone business and was slow to pull the plug on Iridium, even as it cost the company $2.6 billion. He was wowed by the technology, even though there was no market.

In 1998 the company decided to combine all of the telecommunications-related businesses into one group called the Communications Enterprise. Although the decision made sense on the surface—many of the telecommunications devices were closely related and merging into combined products—the resulting unit was too large and bureaucratic to respond to market conditions. The company combined the worst elements of bureaucracy, a bad characteristic in industries that rapidly change, with poor decisions on delegating responsibilities. The unit's leader kept Galvin in the dark about declining performance. But when decisions did make their way up to Galvin, he was deliberate and methodical to a fault. He eventually fired the head of the Communications Enterprise, restructured the group into six units, and eliminated one level of managers, but the damage was done. Competitors had leaped ahead on several fronts.

Questions remain about the right person to lead Motorola and the right structure for the company. Some analysts suggest that Galvin should step down from the position of CEO and just assume the position of chairman of the board. He is smart and experienced in the industry, despite questions about his ability to lead the company on a day-to-day basis. Perhaps it is time to bring in an outsider for a fresh perspective on the company. Some have also asked what the appropriate structure is for the company. Should the company become flatter and more flexible? Should it shed some of its less profitable businesses to concentrate on core business? How do you compete in the rapidly changing and highly competitive high-technology businesses that are central to Motorola? ■

*This case is based largely on the following article: Roger O. Crockett, "Motorola: Can Chris Galvin Save His Family's Legacy?" *Business Week* (July 16, 2001), 73–78.

QUESTIONS FOR DISCUSSION

1. Research Motorola (www.motorola.com) and the telecommunications business. What are some of the key environmental conditions that the company faces? How should it structure to meet those conditions?

2. If Motorola restructures, what is likely to be the next change it would have to enact? Why?

PART
V
Integrative Cases

In this, the last section of the book, we present four cases that illustrate and integrate many of the concepts that have been covered in this text. Each case requires the reader to apply various organization theory concepts in an analytic framework.

The cases are based on actual incidents experienced by real organizations. Questions that follow the cases help the reader focus on key issues. However, these questions do not address all of the issues presented in each case. As you try to answer these questions you may want to think of other important points raised by the case. Expand your analysis to address the broad organizational perspective presented throughout the text.

The cases cover a variety of organizations—manufacturing and service companies, and successful, growing firms as well as troubled, declining firms. Each organization faces unique circumstances to which it must respond. Our strategic systems framework should allow you to identify and analyze the important variables involved in order to develop your appropriate strategies.

We have attempted to develop timely and relevant cases. However, we must note that events often preempt our best intentions to present current issues. You should go beyond these cases to see whether and how the conditions facing these firms may have changed since the cases were written. What have these companies done? What has changed in the environment?

Well-Connected — The Story of Earthlink, Inc.*

Today, communication plays a dominant role in the everyday lives of all of us. We are so accustomed to instant contact with virtually anyone or any place that we tend to take for granted that this contact will be available quickly, efficiently, and cheaply. Indeed, many of us don't remember the "old days" of operator-assisted phone calls or a time when there were only black-and-white television sets. It even seems eons ago that we were introduced to the "new-fangled" gadget called the computer. Now, of course, the old dial phones have been replaced by multifunction touch-tone phones that don't rely on operators; black-and-white television sets are almost a collector's item; and the computer is no longer a curiosity but an integral part of our lives. We would be hard put to imagine our workaday world without these modern means of staying in touch.

Perhaps no other form of communication affects our lives more than the computer and its connection to the Internet. This connection is a major avenue for communication, both personal and business, and the establishment and maintenance of this connection is truly big business today. One of the rising stars in this business is EarthLink, Inc., a company that is still relatively new in this vital arena of being "well connected" to the Internet but which is, nonetheless, becoming a major player in the field.

COMPANY HISTORY

The company was founded by Sky Dayton in 1994 when he was only 22 years old. Although he never attended college, Dayton had the determination and computer savvy that would have doubtless served him well in a college curriculum. His determination drove him to found EarthLink after spending some 80 hours attempting to configure his computer for Internet access. From this pivotal personal experience with computer-Internet interface has come a thriving business today, with Sky Dayton serving as chairman of its board of directors.

The company has seen phenomenal growth since its first member logged on to its 10 modems in July 1994 and the company generated gross revenue of $100,000 in that first year. An alliance with UUNET in August of 1995 made EarthLink an instant nationwide provider of dial-up access in 98 cities, and the following July a partnership with PSINet brought access to Canada, giving the company full North American coverage.

The year 1996 saw more moves by the company in its efforts to become a more prominent part of the "computer-Internet" world. In September, EarthLink joined with Microsoft to distribute Internet Explorer in return for placement of EarthLink by Microsoft on the Windows95 desktop, and the company began construction on a facility capable of serving over one million users of fiber optic technology. It also saw its membership swell to 200,000 during this time and enjoyed the recognition of being named Internet Company of the Year by the Southern California Software Industry Association.

To provide the additional capital it now needed, EarthLink went public with a listing on the NASDAQ in January of 1997. The number of members using Internet access approached 300,000, and employees numbered 640. The company launched its online mall by forming partnership with 800 Flowers, American Greetings, Barnes and Noble.com., FAO Schwartz, and Travelocity, among others. November saw the offering of 56K connections at some 390 points of presence (POPs) nationwide. The new speed was twice the prevailing 28.8 modem speed.

The year 1998 was also an eventful one for EarthLink. In February, the company entered into a long-term strategic partnership with Sprint that created a unified Internet service, opened up a market of millions of Sprint customers for EarthLink, and gave Sprint access to EarthLink's base of customers. EarthLink became the official Internet service provider for the National Football League as a result. In April, its 500,000 members made the company the largest independent service provider in the world. That month *Money* magazine gave EarthLink the title, "Technology Super Deal," a recognition for best overall value among Internet service providers based on speed, reliability, and widespread availability of local access numbers. The millionth customer signed up, months earlier than expected.

April 1999 saw the company announce Digital Subscriber Line (DSL) market trials in Los Angeles in conjunction with Pacific Bell, and in May, it co-branded high-speed Internet access by using Sprint's DSL network. Next, eBay signed on as a Premier Partner and went live on EarthLink's Personal Start Page, followed by similar action by MarketWatch. The year ended on a high note when *PC Consulting* gave EarthLink it's coveted MVP Award as the best Internet service provider.

A merger with MindSpring in February 2000 and the acquisition of OneMain in September marked further company growth. After moving its headquarters to Atlanta in February, EarthLink announced that it and Sprint would soon make wireless Internet access available to customers. The Time-Warner merger with America OnLine (AOL) offered EarthLink's high-speed Internet services over its cable lines as a condition of the merger, and EarthLink planned to begin providing broadband services in the second half of 2001.

Customer base rose to 4,700,000 in January 2001, and the company added 25 more DSL markets in the United States, to bring its total to 39. Mobile wireless service that allows laptops and other wireless devices to connect at speeds of up to 128 kilobits per second began in Atlanta, Phoenix, and San Diego in February, representing not only continued growth but technology advancement for the company.

This brief history serves as the backdrop for understanding of how EarthLink has experienced quite rapid and varied growth and how this growth has brought the company to its position in the industry. The following sections of the case deal with some of the most prominent areas of impact the company has experienced as a result.

MISSION STATEMENT

Like most modern organizations, EarthLink has found itself enveloped in a turbulent macro environment that has shaped the events that have had a major effect on not only the company itself but also on how and why it does business. As you can see from the brief history of the company, it has seen its meager beginnings mushroom into a complex organization operating in a complex, ever-changing macro environment that appears ever harder to gauge and manage.

The growth of the company has been largely in the form of partnerships and mergers with other organizations in the same or related fields. In order to bring some coherence and symmetry to these arrangements EarthLink has developed a statement of "grand" purpose, which we refer to in the text as a mission statement. It is stated below as an answer to "why" the company exists as an organization.

> To become the leading Internet provider in the world, as measured by the number of members, member satisfaction, and profitability.

The adoption of this statement of purpose is aimed at providing the basic framework for decisions about virtually every aspect of doing business, from designing the organization structure to making choices about future products and alliances. Without this guiding statement, uncoordinated and even contradictory choices might be made that could lead to considerable friction not only within the company but also with its relationship with its macro environment.

The company also believes that this mission statement provides the basis for improving the lives of people by allowing for better communication and enables its employees and shareholders to prosper. It is, thus intended to be a platform for building and maintaining sound internal and external relationships with its various constituencies.

This mission statement flows from a set of core values and beliefs of the company that has come to play a vital role in just how the company does business. These values are expressed here to show how the mission statement flows from them.

CORE VALUES

1. We respect the individual, and believe that individuals who are treated with respect and given responsibility respond by giving their best.
2. We require complete honesty and integrity in everything we do.
3. We make commitments with care, and then live up to them. In all things, we do what we say we are going to do.
4. Work is an important part of life, and it should be fun. Being a good businessperson does not mean being stuffy and boring.
5. We love to compete, and we believe that competition brings out the best in us.
6. We are frugal. We guard and conserve the company's resources with at least the same vigilance that we would use in conserving our own personal resources.
7. We insist on giving our best effort in everything that we undertake. Furthermore, we see the difference in "good mistakes" (best effort, bad result) and "bad mistakes" (sloppiness or lack of effort).
8. Clarity in understanding our mission, our goals, and what we expect from each other is critical to our success.
9. We are believers in the Golden Rule. In all our dealings we will strive to be friendly and courteous, as well as fair and compassionate.
10. We feel a sense of urgency on any matters related to our customers. We are customer driven.

This statement of values is intended to guide management's decisions not only about the "why" of the organization but also about the "how" of its operations. Its implementation can serve as a measure of consistency in all of management's decisions and keep the organization's mission statement in sharp focus for all customers as well as other stakeholders. Value-based consistency, after all, is a mark of quality decision making.

INTERNET BILL OF RIGHTS

At EarthLink the slogan is "It's Your Internet," and the company takes this statement as its marketing mantra for dealing with its customers. It reflects the commitment of the company to provide the kind of service and products that it feels its customers are entitled to as users of the magic tool, the Internet. The vision of the company is reflected in its belief that the Internet exists *because* of customers, not just *for* customers. EarthLink maintains that the values contained in its proposed Internet Bill of Rights are the values that any customer should expect from any Internet service provider, and the company is on record as supporting these values wholeheartedly. It believes that if all members of the industry were to adopt and support this statement, everyone, from companies to customers, would benefit.

PROPOSED INTERNET BILL OF RIGHTS

1. You have the right to pure Internet access—to direct, easy access to the entire Internet, free from the cruel and unusual punishment of pop-up ads when you log on.
2. You have the right to log on and enjoy the Internet, whenever you please, without fear that your enjoyment will be interrupted by arbitrary disconnections.
3. You have the right to counsel, the right to speak with courteous and knowledgeable technical support representatives, toll-free, 24 hours a day, 7 days a week, 365 days a year.
4. You have inalienable right to privacy on the Internet. Your Internet service provider should never sell your personal information for profit, but should commit to protecting the privacy of that information. You also have the right to review the privacy policy of your service provider, which should be posted online for all to see.
5. You have the right to a fast Internet connection no matter where you live. Your service provider should support the latest V.90 standard 56K modems, so that doing what you want and getting what you need is as fast and efficient as possible.
6. You have the right to Internet access from thousands of local numbers nationwide. That protects you from unreasonable access charges—even while you travel.
7. You have the right to a service provider that fights to protect you from spam (all forms of annoying junk e-mail) and provides resources to help you protect yourself.
8. You have the right to an Internet service provider committed to doing everything it takes to help you get the most out of the Internet. You have a right to both the best technology and the best Internet education so that you know how to use that technology to enhance your experience online.
9. You have the right to express yourself to the world and join the Internet community by creating a personal home page, built with the support and assistance of your Internet service. Your service should provide you with all the necessary resources, along with Web space of no less than 6MB.
10. You have the right to be completely satisfied with your Internet service. If at any time, you're not satisfied with EarthLink, call us, and we will work with you to make you satisfied.

These are strong statements, indeed, for any company to make to and about its customers. To adopt and implement them goes a long way toward setting or affirming the direction that the company will take in pursuit of its mission. EarthLink believes just what it says.

COMPANY DIRECTORS AND OFFICERS

To implement company philosophy and to manage the production and marketing of its services, the company has established a seven-member board of directors and a management team consisting of some 14 officials. The following is a brief sketch of this management structure.

Board of Directors

Sky D. Dayton, who only 29 years old, serves as the board's chairman and has been a director since 1994.

Dayton is joined on the board by Charles G. Betty (age 44) who is also chief executive officer of the firm and has been on the board since 1996.

Michael S. McQuary (age 41) is president of Earthlink and has been a director since 2000.

The other directors are Robert M. Kavner (age 57); Linwood A. Lacy, Jr. (age 55); Phillip W. Schiller (age 40); and Reed E. Slatkin (age 52).

The Management Team

This board is supported by a management team whose members' backgrounds are described here:

Sky Dayton: The founder of EarthLink Network in 1994 was its chairman from May of that year till May of 1996. Prior to founding the company, he was a coowner of a computer graphics company; Café Mocha (a coffee house in Los Angeles); and Joe Café (a coffee house in Studio City, California). He also cofounded e-Companies and an Internet incubator and venture fund; he currently serves on a number of boards of directors of private companies.

Charles G. Betty (age 44); Chief executive officer and director; was named to the same post in EarthLink Network and served there until its merger with MindSpring.

Michael S. McQuary (age 41): President and member of the board of directors. He served as president of MindSpring as well as its chief operating officer, and was also a Board member until the merger with EarthLink. He has experience with Mobil Chemical Co. where he held a number of management positions. He is currently a member of the board of directors of Novient Inc, Artisan Network, and MDCM Inc.

Lee Adrean (age 49): Chief financial officer and executive vice president. He previously held positions in First Data Corporation and was president of Providian Corporation Agency Group.

Samuel R. Desimone, Jr. (age 41): Executive vice president, general counsel, secretary. Prior to joining EarthLink, he served in similar capacities with MindSpring. He has also been vice president of corporate development with Merix Corporation (manufacturer of printed circuit boards) and prior to that assignment was in private practice in Portland, Oregon.

William S. Heys (age 51): Executive vice president of sales. He has served as vice president of business development and business services; senior vice president of sales for EarthLink Network and vice president of EarthLink Network's relationship with

Sprint. He has also held a variety of positions in executive sales and management in other computer-related companies.

Brinton O. Young (age 49): Executive vice president, marketing and corporate strategy. He served as senior vice president of marketing of EarthLink Network as well as its vice president for strategic planning. He also had his own consulting firm specializing in high-growth industries.

Linda Beck (age 37): Executive vice president, operations. She is responsible for all of EarthLink's operations groups which includes development, system administration, MIS, and network operations. She has held responsible positions in operations at MindSpring and Netcom, as well as Sybase, GTE, and Amdahl.

Carter Calle (age ?): Executive vice president, call center operations. He has served in this capacity since September 2000 and has served EarthLink in various capacities since 1995.

Jon M. Irwin (age 40): Executive vice president, member experience. He has served in a variety of positions, including executive vice president of operations, senior vice president of broadband services, and vice president of customer support.

Michael C. Lunsford (age 33): Executive vice-president of broadband services. He also served in this capacity for EarthLink Network where he was vice president of special projects. Before joining the management team, Mr. Lunsford was a director.

Veronica J. Murdock (age 37): Executive vice president, acquisitions and integration. She has served EarthLink as executive vice president of member support and vice president of member support and services. Her prior experience is with multimedia companies, visual effects and teleportation, and teleproduction studios.

Gregory J. Stromberg (age 48): Executive vice president of employee services. Prior to joining EarthLink in 2000, he held a number of executive positions at MindSpring.

Lance Weatherby (age 40): Executive vice president, EarthLink Everywhere, which includes responsibility for providing access to the Internet from anywhere in the world and across all platforms, as well as researching and selecting new technologies and bringing them to market. Prior to assuming this position in November 2000 he had held a number of executive positions in EarthLink and has also held marketing positions at Mobil.

From its headquarters in Atlanta, this relatively young and energetic management team oversees the by-now far-flung company that is EarthLink. From its initial venture into the world of the Internet has come a company that offers a rich variety of Internet-related services and has gained widespread recognition as one of the best in the business. Indicative of this recognition is the 1999 PC Computing MVP Award as the Best Internet Service Provider, which the company won in 1999.

As the brief description shows, EarthLink is a young, but well-experienced, group of executives who have been chosen to guide the company's operations.

COMPANY SERVICES

Perhaps the bellwether service that EarthLink offers its customers is dial-up Internet access plans offered under its Home Services umbrella. One of the most popular plans offers ready and reliable access to over 5,000 local telephone numbers in the United States and Canada. The EarthLink Gold plan offers members VIP service, including priority technical support, an additional e-mail account, and additional free software.

EarthLink 800 is a plan that provides toll-free access to the Internet from anywhere in the continental United States through over 2,300 access numbers. This makes

Internet access quite convenient for members who travel frequently and who have a need to stay in touch through the Internet. International roaming is even available for EarthLink Sprint customers for a nominal extra charge.

Additional e-mail boxes are available, as are 6MB of Web space, and a personal start page for each additional box through the Family Pack plan. This offering is aimed at providing Internet access to more users without the necessity of having separate member accounts.

EarthLink has also devised a set of service plans that appeal to the business sector of its membership. These plans are tailored to fit the unique needs of the business client base, although they contain many of the popular features that personal account holders value.

Dial-up Internet access is available to the business client, as is EarthLink Biz DSL (digital subscriber lines) to take advantage of the faster access that it provides. The plan also provides a wide range of other high-speed access options.

The mobile services plan allows the business customer "away-from-the-desk" access to the Internet as well as the use of e-mail. There is no need to be tied down to a telephone line to conduct business.

More and more business customers are beginning to employ broadband technology to speed up their Internet access—dial-up methods are simply not capable of meeting many of today's information needs. Using the broadband technology, the user is "always on," either through wire or custom-built circuits. EarthLink has provided this latter means to over 99 percent of the country.

The ability to have one's own Web page is gaining popularity among all types of users, and many consider the Web page to be a necessity for the business client. EarthLink addresses this need by its simple-to-use Click-n-Build program that lets the user employ a set of templates to put together a personalized page. For clients who demand a more sophisticated page, EarthLink will "broker" arrangements with providers who have expertise in this area because the company does not have a department devoted to this service.

EarthLink Sprint will help its customers register their domain names so that their sites get the maximum exposure. Otherwise, the Web site can easily be "lost in cyberspace."

This brief description shows that EarthLink is more than a "dial-up" Internet company, and it is continuing to expand its list offerings to its customers. The company's marketing efforts take two basic avenues: the Partner Program and direct referrals from present customers.

The Partner Program

The Partner Program is a plan by which EarthLink combines its software with the goods and services of other leaders in the Internet business, in an attempt to maximize benefits for both. About 75 percent of the company's marketing efforts takes this approach.

The OEM (original equipment manufacturers) program component is aimed at combining EarthLink as part of the "package" that manufacturers offer. National retailers promote and distribute EarthLink products and services, and cobranding with companies allows for mutual promotion.

EarthLink's present members can receive Internet access time and other valuable rewards by simply getting others to "join the family." This program involves about 25 percent of the company's marketing efforts and, together with the Partner Program, constitutes the way the company goes about getting its product and services to the market.

Of particular interest to many Internet users, especially to those who use e-mail, is the amount of "junk mail," or spam as it is commonly called, that clutters up the system. It can be quite annoying and even unproductive for the user. To help deal with this undesirable part of the e-mail experience, EarthLink has developed the "Spaminator," an anti-spam device that prevents junk mail from reaching the computer, and it's offered free to EarthLink's customers.

Another free tool offered to customers is a Web-based device that helps the user make sure personal information is safe. Privacy is becoming ever more important to all Internet users as more and more transactions are carried out over the Internet, and so this can be a quite valuable tool. The company even lobbies for privacy rights, in keeping with the company's proposed Internet Bill of Rights.

The company even keeps Web site statistics that will let customers know how many "hits" their Web sites have received. This can certainly be a valuable tool in evaluating the effectiveness of Web sites.

These are representative tools that EarthLink offers, and it appears that the company is committed to keeping them "sharp."

COMPANY CULTURE

The values and beliefs expressed in the company's core values statement, as well as those contained in its proposed Internet Bill of Rights, reflect the basic way the company operates and how it fosters growth and innovation. The whole Internet business is almost by definition one in which "half-life" can be measured in terms of a few years or a few months. A perusal of current literature shows how turbulent the industry is. Internet-related companies have seen unprecedented success (although often not defined in terms of profit) followed almost immediately by failure. Employee layoffs, retrenchments, and bankruptcies mark their tenure in the business.

Perhaps one of the reasons for EarthLink's success in today's Internet world is its culture. The company stresses casualness and friendliness to accompany its professional relationships with its many stakeholders. The management team is relatively young, in a relatively young business. Perhaps this explains the forward-looking attitude that permeates the company. It is simply not bound by precedent; nor is it affected by experience in the old "bricks-and-mortar" world of communication. Indeed, the company was founded almost as an anti–status quo undertaking.

There is an atmosphere that fosters idea-sharing and the encouragement of doing something different — anything that stresses opportunity and professionalism within the company. This is support of the commitment to find ways to bring new technology to the forefront, rather than simply exploring ways to employ existing technology — a fundamentally different orientation where risk-taking is rewarded rather than penalized and where learning is a keynote for literally everyone associated with the firm.

This culture, then, is not unlike the entrepreneurship spirit that values individuality, innovation, and self-reliance. This is the same spirit that underlay much of early American industry, although EarthLink is a far cry from the companies of that era. Maintaining a culture based on these values can be a challenge for the company as it matures, because older, more experienced, companies often find themselves trying to reinvent themselves in order to maintain the values on which they were originally founded.

This culture is doubtless a main plank in the company's success framework and appears to be valued as such. Indeed, it plays a key role in the company's ability to compete with its chief rivals: America OnLine, Microsoft Network, Prodigy, Internet America, AT&T, BellSouth, Netzero, Juno, and Roadrunner.

COMPANY OUTLOOK

Basically, EarthLink expects to continue to improve its broadband business, increase profitability, and show that it can generate cash from its operations in 2001, according to the company. The customer base is anticipated to reach the 5-million mark during that year, with most of the growth coming from the broadband sector, although it expects its narrowband market to be relatively flat.

Continued emphasis on overall cost-containment is expected, as is more reliance on self-installation of broadband applications. Brand advertising is expected to offset the elimination of marketing in the narrowband sector.

To be sure, EarthLink has forged for itself a prominent place in today's wired world. The future belongs to those who are constantly aware of their environments (both micro and macro); who promote innovation, learning, and risk taking; and who can offer the kind and quality of service that meets the needs and tastes of an ever-increasing number of customers who are growing more and more dependent on the Internet. It remains to be seen if EarthLink can retain its place in this industry, but it's probably a good bet that it will. ■

---

*This case is largely based on information contained on Earthlink's Web page: www.earthlink.com

QUESTIONS FOR DISCUSSION

1. What macro environmental force(s) do you suspect might affect EarthLink's performance in the next 5 years? What might be the impact on the company's operations or product lines?
2. Evaluate the current management structure of the company. What suggestions would you make for changes to it?
3. What would you suggest as the standards by which to judge the success of EarthLink in the next 5 years?
4. What new products or services would you suggest for EarthLink?
5. What do you believe have been EarthLink's "keys to success"? Are they likely to change in the near future? If so, how? If not, why not?

Always Low Prices, Always Wal-Mart's Mantra*

Discount stores, such as Wal-Mart, are in fashion today, but that was definitely not the case even a few short years ago. Long viewed as places where shoppers were looking for bargains, not necessarily the latest fashions, discount merchants then appealed to bargain-basement seekers. There was definitely a segmented market based primarily on cheap prices that discount stores, almost by definition, mined. But all that has changed dramatically in the recent past.

With the economic downturn that the U.S. economy is facing, shoppers, many of whom must of necessity seek out bargains, are flocking to discount stores. What's more, it is becoming almost "fashionable" to shop there. No longer are long-time discount-store shoppers the only customers; they are being joined by those who are concerned about or even fearful of a slowing economy. Budget-tightening is affecting almost all income levels. Layoffs and slowdowns have caused many who once only considered purchases at Dillard's or the Gap and who only bought Tommy Hilfiger outfits to enter the movement to "down-shopping" at discount stores.

These "new" customers are buying all sorts of merchandise, from food to clothes, at a pace that has allowed discount stores to fare relatively well in a depressed economy. By some estimates, well over half of U.S. households shopped at dollar stores in 2000, and well-to-do shoppers are no longer surprised to see their neighbors also shopping for bargains. Down-shopping has a new following, and it seems to be growing.

Slow economic times are thus seen by discount stores as an opportunity to capitalize on this phenomenon. Properties once occupied by Montgomery Ward are being bought by Target, and Kmart brought back its famous "Blue Light Specials" in marketing moves it made just prior to declaring bankruptcy in 2002. This has to be bad news for department stores that have traditionally relied on "snob appeal" as their marketing advantage.

So, whether by necessity or reverse "snob appeal," shoppers from virtually all walks of life are making it possible for discount stores to enjoy increased sales while the more traditional department stores are seeing the declining sales and store closings that signal trouble. One of the leaders and prime beneficiaries of the bad fortunes of these department stores is Wal-Mart, a store that has become almost a household word for the new as well as the old discount shoppers.

THE WAL-MART STORY

The merchandising giant that we know today as Wal-Mart had its meager beginnings when its founder Sam Walton, a World War II veteran, opened a Ben Franklin department store in Newport, Arkansas, in 1950. Following a successful operation in that store, Sam founded his first Wal-Mart store in Rogers, Arkansas, in 1962 and later incorporated his operations as Wal-Mart Stores, Inc. on October 31, 1969.

The decade of the 1970s saw the company undergo significant changes. Operating from its headquarters in Bentonville, Arkansas, the company opened its first distribution center there. It offered its stock for trading as an over-the-counter issue and in

1972 was listed on the New York Stock exchange. It was during this decade that the company made its first two acquisitions as a means of expansion: In 1977, it acquired 16 Mohr-Value stores in Michigan and Illinois, and in 1978 it added the Hutcheson Shoe Company. The first pharmacy, auto service center, and jewelry divisions were established in 1978.

The first Sam's Club was begun in 1983, and U.S. Woolco Stores were acquired that same year. Continuing its expansion in the 1980 decade, Wal-Mart acquired Grand Central Stores, and its Supersaver units were established. It was also the decade when the now-famous Wal-Mart Greeters met their first customers at the doors.

Perhaps the decade of the 1990s was the most dramatic in the company's growth and development. It saw more acquisitions: Western Merchandisers, Inc. (1990); McLane Company (1990); Pace Warehouses (1993); Wertkauf (of Germany, 1998); Interspar (of Germany, 1999); and ASDA Group (in the United Kingdom, 1999). It was also the decade when the company became the number 1 retailer in the United States and entered the international market with the first Wal-Mart in Mexico. In 1992, Wal-Mart went to Puerto Rico, and then to Canada with the acquisition of 122 Woolco stores. Shortly thereafter, there were Wal-Mart stores in Argentina, Brazil, China, Germany, and the United Kingdom.

Even though the company received numerous honors during the decade, it also saw the passing of its founder, Sam Walton, on April 5, 1992, less than a month after former President George Bush had presented him with the prestigious Medal of Freedom. It was also the year that S. Robson Walton was named chairman of the board, and Wal-Mart replaced Woolworth on the Dow Jones Industrial Average. The decade ended on a high note when *Financial Times* ranked the Company the ninth most respected company in the world.

In 2000, Wal-Mart continued to receive numerous accolades given in recognition of its success and place in the industry. *Fortune* magazine recognized Wal-Mart as the fifth most admired company in America; as fifth on its Global Most Admired All-Stars list; as eightieth among the best companies to work for, and, in 2001, as the third most admired company in America.

So, the Wal-Mart of today is a far cry from the Ben Franklin store that Sam Walton opened in 1950. This success story must be counted as among the greatest in U.S. industry history. It truly is a testimony to what an idea of discount merchandising coupled with the "gung-ho" spirit that Sam instilled throughout every aspect of his company can produce.

The Company's Organization Structure

Sam Walton guided the company as its official head until his death in 1992, when his assets were divided among his family members, making them among the richest people in the world. Now the company is under the leadership of a 15-member board of directors chaired by S. Robson Walton, while David D. Glass heads the executive committee of the board. The board is supported by a group of 20 company officers who represent the basic divisions of the company and its support functions.

Board members serve on various committees that play vital roles in daily operations. Although Wal-Mart lists its senior officers in its annual report, the reporting relationships and communications channels are deliberately not depicted. According to the public affairs department at Wal-Mart headquarters, the company chooses not to have an organization chart because it would depict rigid relationships that, in fact, do not exist. Open communications—upward, downward, and lateral—typify the Wal-Mart organization. Both individuals and organizational subunits are granted as much authority as possible; senior officials are delegated the authority and autonomy to manage their respective functions as they see fit, provided they do so within the decision parameters set by the executive committee.

Because Wal-Mart is such a large organization with a very loose organizational structure, the integration and coordination of functions are critical. At the senior level, integration and coordination are partially accomplished by senior managers' visits to the local stores where operations are observed; questions are asked; and suggestions are elicited. At the Bentonville, Arkansas, headquarters, it is extremely rare to find even one-half of the senior managers present because most of them are in the field. On Saturdays, senior managers meet with Chairman Walton at headquarters to discuss the previous week's activities and to discuss future plans. Also, some lower-level managers are invited to make presentations about a particular merchandising tactic, new products offered, the success of a particular store, and so on. Generally, the range of topics covered at the Saturday meetings includes, but is not limited to, weekly sales reports on new store construction, distribution center operations, product mixes, and the functioning of company information systems. In short, senior managers' visits, combined with the Saturday meetings, do a good job of keeping everybody up-to-date on Wal-Mart activities.

Retail Divisions

Wal-Mart Operations are divided into four basic concepts or divisions:

Wal-Mart Discount Stores   The approximately 1,700 stores in this division range in size from 40,000 to 125,000 square feet and are organized into departments that offer a wide variety of merchandise, including clothing and shoes, curtains, fabrics and notions, housewares, hardware, electronics, home furnishings, small appliances, automotive accessories, garden equipment and supplies, sporting goods, toys, cameras, health and beauty aids, pharmaceuticals, and jewelry. These stores stock 80,000 items, on average, and employ approximately 150 personnel each.

Sam's Wholesale Clubs   The 470 Sam's Clubs are membership-only wholesale clubs that charge a membership fee of about $30 annually and appeal to small businesses and those looking for good prices on name-brand merchandise. They range in size from 110,000 to 130,000 square feet in size and employ an average of 125 people in each club. These stores offer bulk sales of such items as hard-good merchandise, some soft goods, institutional-size grocery items, jewelry, sporting goods, toys, and tires. The overall idea behind these clubs is to promote high-volume and turnover while minimizing overhead.

Supercenters   The 900 stores in this category range in size from 109,000 to 230,000 square feet; employ 350 associates per store; and are open 24 hours a day. They stock over 100,000 items, 30,000 of which are grocery items. They are aimed at meeting customer needs for "one-stop-shopping" and so their offerings are quite varied. General merchandise is joined by bakery goods, deli items, frozen goods, meat and dairy products, and fresh produce. Banks, hair salons, vision centers, portrait studios, and employment agencies are also to be found in these Supercenters. There are even Tire and Lube Expresses and Radio Grill restaurants located here.

Neighborhood Markets   These units employ 80–100 associates each and offer approximately 28,000 items for sale. The items range from fresh produce, deli foods, fresh meat and dairy products, health and beauty aids, drive-through pharmacies, pet supplies to stationery and paper goods. They are generally located in markets along with the Supercenters to offer a supplement to their food distribution network. They range in size from 42,000 to 55,000 square feet.

When sales of these various retail units of Wal-Mart are added up, the total is $191 billion for the fiscal year that ended January 31, 2001. These sales were generated by more than 1 million associates who operated in more than 3,500 stores in the United States and 1,000 units located in overseas markets. So, the more than one million customers who visit Wal-Mart stores each week seem to be able to find what they want and at prices that are attractive, in keeping with Sam Walton's promise of everyday low prices as a means of bettering the lives not only of the customers but of the communities in which the stores are located. This effort continued into 2001 when in April of that year, Wal-Mart opened two discount centers, one neighborhood store, and 13 supercenters.

Wal-Mart's Commitment to Communities

Sam Walton believed not only in giving customers a fair bargain for their purchases but in also giving back to the communities where his stores were located. He believed that this was a reflection of the values he represented not only as a businessman but as a person as well, and this commitment is being carried on by today's Wal-Mart.

To implement its community involvement, Wal-Mart established its Good Works program through which its associates raised about $190 million in 2000 for local community works. The company has invested $7.3 million in individual college scholarships for its associates, its local communities, and African-American and Hispanic students. More than $77 million has been contributed to these scholarships since 1979. Sam's Clubs and Wal-Mart stores have recognized more than 11,000 Teachers of the Year since 1996 by issuing $6.6 million in grants to their schools in their honor since the beginning of the program.

Wal-Mart also supports such community-based charities as the Salvation Army, whose kettles located at stores raised about $14 million in 2000. Additionally, associates have contributed more than $133-million to the United Way organizations in their communities since 1983. The company is also the largest corporate sponsor of the World War II Memorial Campaign.

Children's health issues also are of major importance to the company. As a leading supporter of these concerns, Wal-Mart has contributed more than $31 million to local hospitals by way of the Children's Miracle Network. The company's Missing Children's Network and its participation in the National Center for Missing and Exploited Children have resulted in the recovery of more than 1,800 missing children.

Cleaning up the environment ranks high on Wal-Mart's list of community concerns. Accordingly, not only has money been donated to local efforts, but the company's recycling efforts resulted in the collection of more than 12 million pounds of plastic and cardboard in 2000.

The company believes that its obligations lie in helping the local communities in which its stores operate, and so it relies heavily on decisions made at the local level to direct its efforts at community betterment. This is done in keeping with the belief that no one knows the local community and its needs better than those associates who live there, so more than 97 percent of the company's community betterment decisions are made locally. In 2001, community involvement funds totaled approximately $190 million.

WAL-MART'S COMMITMENT TO PEOPLE

Another firm commitment that Wal-Mart has made is to its associates. It is the leading employer of senior citizens, employing more than 134,000 of them companywide. A leading employer of disabled people, the company has been recognized as one of the top companies in the United States for providing a positive work environment for them. It also employs more than 140,000 African-Americans and 87,000 Hispanics nationwide. As a matter of fact, the company has been recognized by *Hispanic Magazine* and *Latina Magazine* as one of the best 100 companies in the United States for these employment practices. Its board of directors has two Hispanics and two women as members.

Both full-time and part-time employees are eligible for benefits that include health and dental insurance, stock-ownership, and retirement plans. These help complement the company's commitment to providing the kind of work environment that promotes diversity in the workforce, but one that is aimed at benefiting the associates and the company alike.

COMPANY CULTURE

One of the most valued assets of any company is its culture—the beliefs, attitudes, and customs that bind its members together. The inculcation of culture can create a cohesive group aimed at achieving group objectives.

Concern for the individual, whether the individual is a customer or an associate, is the cornerstone of Wal-Mart's culture. This emphasis is accompanied by open and free communication. Each Friday there are store meetings at which an associate at any level can pose questions and receive answers on subjects ranging from sales, costs, freight charges, to profit margins. There are not many companies that stress this cultural environment more than Wal-Mart.

Wal-Mart's slogan, "Our people make the difference," is more than rhetoric. Sam Walton believed firmly that by treating associates with respect and by showing them that both he and the senior managers cared, they would perform with the highest levels of efficiency, effectiveness, and commitment to the organization. This makes for a flexible, decentralized company that is capable of adjusting to changing conditions rapidly.

One cannot overestimate the role of Sam Walton on the development of this most remarkable corporate culture. Although he was a multibillionaire, Sam Walton was a very down-to-earth person—he drove a 1984 Ford pickup, and lived in a modest house. His work week was normally 6 days long and included his attendance (in his role of cheerleader!) at the Saturday morning senior-level management meetings. During the week he traveled to various Wal-Mart operations throughout the south and midwest where he could be found greeting customers, stocking shelves, or running a cash register. All of this made associates almost believe that they work for Sam Walton, not Wal-Mart, so his influence, once enormous, still can be seen today.

Walton firmly believed in what he called the Sundown Rule, by which he meant that things should not be put off, but should be done by the end of the day, whether it was to satisfy a customer or address the concerns of an associate. Customers were to be looked in the eye and asked if they could be helped if they came within 10 feet of an associate. This "Ten-Foot Attitude" was Sam's way of showing concern for customer satisfaction.

The famous Wal-Mart cheer might be heard at any time in any Wal-Mart store, and perhaps in many different languages. Sam got the idea for the cheer when he visited a tennis ball factory in Korea where the workers did a cheer and exercises together every morning. He modified what he saw to fit his company with his cheer that spells out "W-A-L-'Squiggly'-M-A-R-T-" and ends with "Who's Number One? The Customer!" Even customers are encouraged to join in when they hear this sound of enthusiasm. It is intended to show that people can have a good, relaxed time and get work done at the same time.

Sam Walton wanted to show his stores' customers that they were appreciated and that they could expect every associate to show gratitude for their presence in the stores. Hospitality was the "name of the game," and customer expectations would, indeed, be exceeded. Couple this spirit, gratitude, and service with "everyday low prices" and one can see the manifestation of corporate culture in everyday business transactions. After all, Sam believed that was of major importance to success.

So from the beginning Sam Walton instilled a deep-seated belief in fair treatment for all, in a "fun" environment, with low prices for goods and services in his effort to cultivate a more-than-satisfied group of customers and associates alike. It is a spirit that characterizes the company today, years after Sam Walton's death in 1992.

WAL-MART'S IMPACT ON MAIN STREET BUSINESS

Not all of Wal-Mart's venture into discount merchandising has been met with welcoming arms. In some communities where Wal-Mart stores have opened, they have been accused of siphoning off business from local establishments that have, in some cases been run for generations by the same family. These "traditional" retailers have shown resistance and resentment. Demonstrations against the company's moving into communities have occurred, in spite of Wal-Mart's promise of discount prices and more jobs for the community.

In some communities, Wal-Mart succeeded in repealing local "blue laws" that prevented Sunday operations, which forced local merchants to stay open 7 days a week and pay the required overtime to employees or see the loss of business that would result from resistance. Local customs, such as church attendance, were threatened; indeed, some saw the "Wal-Marting" of their communities as inherently undesirable. One community in Maine was the scene of a referendum to overthrow a zoning decision that would have allowed construction of a Wal-Mart store.

To make peace with those communities that have shown resistance to it, Wal-Mart has in some cases scaled back its "mega-store" plans and worked with locals to help preserve the environment, and, in a few instances, even canceled plans for moving into some communities.

In spite of some local pockets of resistance, the company has generally been quite successful in its efforts to expand its operations, both nationally and internationally, and plans call for this to continue.

WAL-MART'S DISTRIBUTION SYSTEM

Wal-Mart's distribution system is perhaps the most efficient and effective in the entire retail industry. Using the concept of backward integration. Wal-Mart first builds a distribution center in a rural or suburban area. After the distribution center is constructed, 30–40 Wal-Mart stores are constructed within a 600-mile radius. The company then uses its own fleet of trucks to deliver merchandise to the stores within this radius, thus allowing for store orders to be processed and delivered within 1 day.

Logistics, distribution centers, and transportation are the company's keys to being able to compete successfully in the discount market. The private fleet of trucks permits customized, cost-efficient deliveries to the stores, accommodating peak seasonal periods, night deliveries, and accelerated deliveries to maintain in-stock inventory based on just-in-time performance.

This distribution system is finely tuned to the specific needs of stores within a delivery radius and can be considered one of the company's "keys to success."

CUSTOMER SERVICE

Wal-Mart is committed to providing the best customer service in the retail business. Because of its distribution system and supplier relations, customers have the items they want when they want them. Merchandising and distribution experts within the Wal-Mart system identify those items most constantly in demand so that they are made part of the basic stock in both the distribution centers and individual stores.

Courtesy and service to the customer are trademarks of the Wal-Mart organization. Upon entering the store, each customer is welcomed with a friendly greeting by an official greeter, usually a retired person. The greeter, in addition to welcoming the customer, serves as a kind of "store directory" by answering questions about merchandise as well as department location. The company strongly believes that this initial contact goes a long way not in "educating" the customer but in conveying the feeling that the customer is really a valued "guest" in the store.

Beginning with Sam Walton, and continuing to the present, the company has always maintained the absolute necessity of monitoring the macro environment constantly to learn of any shifts there that might affect the company and how it operates. Sam was cognizant that customer needs change over time and that to be successful, the stores must be in a position to adapt to them. In short, his belief was that it was imperative to "know your customer."

COMMUNICATIONS TECHNOLOGY

State-of-the-art communications technology links together all facets of organizational life at Wal-Mart. One could say that Wal-Mart is "married to technology." For instance, right after the Saturday morning senior-level management meetings in Arkansas, executives often relay vital information to stores via the company's six-channel communications system. This system, linked to a mainframe computer, is capable of gathering store data on a daily basis, handling credit card transactions, keeping tabs on inventory and performing other essential functions. Within the distribution centers, bar codes are read by laser scanners to ensure that the right product goes to the right location in the right quantity.

This constant communication between distribution centers and stores makes it possible for management not only to know what's going on in the operations, but also to help ensure that coordination is achieved. This is an important cog in the wheel of communications and supply that lies at the heart of Wal-Mart's operations. This ability to keep stores constantly stocked with appropriate mix of products is a key success factor for the company.

PRODUCT MIX

When customers walk into a Wal-Mart store they immediately see a tremendous amount and variety of merchandise for sale. In general, the merchandise available is a mixture of heavily discounted name brands and even lower-priced "off-brands."

Wal-Mart believes in experimenting with new products or merchandising techniques at a few locations before adopting them for all stores. The new product sales and merchandising techniques are carefully monitored, and should they prove successful, they are then implemented at the other stores.

Wal-Mart has constantly expanded and upgraded the product mix in its stores to include stereos, televisions, microwave ovens, telephones, and other hard goods. Customers can have their film developed or their vision checked at many of the stores. Garden supplies, notions, clothing, cosmetics, and grocery items are just some of the products that are carried in response to customer desires for more "one-stop" shopping.

Because the company believes in allowing autonomy at the local level, store managers have the authority to buy and sell merchandise that reflects local customer preferences in a given area. Examples include crayfish pots in Louisiana stores and school logo items in stores located near colleges and universities. This delegation of decision making about product mix is in keeping with company philosophy that embraces participation by all associates in the everyday operation of the stores.

Store managers spend a considerable portion of each day walking around the stores and talking with associates about a variety of matters. The managers listen to suggestions, such as those about product mix; discuss improvements; and praise these associates for a "job well done." This technique not only is a source of information for management but a chance for them to constantly remind these associates of how important they are to the company and its success.

Wal-Mart has been fortunate in obtaining a steady stream of innovative ideas from its associates. It is common in the stores to have task forces, consisting of both managers and hourly associates, to evaluate new ideas and plan for future operations and products to be carried. This management style is doubtless responsible not only for keeping the product mix current, but also for showing appreciation for all associates regardless of their rank.

FUTURE CHALLENGES

Wal-Mart doubtless must be counted as one of the most innovative and successful merchandising companies in the world. It has changed the merchandising face of rural America as it has brought low-priced quality merchandise to many small towns that would otherwise be left with the necessarily limited stocks of merchandise in "mom-and-pop" stores traditionally found there. It has forced its competitors, such as Sears, for example, to rethink pricing and merchandising policies and techniques as exemplified in that company's "Everyday Low Prices" policy.

Throughout this success story, Sam Walton's management philosophy, especially his appreciation for customers and associates, has been thoroughly instilled throughout the company. Today, customers and associates are truly valued assets of the company, and it is on that basis that Wal-Mart is well poised to meet the challenges that future changes in the micro and macro environments will doubtless bring.

As the pressure for global competition increases, Wal-Mart will doubtless be faced with the necessity of adapting its policies and operations to an array of cultural, legal, and economic environments that are a far cry from those that nurtured its growth in its early stages. This will mean that the company must implement communication and delivery systems that are attuned to values that can be quite different from those in the United States.

The company, as mentioned, has seen exceptional growth in all aspects of its operations and this growth means that management must be kept in tune with an organization whose size will demand a sophisticated management-technology mix. Harnessing information about customer tastes, economic conditions, legal pressures, labor market conditions, and the like are far different for Wal-Mart today than when it began operations, and the pressure of size on management and communications will no doubt increase in the future.

Preserving the environment is also going to continue to be a force in Wal-Mart's future. Although the company has a good record on environmental concerns, note that there is now resistance in some quarters to companies like Wal-Mart, coming into communities and "destroying" what many locals consider sacrosanct lands.

Competitors have taken note of Wal-Mart and its merchandising practices in all but the priciest of department stores whose appeal is other than price. As customers have more choice for their low-price purchases at Sears and Target, for example, Wal-Mart no longer enjoys the luxury of being the "only game in town." The intensity of competition is something that must be counted as a hurdle for the company. Tomorrow's customer will probably buy more goods over the Internet, thus posing a challenge to the bricks-and-mortar stores that are Wal-Mart today, so the company might even have difficulty knowing who its competition is or where it is located.

Changing consumer tastes and habits will have to be monitored. The current practice of "down shopping" that has been a boon to Wal-Mart might prove to be a passing fad, especially if economic conditions permit broad-scale shopping for higher priced goods and services. If that happens in large enough measure, the basic foundation of the company could be undermined. As unlikely as this might appear, the company will be well advised to keep a close tab on consumer behavior, especially on that driven by snob appeal and the seemingly ceaseless demand for anything "new."

The track record of Wal-Mart for keeping Sam Walton's dream alive is a good one, indeed, and there is little, if any, current indication that the company will not be able to monitor its environments and keep abreast of them. It will be interesting to see whether "Always Low Prices, Always" is a mantra that can stand the test of time. ∎

---

*This case is based on information contained on Wal-Mart's Web pages: www.walmartstores.com, with minor portions extracted from "Wall-Mart Stores, Inc.: So Help Me Sam! by Eric Brockmann, Florida State University, which appeared in the fifth edition of this book.

QUESTIONS FOR DISCUSSION

1. What do you believe are the most important factors that have led to Wal-Mart's success?
2. What environmental factors do you think will have the most impact on the company in the next 5 years? Explain.
3. Explain how the company's culture has influenced its past and present success? Do you expect this culture will be more difficult to maintain in the future? Explain.
4. What suggestions would you make for the company to gain further market-share advantage over its competitors?
5. What suggestions would you make for the company as far as expansion is concerned?

Hewlett-Packard: Returning to the Garage

Hewlett-Packard (HP) is a leading global provider of computing, Internet, and intranet solutions; services; and communications products. Each area of operation has been recognized for excellence in quality and support. Taken separately, HP's businesses are individually strong but when put together, they create a powerful competitive advantage and a unique market position.[1]

HP worked hard at reinventing the company during the 1998–2001 period. They went back to their roots of invention, to their radical beginnings in the original HP garage. This "garage" concept refers to the place where Hewlett-Packard was started in 1939. Their goal was to make the total customer experience so engaging and rewarding that customers not only buy from HP again and again, but also enthusiastically recommend HP to others.

HP's overall business strategy is twofold. First, they seek to compete against more narrowly focused competitors in the following product and services categories: servers, software, storage, services and support, PCs and workstations, personal information appliances, and printers and supplies. Second, they seek to leverage the depth and breadth of their product and services portfolio across three business segments through the development of new solutions, markets, and ecosystems at the intersection of e-services, information appliances, and an always-on Internet infrastructure.[2]

BACKGROUND

William Hewlett and David Packard founded Hewlett-Packard in a Silicon Valley garage in 1939. The company was long governed by a few simple maxims: Treat employees with respect, plan for the long term, and hold bureaucracy to a minimum by dividing business units when they get too big.[3] Those ideas served HP well for decades, but by the mid-1990s, the firm was stagnating. In mid-1999 when HP experienced a significant change in management with the hiring of a new CEO, Carly Fiorina, the company had splintered into 83 autonomous businesses that had no overarching strategy. Most of the units exercised nearly total authority over their budgets, often to the detriment of broader goals.[4]

Hewlett-Packard is headquartered in Palo Alto, California. As of 2001, they had over 88,000 employees worldwide working in more than 540 sales and support offices and distributorships in over 120 countries.

HEWLETT-PACKARD CORPORATE OBJECTIVES

Founders Bill Hewlett and David Packard helped craft the first set of corporate objectives in 1957 and the document has remained at the center of the company's management style. Hewlett-Packard feels that the achievements of their organization result from the combined efforts of all individuals in the organization working toward common objectives. They feel that the objectives they established initially and have transformed over the years are realistic, clearly understood, and reflect Hewlett-Packard's basic character and personality.

HEWLETT-PACKARD'S CORPORATE OBJECTIVES[5]

1. PROFIT—"To achieve sufficient profit to finance our company growth and to provide the resources we need to achieve our other corporate objectives."
2. CUSTOMERS—"To provide products and services of the highest quality and the greatest possible value to our customers, thereby gaining and holding their respect and loyalty."
3. FIELDS OF INTEREST—"To participate in those fields of interest that build upon our technologies, competencies, and customer interests, that offer opportunities for continuing growth, and that enable us to make a needed and profitable contribution."
4. GROWTH—"To let our growth be limited only by our profits and our ability to develop and produce innovative products that satisfy real customer needs."
5. OUR PEOPLE—"To help HP people share in the company's success which they make possible; to provide them employment security based on performance to create with them an injury-free, pleasant and inclusive work environment that values their diversity and recognizes individual contributions; and to help them gain a sense of satisfaction and accomplishment from their work."
6. MANAGEMENT—"To foster initiative and creativity by allowing the individual great freedom of action in attaining well-defined objectives."
7. CITIZENSHIP—"To honor our obligations to society by being an economic, intellectual and social asset to each nation and each community in which we operate."

HEWLETT-PACKARD PRODUCTS AND SERVICES

As of October 31, 2000, HP's major business segments included imaging and Printing Systems, Computing Systems, and Information Technology Services.[6]

- *Imaging and Printing Systems* provides laser and inkjet printers (both monochrome and color), copiers, scanners, all-in-one devices, personal color copiers and faxes, digital senders, wide- and large-format printers, print servers, network-management software, networking solutions, digital photography products, imaging and printing supplies, imaging and software solutions, and related professional and consulting services.

- *Computing Systems* provides a broad range of computing systems for the enterprise, commercial, and consumer markets. The products and solutions range from mission-critical systems and software to personal computers for business and home. Major product lines include UNIX® and PC servers, desktop and mobile personal computers, workstations, software solutions and storage solutions.

- *Information Technology (IT) Services* provides consulting, education, design and installation services, ongoing support and maintenance, proactive services like mission-critical support, outsourcing, and utility-computing capabilities. Financing capabilities include leasing, automatic technology-refreshment services, solution financing and venture financing. HP's IT Services strategy reflects today's inextricable linking of business transformation and IT implementation. They offer a complete life cycle of services—planning, implementation, support, and ongoing operations—that customers can choose from to take advantage of emerging technologies and business models.

HEWLETT-PACKARD COMPETITION

Hewlett-Packard encounters aggressive competition in all areas of its business activity. Its competitors are numerous, ranging from some of the world's largest corporations to many relatively small and highly specialized firms. HP competes primarily on the basis of technology, performance, price, quality, reliability, brand, distribution, and customer service and support.[7] Its reputation, the ease of use of its products, the ready availability of multiple software applications, the always-on Internet infrastructure offering, and its customer training, services, and support are also important competitive factors.

The markets for each of the three principal segments are characterized by vigorous competition among major corporations with long-established positions and a large number of new and rapidly growing firms.[8] Product life cycles are short, and to remain competitive HP must develop new products and services, periodically enhance existing products and services and compete effectively on the basis of the factors listed earlier. In addition, the company competes with many of its current and potential partners. The successful management of these competitive partner relationships will be critical to future success. HP also anticipates that it will have to continue to adjust prices on many of its products and services to stay competitive, and thus effectively manage financial returns with correspondingly reduced gross margins.

CEO SEARCH PROCESS AND TRANSITION

The CEO's job is getting harder and more complicated. CEO tenure in office is growing shorter. More CEOs are being recruited from outside the company and the industry. The career paths for the development of CEOs are changing. It is simply a more difficult task to replace a CEO today than it used to be.[9]

The management succession program that brought in Carly Fiorina of Lucent as the new CEO at Hewlett-Packard in mid-1999 was one of the most publicized of its kind—and probably deserved the press attention it received. The retiring CEO, Lewis Platt, had been a vigorous, long-term executive who spent the last few years reorganizing the company and trying out new things and new people. But Hewlett-Packard remained a stolid conservative trying to play catch-up in its explosive industry. Its competition had changed, its products were new, and its customers insisted on radically different services.[10]

The succession and the way it was handled contained some classic moves deserving of special recognition. First, it involved some extremely delicate coordination between the exiting CEO and the board. They apparently worked together harmoniously and constructively, with the board playing the power role. Second, the board did an exhaustive job of preparing a job specification for the kind of incoming CEO they would like to have and what qualities and talents were needed to carry the company into the future.[11] The four attributes the board deemed to be of primary importance for their new CEO were these:

1. The ability to conceptualize and communicate sweeping strategies
2. The operations savvy to deliver on quarterly financial goals
3. The power to bring urgency to an organization
4. The management skills to drive a vision through the company

Third, the board delved deeply into the qualifications of a variety of candidates, both within and outside the company. They reviewed 300 persons, then narrowed the field to four, and ultimately chose Carly Fiorina. Fourth, the board had been so continuously and intimately involved in the whole process that it was fully committed to the support of the new CEO.

CARLY FIORINA

Carly Fiorina is the chairman, president, and chief executive officer of Hewlett-Packard. She was named president and CEO on July 17, 1999, succeeding Lewis E. Platt, who previously had announced his intention to retire. Carly Fiorina was also elected to the company's board of directors on July 23, 1999, and named chairman of the board on September 22, 2000. She is the first woman to hold the three top positions in a computer company.

Background

Prior to joining HP, Fiorina spent nearly 20 years at AT&T and Lucent.[12] She served as president of Lucent's Global Service Provider Business during which time the division dramatically increased its growth rate, rapidly expanded its international revenues, and gained market share in every region across every product line.[13] She also spearheaded the planning and execution of Lucent's 1996 initial public offering and spin-off from AT&T, one of the largest and most successful IPOs ever.

Fiorina holds a bachelor's degree in medieval history and philosophy from Stanford University, a master's degree in business administration from the University of Maryland, and a master of science degree from MIT. For the third year in a row, Fiorina topped *Fortune* magazine's list of the most powerful women in American business.

Fiorina was well aware of the challenges when she joined HP, but she also saw the huge untapped potential.[14] She had grown to admire the company while working as an HP intern during her years studying medieval history at Stanford University. Later, as president of the largest division of telecommunications equipment maker Lucent Technologies Inc., she learned the frustrations of buying products from highly decentralized HP. When HP's board asked her to take over, she jumped at the chance to show off her management abilities.

Thoughts on Leadership

Carly Fiorina brings to Hewlett-Packard years of experience, a passion for change and success, and a heart for people. In a commencement speech she gave at MIT, Fiorina commented on her viewpoints about leadership and what she feels are important qualities for a chief executive to have.

Fiorina believes that leadership in this new landscape is not about controlling decision making. She thinks that no one has time to control decision making. Her opinion is that leadership is about creating the right environment. It's about enablement, empowerment, setting guidelines and boundaries and parameters, and then setting people free. However, Fiorina feels that leadership is not about hierarchy or title or status. She thinks that it is more about having influence and mastering change. Leadership is not about bragging rights or battles or even the accumulation of wealth; it's about connecting and engaging at multiple levels. It's about challenging minds and capturing hearts. Leadership in this new era is about empowering others to decide for themselves in order to reach their full potential. Leaders can no longer view strategy and execution as abstract concepts but must realize that both elements are ultimately about people.[15]

She states, "Now, of course, traditional aspects of being a Chief Executive will continue to be important, like understanding the business or the institution, understanding the numbers or the assets, pushing the right levers to bring about the right results."[16] But the most magical and tangible and ultimately most important ingredient in the transformed landscape is people. The greatest strategy in the world, the greatest financial plan in the world, the greatest turnaround in the world is only going to be temporary if it isn't grounded in people.

Importance of Diversity

Carly Fiorina firmly believes in people and is convinced that diversity nourishes the soul of companies, inspires creativity and inventiveness.[17] She stresses the need to recognize the value in diversity. She states, "Not everyone must be the same. In fact, the opposite is true. To build a great team we need to encourage differences. Whether, as a nation, as an industry, as a company, we must start valuing differences. All the way—not just part way."[18]

Diversity is the existence of many unique individuals in the workplace, marketplace, and community that includes men and women from different nations, cultures, ethnic groups, lifestyles, generations, backgrounds, skills, and abilities. HP welcomes the many dimensions of diversity. HP wants all employees to come to work in an environment that welcomes who they are so that in turn, they can contribute their best to HP's success.

HP has recognized that creating a diverse, inclusive work environment is a journey of continuous renewal. Each step in the process is significant; together the steps have created a diversity value chain upon which they company is building its winning global workforce and workplace.[19] HP has made progressive strides over the years to improve on the diversity within its workplace so that an environment conducive to innovation and creativity can exist.

Diversity is a key driver of HP's success.[20] It is fueled by personal leadership from everyone in the company. A person's behaviors and actions come from conviction; diversity and inclusion are a conscious part of how HP runs its business. Diversity is woven into the fabric of the company; it is an intrinsic part of the corporate nature. Diversity is a key contributor to fulfilling the vision for HP—a winning e-company with a shining soul.

RESTRUCTURING AT HEWLETT-PACKARD

When Fiorina took the reins of HP, it was a company bedeviled by inconsistent financial performance. Seeking to reinvent HP, she evoked its original "garage" spirit and launched a $200 million brand and advertising campaign that included a new logo emblazoned with the word "invent." She also cast aside HP's division into four semi-autonomous business enterprises, each with its own president and CEO, in favor of a more cohesive structure with one chief executive: Carly Fiorina.[21]

At the time of the restructuring Fiorina said, "I could see that HP was at a pivotal point. It's a unique company at a unique time in its history, a company poised to take full advantage of the Internet Age. I want to help the company achieve the right balance between preserving the core values of HP, the soul of the place that has been so special and so revered, but at the same time, reinvent the business in important ways."[22]

Not content to tackle one problem at a time, Fiorina was out to transform all aspects of HP at once, current economic slowdown be damned. That meant strategy, structure, culture, compensation—everything from how to spark innovation to how to streamline internal processes. Such sweeping change is tough anywhere, and doubly so at tradition-bound HP. The reorganization will be "hard-to-do—and there's not much DNA for it at HP," says Jay R. Galbraith, professor at the Institute for Management Development in Lausanne, Switzerland.[23]

To achieve this, Fiorina dismantled the decentralized approach honed throughout HP's 64-year history. Most dramatically, she launched a plan to consolidate HP's 83 independently run businesses into only 12. She also aligned the reduced number of divisions into two "front-end" groups that would focus on customer activities, such as marketing and sales, and two "back-end" organizations devoted strictly to designing and making computer and printer products.[24] One so-called back-end unit develops and builds computers, and another focuses on printers and imaging equipment. The back-end divisions hand products off to two "front-end" sales and marketing groups that attempt to sell the products—one to consumers, the other to corporations. The theory: The new structure will boost collaboration, giving sales and marketing executives a direct pipeline to engineers so products are developed from the ground up to solve customer problems. This is the first time a company with thousands of product lines and scores of businesses has attempted a front-back approach, a strategy that requires laser focus and superb coordination.[25]

In her first 3 months as HP's chief executive, Fiorina unleashed a new advertising campaign, starring herself and emphasizing the HP brand over the former hodgepodge of product names. She tore up the company's profit-sharing program in favor of a strict performance-based bonus system.[26] Ms. Fiorina wants HP eventually to be known for three main specialties: Internet infrastructure such as servers; information appliances, from PCs and hand-held devices to "intelligent" printers; and e-services that will anticipate users' needs.[27]

Fiorina states that the new "HP brand is a promise to our customers and our partners about who we are, where we've been, and where we intend to go. It's a reminder to the people of HP about our inventive capability, returning, in a way, to the "Rules of the Garage"—reflecting the garage in which HP was born. You'll see it in ads, in poster form in employees' cubicles, and it's actually become a popular item among our customers, too. So, we are building very consciously an organization where roles and responsibilities are clear, but where there also is a requirement for interdependence and collaboration—and we're doing that because we think the market demands it. We're doing it because we believe when we really leverage the capabilities of this company we are, I don't want to sound overly aggressive, but we're almost unbeatable."[28]

Since she arrived from Lucent, Carly Fiorina has been consumed with leading this light-speed reinvention. To HP veterans, her impatient approach was "shocking." To Fiorina, it was critical. "A company is a system," she says, contending that HP's tendency toward decentralized decision making cripples the business. "To change the company, you have to operate on the whole system—the strategy, the structure, the rewards, the culture. You have to have the courage and capability to tackle everything at once."[29]

To Fiorina, overhauling an organization requires a sort of mobilization of one's full self. While some gripe that Hewlett-Packard has become "The Carly Fiorina Company," she says, "A company is people—people with brains and hearts and guts. If you're a leader, you've got to capture the whole person. People want to see you get it intellectually and feel it emotionally."[30] Resistant to formula as well as to the status quo, Fiorina has preserved one thing at HP: the team at the top. Four of her seven direct reports are women—which means that HP is the first top-tier *Fortune* 500 company truly run by women.

In speaking about the reinvention at HP, Carly Fiorina has said that reinvention to her is about four things.

> It's about culture, it's about strategy, it's about what you measure and how you reward those measurements, and it's about business process. All of those levers need to be pulled. At a cultural level, we have to be explicit about the values and the behaviors that help us, and explicit about the behaviors that are getting in our way. So our emphasis on reaffirming the core values that have been with this company for 60 years—trust, integrity, teamwork, contribution—is a reaffirmation of the behavior we need to carry forward.[31]

Reinvention also requires some tough strategic choices about how and where HP wants to play.[32] Those choices are particularly difficult for a company with the depth and breadth of capability of HP, because a company like HP honestly can do anything it wants to do. And so the hardest strategy is deciding what not to do.

Reinvention, on the other hand, is not just about creating new efficiencies or wringing out inefficiency. Reinvention requires really new skills, new business models, and indeed, new behaviors. Reinvention is about a focus on growth. It is a focus on fueling the top line, but not at the expense of the bottom line. And in today's world, reinvention for all of us is not a nice-to-do. It is a got-to-do.[33]

Now reinvention is not only about new skills and new behaviors. It is, of course, about new ways of selling your products, new ways of selling your services, new ways of marketing your company, new ways of doing business and of course, also about adding efficiencies to your business. And it certainly is about using technology that wasn't available before, to make life better and to make life at work better.[34]

HP has undergone massive change before. And they are undergoing massive change now. And it certainly won't be the last time that they go through reinvention because vital companies, like vital people, reinvent themselves over, and over, and over. But they have learned a lot about reinvention. And they have learned that in some ways what is perhaps most essential is a new perspective—to be able to see things in a different way.[35]

Hewlett-Packard's choices about what to preserve and what to reinvent are particular to the company—to their particular heritage, to their particular capabilities, to their particular opportunities and challenges. But the need to both preserve and reinvent is universal in the new economy. To embrace change is a healthy rejuvenating process; at the same time companies must recognize that some things are worth keeping. Some things do stand the test of time.[36]

Arguably, the streamlining was intended to aid decision making. But since the changes, it continues to be a logistical nightmare. Managers were slow in getting a sense of their new roles amid the shifting organizational sands.[37] Consternation rippled through the ranks. Managers who had long aspired to run their own autonomous units, known as P&Ls, short for profit & loss, suddenly saw most of those jobs disappear.[38]

Another restructuring red flag is the way Fiorina now sets strategy, a big departure from "The HP Way"—the principles laid out by the founders in 1957. Based on the belief that smart people will make the right choices if given the right tools and authority, "Bill and Dave" pushed strategy down to the managers most involved in each business. The approach worked. Not only did HP dominate most of its markets, but low-level employees unearthed new opportunities for the company. "HP was always the exact opposite of a command-and-control environment," says former CEO Platt. Although Platt wouldn't comment on Fiorina directly, he says, "Bill and Dave did not feel they had to make every decision."[39]

Figures 1 and 2 show the old and new structures for the company, respectively.

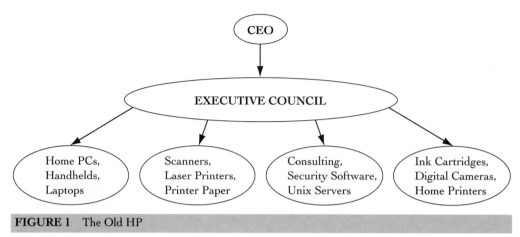

The Old HP

*Each product unit was responsible for its own performance
and was held accountable for its profits and losses.*

FIGURE 1 The Old HP

Source: Adapted from Peter Burrows, "The Radical," *Business Week*, February 19, 2001, pp. 72–73.

THE RESTRUCTURING ASSESSMENT

Business Week offered an assessment of Carly Fiorina's restructuring initiatives.[40] They highlighted the benefits and the risks associated to the changes she had implemented at Hewlett Packard. It is unrealistic to think that a restructuring plan of the magnitude of the one that took place at HP would result in only benefits. Risks and negative factors do exist and must be weighed accordingly.

BENEFITS

1. Happier Customers—Each client will work with only one account team, thus making HP easier to deal with.
2. Sales Boost—Account representatives will be selling all of HP products, not just those from one division; thus HP's selling opportunities should be maximized.
3. Real Solutions—HP can sell its products in combination as solutions to companies facing e-business problems.
4. Financial Flexibility—With all corporate sales under one roof, HP can measure the total value of a customer. Representatives will be allowed to discount some products and still maximize profits.

RISKS

1. Overwhelmed with Duties—With so many products being made and sold by just four units, HP executives have more on their plates and could miss details that keep products competitive.
2. Poorer Execution—When product managers oversaw everything from manufacturing to sales, they could respond quickly to changes. That will be harder with front- and back-end groups synchronizing their plans only every few weeks.

The New HP

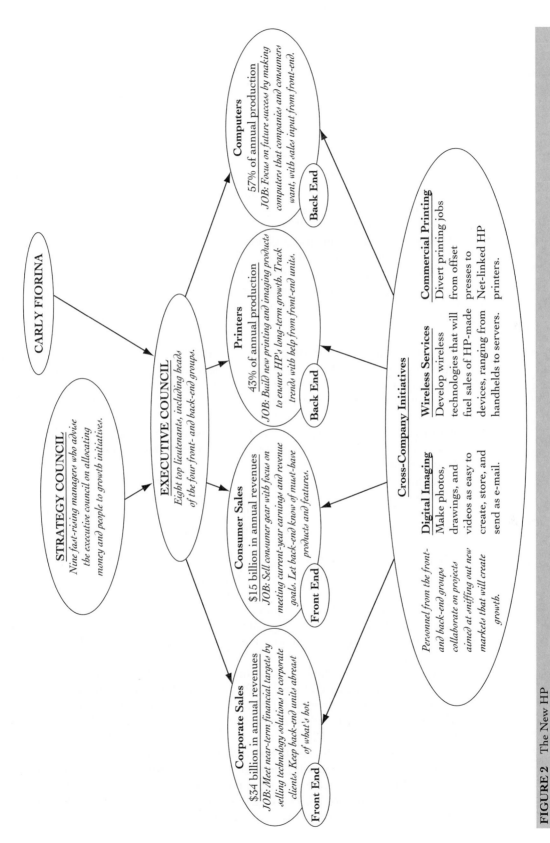

FIGURE 2 The New HP

Source: Adapted from Peter Burrows, "The Radical," *Business Week*, February 19, 2001, pp. 72–73.

3. Less Accountability—Profit-and-loss responsibility is shared between the front- and back-end groups and is no longer the responsibility of one person.
4. Fewer Spending Controls—There are no longer powerful division chiefs regulating and monitoring spending. As lines of command were eliminated, fourth quarter 2000 expenses soared.

CURRENT CHALLENGES

The current fear among all those who have an interest in Hewlett-Packard is that Fiorina is asking too much of the company. This stems from worries that she has spent too much time overhauling HP's broad structure and not enough attending to nitty-gritty operations problems.[41] The streamlining should aid decision making, but for now it continues to be a logistical nightmare. Managers have only started to get a sense of their new roles amid the shifting organizational sands.

Larger strategic challenges loom too. Sure, HP deserves credit for perfecting the art of selling PCs: with 40 percent plus sales growth in recent quarters, it has even out-paced Dell. But unless it can finally make good on promises to gain share in more lucrative e-business markets, it may find itself king of a commoditized market not worth owning.[42]

Initial results of the restructuring were troubling. While Fiorina had early success, the reorganization started to run aground near the middle of 2000. Cushy commissions intended to light a fire under HP's sales force boosted sales, but mostly for low-margin products that did little for corporate profits.

A more fundamental problem stems directly from the front-back structure: It doesn't clearly assign responsibility for profits and losses, meaning it's tough to diagnose and fix earnings screwups—especially since no individual manager will take the heat for missed numbers.[43] And with staffers in 120 countries, redrawing the lines of communication and getting veterans of rival divisions to work together is proving nettlesome. "The people who deal with Carly directly feel very empowered, but everyone else is running around saying, 'What do we do now?'" says one HP manager.[44]

Another problem: Much of the burden of running HP lands squarely on Fiorina's shoulders. Some insiders and analysts say she needs a second-in-command to manage day-to-day operations. "She's playing CEO, visionary, and COO, and that's too hard to do," says Sanford C. Bernstein analyst Toni Sacconaghi.[45]

Most recently, the April 19, 2001, issue of *The Wall Street Journal* reported that Hewlett-Packard would be eliminating 3,000 management positions. The company will also take at least $150 million in write-offs and require its employees to take mandatory vacation time as the computer and printer company warned of an earnings shortfall in the second quarter of 2001. This warning is HP's third unpleasant surprise for Wall Street since late 2000, marking the third quarter in a row that the company will fall short of profit expectations.[46] HP's previous disappointments generally reflected slowing sales growth, whereas HP now expects an actual decline in revenue.

Fiorina blamed the adverse currency effects for part of the slowdown, noting that the strong dollar, which holds down the dollar-denominated value of HP's oversea sales, reduced revenue by about 4 percent compared with the year earlier period.[47] HP plans to continue cost-cutting measures, including cutting 3,000 management jobs in order to boost employee-to-manager ratios across the company. A spokeswoman notes that while many of those 3,000 managers may choose to leave the company, some will likely be redeployed internally.[48] In addition, HP will require employees to take at least 6 days of accrued vacation this year and will write off $100 million in inkjet printer inventories and another $50 million in planned production capacity expansion for inkjet printers.

2000 OBJECTIVES AND RESULTS (PRUDENTIAL SPEECH)

Only a few months after coming in as CEO of Hewlett-Packard, Carly Fiorina set out objectives for the following year (2000). She committed to focus the company on six areas:[49]

1. Accelerate growth in the company's current businesses
2. Streamline the decentralized operating model to fuel growth opportunities
3. Implement a "total customer experience" approach
4. Take advantage of the strong balance sheet to invest in growth opportunities
5. Leverage the company's market position to drive the adoption of next-generation appliances, e-services, and always-on Internet infrastructure in high-growth markets
6. Create e-services ecosystems and place HP at the center

Hewlett-Packard made measurable and important progress in each of the six areas during 2000. Some of the major highlights in each area are listed here.

1. Accelerate Growth in the Company's Current Businesses

Hewlett-Packard recorded overall earnings per share growth of 37 percent in 2000. The company has a long-standing global presence in more than 160 countries. It also has deep roots and established relationships across major geographies—which has led to balanced performance across all regions of the world.

Each of the basic business units also saw growth. In the year 2000, the Imaging and Printing Systems Business led in virtually every category in which it competed. It saw consistent profitability and growth. The Internet is driving more pages to the printer at the same time that it's fueling new applications for printing—newspapers, tickets, stamps, and photos. This business remains the crown jewel of HP.

The Computing Systems and Internet Infrastructure Business continues to deliver enterprise servers, storage, software, and PCs to business customers. The IT and Professional Services Business operates with a public commitment to grow this business aggressively. Their consulting revenues were up 46 percent in the third quarter of 2000, and 600 new consultants were added. And finally HP's Consumer IT Company is the world's largest and occupies 10 percent of all retail shelf space of computer displays.

2. Streamline the Decentralized Operating Model to Fuel Growth Opportunities

HP was restructured as a more focused business, with customer-facing organizations dedicated to serving their business and consumer customers. The company was ahead of schedule in reducing infrastructure costs. It also streamlined human resources (HR) functions by delivering many HR and benefit programs online through a new employee portal.

3. Implement a "Total Customer Experience" Approach

Superdome, the company's new high-end Unix server, was unveiled in September 2000 and is designed to be a complete customer solution—flexible, scalable, reliable, open, and engineered for an always-on, always-connected world. Superdome is a radically different way of going to market at HP and in the industry. For the Superdome customer, everything is delivered from upfront systems assessment; to the system design, tuning, and integration; to installation; to customized service and support offerings to manage and monitor systems performance over time, all from a single point of contact.

4. Take Advantage of the Strong Balance Sheet to Invest in Growth Opportunities

Hewlett-Packard brought on additional key leadership figures during 2000. The company invested in technology and now has the best lineup in its history. HP leveraged its expertise in networking technology supporting storage solutions and made deep investments to create a world-class software business.

HP experienced a large global consumer expansion in Latin America, Asia, and Europe. In Latin America, after only 18 months in Mexico, HP became the number 1 home PC supplier and has now expanded into Chile and Venezuela. In Asia, HP is growing at 60 percent and has a strong market reception. In Europe, HP recently entered Germany's consumer market, the world's third largest and the largest single European consumer market. And finally, outside of North America and Asia, HP is growing 147 percent by staying focused on profitable growth.

5. Leverage the Company's Market Position to Drive the Adoption of Next-Generation Appliances, e-Services, and Always-on Internet Infrastructure in High-Growth Markets

Hewlett-Packard desires to make printers first-class citizens of the Net. New partnerships with stamps.com, encryptix.com, Newspaper Direct, and FedEx have furthered expansion into next-generation markets. The company also has plans to introduce technology that would help make devices like cell phones, pagers, and personal digital assistants (PDAs) print-capable.

6. Create e-Services Ecosystems and Place HP at the Center

Following are four examples of e-service ecosystem offerings that HP undertook in 2000:

1. Ehitex—a high-tech industry parts trading exchange with Hitachi, Compaq, Toshiba, and others

2. SpinCircuit—the high-tech manufacturing and design e-services portal running HP's own e-speak technology

3. E-utilica—the world's first "instant service provider solution," a fully outsourced instant-computing solution for ASPs to purchase as a computer utility and go right into business and right into revenue

4. ResourceLink—the online exchange that helps transfer millions of pounds of food to charities with hungry people to feed

GROWTH OPPORTUNITIES

Hewlett-Packard sees great growth opportunities outside the United States. HP has been a global firm for a very long time. It has been in Asia and Europe for 30 years. It has been in places in Latin America for about the same amount of time. So for HP it's not about building a presence—it has deep roots in countries where longevity matters. Now it's a question of leveraging the relationships and the presence it has.[50]

Carly Fiorina is convinced that HP can grow faster as well as earn more. The company is now poised to capitalize on some real innovations with huge market potential. Digital imaging and e-services are just two of the examples where HP has potential. At the same time, it has to aggressively continued to defend and expand the core businesses. It will do all of this passionately under the control of Fiorina. It has become the world's number 1 consumer IT supplier, and feels that it has just begun.[51]

THE FUTURE

The future of HP and its success depends on its ability to react to changing times. The CEO herself has said, "All the great technology companies got great by seeing trends and getting there first—and they're always misunderstood initially. We think we see where the market is going and that we are perfectly positioned."[52] Regardless of where HP sees itself today, there are multiple factors that Hewlett-Packard believes could affect future results. Realizing that these factors exist is the first step but effectively managing them is entirely different.

The following description of the factors that HP believes could affect future performance were obtained from the October 31, 2000, Form 10-K.

Competition

Hewlett-Packard encounters aggressive competition in all areas of its business. It has numerous competitors, ranging from some of the world's largest corporations to many relatively small and highly specialized firms. It competes primarily on the basis of technology, performance, price, quality, reliability, distribution, customer service, and support. Product life cycles are short. To remain competitive, it must be able to develop new products, services, and support, as well as periodically enhance existing products, services, and support. In particular, the company anticipates that it will have to continue to lower the prices of many of its products, services, and support to stay competitive and effectively manage financial returns with resulting reducing gross margins. In some markets, it may not be able to compete successfully against current and future competitors, and the competitive pressures it faces could harm its business and prospects.

New Product and Service Introductions

If HP cannot continue to develop rapidly and to manufacture and market innovative products and services that meet customer requirements for performance and reliability, it may lose market share, and future revenue and earnings may suffer. The process of developing new high-technology products and services is complex and uncertain. The company must accurately anticipate customers' changing needs and emerging technological trends. It consequently must make long-term investments and commit significant resources before knowing whether the predictions will eventually result in products that the market will accept. After a product is developed, it must be able to manufacture sufficient volumes quickly at low enough costs. To do this it must accurately forecast volumes, mix of products, and configurations. Additionally, the supply and timing of a new product or service must match customers' demand and timing for the particular product or service. Given the wide variety of systems, products, and services that HP offers, the process of planning production and managing inventory levels becomes increasingly difficult.

Reliance on Third-Party Distribution Channels and Inventory Management

HP uses third-party distributors to sell its products, especially printers and personal computers, in order to accommodate changing customer preferences. As a result, the financial soundness of its wholesale and retail distributors, and HP's continuing relationships with these distributors, are important to HP's success. Some of these distributors may have insufficient financial resources and may not be able to withstand changes in business conditions. HP's revenue and earnings could suffer it its distributors' financial condition or operations weaken or if HP's relationships with them deteriorate.

Additionally, inventory management becomes increasingly complex as HP continues to sell a significant mix of products through distributors. Third-party distributors constantly adjust their product orders from HP in response to

- The supply of their competitors' products available to the distributor
- The timing of new product introductions and relative features of the products
- Seasonal fluctuations in end-user demand, such as back-to-school and holiday buying

Distributors may increase orders during times of product shortages, cancel orders if their inventory is too high, or delay orders in anticipation of new products. If HP has excess inventory, it may have to reduce prices and write down inventory, which in turn could result in lower gross margins.

Short Product Life Cycles

The short life cycles of many of HP's products pose a challenge for the company to manage effectively the transition from existing products to new products. If it does not manage the transition effectively, revenue and earnings could suffer. Among the factors that make a smooth transition from current products to new products difficult are delays in product development or manufacturing, variations in product costs, and delays in customer purchases of existing products in anticipation of new product introductions. HP's revenue and earnings could also suffer due to the timing of product or service introductions by suppliers and competitors. This is especially true when a competitor introduces a new product just before HP's own product introduction. Furthermore, HP's new products may replace or compete with a certain number of its own current products.

Intellectual Property

HP generally relies upon patent, copyright, trademark, and trade secret laws in the United States and in certain other countries, and agreements with employees, customers, and partners to establish and maintain proprietary rights in technology and products. However, any of HP's intellectual proprietary rights could be challenged, invalidated, or circumvented. The company's intellectual property may not necessarily provide significant competitive advantages. Also, because of the rapid pace of technological change in the information technology industry, many of the company's products rely on key technologies developed by third parties, and it may not be able to continue to obtain licenses from these third parties. Third parties may claim that HP is infringing on their intellectual property. Even if HP does not believe that its products are infringing on third parties' intellectual property rights, the claims can be time-consuming and costly to defend and divert management's attention and resources away from their business. Claims of intellectual property infringement might also require HP to enter into costly royalty or license agreements. If it cannot or does not license the infringed technology or substitute similar technology from another source, the business could suffer.

Reliance on Suppliers

HP's manufacturing operations depend on its suppliers' ability to deliver quality components and products in time to meet critical manufacturing and distribution schedules. HP sometimes experiences a short supply of certain component parts as a result of strong demand in the industry for those parts. If shortages or delays persist, HP's operating results could suffer until other sources can be developed. In order to secure components for the production of new products, at times the company makes advance payments to suppliers, or it may enter into noncancelable purchase commitments with vendors. If the prices of these component parts then decrease after the company has entered into binding price agreements, earnings could suffer. Furthermore, HP may not be able to secure enough components at reasonable prices to build new products in a timely manner in the quantities and configurations needed. Conversely, a temporary oversupply of these parts also could adversely affect operating results.

International

Sales outside the United States make up more than half of HP's revenues. A portion of the product and component manufacturing, along with key suppliers, is also located outside the United States. Future earnings or financial position could be adversely affected by a variety of international factors:

- Changes in a country's or region's political or economic conditions
- Trade protection measures
- Import or export licensing requirements
- The overlap of different tax structures
- Unexpected changes in regulatory requirements
- Differing technology standards
- Problems caused by the conversion of various European currencies to the Euro
- Natural disasters

Market Risk

HP is exposed to foreign currency exchange rate risk inherent in its sales commitments, anticipated sales, and assets and liabilities dominated in currencies other than the U.S. dollar. It is also exposed to interest rate risk inherent in its debt and investment portfolios. Its risk management strategy uses derivative financial instruments, including forwards, swaps, and purchased options, to hedge certain foreign currency and interest rate exposures. The intent is to offset gains and losses that occur on the underlying exposures, with gains and losses on the derivative contracts hedging these exposures. The company does not enter into derivatives for trading purposes. It is also exposed to equity securities price risk on its portfolio of marketable equity securities. HP typically does not attempt to reduce or eliminate its market exposure on these securities.

Impairment of Investment and Financing Portfolios

HP has an investment portfolio that includes minority equity and debt investments in numerous technology companies. In particular, it has invested in various privately held companies, many of which are still in the start-up or development stage. These investments are inherently risky because the markets for the technologies or products these companies have under development are typically in the early stages and may never develop. Furthermore, the values of HP's investments in publicly traded companies are subject so significant market price volatility. HP may incur losses related to investments in these companies. HP's investments in technology companies are often coupled with a strategic commercial relationship. Its commercial agreements with these companies may not be sufficient to allow it to obtain and integrate such products or technology into the HP technology or product lines, and these companies may be subsequently acquired by third parties, including competitors of HP.

Acquisitions, Strategic Alliances, Joint Ventures, and Divestitures

In the normal course of business, HP frequently engages in discussions with third parties relating to possible acquisitions, strategic alliances, joint ventures, and divestitures. Although completion of any one transaction may not have a material effect on the company's financial position, results of operations, or cash flows taken as a whole, it may contribute to an overall financial result that differs from the investment community's expectations in a given quarter. Divestiture of a part of HP's business may result in the cancellation of orders and charges to earnings. Acquisitions and strategic alliances may require the company to integrate with a different company culture, management team, and business infrastructure. HP may also have to develop, manufacture, and market products with its own products in a way that enhances the performance of the combined business or product line. Depending on the size and complexity of an acquisition, successful integration of the entity into HP depends on a variety of factors:

- The hiring and retention of key employees
- Management of facilities and employees in separate geographic areas
- The integration or coordination of different research and development and product manufacturing facilities

All of these efforts require varying levels of management resources, which may divert HP's attention from other business operations.

Stock Price

HP's stock price, like that of other technology companies, can be volatile. Some of the factors that can affect the stock price are these:

- Announcement by HP or a competitor of new products, services, or technological innovations
- Quarterly increases or decreases in earnings
- Changes in revenue or earnings estimates by the investment community
- Speculation in the press or investment community about HP's financial condition or results of operations

General market conditions and domestic or international macro economic factors unrelated to the company's performance may also affect HP's stock price. For these reasons, investors should not rely on recent trends to predict future stock prices or financial results. In addition, following periods of volatility in a company's securities, securities class action litigation against a company is sometimes instituted. This type of litigation could result in substantial costs and the diversion of management time and resources.

Economic Uncertainty

The revenue growth and profitability of HP's business depend significantly on the overall demand for computing and imaging products and services, particularly in the product and service segments in which the company competes. Softening demand for these products and services caused by worsening economic conditions may result in decreased revenues or earnings levels or growth rates. As of April 2001, the U.S. economy has experienced prior months of weakening. This has resulted in individuals and companies delaying or reducing expenditures, such as for information technology.

HP is currently facing another uncertainty: the much–publicized proposed merger with Compaq. Shareholders are sharply divided over the issue, but, regardless of the outcome of the final vote (still unknown at this writing), it will doubtless have a profound effect on the company and its future. ■

---

*Ann Marie Beyer of Florida State University assisted with this case.

Table 1   Hewlett-Packard Company and Subsidiaries For the Years Ended October 31 (In Millions, Except Per Share Amounts)

	2000	1999	1998	1997	1996
Net revenue	$48,782	$42,370	$39,419	$35,465	$31,613
Earnings from operations	3,889	3,688	3,399	3,405	2,926
Net Earnings from continuing operations	3,561	3,104	2,678	2,515	2,085
Net earnings per share, continuing operations:					
Basic	$1.80	$1.54	$1.29	$1.23	$1.02
Diluted	1.73	1.49	1.26	1.19	.99
Cash dividends declared per share	.32	.32	.30	.26	.22
At year end:					
Assets–Continuing operations	$34,009	$31,764	$28,624	$26,681	$22,934
Assets–Total	34,009	35,297	31,708	29,852	25,977
Long-term debt	3,402	1,764	2,063	3,158	2,579

Source: Hewlett-Packard 2000 Annual Report.

Table 2   Stock History

Date	Stock Event	Average Trading Price
November 6, 1957	IPO	$16.00
September 15, 1960	3 for 1 split	$77.00 on 6/30/60
February 23, 1970	2 for 1 split	$103.28 on 12/31/69
June 27, 1979	2 for 1 split	$89.28 on 3/31/79
June 17, 1981	2 for 1 split	$94.13 on 3/31/81
August 1, 1983	2 for 1 split	$89.88 on 6/30/83
March 24, 1995	2 for 1 split	$100.50 on 1/31/95
June 19, 1996	2 for 1 split	$105.88 on 4/30/96
October 27, 2000	2 for 1 split	$109.25 on 7/31/00

Source: Financial History, www.hp.com/hpinfo/investor/finhist/main.htm.

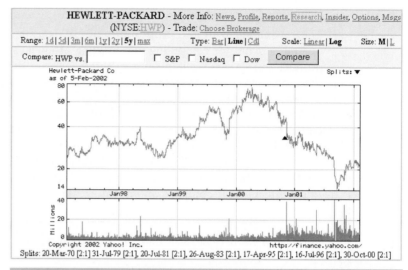

FIGURE 3 3-Year Stock Price History

Source: Yahoo Finance, finance.yahoo.com/?s=HWP&d=c&t=5q&y=on&z=m&q=l.

QUESTIONS FOR DISCUSSION

1. What are the critical issues facing HP at this time?
2. Using concepts from organization theory, how should these issues be resolved?
3. Specifically, what challenges does the pending merger with Compaq pose for HP? Do you think it should be approved by the stockholders of both HP and Compaq? What challenges exist for HP if the merger is not approved?
4. What role is the current HP CEO, Carly Fiorina, likely to have in the future? Explain.

REFERENCES

1. Carly Fiorina, "Prudential Securities Speech," www. hp.com/hpinfo/ceo/speeches/ceo_prudentail_00.htm, accessed on March 8, 2001.
2. "Hewlett-Packard Form 10-K," www.hp.com/ hpinfo/investor/2000form10k/main.htm, accessed on March 31, 2001.
3. David Hamilton, "Inside Hewlett-Packard, Carly Fiorina Combines Discipline, New-Age Talk," *The Wall Street Journal* (August 22, 2000), A1, A18.
4. Ibid.
5. "HP Corporate Objectives," www.hp.com/hpinfo/ abouthp/corpobj.htm, accessed on March 8, 2001.
6. See note 2.
7. Ibid.
8. Ibid.
9. Robert W. Lear, "Succession Reflection," *Chief Executive* (November 1999): 14.
10. Ibid.
11. Ibid.
12. Marie Eve Demers, "Fiorina Named HP Chairwoman," *Electronic News* (October 2, 2000).
13. "Carly Fiorina—Biography," www.hp.com/hpinfo/ ceo/bio/, accessed on March 8, 2001.
14. Peter Burrows, "The Radical," *Business Week* (February 19, 2001): 70–80.
15. Carly Fiorina, "Commencement Address, Massachusetts Institute of Technology," www.hp.com/ hpinfo/ceo/speeches/ceo_mit_commence.htm, accessed on March 8, 2001.
16. Ibid.
17. See note 12.
18. Ibid.
19. "The Diversity Value Chain," www.hp.com/hpinco/ abouthp/div_value.htm, accessed on March 31, 2001.
20. "Our Vision and Strategy," www.hp.com/hpinco/ abouthp/div_vision.htm, accessed on March 31, 2001.
21. "Wake-up Call for HP," *Technology Review* (May/June 2000): 94–100.

22. Ibid.
23. See note 14.
24. See note 3.
25. See note 14.
26. See note 3.
27. Ibid.
28. See note 21.
29. Patricia Sellers, "The 50 Most Powerful Women in Business: Secrets of the Fastest-rising Stars," *Fortune* (October 16, 2000): 130–160.
30. Ibid.
31. See note 21.
32. Ibid.
33. Carly Fiorina, "Art of Reinvention in the New Economy," www.hp.com/hpinfo/ceo/speeches/ceo_reinvention.htm, accessed on March 8, 2001.
34. Ibid.
35. Ibid.
36. Ibid.
37. Peter Burrows, "Can Fiorina Reboot HP?" *Business Week* (November 27, 2000): 59.
38. See note 3.
39. See note 14.
40. Ibid.
41. See note 37.
42. Ibid.
43. See note 14.
44. Ibid.
45. Ibid.
46. David Hamilton, "HP to Cut 3,000 Management Positions," *The Wall Street Journal* (April 19, 2001), B8.
47. Ibid.
48. Ibid.
49. See note 1.
50. See note 21.
51. Ibid.
52. Ibid.

Enron Corp.: Outdistancing the Competition and Then Collapsing*

Up until 2001, Enron's performance was a success by any measure, as the company continued to outdistance and solidify its leadership in each of its major businesses.[1] However, by late 2001, the company filed for bankruptcy under Chapter 11 of the U.S. bankruptcy code. Enron had built a unique corporation and strong businesses with tremendous opportunities for growth. At a minimum, Enron was seeing market opportunities that would triple company size over the next 5 years[2]—but then came the collapse. What happened?

Enron went from a high flyer and a darling of Wall Street to Chapter 11 status in just a matter of months in late 2001. The seventh largest company in the United States, at the time, Enron was the largest company ever to file bankruptcy in U.S. history.

Although at the time of this writing the demise of Enron was still unfolding, it is apparent that Enron had achieved considerable success prior to its failure. It may yet survive as a company, since it failed under Chapter 11 (reorganization) of the U.S. bankruptcy code, but it will be a very different firm.

Enron attempted to have as much to say as possible about the rules governing those markets in which it traded.[3] For years the Houston-based firm simply produced, transported, and marketed natural gas. Then, as energy deregulation threatened profit margins in the gas business, Enron discovered it could make billions by trading and brokering packages of energy. Enron then moved into the telecommunications business, with a national fiber-optic cable network.[4]

BACKGROUND AND OVERVIEW

In 1985, Houston Natural Gas merged with InterNorth, a natural gas company based in Omaha, Nebraska, to form the modern-day Enron Corp. Headquartered in Houston, Texas, the company provided products and services related to natural gas, electricity, and communications to wholesale and retail customers. Enron's operations were conducted through its subsidiaries and affiliates, which were principally engaged in the following activities:[5]

- Transportation of natural gas through pipelines to markets throughout the United States
- Generation, transmission, and distribution of electricity to markets in the northwestern United States
- Marketing of natural gas, electricity, and other commodities; and related risk management and finance services worldwide
- Development, construction, and operation of power plants, pipelines, and other energy-related assets worldwide
- Delivery and management of energy commodities and capabilities to end-use retail customers in the industrial and commercial business sectors
- Development of an intelligent network platform to provide bandwidth management services and the delivery of high bandwidth communication applications

BUSINESS SEGMENTS

Enron divided its operations into the following segments.[6]

- Transportation and Distribution—Regulated industries; interstate transmission of natural gas; management and operation of pipelines; electric utility operations
- Wholesale Services—Commodity sales and services; risk management products and financial services to wholesale customers; development, acquisition, and operation of power plants, natural gas pipelines, and other energy-related assets.
- Retail Energy Services—Sales of natural gas and electricity and related products directly to end-use customers, particularly in the commercial and industrial sectors, and the outsourcing of energy-related activities
- Broadband Services—Construction and management of a nationwide fiber-optic network, the marketing and management of bandwidth, and the delivery of high-bandwidth content

Transportation and Distribution

Enron's Transportation and Distribution business consisted of the company's North American interstate natural gas and transportation systems and its electricity transmission and distribution operations in Oregon. Enron and its subsidiaries operated domestic interstate natural gas pipelines extending from Texas to the Canadian border and across the southern United States from Florida to California. Included in Enron's domestic interstate natural gas pipeline operations were Northern Natural Gas Company (Northern), Transwestern Pipeline Company (Transwestern), and Florida Gas Transmission Company (Florida Gas).

Northern, Transwestern, and Florida Gas were interstate pipelines and subject to the regulatory jurisdiction of the Federal Energy Regulation Commission (FERC). Each pipeline served customers in a specific geographical: Northern, the upper midwest; Transwestern, principally the California market and pipeline interconnects on the east end of the Transwestern system; and Florida Gas, the state of Florida. In addition, Enron held an interest in Northern Border Partners, L.P., which owned a 70 percent interest in the Northern Border Pipeline system. An Enron subsidiary operated the Northern Border Pipeline system, which transported gas from western Canada to delivery points in the midwestern United States.

Enron Transportation Services provided stable earnings and cash flows during 2001. The four major natural gas pipelines had strong competitive positions in their respective markets as a result of efficient operating practices, competitive rates, and favorable market conditions. Enron Transportation once even had plans to continue to pursue demand-driven expansion opportunities.[7]

Wholesale Services

Enron's wholesale business (Wholesale Services) included its worldwide wholesale energy and other commodities businesses. Wholesale Services operated in developed markets such as North America and Europe, as well as newly deregulating or developing markets including Japan, Australia, South America, and India. Enron built its wholesale businesses through the creation of networks involving selective asset ownership, contractual access to third-party assets, and market-making activities. Each market in which Wholesale Services operated utilized these components in a slightly different manner and at a different stage of development. This network strategy enabled Wholesale Services to establish a significant position in its markets.

Wholesale Services managed its portfolio of contracts and assets in order to maximize value, minimize associated risks, and provide overall liquidity. In doing so, Wholesale Services used portfolio and risk management disciplines, including offsetting or hedging transactions, to manage exposures to market price movements (commodities, interest rates, foreign currencies, and equities). Additionally, Wholesale Services managed its liquidity and exposure to third-party credit risk through monetization of its contract portfolio or third-party insurance contracts. In late 1999, Wholesale Services launched an Internet-based e-commerce system, EnronOnline, which allowed wholesale customers to view Enron's real-time pricing and complete commodity transactions with Enron as principal, with no direct interaction.

In 2000, Wholesale Services reinforced its positions in the natural gas and power markets in both North America and Europe. In 2001, Wholesale Services had plans to continue to expand and refine its existing energy networks and to extend its business model to new markets and industries. Wholesale Services also planned to continue to fine-tune its already successful existing energy networks. In key international markets where deregulation was under way, Enron anticipated building energy networks by using the optimum combination of acquiring or constructing physical assets and securing contractual access to third-party assets. Enron also planned to replicate its business model in new industrial markets such as metals, pulp, paper and lumber, and coal and steel. Enron expected to use its e-commerce platform, EnronOnline, to accelerate the penetration into these industries.

Enron's strengths, including its ability to identify and respond to customers needs, access to extensive physical assets, and integrated product offerings, were important drivers of the expected continued earnings growth. In addition, significant earnings were expected from Wholesale Services' commodity portfolio and investments, which were subject to market fluctuations. External factors, such as the amount of volatility in market prices, impacted the earnings opportunity associated with Wholesale Services' business. Risk related to these activities was managed using naturally offsetting transactions and hedge transactions. The effectiveness of Enron's risk management activities had a material impact on future earnings.

Retail Energy Services

Enron Energy Services was a provider of energy outsourcing products and services to business customers. These included sales of natural gas, electricity, liquids, and other commodities, and the provision of energy management services directly to commercial and industrial customers located in North America and Europe. Energy Services provided end-users with a broad range of energy products and services that reduced total energy costs or minimized risks. These products and services included delivery of natural gas and electricity, energy tariff and information management, demand-side services to reduce energy consumption, and financial services, including price-risk management.

Energy Services' products and services helped commercial and industry businesses maximize total energy savings while meeting their operational needs. With a focus on total energy savings, services, and finance capabilities, Energy Services provided outsourcing and other innovative programs. These programs were designed not only to supply electricity and natural gas to businesses but also to manage unregulated energy assets. Their goal was to reduce their customers' energy consumption, delivery, and billing costs, to eliminate inefficiencies of decentralized systems, to reduce energy demand, and to minimize the risk of fluctuating energy prices to the customer.

Enron extended its retail products to Europe. During 2000, significant growth was experienced in marketing commodity services to medium-sized businesses there. At the end of 2000, Enron had approximately 130,000 customers in the United Kingdom and had plans to expand this business model to other European countries. Until the collapse, Energy Services anticipated continued growth in the demand for retail energy outsourcing solutions. Energy Services planned to deliver these services to its existing customers, while continuing to expand its commercial and industrial customer base for total energy outsourcing. Energy Services also planned to continue integrating its service delivery capabilities, extend its business model to related markets, and offer new products.

Broadband Services

During 2000, Enron Broadband Services substantially completed the Enron Intelligent Network (EIN), a high capacity, global fiber-optic network, which through pooling points could switch capacity from one independent network to another and create scalability. Enron Broadband Services provided bandwidth management and inter-mediation services, and high-quality content delivery services. Enron's bandwidth-on-demand platform allowed delivery of high-bandwidth media-rich content such as video streaming, high-capacity data transport, and videoconferencing. The EIN consisted of a high-capacity fiber-optic network based on ownership or contractual access to approximately 18,000 miles of fiber-optic network capacity throughout the United States. As of December 31, 2000, the EIN included 25 pooling points of which 18 were in the United States and one each in Tokyo, London, Brussels, Amsterdam, Paris, Dusseldorf, and Frankfurt, allowing the EIN to connect to most major U.S. cities and a large number in Europe. The breadth of pooling points within the EIN extended its reach by allowing connectivity with a greater number of network and service providers.

Broadband Services extended the Enron business model to the communications industry. In 2001, Enron expected to develop further the EIN. In addition, Enron anticipated further deploying its proprietary Broadband Operating System across the Enron Intelligent Network, enabling Enron to manage bandwidth capacity independent of owning the underlying fiber. Broadband Services expected its intermediation transaction level to increase significantly in 2001 as more market participants connected to the pooling points and transacted with Enron to manage their bandwidth needs. The availability of Enron's bandwidth intermediation products and prices on EnronOnline was expected to impact favorably the volume of transactions. In 2001, Broadband Services expected to continue to expand the commercial rollout of its content service offerings, including video-on-demand. Enron expected the volume of content delivered over its network to increase as more content delivery contracts were signed and as more distribution partner locations were connected. Of course by the end of 2001, it was clear that these expectations could not be realized.

LEADERSHIP

One large reason Enron acted unlike any other utility was that the two men in charge prior to the collapse, Ken Lay and Jeffrey Skilling, acted unlike any other utility executives. Ken Lay, the chairman, previously served as a utility executive. Lay has a doctorate in economics and spent years in the 1970s working at what is now the FERC, surrounded by lawyers and petroleum engineers. "As an economist, I look at how markets ought to operate," he explained. "I spent a lot of time at FERC arguing for new ways to price gas, and got people thinking differently about markets."[8]

Enron's former president and CEO Jeff Skilling is very different from Ken Lay. Skilling, a former McKinsey consultant, was first retained by Enron in 1985 to help the company spot opportunities created by the early deregulation of the gas business. He found it bizarre at first. "I came from a finance background, and here was a commodity controlled by the federal government."[9] One of the tasks he took on was preaching the benefits of creating a liquid marketplace for trading gas to executives and managers in the gas industry. It wasn't easy. "The engineering mindset prevalent in this business was a roadblock. When we first tried to trade gas, the engineers said, 'Let's see the gas.' It was like trying to trade in pork bellies and being asked to see the pigs."[10]

VISION AND VALUES

Enron stated that it operated with a clearly defined vision and strong values, although we now know that this was not the case. The company stated that it believed in the following:[11]

- **Its markets**—The company believed in the inherent wisdom of open markets. It was convinced that consumer choice and competition lead to lower prices and innovation.
- **Innovation**—Enron was a laboratory of innovation. It tried to employ the best and the brightest people and believed that every employee could make a difference.
- **Creativity**—Enron thought the entrepreneurial approach stimulated creativity. It called for new insights, new ways of looking at problems and opportunities, and a strong sense of urgency.
- **Diversity**—Enron valued diversity in people and in thought.
- **Customers**—Success was measured by the success of its customers. Enron was committed to meeting its customers' energy needs with solutions that offer them a competitive advantage—and the company worked with them in ways that reinforce the benefits of a long-term partnership with Enron.
- **Environment**—In everything Enron did, it operated safely and with concern for the environment.
- **Change**—It changed the way energy is delivered, as well as the market for it. It changed the way people thought about energy.
- **Together**—Together, the members of the company created the leading energy company in the world.
- **Respect**—Enron treated others as it would like to be treated. It would not tolerate abusive or disrespectful treatment.
- **Integrity**—Company members worked with customers and prospects openly, honestly, and sincerely. When they said they would do something, they did it; when they said they could not or would not do something, then they didn't do it.
- **Communication**—They had an obligation to communicate. They took the time to talk with one another and to listen. They believed that information was meant to move and that information moved people.
- **Excellence**—Enron was satisfied with nothing less than the very best in everything it did.

It is now quite obvious that Enron did not live up to these values and, in fact, completely ignored most of them. The company's stated vision changed three times since the company's inception. Each change brought broader goals and assisted the company with direction (see Exhibit 1). Since 1995, Enron desired to become the world's leading energy company. This stated goal progressed from focusing on the gas industry to concentrating on the broader spectrum of energy services and enabled Enron to increase the breadth of its operations.

ENRON'S PREVIOUS COMPETITIVE ADVANTAGE

Enron's targeted markets were very large and were undergoing fundamental changes.[12] Energy deregulation and liberalization continued, and customers were demanding reliable delivery of energy at predictable prices. Many markets experienced tighter supply, higher prices, and increased volatility, and there was increasing interdependence within regions and across commodities. Similarly, the broadband industry faced issues of overcapacity and capital constraints even as demand increased for faster, flexible, and more reliable connectivity. Enron was in a unique position to provide the products and services needed in these environments. Its size, experience, and skills gave the company enormous competitive advantages.

Enron believed the following factors formed its competitive advantage:[13]

- Robust networks of strategic assets that Enron owned or had contractual access to gave it greater flexibility and speed to deliver reliably widespread logistical solutions
- Unparalled liquidity and market-making abilities that resulted in price and service advantages
- Risk management skills that enabled the company to offer reliable prices as well as reliable delivery
- Innovative technology such as EnronOnline delivered products and services easily at the lowest possible cost

These capabilities enabled Enron to provide high-value products and services other wholesale service providers could not. It could then take the physical components and repackage them to suit the specific needs of customers. Enron treated term, price, and delivery as variables that were blended into a single, comprehensive solution. The technology and fulfillment systems ensured execution. In those market environments, those abilities made Enron the right company with the right model at the right time.[14]

EARLIER RESTRUCTURING AT ENRON

Enron found that plunging quickly and aggressively into new markets gave it a good shot at outmaneuvering competitors that entered later. The more customers and more suppliers Enron (or any trading company) had, the more options it had in putting together a deal. When Enron agreed to provide electric power to a big utility, it might repackage power it bought from 10 different suppliers under 10 different conditions. The more suppliers it had, the more artfully it could pick out a kilowatt here and another one there before putting them on a plate for the customer. Enron traders compared deal-making to solving jigsaw puzzles—plucking out the kilowatts from its inventory that were configured in ways that fit the customer's needs. The same advantage derived from having more customers than the competition; it meant Enron had more places to unload those kilowatts at good prices.[15]

An issue even more important than the volatility of prices was the continuation of a very fundamental restructuring of the nature of the business. A number of things occurred in the energy business that changed the look of the industry forever and changed the nature of what companies will do as time goes on.[16] Enron believed that rigid vertical integration was costly and inefficient when flexibility and quick response are essential to success. Instead, the company believed that the successful companies in the emerging energy industry would be those that were brain-power intensive, fast-moving, highly networked, and entrepreneurial.[17]

Enron's transformation into a huge energy trading and risk management firm was based on the idea that the vertically integrated business model no longer worked.[18] Since 1974, no nonintegrated major energy company has vertically integrated. The original list consisted of 27 companies, of which 24 were vertically integrated (see Exhibit 2). In 2001, there were 10. As the number and role of vertically integrated majors declined in recent years, other corporate structures grew to prominence.

Analysts expect the vertically integrated oil companies to grow larger but there will be fewer of them. Corporate growth is only one indicator of strategic success. More critical to the prospects for future success are the assessments of the capital markets. Using stock-price appreciation as a measure of investor perception indicates that capital markets favor the energy-service companies [i.e., Enron, El Paso, and Williams Cos.] and mega-merger survivors [i.e., Exxon Mobil and BP].[19] The whole theory of vertical integration is that the information cost is very high. So if a company could own it all, and control it all, that company could reduce those costs. Enron believed the inflexibility created by vertically integrating more than offset the efficiencies of that coordination.[20]

The key to the reversal in industrial structure occurred because the huge costs of interaction and transaction, which formed the basis of the integrated company, were rapidly plummeting because of new technology and communications advances.[21] As an example, the length of time needed to assemble a natural gas transaction changed dramatically during the last two decades. In the early 1980s, before natural gas was deregulated, it easily took 2 to 3 years to put together a contract. By 1989, deregulation had lowered that period to 9 months. When natural gas became a commodity in the mid-1990s, a broker could trade it over the telephone in 2 weeks. Now the transaction could be handled online in less than a second.

PROGRESSION TO THE INTERNET

Creating markets was nothing new for Enron. Seizing on deregulation of the natural gas industry in the late 1980s and electricity in the early 1990s, Enron pioneered telephone-based markets of those products. The company saw that as long as it could create large, diversified pools of supplies in those industries and wire them together, it could ensure liquidity. When the Internet came along, it made that coordination cheaper and easier. Enron entered most industries first with pure financial trades that included derivatives and other instruments that protected companies from big price or supply swings. Then it moved to the physical product, buying mills or building network infrastructure as backup for what it could not acquire in the open market. Enron, however, believed its future was in carrying out e-commerce transactions rather than in owning the infrastructure and commodities themselves.[22]

For each industry it served, Enron figured it needed about 2 percent of the physical product in the right locations. Its rationale was that what it knew was more important than what it owned; Internet connectivity with everyone in the value chain made ownership less important. Enron created markets to ensure that it was getting the lowest-cost components. It then packaged that to sell. That was what the Internet did: It fundamentally was a connection for what were previously vertically integrated structures.[23]

The Internet was perfectly suited for Enron because the company had transformed its business in the late 1980s, just before the gas industry was deregulated. Previously, there was a rigid, vertically integrated business chain. Producers had long-term contracts with pipeline companies. Pipeline companies had long-term contracts with distributors, and distributors with their customers. The kinds of contracts that could be used, and how a company could buy and sell had all been dictated by Washington. Because of deregulation, the chain disintegrated. So when the Internet came along, it was a perfect overlay on that system, because it was a much more effective way of creating those markets.[24]

Enron prided itself on spotting and exploiting new opportunities in the marketplace before anyone else. It was the first energy company to open an e-commerce portal, EnronOnline, and it was a leader in the race to develop a wholesale market for bandwidth, trading Internet capacity the way it did electricity and natural gas. The company's size was its biggest weapon. Like a high school bully, it used brute force to break into new markets and spur deregulation. Then it scooped up market share before its competitors.[25]

EnronOnline was a reinvention of a business that Enron had in energy trading, using new technology. The ability to leverage all the existing Enron expertise meant that the company could build a business of a scale and size in a matter of months that no startup on the planet could match. Very few companies knew how to manage that balance.[26] Via the Web, Enron traded everything from gas to copper to financial instruments that let snowmobile makers and others hedge their risk of bad weather. Enron was building a nationwide fiber-optic network that could zip movie-quality videos across the Web. It created a unit that bought and sold high-speed telecommunications capacity—and it was partnered with America Online Inc. and IBM to market electricity to residential customers with the help of the Web.[27]

The efficiency gains made possible by dynamic pricing and trading were especially suited to the energy industry. If there was ever a place where Internet trading made a lot of sense, it was with energy commodities—mainly because electronic trading could match the speed with which commodity pricing changed. The Web site let buyers and sellers act on prices that could change by the minute. Buyers or sellers could also see real-time price spreads of both the sell price and the buy price. On the telephone, a buyer previously would call to ask about gas prices for each of the next 6 months, but by the time the trader finished reciting the prices, some prices could have changed.[28] The Internet system allowed everyone to see all the prices all the time and make more careful decisions.

Enron's strategy was national in scope. It involved providing the subscriber with a better Internet experience.[29] More specifically, the company aimed to develop an ambitious Internet overlay that would facilitate the delivery of rich multimedia. The plan was to provide speed, prioritization, and quality of service (QoS) on the backbone to keep pace with the capabilities of anticipated local broadband services based on emerging digital subscriber line (DSL) technology. Furthermore, the company proposed to commoditize bandwidth in the same way that gas and electric power had been commoditized within the industries where Enron had been active previously. The goal was to provide wide-area data connectivity.[30]

Success of Enron's Internet Venture

Enron didn't just make markets; it assaulted them.[31] EnronOnline broadened the company's market reach, accelerated its business activity, and enabled it to scale its business beyond its own expectations. By the end of 2000, EnronOnline had executed 548,000 transactions with a notional value of $336 billion, and it was the world's largest Web-based e-commerce system.[32]

With EnronOnline, the company reached a greater number of customers more quickly and at a lower cost than ever before. It was a great new business generator, attracting users who were drawn by the site's ease of use; transparent, firm prices; and the fact that they were transacting directly with Enron. In 2000 the company's total physical volume increased significantly as a direct result of EnronOnline.[33]

Since its introduction, EnronOnline expanded to include more than 1,200 of the company's products by 2001. It also streamlined the back-office processes, making the entire operation more efficient. It reduced overall transaction costs by 75 percent and increased the productivity of the commercial team by fivefold, on average.[34]

THE ROLE OF INFORMATION TECHNOLOGY IN ENRON'S BELIEVED SUCCESS

The Internet, electronic commerce, and information technology (IT) had a dramatic impact on the development of Enron Corp. and on the energy industry in general. In the coming years, these developing technologies are thought to continue to play a vital role in the success of the energy industry as a whole.[35]

When Enron was formed in 1985, the company's pipeline group represented more than 80 percent of its income, with the remaining 20 percent representing exploration and production, gas, liquids, and other energy-related businesses. Before the collapse, about 80 percent of Enron's income was generated from businesses that were new ventures for the company.[36] One of the primary drivers behind this rapid development was the need for companies such as Enron to reduce information transaction costs and the speed at which they were incurred. The Internet, and IT in general, helped to drive information transaction costs to virtually zero. These developing technologies changed both the way business was done and the way Enron organized its various companies. Also increasing was the rate at which these technologies were being introduced into the world economy.[37]

"Our e-commerce strategy can basically be defined as 'making new markets.' Our basic competency is providing reliable delivery of commodities of all types at predictable and lower prices," stated Ken Lay.[38] Enron was finding that many other industries outside of energy still clung to the old methodologies, with very inefficient marketing and delivery systems. "They are not able to keep up with competitors who are using the new model," he said.[39]

IMPORTANCE OF INNOVATION

No company illustrated the transformative power of innovation more dramatically than Enron. Over the past decade Enron's commitment to the invention and later domination of new business categories took it from a $200 million old-economy pipeline operator to a $40 billion new-economy trading powerhouse. In 1985, Enron recognized the opportunities wrought by natural gas deregulation and began to trade it like a commodity. Soon it was opening new markets, trading electric power, pulp, paper, and even broadband. Jeff Shenkman, the chief operating officer of Enron Global Markets, credited the company's culture for its success in building frontier markets. "Challenging conventional wisdom is something we push here," he said.[40]

There is no single way to encourage innovation, but all of the Enron executives recognized its importance. "Innovation is at the heart of sustaining a company's competitive advantage," stated a top Enron executive. "If you do it well, you will be successful in other areas. If it's not embedded in the organization and every employee who works there, how can you ever hope to execute on it?"[41]

Company executives insist this much was true: EnronOnline was conceived months before most top executives were informed. Three hundred-eighty programmers, traders, and managers, many of them working weekends and pulling 18-hour shifts, developed the site in just 7 months. That kind of entrepreneurial autonomy was commonplace at Enron. If an employee had an idea for a new business or process, that person had better be prepared to oversee it himself or herself if the plan was deemed worthy. Employees in the company's analyst training program were measured every 6 months on their "intellectual curiosity" as much as anything else.

CHALLENGES AND RISKS

Before the collapse, some analysts in 2001 pointed out that Enron may be expanding too rapidly and into areas about which it knew little. They questioned the company's ability to trade bandwidth, paper, and metals over the Web like it traded electricity and natural gas. They wondered whether Enron could raise enough capital to fuel all these aspiring e-businesses. If not, which ones would get priority? Top Enron executives noted that skeptics thought Enron was crazy when it dared to make electronic markets in energy. The confidence of these executives rested on their belief in Enron's market-making model.[42] They felt they had a better business model and their success confirmed this notion up until mid-2001.

The use of financial instruments by Enron's businesses exposed Enron to market and credit risks resulting from adverse changes in commodity and equity prices, interest rates, and foreign exchange rates. For Enron's businesses, the major market risks were these:

- Commodity Price Risk—Commodity price risk is a consequence of providing price-risk management services to customers. Enron actively tried to manage this risk on a portfolio basis to ensure compliance with Enron's stated risk management policies.
- Interest Rate Risk—Interest rate risk is also a consequence of providing price-risk management services to customers and having variable rate debt obligations, because changing interest rates impact the discounted value of future cash flows. Enron utilized forwards, futures, swaps, and options to attempt to manage its interest rate risk.
- Foreign Currency Exchange Rate Risk—Foreign currency exchange rate risk is the result of Enron's international operations and price-risk management services provided to its worldwide customer base. The primary purpose of Enron's foreign currency hedging activities was to protect against the volatility associated with foreign currency purchase and sale transactions. Enron primarily utilized forward exchange contracts, futures, and purchased options to deal with this profile.
- Equity Risk—Equity risk arises from Enron's participation in other investments. Enron generally managed this risk by hedging specific investments using futures, forwards, swaps, and options.

Enron evaluated, measured, and believed it could manage the market risk in its investments on a daily basis utilizing value at risk and other methodologies. It soon became apparent, however, that they were wrong.

BANKRUPTCY

By mid-2001, the challenges and risks finally caught up to Enron. In June 2001, as Enron's stock price continued to slide along with increasing allegations of non-disclosure and failure to provide comprehensible explanations of the company's financials, Enron's then president and CEO Jeff Skilling sold his personal equity stake in the company and profited approximately $17.5 million. This fact, combined with stories from countless Enron employees whose 401(k) shares in the company were non-tradable during this period, has been illuminated in the United States Senate Committee on Commerce (December 18, 2001). Two months after liquidating his shares in Enron, Skilling resigned citing "personal reasons." This signaled the frail health of the company and destroyed any remaining positive investor sentiment. In January 2002, Ken Lay resigned as chairman.

The bad continued to get worse when on October 16, 2001, Enron reported a third quarter loss of $618 million and a reduction in shareholder equity of $1.2 billion. The company pointed to Andrew Fastow, the chief financial officer, blaming the company's partnerships under his direction for the significant losses. Just over a week later, the Securities and Exchange Commission opened an investigation into Enron's partnerships and off-balance sheet debt. Even as late as October 24, 2001, Ken Lay had stated that Enron had access to much-needed cash, that the company was performing well, and that Fastow was a good employee whose reputation was being unnecessarily smeared. The very next day Fastow was given a leave of absence.

On November 8 of that same year, investors were provided the news that Enron was restating its earnings for the past 4¾ years. The restatement reduced earnings by almost $600 million, or about 15 percent, and contained warnings that Enron could still find "additional or different information."[43] Three weeks later Enron credit was downgraded to junk status. Finally, on December 2, 2001, the largest bankruptcy in United States' history was filed by Enron.

At the time of this writing, the story of what is to become of the executives who drove the *Fortune* 500's seventh largest company into bankruptcy is still being written. How is it possible that a large, successful, darling of the marketplace could sink so fast? This can be explained in part by the convoluted financials provided by the company and the ultimate effect this had on investor confidence. In order to disguise the off-balance sheet debt and other shortcomings, the financials were made complicated; so complicated that Enron executives had to take a standard defensive approach to handling questions from market analysts who could not decipher the financials. Congressman John Dingell from Michigan illustrated the problem in the December 18, 2001, hearing when he stated, "What we're looking at here is an example of superbly complex financial reports. They didn't have to lie. All they had to do was to obfuscate it with sheer complexity—although they probably lied too."[44]

In December of 2001, Milberg Weiss Bershad Hynes & Lerach filed a suit against Fastow, Skilling, and 27 other Enron executives, claiming they illegally made more than $1 billion from stock sales before Enron fell apart.[45] This suit is one of several class action suits filed thus far. This comes at a time when Enron creditors are clamoring for millions to recoup losses. Enron's auditor, Arthur Andersen, is also a target for civil suit. Probably the most frequently asked question now for those affected by the Enron disaster: What about criminal charges? At present, several U.S. Attorney offices are considering whether to pursue criminal charges against Enron and its officers. ∎

---

*Ann Marie Beyer of Florida State University assisted with this case. At the time of this writing, the Enron collapse was still unfolding.

QUESTIONS FOR DISCUSSION

1. What actions led to Enron's initial success?
2. In what ways did Enron "break the mold" of traditional operations of a gas transmission company?

3. Why did Enron declare bankruptcy?
4. Why was Enron unable to live up to its statement of values?
5. Could the Enron failure and resultant bankruptcy have been prevented?
6. What role should the U.S. government play in resolving the Enron situation?

Suggested Readings

Please note: At the time of this writing, the Enron case was still unfolding. The following are additional readings for review.

J. Berardino, "Enron: A Wake-Up Call," *The Wall Street Journal* (December 4, 2001) p. A18.

C. Bryan-Low and M. Pacelle, "Belfer Family Is a Big Loser as Stock Dives," *The Wall Street Journal* (December 3, 2001) p. C1, C13.

J. Emshwiller and R. Smith, "Behind Enron's Fall, A Culture of Operating Outside Public Views," *The Wall Street Journal* (December 5, 2001) p. A1, A10.

D. Kadlec, "Power Failure," *Time* (December 10, 2001) p. 68–72.

M. Pacelle and R. Smith, "Enron Files for Chapter 11 Bankruptcy, Sues Dynergy," *The Wall Street Journal* (December 3, 2001) p. A3, A10.

R. Smith, "Enron Swoon Leaves a Grand Experiment in a State of Disarray," *The Wall Street Journal* (November 30, 2001) p. A1, A8.

S. Thurm, "Stadium Jinx: What to Call Enron Field? 'Enron Folds,' Maybe," *The Wall Street Journal* (December 4, 2001) p. A1, A10.

J. Weil, "After Enron, 'Mark to Market' Accounting Gets Scrutiny," *The Wall Street Journal* (December 4, 2001) p. C1, C2.

Jeanne Cummings, et al. "Enron Lessons: Firms Need to Have Assets and Auditors Oversight," *The Wall Street Journal* (January 15, 2002) pp. A1, A4.

ENRON BEFORE THE FALL

Table 1   Enron Corp.

In millions, except per share data	2000	1999	1998	1997	1996
Revenues	$100,789	$40,112	$31,260	$20,273	$13,289
Net income					
Operating results	$1,266	$957	$698	$515	$493
Items impacting					
comparability	(287)	(64)	5	(410)	91
Total	$979	$893	$703	$105	$584
Dividends paid per common					
share	$0.50	$0.50	$0.48	$0.46	$0.43
Total assets	$65,503	$33,381	$29,350	$22,552	$16,137
Cash from operating activities					
(excluding working capital)	$3,010	$2,228	$1,873	$276	$742
Capital expenditures and equity					
investments	$3,314	$3,085	$3,564	$2,092	$1,483

Note: By January 2002, Enron stock had fallen to $.25 share.
Source: Enron 2000 Annual Report, www.enron.com, accessed May 18, 2001.

Stock Chart

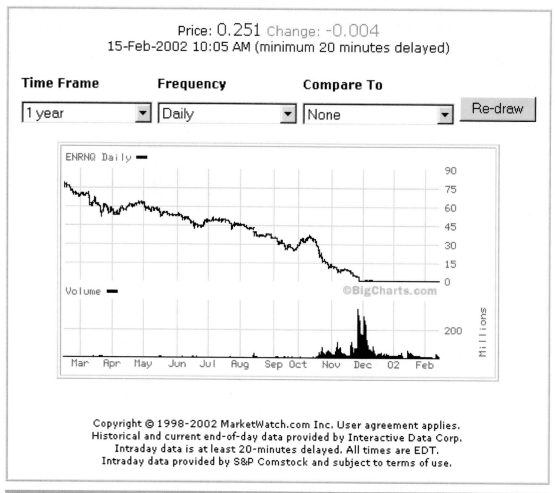

FIGURE 1   Five-Year Stock Price History

EXHIBIT 1

Enron's Visions

1986—To become the premier natural gas pipeline in North America

1990—To become the world's first natural gas major company

1995—To become the world's leading energy company

Source: Enron Online, www.enron.com, accessed May 18, 2001.

EXHIBIT 2

How the EIA's Lineup of Major Energy Companies Has Changed

1980

VERTICALLY INTEGRATED

Exxon
Mobil
Texaco
Chevron
Amoco
Gulf Oil
Shell Oil
Atlanta Richfield
Tenneco
BP America
Conoco
Sunoco
Phillips Petroleum
Getty Oil
Unocal
Occidental Petroleum
Union Pacific Resources
Amerada Hess
Cities Service
Marathon
Coastal
Ashland Oil
Kerr-McGee
Fina

NONINTEGRATED PRODUCERS

Burlington Resources
Superior Oil
Tesoro Petroleum

2000

VERTICALLY INTEGRATED

Exxon Mobil
BP Amoco
Chevron*
Texaco*
Shell Oil
USX (Marathon)
Conoco
Phillips Petroleum*
Amerada Hess
Total Fina Elf

(continued)

(continued)

NONINTEGRATED PRODUCERS

Occidental Petroleum
Unocal
Burlington Resources
Kerr-McGee
Anadarko Petroleum

NONINTEGRATED REFINERS

Equilon Enterprises
Motiva Enterprises
Tosco*
Ultramar Diamond Shamrock
Citgo Petroleum
Sunoco
Valero Energy
Lyondell-Citgo Refining
Clark Refining (Premcor)

ENERGY SERVICES

Enron
The Williams Cos.
El Paso Energy

*Chevron and Texaco merged on October 9, 2001. Phillips Petroleum merged with Tosco on September 17, 2001.
Source: Nissa Darbonne, "Trends and Analysis," *Oil & Gas Investor* (March 2001): 128.

EXHIBIT 3

Enron in Numbers

	ENRON 1985	ENRON 2000
Employees	15,076	18,000 (worldwide)
Countries in which Enron operates	4	30 plus
Assets	$12.1 billion	$33 billion
Miles of pipeline owned	37,000	32,000
Power projects under construction	1	14 in 11 countries
Power projects in operation	1	51 in 15 countries
Fortune 500 ranking	Not ranked	18

Source: Enron Online, www.enron.com, accessed May 18, 2001.

EXHIBIT 4

Mid-2001 Enron Fast Facts Prior to Bankruptcy

Assets	$53 billion
Miles of pipeline	30,000
Miles of fiber	15,000
Number of countries where active	44
U.S. employees	7,388
Total employees	22,120
Headquarters	Houston
Stock Symbol	ENE
Office of the chairman	Kenneth L. Lay, Chairman; Jeffrey K. Skilling, President and CEO
History	Formed in July 1985 as a result of the merger of Houston Natural Gas and InterNorth of Omaha, Nebraska.

Source: Enron Online, www.enron.com, accessed May 14, 2001.

ENRON MILESTONES

July 1985	Houston Natural Gas merges with InterNorth, a natural gas company based in Omaha, Nebraska, to form the modern-day Enron, an interstate and intrastate natural gas pipeline company with approximately 37,000 miles of pipe.
October 1985	FERC Order 436 is issued. Enron's interstate pipelines work to become open-access transporters to allow other entities to transport on our pipelines. Northern Natural Gas successfully transitions to an open-access transportation company through favorable settlements with its customers and the resolution of approximately 5,000 gas purchase contracts, with minimal impact to shareholders between 1986 and 1993. The majority of NNG's settlements on these take-or-pay contracts take place between 1988 and 1990.
July 1987	Florida Gas Transmission's Phase I expansion is completed as a result of growing natural gas needs in Florida. Today, FGT is embarking on the fifth expansion of its pipeline system, more than doubling its overall throughput capacity.
1988	Enron establishes U.K. beachhead at the first signs of energy liberalization and becomes the first company to begin construction of a new power plant when the electric industry is privatized.
1988	The precursor to today's wholesale trading business in North America and Europe, GasBank, is launched and Enron begins trading natural gas commodities. After the deregulation of the U.S. natural gas industry, the market has to revise its methods of contracting for gas in the wholesale market. GasBank allows producers and wholesale buyers to purchase firm gas supplies and hedge the price risk of the new spot market at the same time. Enron is the largest natural gas merchant in North America and the United Kingdom.
October 1989	Transwestern Pipeline Company is the first merchant pipeline in the United States to stop selling gas and become a transportation-only pipeline.
April 1992	FERC Order 636 is issued, separating the merchant function from the transportation function and taking pipelines out of the business of buying and selling gas.
December 1992	Enron acquires Transportadora de Gas del Sur, establishing Enron's first pipeline presence in South America. Since then, Enron has created an energy network in the region that includes natural gas pipelines, electric and natural gas utilities, wholesale commodities trading and energy services
April 1993	The 1,875 megawatt (MW) Teesside power plant, the world's largest gas-fired heat and power facility, becomes operational. After the Channel Tunnel, Teesside is the largest project financing ever completed in the United Kingdom.
June 1994	Enron North America trades its first electron. Today, Enron is the largest marketer of electricity in the United States by a significant margin.
1995	Northern Natural Gas and Transwestern sell their gathering facilities.

Enron Europe establishes a trading center in London and begins trading U.K. power and gas—marking Enron's entry into the European wholesale market. Enron is the largest merchant of natural gas and power in the United Kingdom, the market-maker in the Nordic Region, where Enron is the largest power merchant, and is becoming a leading marketer of electricity throughout continental Europe.

December 1996   The 826 MW Phase I of the Dabhol Power Project, a 2,450 MW power plant located south of Mumbai, India, achieves financial closure and begins construction. It is the first power project in India to involve imported liquified natural gas (LNG) as a fuel source.

January 1997   Enron unveils a new logo and its first global advertising campaign.

Enron acquires Zond Corporation, a leading developer of wind energy power, and forms Enron Renewable Energy Corp.

Construction begins on the 790 MW power station at Sutton Bride, United Kingdom.

June 1997   Enron acquires Portland General Electric (PGE).

Enron announces the settlement of all contractual issues involving the J-Block contract in the U.K. North Sea. Enron records a second quarter nonrecurring charge to income of $450 million after tax, reflecting the full accounting for the effects of the amended contract under current market conditions. The settlement allows the gas to be taken at consistent volumes, assuring a significant long-term supply at favorable fixed prices.

August 1997   Enron announces its first commodity transaction using weather-derivative products. Enron markets a variety of commodities, including coal, pulp and paper, plastics, metals, and bandwidth.

September 1997   Enron Energy Services (EES) is formed. EES is now the only nationwide provider of energy-outsourcing services to commercial and light industrial customers and is expanding its capabilities internationally.

November 1997   Northern Natural Gas initiates a major market-wide expansion project, Peak Day 2000, a 5-year effort that increases the pipeline's contracted capacity by 350,000 million cubic feet of gas per day. Today, this brings Northern's total Peak Day capacity to 4.3 billion cubic feet of gas per day (Bcf/d) compared to 2.8 Bcf/d in 1988.

June 1998   EES transacts its first commercial outsourcing deal with General Cable. In the next 2 years, EES signs outsourcing deals with a total contract value of nearly $20 billion.

July 1998   Enron acquires Wessex Water in the United Kingdom and forms new global water company, Azurix.

Spain and Germany award Enron the first power-marketing licenses granted to new market participants following the passage of national electricity regulations.

December 1998   Northern Border Pipeline completes its third and most ambitious expansion/extension, the Chicago Project. The project involved the construction of 390 miles of 36- and 30-inch-

	diameter pipeline from Iowa to Illinois and eight grassroots compressor stations.
January 1999	Enron Broadband Services introduces the Enron Intelligent Network (EIN), a new Internet application delivery platform.
February 1999	Enron Investment Partners is created to manage private equity funds targeting women and minority-owned businesses in Houston and around the United States.
April 1999	Enron and the Houston Astros announce the name of Houston's new ballpark, "Enron Field," and a 30-year facilities management contract with EES.
May 1999	The 826 MW Phase I of the Dabhol Power Project begins commercial operation, and financing for the 1,624 MW Phase II and India's first LNG receiving facility is completed. When Phase II construction was completed in late 2001, Dabhol became the world's largest independent natural gas-fired power facility.
June 1999	EES transacts its first billion-dollar deal with Suiza Foods. *Sales and Marketing* magazine ranks EES as the No. 1 sales force in America.
July 1999	Enron announces Azurix initial public offering. The 3,000-kilometer Boliva-to-Brazil natural gas pipeline, one of the largest gas projects ever undertaken in South America, begins commercial operation. The pipeline system has a capacity of 30 million cubic meters per day. Enron sells its interest in Enron Oil and Gas, but retains its China and India assets.
November 1999	Enron launches EnronOnline, the first global Web-based commodity trading site. Since EnronOnline's introduction, Enron has become the world's largest e-commerce company. Enron announces the sale of PGE to Sierra Pacific Resources.
December 1999	Enron completes its first bandwidth trade. EES reports its first profitable quarter.
January 2000	In a *Fortune* survey, Enron was ranked No. 24 among the "100 Best Companies to Work for in America."
February 2000	Enron launches EnronCredit.com, the first real-time credit department for corporations. Enron rolls out its "Ask Why" advertising campaign.
March 2000	The Energy Financial Group ranks Enron the sixth largest energy company in the world, based on market capitalizations.
April 2000	Enron Net Works is created to pursue new market development opportunities in e-commerce across a broad range of industries.
May 2000	Enron and strategic investors, IBM and America Online, launch the New Power Company, the first national energy service provider for residential and small businesses in deregulated U.S. energy markets. Through the partnership, Enron provides the New Power Company with energy commodity pricing, risk management services, and government/regulatory expertise.
July 2000	After acquiring MG plc in May, the world's leading publicly traded metals marketer, Enron completes its first physical metals transaction on EnronOnline, providing improved pricing, price-risk management services, and more flexible transactions for customers.

Enron signs a long-term agreement with Blockbuster that will enable consumers to receive high-quality, feature-length movies-on-demand via the Enron Intelligent Network.

December 2001	Enron files for Chapter 11 Bankruptcy.
January 2002	Enron stock drops to less than $1.00 a share. Stock is delisted from the New York Stock Exchange.
February 2002	Enron stock trades at $0.47 a share on February 4, 2002.

Source: Enron Online, www.enron.com, accessed May 18, 2001; www.money.cnn.com, accessed February 4, 2002.

REFERENCES

1. "Enron Annual Report 2000", www.enron.com/corp/investors/annuals/2000/, accessed on May 18, 2001.
2. Ibid.
3. Ken Branson, "To Market, to Market," *Telephony* (February 12, 2001): 46–58.
4. Frank Gibney, Jr., "Enron Plays the Pipes," Time.com, August 28, 2000.
5. Enron Annual Reoprt 2000.
6. Ibid.
7. Ibid.
8. Brian O'Reilly, "The Power Merchant," *Fortune* (March 17, 2001): 148–68.
9. Ibid.
10. Ibid.
11. "Enron's Vision and Values," www.enron.com, accessed on May 14, 2001.
12. See note 5.
13. Ibid.
14. Ibid.
15. See note 8.
16. Jeff Share, "Integrated Energy Companies Becoming Archaic, Skilling Says," *Pipeline and Gas Journal* (January 2001): 37.
17. Ibid.
18. Nissa Darbonne, "Trends and Analysis," *Oil & Gas Investor* (March 2001): 128.
19. Ibid.
20. "A Better Business Model?" *InternetWeek* (October 30, 2000): 22.
21. See note 16.
22. Robert Preston and Mike Koller, "Enron Feels the Power," *InternetWeek* (October 20, 2000): 20.
23. Ibid.
24. See note 20.
25. Margaret Boitano, "Is Dynegy the Next Enron?" *Fortune* (December 18, 2000): 166–72.
26. Gary Hamel and Thomas A. Stewart, "Today's Companies Won't Make It, and Gary Hamel Knows Why," *Fortune* (September 4, 2000): 386–87.
27. Wendy Zellner, "Enron Electrified," *Business Week Online,* July 24, 2000.
28. Theo Mullen, "Enron Breaks into E-Biz Big Leagues," *Internet Week Online,* May 11, 2000.
29. Dan Sweeney, "Burning the Bulb at Both Ends," *America's Network,* February 1, 2000.
30. Ibid.
31. See note 22.
32. See note 5.
33. Ibid.
34. Ibid.
35. Steve Poruban, "Enron's Lay Sees More E-Commerce Changes for Industry," *Oil & Gas Journal* (April 16, 2001): 32–34.
36. Ibid.
37. Ibid.
38. Ibid.
39. Ibid.
40. Nicholas Stein, "The World's Most Admired Companies," *Fortune* (October 2, 2000): 182–89.
41. Ibid.
42. See note 23.
43. See note 5.
44. Bethany, McLean, "Why Enron Went Bust" *Fortune* (December 24, 2001): 58–68.
45. Zellner, Forrest, Thornton, Coy, Timmons, Lavelle, and Henry, "The Fall of Enron," *Business Week* (December 27, 2001): 30–36.

Index